ENGLISH CASTLES

A Guide by Counties

Dedicated to Ian

ENGLISH CASTLES

A Guide by Counties

ADRIAN PETTIFER

THE BOYDELL PRESS

First published 1995
The Boydell Press, Woodbridge

ISBN 0 85115 600 2

The Boydell Press is an imprint of Boydell & Brewer Ltd
PO Box 9, Woodbridge, Suffolk IP12 3DF, UK
and of Boydell & Brewer Inc.
PO Box 41026, Rochester, NY 14604–4126, USA

British Library Cataloguing-in-Publication Data
Pettifer, Adrian
English Castles:Guide by Counties
I. Title
914.104859
ISBN 0–85115–600–2

Library of Congress Cataloging-in-Publication Data
Pettifer, Adrian, 1959–
English castles : a guide by counties / Adrian Pettifer.
p. cm.
Includes bibliographical references (p.   ) and index.
ISBN 0–85115–600–2 (hardback : alk. paper)
1. Castles – England – Guidebooks. I. Title.
DA660.P48 1995
914.204'859 – dc20   95–22530

The paper used in this publication meets the minimum requirements
of American National Standard for Information Sciences –
Permanence of Paper for Printed Library Materials, ANSI Z39.48–1984

Printed in Great Britain by
St Edmundsbury Press Ltd, Bury St Edmunds, Suffolk

CONTENTS

ILLUSTRATIONS

Copyright material is reproduced by permission, as listed under Acknowledgements.

PLATES

PLANS

ACKNOWLEDGEMENTS

The castle plans are closely based on copyright material which has only been modified as much as has seemed necessary for relatively small-scale reproduction in this volume. Permission to reproduce the plans is gratefully acknowledged, as follows:

Aydon, Brougham, Carisbrooke, Carlisle, Castle Rising, Conisbrough, Dartmouth, Deal, both plans of Dover, Farnham, Framlingham, Goodrich, Kenilworth, Old Wardour, Orford, Portchester, Restormel, Richmond, Rochester, Stokesay, Warkworth: by permission of English Heritage.

Bodiam, Compton, Sizergh, Tattershall: by permission of the National Trust.

Colchester: by permission of Colchester Museums.

Lewes: by permission of Sussex Archaeological Society.

Ludlow: by permission of Powis Castle Estate.

Newcastle: by permission of the Society of Antiquaries of Newcastle upon Tyne.

Barnwell: reproduced from the *Victoria County History, Northamptonshire*, vol. III, p. 70, by permission of the General Editor.

Bolton: reproduced from the *Victoria County History, Yorkshire North Riding*, vol. I, facing p. 270, by permission of the General Editor.

Buckden: reproduced from the *Victoria County History, Huntingdonshire*, vol. II, p. 263, by permission of the General Editor.

Durham: reproduced from the *Victoria County History, County Durham*, vol. III, facing p. 64, by permission of the General Editor.

Herstmonceux: reproduced from the *Victoria County History, Sussex*, vol. IX, facing p. 132, by permission of the General Editor.

Maxstoke: reproduced from the *Victoria County History, Warwickshire*, vol. IV, p. 134, by permission of the General Editor.

Pleshey: reproduced from the *Victoria County History, Essex*, vol. I, p. 298, by permission of the General Editor.

Warwick: reproduced from the *Victoria County History, Warwickshire*, vol. VIII, p. 454, by permission of the General Editor.

Permission to reproduce the plates is gratefully acknowledged as follows:

Belsay Castle, Castle Rising, Carisbrooke Castle, Deal Castle, Dover Castle, Dunstanburgh Castle, Framlingham Castle, Goodrich Castle, Orford Castle, Rochester Castle, Stokesay Castle: by permission of English Heritage.

Alnwick Castle, Bodiam Castle: courtesy of the Royal Commission on the Historical Monuments of England.

Tattershall Castle: copyright the National Trust Photographic Library/Brian Lawrence.

The Tower of London: courtesy of Aerofilms Limited.

York, Micklegate Bar: courtesy of Arnold Taylor.

FOREWORD

Every castle writer begins by apologising for yet another book on the subject. My own justification for adding to the pile is the need for a comprehensive guide to the medieval castles of England. Some excellent books describe the historical and architectural development of the castle (see bibliography), but there is no descriptive gazetteer suitable for the castle enthusiast or the general reader. This book attempts to fill the vacuum. While giving due weight to the well-known castles, I have tried to show the full depth of our inheritance.

English castles are a very diverse group, and consequently it is hard to do them justice. They range from massive edifices which still dominate the landscape to 'motte-and-bailey' earthworks and Border pele towers. Castellated mansions of the later Middle Ages are often dismissed as castles altogether because of the concessions made to comfort, but castles always display a compromise between the requirements of defence and domestic convenience. I have adopted a more tolerant approach and accepted all sites with enough defensive characteristics. In a few later medieval cases the decision was a borderline one. My aim is to give a brief description and history of every masonry castle except the most fragmentary. I have been more selective with earthwork castles because they are so numerous. Only the more impressive and historically important ones are included.

Real castles are a medieval phenomenon, spanning the centuries from the Norman Conquest to the Tudor era, and that sets the limits for this book. Buildings and earthworks of other periods fall outside its scope, even if they are popularly called 'castle' like many ancient hillforts, Roman forts and stately homes. I *have* included the small proportion of medieval fortifications which are not actually castles, these being walled towns, defended monasteries and Tudor coastal forts. They are too closely related and it would be a pity to ignore them. For the sake of clarity a few sites which do not strictly merit inclusion have been allowed in, namely sham castles on genuine sites and medieval manor houses which bear the name of castle but do not actually deserve the title.

My main qualification for writing this book is having visited many of the sites. I have tried to be as accurate as possible, given the conflicting demands of brevity, but I apologise in advance for the inevitable mistakes. Hopefully this book will provide a useful summary of every English castle you are likely to visit, more convenient to digest on the spot than a detailed guidebook and supplying a few key facts for all those places where no information is readily available. The text is complemented by a short historical introduction and a glossary covering all aspects of castles in some detail.

HISTORICAL INTRODUCTION

The English medieval castle was seldom an impregnable fortress. It served both as fortification and residence, and there was always a degree of incompatibility between the two roles. Military emergencies were unusual, even in the Middle Ages, and to keep up with the latest initiatives in siege warfare would have imposed an unjustifiable burden. One can often observe the dilemma between making a castle strong against assailants without rendering it inconvenient to those who lived there. Even the siting of castles was dictated not by defensive considerations alone, but by the need to dominate the town or control the highway. The dynamic role of the castle – forming the seat of a lord who commanded the surrounding territory – was more important than the strongest defences.

Although castles are similar in overall conception they can be highly individual and no two are alike. Each was purpose-built according to the site, the circumstances, the builder's preferences and the funds available. Contrasting schools of thought helped to create variety in numerous ways, e.g. keep or no keep, round or square towers, regular or irregular layout, etc. There is an element of evolution in these respects but it should not be overstated. Conversely the view that castles cannot be categorised meaningfully into types is unhelpful.

Origins

Although this book deals with English medieval castles, it must be emphasised that most of the defensive features employed in the Middle Ages had already existed for a long time, and very little is native to this island. Towns have always needed defending and from ancient times there was sometimes a citadel providing an inner line of defence. Such was the ancient Greek *acropolis*, though it should be noted that this was a state fortress as opposed to a private residence. In Britain mighty hillforts protected the Iron Age populace; their earth ramparts are still impressive at sites such as Old Oswestry and Maiden Castle. The Roman invaders built forts which were garrison bases designed to house a professional army. The later Roman forts of the 'Saxon Shore' are more geared for defence, with thick walls and flanking bastions – a sign that Rome was losing the initiative to Teutonic invaders. As the western half of the Roman Empire fell apart in the fifth century AD, wealthy senators fortified their country villas against barbarian attack. These were arguably the forerunners of the medieval castle, though there are no known examples in Britain.

The castle proper originated in Dark Age Europe. With the break-up of the Carolingian Empire in the ninth century there emerged the pragmatic system of feudalism, with its emphasis on loyalty to one's immediate superior in place of the old ties to a remote central authority. Lords great and small carved out estates for themselves and raised private fortresses to live in. This process can be seen most clearly in northern France, where a number of dukes, counts and lesser warlords wielded power without effective restraint from the weak French monarchy. By the year 1000 castles were becoming a familiar sight in western Europe, though almost all of them were modest affairs of earth and timber.

Different conditions prevailed on the English side of the Channel, however. After the Danes had been rebuffed England emerged in the tenth century as a relatively unified kingdom. This unity contrived to keep feudalism and the castle at bay. Defence remained purely communal, as in the 'burghs' or fortified towns founded by Alfred the Great and his successors. A few castles were in fact raised in England before the Norman Conquest, but they were the product of Norman adventurers invited across by Edward the Confessor to assist in the wars against the Welsh. These Normans were not popular and their stay was brief. Whether the English would eventually have adopted castles of their own accord is an open question. It is difficult to see how they could have resisted such a pervasive European trend in the long term, but we shall never know as the Battle of Hastings was about to change their destiny dramatically.

Castles of the Conquest

Castles finally appeared in England as instruments of foreign conquest. The chronicler Orderic Vitalis observed with some justice that England's lack of castles made the Norman Conquest easier, since the defeated Saxon thanes had no private fortresses to retreat to. William the Conqueror is said to have brought a ready-to-assemble wooden fort across the Channel with him, and his march upon London was accompanied by the foundation of several impromptu castles en route. William erected castles at key places (primarily the old Saxon burghs) all over England in the years following 1066. Most of these castles were formidable earthworks, consisting of one or more enclosures (baileys) defended by massive ramparts, ditches and wooden stockades. Such castles were often dominated by a huge artificial mound or 'motte'. William's chief followers, who had been rewarded with vast estates, also began to raise castles. All the early castles acted as administrative centres, barracks, prisons and places of justice, but their primary function was to protect the small Norman households who lived in them from the defeated but resentful English.

By the end of William's reign the castle had become a well-established – and much hated – symbol of Norman domination. The Domesday Book (1086) mentions about sixty English castles but the real total must already have been considerably larger. As a taxation document Domesday only mentions castles incidentally, for instance if houses had been destroyed to make way for them. At least half were under William's direct control, and the rest were held by trustworthy tenants-in-chief. William Rufus was less cautious than his father, so castle building increased. Nevertheless, only on the Welsh Border did castles begin to proliferate, because here William I had delegated his powers to three 'palatine' earls who enjoyed a free hand in return for invading Wales. They and their sub-tenants built castles in considerable numbers to defend the newly-won 'Marcher' lordships. There was no comparable militarisation of the Scottish Border. Territorial disputes arose from time to time but, on the whole, England and Scotland coexisted peacefully for the next two centuries.

Transition to Stone

Earthwork castles of the 'motte-and-bailey' type continued to be the norm well into the twelfth century. However, as the Norman conquerors settled down some of them began to reconstruct their castles permanently in stone. Defence was no doubt the primary consideration: earthworks can quite easily be dug away by an attacking force and wooden stockades are extremely vulnerable to fire. Nevertheless status was an important factor even at this early stage. Norman lords sought monumental buildings to rival the great churches which were beginning to dominate the landscape. Stone tower keeps had originated in northern France in the late tenth century. Naturally, the King was the first to build such keeps in England. William the Conqueror himself began the White Tower which forms the heart of the Tower of London. Designed as a palace-fortress truly fit for a king, it set the pattern for the next hundred years. In fact, few tower keeps ever rivalled it. A simpler form of keep was the so-called shell keep, consisting simply of an embattled wall around the motte top. Even before 1100 a few enterprising barons had built stone 'curtain' walls around their baileys in place of wooden stockades.

Castles feature prominently in the sporadic revolts of the period. Indeed, Norman warfare was characterised by few battles but many sieges. Hence William II had difficulty besieging the Northumbrian castles of Robert de Mowbray in 1095, and seven years later Robert de Belleme defied Henry I from his Shropshire strongholds. Henry I rebuilt the more important royal castles in stone – one of several measures aimed at keeping the barons in check. A number of keeps are convincingly attributed to him, though documentary proof is lacking. Royal control broke down following the disputed accession of King Stephen. Many barons, particularly in the South-West, preferred the rival claims of the Empress Matilda, and an inconclusive civil war known to history as the 'Anarchy' lasted for most of Stephen's reign. Ambitious lords took advantage of the situation to build castles without authority. As the Anglo-Saxon chronicle complains: 'They filled the land with castles . . . and filled them with devils and wicked men'. A considerable number of England's more obscure earthwork castles can no doubt be assigned to this period, but some fine stone keeps rose as well. By contrast, Stephen exhausted his resources in fruitless campaigns to defeat his rival. Hence he was not a great builder of castles, although no one besieged more!

The breach was healed when Matilda's son assumed the throne as Henry II. Henry ordered the demolition of many (though by no means all) of the 'adulterine' castles, while taking some of the more important ones into royal hands. Henry proved himself the master of his barons but not of his own family, as shown by the great revolt of his son (Prince Henry) in 1173–74. Some disgruntled English lords took part in this abortive rebellion, and as a result more baronial castles were destroyed. Meanwhile Henry did much to strengthen his own castles, consolidating a vast personal empire which stretched from the Tweed to the Pyrenees. For the first time we have yearly records of royal expenditure in the Pipe Rolls, and Henry built on a prodigious scale. He spent over £7000 on Dover Castle alone – a vast amount of money in those days. By the time of his death the King's authority was reinforced by a series of masonry castles throughout England.

Henry II also endeavoured to control private castle building. A system of royal approval emerged, whereby barons were required to apply for a licence to 'crenellate', or fortify, their manor houses. Despite this restriction the greater barons frequently strengthened their castles in stone without interference. Most castles of this era, whether royal or baronial, had a plain curtain around the bailey and a keep for inner defence – either a shell keep on a motte or a big square tower. Even Henry II's great keep at Dover is a massive cube in the tradition of William I's White Tower. However, there was a gradual shift towards more dynamic defensive forms in the second half of the twelfth century, in response to the rapid improvement in siege techniques.

Castles of Enclosure

The revolution in castle building was triggered to a large extent by the experiences of crusaders, in the Holy Land and (no less importantly) in Spain. Siege warfare became more sophisticated, enabling besiegers to penetrate castle defences in a variety of ways. Scaling ladders and siege towers allowed attackers to go over the wall, catapults and battering rams could breach the wall and, worst of all, undermining could bring a section of wall crashing down. Norman castles, with their lumbering square keeps and relatively low curtains, were vulnerable to such forms of assault, but England was comparatively slow in embracing the remedies. Curtains gradually increased in height and thickness and were strengthened by the provision of flanking towers, which enabled archers to fire laterally upon attackers approaching the wall. Mural towers feature in some early Norman castles, but the concept did not reach maturity until Henry II built curtains at Windsor and Dover which are comprehensively flanked by towers.

These towers are square in the Norman tradition, but the angles of square towers were particularly vulnerable to undermining. This was demonstrated at Rochester in 1215, when King John's sappers brought down a corner of the keep. Castle builders responded by eliminating angles altogether. Mural towers became circular, or at least semi-circular with their curved fronts towards the field. Keeps were also built in rounded form, but there are few English examples because the very concept of the keep was falling out of fashion. Circular rooms must have seemed particularly inconvenient at a time when lords were beginning to move out of their inhospitable keeps in favour of more spacious bailey accommodation. Furthermore, a well-defended enclosure with a number of projecting towers – each of which could serve as a self-contained strongpoint in the event of the bailey being overrun – eliminated the need for a keep as a last resort. Hence there emerged the 'castle of enclosure', consisting of a high curtain with several flanking towers of equal status. The dominant feature of such a castle is likely to be the gatehouse, which developed from a simple tower into a long gate passage flanked by twin towers.

After the glut of castle building in Norman times not many new castles were built in thirteenth-century England. More often there was a piecemeal strengthening of older castles with keeps. Some castles had to be reconstructed after suffering damage during the Magna Carta war (1215–16), when King John attempted to reverse his humiliation at Runnymede and the rebel barons invited the French Dauphin Louis to claim the English throne. Undermining caused devastation at Rochester and Dover, while a number of curtains crumbled before Louis' powerful trebuchets. The siege of Bedford Castle in 1224 demonstrated how even a single castle could be a real nuisance in the hands of a rebel baron. Simon de Montfort's revolt (1264–65) saw long sieges at Pevensey and Kenilworth, but this time the decisive battles were fought in the open. It should be stressed that these wars were short-lived interruptions of a mainly peaceful era. Only in the Welsh Marches was there anything resembling a hostile frontier. Here, Llywelyn the Great and Llywelyn the Last reversed the tide of conquest and put the Marcher lords on the defensive. That is why the new idiom is most apparent in Wales and the Welsh Border districts. One important group of thirteenth-century fortifications should not be overlooked. This was the era in which many English towns received their stone defences.

The kings of England led the way in adapting their castles to the new style. It is estimated that castle building and maintenance accounted for a tenth of royal revenue in this period. Even Henry II had experimented with a round keep at Orford. Richard I's great monument is Chateau Gaillard in Normandy. King John, thwarted by the loss of his continental possessions, lavished attention on his English strongholds instead. Henry III continued the comprehensive programme of strengthening royal castles, leaving an impressive legacy at Dover, Windsor and the Tower of London. Castle building in Britain reached its climax in the reign of Edward I, with the conquest of Wales and the erection of a mighty group of strongholds there. Some of the Welsh castles follow a concentric plan, in which the main enclosure is closely surrounded by a parallel outer curtain. Edward I converted the Tower of London into a concentric fortress but this is the only fully-developed example in England. Combined keep-gatehouses – another characteristic of the 'Edwardian' castle – are nearly as rare.

Fortified Manor Houses

Scotland replaced Wales as the goal of English imperialism in the later years of Edward I, but then the tables were turned. Robert Bruce seized the initiative after his victory at Bannockburn (1314), and for the rest of the fourteenth century there was intermittent warfare between the two kingdoms. The Border counties would languish in an atmosphere of raiding and feuding for the next three hundred years. In this war-torn environment the need for defence was paramount, even among the lesser nobility who were compelled to build pele towers in large numbers. Elsewhere in England the tower house, as opposed to the unfortified manor house, was a rarity and castle building remained in the hands of the greater barons. Owing to the Hundred Years' War (1336–1453) there is one other area where English castles retained a serious defensive role. Although the war was mainly fought on the Continent, the French did manage a number of retaliatory raids across the Channel, especially in the later fourteenth century when they went onto the offensive. New castles on the South Coast, such as Bodiam and vanished Queenborough, were intended to play a part in coastal defence.

Even on the frontiers, however, the nature of the castle was changing. Edward I's Welsh strongholds were exceptional because they had been designed to hold down a conquered people. Contemporary English castles are seldom as formidable. They were no longer instruments of conquest, even if they remained symbols of feudal inequality, and the Scots and French came in raiding parties which were seldom equipped for a long siege. Hence there is a gradual shift in emphasis, castle builders making more concessions to the demands of comfort. The term 'fortified manor house' is often used to describe such castles. Many older castles were brought up to date but some were already being abandoned as residences. In their place we find a resurgence in the building of new castles, many exhibiting great uniformity in design. Previously most castles had been laid out around a conveniently defensible perimeter dictated by the contours of the ground, without much regard to overall symmetry. Now the four-square plan around a quadrangle became fashionable, with towers at the corners and a gatehouse usually located in the middle of one side. This quadrangular layout was efficient from a defensive point of view. It also allowed the domestic buildings to be ranged conveniently against the four surrounding walls.

Some castle builders of this era were professional soldiers who earned their reputation during the long-running wars with France and Scotland. They made a fortune out of ransom money and plunder, erecting impressive castles which emphasised their soldierly status. Fourteenth-century castles also reflect the chivalrous aspirations of the aristocracy at a time when knightly virtues were highly valued, if not always practised. Some developments appear to put the clock back to the Norman era. One is the reappearance of the square flanking tower. Most later medieval towers contained suites of apartments instead of being purely defensive platforms, and from a domestic point of view circular rooms were never popular. Another seemingly archaic development was the revival of the keep. Scholars prefer the Scottish term 'tower house' to distinguish these structures from the keeps of Norman times. They were not so much a defensive last resort against outsiders, it is argued, as a secure place for the lord against his own retainers, at a time when the French wars had caused the old system of feudal levies to be replaced by one of recruiting untrustworthy mercenaries. Tower houses, including the many small pele towers, are most common in the Northern counties but they can be found all over England. It should be noted that there was much less royal castle building in the fourteenth century and beyond. Edward III strengthened some South Coast castles against the French but his biggest castle expenditure, at Windsor, was mainly of a domestic nature.

Impact of Artillery

Under Henry V there was a renewed tide of conquest in France. The fruits of victory – admittedly short-lived – created another generation of veterans eager to advertise their soldierly status by building castles. The main themes of the fourteenth century – quadrangular castles and tower houses – carried on into the fifteenth. A new development was the frequent use of brick as the main building material. Castles maintained that cautious divide between the lord and his hired retainers, the latter sometimes being confined to an outer or 'base' court. However, except perhaps in the North there was less castle building in the fifteenth century, and the concessions made for comfort at the expense of security reached a point where the castle turned into a castellated mansion. Great piles like Herstmonceux and Tattershall, although they look impressive enough, have serious defensive flaws. The quadrangular castle, with its ranges backing onto the curtain, was on its way to becoming an unfortified courtyard house. Such tendencies increased after the middle of the century, which is surprising in view of the dynastic struggle which erupted between the Houses of Lancaster and York. In fact the Wars of the Roses (1455–87) were an intermittent series of field campaigns in which castles played little part. A few Northumbrian strongholds were besieged by the Yorkists but the castle had ceased to have a significant role in warfare. Few castles of the late fifteenth century show any genuine defensive capability, and small gun ports are the only admission that artillery was introducing a new dimension to warfare.

Cannon first appeared in England in Edward III's reign but their impact on siegecraft was minor owing to their unreliability. In the fifteenth century guns became more powerful, and the French made devastating use of the new weapon in the last stages of the Hundred Years War. On the Continent and even in Scotland attempts were made to adapt castles to artillery, but the English resisted these developments. Hence, although the rise of artillery coincided with the decline of the English castle, it seems that the one did not actually cause the other. If castles had become status symbols, it was because their high towers and embattled parapets conveyed an image of baronial pride. The response to artillery demanded a squatter profile which failed to appeal to the nobility.

The End of the Castle

It is not strictly true that castle building was forbidden under the Tudors. Licences to crenellate were still issued occasionally but they had become a symbolic gesture, permitting a favoured subject to put battlements on top of his house. Tudor legislation abolishing private armies did more to bring the aristocracy to heel. This and other incentives encouraged their transition from war lords to courtiers. The North took longer to adjust and pele towers continued to rise near the Scottish Border well into the sixteenth century. This was due to general lawlessness as much as the periodic clashes between England and Scotland. Conditions did not really improve until the union of the two realms in 1603.

Frontier defences were needed more than ever in the sixteenth century. Henry VIII's breach with Rome and the alliance of the chief Catholic powers against him led to a short-lived threat of invasion in the 1540s, and this prompted Henry to embark upon the first comprehensive scheme of coastal defence since Roman times. With their thick walls and geometrical layouts Henry's forts were designed to withstand the artillery of the day. They also differ from castles proper in being garrison posts rather than residential fortresses, so we have strictly reached the end of our story. However, by Elizabeth I's reign low ramparts and arrow-headed bastions (as at Berwick) had become the staple defence for artillery, and Henrician forts have more in common with the medieval castle than with that kind of fortification. How effective these coastal fortifications would have been in stopping an invasion is doubtful. The scare of the 1540s did not materialise, while the Spanish Armada was defeated by weather and aggressive seamanship.

Many older castles were abandoned for up-to-date residences in the Tudor period. Others were modernised to the detriment of their old defensive strength. Ironically, the medieval castle had long ceased to be a fortress when the stability of England temporarily broke down in the conflict between Charles I and Parliament (1642–46). As in previous wars the outcome of the Civil War was determined primarily on the battlefield, but many castles were hastily refortified to act as garrison posts. As a result the Civil War is remarkable for its many sieges. Some castles held out surprisingly well against the artillery of the day, but the victorious Parliament ordered the 'slighting' of many to prevent their future use by the Royalists. It is a pity that so much damage was done during a crisis which only lasted a few years.

Recent Times

In the post-medieval centuries English castles have suffered a variety of fates. A number of royal strongholds declined to utilitarian functions, such as garrison posts on the frontiers or gaols and court houses in the county towns. Other castles lost their defensive role but remained inhabited. This often entailed sweeping changes to the fabric, particularly if their owners could afford to keep up with changing tastes. Only where there was impoverished occupancy, as at Stokesay, has a castle survived more or less in its original form. The majority of castles, abandoned both as fortifications and residences, were regarded as white elephants and often became convenient sources of building stone for the local populace. Many castles have vanished in this way. Ironically, as genuine castles were being destroyed there emerged a new interest in castellated architecture. Sham castles became fashionable in the eighteenth and nineteenth centuries, both to live in and to have as romantic ruins in landscaped parks.

It is only in the last century that society has begun preserving historic monuments for their own sake. Interest has been growing since the Victorian era and a great deal of progress has been made in the sympathetic restoration of old buildings. For many castles the process of decay has been halted, temporarily at least. Today they are enjoying a new lease of life as tourist attractions. While the public continues to be fascinated with the past they may stand for a long time yet, if we can master the environmental problems which threaten to engulf us.

INTRODUCTION TO THE GAZETTEER

About nine hundred castles and other medieval fortifications are mentioned in this book. More than half are main entries, containing a brief history and description aimed at visitors or just for armchair reference. At the foot of each entry are access details, references and any related sites. References (see bibliography) are omitted for the shortest entries and, exceptionally, where I could find no substantial source. Relations may be historical or typological but they are only cited where a few close comparisons can be made. It is impractical to cross-refer, for example, to all other shell keeps, or all castles built by certain kings.

Accessibility has not been a criterion for inclusion but I have tried to indicate at the end of each entry whether a site is open, and to what extent. I must stress that the information is a guideline only. Complete accuracy is not possible and specific opening times have been avoided because they are so changeable. To keep up to date with times and admission charges consult one of the annual publications: *Historic Houses, Castles and Gardens* or the Automobile Association's *2000 Days Out in Britain*.

The biggest collection of castles is that maintained by English Heritage (**EH** in the text). Membership of this organisation is a must for any serious castle-hunter. Relatively few castles are owned by the National Trust (**NT**). A third category which may be singled out is the diverse group in the care of local authorities (**LA**). Everything else is basically in private hands. I have not attempted to identify the owner, though this class includes major landholders such as the Crown. Most of the really worthwhile castles, whether ruined or still habitable, are open to the public to some extent. Happily the trend is still towards more becoming accessible though there have been some reversals over the years. Opening times can vary tremendously, from all day every day to occasional afternoons in the height of summer. English Heritage properties are generous in this respect: 'standard' opening hours are 10am to 6pm, April to September, and 10am to 4pm, October to March. Many of their properties are closed on certain days in winter and a growing number are only open during the summer season. Even published opening times can be subject to sudden change so it is advisable to check in advance if you are travelling some distance.

Some castles which do not open normally have occasional open days, perhaps to raise money for charity. Others may accept visitors by appointment, whether singly or in groups. I have indicated in the text where I know such arrangements exist but it is worth enquiring if you want to visit a particular castle. A limited view from outside is the most you will get at many of the lesser sites, and even that will not be possible at some. This is inevitable when so many castles are still private homes. There is also a rather sorry group of castle ruins which have not been preserved as ancient monuments and are slowly crumbling away. There are still too many of this kind, even if they are seldom first-rate examples. Often they are mouldering in farmyards or fields and you may need to obtain permission to take a closer look. Lovers of romantic ruins will find such ivy-clad jumbles more appealing, while they last, than those carefully tended English Heritage sites. All the same I hope that more of them will be rescued before it is too late. Meanwhile you enter at your own risk, and beware of falling masonry!

This book is structured alphabetically, but within county order as some sort of regional organisation seemed desirable (Carisbrooke next to Carlisle is not helpful to the prospective visitor!). I preferred to stick to the traditional counties, especially since the reorganised counties of 1974 have a doubtful future. Some adjustments have been made for geographical convenience. Each section ends with an 'other sites' section which is a sort of dumping ground for masonry fragments and unexceptional earthworks; also any vanished strongholds of particular importance.

It is assumed that most visitors nowadays will arrive by car. Indeed, some of the remoter sites would be difficult to visit without one. However, the majority of our castles are located in towns or villages of a reasonable size. It is still possible to get by on public transport but you need to be an organisational genius to plan a tour of several places under such constraints!

Some of the castles in this book can be surprisingly difficult to find. Space has prevented me from giving detailed directions, though Ordnance Survey grid references are supplied in the index. Ruins (particularly the farmyard variety) can be messy places, so dress for muddy paths and rain-soaked fields. Finally I would implore you to follow the country code and respect the privacy of owners.

THE COUNTIES OF ENGLAND AS USED IN THIS VOLUME
based on the traditional counties

The Gazetteer

Bedfordshire

Owing to the loss of Bedford Castle – destroyed as early as 1224 – there are no castles in Bedfordshire with any masonry remains, if we exclude the late medieval brick ruin of Someries. However, the county does preserve some good motte-and-bailey castles, such as Cainhoe and Yelden.

BEDFORD CASTLE Bedford was one of the burghs fortified against the Danes by King Edward the Elder, Alfred the Great's son. It is likely that this county town was saddled with a castle soon after the Norman Conquest, but there is no actual evidence of one until *circa* 1130, when it was held by Payn de Beauchamp. In 1138, when besieged by King Stephen, its strong keep and curtain are mentioned, the implication being that they were already of stone. During the Magna Carta war the castle was seized by Fawkes de Breaute and became the base for that notorious baron's misdeeds against his neighbours. In 1224 he overreached himself by abducting one of the King's justiciars and holding him prisoner here. The young Henry III responded by laying siege to the castle in person, bringing with him a tall siege tower, powerful catapults and a contingent of miners to tunnel beneath the curtain. Each obstacle was successively battered down or undermined, and when the keep fell the garrison had to surrender. Some of them were hanged but De Breaute himself obtained a pardon. The King ordered the total destruction of the castle, as a result of which the walls were demolished and the ditches filled in. Only the oval motte remains, near the bridge across the River Ouse, and even this has been truncated.

> *Access:* Freely accessible (LA).
> *Reference:* VCH *Bedfordshire* (III). *The Siege of Bedford Castle* by M. Greenshields.
> *Relations:* For notable sieges of the thirteenth century see Dover, Rochester and Kenilworth.

CAINHOE CASTLE In a field just to the south-east of Clophill are the earthworks of a castle probably raised by Nigel d'Albini, who is recorded as the tenant in the Domesday Book. A motte dominates the site and there are three baileys defined by well-preserved ramparts and ditches. Though never rebuilt in stone it remained occupied until the Black Death, which wiped out the inhabitants of the castle and the village which lay alongside.

> *Access:* Freely accessible.

SOMERIES CASTLE stands two miles out of Luton, approached by a minor road off the road to Wheathampstead. The ruin is the earliest brick building in a county which later became a major producer of bricks. Its builder was probably John, Lord Wenlock, who fell – struck down in a squabble with a fellow Lancastrian – at the Battle of Tewkesbury in 1471. The mansion followed a quadrangular plan but only the range containing the gatehouse and chapel now stands, the rest having been pulled down in 1742. Despite its polygonal flanking turrets the gatehouse has no pretensions as a defensive structure. The large and small gateways were for the convenience of horse and foot traffic at the expense of security. Someries is thus a castle in name only, though there is a tradition of a tower house.

Access: Freely accessible (LA).
Reference: VCH *Bedfordshire* (II).

TOTTERNHOE CASTLE   overlooks the village from a chalk spur of the Chiltern Hills, two miles west of Dunstable. Its motte and two baileys are strongly situated – one side has no artificial defences because the ground drops away so steeply. The castle's Norman origin has been confirmed by excavation but its history is quite obscure. It is probably an adulterine castle of the Anarchy.

Access: Freely accessible.

YELDEN CASTLE,   by the River Til three miles east of Rushden, features an impressive motte between two baileys. Built by the De Trailly family, the castle is first mentioned in 1174 during Prince Henry's revolt. It was in ruins by 1361. Excavations have uncovered a thirteenth-century stone curtain with a circular corner tower, and another round tower curiously rising out of the ditch, but no masonry is visible on the site now.

Access: Visible from the road.

OTHER SITES   The motte-and-bailey castles at *Meppershall* and *Podington* are accompanied by remains of village enclosures – evidence of planned Norman boroughs which failed to thrive. Other mottes may be seen at *Risinghoe* (near Bedford), *Thurleigh* and *Toddington* (Conger Hill). There is an extensive site of several baileys from a Norman castle of the Beauchamps at *Eaton Socon. Bletsoe Castle* is an Elizabethan house on the site of a castle licensed in 1327. The site of *Ampthill Castle* is marked by a cross in Ampthill Park. It was a fifteenth-century quadrangular stronghold, built by Sir John Cornwall and occupied by Catherine of Aragon after her breach with Henry VIII.

Berkshire

Windsor overshadows everything else in the county. Wallingford Castle, another royal stronghold on the Thames, was nearly as important in its heyday, but it endured a battering in the Civil War and is now reduced to earthworks. The town of Wallingford is notable for its Anglo-Saxon rampart. The only baronial castle of any substance is Donnington, which is chiefly remembered for its Civil War siege.

DONNINGTON CASTLE crowns a hill above the River Lambourne, a mile north of Newbury. Sir Richard Abberbury, the queen's chamberlain, obtained a licence to crenellate this place in 1386. In 1415 the castle was purchased by Thomas Chaucer, son of the poet, and through him it passed to the De la Pole dukes of Suffolk. Donnington is notable for its stirring role in the Civil War. After the first Battle of Newbury Charles I entrusted the castle to Colonel (later Sir) John Boys. The Roundheads laid siege in July 1644 but were unable to take it in spite of a fierce artillery bombardment. The King marched to the relief of the castle and the second Battle of Newbury was fought around it in October. This did not achieve the desired result and the Royalist army had to withdraw, but Sir John still resisted the ultimatum delivered to him by Sir William Waller. Defence continued in appalling conditions for the next eighteen months. It was only when all hope of relief had finally vanished (in April 1646) that the garrison accepted honourable terms for surrender. They were permitted to march to Wallingford to join the Royalists still holding out there.

It must be said that the old walls could not have sustained such a pounding on their own. Donnington was a comparatively modest stronghold and certainly not designed to withstand powerful artillery. In preparation for the siege Sir John Boys constructed a series of earthworks on the slopes around the castle. These, with their projecting bastions, are rare survivals of Civil War fortification. The castle followed a quadrangular layout except that the rear bowed outwards in short, straight sections. There were round corner towers and two intermediate square towers on the longer sides. Owing to the siege or subsequent slighting only the footings of the curtain and its towers remain, but the handsome gatehouse has come down to us virtually intact, lacking only its roof and floors. The outer angles are clasped by boldly projecting, cylindrical towers which rise considerably higher than the main body of the gatehouse. A large brick patch in one of them fills a gaping hole made during the siege. The gate passage is crowned by an elaborate vault, and in front of the entrance are the side walls of a barbican.

Access: Freely accessible (EH).
Reference: Guidebook by M. Wood.
Relations: For the De la Poles see Wingfield Castle. Compare Henry Yevele's gatehouse at Saltwood.

WALLINGFORD CASTLE AND TOWN DEFENCES The historic little town of Wallingford lies within an earth rampart first thrown up in the reign of Alfred the Great or Edward the Elder, as a precaution against Danish attack. Many towns were fortified during the great fight back against the Danes but this is one of the few places where Anglo-Saxon town defences can still be seen. Wallingford was once believed to be a Roman town because the rampart encloses a rectangular area and the streets follow a grid pattern. It shows that the Saxon planners were not ignorant of Roman models. The town, commanding an important crossing over the Thames, was one of the largest of the Saxon burghs. The rampart can still be followed on the three landward sides but, as at Wareham, there is no evidence of any man-made defences facing the river. In the Norman period the rampart was heightened, but the town then fell into economic decline so the timber stockades which lined the summit were never replaced in stone.

The north-east quarter of the town enclosure became the site of Wallingford Castle. William the Conqueror crossed the Thames here in 1066, during his march on London, and he may have founded the castle in passing. It certainly existed by 1071. This important royal fortress fell into the Empress Matilda's hands during the Anarchy and resisted King Stephen in three great sieges. The platform of a siege fort from this time can be seen across the river. The castle showed its strength again in the Civil War. It resisted the might of Parliament until July 1646 – virtually the end of the war – and even then surrendered honourably. Six years later it was destroyed as a potentially dangerous stronghold. The earthworks, comprising a large motte between two baileys, are still quite impressive but almost all the masonry has disappeared. A number of English kings contributed to the defences, notably Henry II and John, resulting in an impressive castle with a shell keep on the motte and two towered curtains. A section of the outer rampart has been turned into a public garden and this carries an excavated length of wall and one round tower. The inner bailey is now occupied by Castle House.

> *Access:* The town rampart is freely accessible (LA). Most of the castle lies on private
> land, though visible from the public section.
> *Reference:* VCH *Berkshire* (III). *HKW* (II).
> *Relations:* The Saxon rampart at Wareham. William I's Thames-side castles at Wind-
> sor, Oxford and the Tower of London.

WINDSOR CASTLE is one of England's largest, containing thirteen acres within its walls. It has enjoyed favour as a royal residence from Norman times to the present, and is the only royal castle to have made the transition to palace. Most monarchs have contributed in some way to its splendour and every century except the eighteenth has left its mark on the fabric. The result is a magnificent but extremely mutilated stronghold. In particular, George IV and his ambitious architect, Sir Jeffry Wyatville, beautified the castle at the expense of its historic architecture. Their refacing of the outer walls and towers has concealed the original masonry beneath a smooth veneer that gives the whole castle the appearance of a sham. Nevertheless in general outline the castle remains the creation of medieval kings, and a vast amount has survived the whims of fashion.

The castle owes its position to William the Conqueror. He chose the elevated site on a chalk cliff above the Thames in 1067 and his earthworks have since dictated the layout of the castle. Although raised on the grand scale Windsor is a typical motte-and-bailey fortress, with two baileys or wards of roughly equal size on either side of a motte fifty feet high. Henry II began a stone palace in the upper ward in 1165, and followed this with a reconstruction of the defences in 1173–79. The 'Round Tower' on top of the motte is basically his shell keep, and the upper ward is surrounded by his towered curtain. The walling of the lower ward resumed at a slower pace, and was still incomplete when the castle withstood a three-month siege from the Dauphin Louis' supporters in 1216. Windsor and Dover were the only castles strong enough to resist them. The striking west front of the castle facing Thames Street takes us into the 1220s and Henry III's reign.

To appreciate the medieval castle it is best to start off by examining this west front, with its three D-shaped towers (named Curfew, Salisbury and Garter). Curfew Tower, on the left, is particularly impressive, though its picturesque roof is a Victorian addition by Salvin. The side facing Castle Hill has been altered too much to appreciate. Henry VIII rebuilt the gatehouse leading into the lower ward in 1510 but it deliberately adheres to a medieval style, having polygonal flanking towers and a row of genuine machicolations over the gateway. The heavily restored Henry III and Edward III towers (both thirteenth century) rise at the foot of the motte. Wyatville reinforced the Round Tower to support the phoney machicolated crown which dominates the castle. Without it, the keep would only rise as high as the pilaster buttresses. Home Park is not open to visitors so you cannot get a close view of the upper ward curtain, and it has been altered beyond recognition in any case, but it is interesting for its Norman flanking towers. Only five now remain (the York, Augusta, Clarence, Chester and Prince of Wales towers) intermixed with other towers by Wyatville. Mural towers were by no means a new invention, but Windsor's are spaced closely enough to methodically flank the curtain. These simple, square-fronted towers may be compared with the round towers flanking Windsor's west front to appreciate the progress of fifty years.

The lower ward has become a sort of close around St George's Chapel. The chapel is actually a cruciform church, one of the greatest achievements of Perpendicular Gothic and by far the largest ecclesiastical building to be found within a castle. Commenced in 1472 by Edward IV to celebrate his return from temporary exile, it was completed by Henry VIII in 1528 following a pause in Henry VII's reign. The chapel became a royal mausoleum second only to Westminster Abbey, and its treasures are far too numerous to describe here. It is an apt setting for the ceremonies of the Order of the Garter, that fantasy creation of Edward III for the chivalry of Christendom. Edward aspired to recreate the Round Table under a new guise, with Windsor as his Camelot. In 1348 he established a college of secular canons to perform the services, which were originally held in a smaller chapel to the east, now embodied in the Albert Memorial Chapel. Two cloisters lie to the north of it. The wooden Horseshoe Cloister was added in 1478 in front of St George's Chapel. As there is no bell tower the nearby Curfew Tower was adapted for this purpose, and the massive bell frame is an unexpected feature of the tower's interior.

The route towards the upper ward passes the Winchester Tower overlooking the river, occupied by Geoffrey Chaucer when he was Clerk of Works here. At the foot of the motte is the so-called Norman Gate which leads from the lower ward into the upper. This gatehouse has the veneer of newness characteristic of all the castle's defences, but the vault of the gate passage, the portcullis (a rare survivor) and one of the twin flanking towers go back to Edward III's reign (1359). The keep contains some over-restored timber-framed buildings around a central courtyard, but the principal buildings of the royal palace have always occupied the north side of the upper ward, where the terrain afforded some natural protection from attack. Henry II's palace was built around two oblong courtyards, later roofed over to form the Grand Staircase and the Waterloo Chamber. Wyatville created the immense St George's Hall by combining the great hall and private chapel. Medieval undercrofts still underlie some of the state apartments but the transformation above has been complete. The magnificent rooms at the west end are very much as Charles II left them, but Wyatville must take the credit – or blame, if you prefer – for the remainder. He turned the upper ward into a unified quadrangle, and although his work has been much maligned it is a tragedy that so much of it was gutted in the terrible fire of 1992. Note that the private royal apartments on the other two sides of the ward, linked by Wyatville's Grand Corridor, originated in Edward III's time as accommodation for the vast retinue which accompanied royal visits to Windsor. Although there is not a great deal left to show for it, Edward spent £50,000 – a vast sum in those days – on improvements to his birthplace.

> *Access:* The lower ward and St George's Chapel are open daily. Curfew Tower can be visited at certain times. The state apartments are closed pending restoration.
>
> *Reference: The Architectural History of Windsor Castle* by W. St John Hope. VCH *Berkshire* (III). *HKW* (II). Souvenir guides.
>
> *Relations:* Dover and the Tower of London were the other principal royal castles. For late Norman castles with square flanking towers see Dover and Framlingham. Oxford, Hastings and Leicester are other castles with collegiate chapels.

OTHER SITES *Hamstead Marshall,* once held by the earls Marshal, preserves a motte-and-bailey site near the parish church and two more Norman earthworks – possibly siege forts – close by. Another motte-and-bailey can be seen at *Hinton Waldrist. Brightwell's* motte was apparently raised as an outpost to Wallingford Castle during the Anarchy.

Buckinghamshire

Buckinghamshire, like a few other East Midland counties, was never a good place for castles. There are several long-abandoned Norman earthworks, notably Castlethorpe, but Boarstall is the only stone structure. Even here only the gatehouse has survived in an altered state.

BOARSTALL TOWER, between Thame and Bicester, is the gatehouse of a castle which has otherwise disappeared. Sir John de Handlo, Sheriff of Oxfordshire, obtained a licence to crenellate in 1312. However, the appearance of the gatehouse suggests a date about a century later when the manor was held by the Rede family. The gatehouse is an oblong block, with a central gate passage and hexagonal towers at the four corners. The outer towers are pierced by cross-slits while the more slender turrets at the rear contain spiral stairs. A large chamber occupies the top floor. Boarstall followed the quadrangular plan but everything else was swept away in the eighteenth century. The castle withstood two Roundhead assaults in 1645 and only succumbed in June 1646 after a two-month siege. Perhaps as a result of damage sustained, the gatehouse was given a considerable facelift shortly afterwards. The alterations include the bay window above the outer archway and a balustrade in place of the parapet. An eighteenth-century bridge crosses the surviving portion of wet moat.

    Access: Exterior visible. Interior by appointment only (NT).
    Reference: Guidebook by S. Hall. VCH *Buckinghamshire* (IV).
    Relations: Late castle gatehouses such as Bickleigh and Dunster.

BOLEBEC CASTLE is a motte-and-bailey site overlooking the village of Whitchurch. It takes its name from Hugh de Bolebec, whose illegal castle building attracted criticism from the Pope in 1147. Despite its adulterine origin the castle survived Henry II's accession, passing to the De Vere earls of Oxford. They rebuilt it in stone, but the castle was destroyed by Parliament after the Civil War and all traces of masonry have vanished.

    Access: Freely accessible.
    Relations: For the De Veres see Hedingham.

CASTLETHORPE This impressive earthwork by the River Tove has passed its name on to the village (it is sometimes referred to as Hanslope Castle). A deep ditch marks the original bailey but the motte appears to have been left unfinished. The parish church (part Norman) stood within the enclosure and no doubt doubled up as the castle chapel. King John destroyed the castle to punish Robert Mauduit, one of the Magna Carta barons, but it rose again in 1292 when William de Beauchamp obtained a licence to crenellate. He created a new bailey to the west, bounded by a straight rampart with a broad ditch in front.

    Access: Freely accessible.

OTHER SITES Motte-and-baileys exist at *Cublington*, *Wing* and *Weston Turville*, the latter beside the manor house. A motte at *High Wycombe* (in the grounds of Castle Hill House) is crowned by an eighteenth-century folly. *Lavendon* preserves the earthworks of three baileys but has lost its motte. *Buckingham Castle* was founded early enough to receive Hereward the Wake as a prisoner (1071), but its motte was flattened in 1771 to make way for the parish church.

Cambridgeshire and Huntingdonshire

Cambridge Castle, as rebuilt by Edward I, would have been a worthy sight if it had survived, but Cambridgeshire is another East Midland county which has lost the few stone castles it once possessed. Only Norman earthworks remain. The same would be true of Huntingdonshire were it not for two surprisingly late fortified mansions from the Yorkist era: Buckden Palace and Elton Hall. For the Soke of Peterborough see Northamptonshire.

BOURN HALL, overlooking Ermine Street (A14), is a late Elizabethan mansion standing within the rampart of a Norman ringwork. The ringwork already existed at the time of the Domesday Book, which records that Picot, Sheriff of Cambridgeshire, granted the chapel in his castle to the forerunner of Barnwell Priory. Henry III destroyed the castle during the Barons' Wars of 1264–66.

Access: Now a private clinic.

BUCKDEN PALACE was a residence of the medieval bishops of Lincoln, allowing a midway break on the journey from London to their cathedral city. This episcopal palace was entirely rebuilt in brick by Thomas Rotherham, who became bishop in 1472. After his transfer to York in 1480 it was completed by Bishop Russell. The dominant feature is a tower house modelled on the great brick tower at Tattershall Castle. Buckden's tower house is oblong in plan with octagonal corner turrets rising above parapet level. However, it is less ambitious in scale and lacks the machicolated crown which gives Tattershall such distinction. The broad chimney-breast is a prominent and altogether domestic feature. Another obvious weakness is the tower's proximity to the steeple of the parish church. They are separated only by the width of the former moat. This is typical of the castellated mansions of the later Middle Ages and shows that the builder was more interested in status than defence, though such towers must have had some value as a refuge in the event of local danger. Catherine of Aragon was detained here for a while following her divorce from Henry VIII.

The tower house could serve as a self-contained residence but the palace buildings were far more extensive. The inner courtyard contained a lavish suite of residential buildings and it is a pity they have all vanished. It is unusual to find a courtyard of this era which is not quadrangular, so the layout was probably dictated by an older moated enclosure. As well as the tower house, the inner courtyard preserves its

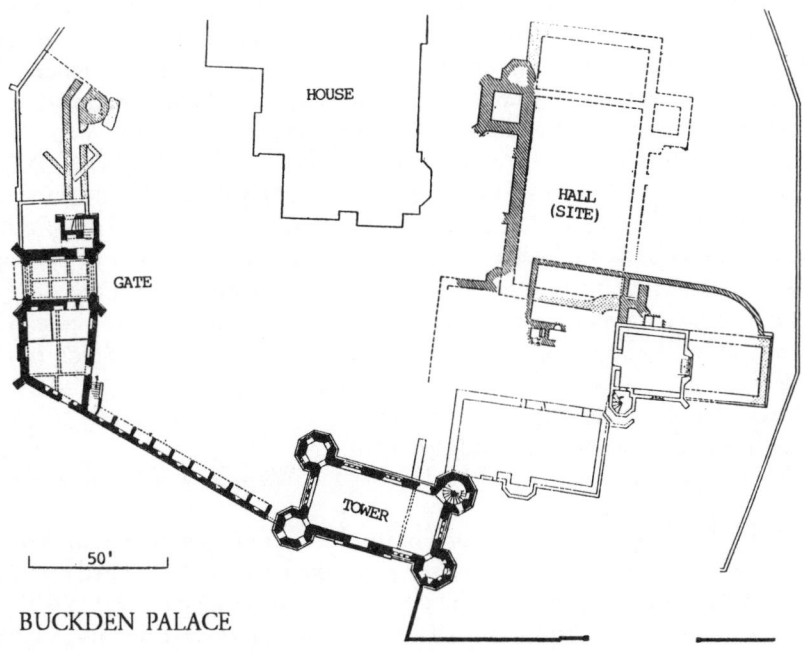

HOUSE

HALL
(SITE)

GATE

TOWER

50'

BUCKDEN PALACE

diapered gate tower, with a range of ancillary buildings attached and the length of wall connecting the gatehouse to the tower house. The wall is pierced by arrow-slits but is too thin for a genuine curtain – the wall-walk is carried on a row of arches. The courtyard was surrounded by a large outer enclosure subdivided into several areas. There was an outer courtyard for retainers, an orchard, a park, and the churchyard too forms part of the ensemble. Much of the precinct wall survives, as well as an outer gate giving access from the High Street. Buckden remained episcopal property until 1837. The religious link has been re-established because it is now occupied by a modern religious order, the Claretian Missionaries.

Access: Grounds open regularly.
Reference: VCH *Huntingdonshire* (II). RCHM *Huntingdonshire*.
Relations: Tattershall. Newark was another castle of the bishops of Lincoln.

BURWELL CASTLE West of the splendid parish church is a small, rectangular earthwork bounded by a wide ditch. It is not a typical Norman earthwork by any means and was one of a group of strongpoints raised by King Stephen in 1143 to contain the revolt of Geoffrey de Mandeville, Earl of Essex. It was probably this castle which Geoffrey besieged the following year, only to be struck dead by an arrow. It seems that the castle was garrisoned more permanently because excavations have uncovered a stone gate tower (not visible). The site was later held by Ramsey Abbey.

Access: Freely accessible.
Relations: Compare Lidgate.

CAMBRIDGE CASTLE Cambridge originated as a Roman town on the west bank of the River Cam. A Saxon burgh flourished within the Roman defences, but William the Conqueror established his castle on the site in 1068 and the townsfolk migrated to the other side of the river. In 1284–99 Edward I completely rebuilt the castle to a square plan, with round corner towers and an oblong gatehouse. The Norman motte was retained and one of the corner towers – in effect a keep – was placed on top. It would have offered an interesting comparison with Edward's Welsh castles, but not a stone remains. Cambridge remained a royal castle but degenerated into a court house and gaol, the defences being robbed to provide material for the town and colleges. In 1643 the staunchly Parliamentarian town threw artillery-proof earthworks around the castle in preparation for a Royalist attack which never came. The last ruins were swept away in 1842. Today the only remains are the high motte beside the Shire Hall, commanding a fine view over the city, and a section of the Civil War rampart.

> *Access:* Freely accessible (LA).
> *Reference:* VCH *Cambridgeshire* (III). *HKW* (II).
> *Relations:* William I's motte castles at Huntingdon, Warwick, Windsor and York.

ELTON HALL, the rambling mansion of the Proby family, has been transformed by a series of reconstructions. However, the gatehouse is part of the original mansion built by Sir Richard Sapcote about the year 1477. It is rectangular with a shallow projection in the middle, resulting in a T-shaped structure which contains a vaulted gate passage. The gatehouse is surmounted by a machicolated parapet which goes all the way round, even following the pitch of the gentle gables which crown the three ends of the 'T'. This elaboration is quite rare in England, where machicolations were generally used sparingly. Paradoxically their appearance in such force suggests a building in which display was more important than defence, but this is only to be expected in the late fifteenth century. Presumably the original mansion was quadrangular but the only other fifteenth-century work is the chapel undercroft in the range alongside the gatehouse.

> *Access:* Limited opening times in summer.
> *Reference:* VCH *Huntingdonshire* (IV). RCHM *Huntingdonshire*.
> *Relations:* Machicolated gatehouses at Lancaster and Hylton.

ELY CASTLE lies in the park to the south of the cathedral. William the Conqueror established some kind of fortification here after driving Hereward the Wake from the Isle of Ely. Whether the existing motte and bailey date from that time is uncertain, because Nigel, Bishop of Ely, raised a new castle here during the Anarchy. It was soon abandoned – perhaps at Henry II's instigation. The cathedral monks later utilised the large motte, known as Cherry Hill, to carry a windmill.

> *Access:* Freely accessible.

HUNTINGDON CASTLE William the Conqueror founded a castle in this Saxon burgh in 1068. It guarded the bridge across the River Ouse. The motte-and-bailey earthworks are still clear enough, though the motte has been truncated and the bailey is cut into by a disused railway line. The castle belonged to the kings of

Scotland who held the earldom of Huntingdon. In 1174 William the Lion invaded England in support of Prince Henry's revolt. He was captured at Alnwick, and Huntingdon Castle was besieged and destroyed by Henry II's forces. It never rose again. A mound on Mill Common may be a siege fort from that episode.

Access: Freely accessible (LA).

OTHER SITES *Ramsey Abbey* suffered during the Anarchy, because Geoffrey de Mandeville turfed out the monks and fortified the site in spite of the abbot's attempts at sabotage. The ringwork at *Wood Walton* was another of De Mandeville's castles, while the square mound at *Rampton* may represent one of the castles raised by King Stephen to check his revolt (see Burwell). The large, ditched enclosure at *Castle Camps* marks the site of a De Vere stronghold. *Wisbech Castle*, founded by William the Conqueror, became a seat of the bishops of Ely, but the castle and the seventeenth-century mansion which replaced it have been destroyed. The present *Kimbolton Castle*, one of Vanbrugh's masterpieces, stands near the site of an older stronghold.

Cheshire

Medieval Cheshire was a palatine county. Its Norman earls enjoyed regal powers in return for a free hand against the Welsh, though their attempts at conquest met with stern resistance. From 1237 the earldom was vested in the person of the King or his heir, so its autonomy ceased in practice. Unlike the other Welsh Border counties Cheshire is not rich in castles. The earls prevented it from becoming a free-for-all like the Marcher lordships. The one significant monument is Beeston Castle on its mighty rock. Not much of Chester Castle has survived. Chester's city wall is one of the most complete in England though it has suffered considerably from restoration.

ALDFORD CASTLE commanded a crossing of the River Dee. It is one of a group of earthworks marking the early frontier between the Norman palatinate and the Welsh principalities. The castle was founded by a sub-tenant of the Earl of Chester whose descendants adopted the name of De Aldford. It comprises a flat-topped motte and a bailey surrounded by a wide rampart. Remains of a shell keep have been found on the motte but no masonry is visible now.

Access: Visible from the churchyard.

BEESTON CASTLE was begun by Ranulf de Blundeville, the most powerful of the palatine earls of Chester, in 1225. Prompted by the King's growing mistrust, he built several strong castles to protect his territories. It is possible that Beeston was intended as an impressive new seat of administration away from the mercantile bustle of Chester. As an experienced soldier and crusader Ranulf clearly appreciated castles built in the new idiom – i.e. round flanking towers and no keep – and the great rock of Beeston provided a wonderful situation for one. He died in 1232 leaving the castle unfinished. Henry III used Beeston as a base in his wars with the two Llywelyns, but it was left to Edward I to complete the defences in 1303. After that the story is one of slow decay, enlivened by its only military activity during the Civil War. Initially occupied by the Roundheads, the castle was seized by a band of Royalists who allegedly scaled the cliff. However, as the tide of the war turned the garrison found itself under siege, and was forced to surrender in November 1645 after a year-long bombardment. The slighting which followed reduced the castle to its present ruinous state.

An Iron Age fort occupied this site, two miles south of Tarporley, but Beeston is a product of the time when castle building was approaching its zenith. It occupies a huge sandstone hill rising dramatically out of the Cheshire plain. The castle does not have a keep as such but its compact inner bailey occupies the highest corner of the rock, so the Norman motte-and-bailey concept had not been entirely forsaken. The outer bailey follows the contours of the hill and is large enough to have accommodated a vast retinue. A nineteenth-century gatehouse forms the entrance to the site, and some ascent is necessary before the real outer gatehouse is reached. More than half of the outer curtain has disappeared but the long section on the east side of the hill has seven towers, spaced closely together to provide effective flanking fire. These towers are the semi-circular, open-backed variety often found on town walls at this period.

A long ascent through the outer bailey takes us to the summit. The inner bailey is cut off by a rock-cut ditch of exceptional width and depth, now spanned by a modern bridge. A squat gatehouse, perhaps the earliest in England to be equipped with round-fronted flanking towers, guards the entrance. The gatehouse is tolerably preserved but the curtain, with its three D-shaped towers fronting the ditch, is badly ruined. The wall to the rear of the courtyard is thin and tower-less, because the hill terminates abruptly here in a cliff dropping to the plain. The site commands magnificent views – note Peckforton Castle on a neighbouring hill. The well near the gatehouse descends through the rock to a depth of nearly four hundred feet.

Access: Standard opening times (EH).

Reference: Guidebook by J. Weaver.

Relations: Chester was the chief castle of the earls. For other castles of Ranulf de Blundeville see Bolingbroke and Chartley.

CHESTER CASTLE AND CITY WALL   Chester originated as the Roman legionary fortress of *Deva*. Stone defences first rose around AD 100 and for the next three centuries it housed the Twentieth Legion. When the Roman occupation came to an end the site appears to have been deserted, but the Danes took refuge one winter behind the old walls and withstood a Saxon attempt to dislodge them. This prompted Ethelred, Earl of Mercia, to establish a burgh here on the Wessex pattern in 907. It put up a rare resistance to William the Conqueror but fell in 1070. The present city wall is largely of the thirteenth century, a period when most English towns rebuilt their defences. There was a particular need here because of the threat from the Welsh, united under Llywelyn the Great and Llywelyn the Last. It is likely that the rebuilding was at least begun in the time of the palatine earls. The first murage grant was made in 1249, after Chester had defaulted to the Crown. Building continued beyond 1300 but Chester lost its strategic importance after the Edwardian conquest of Wales. The silting up of the River Dee exacerbated its economic decline. In the Civil War Chester held out staunchly for the King and was besieged, on and off, for nearly three years. Earthen redoubts were constructed beyond the old defences and these kept the Parliamentary army at bay initially. After the defeat of a Royalist relieving force at Rowton Heath, however, the Roundheads under Sir William Brereton got closer and inflicted a heavy bombardment. Resistance continued nevertheless, breaches were hurriedly patched up and it was starvation which forced the city to surrender in February 1646.

Underlying the medieval defences are the remains of the legionary fortress. This had the usual rectangular plan of Roman forts, with rounded corners and a gate on each side. The city wall follows the Roman alignment on the north and east, i.e. between St Martin's Gate and Newgate, but little Roman work is actually visible. The medieval city expanded beyond the Roman line to the south and west, and the wall here follows the course of the river as it was in the thirteenth century. Near Newgate can be seen the foundations of the Roman angle tower where the two walls parted company.

The city wall is virtually intact and a walk around the two-mile circuit is one of Chester's great attractions, though it should be pointed out that this is only possible thanks to considerable restoration. Following the Civil War the defences were slighted, but in the eighteenth century the wall became an object of curiosity and a popular promenade. Consequently, at a time when most towns were pulling down the defensive girdles which confined them, in Chester the trend was reversed. The citizens restored the parapet walk and rebuilt the gaps made in the Civil War. This spirit of preservation did not extend to the four main gatehouses, which were pulled down for the convenience of traffic and replaced by wide arches to preserve the continuity of the wall-walk. The only medieval gates are two small posterns on the east side, one beside Newgate and the other leading into the cathedral precinct. Furthermore, less than half of the old flanking towers survive, and most of the remaining ones have been interfered with. About thirty towers once existed, most of them semi-circular and spaced unevenly along the north and east walls. No towers guarded the south and west sides, and the wall is lower here because of the protection once afforded by the river.

King Charles' Tower, at the north-east corner, is the best of the mural towers. From here Charles I watched the Battle of Rowton Heath. However, an even more impressive tower is the cylindrical Water Tower, added in 1322–26 at the end of an embattled spur wall which projects from the north-west corner of the circuit. The tower, seventy-five feet high, originally rose from the waters of the Dee and controlled access to the quay, but the river has since receded leaving the big loop known as the Roodee between it and the western city wall. Generally speaking, the wall is at its most impressive on the north side, between King Charles' Tower and the Water Tower. The moat survives here, utilised as a canal, and enough flanking towers are left to convey an impression of strength. Furthermore the only substantial Roman masonry (a fourth-century reconstruction) is to be found between King Charles' Tower and the North Gate.

Chester Castle occupies a knoll overlooking the river at the south end of the walled city. Before the defences were extended it stood outside their circuit. William the Conqueror founded the castle after the city had fallen, but he soon made Hugh d'Avranches Earl of Chester and granted the castle to him. It was the principal seat of the palatine earls. After passing to the Crown in 1237 the defences were brought up to date – Ranulf de Blundeville having neglected Chester Castle in favour of Beeston – but in the later Middle Ages it fulfilled the usual urban functions of court house and gaol. The remains were quite substantial until 1793, when they were largely swept away to make room for the present assize buildings. An eighteenth-century plan shows no keep but two walled baileys. Small, internally-projecting towers stood along the inner curtain. The surviving one is known as the Agricola Tower after the Roman governor. Originally it was a gate tower, as the blocked archway shows, but it was later superseded by a new gatehouse (vanished) alongside. The tower is perhaps an early work of Ranulf de Blundeville. Its upper floor contains a vaulted chapel in Norman Transitional style, adorned with the remains of newly-discovered frescoes. A length of much-restored inner curtain also survives, together with Henry III's half-round Flag Tower.

>*Access:* The city wall parapet is freely accessible (LA). There is a Civil War exhibition in King Charles' Tower. The Agricola Tower is sometimes open (EH).
>
>*Reference:* BOE *Cheshire. HKW* (II) for the castle.
>
>*Relations:* Beeston. York also originated as a legionary fortress. Chichester has a similar city wall.

DODDINGTON CASTLE stands in the park of Doddington Hall, the eight-eenth-century mansion of Sir Thomas Broughton. It is an example of an antiquity preserved as a landscape feature. The castle is a free-standing tower house, quite intact, with a vaulted ground floor and corner turrets which rise higher than the rest. The entrance is at first-floor level (rare for a later medieval tower house), now reached by a Jacobean staircase. Licences to crenellate were granted to Sir John Delves in 1365 and a descendant of the same name in 1403. Either date would fit. The elder John distinguished himself at the Battle of Poitiers as one of Lord Audley's squires, so the tower may have been built with his share of the booty. Doddington lies five miles south-east of Nantwich.

>*Access:* In school grounds.
>
>*Reference:* BOE *Cheshire.*

HALTON CASTLE occupies the summit of a rocky hill. The setting is reminiscent of Beeston, though the view – over Runcorn and the Mersey estuary – is tainted by industry. The castle may have been founded by Nigel de Halton, a tenant of the first Earl of Chester, but the existing ruins belong to a rebuilding by Henry de Lacy, Earl of Lincoln. Henry died without an heir in 1311 – his only son drowned in the well at Denbigh Castle – and the extensive De Lacy estates passed to Thomas, Earl of Lancaster. Since then Halton has been a dependency of the Duchy of Lancaster. The castle's two baileys were surrounded by towered curtains. However, destruction by order of Parliament after the Civil War has left the castle in a fragmentary state. Most of the enclosure wall is relatively modern but it incorporates a genuine piece of curtain pierced by two cross-slits. It is flanked by a square flanking tower pierced by a later Perpendicular window, and another fragment of curtain nearby preserves an ornate window. The castle was plundered for stone in the eighteenth century to build the court house (now a pub) which occupies the site of the gatehouse. The 'ruin' beside it is a contemporary eye-catcher built to improve the view from Norton Priory.

Access: Exterior only.
Reference: Mackenzie (II).
Relations: Beeston. For the De Lacys see Longtown, Clitheroe and Pontefract.

OTHER SITES Norman frontier strongholds at *Dodleston, Malpas, Pulford* and *Shocklach* have been reduced to grassy mottes. The earls of Chester had a castle at *Frodsham*, its stones utilised in the house called Castle Park. *Shotwick Castle* was another Ranulf de Blundeville stronghold, with a hexagonal layout resembling his castle at Bolingbroke (Lincolnshire). It overlooked the marshes of the Dee estuary but nothing is left. *Brimstage Hall* incorporates a truncated pele tower. *Peckforton Castle*, though built only in 1844 by Anthony Salvin, deserves a mention as an unusually good Victorian reproduction of a medieval castle.

Cornwall

Cornwall was already accustomed to foreign domination – by the English – before the Norman Conquest. Norman penetration was slow and the Cornish castles mentioned in the Domesday Book are both near the Devon border. They are Launceston and Trematon, typical motte-and-bailey strongholds with shell keeps on top. Restormel Castle is a circular enclosure backed by residential buildings, while Tintagel takes the prize for spectacular setting and romantic associations. These four ended up as castles of the Duchy of Cornwall. There is a curious shortage of later medieval castles, but the vulnerability of the coastline led to a new spate of fortifications in Tudor times. The defences around Fowey are interesting as a rare example of local initiative, while Pendennis and St Mawes are two splendid coastal forts from the chain erected by Henry VIII.

CARN BREA CASTLE Carn Brea is a stark granite hill rising a mile south-west of Redruth (not to be confused with the hill of the same name near Land's End). Around the summit is the rampart of an Iron Age hillfort, and the castle lies on a rocky outcrop at one end. The castle is just a restored square tower, in essence a Cornish pele tower. Its date is indeterminable, but it is first mentioned as a possession of the Bassett family in the late fifteenth century.

Access: Now a restaurant.

FOWEY BLOCKHOUSES   Now an idyllic harbour town, Fowey was once a port of some consequence and its seafarers were perhaps the most notorious on either side of the Channel. The 'Fowey Gallants' regarded piracy as a legitimate form of enterprise and took advantage of the Hundred Years War to indulge in raids on Britanny. In 1457 the Bretons took revenge and sacked the town. It was probably this event which prompted the inhabitants to defend the approach to their harbour up the estuary of the River Fowey. At the narrowest point they erected twin square towers for defence by cannon, connected by a boom chain which could be raised to prevent the passage of enemy vessels. The tower called Fowey Castle stands beneath the cliffs on the west or townward side, but half of it has collapsed. A better idea can be obtained by taking the ferry to its twin at Polruan (see below). They are interesting as early examples of artillery defence, built publicly rather than privately. The end of war with France did nothing to change conditions here and Fowey ignored a royal command to stop raiding. During Henry VIII's reign the town erected a more advanced blockhouse in an elevated position a little further south. Known as St Catherine's Castle, it is a U-shaped tower with two rows of large gun ports in the curved wall facing the sea.

> *Access:* Fowey Castle is visible from outside. St Catherine's Castle is freely accessible (EH).
> *Relations:* Polruan. The early artillery fortifications at Dartmouth, Kingswear and Portsmouth.

LAUNCESTON CASTLE AND TOWN WALL   The keep of Launceston Castle dominates the town and surrounding countryside. Most Saxon burghs had castles forced upon them within a few years of the Norman Conquest, and the castle of 'Dunhevet' is recorded in the Domesday Book. At that time it was held by William the Conqueror's half-brother Robert, Count of Mortain, who had been created Earl of Cornwall in return for his support. So it is likely that he is the founder, unless he inherited a castle already raised by William. Its elevated situation above the River Kensey, controlling the main route into Cornwall, gave it an early strategic importance. The castle is a powerful motte-and-bailey, the motte (built up from a natural mound) being positioned to overlook and overawe the town.

Initially the castle passed through a variety of hands, and the only Norman masonry is the shell keep on the motte. In 1227 Henry III granted the Earldom of Cornwall to his brother Richard, and he must have been responsible for most of the existing masonry. Richard was elected 'King of the Romans', making him heir presumptive to the Holy Roman Empire, but he died in 1272 without attaining this dignity. His son Edmund transferred the administration of the earldom to Lostwithiel, and Launceston fell into decline. The castle fell into the common rut of being used as a court house and gaol for the duchy, and the defences decayed. By the end of the Civil War, during which it changed hands several times, it was a total ruin.

Earl Richard built a stone wall on top of the bailey rampart, but only the lower courses survive. It was a curiously plain curtain for the thirteenth century, without towers except for the drums flanking the southern gatehouse. The latter are still quite impressive and the simple gate tower at the far end of the bailey has also survived destruction. Otherwise it is the keep which commands our attention. The only approach is via the stretch of curtain ascending the side of the motte, controlled at its foot by a ruinous tower. Launceston's unique 'triple crown' keep is the result of three phases: A stone revetment around the upper part of the motte; the late Norman shell keep on top; and Richard of Cornwall's cylindrical tower rising up within it. This arrangement appears to constitute an early example of concentric planning, though it is clear from the joist holes in the walls that the narrow space between the tower and the shell was roofed over. The inner keep is an austere building with little evidence of domestic comfort. The main apartments were always in the bailey, and the foundations of a large hall are on display there.

The town of Launceston was important enough to be walled in stone. No date is recorded but it was probably done under the patronage of Earl Richard. The wall linked up with the castle but the only surviving portion is the South Gate. This gate tower has a tall entrance passage and a drawbridge recess. It survives intact because of its later use as the borough's 'lock-up'.

Access: The castle is open at standard times in summer (EH). The South Gate houses an art gallery (LA).

Reference: Castle guidebook by A. D. Saunders.

Relations: Robert of Mortain founded Trematon, Castle Neroche and Berkhamsted. Tintagel was also rebuilt by Richard of Cornwall.

PENDENNIS CASTLE crowns a headland a mile east of Falmouth. The name suggests a Dark Age hillfort but any remains are buried beneath the later rampart. What now stands is an Elizabethan artillery fortress surrounding one of Henry VIII's coastal forts. Erected in 1540–45, when the Reformation had made England a target for invasion, the castle protected the entrance to Carrick Roads, the large inlet of the sea which could have offered a sheltered landing place to the fleet of the Catholic powers. St Mawes Castle was placed on the opposite shore and the guns of the two forts commanded the mile-long sheet of water between them. Pendennis is unusual among the Henrician coastal forts in having such an elevated situation. On the rocks below is a semi-circular blockhouse ('Little Dennis') which would have been of value in repelling ships invisible from the castle. As originally conceived Pendennis was one of the smaller coastal forts, just a squat round tower with gun ports at all three levels. The walls were thick enough to withstand the artillery of that time and the merlons of the parapet are rounded off to deflect any well-aimed cannon balls. A square forebuilding was added before completion, housing the governor's quarters and a complicated entrance passage involving two right-angled turns. The portcullis remains in position and the slots for drawbridge chains can still be seen. Over the entrance is a handsome panel bearing the royal arms. The low chemise wall with gun emplacements surrounding the tower must also have been an afterthought, as it blocks the gun ports on the ground floor of the tower. Henry's 'castles' were purely defensive units, but the quality of masonry here is high and there was clearly a lot of pride in the workmanship.

The threat of invasion revived under Elizabeth I and did not disappear after the fiasco of the Spanish Armada. Spanish ships raided the Cornish coast in 1595 and this incident led swiftly to the expansion of Pendennis. The summit of the headland was enclosed within a stone-encased rampart, defended by arrow-head bastions at the corners and in the middle of the two longer sides. A Classical entrance commemorates the completion of the defences in 1611. The enlarged castle was garrisoned as part of the coastal defence system until the Second World War, but the only serious fighting took place during the Civil War. Garrisoned for the King by the elderly Colonel John Arundell, Pendennis withstood a six-month bombardment from the Roundheads. Besieged by land and blockaded by sea, the garrison was starved of supplies and finally surrendered on honourable terms in August 1646.

Access: Standard opening times (EH).

Reference: Guidebook by B. Morley (includes St Mawes). *HKW* (II).

Relations: St Mawes. Carisbrooke and Berwick are other Elizabethan fortifications.

PENGERSICK CASTLE, near the coast between Germoe and Praa Sands, is a tower house with a projecting stair turret. The embattled parapet and ground-floor arrow-slits are not just for show, but for its date (Henry VIII's reign) these features are remarkable in a private house. It suggests how insecure the western tip of Cornwall was in Tudor times, and coastal raids are no doubt the reason for this apparent anachronism. The tower lay on the estates of the Godolphin family, of nearby Godolphin House.

Access: Visible from the road.

POLRUAN CASTLE is the companion of Fowey Castle (see above), rising from the rocks on the east side of the River Fowey estuary. Unlike its neighbour this blockhouse stands virtually intact, though now a shell. It is interesting as an early example of coastal defence, probably predating the more advanced blockhouses protecting Dartmouth. The tower is only two storeys high and the two 'keyhole' gun ports seem inadequate for their purpose. Given the limited cannon of the mid fifteenth century the towers cannot have provided very effective fire power across the estuary, and the boom chain was probably a more serious barrier. In spite of its shortcomings the tower was garrisoned until the Dutch invasion scare of 1667.

Access: Freely accessible (LA).

Relations: Fowey and Dartmouth.

RESTORMEL CASTLE occupies a knoll above the River Fowey, a mile north of Lostwithiel. Its plan is quite a curiosity: A perfectly circular bailey with a set of internal buildings arranged concentrically against the curtain. The domestic buildings are ruined but the curtain is virtually intact. The sense of compactness is heightened by the absence of any outer bailey, because although one existed every trace has disappeared.

There is no historical reference to the castle until 1264, when Simon de Montfort seized it, but Restormel is clearly older than that. From outside the embattled curtain appears to crown a motte, and the structure is often described as a large shell keep, but the 'motte' is really a ringwork. Furthermore the inner bank was removed when the curtain was built, so the rampart now looks as if it has been heaped against the outside. The curtain is attributed to Robert de Cardinham, lord of the manor *circa*

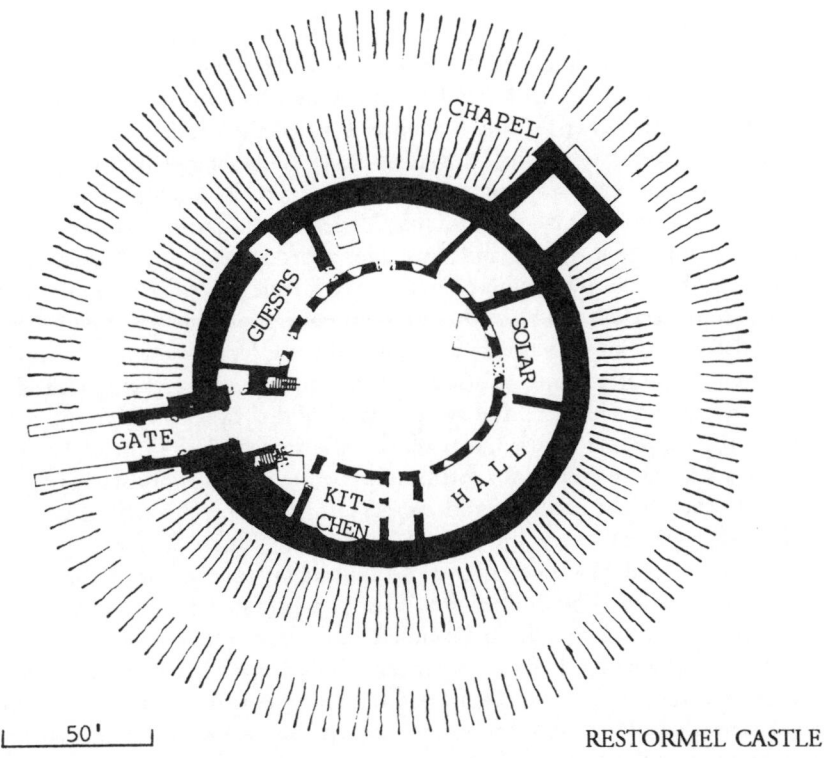

CHAPEL

GUESTS

SOLAR

GATE

HALL

KIT-
CHEN

| 50' |

RESTORMEL CASTLE

1192–1225. However, the square gate tower goes back a century further to the era of Baldwin Fitz Thurstan, who probably founded the castle. Gates were often the first element of a castle to be rebuilt in stone. This gate tower was an elementary structure and is now the most ruinous part of the defences.

In 1270 the castle passed to the earls of Cornwall and enjoyed a brief ascendancy. Earl Edmund chose Lostwithiel as his administrative centre and Restormel became his residence. It is to this era that we owe the interesting apartments which back onto the curtain, resulting in a bewildering group of curved chambers. An inventory of 1337 – when the Duchy of Cornwall was created – identifies these apartments as the kitchen, hall, solar, ante-chapel and two large guest chambers (proceeding anti-clockwise from the gate tower). Apart from the kitchen the main apartments all stood at first-floor level over cellars. The chapel, reached from the ante-chapel, occupied a contemporary square tower which projects boldly from the line of the curtain. A square mural tower in the Edwardian age is typical of Cornish conservatism. At the death of Edmund in 1299 the earldom reverted to the Crown, and with the creation of the duchy the castle was seldom visited. The only military episode was a siege in 1644, when it fell briefly into Royalist hands.

Access: Standard opening times in summer (EH).
Reference: Guidebook by C. A. Ralegh Radford.
Relations: The duchy castles of Launceston, Tintagel and Trematon.

21

ST MAWES CASTLE   guards the eastern entrance to the estuary known as Carrick Roads. It is the companion of Pendennis and exactly contemporary (1540–45). These two Henrician coastal forts offer some interesting contrasts. In each a squat round tower is the chief feature, but instead of having a square residential block slapped on in front of it, the St Mawes tower is elaborated by three attached, semi-circular bastions with parapets at a lower level. The tower is capped by a distinctive stair turret. St Mawes is unlike Pendennis but like the majority of Henry VIII's forts in being low lying and thus able to challenge enemy shipping at close quarters. Both castles share with Henry's other fortifications the rounded merlons designed to deflect cannon balls, the large embrasures for guns at several levels, and the emplacements for drawbridge and portcullis, the latter showing that the forts were intended to offer some resistance at close quarters if the enemy ever landed. Above the entrance we encounter again a panel of the royal arms. On the rocks in front of the castle is a semi-circular blockhouse matching the one at Pendennis, perhaps erected as an emergency fortification before the real work started.

In terms of size the castles would appear to have been conceived as equals and their early governors were bitter rivals. With the Elizabethan enlargement of Pendennis, however, St Mawes shrank into a subsidiary role. Its part in the Civil War typifies this. In contrast with Pendennis Castle's heroic stance, the royalist governor here wisely judged the castle to be indefensible from the land and surrendered without a shot being fired. The insignificance of St Mawes has allowed it to survive in a very unspoiled condition, despite continuous military occupation. Not only has the stonework suffered very little modification, but within there is a surprising amount of original woodwork in the form of partitions, beamed ceilings and ornate doorways. The quality of carving here seems decidedly at odds with our vision of Henrician coastal forts as utilitarian garrison posts. The castle is also notable for the series of verse inscriptions (composed by Leland) heaping sycophantic praise upon His Majesty.

Access: Standard opening times (EH).
Reference: Guidebook by B. Morley (includes Pendennis). *HKW* (II).
Relations: Pendennis.

ST MICHAEL'S MOUNT   The great conical rock rising out of Mount's Bay just off the coast at Marazion is an astonishing sight. At low tide the Mount is accessible along a causeway first constructed in the fifteenth century, but at other times it is an island. Dark Age legends of St Michael appearing here turned the rock into a place of pilgrimage. A Benedictine priory was founded on the summit after the Norman Conquest, its parent house being the abbey crowning that other great island rock across the Channel, Mont St Michel. The priory was never a large establishment and the existing church and monastic quarters were erected following an earthquake in 1275. These buildings are mixed up with the dramatic additions made by the St Aubyn family in Victorian times, which turned the Mount into a large mansion as well as giving it a castellated appearance.

Although not a fortification by intent, the strong position of the priory caused it to be used as a last resort by desperadoes. In 1193 Henry de la Pomeroy seized the Mount and fortified it in the name of Prince John. It took the arrival of a large force

22

under the Archbishop of Canterbury to persuade him to surrender. Again in 1473 John de Vere, Earl of Oxford and last champion of the Lancastrian cause, captured the Mount by disguising his men as a band of pilgrims. They defied Edward IV's army of six thousand men for six months. The embrasured length of wall overlooking the approach – the only sign of man-made fortification on the Mount – is probably a late medieval defence against raiders. Following the dissolution of the priory a royal garrison was installed as part of Henry VIII's coastal defence network. The Mount was stormed during the Prayer Book rebellion of 1549.

Access: Open regularly (NT). A boat service is available when the tide is high.
Reference: Guidebook by J St Aubyn.
Relations: The fortified monasteries at York, Tynemouth and Lindisfarne.

TINTAGEL CASTLE The legend of King Arthur has made Tintagel a hallowed place. Geoffrey of Monmouth, writing about the time when the castle was in fact founded, chose it as the setting for Arthur's conception. That is his only link with Tintagel, but it has lasted in the popular imagination. The beauty of the site is no doubt the reason why. This rocky, sea-battered headland is an unusual setting for a medieval castle but a very likely one in which to find an ancient hillfort. It comes as a surprise to discover that no evidence has been found of any fortification before the Norman period. Instead, the headland first became the retreat of Dark Age monks who were drawn to such inaccessible spots. The foundations of several groups of monastic buildings are scattered across the summit of the headland and its eastern slope.

The Tintagel headland is nearly an island, but is connected to the mainland by a narrow neck of rock. The castle occupies the junction of the two and has a bailey on either side of the isthmus. Originally the narrow chasm between them was connected by a bridge, but over the centuries the causeway has eroded and the castle is now divided into two distinct halves, connected by precipitous stairways. Today the castle is very ruinous, as is only to be expected on such an exposed site. Both baileys are protected by simple curtains, at least on those sides where the natural defence is merely a steep fall as opposed to a sheer drop. There is no keep. The walls are attributed to Henry III's brother Richard, Earl of Cornwall, around 1240. The shattered gate tower leading into the outer (mainland) bailey is preceded by a narrow passage. This is overlooked by an elongated walled enclosure on an outcrop of rock, so that attackers (if they ever came) could have been showered with arrows from above. In the inner bailey on the headland are the ruins of a fourteenth-century hall within the footings of a Norman predecessor. The latter goes back to the foundation of the castle by Reginald de Dunstanville, a previous Earl of Cornwall (d.1175). A gateway at the rear of the inner bailey leads to the summit of the headland and the Dark Age monastic remains. That Tintagel was not just an uncomfortable fortress is shown by the medieval walled garden on the headland. The path descending to the sea is barred at its far end by the Iron Gate, controlling access from the landing place beyond.

Access: Standard opening times (EH).
Reference: Guidebook by C. Thomas.
Relations: For the Dunstanvilles see Trematon. Richard of Cornwall also rebuilt Launceston.

TREMATON CASTLE stands on an eminence rising steeply above the River Lynher, two miles south-west of Saltash and the Tamar estuary. The castle was probably founded by Robert, Count of Mortain and Earl of Cornwall. It is referred to as his in the Domesday Book. At that time Trematon was a place of some importance whereas now it is scarcely a village. Robert's son William took the wrong side in the showdown between Henry I and Robert Curthose (1106), forfeiting his estates as a result. Henry I's illegitimate son Reginald de Dunstanville later became earl. He was not allowed to pass the title on to his own illegitimate son Henry, but Henry inherited Trematon. After he died in 1220 it passed to the De Valletorts and ultimately became part of the Duchy of Cornwall. The castle saw action in the Civil War and, earlier, in the course of Kilter's Insurrection which broke out in Cornwall in 1594. The rebels laid siege to the castle and managed to lure out and capture its defender, Sir Richard Grenville.

Trematon is a fine example of a motte-and-bailey castle. It is even more notable for the excellent preservation of its late Norman masonry, almost certainly the work of Henry de Dunstanville. An oval shell keep crowns the motte and the bailey is surrounded by a plain curtain. Both keep and curtain retain their crenellations, the latter having unusually narrow merlons. Until 1807 the curtain stood complete, but in that year a long portion was removed to supply materials for the house which stands in the bailey. Consequently there is now a long gap between the gatehouse and the south-west corner of the bailey. At the foot of the motte is an original postern. The main entrance is through a perfectly-preserved gatehouse added by Reginald de Valletort *circa* 1250. Its square plan is decidedly old-fashioned at a time when round-towered gatehouses predominated. Nevertheless, the gatehouse projects entirely outside the line of the curtain, so that it acts as a powerful flanking tower, and the gate passage was defended by two portcullises and a pair of gates between them. The steep ascent through the gate passage is an obstacle in itself. Note the fine arrow-slits of the castle, both the cross-slits on the keep parapet and the slits with roundels in the gatehouse.

Access: Private, and barely visible from outside. Open by appointment only.

Reference: Archaeologia (LXXXIII).

Relations: Robert of Mortain's castles at Launceston and Berkhamsted. For the Dunstanvilles see Tintagel and Castle Combe.

OTHER SITES There are a Norman earthwork enclosure at *Cardinham* and a motte at Boscastle (a corruption of *Bottreaux Castle*). *Ruan* Lanihorne had an impressive fourteenth-century castle with numerous towers, but only a scrap of wall survives.

County Durham

Medieval Durham was a palatinate ruled by the bishops of Durham. It was the longest lasting of the English palatine counties and the only one in ecclesiastical hands. The 'prince-bishops' enjoyed their autonomy in return for a leading role in the defence of the Scottish Border. As a result some bishops, such as Anthony Bek and Thomas Hatfield, were soldiers first and foremost. County Durham was vulnerable to Scottish raids, especially in the decade after Bannockburn when English confidence collapsed. The bishops were empowered to grant licences to crenellate and this is a good county for castles. Norman castles are surprisingly few, with masonry only at Barnard Castle and the prince-bishops' chief castle in Durham. The barons of the county indulged in a flurry of building in the late fourteenth century. Raby, Brancepeth, Lumley, Hylton and Witton castles all date from this time, their machicolations and turrets evocatively piercing the skyline. They have all been affected to varying degrees by making the transition to stately homes. Lower down the social scale, pele towers are surprisingly few for a Northern county.

AUCKLAND CASTLE The episcopal palace at Bishop Auckland occupies a commanding position above the River Wear, but there is some doubt as to whether it was ever fortified. For Auckland the title of castle is a comparatively new one, and only once do the medieval chronicles call it a castle rather than a palace. One would expect the bishops of Durham to have provided some defences at their chief country seat, but if they did every trace has vanished. Even the old residential buildings have been transformed, in neo-Gothic fashion by the architect James Wyatt. The only exception is the beautiful chapel which was originally the hall. Despite the later conversion this is one of the best medieval halls in England. It is supposed to be a late work of Bishop Hugh de Puiset (d.1195), but the slender, delicately moulded Gothic arcades seem rather sophisticated for his time. Bishop Bek remodelled the hall a century later and inserted the traceried windows in the aisles. It became a chapel after the Restoration when John Cosin was bishop, the original chapel having been demolished by the Puritans. The clerestory windows and roof are his.

> *Access:* Grounds open daily. Interior at certain times in summer.
> *Reference:* Guidebook by G. F. Edwards.
> *Relations:* For the bishops see Durham. Compare the aisled halls at Oakham and Winchester.

BARNARD CASTLE The town takes its name from the castle built by Bernard de Balliol and extended by his son of the same name. Between them they erected a powerful stone castle in the second half of the twelfth century, strongly situated on a rock above the River Tees. In 1216, during the Magna Carta war, the castle withstood a siege from the Scottish King Alexander II. The Balliols became great barons on both sides of the Scottish Border but this was to prove their undoing. John Balliol, Edward I's nominee as puppet King of Scotland, forfeited his estates when he repudiated Edward's overlordship of Scotland. Barnard Castle was then granted to the Beauchamp earls of Warwick. Via them it passed to Richard Neville, the famous 'Kingmaker', and Richard III while he was still Duke of Gloucester. During the Rising of the North in 1569 Sir George Bowes defended the castle against five thousand rebels, but his men eventually mutinied and forced a surrender. In the 1630s Sir Henry Vane dismantled the castle to provide building materials for Raby Castle.

Today the castle is an extensive but very ruinous pile. It possesses an exceptional four baileys, all walled in stone during the period of the two Bernards. From the town a Norman arch – once part of a gatehouse – leads into the northern outer bailey, known as the Town Ward. Much of its curtain still stands as well as the vaulted undercroft of the Brackenbury Tower. The southern outer bailey (not open) doubles the size of the castle but its defences are now fragmentary.

West of the Town Ward are the ditch and curtain of the inner bailey, with two flanking towers added by the Beauchamps. To reach the inner bailey it is necessary to pass through a middle ward, then turn sharp right over a deep ditch hewn out of solid rock. This succession of defences is quite advanced for the twelfth century. Once inside the inner bailey the dominant feature is the Balliol Tower or keep which projects from the curtain. This cylindrical tower of ashlar is actually an early addition to the castle, though it could still be the second Bernard's work as he survived until 1199. As keeps go it is a bit of a fraud, because it was not isolated from the rest of the castle. It was entered directly from the vanished solar at first floor level, and the triangular spur projecting from the keep is not a defensive feature but merely a wedge between the two. All the same the keep is the only part of the castle to survive more or less complete and its ground floor is covered by an unusual domed vault. The solar was the last in a row of fine apartments which stood against the curtain above the steep fall to the river. Their position is marked by the windows piercing the curtain. First appears the oriel window of the solar, bearing the boar emblem of Richard III. Next two traceried fourteenth-century windows mark the site of the Beauchamps' hall. Finally there is the tall, outer face of the Mortham Tower, once a five-storey edifice containing suites of private apartments.

Access: Standard opening times (EH).
Reference: Guidebook by D. Austin.
Relations: For the Beauchamps see Warwick, which has a similar cliff-top situation.

BISHOPTON CASTLE is an impressive motte-and-bailey overlooking the Bishopton Beck about five miles west of Stockton. The site is dominated by a tree-covered motte which stands between two small baileys, and on the side away from the stream there are remains of two much larger enclosures. The castle was raised by Roger de Conyers in 1143 during a dispute over the succession to the bishopric, and here he resisted an attack from the usurper William Cumin. It wasn't occupied for long and a stone curtain never replaced the timber palisade.

Access: Visible from the road.

BRANCEPETH CASTLE, four miles south-west of Durham, was the original seat of the powerful Neville family. It is first mentioned during the Magna Carta war of 1216. In outline the castle may date back to this period but nothing now standing is that old. The castle is similar architecturally to some of its late-fourteenth-century neighbours in the county and the rebuilding is attributed to Ralph Neville, first Earl of Westmorland (d.1425), after Raby was complete. Unfortunately his stronghold has been subjected to drastic alterations. From 1818 there was a heavy-handed restoration in neo-Norman style under the architect John Paterson, whose unin-spired work has been justly criticised. The result is a castle which is a mishmash of original and sham features, best seen from a distance. Nevertheless a considerable amount of medieval masonry has survived and the contrast between the old and the new is clearly apparent.

The castle is situated on a rise overlooking the Stockley Beck. It is a large, irregular enclosure surrounded by a strong curtain. The curtain looks complete but some portions have been rebuilt. Paterson erected the present round-towered gatehouse on the site of the original. Most of the mural towers are authentic and have suffered comparatively little interference. These massive, oblong structures are unusual for the diagonal buttresses clasping their outer corners. Proceeding clockwise from the gatehouse we pass the Westmorland and Constable towers which have turrets rather than buttresses. Next comes the Russell Tower, a Paterson insertion, followed by three closely-spaced towers containing vaulted chambers (including the so-called Barons' Hall in Bulmer's Tower). These three towers were attached to the main residential apartments, but the buildings which now lean against the curtain on this side are entirely of the nineteenth century. The curtain returns to the gatehouse via two small turrets. Three Neville monuments can be seen in the adjacent parish church.

Access: Well seen from outside. Interior by appointment only.
Reference: BOE *County Durham* (2nd edn).
Relations: For the Nevilles see Raby, Middleham and Sheriff Hutton.

DALDEN TOWER, to the east of Dalton-le-Dale, is a ruined pele attributed to Jordan de Dalden in the 1320s. Only two sections of wall still stand up high, but set into one at first-floor level is a delicately carved niche which was either a wash basin or a chapel piscina. At one corner are the foundations of a rounded stair turret. The footings of an attached hall have also been exposed.

Access: Freely accessible (LA).

DURHAM CASTLE AND PROMONTORY WALL In the year 995 monks from Chester-le-Street brought St Cuthbert's body here to protect it from the Danes. They chose the naturally fortified site within an incised loop of the River Wear as the setting for their new cathedral. As late as 1075 it rebuffed a Danish attack. The only landward approach to the promontory is guarded by Durham Castle, which was established by William the Conqueror in 1072 but was soon given to Bishop Walcher. The castle remained the chief seat of the bishops of Durham until 1836, when Bishop Van Mildert gave it to the newly-founded university. It now serves as University College.

As seen from across the Wear, castle and cathedral form a magnificent spectacle.

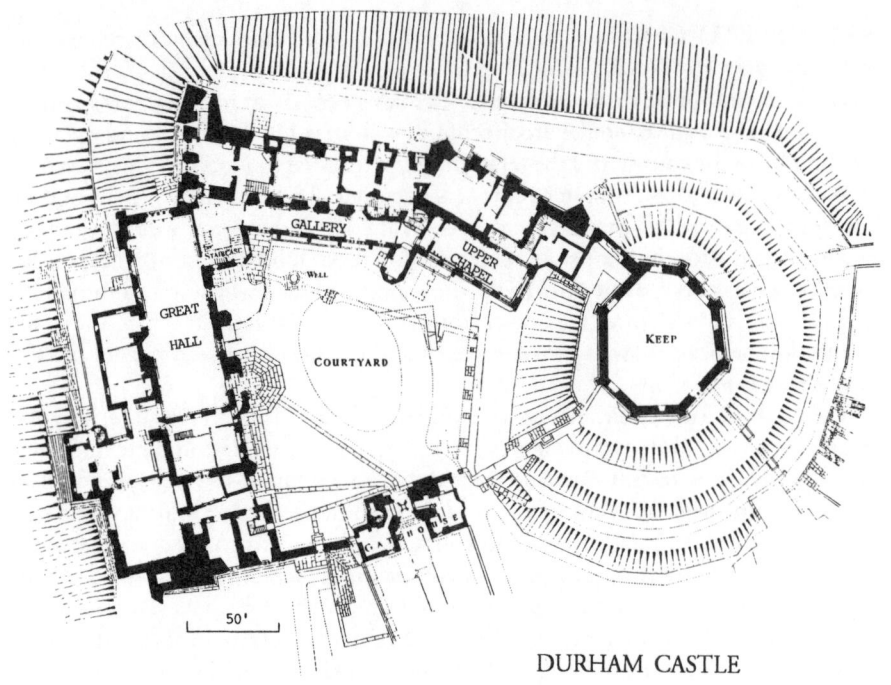

DURHAM CASTLE

It is the cathedral which dominates, but this is only to be expected of England's most celebrated Norman church. Above the river the castle presents a purely residential facade, the domestic buildings protruding from the great hall to the edge of the precipice. Clearly the steep drop was considered protection enough. Whereas Durham Cathedral is still essentially a Norman building the castle exhibits architecture of every century from the eleventh to the nineteenth, reflecting the changing tastes of the bishops, and is memorable as a palace rather than a fortress. In outline, however, the castle is still a Norman stronghold, comprising a triangular bailey overlooked by a large motte.

Palace Green occupies the site of an outer bailey and the main entrance faces the cathedral. The gate tower is basically Norman beneath its neo-Gothic veneer. To the right on top of the motte stands an octagonal shell keep, restored as a tower house under Bishop Hatfield (1345–81) and largely rebuilt by Anthony Salvin in the 1840s. There are ranges of buildings on two sides of the bailey. The north range, opposite the gatehouse, dates largely from the episcopate of Hugh de Puiset (1153–95) but is fronted by a corridor added by Bishop Tunstal in the 1540s. This corridor conceals one of the most elaborate late Norman doorways in England. It led into the lower of two halls, but the halls are no longer recognisable because they were divided into a series of state apartments in the eighteenth century. The 'Norman Gallery' which was part of the upper hall preserves a monumental row of windows with lavish chevron ornament. The chapel at the east end of the north range, with its plain vault supported on columns with crude capitals, takes us back to the early Norman period. It must have been the first part of the castle to be rebuilt in stone and contrasts sharply with Bishop Tunstal's late Perpendicular chapel nearby. Unlike the west range, the north range backs onto a real curtain wall reinforced by several massive buttresses.

The north range housed the bishops' private apartments and the *great* hall has always been in the west range. This is clear from the part-Norman undercroft. Anthony Bek (1283–1311) rebuilt this hall on a magnificent scale. It is a hundred feet long and extended even further until Bishop Fox partitioned off the south end. The hall is crowned by late-fourteenth-century roof beams though most of the other features belong to Salvin's restoration. Bishop Fox (1494–1501) remodelled the domestic offices (again Norman in origin) which project towards the river – the massive brick fireplaces and the timbered partition in the kitchen are his. Bishop Cosin's grand staircase of the 1660s occupies the angle between the west and north ranges.

The promontory within the loop of the Wear was given a stone enclosure wall for extra protection under Bishop Flambard in the early twelfth century. Much of this wall remains in a featureless condition, particularly on the west side beyond the cathedral buildings. Near the southern apex is the Water Gate, rebuilt in 1778. The short gap between the castle motte and the eastern arm of the river was closed by a stronger wall and ditch, and a semi-circular bastion from this part of the circuit can be seen at the end of a passageway off Sadler Street. It stood beside the vanished great gatehouse. This citadel proved impregnable against the Scots on several occasions but it was largely occupied by the cathedral and its Benedictine priory. The city of Durham grew up to the north of the promontory, in the shadow of the castle. It was fortified after an attack by Robert Bruce but nothing is left of the city wall now.

Access: The castle is open regularly (subject to college requirements). The promontory wall can be seen from the riverside walk.

Reference: Castle guidebook by D. Bythell. VCH *Durham* (III).

Relations: The bishops' castles at Auckland, Norham, Crayke and Somerton. Compare the situations of Warkworth and Shrewsbury.

HARTLEPOOL TOWN WALL. The old town occupies a headland which is now something of a backwater, having been eclipsed by West Hartlepool across the bay. In medieval times it was the chief port of the Durham palatinate and its thirteenth-century prosperity can be measured by the splendour of St Hilda's Church. With the Scots taking the initiative after Bannockburn the town hurriedly erected a defensive wall with ten towers. As an afterthought the wall was extended along the quayside to counter the threat of raids from the sea. A long section of this quay wall still stands, rather low and quite featureless except for the arch of Sandwell Gate with its twin pointed turrets. Everything else was destroyed after the Scots captured the town in the Civil War.

Access: Freely accessible (LA).

Reference: VCH *Durham* (III).

HYLTON CASTLE can be found in the estate of that name on the outskirts of Sunderland. It is an improbable find in this suburban landscape: An imposing gatehouse which became the core of an eighteenth-century mansion, was Gothicised in the 1860s and then abandoned, so that today the mansion has disappeared and the gatehouse stands alone as a roofless shell. The gatehouse is a mighty, oblong structure with a machicolated parapet at the wall head on all sides but one. Machicolated turrets rise a short way above the parapet, both at the corners and on either side of the outer entrance, while an annexe projecting at the rear of the gatehouse contained the spiral stair and several chambers. These would have supplemented the main apartments in the body of the gatehouse, but the original internal arrangements have been swept away by the later remodellings. Most of the windows are Victorian, the gateways have been replaced by small doorways and the gate passage has perished. These detract from the appearance of the tower but there is a fine display of twenty heraldic shields on the outer front by way of compensation. They date the castle to the 1390s, making Sir William Hylton its builder.

The gatehouse was intended as a self-contained residence (i.e. a keep-gatehouse) but it makes no sense in isolation. Presumably it was meant to be the focus of a larger stronghold, but the only other building here is the ruin of a free-standing chapel. Sir William was probably too ambitious in his plans and the gatehouse became a splendid entrance leading into nothing.

Access: Freely accessible (EH).
Reference: Guidebook by B. Morley.
Relations: For heraldic displays see Lumley.

LUDWORTH TOWER is a ruined pele three miles east of Sherburn. Only the ground-floor vault and one deeply-fissured wall remain, the rest having collapsed in 1890. Several window openings and the well of the spiral stair are visible, but nothing survives of the hall which adjoined it. The tower was erected by Sir Thomas Holden in 1422 on receipt of a licence from Bishop Langley.

Access: Visible from the road.

LUMLEY CASTLE, in spite of later remodelling, is one of the finest examples of a fully-developed quadrangular castle with ranges of buildings on all sides. Bolton Castle is the best known Northern example and Lumley resembles it quite closely. It has the same oblong corner towers, each one a tower house in its own right, and the same attention to defence within the courtyard as well as outside. But whereas Bolton is largely a ruin, Lumley has come down to us intact and is merely disfigured by some eighteenth-century alterations.

The castle stands a mile east of Chester-le-Street on high ground which suddenly drops to the stream known as Lumley Beck. Ralph, Lord Lumley, obtained permission to crenellate his house here in 1389, the bishop's permit being reinforced by a royal licence three years later. The angles of the towers are clasped by diagonal buttresses – a feature rarely found in military architecture, though common enough in other buildings of the period – and each buttress is capped by a dainty machicolated turret. The original entrance to the castle is in the middle of the east front, overlooking the stream and with its back to the present approach. It is not a gatehouse exactly, rather a gate passage in the middle of the range. A broad machicolation overhangs the outer arch and the wall above is adorned with a display of six heraldic shields and helms. The shields depict prominent local families such as the Nevilles and Percys in addition to the Lumleys themselves, but pride of place is given to the arms of Richard II. Beneath one of the square turrets flanking the gateway is a tiny prison cell reached only by a trapdoor.

In typical Northern fashion the ground floors of the towers and connecting ranges are divided into a series of barrel-vaulted store rooms. The altered hall (with Elizabethan fireplace) is in the west range, flanked by the former solar and kitchen in the adjacent towers. The entrance to the hall range from the courtyard has a portcullis groove and flanking turrets. There are more heraldic shields over the arch but these are Elizabethan additions. Ample accommodation is contained in the other three ranges (including a vaulted chapel in the north-east tower) but later alterations have obscured the original layout. Most of the windows are Tudor and only the south range and its flanking towers are incongruous. During Sir John Vanbrugh's renovation in the 1720s this side was converted into a series of state rooms and a wide corridor was added towards the courtyard. He also erected the grand staircase leading into the castle from the west. Fortunately for the preservation of the older fabric, the Lumleys by this time could not afford a more drastic reconstruction.

Access: Now a hotel. Limited access for non-residents.
Reference: BOE *County Durham* (2nd edn).
Relations: Bolton. The heraldic display at Hylton.

OLD HOLLINSIDE   Perched above the River Derwent a mile and a half south-west of Whickham are the ruins of an unusual, fortified hall-house. The hall occupied the main part of the building but the entrance in the middle of the east front is flanked by oblong towers. These towers are joined together by a tall arch which conceals a wide machicolation on the underside. At the rear of the hall, overlooking the river, are fragments of another tower. A surviving window suggests that the hall was built by the De Hollinsides in the thirteenth century – a period of comparative peace. The defensive towers were added in the next century in response to the threat of Scottish raids, but it is impossible to identify the builder because the house passed through several families quite quickly.

Access: Freely accessible (LA).
Reference: Hugill.

RABY CASTLE   stands within a vast park to the north of Staindrop. Despite the alterations inevitable in a castle which has become a stately home, Raby ranks among the finest of later medieval fortified mansions. It reflects the aspirations of the Neville family, who became the most powerful of the Bishop of Durham's vassals. Ralph, Lord Neville, commanded the English forces at the Battle of Neville's Cross (1346) and probably started building here. His son John obtained a licence to crenellate in 1378 but the castle was probably nearly complete by then.

The irregular layout suggests a piecemeal development around an older residential core. On the east side of the courtyard is the hall range, with a small tower (the original pele) attached to it. This was built up into a pentagonal enclosure surrounded by residential ranges. Massive, oblong flanking towers project at regular intervals. Clifford's Tower is the largest of them, placed at the north-west apex. Next comes the Kitchen Tower at the north-east corner. The east front was peculiar because its towers project deeply from the back of the hall range. There was thus a deep recess between Mount Raskelf, an adjunct of the Kitchen Tower, and the Chapel Tower in the middle of the east front. However, the recess has been filled by an eighteenth-century block. The same has happened to the void between Chapel Tower and Bulmer's Tower. The latter once stood curiously isolated from the rest of the castle and was therefore presumably a tower house. The turreted façade of the Chapel Tower and the pointed south face of Bulmer's Tower are other oddities. On the west front are the Neville Gate and a massive residential block known as Joan's Tower at the south-west angle. Joan's Tower has been heightened and most of the windows are Victorian restorations, but considering the transformation within it is surprising how genuine the outer walls are. Only the castle's south front has been rebuilt. Surrounding the whole complex is an embattled outer curtain inspired by the concentric castles of the Edwardian era. It seems absurdly low, but a low wall overlooked by inner defences is the point of concentric castles. It would have been more formidable when the moat was filled with water (there is now just a lake on the south side of the castle). The outer courtyard is entered through a picturesque but largely-rebuilt gatehouse overshadowed by Clifford's Tower.

The Neville Gate has diagonal flanking turrets and a double row of machicolations above the entrance. Its long, vaulted passage (clearly of two phases) was closed by two portcullises and two pairs of doors. A lot of old masonry survives in the buildings surrounding the courtyard but their magnificent interiors transport us to more recent times. The Nevilles lost their lands after the Rising of the North (1569), a bungled attempt to put Mary Queen of Scots on the English throne. Raby was damaged during the Royalist uprising of 1648 but the Vane family, as earls of Darlington and dukes of Cleveland, embellished it repeatedly in the following centuries. Two campaigns in particular affected the appearance of the castle. The first was the work of the architect John Carr, who in 1782 drove a carriageway through the Chapel Tower and heightened the lower hall at the expense of the great hall and chapel above. The second was the rebuilding of the south range and the extension of the great hall in the 1840s. Because of this the hall is now a Victorian vision of baronial splendour. The only room evoking the medieval castle is the lofty kitchen, which occupies the whole of the Kitchen Tower. Its stone vault is surmounted by an open lantern for the louvre. The Old Lodge in the park surrounding the castle incorporates a pele tower, perhaps intended for the Nevilles' gamekeeper.

Access: Open regularly in summer (grounds and principal rooms).
Reference: BOE *County Durham* (2nd edn). Mackenzie. Souvenir guide.
Relations: The Neville castles at Brancepeth, Danby, Middleham and Sheriff Hutton. The Tower of London is England's only complete concentric castle.

RAVENSWORTH CASTLE lies hidden in a wooded estate on the southern outskirts of Gateshead, just off the A1. The castle was probably erected by Marmaduke Lumley towards the end of the fourteenth century. It was a quadrangular structure, and thus close in date and style to his kinsman's castle at Lumley though less ambitious in scale. A house was built across the courtyard in the eighteenth century, and then in 1808 John Nash was commissioned to design a new Ravensworth Castle nearby. This proud mansion of the Gothic revival was torn down in 1953 and the original castle has not fared much better. The two eastern corner towers still stand as decaying shells, with Nash's neo-Gothic stables between them. They are oblong after the Northern preference, and surprisingly lacking in domestic features.

Access: On private land.
Reference: Jackson, *Castles of Northumbria.*
Relations: Lumley.

WITTON CASTLE overlooks the River Wear, down-river from Witton-le-Wear but on the opposite bank. In 1410 Sir Ralph Eure was pardoned by Bishop Langley for fortifying his house without permission. His stronghold is a rectangular enclosure bounded by an embattled curtain which is virtually intact. It is in effect a simplified version of the quadrangular castles then prevalent. Instead of corner towers there are corbelled turrets at parapet level, two round and one square (the fourth has been displaced by the later mansion). Two simple gateways – both defended by overhanging machicolations – face each other across the courtyard. Astride the north curtain stands a lofty tower house of the usual oblong plan with a vaulted ground floor. The corners are alternately clasped by square projections and diagonal buttresses with crowning turrets – a County Durham motif. After a fire in 1796 the Lambtons gave the tower a neo-Gothic veneer and a projecting porch. They erected the new mansion to the west of the tower house, which displaced part of the curtain and extends some distance beyond the confines of the courtyard. Medieval buildings filled up much of the courtyard but they were destroyed once the new house was complete. There is only a mystifying tower with Elizabethan windows on the opposite side of the courtyard, close to the curtain but not quite touching it. It looks like a smaller tower house but its purpose is unclear.

Access: Open as part of a leisure park.
Reference: BOE *County Durham* (2nd edn).
Relations: Sir Ralph Eure also built Ayton. The tower house at Dacre is similar.

WITTON TOWER is tucked away at the west end of Witton-le-Wear's main street, overlooking Dere Street (A68). What stands is a late medieval pele tower, quite intact but with no original features. Georgian wings stand on either side, and attached to one is a medieval chapel. The history of the house is quite obscure, attention having always focused on the castle across the river.

Access: Private.

OTHER SITES The rectory at *Houghton-le-Spring* was once surrounded by a defensive wall. The rector, John Kelyng, was fined by the bishop in 1483 for erecting it without permission. *Bradley Hall* (near Wolsingham) was another fortified mansion, licensed in 1431, but only a domestic undercroft survives. *Stanhope Castle* is an eighteenth-century sham on the site of a castle of the bishops of Durham. There is a motte at *Middleton St George.*

Cumberland

Cumberland has a stirring past, its history as a frontier zone going back to the days of Hadrian's Wall. This Celtic region was nominally under Scottish rule until 1092, when William Rufus marched in and captured Carlisle. David I of Scotland took advantage of the Anarchy to assert his claim over the disputed territories, but Henry II restored Anglo-Norman rule. Carlisle and Egremont are the only castles to preserve much masonry from the Norman era.

The period of comparative peace which followed was shattered by Edward I's invasion and Robert Bruce's eventual triumph. After Bannockburn (1314) the Scots took the initiative against a disunited England in a series of devastating raids across the northern counties. Cumberland stood in the front line and suffered severely. Although the Scots lost their great strategist when Robert died, and English strength was reasserted under Edward III, the hostility remained and flared up into invasions from time to time. The wars resulted in a border population which thrived upon raids and blood feuds. These activities, encouraged in times of war, became unstoppable in peacetime. Only with the union of the two kingdoms under one monarch in 1603 did the 'reivers' reluctantly embrace a more tranquil lifestyle. A Warden of the Western March was responsible for maintaining law and order of a sort, and he was empowered to grant licences to crenellate which few bothered to apply for. The consequence of those troubled centuries is a profusion of fortifications. The new baronial castles were Cockermouth, Naworth, Penrith and Rose Castle, but many pele towers were erected by the lesser gentry whose counterparts further south lived in unfortified manor houses. Usually there was a hall attached, and sometimes (as at Askerton) a second tower at the service end of the hall. The tower houses at Dacre and Millom are among the most ambitious. A few served the dual role of pele and church tower, as at Great Salkeld.

ARMATHWAITE CASTLE is beautifully positioned beside the River Eden, near Armathwaite bridge. The Eden valley was a regular thoroughfare for raiders and John Skelton is said to have erected this squat tower house around 1445. It stands at one corner of a nineteenth-century mansion but is big enough to dominate. No original features survive because the Sanderson family transformed the interior in the eighteenth century and gave the tower its Classical facade.

Access: Private.

ASKERTON CASTLE lies about six miles north of Brampton on the Bewcastle road. It is one of those fortified houses comprising two towers of equal status flanking a central hall. The hall range goes back to the fifteenth century and retains its original roof, but the modest towers were added by Thomas, Lord Dacre, soon after 1500 (his initials appear high up on the western tower). Thomas was an energetic Warden of the Western March and it appears that Askerton was intended as a small garrison post supplementing Bewcastle. Although the two ranges at the rear are much later their outer sides incorporate Tudor masonry, suggesting a small defensive quadrangle. In Elizabethan times the castle was occupied by Thomas Carleton, a land sergeant who was responsible for keeping watch on the Border. However, he habitually turned a blind eye to raids in return for a share of the booty and allowed the castle to decay.

Access: Visible from the road.
Reference: Curwen.
Relations: Bewcastle. For Thomas Dacre see Drumburgh and Naworth.

BEWCASTLE is celebrated for its churchyard cross, a masterpiece of sculpture from the Dark Ages. Earlier still the Roman army was here, occupying an outpost fort of unusual polygonal plan beyond Hadrian's Wall. Its earth rampart can still be followed. The medieval castle of Bewcastle was also something of an outpost, standing on the edge of the Debatable Lands – a disputed territory inhabited by outlaws. 'Beuth's Castle' is supposed to have been founded after the Norman invasion of 1092 but there is no mention of it until the late fourteenth century. The builder of the present castle is probably Sir John de Strivelyn (d.1378), who became a veteran of the Scottish wars. It became a garrison post controlled by the Warden of the Western March but deteriorated so badly in Tudor times that its role was taken over by Askerton Castle. The castle was raised in one corner of the Roman fort. Its ruins indicate an austere little stronghold, the plain curtain surrounding a square courtyard. Two sides stand to full height but the other two are fragmentary. The only projection is a gate tower, its outer entrance in the side wall so that a right-angled turn is involved. This tower is an addition, usually ascribed to Richard, Duke of Gloucester, during his years as Edward IV's viceroy in the North.

Access: Obtain permission to visit at the farm.
Reference: Curwen.
Relations: Askerton. For John de Strivelyn see Belsay.

BLENCOW HALL, former home of the Blencow family, is a fortified house of the twin-towered variety. The broad but squat towers, now ruinous, date from *circa* 1500. That on the left retains its battlements but has a deep fissure, allegedly caused by Civil War bombardment. Henry Blencow rebuilt the house between them in 1590, recording the date on a fireplace inside. Unlike the towers it is still inhabited. The house stands along the road leading north-east from Greystoke.

Access: Visible from the road.
Relations: Halls with flanking towers at Askerton, Howgill and Nappa.

BRACKENHILL TOWER stands among farm buildings beside the River Lyne, four miles east of Longtown. It is an intact pele tower of moderate size with very little to relieve the grim monotony of its walls. Richard Graham built the tower and inscribed the date 1586 outside. It is surprisingly late, even for Cumberland, but this area was still a wild one in the Elizabethan era and the Grahams were among the most notorious of the reivers. Richard operated a protection racket in the area. The corbelled parapet surrounding a gabled roof reflects the influence of contemporary Scottish tower houses.

Access: Private.
Relations: The similar Graham tower at Kirkandrews.

BRANTHWAITE HALL, midway between Branthwaite and Dean, belonged to the Skelton family from 1422. The pele tower, probably erected soon after that date, preserves its embattled parapet with a stair turret in one corner. Some original windows survive, though now blocked, and the ground floor is unusually divided into two vaulted rooms. The adjoining house was largely rebuilt in 1604.

Access: Visible from the road.
Relations: Armathwaite was another Skelton tower.

BURGH-BY-SANDS CHURCH The village where Edward I died occupies the site of one of the Hadrian's Wall forts. Nothing is left of the fort, nor of the small medieval castle which stood here, but the threat of raids from across the Solway Firth is attested by the fortified tower of St Michael's Church. Added to the church in the early fourteenth century, when such raids were at their height, the tower is basically a vicar's pele. It has a vaulted ground floor entered only from the nave through a doorway which is still closed by an iron-grilled gate, or yett. The floor above was the priest's living room, with a small window looking into the church, but the top stage (pierced by large belfry openings) is a later reconstruction.

Access: The church is usually open.
Reference: Curwen.
Relations: The church peles at Great Salkeld and Newton Arlosh.

CARLISLE CASTLE, CITADEL, CITY WALL AND PRIOR'S TOWER Carlisle is the great fortress city at the west end of the Scottish Border. Roman *Luguvallium* grew up in the shadow of Hadrian's Wall and some vestige of a town remained when William II captured it in 1092. William repopulated Carlisle with Anglo-Norman settlers and founded the great royal castle on a bluff above the River Eden. It reverted to Scottish rule during the Anarchy but Henry II compelled the Scots to withdraw in 1157. Another episode of dynastic strife – Prince Henry's revolt of 1173–74 – gave William the Lion the opportunity to press the Scottish claim again, and the castle suffered the first of its great sieges. For three months it resisted all attempts at assault, the siege ending with the timely capture of the Scottish King at Alnwick. Alexander II was more fortunate, taking city and castle at the second attempt in 1216. The opportunity had again been created by civil war in England, and once the crisis was over the city returned to English rule.

Edward I's designs upon Scotland turned Carlisle into a strategic centre, and with the collapse of the English offensive the city found itself at the forefront of Robert Bruce's retaliatory raids. In 1315 Robert made a determined effort to capture castle and town, employing catapults, scaling ladders and a high siege tower. The garrison put up a valiant resistance under the constableship of Sir Andrew de Harcla, who was later executed for alleged complicity with the Scots. Carlisle was sacked twice by the Black Douglas in Richard II's reign, but the castle held out and being a tough nut to crack the Scots generally preferred to pillage the countryside instead. Further

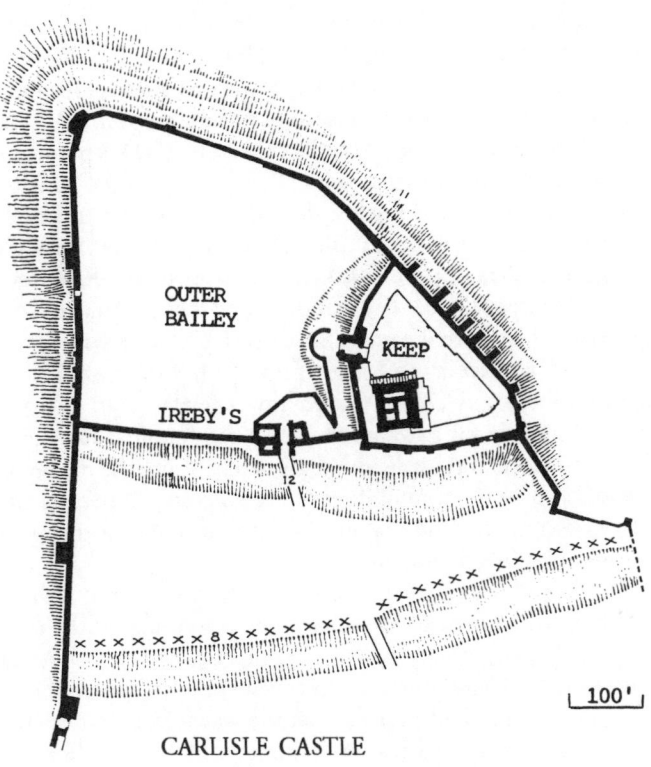

OUTER BAILEY

KEEP

IREBY'S

12

× × × × × × × 8 × × × × × × × ×

|— 100' —|

CARLISLE CASTLE

action came in 1645, when Parliament's Scottish allies forced the city to surrender after a long siege, and finally in 1745, the defences proving too weak to resist the Young Pretender. On their subsequent retreat the Jacobites endeavoured to hold on to Carlisle but the walls soon succumbed to the Duke of Cumberland's artillery.

Carlisle Castle is an impressive reminder of those centuries of strife. It sits grim and squat at the north end of the old walled city, still a medieval stronghold but much patched up after the many batterings it has endured. The layout is roughly triangular, comprising two walled baileys but no motte. The curtain walls are basically Norman. Two flanking towers survive on the west side but the walls are otherwise quite plain. During the Civil War the Scots tore down the cathedral nave to repair the damage wrought during their siege. The outer gatehouse facing the city, known as Ireby's Tower, dates from Henry III's reign but is not a great example of military planning. It consists of two square blocks curiously out of alignment with each other, and a small projection between them containing the entrance. Gloomy barracks now occupy the outer bailey – a reminder of the continuous military presence here down to modern times.

In front of the inner gatehouse is one of Henry VIII's additions – a semi-circular gun battery with a covered fighting gallery facing the ditch. During the invasion scare of the 1540s Henry thickened the inner curtain to support artillery. The wide

37

parapet is partly carried on arcades and there is a ramp for wheeling up cannon. The gate tower projecting from the line of the curtain (Captain's Tower) dates from Edward III's reign but was mutilated during the Tudor remodelling. Within the inner bailey rises a great keep which is virtually a cube. It was already described as 'old' during the siege of 1174 but there is no record of its builder. Henry I is most likely, though the Scottish King David should not be ruled out. The keep is free-standing, though very close to the curtain. As originally conceived its four storeys each contained a single large room, and the keep was entered as usual at first-floor level via a vanished forebuilding. It was drastically remodelled in the late Middle Ages, perhaps in the general shake-up of Northern defences under Richard, Duke of Gloucester. The present cross-wall, vaults and ground-floor entrance were inserted at that time, and the artillery-proof parapet is later still. Utilitarian military structures have replaced the old residential buildings in the bailey, the only relic being the traceried stair turret known as Queen Mary's Tower (*circa* 1390). Mary Queen of Scots was held in the castle for two months when she first fled to England. From early in its history the castle was used extensively as a gaol and the medieval carvings in a window embrasure on the second floor of the keep are supposedly the work of prisoners. In 1596 'Kinmont Willie', a notorious reiver of the Armstrong clan, was rescued by his comrades in a daring raid on the castle.

Between the castle and the city is a third bailey which was never walled in stone. The walls projecting from the castle are actually the beginnings of the city wall. On the west side is Tile Tower, mainly of early Tudor brick. After a short gap a long stretch of the western city wall (known as West Walls) begins. There are no bastions and the only feature is a blocked postern. Carlisle was first defended in earth and timber by the Romans. The medieval wall (built from 1232) followed the same course, but some of the circuit was still wooden when Edward I came here. Possibly the west side, afforded some natural protection by the River Caldew, was only walled in stone after the siege of 1314. On the more vulnerable eastern sector the wall was defended by a series of semi-circular bastions, typical of the thirteenth century, but this stretch has disappeared. West Walls ends at the Citadel, which guarded the south corner of the walled city. Henry VIII added this strongpoint in 1541 as a companion to the remodelled castle. It was designed by Stefan von Haschenperg, the architect of some of Henry's South Coast castles. Originally a triangular enclosure with massive round towers at the angles, most of the Citadel was demolished to make way for the present assize buildings in 1810. Two towers dominate the complex but only the lower part of the eastern one is original. The other tower is a copy on a slightly different site.

West Walls is overlooked by the Prior's Tower, a pele tower on the edge of the cathedral precinct. In medieval times the cathedral was served by Augustinian canons. The tower was part of the prior's house (now the deanery) and its ground-floor vault is carried on a series of arched ribs. The room above is lit by two oriel windows dating from the time of Prior Senhouse (*circa* 1520). His name is inscribed on the painted ceiling which he inserted at the same time. It is often said that Prior Senhouse built the tower but it seems more likely that he remodelled (and effectively de-fortified) an older structure.

Access: The Castle precincts, keep and Ireby's Tower are open at standard times (EH).

The city wall parapet is freely accessible and the Citadel houses the law courts (both LA). There is a key keeper for the Prior's Tower.

Reference: Castle guidebook by C. Platt & M. McCarthy. Turner for the city wall. *HKW* (II & IV).

Relations: Its counterpart as a Border town is Berwick. Keeps at Bamburgh, Norwich, Guildford and Portchester are attributed to Henry I. For Stefan von Haschenperg see Sandgate.

CATTERLEN HALL is not in fact at Catterlen but a mile further south, overlooking Newton Reigny. It belonged to the Vaux family. The earliest part is a pele tower, not large but retaining its fifteenth-century windows. A row of corbels below the parapet at the back of the tower presumably carried a wooden hoarding. The attached hall range was built by Roland Vaux in 1577 and there is a Classical wing beyond.

Access: Visible from the road.

COCKERMOUTH CASTLE crowns a promontory between the rivers Derwent and Cocker. The notorious William de Fortibus acquired the manor in 1215 and built a castle here, possibly on an older site, but Henry III ordered its destruction upon his downfall six years later. It seems to have survived this episode but most of the present complex is the work of Gilbert, last of the Umfraville barons, and Henry Percy, who acquired Cockermouth on Gilbert's death in 1381. As Earl of Northumberland the latter played a major part in the Border struggles of the period, and the unfinished castle was sacked by the Black Douglas (1387). Henry is better known for his revolts against Henry IV, familiar from Shakespeare. The castle remained in Percy hands but drifted into decay. In spite of enduring a Royalist siege during the uprising of 1648 the castle was slighted by Parliament as a potentially dangerous stronghold. Around 1800 Percy Wyndham, Earl of Egremont, built a mansion inside the outer bailey.

The castle has a triangular plan very similar to Carlisle, its apex overlooking the junction of the rivers. There is no keep. Gilbert de Umfraville largely rebuilt the inner bailey though the curtain incorporates portions of William de Fortibus' work. The well-preserved outer curtain is entirely Henry Percy's. Its east front is flanked to the left by the square Flag Tower, now gabled, and to the right by a mighty gatehouse. This massive, oblong structure has the side walls of a barbican in front. A row of shields over the gateway bears the arms of Henry Percy and his allies. The vaulted gate passage was defended by a portcullis and three sets of doors. Within the outer bailey is the Wyndham mansion, built against the curtain. The inner bailey is much ruined and has been distorted to some extent by eighteenth-century 'repairs'. The machicolated inner gatehouse, also preceded by a barbican, stands in the middle of a domestic range dividing the two baileys. The basement of this range occupies the ditch of the original castle, De Umfraville digging a second ditch (now largely filled in) beyond it. To the right is the massive Kitchen Tower with two great fireplaces. Following the curve of the curtain above the River Derwent are the foundations of the hall. A semi-circular tower projects at the western apex of the castle.

Access: Private, and barely visible from outside. Open by appointment only.

Reference: Curwen. BOE *Cumberland and Westmorland.*
Relations: Carlisle. Compare the kitchen tower at Raby. For the Umfravilles see Harbottle and Prudhoe, and for the Percys see Alnwick and Warkworth.

DACRE CASTLE sits in a deep valley overlooking a stream, four miles south-west of Penrith. It is an impressive, free-standing tower house with corner projections. Two of them, at opposite angles, are substantial square towers rising above the embattled parapet, while the other two are smaller turrets projecting diagonally. They contain small chambers, a spiral stair and the latrines. The ground floor is divided into two barrel-vaulted rooms and the floors above served the usual functions of hall and solar. In the hall is an ornate wash basin resembling a piscina – a rare feature in a secular dwelling! The castle may be the 'Dunmalloght' for which William de Dacre obtained a licence to crenellate in 1307. It certainly existed in 1354, when Margaret Dacre received a licence to hold mass here. The castle was restored from dereliction in the 1670s. At that time the large windows were inserted and the original entrance – in the west corner tower – was blocked up in favour of a new doorway leading directly into the hall, approached by an outside stair. A ditched courtyard lay to the west.

Access: Exterior visible. Interior by appointment only.
Reference: Curwen.
Relations: For the Dacres see Kirkoswald and Naworth. Compare the tower house at Witton Castle.

DALSTON HALL stands in its own grounds a mile north of Dalston off the road to Carlisle. The garden front dates mainly from the seventeenth century, but set back to the right of the facade is a squat pele tower of *circa* 1500 with a stair turret at one corner. An inscription in reversed lettering below the embattled parapet tells us that it was built by John Dalston and his wife Elizabeth – note the cat and dog to the left. The entrance to the barrel-vaulted ground floor (incongruously converted into a sitting-room) preserves its iron yett.

Access: Now a hotel (open to non-residents).
Relations: Yetts at Burgh-by-Sands, Great Salkeld and Naworth.

DRUMBURGH CASTLE One of the Hadrian's Wall forts once occupied this knoll overlooking the Solway Firth and the present castle is built from its stones. It was erected in 1518 by Thomas, Lord Dacre, when he was Warden of the Western March, though the walls incorporate masonry from an earlier castle for which Robert le Brun received a licence in 1307. As an Elizabethan survey reports it is 'neither castle nor tower but a house of strength' – in effect a defensible hall-house. Owing to alterations after 1696 the castle now has a purely domestic appearance with large windows and a gabled roof. The first-floor entrance (with a reset panel of Lord Dacre's arms above it) is not the original.

Access: Visible from the road.
Reference: Curwen.
Relations: For Thomas Dacre see Askerton and Naworth.

EGREMONT CASTLE is a pleasant ruin on a hill overlooking the River Ehen and the town. Its foundation is attributed to William le Meschin *circa* 1130 and it would appear to have been a stone castle from the outset. The gate tower and the length of bailey curtain to its left exhibit herringbone masonry characteristic of earlier Norman work. A segmental arch within a round-headed recess leads into the gate passage, once covered by a domed vault. The castle consists of a low motte and a small bailey, surrounded on all sides but one by a narrow outer platform. A circular keep was erected on top of the motte early in the thirteenth century but nothing is left of it. By that time the castle had passed to Lambert de Multon, and it was probably he who built the length of curtain which separates the motte from the bailey. A domestic range backed onto it, tall lancet windows indicating the position of the hall. Other domestic buildings, now reduced to their footings, stood against the bailey curtain opposite the gatehouse. This side of the castle was rebuilt, and the rest repaired, by the Fitzwalters following damage incurred twice during Robert Bruce's incursions. The castle is said to have been slighted as a result of the Rising of the North.

Access: Freely accessible (LA).

Reference: Curwen.

Relations: The Meschin castle at Appleby. Norman gate towers such as Newark, Ludlow and Exeter.

GREAT SALKELD CHURCH Here is a fine example of a vicar's pele which doubles up as a church tower. St Cuthbert's Church is a Norman building with an elaborate entrance portal. The tower was added at the west end of the nave in Richard II's reign, when the Black Douglas was terrorising the neighbourhood. It has small windows, even at belfry level, and a stair turret rises above the battlements. The only entrance is from the nave through an iron yett with wooden panels. A barrel vault covers the ground floor and there is a vaulted basement beneath, giving the tower an exceptional five storeys in all.

Access: The church is usually open.

Relations: The vicars' peles attached to the churches at Burgh-by-Sands and Newton Arlosh.

GREYSTOKE CASTLE stands in a large park. The Howard dukes of Norfolk have owned this place since the fall of the Dacres in 1570. Most of the present mansion is the work of Anthony Salvin in the 1840s, supplanting a seventeenth-century house which in turn replaced the medieval castle. This latter, largely destroyed after its capture by the Roundheads in 1648, is said to have been a quadrangular stronghold with towers at the four corners. All that remains is one of the towers, rising diagonally out of Salvin's ensemble and rather heavily restored to go with it. The top storey is an addition. William, Lord Greystoke, received a licence to crenellate in 1353. His effigy is one of several Greystoke monuments visible in the nearby collegiate church.

Access: Private.

Reference: Curwen.

Relations: The Greystokes' castle at Morpeth.

HARBYBROW TOWER This well-preserved pele, a mile south of Mealsgate, is first mentioned in 1465 when it belonged to Alexander Highmoor. It is likely that he was the builder as the small, two-light windows would be consistent with that date. There is the usual barrel-vaulted ground floor and the walls are unusually thick for a pele tower. The adjoining farmhouse stands on the site of an older hall.

Access: Private.

HUTTON-IN-THE-FOREST This splendid mansion is five miles north-west of Penrith. Its principal features are the long gallery and the main residential block, contrasting works from the seventeenth century when the house belonged to the Fletchers. The old pele tower in the angle between them keeps a low profile. It is attributed to Thomas de Hutton (d.1362) and was restored to a medieval appearance in Victorian times. The ground floor is covered by a barrel vault but the upper levels have been integrated with the rest of the house. Anthony Salvin added the larger tower at the other end of the facade.

Access: Limited opening times in summer.
Relations: For the Huttons see Hutton John.

HUTTON JOHN, like nearby Hutton-in-the-Forest, belonged to the Hutton family in the Middle Ages. It is another L-plan house with a pele tower at the junction. The tower, attributed to Thomas Hutton in the late fifteenth century, has been Georgianised. Its upper floors preserve small chambers within the unusual thickness of the walls. The hall range is Elizabethan in its present form and the larger wing at right angles was added in 1662. It lies six miles west of Penrith.

Access: Open by appointment only.
Relations: Hutton-in-the-Forest.

IRTON HALL, beside the River Irt a mile north-east of Holmrook, commands a fine view into Lakeland. It was occupied for at least seven centuries by the Irton family. Most of the house was rebuilt in 1874 but it incorporates a medieval tower, said to have been built by Adam de Irton in Edward III's reign. This tower, austerely built in the local granite, is relatively tall and slender – too slender, in fact, to be a pele in the usual sense. It is overshadowed by the Victorian clock tower.

Access: Visible from the road.

ISEL HALL is beautifully placed above the River Derwent, three miles north-east of Cockermouth. An earlier tower here was destroyed by the Scots in 1387. The present complex, built by the Leigh family over a hundred years or so, is an ambitious manor house for Cumberland. At the east end stands a fifteenth-century pele tower, such a massive structure that it appears squat in spite of its four storeys. Beside it extends a hall range of the early sixteenth century, preserving a lot of original panelling within.

Access: Open by appointment.

KIRKANDREWS TOWER

KIRKANDREWS TOWER overlooks the River Esk two miles north of Longtown (not to be confused with Kirkandrews-on-Eden). It stood on the edge of the 'Debatable Lands'. Until its partition in 1552 this no man's land was a notorious hive of criminal activity and lawless even by Border standards. The Grahams of Netherby, who built this tower house, were infamous for their shifting allegiance. With its distinctive corbelled parapet enclosing a gabled roof the tower has a Scottish appearance. It resembles nearby Hollows Tower, the old seat of the Armstrongs across the Border. The Grahams and the Armstrongs were deadly enemies. In 1527 their hostility erupted into a mini-war and both Hollows and Kirkandrews towers went up in flames. In its present form the tower probably belongs to shortly after that date. The castellated wall surrounding it is a nineteenth-century embellishment.

Access: Private.
Reference: Curwen.
Relations: Hollows (Scotland). Brackenhill was another Graham pele.

KIRKOSWALD CASTLE

KIRKOSWALD CASTLE Hugh de Morville obtained a licence to crenellate in 1201, but there was a general reconstruction to a quadrangular layout under Ranulf de Dacre after 1317. Ranulf's descendant Thomas rebuilt the residential apartments and widened the surrounding ditch *circa* 1500. However, William Howard abandoned Kirkoswald and used its materials to restore Naworth Castle (an elaborate ceiling from here can still be seen in the Howard Tower). Today the remains (south-east of the village) are meagre, and so overgrown that they are well concealed. The chief fragment is a tall stair turret which projected diagonally from the curtain. The vaulted stump of a corner tower also survives.

Access: On private land.
Reference: Curwen.
Relations: Ranulf de Dacre also built Naworth.

LANERCOST PRIORY

LANERCOST PRIORY In the Irthing valley two miles north-east of Brampton are the beautiful remains of an Augustinian priory founded in 1166. Its position was an unfortunate one and the outbreak of the Scottish wars impoverished it. Most calamitous were the raids led by William Wallace in 1297 and David II in 1346. It is interesting that the prior's house and the guest house were both built in pele tower form. The guest house, close to the west front of the priory church and now attached to the vicarage, is known as King Edward's Tower from the tradition that Edward I lodged here on his several visits to Lanercost. It may well be true since the 'dog-tooth' ornament below the parapet of the little tower is a thirteenth-century motif. As such it is probably the oldest pele tower still in existence. The Prior's Tower is now a ruined shell pierced by Tudor windows. It adjoined the prior's hall in the west range of the cloister, so the arrangement was actually the normal one in spite of its monastic setting. After the Dissolution the Dacres turned this part of the priory into a dwelling for themselves.

Access: Standard opening times in summer (EH).
Reference: Guidebook by J. R. Moorman.
Relations: Carlisle and Hulne have other monastic peles.

LIDDELL STRENGTH is the name given to an impressive motte-and-bailey occupying an elevated site between the River Esk and Liddell Water, which here forms the boundary between England and Scotland. It comprises a high motte and two baileys, the whole encircled by strong ramparts and ditches except where there are steep falls to the river. The castle is first mentioned in 1174 when it fell during William the Lion's invasion. At that time it belonged to the De Stutevilles. Though never rebuilt in stone, Sir Walter Selby led a gallant defence of the place in 1346 during David II's invasion. After four days' resistance the defences were stormed and the garrison of two hundred men was ingloriously slaughtered. There are indications of a later pele tower within the inner bailey.

Access: On private land.
Reference: Curwen.

LORTON HALL stands in the Vale of Lorton on the edge of the Lake District, four miles south-east of Cockermouth. The embattled pele tower is impressive but the masonry has a plaster veneer obscuring all original features. It probably dates from the fifteenth century. Large windows were inserted in the Tudor period and the attached house was remodelled by the Winders family in 1663.

Access: Visible from the road.

MILLOM CASTLE can be found on the northern edge of Millom town beside the old parish church. The church contains monuments to the Hudleston family who lived in the castle. Sir John de Hudleston obtained a licence to crenellate in 1335 and his unusual castle forms a compact rectangular enclosure with buildings against the curtain. The main domestic apartments are now ruinous shells. Steps lead up to a gateway on the east side, flanked by the side walls of a barbican. The blocks to the left and right of the entrance formed the solar and kitchen, with a small yard in between. Behind the kitchen are the outer walls of the hall. Unusually for Cumberland a tower house does not appear to have formed part of the original design, the existing tower being inserted into what little courtyard there was in the fifteenth century, perhaps following the ransack of the castle by the Lancastrians in 1460. It is a mighty structure, as many as five storeys high and divided all the way up by a cross-wall, but the masonry is concealed beneath a roughcast veneer and the parapet has gone. The tower was originally entered on the first floor across the narrow void between it and the solar. Unlike the rest of the castle the tower house is intact and still occupied (a modern house adjoins it). The castle suffered a destructive siege from the Roundheads in 1644.

Access: Exterior only.
Reference: Curwen.
Relations: Small enclosures with tower houses such as Scaleby, Mortham and Edlingham.

MUNCASTER CASTLE, dramatically sited above the River Esk before it enters the sea at Ravenglass, originated as the fourteenth-century pele tower of the Pennington family. Their tower, with a barrel-vaulted ground floor and two spiral stairs, stands at one corner of the present mansion, built for Lord Muncaster by Anthony Salvin in 1862–66. Salvin added the matching tower at the left end of the long facade. Sir John Pennington entertained the deposed Henry VI here following his defeat at the Battle of Hexham (1464).

Access: Open regularly in summer.

NAWORTH CASTLE has become a fine mansion without sacrificing its medieval character. Ranulf de Dacre obtained a licence to crenellate in 1335. His castle, on a promontory two miles east of Brampton, consists of an irregular, quadrilateral courtyard surrounded by a curtain wall. The only level approach is from the south-east and this side has a tower at each end, named Dacre and Howard after the two prominent families who have lived here since the fourteenth century. Dacre Tower is the original tower house. Five storeys high with corner turrets, it flanks the original gateway through the curtain though it does not project at all from the south-east front. The doorway into its vaulted ground floor preserves an iron yett. The Howard Tower is probably one of Thomas Dacre's additions and as a defensive tower it is something of an illusion. It fills the acute angle between two walls and its inner sides are supported on arches above the residential buildings, so it is only a tower at the upper levels. In front of the south-east curtain was a narrow outer bailey, as indicated by the surviving gatehouse (surmounted by a restored panel of the Dacre arms) and the squat tower known as the Boat House.

There are courtyard buildings against the curtain on three sides. They are largely the work of Thomas, Lord Dacre (d.1525), who proved to be a capable Warden of the Western March. The south-east range contained the solar and the chapel, the latter indicated by large windows at the Dacre Tower end. The hall occupies most of the north-east range. This lofty apartment contains four intriguing heraldic beasts: A bull, a gryphon, a dolphin and a sheep. These but little else survived a devastating fire in 1844. As a result of this fire the interiors, while adhering to the old, are the work of Anthony Salvin. He also added the Morpeth Tower near the north corner.

The Dacres lost their lands for taking part in the Rising of the North in 1569–70. Leonard Dacre was defeated in a nearby skirmish with some of the Queen's supporters and Naworth was granted to a branch of the Howard family. William Howard ('Belted Will') zealously enforced law and order on the Border in the Jacobean era. He inserted the magnificent fourteenth-century roof from Kirkoswald Castle in the Howard Tower. His descendants, the earls of Carlisle, still live here.

Access: Limited opening times in summer.
Reference: Curwen. BOE *Cumberland and Westmorland.* Souvenir guide.
Relations: The other Dacre castles of Askerton, Dacre, Drumburgh and Kirkoswald.

NEWTON ARLOSH CHURCH Newton Arlosh was founded by Holm Cultram Abbey in 1305, but this new town failed to flourish in the hostile conditions of its birth. The church of St John illustrates the uncertainties of the period. It is one of the three in Cumberland where the church tower serves as a vicar's pele. It has the usual ground-floor vault and living rooms above. The church was rebuilt on a different axis in 1844 and the tower was restored from ruin at the same time.

Access: The church is usually open.
Relations: Burgh-by-Sands and Great Salkeld.

PENRITH CASTLE The ruins of the castle overlook the town, opposite the railway station. William Strickland, subsequently Bishop of Carlisle, obtained a licence to crenellate his 'chamber' here in 1397. A second licence two years later permitted the expansion of the castle, but this seems to have been completed by Ralph Neville, first Earl of Westmorland, who inherited in 1419. Between them the bishop and the earl created a walled quadrangle typical of the era but without the customary angle towers. Strickland's Tower, the original tower house, flanked the entrance to the castle on the north-east front. Ralph Neville added the Red Tower and a new gatehouse on the north-west. Buildings stood along all four sides. Orders were given to repair the castle from its ruinous condition in 1572 but it was slighted after the Civil War in spite of having been garrisoned by the Roundheads. The castle has been excavated and its foundations are on display, but the only parts to stand up high are the south-east curtain and one side of the Red Tower. Large windows above a row of corbels in the curtain (said to have been inserted by Richard III during his days as vice-regent in the North) mark the position of the hall. Strickland's Tower has been reduced to its vaulted basement. Hutton Hall in Friargate incorporates an altered pele tower of the Hutton family.

> *Access:* Freely accessible (EH).
> *Reference:* Curwen.
> *Relations:* For the bishops of Carlisle see Rose Castle. Compare Ralph Neville's work at Brancepeth and Middleham.

ROSE CASTLE, beside the River Caldew six miles south of Carlisle, has been the chief seat of the bishops of Carlisle since the Border wars broke out. The bishops moved from Linstock Castle in the wake of Edward I's invasion but 'La Rose' soon became a target as well. It suffered on several occasions, notably in the great raids of 1314 and 1322. Bishop Kirkby obtained a licence to crenellate in 1336 and another was granted to Bishop Welton in 1355. The castle took shape between those dates. It was an irregular quadrangle surrounded by a towered curtain. There was a partly-concentric outer enclosure which is still recognisable as a low retaining wall. During the Civil War the castle was twice captured by the Roundheads and a great deal of damage was done. After the Restoration the south and east sides were pulled down as beyond repair and Bishop Rainbow made the other two habitable again. A second, more drastic restoration began in 1829 under the guidance of the architect Thomas Rickman. The present castle is largely his work but three square towers and their connecting walls survive from the medieval stronghold. The towers are named after bishops. Strickland's Tower, now isolated at the north-east corner of the former quadrangle, is the oldest as it is really the work of Bishop Halton (d.1324) some years prior to the first licence. Bell's Tower on the north front was added in the 1480s. Kite's Tower in the west range is an early Tudor gatehouse, overshadowed by Rickman's Percy Tower.

> *Access:* Open by appointment only.
> *Reference:* *Rose Castle* by J. Wilson. Curwen.
> *Relations:* The bishop's castles at Penrith and Bewley.

SCALEBY CASTLE stands in an extensive park south of the village, five miles north-east of Carlisle. The castle is a medieval ruin mixed in with an Elizabethan house. Robert de Tilliol obtained a licence to crenellate in 1307 and the general outline is his. It encompasses a tiny courtyard with buildings on two sides and a curtain bounding the other two, the whole rising within a large circular enclosure surrounded by a wet moat. Much of the masonry goes back to the licence but there was considerable remodelling under the Colvilles in the late fifteenth century. They rebuilt or added the pele tower at the north-east corner. Attached to it is a contemporary polygonal tower which served as a forebuilding. It flanks the entrance to the castle, a simple gateway through the curtain. The gateway has porter's lodges in the thickness of the wall and a portcullis chamber above. The hall, at first floor level above a barrel-vaulted undercroft, is also the Colvilles' work. The south range, which is still occupied, was rebuilt by Sir Edward Musgrave in 1596 and has been restored twice since. Its outer side is actually the old curtain with three projecting turrets. The castle was damaged by the Roundheads, who stormed it in February 1645 after a surprisingly long siege. It had to be captured a second time during the Royalist uprising of 1648.

Access: The exterior may be viewed by appointment.
Reference: Curwen.
Relations: Tower houses with small courtyards at Millom, Mortham and Edlingham.

TRIERMAIN CASTLE overlooks King Water three miles west of Gilsland. It was erected by Roland de Vaux, who obtained a licence to crenellate in 1340. It passed to the Dacres and was a ruin by 1580. The castle was a quadrilateral enclosure with a tower house in one corner and a gate tower in the opposite corner. All that remains is a tall piece of the gate tower, propped up by modern buttresses, together with much of the surrounding ditch.

Access: Visible from the road.
Relations: It must have resembled contemporary Naworth.

WHITEHALL, in its own grounds a short distance south-west of Mealsgate, is a Salvin mansion with a free-standing pele tower close by. An inscription over the entrance records that Lancelot Salkeld built the tower in 1589, but it is more likely that he restored something raised by one of his ancestors a century or so earlier. The austere tower is complete to its embattled parapet and stair turret.

Access: Open by appointment.

WORKINGTON HALL, in a park above the River Derwent, is a once-great mansion which has decayed into a ruined shell. This residence of the Curwens incorporates a few portions of a medieval fortified house. They comprise the hall in the east range, the barrel-vaulted pele tower near the east end of the south range and the gate passage with its flanking rooms on the west side. Sir Gilbert de Curwen obtained a licence to crenellate in 1379. The long north and south ranges were added in the Elizabethan period, but everything was given a thorough overhaul by the architect John Carr in the 1780s. The house is best known as the initial refuge of Mary Queen of Scots, following her escape to England in 1568.

Access: Open regularly in summer (LA).
Reference: Curwen.

OTHER SITES The pele towers listed below are not such good examples. A couple of them are ruined, some are heavily restored and the others have been gabled over or absorbed into later houses so that they are not readily apparent to the casual observer:

Boltongate Rectory (near Mealsgate)
Clargyll Hall (near Alston)
Corby Castle (near Wetheral)
Croglin Vicarage (near Kirkoswald)
Dalemain (near Dacre)
Denton Hall (near Brampton)
Dovenby Hall (near Cockermouth)
Drawdykes Castle (near Carlisle)
Hardrigg Hall (near Skelton – ruin)

Hayton Castle (near Aspatria)
Johnby Hall (near Greystoke)
Linstock Castle (near Carlisle)
Moresby Hall (near Whitehaven)
Netherby Hall (near Longtown)
Newbiggin Hall (near Carlisle)
Randalholm Hall (near Alston)
Thistlewood Tower (near Rose Castle)
Ulpha Old Hall (ruin)

Hayes Castle (near Distington) preserves a piece of curtain from a castle licensed in 1322. The church at *Beaumont* is built on a low motte and there are other Norman mottes at *Irthington* and *Maryport* (Castle Hill).

Derbyshire

The county has suffered several losses and there are few castles left of any real substance. Peveril is the best preserved of the Norman crop though the remains are secondary to its exhilarating Peak District setting. Bolsover has largely been rebuilt and it is a pity that the great keep at Duffield has not survived. More impressive today are the two later medieval mansions of Derbyshire – Haddon Hall and Wingfield Manor – both of which retain limited defensive characteristics.

BOLSOVER CASTLE occupies the summit of a limestone ridge rising steeply from the surrounding plain. It was raised by the Peverel family. The third William Peverel fled into exile accused of poisoning the Earl of Chester and his lands were forfeited to the Crown (1155). Bolsover remained in royal hands until 1553, by which time the castle was a total ruin. Sir Charles Cavendish began building a great mansion around the old castle in 1608, and work continued under his son William, Earl of Newcastle. The dominant feature of the rebuilding is the striking tower known as the Little Castle. It stands near the site of a small Norman keep and is a conscious revival of the medieval keep theme, though in appearance rather than in substance. The thick wall surrounding the oval inner bailey (now the Fountain

Garden) is actually the Norman curtain, refaced by the Cavendishes to such an extent that no medieval masonry is visible. This wall was breached in 1216 when the castle was captured on King John's behalf by William de Ferrers. The chief range of the Cavendish mansion, abandoned in the eighteenth century and now in ruins, occupies one side of the outer bailey.

Access: Standard openings times (EH).
Reference: Guidebook by P. A. Faulkner.
Relations: For the Peverels see Peveril.

CODNOR CASTLE lies in woodland overlooking the River Erewash, a mile east of Codnor town. Soon after 1200 Sir Richard de Grey inherited the manor. He probably built the castle, utilising an older motte-and-bailey of the Peverels. The remains are rather fragmentary and steadily decaying. The best preserved part is the unusual revetment wall which separates the motte from the bailey. It preserves a pointed window and a semi-circular bastion, one of a pair once flanking the entrance. Two other pieces of curtain survive, one in the bailey and one on the motte. Also on the motte is the featureless shell of a later domestic building. The Greys of Codnor were loyal supporters of King John and Henry III during their struggles with the barons, and they later played a prominent role in the Hundred Years' War. On the expiry of their line in 1496 Codnor passed to the Zouche family and the castle soon fell into ruins. The nearby farmhouse was built from its stones in 1640.

Access: Visible from the road.
Reference: Mackenzie (I).
Relations: For the Greys see Grey's Court and Wilton.

DUFFIELD CASTLE was the chief stronghold of the Ferrers earls of Derby. Henry de Ferrers is said to have founded the castle before his death in 1089. William de Ferrers joined Prince Henry's revolt (1173–74), as a result of which the castle was dismantled by order of Henry II. It soon rose again – Earl William managing to regain the King's trust – and the final destruction took place in 1266 after Robert de Ferrers lost his lands for supporting Simon de Montfort against Henry III. The castle lay a mile north of the village, overlooking what is now the A6. On top of a rocky hill which formed a natural motte stood a massive Norman keep, excavated in 1886. At over ninety feet square it was one of the largest in England, divided by cross-walls into three narrow compartments. Unfortunately the royal demolition was very thorough and only the restored foundations can be seen. They show spiral staircases at two opposite corners and a deep well. The keep probably dates from the second half of the twelfth century, but whether it was destroyed by Henry II or Henry III is uncertain. If the latter, then it is reasonable to suppose that it rose after the slighting of 1174. Nothing is left of the bailey.

Access: Freely accessible (NT).
Reference: VCH *Derbyshire* (I).
Relations: Oakham and Tutbury were other Ferrers strongholds.

FENNY BENTLEY OLD HALL, otherwise known as Cherry Orchard Farm, is two miles north of Ashbourne. Attached to the Elizabethan house is an austere little tower house of the fifteenth century. It was the home of the warlike Beresfords and was built either by John, who took part in the Agincourt campaign, or his son Thomas, who fought in France and for the Lancastrians. The latter's shrouded, alabaster monument can be seen in the parish church.

Access: Private.

HADDON HALL stands on a bluff overlooking the River Wye, two miles southeast of Bakewell. The situation and the embattled outline give an impression of strength from a distance, but as a castle Haddon is something of a mystery. Its complex building history suggests a manor house which developed defences but has been effectively de-fortified since. The story goes back to Richard de Vernon, who obtained a peculiar licence in 1195. It allowed him to enclose his house within a wall, but the wall was not to exceed twelve feet in height and was *not* to be crenellated. Some of the wall and part of the chapel survive from that time. What stands today is a rectangular enclosure of the fourteenth century with ranges of buildings on each side. The outer wall is certainly thick enough to qualify as a curtain except on the north side, where the range is a late medieval rebuilding. On the west the curtain remains defensive with a square bastion projecting from the middle. The terrain is strongest here but the insertion of Elizabethan bay windows elsewhere has transformed the appearance of the mansion. The only other towers are the tall gate towers at each end (the inner is fourteenth century, the outer of *circa* 1530). An unaccountable weakness is the chapel which projects from the south-west corner of the enclosure.

There was a general rebuilding under Sir Richard Vernon around 1370. It is likely that he built up the wall into a proper curtain as well as erecting the residential buildings which are the marvel of Haddon. The hall lies across the middle of the enclosure, dividing it into two courtyards. This arrangement allowed the hall to be lit by large windows on either side without weakening the curtain. A fine porch leads from the lower courtyard into the old screens passage. The original wooden screen still exists, though the hall roof is a modern reconstruction. To the north are the kitchen and a row of domestic offices. To the south is a first-floor solar, the former parlour beneath it preserving a painted ceiling of *circa* 1500. Further private apartments are ranged around the upper courtyard to the east. They were remodelled in the Elizabethan period and include a splendid long gallery. The lower courtyard is a typical 'base court' lined with retainers' lodgings. The chapel is a fully-fledged little church with nave arcades, clerestory, chancel and octagonal bell turret. It is especially notable for its fifteenth-century wall paintings. Haddon remained in the hands of the Vernons until 1567 when it passed to the Manners family, subsequently dukes of Rutland. For two centuries they neglected it in favour of Belvoir Castle but allowed its buildings to remain intact, so that Haddon is today one of the most unspoilt medieval mansions in England.

Access: Open regularly in summer.
Reference: Guidebook by K. H. Mantell. BOE *Derbyshire.*
Relations: Belvoir. Walled mansions such as Compton and Penshurst.

MACKWORTH CASTLE, three miles west of Derby, was the residence of the Mackworth family. They were here by 1254 and finally sold out in 1655. Their castle – a quadrangular stronghold with an outer bailey – is said to have been destroyed during the Civil War. Only the outer gatehouse survives, minus its rear wall, beside the village's main street. This gatehouse is an early Tudor addition and not a defensive structure, though the battlements and corner turrets give a misleading impression of strength.

Access: Freely accessible.

PEVERIL CASTLE crowns a steep hill overlooking Castleton in the Peak District. This area was a centre of medieval lead mining and William the Conqueror appointed William Peverel (supposedly his illegitimate son) as bailiff of the royal lands here. The ruined castle which bears his name was usually called the Castle of the Peak in medieval times. It existed by the time of the Domesday survey and comprises a triangular enclosure sloping upwards to a sheer drop at the rear. The very ruinous curtain is probably William Peverel's, since it displays herringbone masonry typical of early Norman work and stone was easy to come by here. It is of some interest as an early stone enclosure with neither keep nor gatehouse originally. It would seem that the north wall, guarding the easiest approach, came first, with the western wall (overlooking a ravine) following. Henry II inserted the present gate arch, facing the town. The precipitous south-eastern side of the bailey was not walled until the thirteenth century and the curtain here has since disappeared. Two round towers stood along it, though why there should have been towers on the edge of the cliff but none elsewhere is difficult to explain.

When the third William Peverel forfeited his estates in 1155 the castle was taken over by Henry II. Expenditure of £184 in 1176–77 – just after Prince Henry's revolt – is just enough to account for the square keep which now dominates the castle. The keep has come down to us in good condition, preserving its ashlar facing except on two of the outside walls. As keeps go it is a modest structure, just two storeys high, though the walls rise higher to protect the vanished roof. The entrance was at first-floor level as usual but there is no evidence for a forebuilding. Clearly the main accommodation was always in the bailey and the foundations of two successive halls can be seen. From 1254 the castle passed through a succession of owners, finally ending up with the Duchy of Lancaster. It has lain abandoned at least since the fifteenth century.

Access: Standard opening times (EH).
Reference: Guidebook by B. Morley.
Relations: Bolsover was another Peverel castle.

WINGFIELD MANOR At South Wingfield are the stately ruins of a mansion erected by Sir Ralph Cromwell in the 1440s. Lord Cromwell was High Treasurer of England and builder of the great brick tower at Tattershall Castle. Unlike Tattershall, Wingfield Manor is all of one period and entirely of stone. It follows the late medieval trend for two courtyards, one containing Cromwell's residential buildings and the other a 'base court' for retainers. This arrangement is often described as a security measure but here the distinction was purely a social one. Neither courtyard can be described as defensive and both are entered through gatehouses which have side arches for pedestrians in addition to the main arch. The flanking turrets cannot make up for such a weakness. In fact the only defensive feature, apart from the commanding position above the River Amber, is an oblong tower house rising at one corner of the inner courtyard. Tattershall's tower was a comfortable residence and a symbol of lordship, but the tower here is a comparatively modest affair and can never have dominated the mansion. Its outer half was blasted down after the Civil War. The tower house is unusual for its distance from the principal apartments, which are situated at the far end of the courtyard. The hall is notable for its porch, its bay window and its vaulted undercroft. It is peculiar to find the solar and the domestic offices lumped together beyond the west end of the hall.

Shortly before his death in 1455 Lord Cromwell sold the mansion to John Talbot, Earl of Shrewsbury. It remained in Talbot hands for over a century. During that time Mary Queen of Scots spent portions of her long imprisonment here, in some discomfort. In 1643 the house was wrested from the Roundheads by the Earl of Newcastle. It became a major source of Royalist resistance and a Parliamentary force was despatched to reduce it. After a lengthy siege in which the besiegers were hampered by lack of artillery a breach was made and the garrison surrendered (1644). Parliament ordered the slighting of the mansion despite its defensive limitations.

Access: Standard opening times (EH).
Reference: Wingfield Manor by W. Hawksley Edmunds. BOE *Derbyshire.*
Relations: Tattershall. For Mary Queen of Scots' execution see Fotheringhay.

OTHER SITES Derbyshire possesses few Norman earthworks. *Bakewell* has a motte-and-bailey castle and another motte is visible at *Castle Gresley. Horeston Castle* (near Horsley) had a square keep built by King John on an outcrop of rock. The base of one wall was excavated in 1888 and is just visible. *Melbourne Castle* is a sad loss. This multi-towered stronghold, licensed in 1311, has been reduced to an ivy-covered scrap of wall at Castle Farm.

Devon

Devon has a representative group of castles, beginning with impressive motte-and-baileys such as Totnes and Plympton, the early Norman gatehouse at Exeter and the keep at Lydford. Exeter also preserves much of its city wall which originated in Roman times. However, the majority of Devon castles are defensive houses of the later Middle Ages, whether arranged irregularly like Okehampton and Berry Pomeroy, or planned on quadrangular lines as Tiverton, Powderham and Compton originally were. Compton is exceptionally late for a private fortification. The Courtenays were the leading family and possessed several of the county's castles. The distribution of castles is curiously uneven with very little in the northern half of the county. There is a particular concentration of castles around Torbay and the Dart estuary, which were convenient landing places for the pirates who plagued the seas during the Hundred Years War and later. Piracy was endemic on both sides of the Channel and the inhabitants of Dartmouth were notorious for it. Eager to protect themselves from the consequences of their own aggression, they pioneered the effective use of artillery in their fortifications. The blockhouses at Dartmouth and Kingswear were innovative in another sense too: they were purely forts as opposed to true castles. In both respects they point towards Henry VIII's chain of coastal defences.

AFFETON CASTLE, or Affeton Barton, lies beside the Little Dart River midway between Cheldon and West Worlington. Only a few ruined walls show where the house stood but the gatehouse, probably added after the Stucleys or Stukeleys acquired the manor in the late fifteenth century, is still intact thanks to a heavy-handed restoration of 1868 which converted it into a residence. There is a square flanking tower beside the blocked gate arch. This is the only feature suggesting defence, and a rather half-hearted one as might be expected at this late date.

Access: Visible from the road.

BARNSTAPLE CASTLE Barnstaple was one of the four Saxon burghs of Devon. Its defences were later rebuilt in stone but nothing is left of them now. The castle has not fared much better because only the high motte survives, overlooking the River Taw. Excavations in 1927 exposed the foundations of a circular shell keep on the summit. Barnstaple was one of the properties granted to Judhael de Totnes and he may have founded the castle before his banishment in 1088. If not, it was raised on Judhael's return after Henry I's accession, since Judhael regained Barnstaple but lost Totnes for good. The castle seems to have been abandoned at an early stage.

Access: Freely accessible (LA).
Reference: BOE *Devon* (2nd edn).
Relations: Judhael's Totnes.

BAYARD'S COVE CASTLE is one of the fortifications protecting Dartmouth. Dartmouth and Kingswear castles stand a mile away towards the mouth of the Dart estuary. In case any hostile ships should get past them the townsfolk of Dartmouth built this small blockhouse commanding the entrance to the harbour. It is probably the tower which was under construction in 1509. The blockhouse is a simple enclosure with a row of large gun ports in the curved wall facing the sea, and a parapet above. It was brought back into commission as a machine-gun post during the invasion scare of 1940.

Access: Freely accessible (EH).
Relations: Dartmouth and Kingswear. St Catherine's Castle (Fowey) is a similar blockhouse.

BERRY POMEROY CASTLE occupies a spur of land falling steeply to the Gatcombe valley, three miles north-east of Totnes. The ruins of a late medieval castle are juxtaposed with those of a great Tudor mansion. The Pomeroys settled here soon after the Norman Conquest but their castle dates only from the fifteenth century. It is probably the work of Henry Pomeroy who held the manor from 1446 to 1487. The new defences were doubtless a response to the menace of French raids, the castle being just a few miles inland from Torbay. Only one side remains of the castle defences, comprising the gatehouse, the D-shaped Margaret's Tower and the length of curtain between them. Enough survives to show that this was no regular quadrangle. The gatehouse has tall flanking towers with pointed fronts and a long machicolation between them. The chamber over the gate passage is divided by an arcade, the narrower part having served as the chapel. A fine fresco here depicting the Adoration of the Magi shows Flemish influence, and its discovery led to the re-roofing the gatehouse during the restoration of the 1980s. The curtain is backed by an earth rampart as a reinforcement against artillery, and the walls are liberally supplied with gun ports.

The big residential block on the east side of the courtyard incorporates the Pomeroys' hall and solar, but it was transformed in the large-scale rebuilding of the following century. In 1547 Sir Thomas Pomeroy sold the castle to Edward Seymour, Duke of Somerset and Lord Protector. As well as converting the eastern block, which survives as a well-preserved shell, he began an ambitious Renaissance mansion centred upon an immense new hall range on the far side of the courtyard, overlooking the valley. Unfortunately it is now too fragmentary to be readily appreciated. Somerset was executed in 1552 and his son, another Edward, completed the work on a reduced scale. If the original scheme had been realised even the surviving portion of the medieval castle would no doubt have been swept away. By 1700 the castle had been abandoned. As a matter of interest there are more ghost stories associated with this castle than any other in England, with the possible exception of the Tower of London!

Access: Standard opening times in summer (EH).
Reference: Guidebook by H. Gordon Slade.
Relations: Compton is another late castle built in response to pirate raids.

BICKLEIGH CASTLE, beside the River Exe, is three miles south of Tiverton. A castle may have existed here in Norman times and the chapel associated with it is a quaint example of Norman work. It stands outside the gates of the present castle, which dates from *circa* 1400. Bickleigh passed from the Pointingtons to the Courtenays around that time so it is uncertain which family built it. In the Civil War Sir Henry Carew held the castle for the King, and after its capture by the Roundheads it was pulled down with the exception of the gatehouse which was allowed to remain as a residence. The gatehouse is a simple, oblong structure with a vaulted gate passage in the middle. A large hall occupies the whole of the first floor, suggesting a variant of the keep-gatehouse theme. Its windows are Elizabethan insertions though original windows still light what used to be the top floor. The gatehouse formed one side of a small quadrangle but nothing else is known about it. The thatched house at right angles to the gatehouse occupies the site of one of the other ranges.

Access: Open regularly in summer.
Reference: BOE *Devon* (2nd edn). Souvenir guide.
Relations: For the Courtenays see Okehampton, Powderham and Tiverton.

COMPTON CASTLE, three miles west of Torquay, has belonged to the Gilbert family – with one long interruption – since the early fourteenth century. The Gilberts are famous for their role in the age of exploration, Sir Humphrey Gilbert discovering Newfoundland in 1583. Occupation descended to impoverished tenant farmers who could not afford any fashionable rebuilding, and for this reason the castle is one of the few to survive more or less intact but remarkably unspoilt. Disregarding its later defences for a moment, Compton originated as a typical West Country manor house. It is centred upon a fourteenth-century hall which, having fallen into ruins, was rebuilt on its original lines in 1955. The west wing containing the solar and a pretty little chapel was added by Otto Gilbert (d.1494). It appears that the tower attached to the solar is older than the others and began as a tower house.

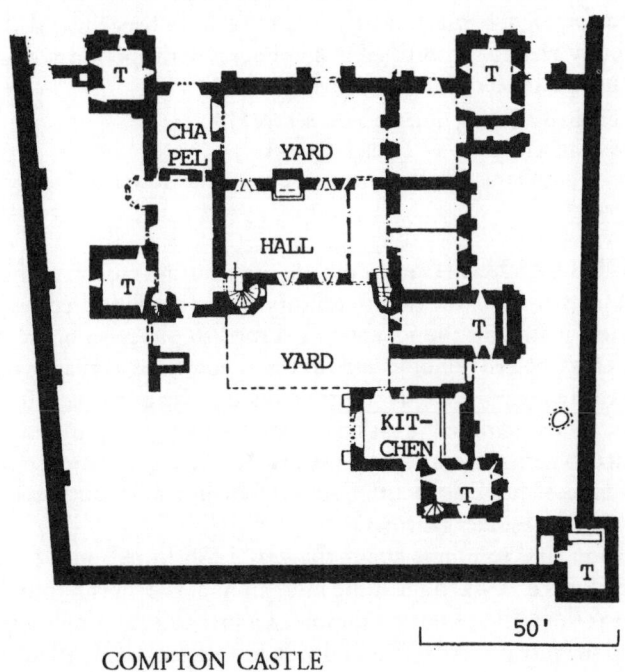

COMPTON CASTLE

The house was transformed into a more extensive complex by Otto's son John. His additions have been dated to *circa* 1520 and if this is accurate then Compton vies with Thornbury as the last true castle ever raised in England (except for a handful of later pele towers). At this time the coast suffered frequent attacks from French pirates and Compton, not far inland, would have been a target. A new wing containing the kitchen and domestic offices was added to the east of the hall. The outer face of this wing, with its projecting towers, is clearly a curtain wall. It is likely that a quadrangle was intended, the hall lying across the middle and dividing it into two. If we imagine the scheme brought to completion there would have been square towers at the four corners and others in the middle of the two longer sides (the older tower is one of the latter). However, the west wing was never extended southwards to match the east wing, so the house follows an H-plan with one of the prongs and the presumed south-west tower missing. The north corner towers are connected by a high curtain, its main weakness being the large chapel window which is made more secure by an iron grille. The gateway through the curtain has a portcullis groove and a machicolated archway high above it. Beyond the corner towers the curtain returns to closely surround the inner castle – a late revival of the concentric theme. One low corner tower projects from an otherwise-plain circuit. The five towers of the inner enclosure are tall and capped by gabled roofs, giving the castle a distinctly Scottish appearance. They have small gun ports at ground level. An outer courtyard lay to the north but nothing survives of it. The defensive nature of the castle is undermined by two serious flaws. On the east the castle is overlooked by higher ground, so much so that the concentric curtain acts as a revetment wall here. Furthermore no trace has ever been found of a moat. Surely one must have been intended, as it was a standard amenity even for unfortified manor houses of the period and without it the walls would not have been a very effective barrier.

Access: Limited opening times in summer (NT).
Reference: Guidebook by W. Raleigh Gilbert.
Relations: Thornbury. For concentric castles see the Tower of London, Dover and Middleham.

DARTMOUTH CASTLE Dartmouth, on the beautiful estuary of the River Dart, was a flourishing port from the twelfth century. When the Hundred Years War made legitimate trading difficult the inhabitants turned to piracy to boost their profits, and the 'Sea Dogs' of Dartmouth were almost as notorious as the 'Fowey Gallants'. Their unfortunate targets were the ports across the Channel. In 1404 the Bretons landed in force and attempted to sack the town in revenge, but they were driven off by the inhabitants with great loss to themselves. According to French sources a second raid was more successful. Dartmouth Castle is actually a mile south-east of the town, at a point where the estuary narrows.

A fortification first rose here about the year 1388 in response to the threat of invasion from France. It was built at the instigation of the mayor, John Hawley, and is interesting as the earliest known example of a fort built by a municipal authority as opposed to the private castle of an individual. It was a simple affair, consisting of a curtain with circular towers cutting off the landward approach to the headland. A tall piece of curtain and one shattered tower can be seen on the high ground over-looking the later defences. In view of the primitive artillery of the day it is difficult to see how this fortification could have interfered with enemy ships. It was also overlooked by much higher ground. Perhaps for these reasons it soon fell into disuse.

The tower which now forms the focal point of the castle crowns the rocks on the edge of the headland. It was built by the townsfolk in 1481–94, though the King approved and contributed an annual subsidy for the garrison. It looks like two connected towers, one square and one oval. In fact the original design was for a free-standing oval tower and the more prominent square portion is an afterthought, but there is no internal division between the two. By the late fifteenth century firearms had improved considerably. It is clear that guns were intended to sweep the estuary and in that sense the castle is revolutionary. The splayed gun ports provided

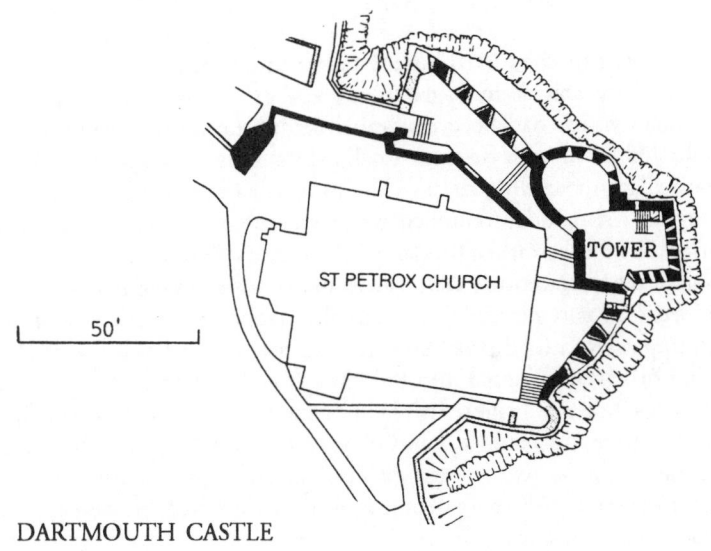

DARTMOUTH CASTLE

a degree of flexibility for cannon fire which was hitherto unknown. They lie in the rock-cut basement. The two floors above provided basic accommodation for the garrison. An opening at ground-floor level received the boom chain which ran across the river to the Kingswear bank. On each side of the building is a thick wall with further gun emplacements (the embrasures here were widened in the eighteenth century). It is basically a screen wall facing the estuary. No defences were provided on the landward side unless the older curtain was still in use. The church of St Petrock (largely rebuilt in 1641) stands immediately behind the tower. Like many other coastal fortifications the castle saw little action in its intended role but became embroiled in the Civil War. The Royalists tried to strengthen the vulnerable rear by digging an earth redoubt (Gallant's Bower) on the high ground behind. However, the castle was stormed by Sir Thomas Fairfax in 1646.

Access: Standard opening times (EH).
Reference: Guidebook by A. D. Saunders.
Relations: Its companions, Bayard's Cove and Kingswear. Compare Fowey.

EXETER CASTLE AND CITY WALL Exeter originated as the Roman city of *Isca.* Occupation continued after the departure of the Romans but it fell to the West Saxons *circa* 658. For the next two centuries Exeter remained on the frontier between Saxons and Celts. Then in 876 the Danes captured the city, only to be driven out by King Alfred three years later. They came again in 1003 but only to plunder and burn. Next in the line of invaders was William the Conqueror, to whom the city offered stout resistance in 1068. It fell after eighteen days, the Normans having undermined the city wall. King Stephen unsuccessfully besieged the city (1138), the pretender Perkin Warbeck captured it twice and in 1549 Exeter resisted the insurgents of the 'Prayer Book' rebellion. This remarkable history of sieges is rounded off by two in the Civil War. To cap it all, the city suffered an aerial bombardment in 1942.

Despite this chequered history Exeter preserves many relics of its medieval past. Even its city wall has managed to survive for the most part and the bombing revealed stretches which had been concealed behind houses for centuries. It is nearly two miles long, but with frequent small gaps and little parapet to walk along it is not a particularly rewarding circuit. The Roman and medieval city occupied a near-rectangular area, today bounded by Northernhay, Eastgate, Southernhay and West Street. Like most other Romano-British cities Exeter was first enclosed by a stone wall in the third century AD. The Roman plinth and regularly-coursed masonry can be seen in many places – it is unusual in fact for so much Roman work to survive. During its eventful history, however, the city wall had to be patched up many times. King Athelstan repaired it in the 930s though nothing of his is now visible. From 1224 the wall was heightened. Half-round flanking towers were added to the circuit at this time but only a handful survive, along Southernhay. Bishop's Bastion, containing a postern which led into the cathedral precinct, is largely a modern reconstruction. All the gatehouses were demolished in the eighteenth century as troublesome obstacles.

The castle of Exeter, often called Rougemont Castle from the red sandstone knoll on which it is built, occupies the northern corner of the city's defences. It was founded by William I straight after the capitulation. The square bailey is protected by the city wall on two sides. Towards the town there is a strong rampart topped by the ruins of a curtain. Towers mark the junctions between the city wall and the curtain and there is a later half-round bastion (Athelstan's Tower) on the north-east (i.e. city) wall. Herringbone masonry is visible in places and the well-preserved gatehouse is almost certainly a relic of the Conqueror's time. Its antiquity is indicated by two triangular-headed windows above the blocked outer archway and another facing the bailey. They suggest Anglo-Saxon work, the only plausible explanation being that English masons were employed and continued to build in their traditional style. The short barbican with its tall arch is contemporary with the rest of the gatehouse and thus the oldest in England. Exeter is one of those early Norman castles which put the emphasis upon a strong gatehouse instead of a keep. Unlike other examples, the gatehouse does not seem to have been converted into a keep during the twelfth century. In the later Middle Ages the administrative functions of this royal castle grew to outweigh its military role and the townward defences were left to decay. A court house (1774) still occupies the bailey.

> *Access:* The city wall remains are freely accessible but the castle can only be viewed from outside (both LA).
>
> *Reference: HKW* (II) for the castle. Turner for the city wall.
>
> *Relations:* There are early Norman gatehouses at Ludlow and Richmond. Compare the town wall at Colchester which is also largely Roman.

GIDLEIGH CASTLE is a fairly complete ruin in the garden of a private house. It may be called a tower house though in fact it is only two storeys high, comprising a single apartment over an undercroft. The windows and doorways resemble those at Okehampton Castle and it is likely that the same master mason was at work. Hence the castle is generally attributed to Sir William de Prouze (d.1316). Gidleigh lies on the edge of Dartmoor, two miles north-west of Chagford.

Access: Private.

Relations: Okehampton.

HEMYOCK CASTLE, in the Culm valley beneath the Blackdown Hills, was licensed in 1380. It was built by Sir William Asthorpe, by all accounts something of a troublesome neighbour, but before and after his time the manor belonged to the Dynhams. The castle was quadrangular with round towers at the corners and in the middle of each side, except on the east where there are twin towers flanking the gate passage. This gate and its flanking towers are now the best preserved part though the upper half has vanished. Apart from that the remains are fragmentary, comprising the ruins of the north-east tower, fragments of three other towers and a few stretches of curtain. It seems that the main house stood free within the bailey as the existing farmhouse incorporates medieval work. The castle may have been reduced to ruins by the Royalists, who stormed it in 1643.

Access: Limited opening times in summer.

Reference: Guidebook by M. Sheppard.

KINGSWEAR CASTLE commands the eastern side of the River Dart estuary. It is the companion of Dartmouth Castle on the opposite bank and thus important as one of the earliest fortifications designed for defence by artillery. The corporation of Dartmouth started work in 1491, when Dartmouth Castle was nearing completion, and it was finished in 1502. Kingswear is simpler than its neighbour, being a plain square tower, but it has identical gun ports on the ground floor. A boom chain could be raised across the estuary, barring enemy ships which would then be caught in the cross-fire. Despite the shutters which covered the gun ports when not in use, the iron cannon quickly rusted and brass replacements had to be brought in. As artillery increased in power Dartmouth Castle was able to sweep the estuary alone and Kingswear fell out of use. It was brought back into service during the Civil War, the landward defences being improved (as at Dartmouth Castle) by the digging of an earthen redoubt, but succumbed to the Roundheads in 1646. In 1855 the tower was restored from ruin and converted into a dwelling.

Access: Private. Best seen from the river (NT).

Reference: Dartmouth Castle guidebook.

Relations: Bayard's Cove and Dartmouth.

LYDFORD CASTLES. Now a small village on the edge of Dartmoor, Lydford was a burgh in late Saxon times. Its situation, on a promontory overlooking the River Lyd, has steep falls on all sides except one. The level approach is defended by a rampart. The first castle at Lydford was the ringwork at the west corner of the promontory, now known as the Norman Fort. It did not stay in use for long and the present Lydford Castle stands nearby, the parish church occupying the space between them. At first sight the castle seems to be a motte-and-bailey earthwork with a square keep on top of the mound. This is an illusion, however, because the keep was built first and earth was then piled around its lower part as if to emulate a motte. It is also questionable as to whether we can regard this building as a keep in the normal sense of the word. In 1195 a strong house for prisoners was erected and the 'keep' has been identified with it. There is a further complication in that only the ground floor is original, the upper storeys being added after a gap in building operations. There is absolutely no refinement in the stonework, resulting in a grim tower which seems to add weight to the prison theory. By the time building resumed a square keep was rather antiquated in any case. Internally there is nothing to suggest that this tower was not a normal keep, though later alterations have been numerous. Even the cross-wall is largely a rebuilding.

Notwithstanding the circumstances in which it was built, the castle subsequently did serve mainly as a court house and prison. This was inevitable because Lydford was the administrative centre of the Forest of Dartmoor and the local tin mines. These provided important revenue for the Crown, and later for the Duchy of Cornwall of which Dartmoor became part in 1337. Royal forests were always harshly administered and the tinners jealously guarded their privileges. 'Lydford law' became synonymous with rough justice, the authorities (it is said) hanging first and sitting in judgement later! Despite its notorious conditions the castle remained a prison until the courts moved to Princetown in the nineteenth century. After this long service the keep is now roofless but otherwise intact.

Access: The castles are freely accessible (EH).
Reference: Guidebook by A. D. Saunders.
Relations: For another prison tower see Hexham.

MARISCO CASTLE can be found on Lundy, a small island in the Bristol Channel. Under the De Mariscos the island was a notorious centre of piracy. This went on until William de Marisco was implicated in a plot to murder Henry III, as a result of which the King despatched a force to take the island. They arrived by stealth in 1242 and captured William, who was taken to London and hanged. The castle which bears the family name was actually constructed on Henry's orders the following year. It stands on a rise at the south end of the island. Two opposite walls of a square keep still rise to a fair height, with Victorian cottages built against them. The form was an antiquated one for Henry's time but quite adequate in this remote location. There are indications of an outer ditched enclosure. During the Civil War the castle was garrisoned by the Royalists but never besieged.

Access: Exterior visible (NT). Lundy can be reached by boat from Bideford or (in summer) Ilfracombe.
Reference: *Lundy* by A. & M. Langham.
Relations: Henry III's keep at York.

OKEHAMPTON CASTLE must have been founded by Baldwin de Brionne, who was made Sheriff of Devon following the Norman conquest of the county. It is mentioned in the Domesday Book. The castle has an impressive position on a spur of land above the West Okement River, a mile south-west of the town. It passed to the Courtenay family who were emerging as major landholders in the county. Hugh

Courtenay rebuilt the castle in its present form sometime after his coming of age in 1297. He was created Earl of Devon in 1335. The castle remained a popular retreat with his successors until the execution (1539) of Henry Courtenay, who fell victim to the intrigues of Henry VIII's court. It was then abandoned and drifted into ruin.

Although the earthworks are Norman, comprising an imposing motte between two baileys, most of the masonry belongs to Hugh Courtenay's time. Only the eastern bailey was ever rebuilt in stone. It was reached via an exceptionally long barbican passage with the remains of square gate towers at each end. The bailey ascends towards the motte and is rendered rather narrow by the domestic buildings on either side. Although very ruinous, these buildings provide a good insight into the extensive accommodation required in a prominent lord's household. The gabled structure on the north side of the bailey contained the hall and solar. Across from the hall is a well-preserved row of retainers' lodgings and next to it a chapel with apartments for the priest attached. The outer wall of this range served as the curtain, but behind the hall was a free-standing curtain which has largely collapsed. Nevertheless, from a defensive point of view the castle relied primarily upon its situation (there is just one small flanking turret on the south side). Crowning the motte are the shattered remains of an oblong tower house, clearly built in two parts. The front portion, with its leaning stair turret, incorporates the base of a small square keep which may go back to Baldwin de Brionne's time.

Access: Standard opening times in summer (EH).
Reference: Guidebook by R. A. Higham.
Relations: Hugh Courtenay also built Tiverton Castle.

PAIGNTON: BISHOP'S PALACE The palace stands close to the parish church and was one of the mansions of the medieval bishops of Exeter. Much of the precinct wall survives, enclosing a rectangular area. The wall is an embattled curtain, doubtless erected in response to French raids but not especially high. Its builder was probably Bishop John Grandisson (d.1369). At an angle of the wall stands the square Coverdale Tower, said to have been occupied by Miles Coverdale, translator of the Bible. It is tall, narrow and does not project beyond the line of the curtain. Evidently the residential buildings were free-standing within the enclosure but nothing is left of them.

Access: Exterior only.
Relations: Fortified episcopal palaces such as Wells and Wolvesey (Winchester).

PLYMPTON CASTLE is an imposing motte-and-bailey, its position affording a fine view. There is a substantial rampart around the single bailey and on top of the motte are a few tall fragments of a circular shell keep. The castle was founded by Richard de Redvers (subsequently Earl of Devon) *circa* 1100, to control what was then a prosperous tin-mining borough. Redvers' son Baldwin joined Matilda's side on Henry I's death, and as a result King Stephen captured the castle in 1136. It is said that Stephen razed the castle to the ground, in which case the existing earthworks and masonry must postdate Baldwin's return from exile under Henry II. However, medieval chronicles tend to exaggerate such matters. The castle remained a Redvers property but on the extinction of their line in 1293 it passed to the Courtenays, who allowed it to decay.

Access: Freely accessible (LA).
Reference: Mackenzie (II).
Relations: The Redvers castles at Christchurch and Carisbrooke.

POWDERHAM CASTLE Sir Philip Courtenay, Lord Lieutenant of Ireland and one of the younger sons of the Earl of Devon, inherited Powderham in 1390. He built the original castle here. The River Exe once came up to it but has since retreated. Before its later transformation the castle was presumably of the quadrangular type. A tall square tower projects from the north-west corner, and the south end of the west range is built up into another, non-projecting tower. The west range itself incorporates a lot of medieval masonry (it probably contained the hall). If the other three sides were ever built they must have vanished by the Elizabethan period, when the west range was replanned as an E-plan mansion with a central porch. By this time Powderham had become the chief seat of the Courtenay earls. In 1645 the castle resisted Sir Thomas Fairfax's troops for several weeks and suffered severe damage. During the eighteenth century it was gradually transformed into a stately home. The west range is now a refined example of Georgian elegance and the two side wings have no connection with the original castle. The western forecourt with its embattled gatehouse is actually Victorian.

Access: Open regularly in summer.
Reference: BOE *Devon* (2nd edn). Souvenir guide.
Relations: The Courtenay castles of Bickleigh, Okehampton and Tiverton.

SALCOMBE CASTLE is strikingly situated on a rock commanding the Kingsbridge estuary, close to the North Sands. It may belong to Henry VIII's coastal defence scheme of circa 1540. However, there is no record of its construction, suggesting local rather than royal funding. This blockhouse comprised a squat, semi-circular gun tower and a curved wall facing seawards, but the tower is now very much a ruin and the wall is fragmentary. In 1646 it put up a stout resistance to the Roundheads, surrendering on honourable terms after four months of siege. It earned the alternative name of Fort Charles and coastal defence did not prevent it from being slighted.

Access: Freely accessible at low tide.
Reference: Mackenzie (II).

TIVERTON CASTLE According to tradition a castle was first raised here by Richard de Redvers, Earl of Devon, around 1106, but if so nothing remains of it. The present stronghold was built by Hugh Courtenay soon after 1300, and the quadrangular plan is very typical of that era but would be unlikely in a Norman castle. We may compare Hugh's reconstruction of Okehampton Castle, where his work was conditioned by the old motte-and-bailey layout. Tiverton's quadrangle was surrounded by a curtain wall which remains on three sides. There were towers at the corners but only the two southern ones have survived. The south-east tower is circular and rather picturesque with its later conical roof; the larger south-west tower is square and ruinous. Windows piercing the curtain between them, some retaining their tracery, show that important buildings stood here, the largest marking the site of the chapel. These windows and the relatively slight projection of the angle towers show that the castle, though a product of the Edwardian age, was not too serious a fortress. This is exemplified by the gatehouse in the middle of the east front. Though undeniably strong it eschews Edwardian defensive principles, being a simple tower with one floor over the vaulted gate passage. The part which projects in front of the curtain is a slightly later extension.

Hugh Courtenay became Earl of Devon and Tiverton was the favourite seat of subsequent earls until their attainder in 1539. On the Courtenays' reinstatement the castle was not restored to them but passed instead to the Giffards. They abandoned the old residential buildings on the south and west and built an Elizabethan house in the north-east corner of the courtyard, backing onto the old curtain. This house still exists in a much-modified form. In the Civil War the castle was garrisoned for the King and withstood the first onslaught by the Roundheads. It was then closely besieged by Fairfax and surrendered in October 1645. Afterwards the west side of the castle, which overlooks the River Exe, was torn down but the rest was left intact out of courtesy to the occupants.

Access: Open regularly in summer.
Reference: BOE *Devon* (2nd edn). Mackenzie (II).
Relations: Hugh Courtenay's Okehampton and the other Courtenay castles of Bickleigh and Powderham.

TOTNES CASTLE Totnes, strongly situated above the River Dart, was one of the four Saxon burghs of Devon. After the Norman Conquest it was awarded to Judhael 'de Totnes', and he raised the castle on its hill-top site. It is an excellent example of a motte-and-bailey stronghold, the great motte intruding aggressively into the old town. Judhael lost his estates for supporting Robert of Normandy against William Rufus, and even when he returned to favour under Henry I he did not regain Totnes. Ownership changed frequently until the Zouche family inherited in 1273. Since their power base was in the Midlands they seldom came here, but the keep on the motte was kept in good repair until the Tudor era. It remains intact today. The keep is a Norman-style shell keep, but although its core contains older masonry the visible stonework dates only from the early fourteenth century and as such is a curious anachronism. The reconstruction is attributed to William, Lord Zouche. It probably took place in 1326 when Edward II ordered the repair of the castle. Two straight stairways in the thickness of the wall lead up to the embattled parapet. A thin foundation visible inside the shell keep supported the wooden tower which first crowned the motte. One ruinous length of bailey curtain also survives. Just outside is a fragment of the town wall, incorporating the simple archway of the North Gate. (The only other relic of the town wall is the rebuilt East Gate.)

Access: Open at standard times (EH).
Reference: Guidebook by S. E. Rigold.
Relations: Judhael of Totnes founded Barnstaple Castle.

OTHER SITES The Royal Citadel of *Plymouth*, built to protect the dockyard in Charles II's reign, takes the place of a castle erected in the 1420s. It followed the standard quadrangular plan but, like the first Dartmouth Castle, was an early instance of a non-residential fortress built by a town for coastal defence. All that can be seen is the base of a small turret off Lambhay Street. The town itself was walled in the fifteenth century but nothing survives. *Bere Barton* at Bere Ferrers incorporates the lower part of a small tower house licensed in 1337. *Colcombe Castle* (near Colyton) is a ruined Tudor mansion taking the place of another Courtenay stronghold. Motte-and-bailey castles can be seen at *Bampton*, *Durpley* and Great *Torrington*.

Dorset

The two main Norman castles of Dorset, Corfe and Sherborne, are now splendid ruins, and dramatic illustrations of the effects of Civil War slighting. Of the two Corfe is the more impressive, not least because of its situation. Wareham preserves a Saxon town rampart but has lost its Norman keep. There is little to show for the turmoil of the Hundred Years War, when the whole of the South Coast was vulnerable to French raids. Rufus Castle is a rare pre-Henry VIII example of public coastal defence. Henry himself erected coastal forts (Portland and Sandsfoot) to protect Portland Harbour.

CORFE CASTLE, midway between Wareham and Swanage, is one of the most dramatic of English ruins. It stands on an isolated hill which forms part of the Purbeck range, towering above the picturesque village of the same name. The late Saxon kings had a palace here and it was outside the gates that Edward the Martyr was murdered in a family coup which put Ethelred the Unready on the throne (979). Nothing is visible from the pre-Conquest era and there is some confusion over its origin as a castle. The Domesday Book mentions Wareham Castle but it is possible that it actually refers to Corfe. Whatever the circumstances behind the two foundations, Corfe soon came to overshadow its neighbour. The site allowed for two baileys of unequal size flanking a steep-sided summit which forms a natural motte. During the Anarchy Baldwin de Redvers seized the castle for Matilda, and King Stephen unsuccessfully besieged it in 1139. The ringwork known as The Rings, a quarter of a mile to the south-west, is probably his siege fort. In 1200–05 King John spent over £1400 on the castle, and expenditure under Henry III amounted to another £1000 over a much longer period. Edward II was held captive here for a while between his abdication and murder. After that the castle was seldom visited by its royal owners and fell into decay. It was sold by Elizabeth I but underwent its most stirring chapter during the Civil War. In 1643 Lady Banks defended the castle against a Parliamentary force. All attempts at assault failed and, after three months, the siege was abandoned. For the next two and a half years Corfe stood out as a Royalist island in Roundhead territory. It was finally captured by a stratagem, some enemy troops entering in the guise of a relieving force (February 1646). Parliament ordered the destruction of the castle and the slighting was carried out with as much thoroughness as the walls would allow.

The marvel of Corfe Castle is the way in which the masonry has held together despite the most determined attempts to blow it up. Walls and towers have bowed outwards, even slid down the hillside, but a great deal stands nevertheless. The approach from the village is through a wide outer gate with rounded flanking towers. This is Edward I's only contribution to the castle. It leads into the large outer bailey, its curtain flanked by seven half-round bastions which are closely spaced on the south-west where the terrain is most vulnerable. The bailey ascends to another round-towered gatehouse (the Middle Gate), still an impressive structure despite having split into two halves during the slighting. This gatehouse, like the outer curtain, is Henry III's work. A stairway from the gatehouse leads upwards in the thickness of a wing-wall to the keep on the summit. Otherwise the route to the top involves passing through the West Bailey which was walled by King John. Its walls converge to a western point, guarded by the octagonal Butavant Tower which has been destroyed to its foundations. Fragments of an early Norman hall – probably the oldest masonry in the castle – lie against the curtain.

A third gatehouse, now vanished, barred the way to the inner bailey on the summit. A ruinous curtain surrounds the perimeter and the castle is dominated by a lofty square keep. The curtain came first and the keep is a later addition – this is clear from the join between them. Nevertheless it is likely that both elements date from Henry I's reign (there is insufficient recorded expenditure to account for the keep under Henry II). The keep was divided by a cross-wall but more than half was blasted down at the slighting. The south face, overlooking the outer bailey, is the best preserved, and on this side there is a projecting annexe which contained latrines – a sophisticated arrangement for its time. At the east end of the bailey are some remains of King John's residential buildings, including a hall. They are arranged around a small, oblong courtyard. The surviving windows indicate a palace of great elegance, but it is too ruined to be really appreciated. Corfe was one of John's favourite residences.

Access: Open regularly except in winter (NT).
Reference: NT guidebook. RCHM *Dorset* (II part 1). *HKW* (II).
Relations: Wareham. King John's work at Odiham, Kenilworth and Scarborough. For Edward II's murder see Berkeley.

CRANBORNE MANOR Cranborne was a royal manor much frequented for the hunting on nearby Cranborne Chase. South-east of the town is a small but well-preserved motte-and-bailey castle which accommodated the Norman kings. In 1207 King John built a new hunting lodge nearby, restored or rebuilt by Gilbert de Clare a century later. It is basically a hall-house, but the embattled parapet with arrow-slits (only surviving on the south front) shows that some consideration was given to defence. Furthermore a square tower projects from the south-west corner. Robert Cecil, Earl of Salisbury, transformed the house in 1608–11, though still to serve as a hunting lodge. He inserted the large windows and added a second tower at the south-east corner for the sake of symmetry.

Access: The exterior is visible when the gardens are open (at certain times in summer).
Reference: RCHM *Dorset* (V).
Relations: Gilbert de Clare's castle at Tonbridge. The fortified hall at Woodsford.

GODLINGSTON MANOR lies two miles north-west of Swanage, off the B3351. Its history is obscure and the main block, which was probably a hall, is much altered. A moulded entrance doorway dates it to the early fourteenth century. The house has the unusual feature of a squat, half-round tower at one end. It was probably added in response to French raids during the Hundred Years War.

Access: Visible from the road.
Relations: Lympne is similar.

PORTLAND CASTLE lies within the naval base at Castletown on the north side of the Isle of Portland. This near-island forms the southern tip of Dorset, connected to the mainland by the long spit known as Chesil Beach. Portland Harbour, in the lee between island and mainland, was a potential landing place for an enemy fleet. Thus, in the years around 1540 when France and Spain were allied and an invasion of Reformation England seemed imminent, Henry VIII built Portland and Sandsfoot castles to defend the approaches. Portland cost nearly £5000 and survives intact. Its form is typically Henrician, with a central tower and a concentric outer curtain, but here the fort is just a segment – nearly, but not quite, semi-circular in plan. The tower, rounded towards the outer wall but octagonal within, is flanked by side wings which join up with the outer wall. The curtain is pierced by large gun embrasures facing seawards and there are further gun emplacements on the parapet, the wide merlons being rounded to deflect cannon balls as usual in Henrician forts. A third tier of cannon fire could have been provided by the higher parapet of the tower. The tower and wings contained accommodation for the governor and officers. The rest of the garrison occupied the narrow space between the tower and the curtain, which was originally roofed over. Like most of Henry's coastal forts, Portland's only real military action came in the Civil War, when it changed hands several times. It lay abandoned for two centuries but new invasion fears led to a second phase of occupation from 1870.

Access: Standard opening times in summer (EH).
Reference: RCHM *Dorset* (II part 2). *HKW* (IV).
Relations: Its precursor, Rufus, and its companion, Sandsfoot.

RUFUS CASTLE, often called Bow and Arrow Castle, occupies a cliff-top position above Church Ope Cove near the eastern tip of the Isle of Portland. Tradition ascribes its foundation to William Rufus and a castle on Portland was captured by Robert, Earl of Gloucester, in 1142. The building rests partly on older foundations which may represent a Norman keep, but the existing ruin is later. It appears to be an irregular, five-sided tower, just two storeys high. The seaward wall was really a cross-wall, but the square portion beyond it has fallen into the sea. Surviving corbels show that the parapet was machicolated. The entrance faces a natural chasm now crossed by a stone bridge. Small gun ports in the walls suggest a fifteenth-century origin, and the absence of any residential features suggests one of those rare pre-Henry VIII forts built purely for coastal defence in an age of cross-Channel raiding. Portland was a royal manor for most of its history, but since there is no expenditure recorded in the royal accounts its construction has been tentatively ascribed to Richard, Duke of York, who received the manor from Henry VI. Presumably it fell into disuse after Portland Castle was built.

Access: Visible from the road.
Reference: RCHM *Dorset* (II part 2).
Relations: Portland. The pre-Henrician coastal defences at Dartmouth, Fowey and Portsmouth.

SANDSFOOT CASTLE, on the cliffs south of Weymouth, was the companion of Portland Castle, guarding the mainland end of Portland Harbour. This Henrician blockhouse was standing by 1541. Unlike its neighbour Sandsfoot is now a ruin, having been abandoned after its capture by the Roundheads in 1646. The part still standing is an oblong block, heavily robbed of its facing stones. With its large Tudor windows it does not look like a Henrician fort at all. This is because it was a residential forebuilding containing the governor's and officers' quarters. Defence was conducted from an octagonal tower behind it, but this has collapsed into the sea.

Access: Exterior only (LA).
Reference: RCHM *Dorset* (II part 2).
Relations: Portland. Pendennis is similar.

SHERBORNE OLD CASTLE It is so called to distinguish it from the 'new' castle, a great mansion first built by Sir Walter Raleigh but much enlarged since. The Old Castle was erected by Roger de Caen, Bishop of Salisbury (1103–39), the most magnificent prelate of his age. He was Chancellor and Justiciar under Henry I and governed England during the King's frequent absences in Normandy. He lost his influence and possessions for supporting the Empress Matilda against King Stephen, and despite the protests of subsequent bishops the castle stayed in royal hands for the next two centuries. Its award to the Earl of Salisbury in 1354 was the final straw, Bishop Wyville declaring that he would take on the earl in combat if necessary. A settlement was reached whereby the bishop regained Sherborne in return for a money payment. In 1592 it was leased to Sir Walter Raleigh, who started to modernise the castle before opting to erect its successor nearby. The abandoned castle was re-occupied on behalf of the King during the Civil War. It was stormed by Sir Thomas Fairfax after a two-week siege (August 1645) and slighted to prevent any further military use.

The castle stood in a large deer park on the banks of the River Yeo. Most of the surviving masonry is Bishop Roger's, since after his time the castle was never anyone's chief residence and its unspoilt antiquity was apparent to John Leland when he visited. However, the damage inflicted at the slighting was heavy and the castle is now very much a ruin. Like some other episcopal palace-fortresses of the Norman period, Sherborne consists of a residential quadrangle surrounded by a defensive outer bailey. The outer bailey covers a large octagonal area, or rather a rectangular area with canted corners, bounded by a deep ditch and curtain. There were five square flanking towers, all but one surviving to some extent. Mural towers were an advanced feature for Bishop Roger's time but there are not enough of them to flank the long curtain comprehensively. The best preserved is the gate tower at the west-south-west angle, which seems to have been the original main entrance into the castle. In King John's reign the tower on the north side became the core of a substantial gatehouse with a narrow outer passage tunnelling through the rampart bank beyond the ditch (only its foundations are visible).

A square keep occupies one corner of the inner quadrangle, though not much above the vaulted ground floor still stands. There are remains of three sides of the quadrangle, especially the north range which contained an ornate chapel over a vaulted undercroft, but the hall opposite was probably pulled down by Sir Walter Raleigh to achieve the fashionable E-plan. To the west are foundations of a second quadrangle added after the castle returned to the bishops of Salisbury.

Access: Standard opening times (EH).
Reference: Guidebook by P. White. RCHM *Dorset* (I).
Relations: Roger de Caen's castles at Devizes and Old Sarum. Similar episcopal palaces at Farnham and Wolvesey (Winchester).

WAREHAM CASTLE AND TOWN DEFENCES Wareham is still contained within an earth rampart which allows an elevated promenade around the town. The rectangular area enclosed by the rampart, and the grid street plan, caused Wareham for a long time to be regarded as a Roman town, but excavations have confirmed its Saxon origin. In the year 875 the Danes seized Wareham and used it as a base for ravaging Wessex. After forcing them to terms Alfred the Great fortified a number of towns in his realm. So Wareham is a burgh showing that the Saxons were also capable of town planning. The preservation of the rampart is remarkable and only matched by the very similar burgh at Wallingford. In both places a river (here the Frome) forms one side of the defences, but there must have been an early form of boom chain to bar the way to Danish ships. Excavations have shown that a stone wall later crowned the rampart, but that it was taken down and the rampart heightened after the Norman Conquest.

The Wareham Castle mentioned in the Domesday Book may be either Wareham or Corfe, but it is clear that both castles existed by the time of the Anarchy. Wareham changed hands five times during that struggle though it was usually in Matilda's hands. Afterwards the castle fell into oblivion, as the town declined and Corfe became the chief royal stronghold of the region. However, enough survived to be captured and destroyed by the Roundheads in the Civil War. All that remains is a large motte, overlooking the river at the south-west corner of the town enclosure. A house on the summit takes the place of a square Norman keep discovered in 1910. Of course, the motte is largely a natural mound, otherwise it could not have supported the weight of this large tower.

Access: The rampart is freely accessible (LA) but the castle site is private.
Reference: RCHM *Dorset* (II part 2).
Relations: Corfe. The Saxon burgh at Wallingford.

WOODSFORD CASTLE was built by Sir Guy de Brien, a licence to crenellate being granted in 1335. He went on to bear the royal standard at Crecy and to command the English fleet in the French wars. His castle was an unusual structure, being a fortified hall-house and peculiarly elongated. The hall and the adjoining solar, on the same axis but at slightly different levels, stood on the first floor above a row of undercrofts. It is difficult to imagine the original appearance of the castle, both outside and within. Square towers projected at each corner and there was a fifth tower in the middle of the east front. However, only the north-east tower survives. It contained latrines. The other towers have vanished though rough walling shows where they stood. Large windows were inserted in the seventeenth century, but what has most muted the defensive nature of the house is the replacement of its corbelled parapet by a thatched roof. These transformations make the castle indistinguishable from an ordinary farmhouse to the casual observer. The castle lies by the River Frome four miles east of Dorchester.

Access: Visible from the road. Interior by appointment.
Reference: RCHM *Dorset* (II part 2).
Relations: The defended hall at Cranborne.

OTHER SITES There are motte-and-bailey castles at *Chelborough* and *Powerstock*, and a promontory site defended by a Norman ditch at *Shaftesbury*. Near Gillingham are the bank and ditch of *King's Court Palace*, a fortified hunting lodge of King John. *Sturminster Castle* (at Sturminster Newton) preserves a fragment of a domestic building on an outcrop of rock, while a motte near *Marshwood* carries the stump of a small square tower. *Chideock* had a fourteenth-century castle of the quadrangular type, recalled by a section of moat in a field. The royal castle of *Dorchester* came to an early end – its site was cleared in 1364 to make way for a friary. A short piece of *Poole's* fifteenth-century town wall survives off St Clement's Lane. *Brownsea Castle*, on Brownsea Island, is a castellated mansion on the site of one of Henry VIII's blockhouses.

Essex

Essex possesses some of the finest Norman castles in England, in earth, stone and even in timber. Ongar and Pleshey are two of the grandest motte-and-bailey earthworks in existence, Mountfitchet has been reconstructed in its original timber form, while the stone keeps at Colchester and Hedingham are exceptional in different ways. The early Norman keep at Colchester would be the largest in England if it were complete. Hedingham on the other hand is difficult to match for attractiveness and the excellence of its preservation. The later medieval period has much less to show: Only the very ruined enclosure at Hadleigh and the brick tower house at Faulkbourne. Colchester also retains most of its remarkable town wall, used throughout the Middle Ages but still largely of Roman masonry.

CANFIELD CASTLE   This strong motte-and-bailey lies beside the River Roding four miles south-west of Great Dunmow, next to Great Canfield parish church. The tall motte rises from its encircling ditch, and there were two baileys with ditches which could have been flooded from the river. Prior to the Norman Conquest the manor was held by Robert Fitz Wymarc, one of Edward the Confessor's Norman friends. Canfield may therefore have been the 'Robert's Castle' to which some of these Normans fled on their downfall in 1052. However, it is likely that the existing earthworks are post-Conquest, when the manor was one of the extensive possessions of the De Vere earls of Oxford.

> *Access:* Visible from the churchyard.
> *Reference:* RCHM *Essex* (II).
> *Relations:* The pre-Conquest castles of Herefordshire. For the De Veres see Hedingham.

COLCHESTER CASTLE AND TOWN WALL   Colchester reached the peak of its importance before the Romans came. Under Cunobelinus it served as the capital of an extensive kingdom covering south-east England, but the Roman invasion changed all that. A city for veterans of the Roman army (*Camulodunum*) was established here, dominated by the temple of the deified Emperor Claudius. Queen Boudicca razed it to the ground in AD 61 but a new city soon rose from the ashes.

The town wall of Colchester is one of the best preserved monuments of Roman Britain. Most of the mile-and-a-half circuit still remains and the amount of visible Roman masonry is astonishing, considering that the wall remained in use throughout the Middle Ages. Inevitably there have been considerable later repairs, but the only substantial addition is a group of late-fourteenth-century bastions along the eastern part of the south wall. The town wall enclosed a near-rectangular area bounded by Balkerne Hill, Northgate Street, Priory Street and Eld Lane. It is best seen today in the castle gardens, along Priory Street (the medieval bastions flank this stretch) and on Balkerne Hill, but three long gaps destroy the continuity. The Balkerne Hill stretch preserves the ruins of the Roman Balkerne Gate. It survives because it went out of use and was blocked up in the late Roman period. The other town gates were rebuilt in the Middle Ages and pulled down as obstacles after the Civil War. The wall, first built in the second century AD, saw an active life of fifteen hundred years. Then, during the Royalist uprising of 1648, Colchester was seized by the King's supporters and besieged by Sir Thomas Fairfax. After its capture the defences were slighted.

Colchester Castle, near the centre of the walled town, has by far the largest ground area of any keep in England, measuring 150 by 110 feet. William the Conqueror founded a castle here soon after the Norman Conquest and the keep may have been started following a Danish raid on the town in 1071. The masonry is certainly early Norman – note for example the herringbone work in the fireplaces. The keep has affinities with the Tower of London's White Tower, so much so that the builder of the latter, Bishop Gundulf of Rochester, is often credited with the design. However, it is possible that a destroyed keep at Rouen provided the model for both. The chief similarity is the apsidal projection at the south end of the east wall. In some respects the Colchester keep is quite different: it is much more rectangular in plan, there are projecting towers rather than mere buttresses at the corners and the keep was originally divided by two cross-walls, so that the eastern half contained two curiously

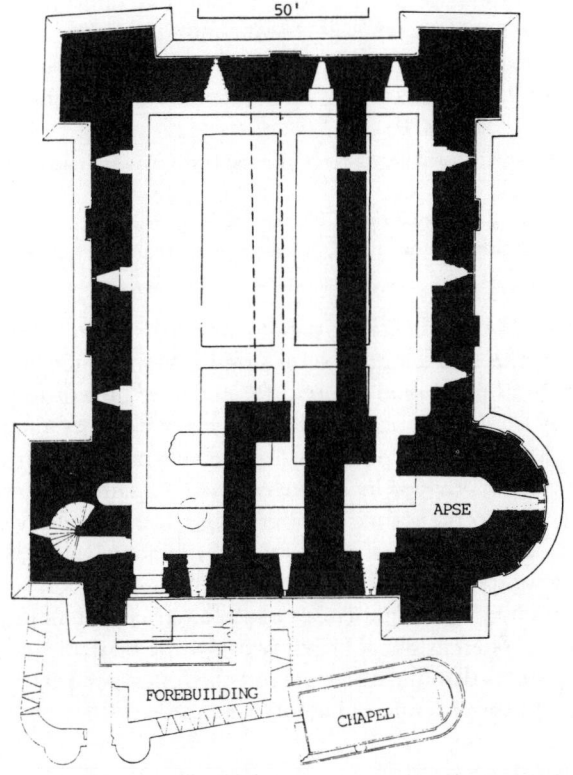

COLCHESTER CASTLE: KEEP AT GROUND LEVEL

long and narrow apartments. Only the eastern cross-wall still stands. The apse shows where a chapel was intended, but the keep now appears peculiarly squat in relation to its area because only the two lower floors survive. Traces of walled-up battlements (best seen on the east side) reveal that, when only one storey high, the keep was capped by an embattled parapet. This may have been done as an emergency measure in 1083 when a Danish invasion seemed imminent. The next level must have followed soon after. An old drawing appears to confirm that the upper half – i.e. the principal residential floor – *was* built, so it must have been taken down in 1683 when an attempt was made to demolish the keep. This proved too great an effort and the lower half was left a roofless shell. The round turret at the head of the spiral stair is an addition of the 1750s. The present roof was installed in the 1930s, enabling the keep to display the Romano-British exhibits of the Colchester and Essex Museum. Its Roman contents are appropriate, because the walls contain a lot of re-used Roman materials and beneath the keep is the vaulted substructure which supported the Temple of Claudius.

The ornate doorway into the keep – unusually situated at ground floor level – is an insertion of the twelfth century. There are foundations of a forebuilding in front of it, and of a barbican with round flanking turrets in front of that. The rampart of

71

the bailey is still impressive but its stone curtain has vanished. An outer bailey extended northwards to the town wall. Throughout its history the castle was a royal stronghold, but the keep increasingly came to be used as a prison. Its one military event occurred in 1216, when King John captured it from the Dauphin Louis' supporters.

Access: The castle is open regularly while the town wall remains are freely accessible (both LA).
Reference: Castle guidebook by D. Clarke. RCHM *Essex* (III).
Relations: Tower of London. Exeter has another Roman city wall which stayed in use.

FAULKBOURNE HALL, in a large park to the north-west of Witham, is a picturesque mansion of fifteenth-century origin. Sir John Montgomery obtained a licence to crenellate in 1439 and began the transformation of an existing timber-framed manor house. He encased the outer walls in brick and extended the house around a tiny courtyard. Much of the house has been rebuilt but the west front preserves octagonal corner towers capped by crocketed spires – a rather eccentric feature in a secular dwelling! Despite the licence, Sir John's house was not defensive. The imposing brick tower house at the north-east angle was probably added by his son, Sir Thomas, in the insecure atmosphere prevailing during the Wars of the Roses. It is one of the last medieval tower houses, no doubt inspired by Tattershall but meant to be imposing rather than secure. There is blank arcading below the battlements, as if to mimic machicolations, and small round turrets are corbelled out at parapet level. The staircase at one corner of the tower is interesting for being made entirely out of brick.

Access: Private.
Reference: RCHM *Essex* (II).
Relations: Tattershall.

HADLEIGH CASTLE overlooks the marshes of the Thames estuary to the west of Leigh-on-Sea. This very ruinous stronghold was first raised by Hubert de Burgh, Earl of Kent and Chief Justiciar, a licence to crenellate being granted in 1230. De Burgh had been one of the most influential barons in the realm during Henry III's troubled minority but by this time he was falling out of favour. In 1232 his enemies engineered his disgrace and imprisonment, with the consequential loss of his estates. Even after his exoneration De Burgh did not regain Hadleigh. The castle remained in royal hands but it was granted to favoured subjects from time to time. It enjoyed a revival under Edward III, who did a considerable amount of rebuilding here in the 1360s. At this time French raids were causing great alarm and the King sought to defend the approaches to London. Hadleigh was conveniently placed to command the estuary in conjunction with Queenborough on the opposite side. The Crown finally sold off the castle in 1551 and by the next century it was ruinous. Constable's paintings have given it a measure of fame.

The castle was an oval, keep-less enclosure surrounded by a curtain. Much of the wall goes back to Hubert de Burgh's time but it is likely that he left the castle incomplete. Edward III built the two handsome round towers on the east curtain, which are the only portions still standing almost to full height. Little more than footings survive elsewhere though excavations have exposed the entire layout. On the north Edward erected another tower and a new gateway with barbican alongside. Two other half-round towers may be original. The west curtain had to be rebuilt a few times owing to the unstable clay on which it stands, while the south curtain has tumbled down the hillside. On the west side of the bailey are the foundations of two successive halls and solars.

Access: Freely accessible (EH).
Reference: RCHM *Essex* (IV). *HKW* (II).
Relations: Queenborough (destroyed). See Hubert de Burgh's defence of Dover Castle.

HEDINGHAM CASTLE The village of Castle Hedingham is dominated by one of our finest keeps. Faced with ashlar masonry brought all the way from Barnack, it is almost perfectly preserved, lacking only its battlements. The sloping plinth and pilaster buttresses are typical Norman motifs but the turrets rising at two opposite corners are a distinctive feature. From outside the keep is seen to have five stages. This translates to four storeys within, because the hall – as usual in the larger Norman keeps – is twice the height of the other rooms and its upper windows are at gallery level. The top floor, or solar, is just below the parapet, so there is no blank space to protect a steeply-pitched roof as in many Norman keeps. It is interesting to see how the windows graduate from narrow slits at ground level to larger and more elaborate openings above, though being Norman they are all relatively small. Note the even rows of putlog holes used in the construction. A forebuilding preceded by a flight of steps guarded the way in. This has been allowed to decay into a ruinous stump, but the first-floor entrance (with chevron ornament and portcullis groove) is still in use. The room within is bisected by a wide archway which prepares us for the loftier, moulded arch at hall level. These cross-arches are a unique feature. They helped support the wooden floors without dividing the keep into smaller rooms as a cross-wall would have done. A mural gallery runs all the way around the keep at the upper level of the hall. It is pierced by frequent window recesses so the hall benefits from light at two levels. The present floors and roof are modern, the older ones having been consumed by a fire in 1918. The keep stands on top of a large, low mound which formed a natural motte. It was once surrounded by a stone curtain.

In certain respects – especially the five levels – this keep resembles the larger keep at Rochester and the same architect is a possibility. If the two are contemporary then Hedingham must be the work of Aubrey de Vere, who met his death in 1141 during the riots which accompanied the Empress Matilda's ejection from London. However, it is possible that his son (another Aubrey) was the builder. He was created Earl of Oxford as a reward for his loyalty to Matilda, and his support ensured the survival of this adulterine keep after the accession of her son as Henry II. The only military episode on record took place in the aftermath of Magna Carta, Robert de Vere being one of the rebel barons. King John captured the castle after a long siege (1216), but the Dauphin Louis retook it after an equally lengthy struggle. The De Veres played their part as one of the chief families of medieval England, active in England's wars with Scotland and France. John de Vere lost his estates and title for supporting the Lancastrian cause against Edward IV, and played an important part in Henry VII's invasion. He regained all his honours and more besides, but made the mistake of showing off his vast body of retainers while entertaining the King here. This flouting of Henry's laws cost him a heavy fine. Nevertheless he was wealthy enough to rebuild much of the castle as a Tudor palace. Unfortunately the only memento of his work is the handsome brick bridge which crosses the broad ditch between the motte and the outer bailey. Hedingham's link with the De Veres was severed in 1625 and the rest of the castle was destroyed. The present house in the outer bailey dates from 1719.

Access: Open regularly in summer.
Reference: Guidebook. RCHM *Essex* (I).
Relations: Rochester. For John de Vere see St Michael's Mount.

MOUNTFITCHET CASTLE

The motte-and-bailey at Stansted Mountfitchet is not the equal of Ongar or Pleshey but it has been reconstructed in wood to give some idea of what an earth-and-timber Norman castle looked like. The reconstruction (of the 1980s) is a conjectural one but it is the only place in England where you can still see a motte and a bailey rampart crowned by a wooden stockade, and various timber buildings inside, evoking what must have been a common sight in the century after the Norman Conquest. That the original Mountfitchet Castle developed into something more substantial is shown by a knob of masonry on the side of the motte. It seems to be part of a curtain around the outer bailey, and if the outer bailey was walled in stone then the motte and the inner bailey presumably also had stone defences. The castle takes the name of the Montfitchet family who settled here after the Norman Conquest. Richard de Montfitchet joined the first wave of opposition to King John, as a result of which the castle was destroyed in 1212.

Access: Open regularly except in winter.
Reference: Souvenir guide.
Relations: Ongar and Pleshey.

ONGAR CASTLE

lies north-east of the parish church at Chipping Ongar. Eustace, Count of Boulogne, received the manor after the Norman Conquest and may have raised the castle. It certainly existed by 1162, when it was granted to Henry II's justiciar, Richard de Lucy. Only the motte-and-bailey earthworks remain but their scale is prodigious. The motte, some fifty feet high, is surrounded by a water-filled moat, and much of the bailey ditch holds water still. Some flinty fragments mark the site of a stone gatehouse filling a gap in the bailey rampart opposite the motte, and more stonework (probably from a shell keep) used to be visible on the motte. Occupation continued throughout the Middle Ages, the castle being abandoned in the Elizabethan era for a nearby mansion. Another moated bailey lay behind the motte. Traces of a larger enclosure to the west probably indicate a planned Norman town which failed to take off.

Access: Now a nature reserve – no admission.
Reference: VCH *Essex* (IV). RCHM *Essex* (II).
Relations: The motte-and-baileys at Canfield, Pleshey and Rayleigh.

PLESHEY CASTLE is a mighty earthwork, one of the strongest motte-and-bailey castles not encumbered by masonry. Its motte, sixty feet high, has an oval summit and a deep, water-filled moat around it. The bailey is protected by a high rampart and part of its surrounding ditch is also full of water. In fact Pleshey was once a substantial stone fortress but its walls disappeared long ago. It is amazing how un-controlled stone-robbing can destroy so much. Little is known of the defences but excavations have uncovered a hall on the motte and a chapel in the bailey. The only structure left standing is a brick bridge crossing the moat between motte and bailey. On the opposite side of the motte is a well-preserved rampart large enough to enclose much of the present village. It defended a Norman borough founded under the patronage of the Mandevilles, but Pleshey did not flourish as a town for long.

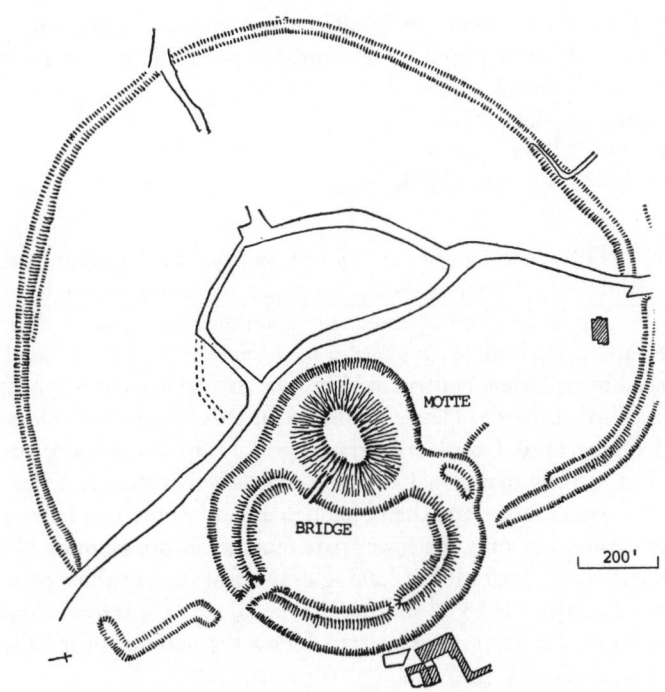

PLESHEY CASTLE AND VILLAGE ENCLOSURE

Pleshey was one of the adulterine castles raised by Geoffrey de Mandeville, Earl of Essex, during the Anarchy. They were destroyed after Henry II came to the throne but Henry later allowed William de Mandeville to refortify Pleshey. The castle passed to the Bohun earls of Hereford and from them to Thomas of Woodstock, Duke of Gloucester. He was leader of the opposition to his nephew, Richard II. In 1397 the

King's men quietly seized him here and took him to Calais for summary execution. Henry VI's unpopular Queen, Margaret of Anjou, gave the castle a new lease of life in the 1450s (the bridge is probably hers), but after that it fell into decay. The village is five miles north-west of Chelmsford.

Access: Limited opening times in summer.
Reference: VCH *Essex* (I). RCHM *Essex* (II).
Relations: For Geoffrey de Mandeville see Walden. Ongar, Haughley and Thetford have comparable mottes.

RAYLEIGH CASTLE is another of the great motte-and-bailey sites of Essex. In plan it resembles Ongar and Pleshey though there is no rampart around the bailey. Instead the castle is surrounded by a wide rampart beyond the ditch, broadening into an outer bailey on one side. Excavations have shown that the slopes of the motte were, unusually, encased with rubble – presumably this great mass of earth needed reinforcing. A stone curtain was also found around the inner bailey. The castle already existed at the time of the Domesday Book. This records its foundation by Sweyn, son of Robert Fitz Wymarc whom we encountered at Canfield. Occupation lasted until the thirteenth century.

Access: Freely accessible (NT).
Reference: RCHM *Essex* (IV).
Relations: Canfield, Ongar and Pleshey.

WALDEN CASTLE The handsome town of Saffron Walden, dominated by its magnificent church, also preserves the ruin of a square Norman keep. It is the work of Geoffrey de Mandeville, Earl of Essex, an adventurer who played off both sides during the Anarchy. He built several castles to strengthen his power base but King Stephen forced him to surrender them in 1142. De Mandeville rebelled the following year and was killed in battle. Henry II ordered the destruction of his castles but Walden evidently escaped. Considering the length of time that a major keep would take to build, it is likely that it had been left unfinished at the Earl's death in any case. The keep covers a larger area than Hedingham and would clearly have been an impressive structure, but only the lower part remains in the grounds of the local museum. Its walls have been robbed leaving only a featureless rubble core, and the corner which contained the spiral staircase has collapsed. Excavations have uncovered a forebuilding. The surrounding streets follow the outline of the bailey.

Access: Freely accessible (LA).
Reference: RCHM *Essex* (I).
Relations: Hedingham. Pleshey was another of Geoffrey de Mandeville's castles.

OTHER SITES Although Canfield was suggested above as the pre-Conquest castle of Robert Fitz Wymarc, another possible contender is the earthwork enclosure at *Clavering*. There is a motte-and-bailey castle in the grounds of *Great Easton* Hall, and another motte can be seen at *Mount Bures*. *Tilbury Fort*, a coastal fortification of the Restoration period, occupies the site of one of Henry VIII's blockhouses.

Gloucestershire

Gloucestershire is one of the Welsh Border counties, but only just. The short frontier is marked by the River Wye and reaffirmed by Offa's Dyke. The Normans quickly penetrated into Gwent and Glamorgan, so Gloucestershire did not become Marcher lordship territory. Castles are correspondingly fewer, though the shell keep at Berkeley and the gatehouse at St Briavels are good examples of military architecture. There would have been more if the important castles at Bristol and Gloucester had not perished. Later medieval castles are represented by Beverston and the rebuilding of Berkeley, both reflecting the local importance of the Berkeley family. Sudeley is a late quadrangular castle while Thornbury Castle, later still, is a unique amalgam of medieval castle and Tudor mansion.

BERKELEY CASTLE rises on a low hill in sight of the Severn estuary. The castle is an appealing blend of Norman fortress and later medieval mansion, still remarkably unspoilt despite its continuous occupation by an aristocratic family, who might have been expected to rebuild or drastically modernise it in more recent centuries. Domesday Book records that William Fitz Osbern, Earl of Hereford, founded the castle. He was killed in 1071 so the castle must have existed by then. Fitz Osbern's sub-tenant adopted the name of De Berkeley. The Berkeleys have held the castle – with one interruption – ever since, although it has sometimes been contested by different branches of the family. The one break in the Berkeley ownership arose from their loyalty to King Stephen. After gaining the throne Henry II granted the castle to Robert Fitz Harding, a Bristol merchant who had helped finance his campaigns against Stephen. Henry is said to have strengthened the castle on Fitz Harding's behalf, which suggests that this was one of the castles which Henry controlled indirectly. Fitz Harding's son Maurice healed the breach by marrying the dispossessed heiress and adopting the Berkeley name.

The motte-and-bailey layout may go back to William Fitz Osbern but the oldest masonry here is the unusual keep. If it dates from Henry II's contract with Robert Fitz Harding (*circa* 1155) then the three semi-circular projecting bastions are remarkably early, though the plinth and pilaster buttresses are consistent with that date. One of the bastions contains a well chamber and another formed the apse of a chapel. The keep belongs to the shell keep type but its high wall actually encases the motte instead of rising from the summit. A feature taken from the tower keeps of the period is the forebuilding. This is an afterthought, enclosing a narrow staircase which ascends to the keep entrance. A deep breach in the keep wall, facing the outer bailey, is the only damage wrought by the Roundheads following a brief siege in 1645. The oblong Thorpe Tower beside it dates from the fourteenth century. The keep is infamous for the murder of Edward II by his jailors, Sir John Maltravers and Sir Thomas Gurney, in 1327. According to tradition the deed was done – with or without the infamous red-hot poker – in the chamber above the forebuilding. Edward had been sent to Berkeley for 'safe keeping' following his abdication, but dethroned monarchs seldom remain alive for long.

The keep stood between two baileys. Only a restored gatehouse survives from the outer bailey but the inner is still intact. It is reached via a fourteenth-century gateway flanked on one side by the keep and on the other by a narrow, oblong tower. The machicolated gallery at the inner end of the gate passage comes as a surprise, but it is not authentic. Residential buildings surround the compact courtyard except where the keep interrupts them. They are mainly the work of Thomas, Lord Berkeley, in the 1340s, though there have been many minor alterations in the ensuing centuries. Note the distinctive 'Berkeley' arches – a hallmark of Thomas' work. Thomas lived here during Edward II's captivity but was absolved of any complicity in his murder, and actually enjoyed favour in the reign of his son. The buildings centre upon a hall on the east side of the bailey, opposite the gatehouse. On the south there is a long range containing private apartments, while to the north lie the kitchen and a labyrinth of domestic offices. Most evocative is the hall itself, preserving its original timber roof. (The painted Tudor screen came from elsewhere.) Otherwise the finest room is the old chapel of St Mary (now the Morning Room). It preserves two traceried windows and a painted wooden ceiling. The wooden gallery now in the room next door formed an elevated pew for the family. The shape of the residential buildings is determined by the heavily-buttressed curtain behind them. It is Norman at least in parts.

Access: Open regularly in summer.
Reference: BOE *Gloucestershire – The Vale and the Forest of Dean.* Mackenzie (I). Souvenir guide.
Relations: Beverston was another Berkeley stronghold. The shell keeps at Farnham and Eynsford also surround a motte. Compare Richard II's death at Pontefract.

BEVERSTON CASTLE, in the Cotswolds two miles west of Tetbury, was another Berkeley seat. Maurice de Berkeley (d.1281) first raised the castle, Henry III pardoning him for building it without a licence, but it was remodelled by Thomas, Lord Berkeley, in the following century. Thomas also reconstructed Berkeley Castle. According to tradition Beverston was rebuilt with booty won at the Battle of Poitiers, which would date it between 1356 and Thomas' death in 1361. The castle was a small quadrangular stronghold but only the west range and its square flanking towers survive. They are roofless but otherwise well preserved. The west range contained the solar above a vaulted undercroft. Thomas added an upper floor and built (or rebuilt) the towers. The gabled North Tower projects diagonally. The larger South Tower contains a chapel at first floor level, with an elaborate vault and delicately-carved sedilia. There is also a small oratory in the chamber above. A seventeenth-century house occupies the site of the south range, which contained the hall. One other survival is the ruinous outer gatehouse with rounded flanking towers. The Berkeleys sold Beverston in 1597 and everything else was torn down after the Civil War. In 1644 the castle withstood a fierce assault from the Roundheads but surrendered following the capture of its governor, who had strayed into the village to visit his mistress. The present house was built soon after.

Access: Visible from the road. The garden is open occasionally.
Reference: BOE *Gloucestershire – The Cotswolds.*
Relations: Berkeley.

BRISTOL CASTLE AND CITY WALL Bristol emerged as a major port in Norman times. Its first defences were of earth and timber, replaced by a stone wall soon after 1200. Within a few decades the circuit had to be extended, both to the west and across the River Avon to include the prosperous suburb of Redcliffe. Little of the city wall remains above ground but there is one surviving gatehouse – St John's Gate – astride Broad Street. Rebuilt in the mid fourteenth century, it is a simple gate passage with a portcullis groove and an early fan vault. The gate is crowned by the tower and spire of St John's Church. The body of the church, rebuilt about the same time, stands on the line of the city wall, its large windows suggesting that the wall no longer had a serious defensive role.

It is not surprising that a big city like Bristol should have shaken off its defences, but the destruction of the castle is a great pity. It lay beside the river to the east of the walled city. As rebuilt by Robert, Earl of Gloucester, in the 1120s the castle comprised two walled baileys dominated by a tall square keep. King Stephen was a prisoner here in 1141 following his capture at Lincoln. From Henry II's reign it was a royal stronghold, but Oliver Cromwell ordered the destruction of the castle after the Civil War. Bristol had been a vital port for the Royalists and its capture by Sir Thomas Fairfax in 1645 was a severe blow. Some of the keep plinth has been left uncovered in Castle Park. The only other remains are two undercrofts from Henry III's residential buildings, off Castle Street.

Access: St John's Gate is visible from outside. The castle site is freely accessible (LA).
Reference: HKW (II) for the castle.
Relations: The town gates fused with churches at Langport and Warwick.

GLOUCESTER CITY WALL Gloucester originated as a city for Roman legionary veterans. *Glevum* survived the departure of the Romans, becoming a Saxon burgh. The Roman city followed the rectangular plan of its fortress predecessor, but medieval Gloucester expanded westwards to the River Severn. Gloucester supported Parliament in the Civil War, surviving a month-long siege in 1643. After the Restoration the city's defences were destroyed in punishment. The work was thorough and nothing of the city wall survives above ground. However, excavations in 1979 revealed the East Gate and its footings have been left on display inside a protective glass building. The round-towered, thirteenth-century gatehouse can be seen overlying the foundations of its Roman predecessor. Part of the Roman city wall and a flanking bastion have also been uncovered beneath King's Walk.

Nothing survives of the royal castle which lay beside the river at the west end of the city. Founded by William the Conqueror, it also fell victim to Charles II's vengeance and the site is occupied by Gloucester Prison (1821). It seems to have resembled Bristol Castle, with a large keep built by Henry I and two walled baileys. A fourteenth-century sketch depicts a typical square keep with angle turrets.

Access: The East Gate is open at certain times in summer (LA).
Reference: VCH *Gloucestershire* (IV).
Relations: Bristol.

MISERDEN CASTLE is a substantial motte-and-bailey earthwork beside the River Frome in Misarden Park, between Gloucester and Cirencester. Excavations have uncovered a shell keep (no longer visible) on the tree-clad motte. Its probable builder, Robert Musard, was ambushed by King Stephen's men in 1146 and forced to surrender the castle on threat of death. The castle survived Henry II's accession, but by 1289 it had been abandoned for a manor house on the site of the present mansion.

Access: On private land.

ST BRIAVELS CASTLE occupies an elevated site overlooking the Wye valley and the Welsh Border. Miles Fitz Walter, Earl of Gloucester, first built the castle during the Anarchy, but Henry II took possession in 1160 and it remained a royal stronghold thereafter. Kings (especially John) came here to hunt in the Forest of Dean. In between it served as the administrative centre of the forest, which was important for its iron forges, and the castle became a storehouse for the innumerable crossbow bolts made there.

A massive gatehouse dominates the castle. Built by Edward I in 1292–93, it must have been a good example of the keep-gatehouse theme and a worthy counterpart to the gatehouses of Edward's Welsh castles. The effect is marred now by the loss of the parapet, long since displaced by pitched roofs, and the destruction of one side of the long gate passage. Semi-circular flanking towers rise from square bases which retreat back into the wall as short pyramidal spurs. This strengthening of the wall base achieved popularity in the Welsh Marches as a deterrent to undermining. Three portcullises closed the gate passage, and smaller portcullises even barred the doorways leading into the porters' lodges. Beneath one of these lodges is a pit prison, and later the entire gatehouse served as a prison for those who had fallen foul of the harsh forest laws. Originally, however, the two upper floors of the gatehouse contained a hall and other apartments for the constable.

The gatehouse forms one end of the present house, which originated as a suite of royal apartments. Though much altered in the Jacobean period and later, the house preserves a lot of masonry from King John's time, notably a reset fireplace in the so-called Jury Room. An altered chapel projects into the bailey, but the hall which stood opposite has vanished. The surrounding curtain (probably Norman) only partly stands to full height. Fitz Walter's square keep dominated the bailey, but it collapsed in 1752 and only some fallen blocks of masonry marks the site.

Access: Open regularly in summer (EH).
Reference: St Briavels Castle by A. Clark. HKW (II).
Relations: Edward I's gatehouses at Rockingham and the Tower of London, and other Edwardian gatehouses such as Tonbridge and Dunstanburgh.

SUDELEY CASTLE stands in beautiful gardens to the south-east of Winchcombe. A castle here was besieged during the Anarchy but the present structure is an amalgam of a late medieval castle and an Elizabethan mansion. It was built by Ralph Boteler, commander of the English fleet in Henry VI's reign, reputedly with the ransom of a captured French admiral. In 1458 Boteler received a pardon for crenellating

Sudeley without a licence but he did not find favour with the new Yorkist regime. He was compelled to sell the castle to Edward IV, who granted it to his brother Richard, Duke of Gloucester (later Richard III). Katherine Parr, Henry VIII's widow, lived here as the wife of Thomas Seymour. She is buried in Boteler's chapel which stands just outside the castle. In the 1570s Lord Chandos rebuilt the outer courtyard as an up-to-date mansion, and the inner courtyard was slighted following the surrender of the castle to the Roundheads in 1644.

The castle's two quadrangles were not quite in alignment with each other. Ralph Boteler's outer quadrangle was probably a 'base court' with lodgings for retainers, but the existing ranges around it date from the Elizabethan reconstruction. Only the gate passage is original. His inner courtyard has fared better, though not much better because of the slighting. The western corner towers (both square) survive along with the much-restored curtain between them. The slender Portmare Tower is named after that French admiral. Dungeon Tower is considerably larger, its name suggesting that it served as a donjon or tower house. The only other remnant is part of the east wall which clearly belonged to a very fine building, often assumed to be the hall but more probably a suite of state apartments. Because this work is superior to the rest it is believed to date from Richard of Gloucester's tenure. The great traceried windows piercing what was an outer wall show indifference to any defensive considerations. Sudeley thus changed quickly from a late medieval fortified mansion into an unfortified palace.

Access: Open regularly in summer.
Reference: BOE *Gloucestershire – The Cotswolds.* Souvenir guide.
Relations: For other work of Richard III see Warwick and Penrith.

THORNBURY CASTLE has been described as the last genuine castle, or rather private house with defensive features, ever raised in England. This is probably true if we ignore Scottish Border territory. It is a testimony to the ambition of Edward Stafford, Duke of Buckingham, who began building here in 1511. Ten years later Henry VIII had him executed on a charge of treason. It was alleged that the duke had raised a private army in the Welsh Marches, in defiance of the Tudor laws against such practices, and Thornbury Castle may have been another factor weighing against him. No licence was obtained for its construction and it seems to have been inspired by a nostalgia for the 'good old days' of baronial autonomy. Admittedly, the castle was really just a defensive facade concealing a comfortable mansion behind it. Furthermore it made no attempt to adapt to the growing power of artillery, and the gun ports which pierce the outer walls are no more advanced than their late-fourteenth-century prototypes. Nevertheless Thornbury would have been strong enough to alarm a suspicious monarch. After Buckingham's death the unfinished complex lay abandoned for almost two centuries, until the Howard family decided to make the inner courtyard habitable.

The castle follows the standard quadrangular layout of later medieval times, and is provided with an outer courtyard large enough to house a sizeable body of retainers. So here as elsewhere the hired levies were kept away from the duke and his personal household, though whether this arrangement reflects mistrust or the social hierarchy is a moot point. Two long ranges of retainers' lodgings back onto the outer curtain.

This curtain has three square flanking towers (the angle tower is set diagonally), several intermediate turrets and a liberal supply of gun ports and arrow-slits. The main entrance, flanked by semi-octagonal turrets to front and rear, was furnished with a portcullis in traditional fashion. The south wall of the outer courtyard was never built and on the east lies the inner quadrangle.

Clearly the west facade of the inner curtain was intended to look uncompromisingly defensive, with massive octagonal towers at each end and a twin-towered gatehouse in between. However, this front appears woefully squat because it was left in 1521 at less than half its intended height. The north range (with square flanking towers) is similarly truncated and the east range, which would have contained the hall, was never even begun. Only the south range and the machicolated Lord's Tower at the south-west angle reveal the scale of Buckingham's intentions. As a matter of fact the south range reveals the defensive limitations of the castle, because here martial pretensions were abandoned in favour of luxury. Bay windows and ornamental brick chimneys show that the Tudor age had arrived. In front of the south range was a walled garden connecting with the churchyard, and the proximity of the splendid church tower is another obvious weakness. The castle lies in a park to the west of the town.

Access: Now a hotel. Limited access for non-residents.
Reference: BOE *Gloucestershire – The Vale and the Forest of Dean.*
Relations: Compton is a rival for the title of last English castle.

OTHER SITES Motte-and-bailey castles can be seen at *Dymock, English Bicknor* and *Upper Slaughter.* Excavations in 1930 on Little Camp Hill at *Lydney* revealed the curtain of a Norman castle, its entrance flanked by a small, square keep. Unfortunately the foundations have not been left on view. *Brimpsfield* had a thirteenth-century castle belonging to the Giffards, demolished after they joined the Earl of Lancaster's revolt against Edward II (1322). The overgrown ditch remains and grassy mounds mark the position of the curtain. *King John's Castle* in The Mythe, outside Tewkesbury, is a tower which formed part of a residence of the abbots of Tewkesbury. It is not a fortification and has no connection with King John.

Hampshire

The calm waters of the Solent offer an ideal approach for an invading fleet. For this reason you can trace the history of coastal defence in Hampshire from Roman times to the present. Portchester has an impressive 'Saxon Shore' fort which became one of the chief medieval castles of the county, dominated by its great Norman keep. Otherwise there was (as usual) no organised coastal defence in the Middle Ages, though the inhabitants of Southampton and Winchester strengthened their defences in response to French raids during the Hundred Years War. Although incomplete, Southampton's town wall is one of the best in England. Portsmouth emerged as a naval base in the fifteenth century and its defences are intermixed with Tudor and later fortifications. The invasion scare of the 1540s resulted in the concentration of several Henrician forts on this coastline. Calshot and Hurst have rounded layouts typical of the early 1540s whereas Southsea Castle shows the sudden change to angular forms. A different theme is the group of castle-palaces (Bishop's Waltham, Merdon and Wolvesey at Winchester) built by the powerful Henry de Blois, Bishop of Winchester. There is some important domestic architecture, such as the Norman hall at Christchurch, the fine hall of Henry III at Winchester and the royal palace inside Portchester Castle. Odiham's rare octagonal keep is virtually the only Hampshire castle which is far inland.

BASING HOUSE, just outside Basingstoke, combines a powerful Norman ringwork with the sorry fragments of a great Tudor mansion. The union is a peculiar one and the polygonal layout of the mansion is dictated by the ringwork. Even more surprisingly, the mansion occupying the site of the De Ports' castle was one of the last to be built with a licence to crenellate. This licence was granted in 1531 to William Paulet, Comptroller of the Royal Household and later Marquis of Winchester. However, the Tudor Basing House was not intended as a genuine fortification in spite of all this. The licence and the crenellations themselves had only a symbolic value by Henry VIII's reign. Nevertheless the old earthworks, augmented by bastions suitable for mounting artillery, were to stand the house in good stead when it endured a momentous siege during the Civil War. Oliver Cromwell commanded the final, bloody assault on this staunchly Royalist stronghold in October 1645, thus ending two years of resistance. The Roundheads slaughtered many of the Catholic sympathisers who had taken refuge here, and the burnt-out mansion was then ruthlessly torn down.

Access: Open regularly in summer.
Reference: VCH *Hampshire* (IV). Souvenir guide.
Relations: Notable Civil War sieges at Donnington, Ashby, Pontefract, etc.

BISHOP'S WALTHAM PALACE was a favourite retreat of the medieval bishops of Winchester. King Stephen's episcopal brother, Henry de Blois, first built a palace on this site *circa* 1135. Only the foundations of an apsidal chapel can be seen from that period. When the Anarchy broke out Henry fortified his houses and a stone curtain (not visible) has been found beneath the present buildings. Bishop Henry enjoyed great power during his brother's reign but was forced into temporary exile on Henry II's accession, his castles being demolished as adulterine. He was allowed to return in 1158 and proceeded to rebuild them in a manner which invited the admiration of contemporary chroniclers. The palace here must have been quite splendid but, unlike his other residences, is largely devoid of defensive features. It occupied a large, irregular quadrangle surrounded by a moat. The main apartments, including a spacious hall, lay on the west side of the quadrangle. These form the principal remains. Although still Henry's work in essence they were remodelled several times by later bishops, particularly Thomas Langton (d.1501). It was he who inserted the large windows of the hall block and united its two floors into one. The one concession to defence is a square, keep-like tower at the south-west corner of the quadrangle. It rises to full height except for one collapsed corner. The tower contained a self-contained suite of apartments offering a degree of security to its occupier, rather like the tower houses of the later Middle Ages. A narrow gallery connected the tower to the hall. The palace was badly damaged during the Civil War and has been in ruins ever since.

Access: Standard opening times in summer (EH).

Reference: VCH *Hampshire* (III).

Relations: Henry de Blois' fortified palaces at Merdon, Wolvesey (Winchester), Farnham and Taunton.

CALSHOT CASTLE is positioned at the end of a shingle spit commanding the entrance to Southampton Water. Erected in 1539–40, it formed part of Henry VIII's extensive chain of coastal fortifications, providing an inner line of defence against enemy vessels which had survived bombardment from the forts guarding the Solent. Since the threat of invasion was sparked by the Reformation it is fitting that much of the stone came from the recently-dissolved Beaulieu Abbey. The castle is really just a blockhouse, comprising a squat round tower typical of Henry's earlier forts. There is no outer ring of bastions, just a low chemise wall with widely-splayed embrasures for cannon. Further guns could have been placed in the two upper floors of the tower and on the roof (the existing parapet is not the original). The entrance, with its Tudor arch and drawbridge slots, is typically Henrician. Calshot saw little action but remained a garrison post well into the twentieth century. It is surprisingly unspoilt considering its long occupation.

Access: Standard opening times in summer (EH).

Reference: EH guidebook.

Relations: The Henrician part of Pendennis. Hurst occupies a longer spit.

CHRISTCHURCH CASTLE Christchurch was originally called Twineham and its castle was probably founded *circa* 1100 by Richard de Redvers, Earl of Devon. The town is noted for its priory church, a gem of Norman architecture, but close by stands the Norman House which is also of great interest. This ruined building contained the hall and solar of the castle, both apartments standing above an un-vaulted undercroft. The original doorway, once reached by an outside staircase, marks the junction between the two rooms which were only divided by a wooden partition. The hall was lit by several two-light windows enriched with chevron ornament. Two of them pierce the wall facing a stream, i.e. the outside wall of the castle. Though positioned at first-floor level they are too low and too large for real security, so here we find an early instance of domestic convenience intruding upon defence. Between these two windows is a tall, circular chimney – one of the oldest in England. The architecture of the hall suggests the 1160s, making it the work of Richard de Redvers, grandson of the founder, or his son Baldwin. The only other remnant of the castle is the motte, bearing two featureless walls of a square tower. It may have been a Norman keep though the canted corners suggest at least a remodelling in the later Middle Ages when the castle belonged to the Montagu earls of Salisbury. In 1645 the derelict castle became the last resort of some Roundhead soldiers who managed to hold out here when the Royalists attacked the town. Afterwards the defences were destroyed by order of Parliament.

Access: Freely accessible (EH).

Reference: Leaflet guide by M. Wood.

Relations: For the Redvers family see Carisbrooke and Plympton. Compare the Norman halls at Oakham and Richmond.

HURST CASTLE Its nucleus is one of the coastal forts of Henry VIII, expanded as a result of another invasion scare in Victorian times. The original castle was built in 1539–44 and the master mason, Thomas Bertie, later became captain of the garrison here (a curious but not uncommon reward for a castle builder). Like Calshot it lies at the end of a spit of shingle, well over a mile long and projecting into the middle of the Solent. The Isle of Wight is little more than a mile away and, along with its counterpart at Yarmouth, the castle's guns could effectively command the western entrance to the Solent. Hurst was garrisoned almost continuously until the Second World War. Its situation also made a secure prison, used mainly for the incarceration of Catholics though its most famous inmate was Charles I en route to his trial and execution. The Henrician fort is now flanked by two long batteries added in 1861–73, when the fear of a resurgent France under Napoleon III led to that vast array of defensive works known as 'Palmerston's Follies'.

Henry's castle consists of a central tower, polygonal outside but circular within, surrounded by a thick curtain with three semi-circular projecting bastions. Large gun ports originally pierced the curtain and further cannon could have been mounted on the parapets of the curtain and the higher central tower. Later modifications have obscured much of the original layout. The central tower has a spiral stair turret at its nucleus, probably an original feature though it was rebuilt in the Napoleonic period when the tower's brick vault was inserted. One bastion and the seventeenth-century barracks against the curtain were filled with concrete during the Victorian reconstruction as a reinforcement against the artillery of the time. Another bastion has largely been hidden with the addition of the eastern battery. Only the north-west bastion, which is higher than the others, preserves its original appearance. Beside it is the entrance gateway, retaining its portcullis groove and slots for the drawbridge chains.

Access: Standard opening times in summer (EH). The castle can be reached by boat from Keyhaven.

Reference: Guidebook by O. E. Craster. *HKW* (IV).

Relations: The other Solent forts at Calshot, Netley, Southsea and Yarmouth.

MERDON CASTLE lies on the northern edge of Hursley Park, about five miles south-west of Winchester. It is one of the group of castles built around 1138 by Henry de Blois, Bishop of Winchester, and destroyed as adulterine when Henry II came to the throne. Evidently Merdon was not totally destroyed but it was not one of the palaces Bishop Henry rebuilt on his return from exile in 1158. The site is a triangular enclosure defended by a bank and ditch. It occupies part of a larger earthwork possibly dating from the Iron Age. That there was a stone curtain is shown by surviving fragments, but the main feature is the ruined gatehouse. Only the outer gateway and a narrow chamber which flanked the gate passage still stand. It is likely that this was one of those Norman castles in which a strong gatehouse was provided instead of a keep.

Access: On private land.
Reference: VCH *Hampshire* (III).
Relations: Bishop's Waltham and Wolvesey (Winchester).

NETLEY CASTLE stands near the beautiful ruins of Netley Abbey. The abbey was newly dissolved when this blockhouse was being built and many of its stones are said to have been utilised. That was in 1542, when Henry VIII augmented his chain of fortifications guarding the Solent. Netley was placed to control the passage of vessels along Southampton Water a few miles ahead of Southampton itself. It was one of Henry's smaller fortifications – just an oblong block with an embrasured wall facing the sea and a parapet consisting of rounded merlons. The seaward wall is embedded in the seaward facade of the present 'castle', which is a large Victorian mansion.

Access: Now a hospital.
Reference: VCH *Hampshire* (III).
Relations: Calshot also guarded Southampton Water.

ODIHAM CASTLE was a royal foundation, built by King John in 1207–12 and costing £1200. As usual, John was attracted by the hunting. The castle stands not in Odiham but close to the neighbouring village of North Warnborough. It is sited in a bend of the River Whitewater and the earthworks consist of three rectangular baileys, the ditches still partly filled with water. None of them appear to have been walled in stone but in the middle of the inner bailey stands an unusual octagonal keep. Round towers were superseding square ones during John's reign and a handful of round keeps were built. An octagonal plan is a rare compromise for this period, though Henry II had built a smaller keep at Chilham and octagonal towers were to enjoy popularity later. Unfortunately the keep here is now in a very ruinous condition and being allowed to decay further. Part of its circumference has entirely collapsed and what remains is the rubble core, though much of it stands to full height. Enough is left to show that the keep was three storeys high with fireplaces warming the two upper floors, which no doubt formed the hall and the solar.

The castle saw fighting soon after its completion. In 1216 thirteen men defended it against a large besieging force under the Dauphin Louis. After two weeks the garrison negotiated an honourable surrender. Henry III granted the castle to his future adversary Simon de Montfort. David II of Scotland spent much of his eleven-year imprisonment here following his capture at the Battle of Neville's Cross in 1346. By the Elizabethan era the castle was a ruin.

Access: Freely accessible.
Reference: VCH *Hampshire* (IV). *HKW* (II).
Relations: Chilham and the early octagonal mural towers at Dover and the Tower of London.

PORTCHESTER CASTLE originated as the 'Saxon Shore' fort of *Portus Adurni*. It is the best preserved of the chain of Roman forts erected along the south-east coast in the late third century AD. The reason for their construction is still debated. Defence against Germanic raiders is the most likely explanation and they were certainly used for that purpose in the following century. However, it is possible that most of the forts were first built as a defence against the Roman Empire by the ill-fated usurper Carausius, who set himself up as an independent ruler in Britain. The fort wall stands complete and to full height, enclosing a nine-acre square. Owing to later patching six of the original bastions have perished but fourteen still project from the circuit. These bastions are all U-shaped and hollow. Portchester is also fortunate in being the only Saxon Shore fort to preserve its original relationship with the coast. The waters of Portsmouth Harbour almost lap against its east side.

The fort survives in such good condition because of its continued use after the Roman departure, first sheltering a Saxon burgh and then becoming the outer bailey of the medieval castle. This large enclosure could conveniently accommodate the retinues accompanying kings on their frequent journeys across the Channel. Its potential was not recognised until the time of Henry I. He is believed to have founded the castle in the 1120s, the site being in royal hands during a minority. After the estates were returned to their feudal holder the castle seems to have retained a royal garrison, at least until the Anarchy broke out. Henry II placed it under his direct control following Prince Henry's revolt (the prince was held prisoner here for a short while) and Portchester remained a royal castle thereafter.

Henry I restored the fort's crumbling walls, built the present gate towers (called Land Gate and Water Gate) and created a rectangular inner bailey in the north-west corner of the fort. It is defended by the Roman wall on two sides, and on the other two by a stone curtain with a projecting gate tower. Another square tower is positioned diagonally at the vulnerable south-east corner. Portchester is thus an early example of a castle employing flanking towers, perhaps inspired by the Roman bastions. The inner curtain is overshadowed by the lofty square keep which has displaced some of the Roman wall at the north-west corner of the castle. It is the product of two phases, as shown by the pilaster buttresses which disappear two-thirds of the way up. Evidently Henry I's keep comprised only two storeys plus roof space. Its heightening to four storeys is ascribed to the Mauduits who held the castle prior to Henry II's seizure. The keep is divided by a cross-wall and entered via a forebuilding which is another addition of the second phase. Originally the entrance was at first-floor level, the ground floor doorway being a later insertion.

After the loss of Normandy in 1204 Portchester's importance diminished. It was nearly destroyed in 1217 following its capture by the Dauphin Louis. However, the Hundred Years War gave it a new lease of life, both Edward III and Henry V preparing their French invasions here. Richard II built a palace in the castle during the last few years of his reign, but he was overthrown before its completion. Though roofless the buildings are a fine example of the domestic architecture of the period. They back onto the inner curtain, the principal rooms being at first-floor level. The hall stands to the left of the gatehouse and the solar occupied the range at right angles to it, connecting with the keep. Lodgings on the east side of the bailey adjoin Assheton's Tower, built by the constable of that name *circa* 1380. The only other post-Norman

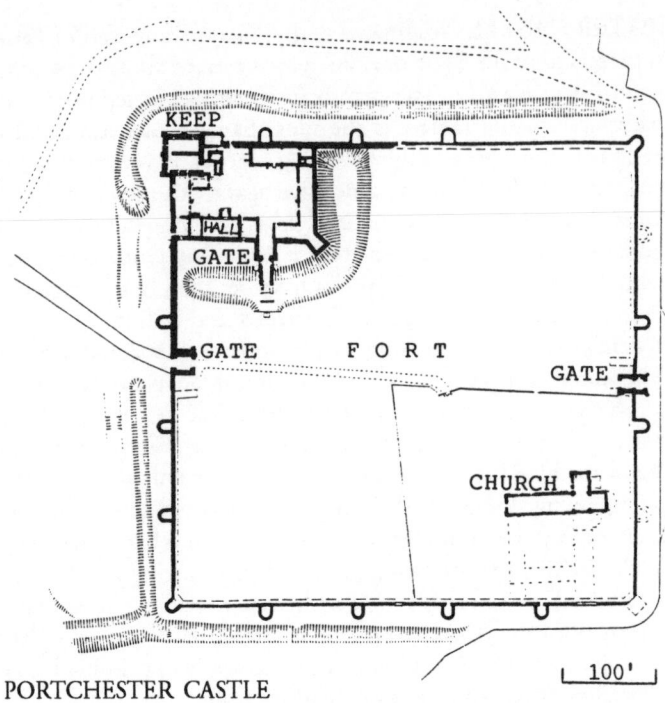

PORTCHESTER CASTLE

work of any significance is the long barbican in front of the inner gatehouse, of three successive periods (Edward II, Richard II and Jacobean). Generally the castle is well preserved though only the keep and the Land Gate are not in ruins.

From the fifteenth century Portchester was eclipsed by Portsmouth and the castle came to be used chiefly as a prison. During the Napoleonic wars the outer bailey served as a compound for French prisoners. Today it is empty except for the parish church of St Mary which occupies the south-east quadrant. Although several castles had collegiate churches attached to them, this was the only monastic foundation inside castle walls and it did not last long. Founded as a small Augustinian priory in 1133, the canons moved to Southwick a decade or two later. The transfer did not take place before their cruciform church had been completed. A fine piece of Norman architecture, it survives more or less as the canons left it, minus the south transept.

Access: Standard opening times (EH).
Reference: Guidebook by J. Munby. *HKW* (II).
Relations: Keeps attributed to Henry I at Guildford, Norwich, Carlisle and Bamburgh. Pevensey Castle is also inside a Saxon Shore fort.

PORTSMOUTH TOWN DEFENCES Portsmouth's historic role as a naval base derives from its position guarding the narrow entrance to Portsmouth Harbour. Richard I built the first dockyard here. Its importance increased with the Hundred Years War and the town which developed around it (now Old Portsmouth) inevitably became a target for French attacks. Following a royal survey in 1386 an earth rampart was raised around the landward sides of the town (there was never a castle). From 1560 the rampart was continued along the sea front and strengthened elsewhere by a series of arrow-head bastions. Portsmouth was thus fortified at a time when most towns were secure enough to shed their defensive circuits. More works were undertaken by Charles II's engineer, Bernard de Gomme. The defences were further elaborated over the next two centuries but Lord Palmerston's astonishing ring of fortifications, built in the 1860s, rendered them obsolete. The complex of ramparts, bastions and outworks facing inland was demolished and only the seaward defences remain.

The oldest of the visible defences of Portsmouth is the Round Tower, on the promontory known as The Point. Here the entrance to Portsmouth Harbour is just a few hundred yards wide and a boom chain ran across from this tower to another on the Gosport side. One of the earliest buildings devised for defence by artillery, the Round Tower was built in 1415 – a year which brought victory for England but alarm in Portsmouth. The present gun embrasures, widely-splayed for greater range, were inserted in Henry VIII's reign and the upper part of the tower was rebuilt during the Napoleonic Wars. From the Round Tower a Victorian gun battery leads towards the Square Tower, built in 1494 but refaced in 1827. It is here that the town's perimeter defences began. Beyond another gun battery is the Saluting Battery, a stone platform for cannon which projects out a little from the rest of the defensive line. It is the only unspoilt bit of Elizabethan work remaining. The rampart which continues from here is all De Gomme's, terminating in the King's Bastion which occupies the site of a Tudor predecessor.

Access: The defences are freely accessible (LA).

Reference: Fortifications in Old Portsmouth by A. Corney. *HKW* (IV).

Relations: God's House Tower at Southampton is another early artillery defence. For more complete Elizabethan town defences see Berwick.

SOUTHAMPTON CASTLE AND TOWN WALL One of the chief ports of medieval England, Southampton preserves a wealth of medieval domestic architecture. Its flourishing Dark Age predecessor was abandoned in favour of the present site in the tenth century, and excavations have shown that this new town had earth and timber defences from the beginning, no doubt as a defence against the Danes. The present town wall, though far from complete, is one of the most rewarding in England. Construction started on the north and east sides in 1260 but work dragged on until the end of the century. On the south and west the estuary of the River Test was considered sufficient protection. Naturally it proved no defence against seaborne attack and in 1338 – soon after the outbreak of the Hundred Years War – the French descended upon the town and sacked it. In spite of that, work on the other two sides did not begin until the 1360s, when the French became a more frequent menace in the Channel. With the revival of the French war under Henry V various improvements were made, taking into account the growing power of artillery. Southampton has served as the chief embarkation point for many armies crossing to France. This was as true in the Middle Ages as it was in 1944, and the expeditions which led to Crecy and Agincourt set off from here.

Over a mile in length, the walled circuit enclosed a roughly rectangular area. It had numerous bastions, mostly semi-circular, and larger towers at the angles. Today only the west wall survives, along with parts of the north wall and a length near the south-east corner of the circuit. A tour of the wall may conveniently begin at the Bargate, the northern entrance to the old town and a very imposing one. The machicolated front is an early fifteenth-century addition. Behind it are twin half-round towers a century or so older, while the gate passage retains a Norman archway from an older structure. In contrast with the fortress-like outer face, the side facing the town has large windows lighting the storey above the gate. This spacious chamber served as the guildhall in medieval times and later civic uses saved the gatehouse from demolition in later centuries. It was a major obstruction to traffic until the construction of a by-pass in the 1930s, which relieved the problem but resulted in the destruction of the stretches of town wall on either side.

Beyond the Bargate the wall leads west to the circular Arundel Tower, then southwards to the old quay. Shortly a kink in the circuit denotes the junction with the older castle wall. Southampton Castle was a royal stronghold first mentioned in the 1180s. Richard I and John rebuilt it in stone. The west curtain survives as the town wall, with a postern leading into a cellar from the castle's domestic buildings. The north curtain – supported on an arcade which was originally buried in an earth rampart – can also be seen. It terminates in the footings of a gatehouse with round flanking turrets. However, there is no sense of a castle now because the motte has been flattened and the bailey has been built over. Richard II commissioned the architect Henry Yevele to erect a round keep on the motte, as part of a general strengthening of the castle when there were renewed fears of French raids.

The western wall of the town stands mostly to full height. Beyond the castle wall is the start of the quayside stretch which was not begun until the 1360s. Work then proceeded in haste, as shown by the incorporation of several house facades. They include the fine Norman house known as King John's Palace. In addition to the traditional arrow-slits the walls are pierced by simple gun ports, and if these are original they are the earliest in England. The portion just before the West Gate is distinguished by a projecting arcade of nineteen arches, each bearing a machicolation on the underside. This feature suggests influence from the South of France, but that is not surprising in mercantile Southampton. The West Gate – a simple gate tower – led to the quays, and was therefore the embarkation point for medieval armies.

Beyond the West Gate the wall curves eastwards, following the old line of the estuary (the land was reclaimed in the nineteenth century). There is then a long gap until we reach the South Gate at the south-east corner of the old circuit. It is flanked by a corridor terminating in God's House Tower, a sturdy square structure which projected well in front of the town's eastern defences. Both gatehouse and tower are additions of Henry V's reign and the corridor between them, as well as serving as a sluice gate for the moat, was designed for artillery defence – in effect the first gun battery. Turning northwards, the wall disappears at Briton Street and only one other fragment survives from the long eastern stretch. Polymond's Tower still stands at the north-east corner and the wall then returns to the Bargate.

> *Access:* The town wall and castle remains are freely accessible (LA). The Bargate and God's House Tower both contain museums.

Reference: VCH *Hampshire* (III). Turner for the town wall. *HKW* (II) for the castle.
Relations: Impressive but incomplete town walls such as Canterbury, Oxford, Great Yarmouth and Newcastle.

SOUTHSEA CASTLE lies at the southern tip of Portsea Island, commanding the approach to Portsmouth. It was built by Henry VIII in 1544, a slightly later addition to his chain of coastal forts and very different from its predecessors. Henry's earlier forts are distinguished by their rounded profiles employing principles devised in northern Europe. Stefan von Haschenperg, the mastermind behind this group, had been dismissed the previous year and Southsea Castle shows the arrival of new theories of artillery defence. Here the inspiration was Italian, resulting in a fort with straight sides and angles. The castle followed an oblong plan with triangular gun platforms in the middle of the two longer sides. They seem to be precursors of the arrow-head bastion which made its first appearance in England at Yarmouth a couple of years later. As at most Henrician forts there is a central tower, though here it is square in keeping with the overall design.

In 1545, just after its completion, the castle saw action when the French made an unsuccessful attack on Portsmouth. Henry watched the fighting from here and witnessed the sinking of his favourite warship, the *Mary Rose* (resurrected from its watery grave in 1982). Apart from that the only real fighting took place in 1642, when the castle was stormed by Parliamentary troops during a night raid. However, it remained garrisoned as part of the increasingly complex defences around Portsmouth until 1960. As a result it has undergone considerable modification. The whole of the landward side dates from an enlargement of 1814, along with the brick vaults in the central tower and the barracks in the courtyard. Although the seaward front is original in its core, the point of the gun platform has been rounded off and the rest of the walling has been refaced to match. The parapet contains emplacements for the powerful artillery of the nineteenth century.

Access: Open regularly (LA).
Reference: *Southsea Castle* by A. Corney. *HKW* (IV).
Relations: Yarmouth. Henry VIII's other Solent forts at Calshot, Hurst and Netley.

WINCHESTER CASTLE, WOLVESEY PALACE AND CITY WALL As the capital of the kings of Wessex, who brought the whole of England under their sway in the tenth century, Winchester enjoyed the status of capital long into the Norman period, though eventually the pull of London proved too strong. It is therefore inevitable that William I should have founded a castle here soon after the Norman Conquest. The castle occupied a curiously elongated site on high ground at the western edge of the walled city. It received stone buildings in the twelfth century but much restoration was necessary following the city's capture by the Dauphin Louis in 1216. The defences were pulled down after Winchester fell to Parliament in 1645 and the outer bailey is now occupied by barracks. The only building left standing is a very important one, since after Westminster Hall it is acknowledged as England's finest medieval hall. It survived because of its use as a court house. Sir Walter Raleigh was its most famous defendant. As reconstructed by Henry III in 1222–36 the hall is a splendid apartment, 110 feet long and exactly half as wide and high. The castle was Henry's birthplace. Slender five-bay arcades with columns of Purbeck marble divide the main body of the hall from the aisles. The present entrance is Victorian. Despite its architectural importance the hall is best known for the Round Table which hangs at one end. It may be a disappointment to learn that the table dates only from Edward III's reign. The portrait of King Arthur and the names of twenty-four of his knights were painted on in 1522 in preparation for a visit by the Emperor Charles V. Behind the hall some foundations have been uncovered and left on view. They comprise part of the inner curtain, a round tower at the northern apex and a square keep of medium size.

The early history of the castle is confused because a royal palace with another Norman keep stood near the cathedral. It existed until 1141 when Henry de Blois, Bishop of Winchester, pulled it down during his battle with the Empress Matilda for control of the city. During those troubled years Henry partially fortified his own palace which occupied the south-east corner of the city, counterbalancing the royal castle on the west. Wolvesey Palace (often called Wolvesey Castle to distinguish it from its successor) remained the chief seat of the bishops throughout the Middle Ages. It was finally abandoned in 1684 by Bishop Morley, who built the present Baroque palace alongside. The fine chapel (rebuilt by Cardinal Beaufort in the 1440s) is incorporated but the rest of the old palace is very much a ruin. Excavations in 1963–74 have revealed what a lavish complex it was. Prior to the Anarchy Wolvesey consisted of two large hall blocks facing each other. From *circa* 1138 Bishop Henry connected the two blocks to form a closed courtyard. On the south there was a definite curtain wall entered through a sequence of gateways. Henry went on to build two square towers against the eastern hall block, creating an illusion of strength on this side. It *is* an illusion, for despite the circumstances of its origin Wolvesey's defences are really more for show than anything else. The so-called keep is really just a symbolic imitation of a keep as it housed a vast kitchen, and the smaller Wymond's Tower served as a latrine block for the adjoining solar. The gatehouse on the north side of the courtyard was erected following Henry's return from exile in 1158. Today the palace is fragmentary and only the end walls of the eastern hall block, the two towers on the east front and the gatehouse stand to any height.

A large outer courtyard surrounded the palace, bounded on the south and east by the city wall. The city wall enclosed a strictly rectangular area except on the east where its line deviated to follow the course of the River Itchen. The layout recalls Winchester's origin as the Roman *Venta* but no Roman masonry remains visible. Indeed, the Wolvesey stretch is the only part of the city wall still standing, because the bishops kept it in good repair even when the rest of the circuit was disappearing. This section was rebuilt by William of Wykeham in the 1370s, when fear of French raids was not just confined to the coastal towns. The wall runs along College Street past Winchester College. Kingsgate beyond is one of the two surviving gatehouses from the walled circuit. It led into the cathedral precinct and its upper floor has long been used as the church of St Swithun. The West Gate stands on the High Street near the castle hall. This oblong structure is essentially of early-thirteenth-century date though the outer front, with machicolations and gun ports, is another improvement of the 1370s or thereabouts.

Access: The castle hall and the West Gate are open regularly (both LA). Wolvesey Palace is open at standard times in summer (EH). The city wall is visible from the road.

Reference: VCH *Hampshire* (IV). *HKW* (II) for the castle. Wolvesey Palace guidebook by M Biddle.

Relations: The Palace of Westminster and halls such as Penshurst, Oakham and Auckland. Henry de Blois' castle-palaces at Bishop's Waltham, Farnham and Taunton. Compare Southampton's extensive town wall.

OTHER SITES The ringwork at *Ashley* (near Winchester) may date from as late as 1200 when a licence to crenellate was awarded. Another ringwork (*Barley Pound*) can be found south of Crondall. *Gosport's* fifteenth-century gun tower has vanished. It commanded the entrance to Portsmouth Harbour in conjunction with the Round Tower at Portsmouth.

Herefordshire

Castles actually came to Herefordshire *before* the Norman Conquest. Edward the Confessor invited over his Norman nephew Ralph 'the Timid', making him Earl of Hereford in return for guarding this section of the Welsh Border. Ralph and his followers erected castles, hitherto unknown in England, at Hereford, Ewyas Harold and Richard's Castle. After 1066 Herefordshire briefly became a palatinate under William Fitz Osbern. The barons of the county erected castles at an accelerated rate, especially in the western districts which they had seized from the Welsh. These formed part of Marcher lordship territory, where barons enjoyed freedom from royal interference until the Tudor period. Under threat from the two Llywelyns (Great and Last) for much of the thirteenth century, the castles of this area were upgraded to the demands of contemporary warfare, with round towers and twin-towered gatehouses. This is demonstrated at Clifford, Longtown, Pembridge and Wilton. The trend culminates in the mighty Edwardian castle at Goodrich, which is now a splendid ruin. Wigmore, another important stronghold of this era, has decayed rather more. The chief castle at Hereford has unfortunately perished though some of the city wall survives. With the conquest of Wales under Edward I Herefordshire's castles lost their strategic value and most of them have fallen into a sad state of decay. A few fortified mansions of the later Middle Ages, such as Croft, Kentchurch and Hampton Court, have not suffered this fate but have succumbed to later transformations instead.

BRAMPTON BRYAN CASTLE is attributed to Robert Harley, who inherited the manor in 1309. Today the castle has been reduced to the ruins of the gatehouse and the hall range, which are separated by a narrow courtyard. Only one wall of the hall stands, with an Elizabethan porch projecting from it. The gatehouse proper is fragmentary but the barbican, which was added as an afterthought, is a handsome and well-preserved feature. Twin round towers flank the entrance and the long gate passage shows two portcullis grooves. In 1643 the castle was defended by Brilliana Harley in the absence of her husband. Here, the dramatic roles normally associated with the Civil War were reversed, as Lady Harley was a Parliamentarian endeavouring to keep the King's forces at bay. She forced the besiegers to withdraw after two months, but the strain of the siege hastened her death and the following year the Royalists captured and slighted the castle. The remains stand in the gardens of Brampton Bryan Hall.

Access: Open occasionally.
Reference: RCHM *Herefordshire* (III). Salter.
Relations: Barbicans such as Warwick, Arundel and Lewes.

BRONSIL CASTLE lies in Eastnor Park, a mile east of neo-Gothic Eastnor Castle. Richard, Lord Beauchamp, obtained licences to crenellate in 1449 and 1460. In those years he was High Treasurer of England. The castle followed the quadrangular plan with octagonal corner towers and intermediate towers, the whole being surrounded by a broad moat. The moat is still full of water and one of the semi-octagonal towers which flanked the gatehouse survives in an overgrown state. Everything else was pulled down in the eighteenth century and the area of the courtyard is now covered in trees.

Access: On private land.
Relations: The Beauchamp castles of Elmley, Holt and Warwick.

CLIFFORD CASTLE Its name is appropriate, as the castle is perched on a steep slope above an old crossing of the River Wye, two miles north of Hay-on-Wye. The Domesday Book records that William Fitz Osbern, palatine Earl of Hereford, built a castle here before his death in 1071, though this may have been the motte-and-bailey further east at Old Castleton. If so, the move to the present site probably occurred under the De Cliffords early in the twelfth century. This family played an important part in the Marcher struggles of the period though the best known of their line is Henry II's mistress, 'Fair Rosamund'. The castle probably remained an earth and timber affair until the 1220s when Walter de Clifford built the stone curtain on the motte. It is an up-to-date version of the shell keep theme, the wall having five semi-circular towers projecting from it, two of them set closely together to flank the entrance. The keep is now very ruinous though one of the towers and part of the hall block stand quite high. Foundations in the middle of the bailey mark the site of a later stone gatehouse, indicating that only half of the bailey was ever walled in stone. In 1233 Henry III occupied the castle after Walter de Clifford refused to pay the debts he owed to his Jewish bankers. Clifford was later inherited by the Mortimers. They neglected the castle in favour of other residences and decay ensued, though it was re-garrisoned at the height of Owain Glyndwr's revolt.

Access: Obtain permission to view at the farm.
Reference: RCHM *Herefordshire* (I). Salter.
Relations: The Northern Clifford strongholds at Appleby, Brough, Brougham and Skipton.

CROFT CASTLE, five miles north-west of Leominster, is the mansion of the Croft family. They were already here at the time of the Domesday Book and have remained (with one long interruption) ever since. The present castle follows the quadrangular plan though the north side is not parallel to the south. Owing to the extent of later alterations it is difficult to date the outer walls with any degree of certainty but some time in the fifteenth century seems most likely. The circular towers at the four corners are so slender that they could not have served any serious defensive purpose. Apart from the north range, which is Elizabethan, the present ranges around the courtyard post-date the acquisition of the castle by Richard Knight in 1746. They are a fine example of Georgian elegance but they tell us little about the original layout. Nor has the exterior fared much better, since the sash windows piercing the curtain and the loss of the parapet have deprived the castle of what little strength it may once have possessed. The entrance porch and its flanking turrets are also Georgian though they probably occupy the site of an older gatehouse. In the chapel just outside the castle is the fine tomb of Sir Richard Croft (d.1509), who enjoyed favour under both Edward IV and Henry VII. It may well have been he who built the castle. Crowning the wooded hill which overlooks the castle is a much older fortification – the Iron Age hillfort of Croft Ambrey.

Access: Open regularly in summer (NT).
Reference: Guidebook by D. Uhlman. RCHM *Herefordshire* (III).
Relations: Treago is similar.

EARDISLEY CASTLE The Domesday Book records a 'fortified house' here, as opposed to a castle proper. At that time it belonged to Roger de Lacy who is thus the probable founder. A low motte occupies one corner of an oblong bailey which is surrounded by a wet moat. However, there is no sign of a rampart within so the inadequate earthworks would appear to justify the Domesday Book description. The castle, rebuilt in stone under the De Bohuns and Baskervilles, was destroyed in the Civil War and an eighteenth-century farmhouse now occupies the bailey. The village is five miles south of Kington.

Access: On private land.
Relations: For Roger de Lacy see Lyonshall and Ludlow.

EWYAS HAROLD CASTLE, on a spur in the Golden Valley, is probably one of the few English castles founded before the Norman Conquest. It may well have been the 'Pentecost's Castle' to which Edward the Confessor's Norman friends fled in 1052 on the return of Earl Godwin from exile. Domesday Book tells us that William Fitz Osbern, Earl of Hereford, refortified the site (i.e. between 1067 and his death in 1071). The existing motte-and-bailey earthworks are probably his, though the impressive tree-covered motte is based on a natural mound. It once supported a shell keep but no masonry is visible now. The decaying stronghold was refortified during Owain Glyndwr's revolt.

Access: On private land.
Reference: RCHM *Herefordshire* (I).
Relations: The pre-Conquest castles at Hereford and Richard's Castle.

GOODRICH CASTLE is the most splendid in the county and one of the best examples of English military architecture. It is still impressive despite its ruinous state. The castle is perched on a rocky spur above the River Wye, four miles south-west of Ross-on-Wye. Godric's Castle – no doubt named after Godric Mappestone, who held land nearby – is first recorded in 1101. Nothing is left of Godric's stronghold but within the bailey, very close to the later curtain, rises a well-preserved though relatively small Norman keep. Henry II took over the castle and the keep is generally attributed to him, but the royal accounts record very little expenditure here. It may therefore have been the work of William Fitz Baderon, Lord of Monmouth, who seized the castle during the Anarchy. The keep is a tall, square tower with pilaster buttresses and Norman windows. The original first-floor entrance was later converted into a window, a new doorway being inserted immediately below.

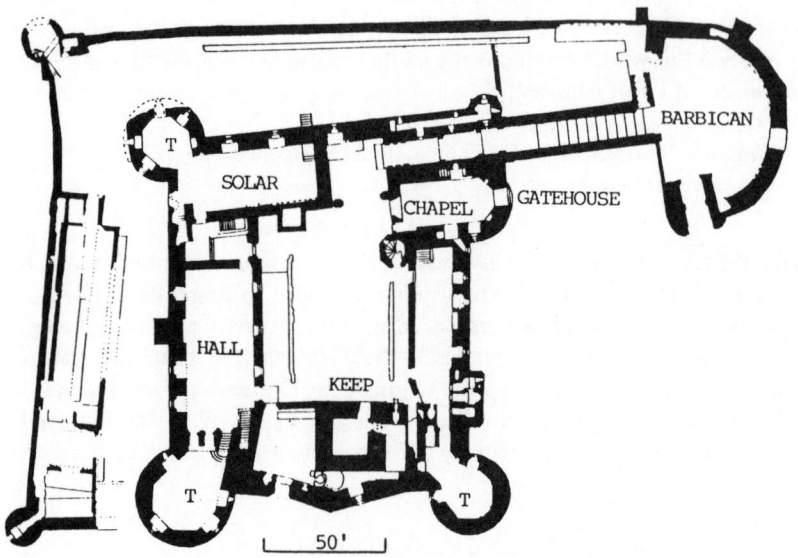

GOODRICH CASTLE

Strangely enough, the existing curtain and corner towers are not the first on the site. King John granted Goodrich to the mighty William Marshal, Earl of Pembroke, and a stone enclosure followed. Some of his masonry is embedded in the present east curtain and the foundations of a round tower underlie the present south-west tower. Whether or not this work was ever completed, it was taken down and replaced by a later Earl of Pembroke, William de Valence. His building here is contemporary and comparable with the Edwardian castles of Wales. Such a castle is a rarity in England. It is square in plan, the more vulnerable south and east sides being protected by a wide, rock-cut ditch. A thick curtain surrounds the bailey, with massive round towers at three corners and a gatehouse occupying the fourth. Each tower rises from a solid square base which sinks back into the cylinder in pyramid fashion, forming spurs. The spurs projecting from the south-east tower are particularly high. Such spur bases, common in castles of the Welsh Marches, were designed to foil attempts at undermining. The gatehouse is a curiously asymmetrical variant of the Edwardian theme, its long gate passage being flanked by one large, U-shaped tower and one small corner turret.

William de Valence probably built the castle in the 1280s, but his son Aymer provided outer defences. To the north and west, where the land falls away but there is no great ditch, he added an outer wall which is concentric to the inner curtain. This wall and its corner turrets have been reduced to little more than foundations. More substantial is the semi-circular barbican which Aymer added in front of the gatehouse. Protected by its own outer ditch, the approach is at right angles to the gatehouse so that an attacking force would have needed to storm the outer entrance whilst under fire from the castle. They would then have to negotiate the causeway across the inner ditch and tackle the complex defences of the main gate passage (a drawbridge, two portcullises and two gates).

An integral part of the original design is the spacious set of domestic buildings surrounding the compact bailey. The main apartments occupy the western half of the bailey, comprising a hall against the west curtain, a solar block on the north side and a kitchen abutting the keep. On the other side of the keep steps descend to a purpose-built prison chamber. The customary three doorways at the service end of the hall lead into the south-west tower which contained the buttery and pantry. The north-west tower, now the most ruinous part of the castle, contained further accommodation. An apsidal chapel occupies the first floor of the large gatehouse tower.

Following Aymer de Valence's death in 1324 Goodrich became a favourite residence of the Talbot family, subsequently earls of Shrewsbury. It was abandoned in favour of more up-to-date residences in the Tudor period. The castle saw no military action until the Civil War. It resisted the Roundheads in 1645 but was closely besieged for two months the following year. With the cutting off of the water supply the garrison was compelled to surrender (July 1646) and the castle was slighted.

Access: Standard opening times (EH).

Reference: Guidebook by D. F. Renn.

Relations: Aymer de Valence's castle at Bampton. Towers with spurs at St Briavels and Tonbridge. The barbican was inspired by a vanished one at the Tower of London.

HAMPTON COURT, set in a large park to the east of Hope-under-Dinmore, was erected by a veteran of the French wars. Sir Rowland Lenthall profited from the victory at Agincourt (1415) and is said to have built Hampton Court with his share of the ransom, though he did not receive a licence to crenellate until 1434. The house is built around a quadrangle and, from the first, was really just a castellated mansion as opposed to a serious fortification. The north front has a quasi-defensive appearance, with square turrets at each end and an oblong gate tower in the middle. This gatehouse preserves its machicolated crown. It may have had something of the keep-gatehouse about it, but the defensive limitations of the rest of the house are only too clear from the way that the chapel projects out of the quadrangle – an exposed building, its large Perpendicular windows inviting assault. The gatehouse, the chapel – with its beautiful roof – and the hall porch are the only relatively untouched parts of the mansion. The rest has been greatly altered since, most drastically under Sir Jeffry Wyatville (of Windsor Castle fame), who gave the mansion the full sham-Gothic treatment from 1817.

Access: Private.
Reference: RCHM *Herefordshire* (III).
Relations: Windsor.

HEREFORD CASTLE AND CITY WALL Hereford means 'army ford', a reference to the turbulent days of its foundation when the Kingdom of Mercia was pushing westwards into Welsh territory. Excavations have uncovered the Saxon town rampart. For centuries the English settlers and the Welsh beyond the River Wye were uneasy neighbours, and in 1055 the town went up in flames. Harold Godwinson (later King Harold) drove back the invaders and rebuilt the shattered defences. In Norman times the enclosed area doubled in size and a walled circuit replaced the earthwork defences from 1224 onwards. Hereford rebuffed a Scottish army in 1645 but fell to Parliament at the end of that year. Damaged during these sieges, the city wall suffered the common fate of demolition and concealment thereafter. However, clearance in the 1960s for the Victoria Street by-pass has led to the re-appearance of much of the western part of the circuit, extending from the river almost to West Street. The wall is much mutilated but it preserves two semi-circular bastions. All the gatehouses have perished, including the one which guarded the medieval Wye Bridge. There was no wall on the riverside but remains of a ditch show that the medieval city had a suburb on the opposite bank.

According to John Leland Hereford Castle was one of the 'largest, fairest and strongest' in England, so its virtual disappearance is a great pity. It lay beside the river at the south-east corner of the city defences. Ralph 'the Timid', the pre-Conquest Norman Earl of Hereford, first raised a castle here in 1051, but it does not seem to have survived the overthrow of the Norman party at court the following year. William Fitz Osbern re-founded the castle soon after the Norman Conquest and it resisted King Stephen for a month in 1138. The castle suffered from too close a proximity to the cathedral. In 1140 the Empress Matilda's supporters fired stones and arrows into the bailey from the central tower (a forerunner of the present one). Henry III found himself a prisoner here after the Battle of Lewes (1264), but his son Edward escaped and rallied the royal forces to victory over Simon de Montfort at Evesham. The defences of this royal stronghold were pulled down at the Restoration. Even the motte, which apparently supported a keep surrounded by a towered curtain, has been levelled. Castle Green was the bailey, a triangular area still bounded by a high rampart except towards the river. Castle Pool is a remnant of the old moat, while the house known as Castle Cliffe incorporates some masonry from the water gate.

Access: The castle site and city wall are freely accessible (LA).
Reference: Salter. Turner for the city wall.
Relations: Ewyas Harold and Richard's Castle are other pre-Conquest castles. Compare the fortified Welsh Border towns of Shrewsbury and Chester.

HEREFORDSHIRE BEACON   Crowning the hump of one of the Malvern Hills above Little Malvern is a rare combination of prehistoric hillfort and medieval castle. The impressive ramparts and ditches of the hillfort, surrounding a citadel and two outer enclosures, date from the Iron Age. Sometime in the twelfth century, probably during the Anarchy, this elevated site was occupied anew, a ringwork being dug at the highest point within the citadel.

Access: Freely accessible.
Relations: Elmley, Old Sarum and Dover are other castles utilising Iron Age defences.

HUNTINGTON CASTLE   originated under the De Braose family. It is likely that they first raised the nearby motte-and-bailey known as Turret Castle, moving to the present site (just north of the village) in the twelfth century. This castle, though much overgrown, is a strong earthwork consisting of a motte and two baileys overlooking a ravine. One tall fragment of curtain crowns the rampart, showing that the inner bailey was once walled in stone. The castle was inherited by the Bohuns in 1248 and was last garrisoned during Owain Glyndwr's revolt. The village is three miles south-west of Kington.

Access: On private land.
Relations: Bramber and Knepp were other Braose castles.

KENTCHURCH COURT   In a park east of Kentchurch village stands the old mansion of the Scudamore family. It was transformed before 1807 by the architect John Nash and the former hall range is now very largely his. The square tower house attached to one corner is genuine, though Nash inserted the large windows and added a fifth storey. The projecting latrine chute is just about the only original feature to survive. Owing to the extent of later alteration there can be little certainty over the date, though the fourteenth century is considered most likely. The tower is known as Owen Glendower's Tower. Glyndwr married Sir John Scudamore's daughter and is said to have been entertained here more than once during his years of struggle against the English. Other medieval portions are the north-east wing (once free-standing) and a gate arch, but it would seem that the tower house was the only defensive feature.

Access: Open by appointment only.
Reference: RCHM *Herefordshire* (I).

KILPECK CASTLE   Kilpeck, off the Hereford-Abergavenny road, is renowned for its Norman church. The marvellous sculpture adorning the church was probably commissioned by Hugh de Kilpeck in the mid twelfth century. The castle of the De Kilpecks lies immediately to the west, on an eminence commanding a fine view. It is a motte-and-bailey earthwork with indications of several outer enclosures, including one around the village. On top of the motte are two pieces of wall from a shell keep, all that survives a slighting by the Roundheads. One of them bears the remains of a Norman fireplace, showing that residential buildings stood against the wall.

Access: Freely accessible.
Reference: RCHM *Herefordshire* (I). Salter.

LONGTOWN CASTLE occupies a spur of land overlooking the River Monnow, in the shadow of the Black Mountains. After the Norman Conquest this area was colonised by Walter de Lacy. It is likely that the motte-and-bailey at Ponthendre formed the original centre of the barony and the present castle is described as new in 1187. The castle is a typical motte-and-bailey earthwork but it overlies the western part of a square enclosure which may be a Roman fort. Early in the thirteenth century another Walter de Lacy, Sheriff of Herefordshire, rebuilt the defences in stone. His work comprised a curtain around the bailey, a cross-wall dividing the bailey into two halves and a circular keep on the motte. The curtain is now very ruinous and the best preserved part is the cross-wall. It is pierced by a gateway with portcullis groove and solid, half-round flanking turrets. The keep is virtually intact apart from one deep breach caused by the collapse of the spiral stair. Note the sloping plinth and the semi-circular buttresses reinforcing the wall where it is weakened inside by a fireplace and a latrine. A third buttresses projected where the breach is. Within, the main apartment was the hall at first floor level. Circular keeps are uncommon in England, since they coincide with that era when the keep-less enclosure was the norm. The castle was probably abandoned in the fourteenth century, and though it was refortified during the Owain Glyndwr rebellion this temporary reprieve did not prevent its collapse into ruin.

Access: The keep is freely accessible (EH).
Reference: RCHM *Herefordshire* (I). Salter.
Relations: The round keeps at Launceston, Conisbrough and (just across the Welsh Border) Skenfrith.

LYONSHALL CASTLE, three miles east of Kington, was probably founded in the 1080s by Roger de Lacy and became the home of the D'Evreux or Devereux family. The site is a moated ringwork near the parish church. Within the ringwork fragments of masonry indicate a curtain, bowing outwards to make room for a circular keep which still stands partly to first floor level. This keep rose from a plinth and preserves the embrasures for three arrow-slits, but the existing ivy-clad masonry is in poor condition and the portion containing the entrance has collapsed. It must have resembled the larger keep at Longtown and is no doubt of similar date, i.e. the early thirteenth century.

Access: On private land.
Reference: RCHM *Herefordshire* (III). Salter.
Relations: Longtown. Roger de Lacy founded the castles at Eardisley and Ludlow.

PEMBRIDGE CASTLE stands a mile north-west of Welsh Newton and just a few miles from Skenfrith Castle across the Welsh Border. It should not be confused with the village of Pembridge which is situated at the north end of the county. The Pembridge family took their name from the village and gave it in turn to the castle. It is an evocative Marcher stronghold, though its completeness is the result of a heavy restoration soon after 1900. The castle had been in ruins since 1644, following its capture and slighting by the Royalists. It originated under Ralph de Pembridge (d.1219). He erected a hall with a circular tower at one end. The hall has been replaced by a seventeenth-century farmhouse though the outer wall survives as part of the later curtain. The four-storey tower may be regarded as a small keep, serving the same function as later tower houses. Towards the end of the thirteenth century another member of the Pembridge family expanded this house into a small quadrangular stronghold. It is still surrounded by a wet moat. The older tower occupies the west corner of the enclosure, though it barely flanks the curtain. At the south corner is a fully-developed Edwardian gatehouse, its round-fronted towers flanking a long gate passage. However, the tower to the right of the entrance, the chamber above the gate and the machicolations belong to the restoration. The embattled curtain beyond is a low rebuilding and only the ends show the original height. It leads to the quarter-round eastern tower which has a round top supported on arches. A tiny turret clasps the north corner. The picturesque courtyard occupies a considerably higher level than the ground outside. As well as the farmhouse there is a rustic Tudor chapel rising curiously above parapet level.

Access: Private.

Reference: RCHM *Herefordshire* (I). Salter.

Relations: Marcher castles of enclosure such as Clifford, Goodrich and Whittington.

RICHARD'S CASTLE The village, four miles south of Ludlow, takes its name from the castle of Richard Fitz Scrob, one of the pioneering Normans who came over with Edward the Confessor's nephew Ralph. These Normans were expelled by Earl Godwin in 1052, but the Domesday Book relates that the castle (then called Avretone) had been restored to Richard's son Osbern. Whether the existing earthworks are pre- or post-Conquest is impossible to determine. The site is a motte-and-bailey on an elevated spur. There are traces of an outer enclosure which protected a small borough, though now only the parish church stands inside. A portion of curtain remains from the bailey defences, continuing up the side of the motte. There is also a precarious fragment of the gatehouse. Excavations in the 1960s uncovered half-round towers flanking the curtain and an octagonal keep on the motte – work of the De Says towards 1200. None of this has been left on view and the site is now overgrown and desolate. Like several other Herefordshire strongholds, the castle was temporarily garrisoned during Owain Glyndwr's revolt.

Access: Freely accessible.

Reference: RCHM *Herefordshire* (III). Salter.

Relations: The pre-Conquest castles at Ewyas Harold, Hereford and Canfield.

SNODHILL CASTLE crowns a hill a mile south-east of Dorstone. Until 1428 it belonged to the Chandos family. This small but strong motte-and-bailey preserves some masonry fragments, all that survives a slighting in 1645. On top of the motte are some remains of a keep. It formed an elongated octagon but would have been too small for a shell keep and rather low for a tower. Towards the bailey it presents a tall round turret, originally one of a pair which flanked the entrance. They suggest a thirteenth-century date. A length of wall and part of a semi-circular tower survive from the bailey defences.

Access: Freely accessible.

TREAGO CASTLE, south-west of the village of St Weonard's, was the residence of the Mynors family from the thirteenth century until 1765. It is a late medieval walled quadrangle, resembling Croft Castle in overall effect and equally altered in later centuries. The architectural features which do survive suggest a date of *circa* 1500, so Treago is either an unusually late fortified house or a remarkably early sham. The cross-slits which pierce the walls are rather antiquated for the early Tudor period and therefore suggest the latter. There are round towers of different sizes at the corners, those on the west being slender turrets as at Croft, while the biggest tower (with a later overhanging cap) is at the south-east angle. A projecting bay covers the site of the original gateway through the east wall, the present entrance being on the north through an Elizabethan porch. The interior of the castle has been rebuilt several times and the small courtyard has been roofed over to serve as a grand staircase.

Access: Private.
Reference: RCHM *Herefordshire* (I). Salter.
Relations: Croft.

WIGMORE CASTLE According to the Domesday Book this was one of the strongholds founded by William Fitz Osbern, Earl of Hereford. Following the rebellion of his son in 1075 the castle was granted to Ralph de Mortimer, founder of a dynasty which became one of the most powerful in the Welsh Marches. Henry II captured the castle from Hugh de Mortimer in 1155, and it was here that Prince Edward obtained refuge following his escape from Hereford Castle in 1265. The most notorious of the line was Roger Mortimer, first Earl of March, who played a leading part in the deposition and murder of Edward II (1327). In concert with his lover, Queen Isabella, Mortimer ruled England for three years until being overthrown by the young Edward III. He died on the gallows at Tyburn and Wigmore was given to the Earl of Salisbury, but the Mortimers regained their lands and title by marriage. They served with distinction during the Hundred Years War, but in 1425 the Mortimer line died out and the castle more or less died with them. It was still habitable in 1461, when the future Edward IV lodged here before his decisive victory at Mortimer's Cross nearby, but after that it lapsed into ruin.

The castle is in a very precarious condition nowadays, its walls overgrown or buried in debris, and threatening to crumble further unless essential work is carried out. If the remains were to be excavated and consolidated Wigmore would be a castle of considerable interest, but at present there is just an atmosphere of desolation. It is a powerfully-sited motte-and-bailey stronghold with a lot of masonry still standing. The oval shell keep on the large motte incorporates Norman portions, but all the other stonework belongs to a reconstruction of *circa* 1300, probably undertaken by the infamous Roger Mortimer. There are three towers on the line of the bailey curtain, two oblong and one half-round. The largest tower contained a suite of chambers and is divided by a cross-wall. Note the arch of the gatehouse, half-buried in an accumulation of earth.

Access: Freely accessible.
Reference: RCHM *Herefordshire* (III). Salter.
Relations: See Roger Mortimer's work at Ludlow and his overthrow at Nottingham Castle.

WILTON CASTLE   commands the bridge across the River Wye between Ross-on-Wye and Bridstow. There may have been a castle here in Norman times but the existing masonry is the product of the Edwardian age and is usually attributed to Roger de Grey *circa* 1300. His descendants styled themselves 'Lord Grey of Wilton' to be distinguished from other branches of the Grey family. The castle remains are mingled with the ruins of an Elizabethan house erected by Charles Brydges. His grandson escaped to Ireland to avoid the Civil War, and the local people burnt the house down as a token of their displeasure. Part of it was made habitable again in the nineteenth century.

The castle covered an irregular oblong overlooking the river. Much of the curtain remains on three sides but the south end is occupied by the Elizabethan house. There are three surviving mural towers of different shapes and sizes. The tower at the north-west corner is octagonal and relatively small. Clearly a north-east angle tower existed but it has disappeared. Next comes the shell of a round tower half-way along the east curtain. Largest of all is the U-shaped tower on the south-west, its inner part incorporated in the present house. This tower is similar to the large gatehouse tower at nearby Goodrich Castle, so perhaps there was an asymmetrical gatehouse of the same sort here. Wilton is roughly contemporary with Goodrich though it does not compare in terms of defensive strength.

Access: Visible from the road.
Reference: RCHM *Herefordshire* (I). Salter.
Relations: Goodrich. For other branches of the Grey family see Codnor and Grey's Court.

OTHER SITES   The county, especially the Marcher territories towards Wales, is rich in motte-and-bailey sites from the Norman years of colonisation. Many are quite small and unimposing – the homes of relatively humble landowners who elsewhere would have lived in unfortified manor houses – so there follows a selective list:

Almeley Castle
Aston Castle (near Ludlow)
Castle Frome
Chanstone Castle (near Vowchurch)
Dorstone Castle
Eardisland Castle
Kingsland Castle
Lingen Castle
Llancillo Castle (near Rowlstone)
Mortimer's Castle (Much Marcle)
Newton Castle (near Abbey Dore)

Oldcastle (near Almeley)
Old Castleton (near Clifford)
Orcop Castle
Ponthendre Castle (near Longtown)
Rowlstone Castle
Stapleton Castle
Staunton Castle (Staunton-on-Arrow)
Tregate Castle (near Llanrothal)
Turret Castle (near Huntington)
Walterstone Castle

Weobley's castle had an oblong keep and a towered curtain but only earthworks remain. At *Ashperton* is the wet moat of a castle licensed in 1292. A fourteenth-century undercroft in a ruined house is the only relic of *Penyard Castle*, near Weston-under-Penyard. Elizabethan *Kinnersley Castle* occupies the site of a medieval predecessor.

Hertfordshire

Hertfordshire preserves several motte-and-bailey castles from the Norman era, including the powerful examples at Anstey and Berkhamsted. Berkhamsted and Hertford retain a lot of Norman masonry as well but both castles are now very ruinous. Hertford and Rye House have late medieval brick gatehouses, but this county was too close to London for uncontrolled castle building to take root.

ANSTEY CASTLE is an impressive motte-and-bailey earthwork, its great motte (relatively low in proportion to its diameter) being surrounded by a water-filled moat. Though it finds no mention in the Domesday Book, the castle is attributed to Eustace, Count of Boulogne, who received the manor after the Norman Conquest. His sub-tenants here adopted the name of the place. Nicholas de Anstey strengthened the castle against King John during the Magna Carta war, but was compelled to destroy his additions once peace returned. No traces of masonry survive though at least one stone building stood on the motte. The motte survived the onslaught of an American bomber which crashed into it in 1944.

> *Access:* Visible from the churchyard.
> *Reference:* VCH *Hertfordshire* (IV).
> *Relations:* Motte-and-bailey sites such as Berkhamsted, Pleshey and Thetford.

BENINGTON CASTLE Four miles east of Stevenage is the Georgian house known as Benington Lordship, set within the raised enclosure of a Norman castle. The earthworks have become the backdrop for a beautiful garden. A twin-towered gatehouse leads into the enclosure but this is a complete sham, having been erected as a folly in 1832. The stump of a small, square keep within the enclosure is a genuine relic but even this has been 'beautified' with neo-Norman doorways. Benington was probably built by Roger de Valognes during the Anarchy. The castle outlasted Henry II's accession and even survived the Valognes' involvement in Prince Henry's revolt, though the keep may have perished because a hundred picks were sent to hack down the walls. It met its final destruction following the banishment of Robert Fitz Walter in 1212.

> *Access:* Limited opening times in summer.
> *Reference:* VCH *Hertfordshire* (III). RCHM *Hertfordshire*.

BERKHAMSTED CASTLE was probably founded by Robert, Count of Mortain and Earl of Cornwall. It was certainly held by him at the time of the Domesday survey. As William I's half-brother Robert did well for himself out of the Norman Conquest, but his son made the mistake of supporting Robert of Normandy against Henry I. As a result the castle was confiscated by the Crown. During the twelfth century it was leased to certain individuals, including Thomas Becket. The only military event occurred during the upheavals of 1216, the castle falling to the

Dauphin Louis after a two-week bombardment. Henry III revived the link with the Earldom of Cornwall by granting Berkhamsted to his brother Richard, 'King of the Romans', and in 1337 it became an outlying possession of the Duchy of Cornwall. The French King, John the Good, was kept here for a while following his capture at Poitiers, but the castle was already in decline. It was finally abandoned in the Elizabethan period.

The castle is a classic example of a motte-and-bailey stronghold, even if its edges have been gnawed at by roads and railway. The motte is tall and conical, and the bailey is surrounded by a double ditch with a rampart in between. Until the 1950s the inner ditch remained full of water. In front of the outer ditch on the north and east sides, following the circumference of the motte, rises a strong rampart. It is probably a concentric defence provided by Richard of Cornwall, though it has been suggested that the earth 'bastions' which project from it could have been raised as platforms for trebuchets during the Dauphin Louis' siege. The shell keep which crowned the motte has vanished but there are remains of the walls which descended to join the bailey curtain. Considerable lengths of this flint curtain survive, especially on the east side. At least some of the masonry dates from the time when Thomas Becket occupied the castle (1155–65), though the money came from Henry II's exchequer. Three semi-circular towers flanked the curtain, and if they date from Becket's tenure they are remarkably early. Little more than foundations are left of the towers now. The stump of a large oblong structure on the west curtain is probably the tower built by Richard of Cornwall in 1254. Foundations show that the north end of the bailey was walled off to form a separate enclosure, in effect a barbican in front of the motte.

Access: Freely accessible (EH).
Reference: VCH *Hertfordshire* (III). RCHM *Hertfordshire*.
Relations: For Robert of Mortain and Richard of Cornwall see the Cornish castles of Launceston, Tintagel and Trematon. Hertford is similar.

HERTFORD CASTLE   Hertford was one of the burghs founded by King Edward the Elder during the English reconquest of the Danelaw. It was no doubt soon after 1066 that William the Conqueror raised the castle beside the River Lea. In general form Hertford Castle resembles Berkhamsted – a motte-and-bailey once surrounded by a double moat, with much of its flint curtain still standing. The earthworks of the castle do not compare favourable, since the motte is surprisingly small and the moats have long been filled in. Royal expenditure is recorded in 1171–74 and the curtain probably dates at least partly from that time. The octagonal tower at the south angle of the enclosure is a later medieval addition.

Like Berkhamsted, the castle endured its only recorded siege in 1216, falling to the rebels during the Dauphin Louis' campaign to win the English throne. A frequent royal residence up to Henry III's reign, the castle declined in favour thereafter. Edward III granted it to his mother, the indomitable Queen Isabella, and those trophies of Edward's military successes – David II of Scotland and John II of France – both saw spells of imprisonment here. An equally reluctant royal visitor was England's own Richard II, who was deposed in the castle before moving on to his death at Pontefract. The castle enjoyed a revival under Edward IV. He built the brick gatehouse in 1461–65. The gatehouse is an oblong structure with shallow angle turrets, the plain surface of the walls being enriched just below parapet level by blank arcades echoing machicolations. This feature is enough to show that the gatehouse was more for show than for defence. However, the original arrangements have been obscured by later adaptation. Occupation of the gatehouse continued long after the rest of the castle had been abandoned, and in the 1790s it was enlarged and converted into a neo-Gothic mansion by the Earl of Hillsborough. This entailed the walling up of the original gateways and the addition of a porch in front. Restoration has uncovered the timber roof beams and partitions on the upper floors.

Access: The bailey is freely accessible (LA). The gatehouse is open occasionally.
Reference: RCHM *Hertfordshire. HKW* (II).
Relations: Berkhamsted. Edward IV's work at Dover.

RYE HOUSE stood beside the River Lea a mile north-east of Hoddesdon. It is remembered for the Rye House Plot of 1683 – a bungled attempt to assassinate Charles II. Sir Andrew Ogard obtained a licence to crenellate in 1443 and Rye is sometimes cited as one of those castles built by veterans of the French wars. However, most of the quadrangle was pulled down in the eighteenth century and its defensive credentials are doubtful. Only the wet moat and the gatehouse still remain. The gatehouse, in fashionable brick except for the stone archway, suggests nothing overtly defensive. It shows a passion for display with its decorative corbels, puny battlements, twin oriel windows and the formation of a diaper pattern in bands of blue brick.

Access: Freely accessible (LA).
Reference: Mackenzie (I).

WAYTEMORE CASTLE overlooks the River Stort at Bishop's Stortford. William the Conqueror established this castle to command the river crossing and later granted it to Maurice, Bishop of London. The castle became a popular retreat of the bishops but in the fifteenth century they transferred to the palace at Much Hadham nearby. Abandoned as a residence, Waytemore achieved notoriety as a gaol for Nonconformists and was pulled down after the Civil War. Earthworks mark the position of the bailey. There is a large motte, oddly rectangular in shape except for one side which bows outwards slightly. On its summit are the foundations of a flint Norman curtain with a square tower – possibly a small keep – at one corner beside the entrance.

Access: Visible from outside (LA).
Reference: VCH *Hertfordshire* (III). RCHM *Hertfordshire*.

OTHER SITES There is a motte-and-bailey site at Great *Wymondley*. *Walkern* preserves the banks of a Norman ringwork. The mottes at *Pirton* and *Therfield* appear to have been left unfinished, unless they were slighted by Henry II.

Isle of Wight

The Isle of Wight saw many foreign incursions, particularly in 1377 and 1545 when the French raided across the island. However, the one medieval castle has a central, inland setting. That castle is Carisbrooke, which illustrates well the development of fortification from Roman times to the Elizabethan era. More immediate coastal defence only appeared under Henry VIII. He built four forts of which Yarmouth is the chief survivor.

CARISBROOKE CASTLE is an extensive fortress situated on a hill about a mile south-west of Newport, virtually in the centre of the Isle of Wight. As a fortification it has a very long history, because the Norman castle is raised on the site of a Roman fort and is surrounded in turn by Elizabethan defences designed to withstand artillery. The Roman fort was probably part of the chain of defences guarding the 'Saxon Shore', both Roman and medieval planners deciding that the defence of a small island with a long coastline is best achieved from the centre. The site became a castle soon after the Norman Conquest, probably under William Fitz Osbern, Earl of Hereford. It is mentioned in the Domesday Book as the castle of 'Alwinestone'. Baldwin de Redvers, Earl of Devon, fled here in 1136 following his defeat at the hands of King Stephen. He planned to hold out in his island refuge but the water supply failed and he was forced to surrender. The Redvers family continued to hold the lordship of the island until their line died out in 1293. After that the castle reverted to the Crown but was granted out to favoured subjects from time to time. It was put to the test during the great raid of 1377 when the invading French were repulsed. Even after Henry VIII's coastal fortifications appeared Carisbrooke remained the centre of the island's defences. The continuing threat from Spain resulted in the construction of an up-to-date rampart around the castle in 1597–1600, designed by the Italian engineer Gianibelli.

The Elizabethan rampart surrounds the two baileys of the Norman castle in concentric fashion. This low, artillery-proof earthwork is encased in stone. There are arrow-head bastions at the corners and a fifth one on the west, commanding the entrance. Beyond the simple gateway through the rampart one is confronted with the main gatehouse. It began as a thirteenth-century gate tower but in 1336, at the start of the Hundred Years War, Edward III extended it outwards. The handsome facade is flanked by round turrets (the 'keyhole' gun ports were inserted a little later) and there is a row of machicolations above the entrance. The long gate passage (with three portcullis grooves) leads into the western bailey, which occupies the site of the Roman fort. Instead of utilising the Roman wall the Normans raised a massive rampart over it and piled up a lofty motte in one corner. Nevertheless the Roman masonry still peeps out from the bank in several places. Before long a polygonal shell keep was placed on the motte and a new wall was built on top of the bailey rampart. The rampart is so powerful that the curtain only needs to be of modest height. During the Elizabethan modifications artillery bastions were added at the south corners of the curtain, but encased within both are square, open-backed towers.

Clearly they are early examples of mural towers and they are too small and too widely-spaced to be effective as flankers. They support the written evidence that the curtain was built by Baldwin de Redvers before his showdown with King Stephen. The curtain ascends the motte to reach the small shell keep, entered through a gate tower which is another addition of 1336. There is a deep well (160 feet) within. The eastern bailey was never walled in stone and its earthworks have been adapted for artillery.

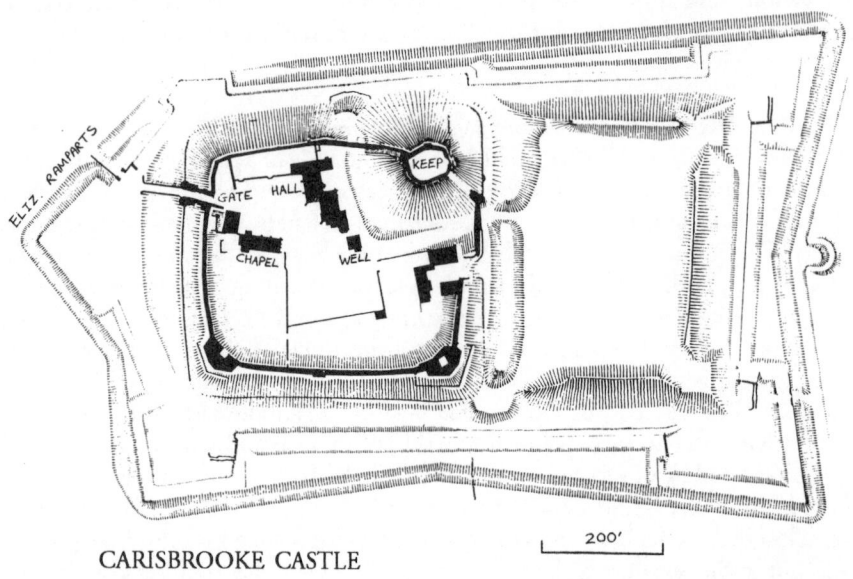

CARISBROOKE CASTLE

Free-standing within the western bailey are the castle's domestic buildings, which remained the residence of the governors of the Isle of Wight until modern times and now house a museum. Charles I's attempts to escape imprisonment in these buildings ended in fiasco (1648). He had arranged to squeeze through a window, then descend by rope to his supporters waiting outside, but when the time came the luckless King discovered that the spaces between the bars were too narrow! The buildings consist chiefly of a hall and solar, with the former St Peter's Chapel (now housing a staircase) in the angle between them. They date from the thirteenth and fourteenth centuries but have been altered beyond recognition since. There are also the ruins of some Elizabethan lodgings against the north curtain. The larger chapel of St Nicholas was rebuilt on its old foundations in 1905. A fascinating glimpse into the domestic life of the castle is provided by the Elizabethan well house, its donkey wheel still regularly trodden for the benefit of tourists.

Access: Standard opening times (EH).

Reference: Guidebook by R. Chamberlain. *HKW* (II & IV).

Relations: Christchurch and Plympton were other Redvers castles. Compare the Elizabethan ramparts at Pendennis and Berwick.

COWES CASTLE Cowes takes its name from the two 'cows' or blockhouses which guarded the estuary of the River Medina. They were built by Henry VIII in 1539–42. Nothing survives at East Cowes. The larger blockhouse at West Cowes is represented by a low, semi-circular bastion facing the sea. The squat round tower behind it has largely been rebuilt. It is incorporated into the present 'castle', built by Anthony Salvin in 1856 to serve as the headquarters of the Royal Yacht Squadron.

Access: Best seen from the river.
Relations: The Henrician fort at Yarmouth.

YARMOUTH CASTLE was begun after a big French raid in 1545. In conjunction with Hurst Castle it guarded the western entrance to the Solent. Completed by September 1547, it is the last of Henry VIII's coastal forts and very different in conception to earlier ones. Like Southsea Castle, Yarmouth is an angular fort – in fact a simple square. The north and west sides are washed by the sea. Southsea is curious for its triangular projections, but here the landward sides are flanked by a single bastion at the south-east corner. This bastion is England's first example of the 'arrow-head' plan which had only recently been devised in Italy. It forms a distinct point and there are gun ports in the 'collar' flanking the walls on either side. However, this bastion is still a masonry tower. Before long bastions would be stone-covered mounds of earth instead. Yarmouth is also unique among Henry's forts in having no central tower.

The fort has been subjected to considerable modification since 1547. Originally the thick curtain surrounded an open courtyard, but the northern half was filled with earth later in the century to form a large gun battery. Since there are domestic buildings against the south curtain the former courtyard has been reduced to a narrow alley. The buildings date from Elizabethan and Jacobean times, containing stores, garrison's quarters and the Master Gunner's House. The kitchen for this house is contained in the arrow-head bastion. Further alterations took place in the 1670s, including the insertion of a new entrance through the south range (the original gate in the east curtain has been opened up again). A garrison remained here until 1885.

Access: Standard opening times in summer (EH).
Reference: Guidebook by S. E. Rigold. *HKW* (IV).
Relations: Hurst and Southsea.

OTHER SITES *Sandown Castle*, one of Henry VIII's coastal defences, was a contemporary of Yarmouth, also possessing an early arrow-head bastion. It was swept away by the sea and a Victorian fort occupies the site.

Kent

Kent is perhaps the most rewarding English county for castles. The reason is partly geographical. Lying so close to the mainland of Europe, this is the corner of England most vulnerable to invasion. As a result coastal defence has been a constant theme along the shoreline. Dover Castle, the 'key of England', is appropriately one of our strongest castles, and the road to London was blocked by the fortified cities of Canterbury and Rochester. It is no coincidence that Dover and Rochester possess two of the finest Norman keeps, and Canterbury's was probably one of the earliest. The Hundred Years War saw the strengthening of old castles such as Rochester and Saltwood, and the erection of new ones like Cooling, Scotney and Westenhanger. Canterbury's city wall is also a rebuilding of this period. Towns on the Kent coast suffered badly during that war, though the damage was small in comparison with the English rape of France. This was due to the maritime supremacy of the Cinque Ports, a confederacy which supplied the ships to carry the English forces across the Channel. The threat of invasion following the Reformation led to a new and ambitious scheme of coastal defence under Henry VIII. Deal and Walmer, just a mile apart, are two of his best forts. Upnor Castle is a rare fort from Elizabeth I's reign.

It would be wrong, however, to attribute all Kent castles to the threat of invasion – a threat which was seldom felt much beyond the coastline. Many of them are too far inland. Tonbridge with its Edwardian gatehouse is the most important piece of military architecture here, though the fortified mansions at Allington, Leeds and Penshurst are perhaps more appealing now. The early Norman masonry of Eynsford Castle and St Leonard's Tower, and the octagonal keep at Chilham, should not be overlooked in the light of such treasures. It should be borne in mind that Kent was densely populated by medieval standards. The number of castles may also reflect the irrepressible spirit of the local peasantry, who led the way in the great revolt of 1381 and resorted to arms again in 1451. Finally it should be said that the county's castles have generally received good treatment in post-medieval centuries, several of them (Allington, Hever, Lympne, Saltwood) being restored in a fairly sensitive manner by antiquaries.

ALLINGTON CASTLE stands beside the River Medway about a mile north of Maidstone. This beautiful, moated castle seems perfect, but the perfection has been contrived in modern times. A Norman castle here was destroyed by Henry II after the revolt of 1173–74. The low mound immediately south-west of the present castle represents the motte and some herringbone masonry is visible in the curtain facing it. Other than that, the existing structure was built by Sir Stephen de Penchester, Constable of Dover Castle and Lord Warden of the Cinque Ports. He obtained a licence to crenellate in 1281 and the original survives. His castle is characteristic of the Edwardian age but is not uncompromisingly military like the contemporary castles of Wales. In design it reflects the quadrangular layout which was becoming popular, but the rear bows outwards in a gentle curve and the distribution of towers is quite irregular. Five D-shaped towers of different sizes project from the curtain, though one or two others existed originally. Solomon's Tower at the south corner is the largest and may be regarded as an early tower house. There is also a gatehouse flanked by simple half-round turrets (the machicolations above the gateway are modern). Some ruins of a barbican survive on the far side of the moat. The range on the south-west side of the courtyard, known as the Penchester Wing, may incorporate a slightly older manor house. However, once the castle was built the main apartments stood opposite, centred on a hall which still exists but is largely a reconstruction. Only its fifteenth century porch is authentic.

In 1492 Allington was granted to Sir Henry Wyatt in recognition of his loyalty to Henry VII. He upgraded the castle by building the narrow range which divides the courtyard into two unequal parts. Its upper floor forms a long gallery. The picturesque, half-timbered house within the smaller enclosure also dates from the Wyatt period. Henry's son was Sir Thomas Wyatt, the poet. The next Sir Thomas organised an abortive rebellion against Queen Mary in 1554. After his execution the castle degenerated into a farmhouse and fell seriously into decay. Sir Martin Conway bought the castle in 1905 and spent the next thirty years restoring it. Much reconstruction was necessary: all the battlements are his work and the hall was rebuilt on the old lines. Today only the rear curtain is still in ruins. Since 1951 the castle has been a retreat house for the Carmelite friars of nearby Aylesford. This is a case of tit-for-tat, since the Wyatts of Allington obtained the original Aylesford Friary at the Dissolution.

Access: Open regularly.
Reference: BOE *West Kent and the Weald.* Guy. Souvenir guide.
Relations: For the Wyatt rebellion see Cooling. Compare the restorations of Hever and Lympne.

CAESAR'S CAMP Tradition has attributed this site to Julius Caesar on one of his two expeditions into Britain. The superb position, on the crest of the North Downs overlooking Folkestone, is worthy of an Iron Age hillfort but the impressive earthworks actually belong to the Norman era. The castle comprises a ringwork and bailey, both surrounded by a strong rampart and ditch. It was probably a castle of the Anarchy but its history is obscure. Excavations have shown that it was occupied long enough for a deep well to be sunk into the chalk, but the defences were never rebuilt in stone.

Access: Freely accessible.

CANTERBURY CASTLE AND CITY WALL Considering the level of bombing sustained by the city in 1942 it is a miracle that so much of medieval Canterbury survives. Among its many attractions are the ruined castle keep and a large part of the city wall. Indeed, though incomplete the wall of Canterbury ranks among the foremost in England. The shape of the defences was determined in the third century AD when Canterbury was the Roman city of *Durovernum.* The Roman wall enclosed an oval area nearly two miles in circumference, and the medieval wall follows exactly the same line. However, very little Roman masonry survives because the wall was rebuilt from the 1370s when a French invasion seemed imminent.

More than half of the circuit is preserved, extending from the site of the North Gate to the castle at the south-west end of the old city. The only gaps in this sector are those left by the demolition of the gatehouses. Eleven bastions survive, notable for their early 'keyhole' gun ports. The four northernmost are square and date from *circa* 1400, but the others are the traditional U-shaped type with open backs. The best stretch of wall, its parapet still intact, can be seen along Broad Street. This sector, bordering the cathedral precinct, was rebuilt by Prior Sellinge in the 1480s. The blocked archway of the Quenin (Queen's) Gate, opposite the gatehouse of St Augustine's Abbey, is the only Roman feature still visible. According to tradition Queen Bertha – a Christian in a pagan land – used to go through this arch to worship in St Martin's Church in the days before St Augustine's mission arrived in 597.

Beyond St George's Street it is possible to mount the wall-walk, but this part of the city was worst affected by the bombing and some of the next stretch is a post-war reconstruction. The wall changes direction at the Dane John, a conical mound now capped by an obelisk. Originally a Roman tumulus, its name is interpreted as a corruption of 'donjon', implying that it served as a ready-made motte for a Norman castle. That may be so but the castle must have soon moved to its present site a little further west. The city wall peters out in the vicinity of its keep.

Canterbury Castle was probably founded soon after the Norman Conquest and certainly existed by the time of the Domesday Book. All that remains is the lower half of a large, oblong keep. Documentary evidence is lacking but there are some grounds for dating the keep to the late eleventh century. The stepped splays behind the narrow window openings suggest an early date. Certainly the £200 spent in the 1170s can only refer to repairs. It may thus be one of the keeps commissioned by William the Conqueror though it bears only a superficial resemblance to his larger keeps at Colchester and London. The plinth and pilaster buttresses are typical Norman features but much of the Caen stone facing has been robbed, leaving the rubble core exposed. The entrance was at first-floor level in the north-west wall – excavations have uncovered a forebuilding. As at Colchester the top floor of the keep was removed in 1817 and the cross-walls (which divided the interior into three main compartments) were taken down at the same time. This attempt to demolish the keep proved too costly. The castle lost its strategic importance at an early stage and the keep degenerated into a prison. Two sieges are recorded. It fell to the Dauphin Louis in 1216, and in 1381 Wat Tyler's peasants stormed the castle, releasing its prisoners and locking up the constable in their place. Nothing remains of the two walled baileys which lay against the city wall.

It is sometimes said that medieval Canterbury relied upon the River Stour for natural protection on its north-west side. However, part of a continuous wall, with two square bastions, can be see along Pound Lane. Another bastion (made habitable as Tower House) survives in isolation. Between them stands the imposing gatehouse which barred the road from London (Watling Street). The West Gate is the only survivor of seven gatehouses in the wall. Archbishop Simon of Sudbury built it in the years preceding his murder during the Peasants' Revolt. The design is attributed to the great master mason Henry Yevele, who went on to build the magnificent nave of the cathedral. The fortress-like outer facade of the gatehouse, with machicolations overhanging the entrance and sturdy drum towers pierced by gun ports, contrasts with a more domestic townward front. Note the portcullis groove in the vaulted gate passage. The West Gate has survived because it housed the county gaol after the castle keep had become too derelict.

Access: The city wall parapet is freely accessible while the West Gate houses a museum. The keep exterior is visible – to get inside apply at the Royal Museum (all LA).

Reference: Renn for the castle. Turner for the city wall.

Relations: Colchester and the Tower of London. Compare town walls such as Southampton, Oxford and Newcastle.

CHILHAM CASTLE stands in beautiful grounds landscaped by Capability Brown. They are entered from the picturesque, half-timbered village square. The castle bailey was demolished in Tudor times and its site is occupied by a brick Jacobean mansion, completed in 1616 by Sir Dudley Digges. Its hexagonal layout was perhaps influenced by the octagonal keep which stands close by. The keep is intact apart from the loss of its parapet. Royal accounts record the expenditure of £400 here in 1171–74 – just sufficient at that time for a keep of this modest size. So Chilham is one of Henry II's castles. The plan is almost unique for its date and octagonal towers did not become common until the thirteenth century. However, this was a period of experimentation away from square Norman keeps and Henry II had just erected another keep of polygonal design at Orford. As at Orford the keep is entered through a forebuilding. This is in two parts: a projecting stair turret and an annexe with much thinner walls. Excavations have shown the annexe to be built on the remains of an early Norman hall, and the blocked archway which is still visible belonged to it. The keep does not stand on a motte and extra security is provided by the low chemise wall enclosing an oblong area around it. Chilham did not remain a royal stronghold for long. King John granted it to his illegitimate son Richard and after that the castle changed hands frequently, later owners including the Earl of Atholl, Bartholomew de Badlesmere and the Roos family.

Access: Grounds open regularly in summer (but the keep interior is only accessible for functions).

Reference: Guidebook.

Relations: Orford. The octagonal towers at Dover, Odiham and the Tower of London.

COOLING CASTLE, a mile east of Cliffe, was built for Sir John de Cobham, a licence to crenellate being granted in 1381. Two years before French raiders had caused devastation on the Hoo peninsula, so Cooling was built at least partly with coastal defence in mind. This seems less credible now because the sea has receded leaving marshland in its wake. A copper plaque fixed to the outer gatehouse – one of the oldest inscriptions in the English language – tells us in verse that Sir John was 'mad in the help of the country' and that his castle is 'charter and witnessing' of the same. Henry Yevele was consulted over its construction though the outer gatehouse is the work of Thomas Crump, a local mason. Sir John did not remain in royal favour, being banished for his part in the baronial opposition to Richard II. He returned after Richard's deposition. Ironically, but not uncommonly where English coastal fortifications as concerned, the castle saw no action against foreign invaders but became embroiled in civil strife. In 1554 Sir Thomas Wyatt sought the aid of Lord Cobham in the rebellion which he was organising to prevent Queen Mary marrying Philip of Spain. When Lord Cobham wisely refused to get involved, Wyatt marched upon Cooling Castle and breached its walls by cannon fire in the space of a few hours. After that episode the castle was abandoned and allowed to sink into ruin.

The castle is one of those later medieval castles which is split into two enclosures, comprising a residential inner quadrangle and a much bigger 'base court' which housed the retainers' lodgings and ancillary buildings. Its low-lying site would have appeared stronger when the moat was full of water. The outer curtain and its rounded angle towers are now very ruinous but the outer gatehouse is well preserved. This is actually just a gateway flanked by open-backed, half-round towers. It is curious that the towers but not the gateway are crowned by machicolated parapets. The inner courtyard is reached through another gatehouse flanked by rounded turrets. 'Key-hole' gun ports appear here and elsewhere in the walls. To the right of the gatehouse the curtain is embellished with alternate panels of stone and flint, creating a chequered effect. The corner tower here has vanished but the round towers at the other three corners, along with much of the intervening curtain, still stand. These towers were machicolated as well. Within the courtyard the only domestic feature to survive is a vaulted undercroft which carried the solar.

Access: Private, but well seen from the road.

Reference: BOE *West Kent and the Weald.* Guy.

Relations: Hundred Years War castles such as Scotney, Westenhanger and Bodiam. John de Cobham's work at Hever.

DEAL CASTLE Henry VIII's impressive scheme of coastal defence – the first planned network since the 'Saxon Shore' forts of Roman times – was precipitated by the alliance between the Emperor Charles V and Francis I of France (1538). Henry had grown accustomed to playing off the one against the other, and perhaps it was inevitable that these great rivals should not remain friendly for long. All the same, with the Reformation barely complete in England and the Pope preaching a crusade against the 'infidel' Henry, there was a genuine threat of combined invasion from these two most Catholic monarchs. It may seem surprising that the most formidable concentration of Henrician fortifications was to be found around Deal. However, the sheltered stretch of water known as the Downs, lying between the east Kent coastline and the Goodwin Sands, offered a potential gathering place for an enemy fleet. Three forts (Deal, Walmer and Sandown) were built along a two-mile stretch of shore to hamper any attempt at landing. They were linked by an earth rampart with intermittent bastions, but that has perished. The whole scheme was finished by the autumn of 1540. At one point the labourers went on strike for an extra penny a day, but they were persuaded to return and the ringleaders suffered imprisonment for their audacity.

Deal Castle, the central fort of the trio, was the largest of all Henry VIII's forts. Here the characteristic geometrical layout of the series attains its most elaborate form. The result, whether by accident or design, is a sexfoil plan reminiscent of a Tudor rose. The Bohemian engineer Stefan von Haschenperg was probably the designer. At the centre is a squat round tower with six semi-circular bastions projecting from

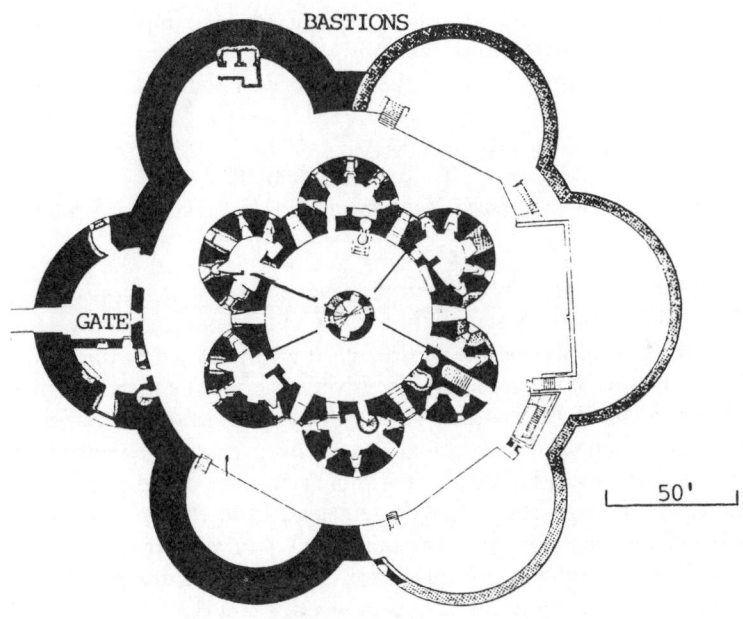

BASTIONS

GATE

50'

DEAL CASTLE

its circumference, and surrounding that is a massive curtain arranged into six projecting lobes. There is thus a return to the concentricity of Edwardian castles, a key feature being the graduated height of the parapets to permit cannon fire from three levels simultaneously. The stone-faced ditch is guarded by fifty-four gun ports set in the curtain, each one in a small chamber reached from a gallery at basement level. The gun ports are widely-splayed embrasures typical of the Henrician era. One of the outer lobes is higher than the rest and contains the entrance, formerly reached by a drawbridge across the ditch. Within the gate passage are all the traditional trappings of defence: Portcullis groove, studded oak gates and murder holes in the vault. To reach the central tower it is necessary to pass though the courtyard, in fact no more than a curving corridor between the central tower and the curtain. It would have been a death trap for attackers attempting to make their way to the the tower entrance while under fire from either side. The central tower had store rooms, garrison's lodgings and the governor's residence crammed into its three floors. Timber partitions radiate from a central stone shaft which contains a spiral stair. Originally the stair was a curious double one, both flights springing from the same post. Two corridors run from the basement to connect with the fighting gallery in the curtain. It is worth mentioning that while the castle is faced in stone throughout, the core is brick.

As a coastal fort Deal saw very little action. The Spanish Armada sailed close by but was already in complete disarray. Instead the castle saw its only real action in the Civil War. During the Royalist uprising of 1648 all three forts were seized by Charles I's supporters and were only retaken with difficulty. The castle was last manned in strength during the Napoleonic wars. Despite its strategic importance Deal is largely unspoilt by later developments. The puny eighteenth-century battlements are the only discordant feature. Originally the parapets were rounded off to deflect cannon balls.

Access: Standard opening times (EH).
Reference: Guidebook by A. D. Saunders. *HKW* (IV).
Relations: Walmer, vanished Sandown and the Henrician fort at Sandgate.

DOVER CASTLE   rises high above the town and harbour, crowning a mighty hill which terminates abruptly at the White Cliffs. This magnificent site was first fortified in the Iron Age and the medieval castle fills the area defined by the ancient hillfort. The castle is thus of extraordinary size (thirty-five acres) and exceptional strength. It had good reason to be. Matthew Paris, the thirteenth-century chronicler, described it as the 'key of England', and throughout its history it has presented a deterrent to all invaders contemplating the shortest route across the Channel. Largely a creation of the early Plantagenets, the castle remained little changed for centuries. The Napoleonic invasion scare forced an upgrading to cater for the powerful artillery of the day. This has resulted in the mutilation of the medieval defences, but the massive alterations are a fitting testimony to the castle's strategic importance. The outer curtain was reduced in height, along with many of the towers, and backed by an earth rampart to support and withstand artillery. Furthermore the mighty ditch in front of the curtain attained its present depth.

It has been suggested that Dover was one of the small group of castles founded under Norman influence before the Norman Conquest. Hence the future King Harold, making his famous oath during his detention in Normandy, promised to surrender the 'castle' of Dover to Duke William. However, medieval terminology is notoriously vague on such matters. It can only be said that, if Dover was not a castle in the strict sense before the Norman Conquest, it became one when William reached Dover during his invasion march. It is known that a Saxon burgh flourished within the ancient ramparts. The cruciform church of St Mary in Castro, still complete despite a heavy Victorian restoration, was built to serve this community about the year 1000. Beside it is a ruined Roman *pharos*, or lighthouse, which guided the vessels of the Roman fleet into the harbour. Church and lighthouse now stand inside the Horseshoe Earthwork, a massive rampart overlying William the Conqueror's original ringwork.

Sometime after the Norman Conquest, whether voluntarily or otherwise, the burgesses left their defended hill and migrated to the harbour below. Henry II was thus able to extend the area of the castle, constructing his mighty keep and inner curtain to the north-west of the original ringwork. The royal accounts known as the Pipe Rolls tell us that they were built in the years 1180–90 at the enormous cost for those days of £6300. The master mason is given as Maurice the Engineer, who had previously built the keep at Newcastle-upon-Tyne. The keep is one of the latest and greatest of the square Norman keeps. It is a mighty cube nearly a hundred feet long in each direction, with square corner turrets and the most elaborate of forebuildings. This forebuilding is an L-shaped structure appended to the main body of the keep,

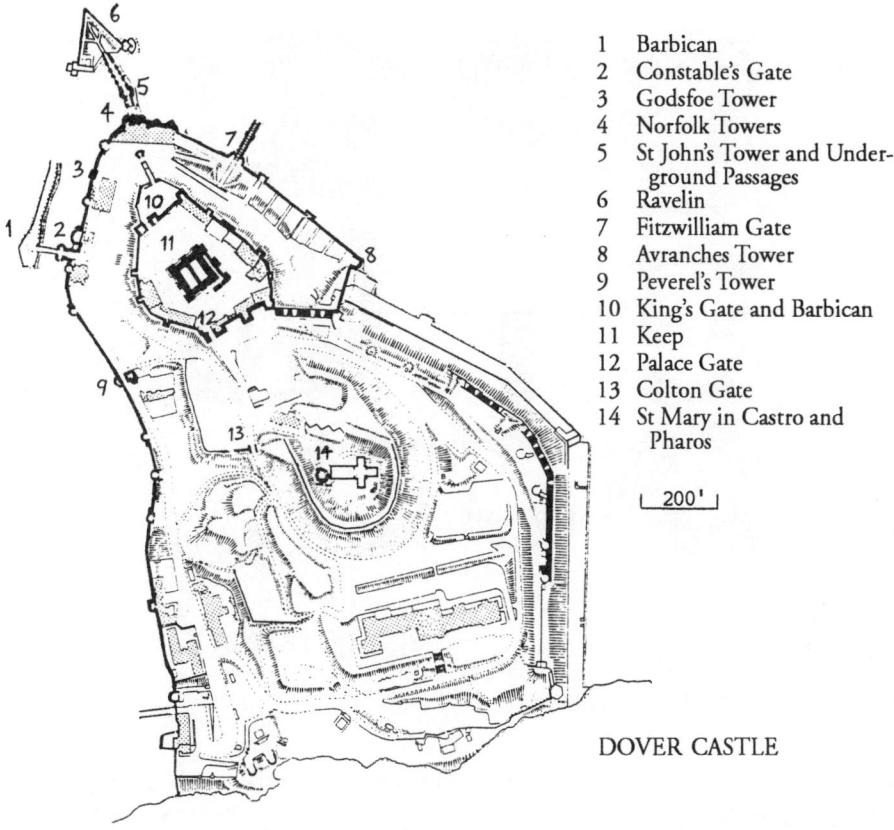

1	Barbican
2	Constable's Gate
3	Godsfoe Tower
4	Norfolk Towers
5	St John's Tower and Underground Passages
6	Ravelin
7	Fitzwilliam Gate
8	Avranches Tower
9	Peverel's Tower
10	King's Gate and Barbican
11	Keep
12	Palace Gate
13	Colton Gate
14	St Mary in Castro and Pharos

└ 200' ┘

DOVER CASTLE

with three projecting turrets of its own. The forebuilding was originally roofless so that assailants would be exposed to projectiles hurled from the parapet. Where the ascent changes direction is an ornate little Romanesque chapel occupying one of the forebuilding turrets.

The staircase leads to a grand entrance portal at second-floor level – one floor higher than usual and another parallel with Newcastle. No doubt this arrangement provided an extra degree of security, but it also means that the forebuilding took the form of a grand staircase communicating directly with the principal apartments, as this floor contained the royal hall and solar. As in other major Norman keeps, this level actually forms a double storey with a mural gallery running most of the way around the upper stage. The precise reason for such galleries is conjectural but, as it lay below the original roof line, its function seems to be residential rather than military. A number of private chambers are contrived within the great thickness of the walls off the hall and solar. One of them contains a well, the shaft of which sinks 350 feet into the underlying chalk. A passage leads to another chapel, even more delicate that the one immediately below it and showing signs of the transition to Gothic architecture. The floor beneath is similar in layout, including the mural chambers. It was probably intended as the constable's residence, while the ground floor was used for storage. Two broad spiral stairs connect all floors. While the keep

117

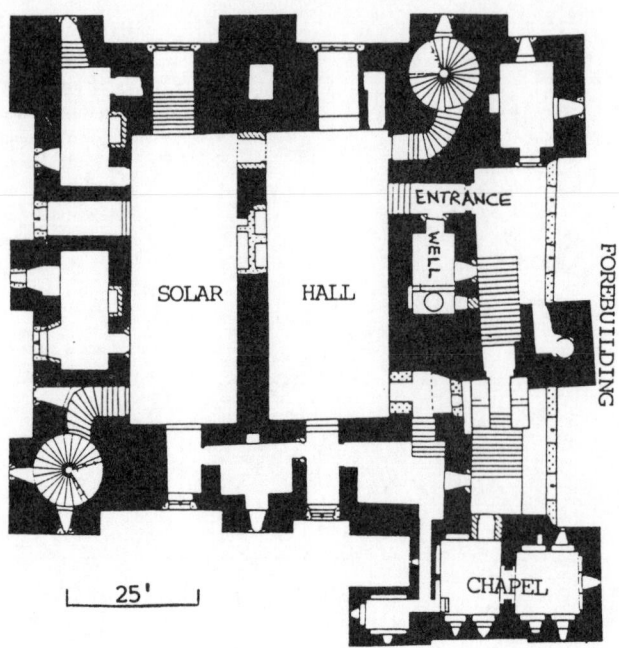

DOVER CASTLE: KEEP AT SECOND-FLOOR LEVEL

retains its Norman proportions, many of the doorways and windows date from a remodelling in Edward IV's reign while the brick vaults were inserted during the Napoleonic era to allow the mounting of guns on the roof.

As a tower keep large enough to contain the chief apartments on a single floor, Dover owes its conception to London's White Tower which is a century older. That keep has the same cross-wall, the same double storey, the same mural gallery. Dover shows progress in its forebuilding and its considerably thicker walls, partly for defence but also to make room for the mural chambers which allowed much more privacy. Nevertheless the keep at Dover is quite conventional when it is recalled that Henry II had experimented with new shapes of keep elsewhere. By contrast, the inner curtain which surrounds the keep is one of the earliest to be comprehensively defended by flanking towers. There are fourteen in all, each square-fronted and open-backed though they vary in size and depth. Two pairs of these towers are placed closely together to form twin-towered gatehouses – the earliest in England – known as King's Gate and Palace Gate. There are ruins of a barbican in front of the King's Gate. The inner curtain has lost its battlements and has suffered from refacing. Eighteenth-century barracks in the inner bailey incorporate a lot of walling from Henry III's residential buildings.

The outer curtain follows the crest of the Iron Age rampart. A portion of it also dates from Henry II's time, apparently 1168–74, i.e. before the keep and inner curtain were constructed. His work begins to the east of the inner bailey at the Avranches Tower, blocking the original entrance to the hillfort. Its octagonal plan and the two closely-spaced rows of arrow-slits are remarkable for their date. The next two towers are square and open-backed, like those of the inner curtain. After that there was a pause. Henry II erected his keep and inner curtain, while Richard I was too preoccupied with his foreign wars and Chateau Gaillard. King John resumed work in 1207 following the loss of Normandy. He continued the curtain around the northern tip of the hillfort as far as Peverel's Tower on the west. As the outer curtain runs parallel to the inner and at no great distance from it, Dover qualifies as the first concentric castle in Britain, though whether by accident or design is debatable. The closely-spaced bastions along this stretch (mostly named after constables of the castle) are mostly semi-circular in accordance with the latest military developments. However, they are still small flankers with a purely defensive role. Godsfoe Tower, the only square one, is a fifteenth-century rebuilding. At the northern apex of the site two bastions were set together to flank the main entrance.

A momentous siege took place in 1216, during the Dauphin Louis' campaign to win the English throne. His men drove a mine beneath King John's gatehouse, causing one of its flanking towers to collapse. The constable, Hubert de Burgh, filled the breach with timber and managed to hold out until John's death resolved the issue. Early in Henry III's reign elaborate measures were taken to make the northern approaches more secure. The undermined tower was rebuilt but John's gateway was blocked forever with a pointed bastion, thus creating the trio known as the Norfolk Towers. An earthwork was dug to the north of them to force an oblique approach, and two new gatehouses were constructed at less accessible points of the outer curtain. The Fitzwilliam Gate with its pointed flanking towers lies on the east wall close to the junction between Henry II's and King John's work. It is reached via a tunnel through the rampart on the far side of the ditch. On the west wall is the massive Constable's Gate which, as its name suggests, replaced the first floor of the keep as the constable's residence. This gatehouse has suffered many alterations but its outer front is largely as conceived. It has an unusually elongated plan, a cluster of four half-round towers of different sizes rising from square bases. One of them contains the gate passage and is fronted by an oval tower. The Constable's Gate could only be approached along the crest of the rampart beyond the ditch, and as a further protective measure a long barbican (of which only the lower walls survive) closed off this approach.

All this was not the end. As a further protection against attacks from the north a series of underground passages was dug to connect the castle with the earthwork beyond the north curtain. These passages still remain, though enlarged and extended during the Napoleonic period. They would have allowed a strong garrison to emerge behind enemy lines and surprise attackers from the rear. As a precaution against outsiders getting in by the same method, access to the main passage is controlled by the cylindrical St John's Tower which rises unexpectedly out of the castle ditch.

Henry III spent £7500 on the castle, i.e. more than Henry II but over a longer period. After strengthening the north side of the castle in the 1220s Henry III continued the outer curtain southwards, still with bastions, from Peverel's Tower to the cliff's edge. Peverel's Tower was enlarged into a gatehouse communicating between the northern and southern outer baileys. There was once a corresponding eastern curtain running to the cliff from the Avranches Tower. Henry's last work at

Dover was the Horseshoe Earthwork (see above), topped by a curtain now reduced to foundations. This created a fourth, intermediate bailey, reached from the large southern enclosure through the octagonal Colton Gate.

Dover Castle stood aloof from the French raids of the Hundred Years War. A great deal was spent on the town defences during that epoch but nothing is left to show for it.

Access: The precincts, keep and underground passages are open at standard times (EH).
Reference: Guidebook by R. Allen Brown. *HKW* (II).
Relations: The Tower of London and Newcastle. For earlier flanking towers see Framlingham and Windsor. Other castles occupying ancient hillforts are Old Sarum, Elmley and Almondbury.

EYNSFORD CASTLE is an early example of a Norman masonry stronghold, all the more remarkable because it was not the work of some great baron but of a relatively humble knight. The Domesday Book tells us that William de Eynsford held the manor as a tenant of the Archbishop of Canterbury. He raise a low mound beside the River Darent, and excavations have found the wooden tower which he built on top. Soon afterwards, almost certainly before 1100, William erected a flint curtain with a plain parapet around the foot of the mound, filling the space between them with earth. Hence, although Eynsford's 'motte' is low and irregular in shape, it may be compared with the stone-cased mottes at Berkeley and Farnham. The curtain remains in good condition for most of its length though one section has collapsed. Much of the flint is laid in herringbone fashion – a sign of early Norman work – and the grim austerity of the wall is relieved only by three featureless openings at the western apex, marking the site of latrines. A walled-up parapet shows that the curtain was raised to its present height in two stages, but there cannot have been long between them. In the twelfth century a gate tower (reduced to its foundations) was added to strengthen the entrance. About the same time a stone hall took the place of the original wooden tower. It is now very ruinous. In spite of the forebuilding which led to a first-floor entrance, the hall was purely residential and cannot be described as a keep. Indeed, the absence of a keep is quite unusual for the twelfth century. The Eynsford family died out in 1261 and the castle was later ransacked during a dispute over possession. It was abandoned thereafter though a Tudor house occupies the outer bailey.

Access: Freely accessible (EH).
Reference: Guidebook by S. E. Rigold.
Relations: Farnham and Berkeley.

GODARD'S CASTLE occupies a commanding site on a spur of the North Downs overlooking Thurnham village, four miles east of Maidstone. In Norman times it was successively the residence of the De Says and the De Thurnhams. The site is extremely overgrown but the large oval motte, with buried footings of a shell keep on top, is still impressive. There was a small bailey with a stone curtain, of which some foundations and rubble fragments remain. At the foot of the motte are the side walls of a long gate passage, once covered by stone vaulting but now crumbling badly and obscured by bracken.

Access: Accessible from a public footpath.

HEVER CASTLE, beside the River Eden two miles east of Edenbridge, is set within a wet moat between beautiful gardens and what appears to be a Tudor village. Gardens, 'village' and the splendid interior of the castle are all the creation of a rich American, William Waldorf Astor. He purchased the castle in 1903 and immediately set about its transformation, which thus went on at the same time as Lord Conway was restoring Allington Castle. To his credit, Viscount Astor did not interfere with the exterior, which remains largely authentic.

There is some doubt as to the original builder. William de Hever obtained a licence to crenellate in 1340 and Sir John de Cobham obtained another in 1384. The latter date is favoured though Sir John may just have added the gatehouse. The castle is a simple, square enclosure, its embattled curtain enlivened by Tudor windows, chimneys and gables. Square turrets project at each end of the entrance front and between them is the handsome, oblong gatehouse. This dominates the rest and is no doubt an echo of the old keep-gatehouse theme. The gateway, surmounted by carved tracery and a row of machicolations, is placed off-centre so that there is a large room on one side of the gate passage but just a tiny chamber on the other. Two original wooden portcullises (one still in working order) hang in the gate passage; the drawbridge is a restoration. Timber-framed ranges occupy three sides of the tiny courtyard, early Tudor in origin but heavily restored by Viscount Astor. They recall the castle's famous association with the Bullen family. Sir Geoffrey Bullen, an aspiring merchant and Lord Mayor of London, purchased Hever in 1462. It was here that Henry VIII came to court Anne Bullen, who changed her name to Boleyn. Her life as queen was cut short by the executioner's sword (1536) and her dynasty-making father Sir Thomas died soon after. His elaborate brass can be seen in the parish church. The castle reverting to the Crown upon his death, Henry conferred it on another discarded wife – Anne of Cleves.

Access: Open regularly except in winter.
Reference: Guidebook by G. Astor. Guy.
Relations: Allington. For Sir John de Cobham see Cooling.

LEEDS CASTLE rises serenely from the waters of its surrounding lake. The lake is an artificial one created by damming the River Len. Leeds was held in Norman times by the De Crevecoeurs. The castle existed by 1139 because in that year King Stephen wrested it from Matilda's supporters. In 1278 William de Leybourne made a gift of Leeds to Edward I, who rebuilt the castle in its present form. Edward granted the castle in turn to his two wives, Eleanor and Margaret, and this began a tradition whereby it was often held by the queens of England. The castle proved less than hospitable to Edward II's Queen Isabella. In 1321 the constable, Bartholomew de Badlesmere, refused to let her in, and the King assembled a large besieging force to bring the castle back under royal control. Lord Badlesmere paid for his impudence with his head. Henry VIII augmented the palace buildings but after his death the castle ceased to be a royal possession. It has been occupied by various families since.

The two islands on which the castle stands suggest a motte-and-bailey origin, and the lake itself existed by 1272. In terms of masonry, however, the castle is essentially the work of Edward I, with additions by Henry VIII and much nineteenth-century beautification. Around the entrance the lake decreases to a narrow moat. On the near side of the moat are the ruins of a peculiar barbican which had three gateways because three roads converged here. The gatehouse is a squat tower, Edwardian in date but not at all in spirit. It has a recess for the drawbridge and a later row of machicolations above the entrance. Except for one of the four D-shaped flanking bastions the curtain was reduced to a low retaining wall in the nineteenth century, to allow an unimpeded view across the lake. Foundations of an earlier curtain enclosing a slightly narrower area have come to light, so Leeds may have been a concentric castle though there is no proof that the two walls stood simultaneously. There are two separate residential blocks within the bailey: Maiden's Tower, one of Henry VIII's additions, and the neo-Gothic mansion built by Fiennes Wykeham-Martin in the 1820s. It occupies the site of lavish medieval apartments.

From the back of the mansion a stone corridor (replacing a wooden causeway and drawbridge) leads to the keep on the smaller island. It is known as the Gloriette. This peculiar, D-shaped structure is built around a tiny courtyard in shell keep manner. Its lower part, including the tall plinth which rises straight out of the water, is Edward I's work though a keep located passively at the rear seems strangely out of character for his time. The upper floor is a rebuilding of Henry VIII. Although some original woodwork remains the interior of the Gloriette has been transformed by later alterations.

Access: Open regularly in summer.
Reference: Guidebook by L. Geoffrey-Lloyd & P. Wilson. *HKW* (II).
Relations: Edward I's work at the Tower of London and St Briavels. Kenilworth Castle had a much bigger lake.

LEYBOURNE CASTLE stands on a low hill a mile north of West Malling. Today it consists of a ruined gatehouse and part of a round angle tower, linked by a house built as recently as 1930. Though sadly truncated the gatehouse is a good piece of Edwardian military architecture, comprising a long gate passage flanked by half-round towers. It is well provided with arrow-slits and preserves two unusual features. Firstly the portcullis groove is situated not within the passage but just in front of the outer gateway, thus keeping the chamber over the entrance free from the clutter of winding gear. Secondly there is a narrow slot just above the gateway. It has been suggested that, in the event of a siege, water could have been poured through it to extinguish burning faggots placed against the gates. Something similar can be seen in one of the gatehouses at Caerphilly Castle, the great Welsh stronghold of Gilbert de Clare. Leybourne was no doubt inspired by De Clare's mighty gatehouse not far away at Tonbridge. It is likely that the builder was Sir William de Leybourne, commander of the fleet. It must have been newly built when Edward I visited in 1286. Another relic of the medieval castle is a building which stands opposite the present house. It may have been the hall but no features survive to confirm this.

Edward III granted the castle to St Mary Graces Abbey, his new foundation in London, and it stayed in religious hands until the Dissolution.

Access: Private.

Reference: Guy.

Relations: Tonbridge and Welsh Caerphilly. Barnwell Castle also passed into monastic hands.

LYMPNE CASTLE occupies the edge of an escarpment overlooking Romney Marsh. The Norman parish church, which is as big as the castle, stands alongside. Down below are the broken walls of Stutfall Castle, one of the 'Saxon Shore' forts, showing that the sea came this far in Roman times (it has now receded two miles). There is a tradition that the square tower forming one end of the present castle originated as a Roman signal tower. No proof is forthcoming but its date is a matter for conjecture (perhaps thirteenth century). It formed a squat tower house keeping watch on the coast. Around 1360 a spacious hall block was added, the older tower being converted to contain the kitchen and domestic offices. The hall is a lofty chamber, somewhat restored though the crown-post roof is authentic. Beyond it, the first-floor solar also preserves its original roof. Later, perhaps as a result of renewed invasion fears in the 1430s, a tall U-shaped tower was added beyond the solar. The castle is thus a hall-house standing between defensive towers, like some fortified houses in the North. The large windows of the hall invited assault but the escarpment and a terrace wall rendered attack difficult from the south, while some sort of courtyard may have existed on the north. From the Norman Conquest until 1860 Lympne belonged to the archdeacons of Canterbury, and its proximity to the archbishops' castle at Saltwood is significant. Sir Robert Lorimer was commissioned to restore the castle from decay from 1905.

Access: Open regularly in summer.

Reference: Guidebook.

Relations: Saltwood. Nappa Hall is the best Northern example of a twin-towered hall.

PENSHURST PLACE At the heart of this great mansion is one of England's finest medieval manor houses. It was built by Sir John de Pulteney, four times Lord Mayor of London, after he purchased the manor about 1338. His house conforms to the usual domestic layout of the later Middle Ages, the hall being flanked on one side by service rooms and on the other by the solar block. Porches from both north and south lead into the screens passage of the hall. This magnificent chamber is virtually untouched by time and its chestnut roof is one of the glories of medieval carpentry. Its main beams are supported on carved figures, other authentic features being the tiled floor, the step up to the dais and the central hearth (the 'louvre' in the roof has been cunningly eliminated). The carved Tudor screen conceals three doors leading to the buttery, the kitchen corridor and the pantry (the kitchen itself has perished). The large solar, now equipped as a dining room, lies over a vaulted undercroft of unusual grandeur. At right angles to the solar is the so-called Buckingham Wing, added to augment the accommodation by John, Duke of Bedford. He bought Penshurst in 1430, while Regent of England on behalf of his young nephew, Henry VI.

It is not immediately apparent that Penshurst developed into a fortified mansion. Sir John de Pulteney obtained a licence to crenellate in 1341 but the battlements around his house are purely symbolic. Sir John Devereux obtained another licence in 1392, but he died the following year and it may have been the Duke of Bedford who enclosed the manor house within a great square of walls and towers. There were towers at each corner and probably in the middle of each side. The house stood well inside the enclosure so comfort did not have to be compromised. Eighteenth-century demolition has robbed Penshurst of its surrounding curtain, deliberately restoring a purely domestic ambience. Only four of the oblong towers survive. The western corner towers form part of the present mansion, linked to the older core by long wings of Elizabethan origin. The other two are gate towers, Garden Tower barring the entrance from the south and King's Tower in a corresponding position on the north. The latter was remodelled in the 1570s, when Sir Henry Sidney created a new residential quadrangle to the north of the hall.

Access: Open regularly in summer.
Reference: BOE *West Kent and the Weald.* Souvenir guide.
Relations: Fortified manor houses with halls across the courtyard such as Compton and Haddon.

ROCHESTER CASTLE, CITY WALL AND GUNDULF'S TOWER

Castle and cathedral stand close together beside the River Medway. For once it is the castle which dominates, the squat cathedral tower seeming insignificant alongside the magnificent keep. This is the tallest of the Norman keeps, rising 115 feet to the top of its corner turrets. Rochester originated as the Roman town of *Durobrivae*, positioned where Watling Street crossed the Medway. Soon after the Norman Conquest a castle was founded here on Boley (i.e. Bailey) Hill, just to the south of the present site. It was probably this castle which existed when Rochester was held against William II in 1088, during the revolt of Bishop Odo of Bayeux. The King assembled an army of native Englishmen to subdue his Norman rebels, and when the city fell Odo went into exile. After the siege Gundulf, Bishop of Rochester, undertook to rebuild the castle in stone at his own expense, in return for the King's confirmation of the cathedral's right to a certain manor. Gundulf was noted for his skill as a builder, an unusual qualification for a bishop. He resited the castle in a more secure position at a corner of the Roman city defences. Part of the curtain dates from Gundulf's time but the great keep is the work of another prelate. In 1127 Henry I placed the castle under the guardianship of William de Corbeil, Archbishop of Canterbury, and it was he who built the keep in the decade which followed.

The archbishops of Canterbury acted as constables until 1215, when Stephen Langton handed the castle over to the Magna Carta rebels. There followed one of the most gripping of medieval sieges, King John assembling a large force to regain this key stronghold. Having failed to breach the walls by a prolonged catapult bombardment, John's sappers drove a mine beneath the south angle of the curtain and caused it to collapse. The garrison fell back into the keep, but the mine was extended and the adjacent corner of the keep came crashing down. Even this did not compel the defenders to surrender. They retreated behind the cross-wall and continued to hold out, but lack of provisions forced them to surrender on terms.

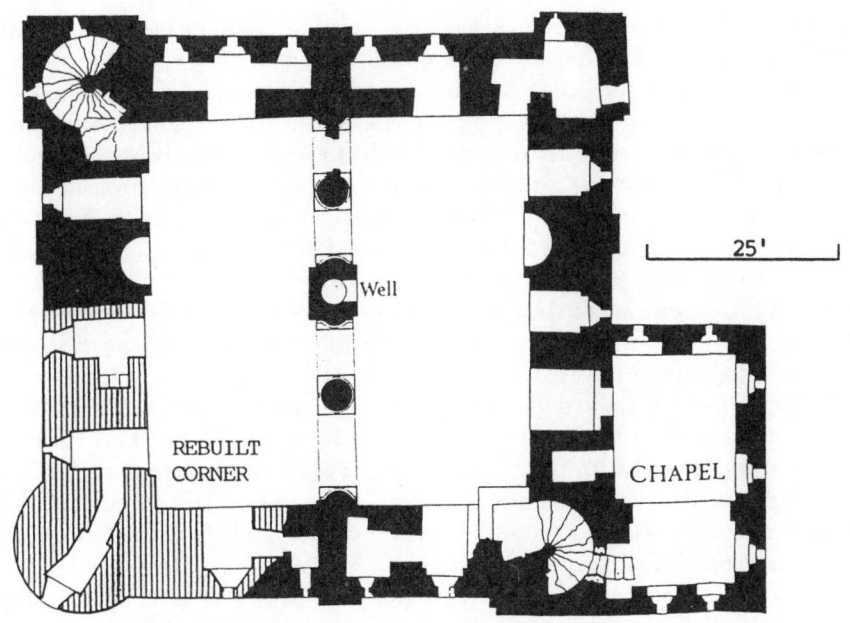

ROCHESTER CASTLE: KEEP AT SECOND-FLOOR LEVEL

Henry III repaired the damaged stronghold in the 1220s but Rochester Castle endured another battering in 1264, this time at the hands of Simon de Montfort. The curtain was breached once again but the keep was saved by the arrival of a royal relieving force. The damage sustained on this occasion was left unchecked until the later years of Edward III, who refortified the castle in response to the growing threat of French raids.

Archbishop Corbeil's keep is intact save for the loss of its roof and floors. The height is accentuated by its relatively small floor area, small that is when compared with an immense cuboid keep such as Dover. The keep is five stages high, including the 'double' storey which contained the hall and solar. Originally the only entrance was at first-floor level via a forebuilding. The forebuilding is a tall and narrow projection, higher than most forebuildings though it does not rise the full height of the keep. It contains a vaulted prison chamber beneath the entrance vestibule and an austere chapel – which was reached from the body of the keep – above it. At this level the cross-wall is pierced by a four-bay arcade. In the middle of the cross-wall a well shaft rises the full height of the keep so that water could be drawn at each level. Rochester is one of those ambitious keeps with a mural gallery at the upper level around the hall and solar. The windows here are unusually large for a Norman keep – presumably at this height they were considered to be out of the reach of siege towers. The top floor above gallery level, also well lit, is a luxury matched among Norman keeps only at Hedingham Castle, which may have been designed by the same architect. Three of the corner turrets, rising well above parapet level, are square but the south corner turret is circular. This whole corner belongs to Henry III's reconstruction after the siege of 1215. The junction between the Norman masonry and Henry III's more perfunctory work is clear enough.

Large portions of the bailey curtain also survive. Towards the river, where the curtain follows the line of the Roman city wall, can be seen some herringbone masonry characteristic of Gundulf's time. Evidently in the period between Gundulf and Corbeil the castle was a keep-less enclosure. At the south corner, overshadowed by the keep which stands just within the curtain, a round tower marks Henry III's patching after the siege of 1215. Facing the cathedral the curtain is all Edward III's work of 1367–70. It preserves two square flanking towers but the gatehouse has perished. The present entrance at the north corner of the bailey is through a neo-Norman gateway of 1872, piercing a bastion built to command the once-fortified bridge across the Medway.

Bishop Gundulf was also responsible for Gundulf's Tower, originally free-standing but now attached to the north transept of Rochester Cathedral. There is some disagreement as to whether this buttressed square tower was erected as a small keep – perhaps a refuge for the cathedral monks – or as a bell tower. Regardless of its origins, the tower was later capped by a machicolated parapet, though this disappeared in the eighteenth century when the top floor was taken down.

Medieval Rochester occupied the same ground as its Roman predecessor, except on the south-west where the cathedral precinct was enlarged. Part of the castle curtain doubled up as the city wall. Otherwise the remains of the city wall belong to the south-east part of the circuit, rebuilt on the Roman line in the 1340s after the outbreak of the Hundred Years War. The mighty East Gate which once straddled the High Street has long vanished, but demolition has exposed lengths of wall to either side, culminating in a circular tower from the east corner of the circuit.

Access: The castle is open at standard times (EH). Gundulf's Tower and the city wall (LA) are visible from outside.

Reference: Castle guidebook by R. Allen Brown. *HKW* (II).

Relations: The keeps at Dover and Hedingham. Compare the undermining of Bungay.

ST LEONARD'S TOWER   Rising from a rocky platform at the south end of West Malling stands a tall and unspoilt Norman tower, now an empty shell but virtually intact. Its walls are enlivened by pilaster buttresses, a row of blank arches and tall window openings on the top floor. The tower is attributed to Gundulf, Bishop of Rochester and architect (d.1102), but there is some debate over its function. A chapel and cemetery existed here later in the Middle Ages so it has been argued that this tower was always a bell tower. However, it seems rather a grand accompaniment for a small chapel and it is doubtful if Gundulf intended any more important religious foundation here, so close to his abbey at West Malling. Although the entrance has always been at ground floor level and there is no trace of a bailey, this tower resembles the smaller Norman keeps in other respects. Similar uncertainty surrounds Gundulf's other keep-like tower adjoining Rochester Cathedral.

Access: Freely accessible (EH).

Reference: Guy.

Relations: Gundulf's work at Rochester and the Tower of London.

SALTWOOD CASTLE, part ruined and part restored, occupies a hill above the old Cinque Port of Hythe. From 1026 the manor belonged to the archbishops of Canterbury but in Norman times Saltwood was held by sub-tenants. Henry de Essex, Constable of England and Lord Warden of the Cinque Ports, is credited with the building of the castle (at least in its stone form) during the Anarchy. His illustrious career ended in disgrace and dispossession in 1163. By then advanced in years, he was accused of fleeing during a skirmish with the Welsh and letting the royal standard fall into their hands. The castle should have reverted to the archbishop but, mindful of his growing rift with Thomas Becket, Henry II granted it instead to Becket's enemy, Ranulf de Broc. According to tradition, it was at Saltwood that Becket's four murderers made their plans, setting off from here to carry out the infamous deed in Canterbury Cathedral (1170). One of Henry II's acts of atonement was the restoration of Saltwood to the custody of the archbishops, who henceforth retained it as a retreat. Archbishop William Courtenay favoured the castle as a residence and undertook a thorough remodelling from 1382. The defensive nature of his work suggests that he was affected by the prevailing fear of a French invasion. Many Lollards were imprisoned here in the later Middle Ages. At the Reformation Thomas Cranmer ended the archbishops' link with Saltwood by handing it over to Henry VIII.

The inner bailey occupies an oval ringwork surrounded by a curtain wall of Norman masonry. The two square towers which project from the south curtain were added by Archbishop Courtenay, but three odd Norman towers also remain. They project *internally* like the interval towers of Roman forts, which seems to confirm a date around the mid twelfth century when there was room for experimentation in such matters. The eastern tower was later adapted to form the inner part of Archbishop Courtenay's handsome gatehouse (the entrance from the bailey is now blocked). This gatehouse, probably designed by the celebrated master mason Henry Yevele, has tall, cylindrical towers at the outer corners and a row of machicolations between them. It is big enough for a keep-gatehouse and it remains the inhabited part of Saltwood Castle, supplemented by more recent wings on either side. Within the bailey there are, unusually, two halls. The ruined hall backing onto the curtain dates from the early fourteenth century as its window tracery reveals. The other is said to have been Archbishop Courtenay's audience chamber. It is largely a modern reconstruction though the vaulted undercroft is original. Courtenay is also credited with the walling of the triangular outer bailey, though the so-called Roman Tower incorporates older masonry. The outer curtain is now very ruinous but it preserves two round flanking towers and the lower part of a gate tower. The approach to the latter is commanded by one of the towers of the inner curtain.

Access: Open by appointment only.
Reference: Guidebook by A. Clark. BOE *North-East and East Kent.*
Relations: Henry Yevele's work at Canterbury (West Gate), Cooling and the Palace of Westminster. See the archbishops' palace at Lambeth.

SANDGATE CASTLE Beside the beach two miles west of Folkestone is one of Henry VIII's coastal forts. The building accounts, which survive in full, tell us that it was built between March 1539 and October 1540 at a cost exceeding £5500. They also reveal that the designer was Stefan von Haschenperg. Little is known about this

Bohemian engineer, who was dismissed from the royal service in 1543 for extravagance and 'lewd behaviour'. It is generally accepted that he designed Henry's chain of fortifications along the South Coast, but only for Sandgate is there any documentary proof. The castle was one of the most intricate Henrician forts, following a triangular plan with two concentric curtains surrounding a cylindrical tower. There were smaller round towers at the angles of the inner curtain, the outer curtain forming lobes around them. The castle is badly mutilated now owing to modifications undertaken in 1806 during the Napoleonic wars. The inner curtain, its towers and the seaward lobe of the outer curtain were pulled down in order to give the central tower an uninterrupted view seawards. It thus came to serve as a ready-made Martello tower. So today only the central tower and the two landward lobes of the outer curtain survive. A novel feature is the D-shaped entrance tower which stands in advance of the outer curtain, the two being linked by a walled passage. The entrance doorway is contrived at the back – an inaccessible position which would have rendered it difficult to batter or burn down.

Access: Exterior only.
Reference: HKW (IV).
Relations: The Henrician forts at Deal and Walmer. Von Haschenperg also designed Carlisle Citadel.

SANDWICH TOWN DEFENCES Sandwich was one of the Cinque Ports but its prosperity depended on its position by a haven open to the sea. A series of storms in the late thirteenth century began the silting up of this haven and ushered in the town's decline. During the Hundred Years War Sandwich was still important enough to be a target for French raids, and the invasion scare of the 1380s led to the construction of a defensive circuit. Since attack was most likely to come from the sea, a stone wall (now destroyed) was constructed facing the River Stour. The two surviving gatehouses are to be found here. Fishergate, leading to the quay, is a simple gate tower with a gabled Elizabethan top. The other gate, known misleadingly as the Barbican, stands nearby. It comprises the lower part of two round flanking towers, built in chequers of flint and stone, and now linked by a modern superstructure. Away from the river Sandwich only had an earth rampart for its protection, but this survives and provides a splendid raised promenade around the town. There are also references to a castle but even its site is unknown. Sandwich was sacked by the French in 1438. The end of the Hundred Years War did not prevent them coming again in 1457 under Marshal Pierre de Breze. The narrow streets of the old town became the scene of furious fighting, but the inhabitants held out long enough for reinforcements from the other Cinque Ports to arrive, and this forced the French to withdraw.

Access: The defences are freely accessible (LA).
Reference: Turner.
Relations: The defended Cinque Ports of Rye and Winchelsea.

SCOTNEY OLD CASTLE, just south of Lamberhurst, occupies a wooded valley overlooked by the 'new' castle which is a Salvin mansion. The view from the one to the other, made glorious by the surrounding gardens, was created by quarrying away some of the hillside for stone. Scotney is thus a classic example of a monument preserved and 'perfected' as a landscape feature on a country estate. The Old Castle, surrounded by a broad, wet moat, consists today of a single, round tower (the Ashburnham Tower), linked by a brick Elizabethan house to a ruined wing. Though not very tall, the tower gains effect from its heavy machicolated crown and later conical roof. Originally it was one of four angle towers belonging to an irregular quadrangle. The emplacements of the other three towers can still be seen, but the curtain is now no more that a revetment to the moat and the gatehouse has been reduced to the stumps of its pointed flanking turrets. Though remodelled by William Darell in the 1630s, the ruined wing embodies the medieval hall range which lay across the courtyard, free of the outer walls. The moat also encloses an outer courtyard which was never walled in stone. Scotney is the work of Roger de Ashburnham, Conservator of the Peace in Kent and Sussex. Though miles from the sea, the castle was probably built in anticipation of a French invasion. The favoured date is 1378, following a severe coastal raid the previous year.

Access: Open regularly in summer (NT).
Reference: NT guidebook.
Relations: Contemporary Hundred Years War castles at Cooling, Westenhanger and Bodiam.

STARKEY CASTLE, three miles south-west of Rochester, is a castle in name only. At least there is no evidence of any fortification. It is a fourteenth-century hall with a latrine block attached at one corner. Various alterations have been made in more recent times and the hall is now subdivided. The house takes its name from Sir Humphrey Starkey, Recorder of London. He enlarged it in the 1470s but none of his additions have survived.

Access: Visible from the road.

STONE CASTLE, south of the village, is a Victorian house incorporating a much older square tower of flint. Apart from a couple of arrow-slits the tower preserves no original features and its date is a mystery. It may be a small Norman keep, but it is more likely to be a tower house of the Northwood family who lived here in the fourteenth century. A later occupant was Sir John Wiltshire, Comptroller of Calais (d.1526), whose monument can be seen in the marvellous parish church of Stone.

Access: Private.

SUTTON VALENCE CASTLE A small square keep stands on the edge of an escarpment overlooking the Weald. It was built about the middle of the twelfth century by William le Gros, Count of Aumale, or his successor, Baldwin de Bethune. The keep is now very ruinous, only one wall standing to any significant height. This wall preserves the remains of a passage at first floor level. The angles of the keep are clasped by pilaster buttresses in typical Norman fashion and excavations have uncovered a forebuilding. There was once a stone curtain around the bailey but no traces survive. The castle was later held by the Valence earls of Pembroke, hence the name of the village, but it has been in ruins at least since the fifteenth century.

Access: Freely accessible (EH).
Reference: Guy.
Relations: Castle Bytham and Scarborough are other foundations of William le Gros.

TONBRIDGE CASTLE Guarding a crossing over the River Medway, the important castle of Tonbridge was founded by Richard Fitz Gilbert. It existed by 1088, when William Rufus stormed the castle with the help of a native English army raised to quell the rebellion of Bishop Odo of Bayeux. Despite his involvement in this revolt, Fitz Gilbert retained possession. His descendants adopted the name of De Clare from their estates in Suffolk, acquired the earldoms of Hertford and Gloucester and played a major part in the Anglo-Norman invasions of Wales and Ireland. The castle was captured by royal forces again in 1215, when Gilbert de Clare was prominent among the Magna Carta barons. His grandson, another Gilbert, was the most formidable of this powerful line. The 'Red Earl' championed the interests of the barons in their clashes with Edward I, and at Caerphilly he erected a fortress which even that castle-building monarch could not outdo. It was this Gilbert who erected the mighty gatehouse at Tonbridge Castle. The De Clare line came to an end with his son, who fell at Bannockburn. Tonbridge passed to the Stafford family, later dukes of Buckingham, but the castle fell into decay. In spite of this, it withstood a brief siege from the Royalists in 1643.

The castle is an impressive example of a Norman motte-and-bailey – a layout curiously rare in Kent. On top of the great motte are the lower courses of a round shell keep. The bailey curtain dates from thirteenth century, probably from the time of the earlier Gilbert de Clare mentioned above or his son Richard. Owing to later stone-robbing it is now very ruinous and none of the flanking towers survive. The curtain is best preserved where it overlooks the river, four latrine chutes showing that residential buildings once stood here. The Red Earl's gatehouse, by contrast, is still an imposing structure. Newly built in 1275, when Edward I visited the castle, the gatehouse is an outstanding example of Edwardian military architecture, as one might expect from the builder of Caerphilly Castle. Massive U-fronted towers (rising from square bases) flank the long entrance passage, which was protected by two portcullises, two pairs of gates and three rows of murder holes in the vault. Circular stair turrets clasp the rear corners. The building is a classic example of a keep-gatehouse which could be defended independently if the rest of the castle fell. Hence the inner gates barred access from the bailey and even the doors leading to the curtain wall-walks were sealed off by portcullises. A hall occupied the whole of the second floor of the gatehouse. This awkward arrangement was necessary, since the chamber immediately over the gate passage would be clogged with drawbridge and portcullis winding gear. An eighteenth-century house stands beside the gatehouse.

Portions of a defensive bank and ditch around the town can still be seen, chiefly behind the Cattle Market and between East Street and the river. A town wall was licensed in 1259.

Access: Open regularly (LA).

Reference: Tonbridge Castle by J Hilton. Guy.

Relations: Caerphilly (Wales) and the ancestral castle at Clare. Compare the Edwardian gatehouses at St Briavels and Dunstanburgh.

UPNOR CASTLE belongs to the genre of Henrician coastal forts but is an Elizabethan addition to the chain. It was begun in 1559 to guard the approach to the new dockyard at Chatham, lying two miles away near the estuary of the River Medway. Sir Richard Lee interrupted his work on the fortifications at Berwick-on-Tweed to come and design this fort, but construction dragged on for eight years. In 1599–1601 Upnor was enlarged but it had to wait until 1667 to face enemy action. In that year the Dutch under Admiral de Ruyter sailed into the Medway and set fire to much of the English fleet. The castle was unable to offer any effective resistance and in the following year a new chain of defences was begun, Upnor being relegated to the role of storehouse and magazine. Military occupation of one kind or another continued until the Second World War.

As originally conceived the castle comprised an oblong blockhouse, set in the middle of a curious screen wall terminating at each end in a stair turret. This building provided accommodation for the garrison, defence being concentrated upon the low, pointed bastion facing the Medway. Pointed bastions were devised as a defence against artillery in Renaissance Italy. Sir Richard Lee built several along his new ramparts at Berwick, but the Upnor bastion does not have the characteristic 'arrow-head' plan resulting from a narrow collar. Its riverside setting made that unnecessary. However, since only one side of the bastion faces upriver, there were insufficient gun emplacements to fire effectively on an approaching fleet – this was the problem in 1667. The late Elizabethan enlargement provided defences on the landward side. A walled courtyard was created in front of the blockhouse, with towers where the new curtain joins the screen wall. The courtyard is entered through a gate tower retaining the traditional obstacle of a drawbridge. This archaic curtain may have kept out unauthorised personnel but it cannot have had any serious defensive role. Today the exterior of the castle is surprisingly unspoilt but the interior bears the scars of its varied uses.

Access: Standard opening times in summer (EH).

Reference: EH guidebook. *HKW* (IV).

Relations: Berwick. Other Elizabethan defences at Carisbrooke and Pendennis.

WALMER CASTLE is the most southerly of the three Henrician coastal forts which protected the Downs, that sheltered strait lying between the coast and the Goodwin Sands. It stands a mile from Deal Castle, to which it was originally connected by earthworks, and was built at the same time (1539–40). Though resembling Deal in principle it is simpler in design, consisting of a squat cylindrical tower closely surrounded by a lower curtain, the latter projecting outwards in four big semi-circular lobes to form a quatrefoil plan. It was a plan shared by Sandown Castle, the northern member of the group and now almost totally destroyed. Fortunately, Walmer Castle stands in its entirety but, in contrast to Deal and most of the other Henrician forts, its austerity has been mellowed by conversion into a stately home. In 1708 the militarily-redundant castle became the official residence of the Lord Warden of the Cinque Ports, a medieval office which has survived to the present day as an honourable sinecure. The transformation to a mansion is all the more remarkable given that the low, curved, immensely thick walls cannot have lent themselves easily to such a purpose. Fine gardens now surround the castle and encroach upon its deep, stone-faced ditch, while many of the gun embrasures have been converted into windows.

When first built Walmer exhibited the usual Henrician defensive arrangements. Cannon would have been mounted on the parapets of the central tower and outer curtain, a third tier of fire being provided at the level of the ditch by gun ports in the curtain. These gun ports are linked, as at Deal, by a continuous fighting gallery in the thickness of the wall. The central tower provided the main accommodation for governor and garrison. During the eighteenth-century alterations some of the circumference of the central tower was removed to provide access to a new wing of state apartments, blocking the narrow courtyard between this tower and the curtain. The lobe containing the entrance (another similarity with Deal) was heightened in the 1860s to provide further accommodation. Its battlements are pure sham and quite unlike the originals, which would have been rounded off to deflect cannon balls. There are further apartments in the south lobe, including the room in which the Duke of Wellington died in 1852. As Lord Warden Wellington lived at Walmer for much of his later life and the room has been preserved as he left it.

Access: Open regularly (EH).
Reference: Guidebook by J. C. Coad & G. E. Hughes. *HKW* (IV).
Relations: Deal and the destroyed fort at Sandown.

WESTENHANGER CASTLE, close to the castles of Saltwood and Lympne, stands between Folkestone Racecourse and a railway line. John de Criol obtained a licence to crenellate in 1343 and the remains represent a quadrangular stronghold, no doubt erected with coastal defence in mind at a time when the French had unleashed a series of raids along the South Coast in retaliation to the English invasion of France. Like the classic quadrangular castle at Bodiam, Westenhanger had cylindrical towers at the four corners and an intermediate square tower in the middle of each side, except on the west where a twin-towered gatehouse took its place. Today only the northern half of the castle still stands. Crumbling, ivy-clad lengths of wall run from the intermediate tower on the east side, past the three towers on the north to the remains of the gatehouse on the west. The north-east tower, crowned by a conical roof, is the only part of the castle to survive intact because of its later use as a dovecote. The gatehouse is now represented by the side walls of the entrance passage, its vault having long since fallen in. Everything else was pulled down in 1701 for the sake of its building materials, and the present farmhouse was built soon after.

Access: On private land.
Reference: BOE *West Kent and the Weald.* Guy.
Relations: Bodiam and the Hundred Years War castles at Cooling and Scotney.

OTHER SITES Kent's greatest loss is *Queenborough Castle* on the Isle of Sheppey, built by Edward III in 1361–77. It was the last new royal castle of the Middle Ages and its coastal defence role foreshadowed the coastal forts of Henry VIII. The castle followed an unconventional circular plan, with six rounded towers projecting from the inner curtain and a concentric outer wall. Tudor adaptations made the castle suitable for artillery, but it was pulled down in 1650 and only a low mound marks the site.

There are motte-and-bailey castles such as *Binbury* (near Thurnham), *Castle Toll* (near Newenden), *Stockbury* and *Tonge* (near Sittingbourne). Of later medieval castles, *Coldbridge* (near Egerton) preserves only earthworks while *Shoreham Castle* is marked by a piece of wall built into a farmhouse. *Knole* at Sevenoaks is the supreme example of a late medieval palace which is towered and embattled but not at all defensible. It was built by Archbishop Bourchier during the Wars of the Roses. *Sandown Castle*, one of the three Henrician forts around Deal, has been washed away by the sea except for a fragment of the outer wall. It was identical to Walmer.

Lancashire

In 1351 the Duchy of Lancaster was created as a palatinate on the model of Cheshire and County Durham. Lancashire lies far enough north to have suffered from Scottish incursions but it is not a great county for castles. Lancaster Castle, though much mutilated, is by far the most important. There is also the small Norman keep at Clitheroe, but we are otherwise left with a handful of pele towers. The Furness district, which formed an outlying part of the county, has been included under Westmorland.

ASHTON HALL overlooks the estuary of the River Lune, three miles south of Lancaster on the Cockerham road. Until 1514 it belonged to the Lawrence family. Their tower house, long and squat, dates from the fourteenth century. It has diagonal corner turrets rising above parapet level but the windows and most other features are neo-Gothic insertions. The adjoining house dates only from 1856.

Access: Private.

BORWICK HALL The oldest part is the fifteenth-century pele tower of the Borwick family. This plain tower has been refitted in more recent centuries. The attached house was built, or more probably rebuilt, by Robert Bindloss, a Kendal clothier who purchased the manor in 1590. A handsome gatehouse of 1650 completes the ensemble. It lies by the River Keer three miles north-east of Carnforth.

Access: Open occasionally.

CLITHEROE CASTLE is perched on a limestone outcrop overlooking the town and the River Ribble. It is probably the castle of Roger de Poitou mentioned in the Domesday Book; it certainly existed by 1102. In that year Roger lost his lands for joining the revolt against Henry I. His estate, known as the Honour of Clitheroe, passed to Robert de Lacy. The site was ideal for a Norman castle, the highest part of the outcrop forming a ready-made motte. On top of this motte stands the ruin of a square keep with corner buttresses, erected in the twelfth century by one of the De Lacys. This keep – supposedly the smallest Norman keep in England – can never have been very hospitable. The summit was enclosed within a curtain, a considerable length of which survives, so the keep was presumably just an adjunct to more spacious accommodation which has disappeared. As well as the usual first-floor entrance, the keep could also be reached (via a movable bridge) from the parapet of the curtain. Eighteenth-century Castle House (now a museum) occupies the far end of the bailey.

When Henry de Lacy died in 1311 Clitheroe was inherited by the powerful Thomas, Earl of Lancaster, and hence remained a possession of the Earldom, then Duchy, of Lancaster. The castle was kept in good repair until the dawn of the Tudor era. Its decay was hastened by deliberate dismantling in 1648, to prevent it from falling into Royalist hands.

Access: Freely accessible (LA).
Reference: VCH *Lancashire* (VI).
Relations: The De Lacy strongholds of Halton, Pontefract and Almondbury.

GREENHALGH CASTLE On a hill just to the north-east of Garstang is the surviving fragment of a castle built by Thomas Stanley, Earl of Derby and 'King' of Man. The licence was granted in 1490, making it an unusually late one, but this was one of several honours conferred by a grateful Henry VII. Stanley's betrayal of Richard III at Bosworth did not endear him to his Northern neighbours and, to make matters worse, he had been rewarded with the lands of several dispossessed Yorkists. In 1646 the castle put up a determined resistance to the Roundheads and was slighted. The castle was a small quadrangular stronghold but it is said to have had as many as eight square towers. All that remains is a tall piece of one of the towers.

Access: On private land.
Reference: VCH *Lancashire* (VI).
Relations: Lathom House (destroyed).

HORNBY CASTLE rises above the River Wenning, a tributary of the Lune. The De Montbegons or their successors, the Longuevillers, moved from the nearby motte-and-bailey site at Castlestede sometime in the thirteenth century. When the ground was being cleared for the present mansion a length of curtain and two round towers were uncovered. However, the only medieval survivor now is a tall tower house. Its lower part dates from the fourteenth century, by which time Hornby belonged to a branch of the Neville family. Sir Edward Stanley, son of Henry VII's supporter Thomas, rebuilt the upper part of the tower soon after 1500. It bears his shield and an oriel window. Sir Edward was created Lord Mounteagle after distinguishing himself at the Battle of Flodden. He erected the octagonal tower of Hornby church as a thank-offering. The castle was destroyed by order of Parliament following its capture in 1643. The tower house now forms part of a castellated mansion built for the financier Pudsey Dawson in 1849–52.

Access: Visible from the bridge.
Reference: VCH *Lancashire* (VIII).
Relations: For the Nevilles see Middleham, Sheriff Hutton, Raby and Brancepeth. See Greenhalgh for the Stanleys.

LANCASTER CASTLE and its distinguished neighbour, the priory church, crown the summit of a hill overlooking the River Lune. A Roman fort occupied the site. Following the arrival of the Normans Lancaster became part of the vast estate granted to Roger de Poitou and the first castle is very likely to have been his foundation. Lords of Lancaster in the twelfth century included two future kings of England, Stephen and John. However, the dynasty which is most closely associated with Lancaster appeared in 1265 when Henry III granted the Earldom of Lancaster to his younger son, Edmund 'Crouchback'. The castle became the chief seat of the powerful lords who followed, including Thomas, ringleader of the baronial opposition to Edward II; Henry, the first palatine duke; and John of Gaunt, who married his way into the duchy. This was also the period of Scottish raids. Lancaster was pillaged several times though the castle was never attacked in earnest. After John of Gaunt's son seized the throne as Henry IV in 1399, and the consequent union of the Duchy of Lancaster with the Crown, the castle fell into decline as a residence but remained the administrative centre of the Duchy. It remains very much a 'working' castle, still serving as a court house and prison.

The existing castle is largely a reconstruction of 1788–1823 by Thomas Harrison, designed to meet the growing requirements of the county gaol and the courts. The phoney curtain and towers enclose an area roughly corresponding with the medieval bailey, except on the north side where the prison juts out in a big arc. Furthermore a series of assize buildings, notably the semi-circular Shire Hall, projects on the west. Fortunately, a few important pieces of the medieval castle have been preserved. The finest of these is John of Gaunt's Gate, one of the most majestic of medieval English gatehouses. It is a massive and rather austere-looking block as befits the entrance to a prison. There is a continuous machicolated parapet around the wall-head and the well-proportioned gateway preserves its original portcullis. It is flanked by semi-octagonal towers which carry inner turrets above parapet level. Despite its name the gatehouse was actually built by Henry IV from 1402, and it bears his arms. To the right of the gatehouse stands the Well Tower, a square Norman tower also remodelled under Henry IV. At the back of the castle stands the Lungess Tower, a square Norman keep. Though attributed to Roger de Poitou it is probably not quite that old. The top floor and parapet belong to the Elizabethan age and centuries of prison use have left their scars. Finally the circular Hadrian Tower (largely rebuilt) forms part of the Shire Hall complex.

Access: The Shire Hall is open regularly in summer but the medieval portions are only visible from outside (LA). More will be open when the castle ceases to be a prison.

Reference: VCH *Lancashire* (VIII).
Relations: Work of the Lancastrian kings can be seen at Tutbury and Leicester. Compare the castle-prisons at Lincoln and Oxford.

RADCLIFFE TOWER is an oblong pele for which James Radcliffe obtained a licence to crenellate in 1403. Not much of the tower stands above ground-floor level and the vault which once covered this floor has fallen in. Originally a timber-framed hall stood alongside – apparently one of the finest in a county noted for its half-timbered buildings – but it has vanished. The ruin stands in Tower Street, close to the parish church.

Access: Freely accessible (LA).

TURTON TOWER Four miles north of Bolton is a timber-framed mansion dominated by a pele tower. The pele was built by a member of the Orrell family, who inherited the manor in 1420. In the 1590s William Orrell heightened the tower, modifying the floor levels and inserting the large windows. It now contains a handsome apartment on each of its three floors, evocatively furnished in Jacobean style. The rest of the house, which consists of a range at right angles to the tower and a later connecting block, is basically Tudor, though much of the 'black and white' timbering on show is actually Victorian.

Access: Open regularly in summer (LA).

OTHER SITES Motte-and-bailey earthworks can be seen beside the River Lune at *Castlestede* (the forerunner of nearby Hornby Castle) and *Halton*. Castle Hill at *Penwortham* is the site of another Norman castle, established by Roger de Poitou (founder of Lancaster and Clitheroe castles) and mentioned in the Domesday Book. A large Norman keep has been uncovered at *Bury*. *Liverpool* had a royal castle from King John's reign but it was torn down during the Commonwealth. The same fate overtook a tower house of the Stanleys which stood close by. A sad loss is *Lathom House*, a multi-towered edifice built (like Greenhalgh) by Thomas Stanley, Earl of Derby. Despite its late date this was evidently a serious stronghold with some provision for defence by artillery. In one of the most memorable of Civil War sieges the Countess of Derby resisted the forces of Parliament here for two years. Afterwards the house was demolished and the site is marked by part of an eighteenth-century successor mansion. *Thurland Castle* at Tunstall is a Victorian rebuilding (re-using much original material) of a moated castle licensed in 1402. *Hoghton Tower*, often described as fortified, is really a hilltop Tudor mansion which was castellated later.

1

2 Dover Castle. The great Norman keep

3 Rochester Castle. Another square Norman keep

1 Carisbrooke Castle. A motte with a shell keep on top

5 Orford Castle. The round keep

4 Castle Rising. The Norman hall keep

8 The Tower of London. A concentric castle enclosing the White Tower

9 Dunstanburgh Castle. A keep gatehouse

10 York, Micklegate Bar

11 Stokesay Castle. The Great Hall

13 Alnwick Castle. The barbican

15 Tattershall Castle. The brick tower house

14 Belsay Castle. A Northern tower house

16 Deal Castle. A Henrician coastal fort

Leicestershire and Rutland

These counties possess a number of motte-and-bailey sites. There are Norman halls at Leicester and Oakham but, with the loss of Belvoir, all the defensive architecture belongs to the late Middle Ages. Leicester Castle was refortified under the Lancastrian kings and Leicestershire would be a poor county for castles were it not for William, Lord Hastings. This Yorkist magnate graced his native county with two very different fortified mansions: Ashby and Kirby Muxloe.

ASHBY CASTLE Ashby-de-la-Zouche takes its name from the Zouche family, whose line died out in 1399. In 1464 Ashby was one of the estates granted to William, Lord Hastings, as a reward for his services to Edward IV. Hastings held the office of Lord Chamberlain and in 1474 he obtained a licence to crenellate his houses at Ashby and Kirby Muxloe. Unfortunately, Lord Hastings did not outlive his royal patron for long, falling victim to the coup organised by Richard, Duke of Gloucester. In a scene familiar from Shakespeare, Hastings was accused of treason and dragged off to summary execution in the Tower of London. His family, however, retained possession. During the Civil War Henry Hastings strengthened the castle with earthen redoubts and turned it into the chief centre of Royalist resistance in the county. The garrison endured over a year of siege before surrendering on honourable terms in February 1646. The Hastings Tower was slighted by order of Parliament but the rest of the castle remained habitable into the eighteenth century. It is now all ruined.

Before Lord Hastings there was only a manor house here, though it was a fine one in keeping with the status of the Zouches. Hastings made the older buildings the core of his mansion. They form a range centred upon a late Norman hall, flanked by the solar and a buttery and pantry wing. In the fourteenth century the massive kitchen was added to the complex. Lord Hastings modernised these buildings and extended the range with the addition of a fine chapel in the prevailing Perpendicular style. Following the licence to crenellate he built a curtain around the manor house and raised the mighty square tower which is named after him. The curtain cannot have been a very formidable obstacle – only a portion survives – but the Hastings Tower is still impressive. It is one of the best examples of a late medieval tower house, providing its owner with a dignified but secure residence. It stands detached from the manorial buildings, facing them across the courtyard. The tower is built in fine ashlar masonry, its four storeys consisting from the bottom upwards of a storeroom, kitchen, hall and solar. Additional accommodation was provided in the seven-storey annexe which is not quite as wide as the main body of the tower. The tower has its own well to ensure complete self-containment. The courtyard front of the tower stands to full height (ninety feet), with traceried corner turrets and a row of corbels which carried a machicolated parapet. The ground-floor entrance was protected by a portcullis. Unfortunately the courtyard front is now little more than a facade, because the rear of the tower was blasted down at the slighting. An underground passage links the tower with the cellar beneath the kitchen. This is a great rarity, since underground passages in castles are generally the stuff of legend.

Access: Standard opening times in summer (EH).
Reference: Guidebook by T L Jones.
Relations: Lord Hastings' castle at Kirby Muxloe.

BELVOIR CASTLE   There has been a castle on this hilltop site since Robert de Todeni raised one after the Norman Conquest. From 1247 it belonged to the De Roos family. A medieval seal still in the castle depicts a large, square keep and an embattled curtain. This castle has dictated the shape of the present mansion but hardly any medieval work is visible now. Edward IV stormed the castle in 1461 and Lord Hastings robbed its stones for Ashby Castle. Thomas Manners, Earl of Rutland, erected a Tudor mansion on the site and this in turn was largely destroyed during the Civil War. What stands today was erected in the 1660s and heavily Gothicised by the architect James Wyatt from 1801. It is a spectacular piece of castellated fantasy and only the south range incorporates some medieval masonry.

Access: Open regularly in summer.
Reference: BOE *Leicestershire and Rutland* (2nd edn).
Relations: Ashby. The Roos strongholds at Helmsley and Wark-on-Tweed.

ESSENDINE CASTLE   Four miles north of Stamford is a square enclosure still largely surrounded by a deep ditch. It may have been dug by Gilbert de Gant after the Norman Conquest or by the Busseys in the following century. Inside the enclosure stands the parish church of St Mary which presumably originated as the castle chapel. This simple little church is now largely of the thirteenth century but it retains a fine Norman entrance portal, surmounted by a panel depicting Christ flanked by angels.

Access: Freely accessible. The church is usually open.

HALLATON CASTLE,   to the west of the village, is an impressive Norman earthwork with a classic 'figure of eight' plan, the large motte being complemented by a small bailey. It is one of those sites with no recorded history and in the absence of any hard facts it is plausible to regard it as a short-lived castle of the Anarchy. The Earl of Leicester agreed to destroy adulterine castles around Leicester towards the end of Stephen's reign.

Access: Freely accessible.

KIRBY MUXLOE CASTLE,   four miles west of Leicester, is the companion of Ashby Castle, being the work of William, Lord Hastings. Although a licence to crenellate was granted in 1474 construction did not commence until October 1480, by which time Ashby was nearing completion. The building accounts, which survive in full, give a total expenditure of £1088 on the incomplete castle. Roger Bowlett was appointed controller of works and John Cowper was the master mason. Lord Hastings' executing in June 1483 did not bring construction to a halt immediately.

His widow continued the work but very little was done in 1484, after which the project was abandoned. The castle remains an unfinished symbol of a great baron's fall from grace.

An older manor house occupied the site and some of its foundations are visible in the courtyard. Unlike Ashby, where Lord Hastings utilised existing buildings, Kirby Muxloe was completely rebuilt on quadrangular lines. It is oblong rather than square in plan. Kirby also differs from Ashby in the choice of brick as the main building material, stone being used only for doorways and windows. The low revetment wall which defines the courtyard, rising out of a water-filled moat, marks the position of the intended curtain and its square angle towers. Only two portions – the gatehouse and the west corner tower – now stand, though more must have been built. The gatehouse is a ruin and is known to have been left incomplete. It is a sturdy, oblong structure with semi-octagonal flanking towers and stair turrets at the rear. The angle tower has fared better because it is still intact, including the battlements, though now a shell. Kirby Muxloe was one of the last castles built with some serious regard for defence. Its gate passage was defended by a drawbridge, a portcullis and two pairs of gates, and both the gatehouse and the surviving tower are pierced by gun ports. These gun ports, however, are the primitive type which had been in use for over a century: small roundels permitting only a limited range of fire.

Access: Apply to key keeper (EH).
Reference: Guidebook by C. Peers.
Relations: Ashby.

LEICESTER CASTLE   Leicester originated as the Roman *Ratae*, was occupied by the Danes as one of their Five Boroughs, then fortified against them following the English reconquest of the Danelaw. Hugh de Grantmesnil became Sheriff of Leicester after the Norman Conquest and he probably founded the castle on the King's behalf. Under Henry I it became the fief of Robert de Beaumont, Earl of Leicester. His grandson, another Robert, was one of the ringleaders of Prince Henry's revolt in 1173. As a consequence Leicester was sacked by Henry II's supporters and the castle was demolished. However, the town rose again under the patronage of Simon de Montfort, and following his death at Evesham Henry III awarded the earldoms of Leicester and Lancaster to his younger son Edmund 'Crouchback'. Leicester thus became a possession of the illustrious House of Lancaster and the rebuilt castle emerged as one of the earls' chief residences. After the fusion of the Duchy of Lancaster with the Crown in 1399 the castle lost its importance, being relegated to the role of administrative centre and gaol. Leicester saw action in the Civil War, being stormed by Prince Rupert and recovered by Parliament after the Battle of Naseby.

Nothing is left of Leicester's Roman and medieval town wall. Furthermore the castle has only survived as a number of isolated fragments. It stood beside the River Soar. Castle Yard marks the site of the inner bailey and the truncated Norman motte can still be seen there. The defences of the bailey have perished but there are two interesting domestic survivals. The seventeenth-century façade of the Court House conceals a remarkable Norman hall. It was originally divided into aisles by two lines of wooden posts, but only one carved capital remains in place and the building has suffered from later partitioning. The adjacent church of St Mary de Castro originated as an unusually sumptuous castle chapel, founded as a collegiate establishment *circa* 1107 by the first Robert de Beaumont. Portions of elaborate Norman work have survived a heavy Victorian restoration. The church stood within its own precinct, entered through the surviving timber-framed gatehouse.

The castle was enlarged in the 1330s by Henry, the blind Earl of Lancaster. He added a large outer court known as the Newarke ('new work'), enclosing a religious complex comparable to the lower ward of Windsor Castle. The centre of this complex was a second and larger collegiate church. This no longer survives but Trinity Hospital is still in use as an almshouse, preserving its chapel and infirmary arcades. Two gatehouses nearby are the only remnants of the defences, both the legacy of a rebuilding programme under the Lancastrian kings. Turret Gate (1422), a simple ruin, led from the Newarke into the inner bailey. The Magazine Gate, of Henry IV's reign, was the main entrance into the Newarke. An oblong bulk with a vaulted gate passage, it stands intact but much restored, and isolated by the road network. The large and small entrance arches, one for horse traffic and one for pedestrians, were popular in the later Middle Ages but hardly compatible with security.

> *Access:* The Magazine Gate housed a regimental museum and the Court House is sometimes open (both LA). St Mary's Church is usually locked.
> *Reference: Leicester Castle* by L. Fox. VCH *Leicestershire* (IV).
> *Relations:* Windsor. The Norman hall at Oakham.

OAKHAM CASTLE is notable for its hall, a gem of late Norman craftsmanship. The building has been relatively little altered since its completion and the Romanesque proportions can still be admired. Four-bay arcades divide the hall into a nave and two aisles, and the sculptural decoration on capitals and corbels is of an extremely high quality. Note the figures of musicians (now headless!) which are carved between each arch. The foliated capitals bear a strong resemblance to those in the choir of Canterbury Cathedral, so it is more than likely that the same French masons were responsible. Presumably they came here upon completion of their work at Canterbury in 1184, when Walkelin de Ferrers was lord of the manor. The hall formed the centre of a complex of manorial buildings which are detailed in a survey of 1340. The rest has vanished and the hall only survives because of its use into modern times as a court house for the small county of Rutland.

By itself the hall gives the impression of an unfortified manor house, but the rectangular rampart surrounding it shows that the castle did have defences. The rampart, which was heightened at least once during the Norman era, received a stone curtain in the thirteenth century. Portions are still visible, including the rubble core of two semi-circular flanking towers on the west side, facing the beautiful parish church of Oakham.

> *Access:* Open regularly (LA).
> *Reference:* Guidebook by T. H. Clough.
> *Relations:* The Ferrers family also held Tutbury and Duffield castles. Compare the Norman halls at Leicester and Christchurch.

SAUVEY CASTLE is strongly situated on a spur overlooking the confluence of two streams, which were once dammed to form a moat. The only approach is cut off by a deep ditch, and beyond the rectangular outer bailey is an elongated mound surrounded by a rampart. King John spent £440 here in 1210–11 and if the earthworks date from his time then it shows how long the motte-and-bailey castle survived. Presumably the buildings were all of wood. It remained a popular royal hunting lodge under Henry III but fell into decay thereafter. The site lies about two miles east of Tilton, near Launde Abbey.

Access: On private land.

OTHER SITES There are several other Norman castle sites, surviving as rough earthworks (*Uppingham* and *Alstoe Mount* near Burley) or as isolated mottes (*Earl Shilton* and *Whitwick*). *Hinckley* preserves a ringwork near the parish church and *Mountsorrel Castle* is a promontory site cut off by a ditch. *Groby Old Hall* is the early Tudor successor of another Norman castle, its motte surviving close by. The site of the De Lacy stronghold at *Castle Donington* has been built over.

Lincolnshire

Lincolnshire once had its fair share of castles but few are well preserved. Stone robbing has led to the destruction of several major strongholds. Only at Lincoln Castle does much Norman masonry survive, and thirteenth-century towered enclosures such as Bolingbroke, Castle Bytham and Tattershall have been ruthlessly torn down for their materials. Somerton has survived better, though not much better. Tattershall Castle at least preserves the remarkable tower house which Lord Cromwell added in the fifteenth century. It makes a striking feature in this flat landscape. Thornton Abbey possesses a genuinely defensive gatehouse, which is rare for a monastic establishment. Both Thornton and Tattershall are important examples of early brickwork.

BOLINGBROKE CASTLE occupies a low-lying site at Old Bolingbroke. William de Roumare, created Earl of Lincoln by King Stephen, first raised a castle here during the Anarchy. The site was utilised for the construction of a stone castle by Ranulf de Blundeville, Earl of Chester, in the 1220s. It was one of several castles raised by this powerful baron. Bolingbroke followed a hexagonal plan, with semi-circular flanking towers at five corners and a round-towered gatehouse (one of the earliest of this kind) occupying the sixth. It passed via the De Lacys to the earls and dukes of Lancaster. The future Henry IV – Henry of Bolingbroke – was born in the castle in 1367. The Lancastrian kings spent over £1000 on improvements to the castle and new lodgings were erected here as late as Elizabeth I's reign. Disaster came with the Civil War. The decaying castle fell to the Roundheads in 1643 and the subsequent slighting was a severe one. Later stone robbing was so thorough that the castle had all but disappeared, but excavations in the 1970s have revealed the layout. The lower courses of the curtain and its towers are visible throughout their circuit. Beyond are the earthworks of a large outer bailey.

Access: Freely accessible (EH).
Reference: Mackenzie (I). BOE *Lincolnshire* (2nd edn).
Relations: Ranulf de Blundeville's castles at Beeston and Chartley.

BOURNE CASTLE may have been founded by Baldwin, Count of Brionne, before 1100. In the twelfth century it passed to the De Wakes who claimed descent from Hereward the Wake. The site lies on the south side of the town and consists of two concentric baileys following a roughly oblong plan. Deep ditches (once water-filled) show the extent of the castle, but the motte has been flattened and no masonry remains. A square keep and a round-towered gatehouse are known to have stood here.

Access: Freely accessible.

CASTLE BYTHAM overlooks the village of the same name. It is first mentioned in 1141 when William le Gros, Count of Aumale, held it. Perhaps he was the founder. William de Fortibus, a notorious robber baron, was probably responsible for the stone defences. Captured and destroyed by the young Henry III in 1221, the castle rose again under William de Colville but was a ruin by the Tudor era. Now only powerful earthworks remain. The site is an oblong enclosure surrounded by a ditch, but the rampart is placed rather curiously on the far side of the ditch. Hummocks indicate the position of the towered curtain which crowned this rampart, while a low mound at a gap in the rampart probably marks the site of a circular keep. On the level approach away from the village the rampart is double and preceded by an outer bailey.

Access: On private land.
Reference: Mackenzie (I).
Relations: For William le Gros see Scarborough, and for William de Fortibus see Cockermouth.

GRIMSTHORPE CASTLE Set within a landscaped park four miles north-west of Bourne, this ancestral seat of the earls of Ancaster has been repeatedly embellished through the centuries but still follows the outline of a medieval quadrangular castle. The original castle is believed to have been built by Gilbert de Gant in the late thirteenth century. His angle towers still exist but they are all oblong in plan and therefore rather conservative for their date. The oddly-tapering King John's Tower at the south-east corner is the largest, containing vaulted chambers. The other three are quite slender in relation to their height, and clearly too small and widely-spaced to be very effective as flankers. The walls which must have connected these towers no longer exist. Charles Brandon, Duke of Suffolk, hurriedly erected new residential ranges in their place in order to entertain Henry VIII here in 1541. Three sides of the present quadrangle are basically still his, albeit much altered, but Sir John Vanbrugh was commissioned to rebuild the north front in the 1720s. His Classical facade has monumental towers at either end, concealing the medieval angle towers which lie behind them.

Access: Limited opening times in summer.

Reference: BOE *Lincolnshire* (2nd edn). Souvenir guide.

HUSSEY TOWER, sadly derelict, is a relic of medieval Boston. It stands off the Skirbeck Road to the south of the old town. The embattled tower, with a vaulted ground floor and thin corner turrets at parapet level, is believed to date from 1500 or thereabouts – decidedly late for a tower house so far south. It takes its name from the Hussey family. John, Lord Hussey, enjoyed favour with Henry VIII but was executed in 1539 for his part in the Northern rebellion known as the Pilgrimage of Grace. The mansion which adjoined the tower then fell into neglect and was pulled down in 1565.

Access: On private land.

Relations: Nearby Rochford Tower.

LINCOLN CASTLE, CLOSE AND CITY WALL The Romans first took advantage of this spectacular site, *Lindum* becoming a settlement for army veterans. It survived the Roman departure and by the Norman Conquest had emerged as one of the largest towns in England. Medieval Lincoln reflected its Roman origins, with an oblong citadel occupying the site of the hilltop fortress and a lower town on the slope towards the River Witham. The Roman wall remained in commission throughout the Middle Ages but now only a few fragments survive, notably the precious Newport Arch in Bailgate. Spanning the High Street at the lower end of town stands a gatehouse known as the Stonebow, rebuilt before 1500 and housing the guildhall on its upper floor. However, it is a monumental entrance rather than a piece of fortification and rare as such for a city gate, erected at a time when town defences were no longer really necessary.

Castle and cathedral have faced each other across the hilltop since Norman times. Lincoln Castle was raised over the south-west quarter of the citadel by order of William the Conqueror in 1068. The site had previously been densely occupied – Domesday Book tells us that 166 houses were destroyed to make way for the castle. Its stone wall is mentioned as early as 1115 and Henry I is regarded as the likely builder. The high curtain, still intact though frequently patched up in later centuries, preserves portions of herringbone masonry confirming its early Norman date. It stands on top of an earth rampart surrounding a large, roughly square bailey. A rare feature is the presence of not one but two mottes, both on the southern edge of the bailey. Why they should stand so close together is a mystery, since they seem to threaten each other from a defensive point of view. The larger motte is crowned by a polygonal shell keep known as the Lucy Tower, evidently a later Norman addition and possibly erected by the Earl of Chester, who held Lincoln for the Empress Matilda. Lincoln was the scene of much fighting during the Anarchy – King Stephen was taken prisoner during a battle outside the walls in 1141. The smaller motte carries the so-called Observatory Tower, an early Norman structure extended in the fourteenth century and capped by a Victorian turret. Cobb Hall, a horseshoe-plan tower flanking the vulnerable north-east corner of the walled circuit, is a defensive improvement made after an unsuccessful siege by the Dauphin Louis' supporters in 1217. There are two gatehouses. The West Gate, now blocked, is a simple Norman gate tower. The East Gate was re-fronted in the fourteenth century with a lofty gate arch and round turrets corbelled out higher up. Foundations of a barbican can be seen in front but the courtyard extension of the gatehouse is another Victorian embellishment. (It incorporates an oriel window from a medieval house in the city).

In Norman times the castle was usually a royal stronghold but the De la Haye family acquired a hereditary constableship. This office was inherited by the earls and dukes of Lancaster and thus reverted to the Crown in 1399. None of the medieval residential buildings survive because the bailey is occupied by dour assize and prison buildings recalling the castle's long use (until 1878) as the county gaol. The prison chapel with its isolated pews, and the graves of hanged prisoners inside the shell keep, are poignant reminders of that grim era.

A fine view of the cathedral can be obtained from the castle battlements. The cathedral close occupied the south-east quarter of the citadel but the addition of the magnificent Angel Choir in 1255–80 caused the cathedral to project beyond the line of the Roman wall. In 1285 a licence was obtained to crenellate the expanded cathedral close. A second licence in 1319 permitted the erection of flanking towers along the line of the wall. Portions of the close wall survive to the south and east of Minster Yard. Two square towers are visible from Winnowsty Lane and another is incorporated into the house known as The Priory. The towers are located on that part of the circuit which doubled up as the city wall. So is the Potter Gate, a gate tower of simple defensive character. By contrast the Exchequer Gate, the main entrance from within the city, is monumental rather than defensive in character. Evidently there was no real intention to fortify the close against the city.

> *Access:* The castle is open regularly and the Stonebow can be visited at certain times (both LA). Some of the close wall is visible.
> *Reference:* BOE *Lincolnshire* (2nd edn). Castle guidebook.
> *Relations:* Lewes is the only other castle with two mottes. Compare the fortified religious precincts at Bury and Lichfield.

ROCHFORD TOWER, sometimes called Kyme Tower from its later owners, is named after the Rochford family who built it. The tower stands midway Boston and Freiston, closely resembling nearby Hussey Tower in date and form. It is a late medieval tower house built of brick, with angle turrets projecting from the crenellated parapet. The ground-floor room is vaulted in brick and there are still traces of religious frescoes in the chamber above.

> *Access:* Visible from the road.
> *Relations:* Hussey Tower. The wall paintings at Longthorpe.

SOMERTON CASTLE lies off a minor road two miles west of Boothby Graffoe which, in turn, is several miles south of Lincoln. Only a few portions stand of the castle licensed to Anthony Bek in 1281. Two years later he became Bishop of Durham and later handed the castle over to Edward I as a goodwill gesture. Typically Edwardian, the castle enclosed a rectangular courtyard with circular towers at the four corners.

Today the most substantial features are the south-east tower and its square annexe, both preserved to full height and now forming part of an Elizabethan house. Everything else has vanished except for the vaulted ground floors of two other corner towers and a bit of curtain attached to one of them. The tower vaults are interesting: two are domed and one springs from a central pillar. Extensive moats (now drained) surround the castle, and these in turn are enclosed by a curious outer rampart. The rampart may have been raised for the confinement of John the Good, the French King captured at Poitiers. He was brought here for greater security in 1359 and stayed for six months before returning to France. This was no grim confinement, however, the King being attended by an entourage in keeping with his status.

Access: Private.
Reference: BOE *Lincolnshire* (2nd edn). *HKW* (II).
Relations: Bishop Bek's work at Auckland and Durham.

SOUTH KYME TOWER The unusually slender proportions suggest a church tower but it was actually a secular building. Perfectly preserved, though now an empty shell, this tall tower is distinguished by its ashlar masonry and the regular distribution of small traceried windows. It rises to an embattled parapet with a stair turret in one corner. The ground-floor vault bears the arms of the Umfraville family and the architecture points to Sir Gilbert, last of the Umfravilles (d.1381), who was lord of the manor for much of the fourteenth century. The tower did not originally stand alone. It belonged to an extensive manor house but it is doubtful whether it was spacious enough to be regarded as a tower house proper. Everything else was pulled down in the 1720s and replaced by the house which stands nearby.

Access: Visible from the road.
Reference: BOE *Lincolnshire* (2nd edn).
Relations: The Umfraville castles at Cockermouth, Harbottle and Prudhoe.

STAMFORD CASTLE AND TOWN WALL This handsome, stone-built town first came to prominence as one of the five chief boroughs of the Danelaw. Danish Stamford embraced both banks of the River Welland but the Northamptonshire bank (Stamford Baron) was excluded from the later medieval defences. A stone wall was built from 1261 but the remains are now quite fragmentary. The only remnant of the town wall worth seeking is a large semi-circular bastion in Petergate, marking the western extremity of the circuit. Despite the defences Stamford was pillaged by a Lancastrian army in 1461.

The castle was in ruins by then and has since fared almost as badly. It was a royal foundation mentioned in the Domesday Book but was never of any great importance. The town has encroached on the bailey and in 1932 the motte (which carried a round keep) was levelled to make way for a car park. The site lies by the river between Castle Dyke and St Peter's Vale and the surviving fragments are scattered. They comprise a couple of pieces of bailey curtain, one pierced by a postern. There is also the end wall of a domestic building, probably a chapel, with three blank arches of thirteenth-century date.

Access: The remains are freely accessible (LA).
Reference: RCHM *Town of Stamford.*

TATTERSHALL CASTLE possesses one of the most splendid of later medieval tower houses. It has justly been described as the finest piece of medieval brickwork in England. This magnificent tower was erected by Ralph, Lord Cromwell, in the years 1434–46. Rising over a hundred feet to the top of its corner turrets, with a view stretching from Lincoln Cathedral to Boston Stump, it dominates the surrounding fenland, all the more so because the rest of the castle has perished. There had in fact been a castle here since 1231, when Robert de Tattershall obtained a licence to crenellate. Wet moats enclose an inner bailey and a concentric platform which is divided into two outer baileys. Unfortunately the thirteenth-century curtain has been totally destroyed, though excavations have left on view the stone bases of two rounded flanking towers.

Lord Cromwell erected his new tower on the edge of the bailey, projecting into the moat. During its construction Cromwell was Lord High Treasurer of England and the tower house was intended to be commensurate with his status. The choice of brick was dictated by fashion rather than the shortage of local stone, since he used stone for the fine collegiate church which stands nearby. Stone is in fact used for the door and window surrounds, the spiral staircase and the machicolations. Surviving building accounts reveal that the bricks – over a million of them – were made locally but that many of the craftsmen were foreign, including the supervisor, Baldwin 'the Dutchman' (probably a German). This explains the continental appearance of the tower, although the plan – rectangular with octagonal corner turrets – is conventional enough.

The corner turrets rise well above parapet level and are finished off with decorative brickwork emulating machicolations. Between the turrets on all four sides is a covered fighting gallery projecting outwards on genuine machicolations. The gallery has embrasures in its outer wall and there is an embattled parapet above. This elaborate crown gives Tattershall its unique dignity but the present isolation of the tower is misleading. Originally it was connected to the main residential buildings of the castle and that is why the angle turrets do not project at all on the bailey side. The tower basically formed a magnificent suite of apartments for Lord Cromwell's personal use so it was not a self-contained keep in the old sense. There are five storeys including the vaulted basement, each level comprising one grand apartment with extra accommodation provided in the angle turrets. The first floor contained a hall. The second-floor room, approached along a tall vaulted corridor, is conjectured to have been Lord Cromwell's audience chamber. Above that was the solar. One defensive flaw is the presence of no less than three entrance doorways, one for the basement, one for the ground floor and one for the spiral stair leading to the upper floors. Furthermore, the massive walls of the tower are weakened by traceried windows which are nearly as big at ground level as they are on the top floor, with only the width of the moat to keep an enemy at bay. This demonstrates the triumph of domestic comfort and the tower's corresponding limitations as a serious fortification.

A single retainer's lodging (once part of a range) and the ruins of the stable block are the only other relics of Tattershall Castle. They are again Lord Cromwell's brickwork, located in the outer baileys. After Cromwell's death the castle fell into disuse and demolition took place in the eighteenth century. Even the great tower

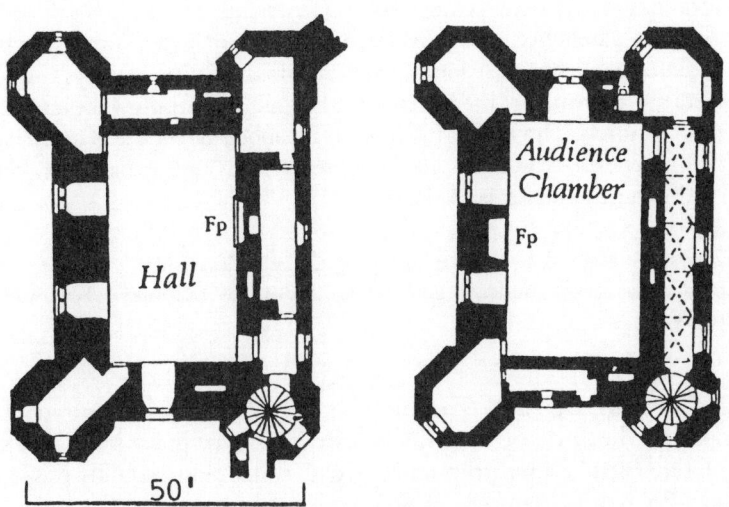

TATTERSHALL CASTLE: TOWER HOUSE AT FIRST-
AND SECOND-FLOOR LEVELS

was in a ruinous state by 1911, but in that year the castle was purchased by Lord
Curzon. He embarked upon a thorough but scholarly restoration of the fabric,
putting in new floors and reinstating the magnificent heraldic fireplaces which had
been ripped out of the tower for shipment to America.

Access: Open regularly in summer (NT).

Reference: Guidebook by M. W. Thompson. *Tattershall Castle* by Lord Curzon & H.
A. Tipping.

Relations: Wingfield Manor is Lord Cromwell's work. Derivatives such as the tower
house at Buckden and Oxburgh's gatehouse. Lord Curzon also restored Bodiam.

THORNTON ABBEY Six miles south-east of Barton-upon-Humber are the
remains of an abbey of Augustinian canons founded in 1139. Little is left of the
church and claustral buildings but the magnificent gatehouse has survived the
centuries unscathed. It was erected by Abbot Thomas de Gretham following the issue
of a licence to crenellate in 1382. A number of monasteries built elaborate gatehouses
in response to such licences but Thornton is one of the few with some serious regard
towards defence. The outer front has intricate niches containing statues, but there
are no compromising window openings and the ornate entrance portal was closed
by a portcullis. The elaborately vaulted gate passage preserves its original oak gates
and the gatehouse is preceded by a long barbican added in 1389. It consists of two
parallel walls, both pierced by thirteen arrow-slit embrasures and terminating in a
round turret. Curiously enough there is no cross-wall between the turrets. The
barbican is built entirely of brick and the gatehouse is largely of the same material,
stone being reserved for the window dressings and other decorative elements. Wing
walls project on either side of the gatehouse, as if to discourage attempts to by-pass

it, but the monastic precinct was much too big to defend. The building must be seen as a sort of keep-gatehouse, normally serving as a court house and exchequer but capable of acting as a temporary refuge when required. Its upper storeys contain two large and stately apartments, the lower graced by an oriel window looking towards the site of the church. The reason for this strong abbey gatehouse is uncertain, but even the Humber estuary was not safe from French raids and perhaps the abbey had suffered badly during the Peasants' Revolt.

Access: Standard opening times (EH).
Reference: Guidebook by A. Clapham & P. K. Baillie Reynolds.
Relations: Defensive monastic gatehouses at Bury St Edmunds, Tynemouth and Alnwick.

TOWER ON THE MOOR The 'moor' is Edlington Moor, where most of the clay was dug for the bricks of Tattershall Castle. The tower house here was a smaller version of Tattershall's, fifteenth-century in date and almost certainly raised by the same man. Why Lord Cromwell should erect a similar tower just five miles away is a mystery and posterity has treated it less kindly. Only one of the octagonal corner turrets still stands, built of the local brick and originally containing the spiral stair. This turret overlooks a golf course about a mile north-east of Woodhall Spa.

Access: Visible from the road.
Relations: Tattershall.

OTHER SITES Only some disturbed earthworks remain of *Sleaford Castle*, erected *circa* 1130 by Alexander, Bishop of Lincoln. Like his surviving castle at Newark (Nottinghamshire) it had an oblong plan anticipating the quadrangular castles of later times. Lincolnshire's motte-and-baileys include the site known as 'The Castles' at *Barrow-upon-Humber*, overgrown *Castle Carlton* (near South Reston) and another at *Wrangle*. *Swineshead Castle* is a low-lying fenland earthwork, its bailey surrounding a central motte. Isolated mottes appear at *Corby* Glen and *Owston* Ferry, while ringworks exist at *Gainsborough, Heydour, Welbourn* and Wyberton (*Wybert's Castle*). *Folkingham Castle* is a deeply moated site.

Middlesex

London's mighty city wall has been reduced to a few pieces but the Tower of London – a misnomer in view of its great extent – is one of the greatest of medieval castles. It possesses one of the oldest and largest of Norman keeps, a towered curtain second to none and an outer wall which makes it England's best example of a concentric castle. The Palace of Westminster retains its Jewel Tower, which was strong enough to house the royal treasure. The rest of Middlesex is virtually a castle-free zone.

LONDON CITY WALL London was first enclosed by a defensive wall around AD 200. Starting at the Thames in the Blackfriars area, the city wall ran for two miles before rejoining the river further east where the Tower of London now stands. A large 'kink' on the north side of the circuit was caused by the junction with an earlier Roman fort. In the last decades of Roman occupation, when London lay exposed to the incursions of sea-borne barbarians, the wall was extended along the riverside. Alfred the Great repaired the decaying city wall after driving the Danes out. Later the Danes occupied the city again, culminating in the memorable siege of 1014 when London Bridge was pulled down. On the approach of William of Normandy in 1066 the citizens barred their rebuilt bridge against him, forcing the Normans to harry the south bank of the Thames as far as Wallingford before crossing. The English then came to terms with their invader and the Conqueror entered London unopposed.

William erected his mighty Tower to overawe the Londoners. By the year 1111 a second castle had appeared beside the river near the western end of the walled city. Baynard's Castle was rebuilt later in the Middle Ages as a royal palace and succumbed to the flames of the Great Fire in 1666. Plans to expose the foundations of its river frontage have not come to fruition. (Two other Norman castles within the city did not last long.) London established itself as the capital of England in Norman times and the city appointed its first mayor in 1193. Soon after this date the new spirit of civic independence led to a major overhaul of the city wall. Building had commenced by 1215 at the latest. The wall was increased in height and provided with a set of semi-circular flanking bastions (twenty-two are known). The Roman circuit was more than large enough for the London of this era, the only extension coming in 1276 when the important Blackfriars monastery was incorporated. There were six main gatehouses with familiar names: Ludgate, Newgate, Aldersgate, Cripplegate, Bishopsgate and Aldgate. Moorgate was added in 1415. The old London Bridge was defended by twin gate towers, though the late Roman riverside wall was allowed to crumble. By Tudor times London had far outgrown its ancient limits. When Parliament fortified the city against a possible Royalist attack in 1643 a much bigger circuit of earthworks was called for, and the old wall suffered the common fate of piecemeal demolition.

In the twentieth century – largely as a result of the Blitz – portions of the city wall have been rediscovered and preserved. The remains all belong to the eastern part of the old circuit, north of the Tower, and the north-western sector in the Cripplegate district, where the Roman fort stood. The surviving fragments generally exhibit medieval work on top of Roman, the difference in masonry being clearly discernible. Many fragments are hidden in private yards and cellars, so this brief summary is confined to the better and more accessible pieces. Starting on Tower Hill, just beyond the Tower of London's moat, are the excavated footings of a postern tower (*circa* 1300) and a well-preserved length of wall. A little further north is the fine stretch in Cooper's Row, standing to full height with a row of arrow embrasures below the parapet. In the north-western sector the first piece (with late medieval brick battlements) stands in St Alphege's churchyard on London Wall. There follows a long stretch of wall amid the concrete of the Barbican complex. It incorporates the only surviving medieval bastion, which guarded the north-west corner of the circuit.

The last stretch, off Noble Street, shows how the original Roman fort wall was thickened when the city wall was built.

Access: These remains are freely accessible (LA & EH).
Reference: RCHM *London* (III).
Relations: Roman city walls at Canterbury, Colchester and Exeter.

PALACE OF WESTMINSTER The Houses of Parliament occupy the site of a royal palace which flourished from the time of Edward the Confessor until Henry VIII moved to Whitehall and St James's. Although the Tower of London could accommodate the royal entourage, most kings found Westminster more congenial than the volatile city of London. There was convenient transport between the two by barge along the Thames. Parliament's relationship with the palace is an old one, since the House of Lords regularly met in the private royal apartments from the fourteenth century and the House of Commons used the collegiate chapel of St Stephen after the Reformation. Unfortunately these were consumed in the great fire of 1834 and in their place we see Sir Charles Barry's vast complex. Fortunately the incomparable Westminster Hall survived the inferno. It is by far the best of England's medieval halls and its dimensions (240 feet long by ninety feet high) make it one of the largest in Europe. This is all the more surprising considering its early Norman origin. The side walls go back to William II but the hall was remodelled in 1394–99, i.e. the last years of Richard II. The celebrated Henry Yevele, architect of Canterbury Cathedral nave, was master mason. Hugh Herland, as master carpenter, constructed the magnificent hammerbeam roof which spans the hall's great width (the Norman hall was aisled). Elegant sculpture can be seen in the angels at the ends of the hammerbeams and the statues of kings lining the walls. The hall was primarily a venue for state ceremonial though its everyday use passed into the hands of the royal courts. Coronation banquets and treason trials (notably Charles I's) took place here.

Several royal palaces were unfortified even in Norman times and Westminster was one of them. The precinct wall which surrounded the palace never quite developed into a defensive curtain, though Edward III commissioned a youthful Henry Yevele to build two towers along its line in 1365. One of them, the original Clock Tower, has disappeared beneath its famous successor. The Jewel Tower survives owing to later use as a repository for Parliamentary records. Now an isolated structure facing (and overawed by) the Victoria Tower, it occupied the south-west corner of the medieval palace precinct. The present windows, enlargements of 1718, do not conceal the defensive character of the tower, and the ground floor is covered by a vault with beautifully carved bosses. As a matter of fact the Jewel Tower, as its name suggests, was built as a secure place for the extensive treasures of the King's privy wardrobe. The tower is a rectangular structure with a smaller wing at right angles, carefully contrived to stand completely outside the angle of the precinct and thus not encroach upon the King's private garden which lay behind. The moat (reinstated at this point) had to be pushed out onto a piece of land appropriated from Westminster Abbey, much to the annoyance of the abbot and monks.

Access: The Jewel Tower is open at standard times (EH). Westminster Hall (and the Houses of Parliament) can only be visited by arrangement with an MP.

Reference: *Westminster Hall* by H. Saunders. Jewel Tower guidebook by A. J. Taylor. *HKW* (I).
Relations: The Tower of London. Henry Yevele's work at Canterbury and Saltwood.

TOWER OF LONDON The Tower of London and Dover Castle were the strongest castles of medieval England. There are those who would put Dover first and London second but this is a matter of preference. Both castles retain their majesty in spite of extensive later mutilation. It must be admitted that Dover makes the most of its glorious position whereas the Tower derives no advantages from its site. Squatting on the north bank of the Thames, and now overshadowed by the glass skyscrapers of the City, the grandeur of the complex is not immediately apparent. Nevertheless its sheer size – eighteen acres – cannot fail to impress and the majestic keep and concentric curtains are visible from all directions. The prime role of the Tower was to overawe the defiant citizens of the capital. This may seem less strategic than Dover's coastal defence but English kings generally had more to fear from their own subjects than from external attack. One claim can never be denied, that in terms of historic intensity the Tower has no equal.

William the Conqueror founded a castle here as soon as London surrendered in 1066. The south-east angle of the city wall (see above) formed a ready-made defence on two sides, and a ditch was dug elsewhere to separate the castle from the city. This first castle covered a much smaller area than the present one, corresponding with the inner bailey to the south of the White Tower. The White Tower itself was commenced in William's lifetime, traditionally in 1078. Work must have continued into William II's reign though it was presumably complete by 1097, when a curtain was being built around the bailey. Although it is the prototype for those which followed, the White Tower is one of the grandest of all Norman keeps and its impact upon the subdued Londoners no doubt explains why this keep has become synonymous with the entire castle. Later Norman kings, even Henry II, saw no need for improvement. There was a lull in building activity until 1190, when William Longchamp, Bishop of Ely, added an outer bailey to the west, thus encroaching upon the city. Longchamp was the unpopular regent appointed to govern England during Richard I's absence on crusade. Before his work was finished Longchamp found himself besieged in the Tower by Prince John's supporters, and subsequently driven into exile.

In the early years of his reign Henry III rebuilt the defences of the inner bailey and constructed a lavish palace within. From 1238 he undertook a vast enlargement of the Tower, supplanting Longchamp's outer bailey by a much bigger enclosure extending northwards to Tower Hill and eastwards beyond the line of the city wall. Hence the White Tower now occupies a central position. This further inroad upon the city was not welcomed and the citizens were delighted when Henry's main gatehouse twice fell down. Building continued nevertheless for the rest of Henry's reign. The total cost exceeded £10,000 but Edward I managed to spend twice as much as his father in a single decade (1275–85). He surrounded Henry's great curtain with an outer wall which converted the Tower into a concentric fortress, outshining even his own Welsh castles in scale. In accordance with the principles of concentric planning the outer curtain is lower than Henry's and there is a relatively narrow space between the two, so that bow-fire could be directed an at enemy from both parapets simultaneously. Much of the cost was incurred by having to fill in Henry III's moat and dig a new one beyond the outer curtain. (The moat, fed by the river, was drained in 1843 by order of the Duke of Wellington, who was then constable of the Tower.) The two bastions at the northern corners of the outer curtain – Legge's and Brass Mounts – are artillery platforms attributed to Edward IV.

Edward I contrived a series of obstacles to make the Tower difficult to enter from the city. First there was a semi-circular barbican, now reduced to footings. It was known as the Lion Tower because for centuries it housed the beasts of the royal menagerie. Next there are two round-towered gatehouses, one behind the other. The Middle Gate was refaced in 1717 but the Byward Gate is more authentic and retains a portcullis with winding gear. The alternative and more convenient approach to the Tower was from the river through St Thomas' Gate, better known as Traitors' Gate from the many prisoners who passed beneath its wide archway after conviction in Westminster Hall. This oblong projection has slim round turrets at the outer corners. Before the construction of Tower Wharf in the fourteenth century the Thames flowed directly into the gate chamber and washed the outer curtain. This resulted in undercutting and the entire riverside wall east of Traitors' Gate had to be rebuilt in the next reign. The smaller water gate further east (Cradle Tower) was added by Edward III in the 1350s.

Henry III's great curtain is flanked by twelve towers, all rounded in accordance with the defensive principles of the era. The only exception is the octagonal Bell Tower at the south-west corner, its lower half quite solid. The plan is surprising considering that this tower is older than the rest, being the chief relic of William Longchamp's extension of the 1190s. Its size is remarkable too for a mural tower of the late twelfth century. It is larger than some keeps. Henry III's big towers followed suit in being for residence as well as defence. In that respect they are an improvement on the purely defensive bastions at Dover. East of the Bell Tower there comes first the cylindrical Wakefield Tower, which occupied one corner of the inner bailey. Its upper floor housed the King's bed chamber, once communicating with the buildings of royal palace. From here the rest of the great curtain along the riverside, including the Lanthorn Tower, is a Victorian reconstruction, the original having been pulled down in 1777. On the other three sides the curtain is still complete and its towers are mostly D-shaped. Three of them (the Constable, Brick and Flint towers) have been rebuilt and most of the others have suffered from later alterations to a greater or lesser extent. The curtain on the west, with its many arrow-slits, is deliberately the most brow-beating as if to intimidate the city. Henry III's mighty Devereux Tower stands at one end, the older Bell Tower guards the other and a single tower is placed midway between them. This, the Beauchamp Tower, is the most impressive of the wall towers. It is actually Edward I's work, named after a captive Earl of Warwick and closing the gap formerly occupied by Henry III's main gatehouse.

Sir Walter Raleigh was a prisoner in the infamous Bloody Tower for thirteen years. This tower, an adjunct of the Wakefield Tower, contains a gate passage leading into Henry III's great courtyard. Once inside, the ruined stretch of loopholed curtain on the right is the only relic of the inner bailey (Henry III's palace was torn down during the Commonwealth). The present buildings in the great courtyard mainly belong to recent centuries, but two Tudor survivors are the timber-framed Queen's House (once the lodging of the lieutenant, or deputy constable) and the collegiate chapel of St Peter ad Vincula, a fine example of Perpendicular architecture from Henry VIII's reign. Tower Green, in front of the chapel, is the place where a handful of unfortunates – including Anne Boleyn and Jane Grey – were spared the ignominy of a public execution.

Once inside the great courtyard, however, it is the White Tower which commands our attention. Its name recalls the fact that it was whitewashed, at least from the thirteenth century. William I entrusted the construction of this keep to Gundulf, Bishop of Rochester, who was renowned for his architectural skills. He created one of the most splendid keeps of the Middle Ages and set a pattern for the major keeps of the Norman era. Whether the design was Gundulf's, or whether it derived from a vanished keep of the dukes of Normandy at Rouen, is unknown. So accomplished a building surely had its prototypes. It was a palace-fortress on the grand scale, with all the requirements of a Norman king's household arranged into a massive oblong structure. Its ground dimensions, 120 by 110 feet, are excelled only by the contemporary keep at Colchester. The keep is divided into two by a cross-wall. A smaller subdivision accommodates the chapel of St John, its sanctuary projecting as an apse from the south-east corner of the keep. An apse appears in the same position at Colchester but later Norman keeps dispensed with this feature.

St John's Chapel is a gem of early Norman religious architecture. It has round-headed arcades on circular columns and side-aisles which continue around the apse to form an ambulatory. The chapel stands on the second floor of the keep, i.e. the principal level which contained the royal apartments. The gallery surmounting the chapel arcades continues around the outer wall of the keep and once looked down upon the hall and solar below. A 'double' storey containing the chief accommodation, with a gallery at the upper level, became a standard amenity in the larger keeps of the twelfth century. Unfortunately, the arrangement is no longer apparent here because a third floor has been inserted at this level. Tall corner turrets, rising to 110 feet, are capped by distinctive cupolas of the seventeenth century. The turret containing the main spiral stair is circular, and therefore ahead of its time. The original first-floor entrance to the keep has been reinstated in modern times, but the forebuilding which protected it no longer exists. It was an addition to the original structure, so the forebuilding is one keep component which the White Tower did not pioneer. High above the entrance doorway (at gallery level) can be seen two small pairs of windows which are the only Norman ones left in the keep. All the others are enlargements attributed to Sir Christopher Wren. The sloping plinth and pilaster buttresses are characteristic of Norman architecture.

The interior of the White Tower is somewhat obscured by the vast array of arms and armour on display. This magnificent collection recalls one of the chief functions of the Tower of London as its use as a palace declined – that of arsenal and armoury for the realm. Until 1812 it housed the mint and the Crown Jewels are still entrusted to the Tower's safe keeping. Above all, the Tower is celebrated for the sinister events arising from its use as a prison for illustrious captives, many of whom languished here en route to the block. Indeed, imprisonment within the Tower – and decapitation on Tower Hill – were jealously guarded privileges of the nobility! A list of victims reads like a roll call of tragic heroes and villains, ranging from the Scottish patriot

Sir William Wallace (1305) to the Jacobite Lord Lovat (1747). The Tower reached its zenith as a political prison in Tudor and early Stuart times. Dethroned monarchs have also suffered within its walls: Richard II was forced to abdicate and Henry VI and Edward V were murdered. Despite its strength, the Tower has a rather undistinguished military history. As well as falling to Prince John, it was ransacked during the Peasants' Revolt and bombarded into surrender by the Yorkists in 1460. Edward IV was the last monarch to spend much time in the Tower, though the tradition of lodging here before coronation lasted until James I's accession.

> *Access:* The precincts, White Tower and certain wall towers (Beauchamp, Bloody and Wakefield) are open daily. Other portions can be visited on guided tours.
>
> *Reference:* Guidebook by R. Allen Brown & P. E. Curnow. *The Tower of London* by G. Parnell. *HKW* (II).
>
> *Relations:* Dover and Colchester. Dover was one of the other castles strengthened by Henry III, along with Windsor, Corfe and York. Dover also has a prototype concentric curtain.

OTHER SITES Geoffrey de Mandeville's castle near *South Mimms* appears typical of the motte-and-bailey type, but excavations have demonstrated that the 'motte' was thrown up around the base of a wooden tower.

Norfolk

In the Middle Ages Norfolk was one of the most populous of English counties, as the vast number of ancient churches still testifies. Considering its size Norfolk has only an average number of castles but some fine examples survive. As usual, the story begins with the Normans who have left some mighty earthworks behind: Castle Acre, Castle Rising, New Buckenham and Thetford are quite formidable. The Norman contribution in stone is noteworthy too, with unusually ornate keeps at Castle Rising and Norwich and our earliest circular keep at New Buckenham. There was a lengthy pause in castle-building after the Norman era – a sign of peace and prosperity, though this affluence has left us with the town walls around Norwich and Great Yarmouth. Castles revived in the late Middle Ages, when the coastal areas lay exposed to foreign raids and the Norfolk gentry frequently indulged in attacks upon each other. The Paston Letters give an insight into their feuding way of life. The Pastons lived in Caister Castle, one of a group to be built of brick. This material gained swift acceptance in the county owing to the lack of good building stone. The brick gatehouses of Middleton and Oxburgh contrast well with flinty Baconsthorpe.

BACONSTHORPE CASTLE, three miles east of Holt, is the work of John Heydon, a somewhat dubious lawyer who rose to local prominence as a supporter of the Yorkists during the Wars of the Roses. Such a man had many enemies and it is not surprising that he should choose to build a house offering more than token defence. It was in fact one of the last true castles. As originally conceived the castle followed a quadrangular plan with square towers guarding the corners, except at the angle occupied by the gatehouse. John's curtain survives on two sides. It is a serious piece of defensive work with two intermediate, semi-circular towers facing west and a row of arrow-slits on the south. Later, perhaps after the castle had been inherited by his son Sir Henry in 1480, the courtyard was expanded to the north and east, leaving the gatehouse in the centre of the south front. Strangely enough the moat (now drained) always enclosed this larger area. The new curtain to the north was built in a much less sturdy fashion, though it still has flanking towers. On the east no curtain was ever built, perhaps because the moat expanded into a protective lake here. In its place are the remains of a building which was used for processing wool into cloth – a reminder of Norfolk's medieval economy. The oblong gatehouse is the most impressive feature of the castle, though very much a ruin like everything else. It was large enough to serve as a self-contained residence, at least in times of danger. In front of the outer gateway is a tall but shallow porch – 'barbican' would be rather too grand a term for it. The outer gatehouse dates only from Elizabethan times. It was occupied until 1920 – much longer than the rest of the castle – but is now an empty shell.

Access: Freely accessible (EH).
Reference: Guidebook by S. E. Rigold.
Relations: Kirby Muxloe is another late castle, and Compton is later still.

CAISTER CASTLE stands three miles north of Great Yarmouth, not at Caister-on-Sea but a little inland at West Caister. This brick stronghold is a monument to Sir John Fastolf. Fastolf was a distinguished veteran of the Hundred Years War, a knight of relatively humble origin who played an important part in the Lancastrian conquest of northern France. He is well known in the distorted guise of Shakespeare's Falstaff. Fastolf built this castle in 1432–46, when he was enjoying a prosperous retirement. On his death in 1459 Caister passed to the Paston family, whose letters give a first-hand portrayal of life in fifteenth-century Norfolk. Unfortunately for the Pastons, the Duke of Norfolk also laid claim to the castle and, when legal means had failed, he set about making good his claim by force. In 1469 he brought a considerable force to lay siege to the castle, which creditably held out for several weeks against the duke's cannon before the inevitable surrender. Although the castle was temporarily lost to the Pastons, on the duke's death they successfully claimed it back. In 1599 they abandoned Caister in favour of a new mansion nearby and the castle soon sank into ruin.

Most fifteenth-century castles were built by veterans of the French wars and a number were in fashionable brick. They tended to be showplaces, combining lavish accommodation with a show of strength. Some had a secondary role in coastal defence and Caister did repulse French raiders shortly after its completion. Caister was one of the finest of its kind but rather too much was pulled down in the eighteenth century. The castle stands in a wide moat still full of water. It is one of those with an inner quadrangle and a subsidiary 'base court' for retainers. (This is less obvious now because the arm of the moat between the two courtyards has been filled in.) There is also part of a third courtyard behind, attested only by a circular corner tower incorporated in a later house. The base court, of inferior brick, is now fragmentary and the main quadrangle had suffered so much destruction that only its north and west walls still stand. These lengths of curtain (quite remarkably) had machicolated parapets all the way along, partly surviving on the north. Originally there were domestic buildings on all four sides and their foundations can be seen. In the north-west angle rises the great cylindrical tower which is Caister's principal feature. This tower (ninety feet high) contained five storeys of living apartments. It was clearly the builder's private retreat, communicating directly with the hall which lay against the west curtain. The tower is pierced by gun ports and crowned by more machicolations. A tower house of these slender proportions is quite rare for England though the type is common enough in northern Europe. The layout of the castle has also been likened to the moated castles of the lower Rhine, suggesting (as at Tattershall) a continental architect.

>*Access:* The castle is open regularly in summer. There is a vintage car museum in the grounds.
>
>*Reference:* Guidebook by E. D. Smith.
>
>*Relations:* The Paston castle at Gresham. Brick castles such as Tattershall, Kirby Muxloe and Herstmonceux.

CASTLE ACRE: CASTLE AND TOWN DEFENCES The village of Castle Acre is a classic medieval township above the River Nar. The castle was first raised by William de Warenne, Earl of Surrey and Chief Justiciar to William the Conqueror. As at Lewes the De Warennes accompanied their castle with a priory for monks of the new Cluniac order. It is recorded that the monks were temporarily lodged in the castle bailey (more probably the town enclosure). Today the priory remains are the most notable feature of the village and a textbook example of a medieval monastery. The castle ruins are scanty in comparison but the earthworks are still impressive. A ruinous Norman curtain encircles the summit of a large, low motte with the stump of a keep inside. Its complicated building history was revealed by excavation in the 1970s. The keep began as William de Warenne's hall, standing within a modest ringwork bank. The castle became something more formidable as a result of the Anarchy. About 1140, under the third William de Warenne, the ringwork was raised into a motte and the hall became the base of a strong keep (note the thickening of the walls). A square tower divided by a cross-wall was intended, but before completion it was reduced to a narrow oblong structure. Soon afterwards the keep was demolished, probably as an adulterine castle after Henry II's accession. Evidently the keep was considered a threat but the rest of the castle was not. A portion of bailey curtain also survives, crowning the rampart bank, and the gatehouse has been uncovered. The castle seems to have been abandoned following the death of the last Warenne earl in 1347.

The bulk of the village stands within a ditched enclosure once believed to be of Roman origin owing to its rectangular outline. It is now clear that the earthwork is contemporary with the castle, showing that the Warennes founded a town alongside. Many of these Norman castle boroughs did not prosper but Acre seems to have flourished initially. A piece of wall crossing the castle ditch shows at least an intention to wall the town in stone, and a stone gatehouse survives. Known as the Bailey Gate, this simple structure has a tall gate passage and rounded corner turrets (*circa* 1200).

Access: The castle and Bailey Gate are freely accessible (EH).

Reference: Guidebook by J. G. Coad.

Relations: Lewes and the other Warenne castles at Reigate, Conisbrough and Sandal.

CASTLE RISING The village, four miles north-east of King's Lynn, takes its name from the Norman castle which dominates it. William d'Albini (or d'Aubigny), Earl of Sussex, started building here *circa* 1139. One of the foremost barons of his time, he was loyal to King Stephen but consolidated his own power during the Anarchy. William had married Henry I's widow and his keep was truly fit for a queen. Fortunately this one survived Henry II's accession. The D'Albini line died out in 1243. Edward III granted the castle to his mother, Queen Isabella. Despite her complicity in Edward II's death she was not a prisoner and lived here in great splendour. Unfortunately her domestic additions have left little trace. Following Isabella's death in 1358 the castle passed to the Black Prince and henceforth declined as an appendage of the Duchy of Cornwall. By Elizabethan times it was sinking into ruin.

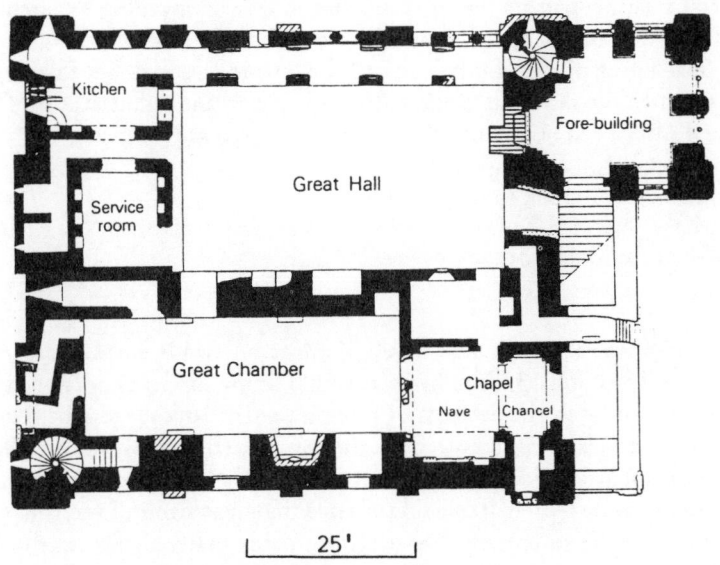

CASTLE RISING: KEEP AT FIRST-FLOOR LEVEL

Castle Rising's earthworks are prodigious, comprising an oval ringwork and a smaller bailey in front. Such is the height of the ringwork bank that it almost conceals the splendid keep within. This keep is the sole building of any substance left, though there was once a well-appointed group of residential buildings alongside. The only other masonry remains are the truncated gate tower and the ruin of an early Norman church. Set in a gap in the ringwork bank, the gate tower is contemporary with the keep but the surviving fragment of wall is later medieval. The church originally served the village. William d'Albini buried it in his rampart and built the beautiful church which still stands nearby in recompense.

The keep stands virtually intact, though long deprived of its roof and floors (except in the forebuilding tower). It is a rectangular structure which is considerably longer than it is high – in other words a hall-keep and the best example of this rare type. The ground floor was just an undercroft for storage, the principal accommodation lying on the floor above. Owing to its importance the first floor rises through two stages, giving the illusion of three storeys in all. The keep is divided longitudinally by a cross-wall, thus separating the hall from the solar at first-floor level. Stone vaults support a kitchen and pantry at one end of the hall, and another vault supports a chapel beyond the solar. Unlike other keeps with a 'double' storey there is no upper gallery, though a gallery does run along one wall at hall level.

There is the usual first-floor entrance, reached via an elaborate forebuilding which is divided into two parts: a square entrance tower rising the full height of the keep and a narrower annexe containing the staircase up to it. The original portal into the hall from the forebuilding tower is a sumptuous piece of Romanesque. It was later bricked up to form a fireplace. For some reason the staircase annexe is singled out for special treatment in its use of blank and interlaced arcading for architectural effect. Otherwise the exterior is typically severe, though handsome enough with its regular spacing of pilaster buttresses and the latrine chute arches forming a tidy composition on the west wall. Both in domestic layout and architectural refinement William d'Albini was no doubt influenced by the keep at Norwich.

Access: Standard opening times (EH).
Reference: Guidebook by R. Allen Brown.
Relations: Norwich. William d'Albini's work at New Buckenham and Arundel. The hall-keeps at Middleham and Bowes.

CLAXTON CASTLE was built by the Kerdistons. Two licences to crenellate are recorded, for 1341 and 1377. Either date would fit the surviving portion, a ruinous length of curtain with the remains of three rounded flanking towers. Two of the towers are placed close together to flank the entrance (the gateway is now blocked). Flint is the principal building material but a lot of early bricks are incorporated. The remains presumably represent one side of a quadrangular layout. Everything else was pulled down in the seventeenth century to provide materials for nearby Claxton Hall. The castle lies seven miles south-east of Norwich.

Access: On private land.

ELMHAM CASTLE At North Elmham is the ruin of a church which was once believed to be a Saxon cathedral but is now, rather disappointingly, regarded as an early Norman chapel. After it fell into disuse Henry le Despenser, a haughty and bellicose bishop of Norwich, converted the church into a hunting lodge, making a hall and solar out of the old nave and transept. In 1388 he obtained a licence to crenellate and dug the surrounding ditch. There is a large outer enclosure bounded by a wide ditch. Excavations have shown that no curtain was ever built, so these ditches were the only defence.

Access: Freely accessible (EH).

GREAT YARMOUTH TOWN WALL Modern Yarmouth embraces the sea but the old town turns its back on the coast. Instead it faces the River Yare which runs parallel to the coastline a short distance inland. The town rose to prominence as a port in medieval times and its defensive wall is unusually complete, though not intact. The right to collect murage was first granted in 1261 when the town was at the peak of its prosperity. However, building did not begin until 1285 and dragged on for most of the following century. Nothing survives of the accompanying castle. In contrast to most, the town wall was maintained and even strengthened in Tudor times to counter the threat of foreign invasion. Ironically the only siege came during Kett's Rebellion in 1549. The town was a Roundhead stronghold throughout the Civil War. Old Yarmouth was centred upon its quays so the area enclosed is correspondingly long and narrow. No wall was ever built along the river front but even so the circuit stretches for well over a mile. In places it is clear that the parapet is supported on arcades, the thin wall beneath each arch being pierced by an arrow-slit. More often the original arrangement has been obscured by the provision of an earth rampart against the inner face of the wall – a Tudor reinforcement against artillery. The wall was flanked by half-round bastions in the Edwardian manner and there are several larger towers at more salient locations. Altogether eleven towers remain but the ten gatehouses have all been demolished.

The circuit begins on North Quay with the circular North-West Tower, which stands intact though its parapet has given way to a conical roof. This tower is now isolated owing to the demolition of the stretch of wall to the east along Rampart Road, and the actual wall is first encountered beyond Northgate Street. Skirting St Nicholas' churchyard, the wall turns southwards at the octagonal stump of King Henry's Tower. It continues (with a few gaps) past several bastions and beneath a shopping complex. Further on is a triangular earthwork projection, added in the Elizabethan period to sweep the long east wall by artillery fire. The wall changes direction again at the South-East Tower, a handsome D-shaped structure enriched with chequer panels of flint and brick. There follows the best preserved stretch of wall, partly rebuilt after a collapse in 1557. Its parapet is pierced by frequent arrow-slits. The wall turns westwards at the Blackfriars' Tower. Near this tower the Tudor rampart is best preserved. The wall vanishes just before South Quay. Here stood the South Gate, barring the road to London. A tower stood on the edge of the river and from here a boom chain could be raised to prevent the incursion of unwelcome vessels.

Access: The remains are freely accessible (LA).
Reference: Turner.
Relations: The town walls of Canterbury, Southampton, Oxford and Newcastle. York's city wall is also mounted on arcades.

GRESHAM CASTLE was licensed in 1319. Sir Edmund Bacon was the builder but the Paston family later acquired it. The unfortunate Pastons, later forced out of Caister Castle by the Duke of Norfolk, also suffered disputed ownership here. In 1450 Lord Moleyns ransacked the castle while Sir William Paston was away. Today the castle is an overgrown tangle of masonry fragments rising out of a deep, dry moat. Clearance would reveal a lot more. It formed a small quadrangle with circular angle towers of different sizes, as shown in a fifteenth-century plan.

Access: On private land.
Relations: Caister.

KING'S LYNN TOWN WALL King's Lynn (or Bishop's Lynn as it was before the Reformation) grew up beside the Great Ouse near its exit into the Wash. Like Great Yarmouth, the town depended on its riverside wharfs and thrived on the profits of the wool trade. Unlike Yarmouth, its town wall (built from 1266) has virtually disappeared. The destruction began in 1643 when Lynn, alone among the ports of the East Coast, declared for the King and was besieged by Parliamentary forces. Apart from a low stretch in the gardens known as The Walks all that survives is the town's South Gate on London Road, preserved because of its later use as a gaol. This oblong structure with turrets and side-passages was built of brick in 1437. Its outer face was encased in stone early in the following century. There was never a castle here.

Access: The South Gate is visible from outside (LA).
Reference: Turner.
Relations: Great Yarmouth.

MIDDLETON TOWERS This mansion is still enclosed by a wet moat. Most of the present complex is the result of a rebuilding by Sir Lewis Jarvis in the 1860s but the brick gatehouse formed part of the original castellated house on the site. It was begun by Thomas, Lord Scales, and completed by Anthony Woodville, Earl Rivers. Both men were victims of the Wars of the Roses but on different sides. Lord Scales died fighting for the Lancastrians in 1460 and Earl Rivers lost his head when Richard III seized the throne in 1483. With its octagonal corner turrets rising a little above parapet height the gatehouse clearly owes a debt to Lord Cromwell's great tower at Tattershall. Appearance was as important as defence, hence the oriel window above the outer gate arch (the second oriel is Victorian). In all likelihood the rest of the complex would have been light on defensive features, with the gatehouse acting as a strongpoint, but this is just conjecture. Nearer Middleton village, a mile to the south, rises the motte of a Norman predecessor.

Access: Private.
Reference: Mackenzie (I).
Relations: Tattershall and the gatehouse at Oxburgh.

MILEHAM CASTLE is a substantial though overgrown Norman earthwork consisting of a motte and two semi-circular baileys, the one preceding the other. Both baileys are enclosed by ditch and rampart, and on top of the motte are some flint fragments of a square Norman keep. The castle existed by 1153 but its history is quite obscure. It was probably an unlicensed castle of the Anarchy, destroyed after Henry II's accession.

Access: On private land.

NEW BUCKENHAM CASTLE

NEW BUCKENHAM CASTLE A predecessor of the castle lay at Old Buckenham. About 1146 William d'Albini, Earl of Sussex, founded a priory on the site and erected this stronghold nearby. The massive ringwork is comparable with that of Castle Rising, D'Albini's seat in western Norfolk, though here for once the ringwork really is circular and the mighty rampart is surrounded by a water-filled moat. Just inside the ringwork bank lies the stump of a large circular keep. Only the bottom storey survives but if it dates from D'Albini's time then it is the oldest of England's surviving round keeps. Round towers for defensive purposes did not catch on in England until the late twelfth century. It is significant that this keep should be found in Norfolk, a county with many round church towers of Norman date. This was a pragmatic solution in the absence of good stone for making corners. The keep is built entirely of flint and as such is a very plain structure when compared with D'Albini's ashlar keep at Castle Rising. An incongruous feature imported from contemporary square keeps is the cross-wall, dividing the interior into two semi-circular apartments. To the east of the ringwork lies a strong outer bailey surrounded by its own rampart and ditch. Beyond it a length of ditch shows that William d'Albini intended a fortified borough beyond the castle. West of the ringwork is a second outer bailey preserving a part-Norman chapel which now serves as a barn.

Access: Apply to key keeper.
Reference: *New Buckenham Castle* by N. Holland.
Relations: Castle Rising. The round keeps at Orford and Conisbrough.

NORWICH CASTLE, CITY WALL AND COW TOWER

NORWICH CASTLE, CITY WALL AND COW TOWER Norwich and York were the biggest towns of medieval England after London, and Norwich was saddled with a royal castle within a year of the Norman Conquest. The site, at the heart of the old city, is a natural hillock which was scarped into a formidable motte – though a motte large enough to be regarded as an inner bailey. A car park occupies the site of the outer bailey. The strength of this earth and timber fortification is attested in 1075 during the rebellion of some disaffected barons. On the failure of the revolt the Earl of Norfolk fled abroad leaving his wife to hold the castle against William I's supporters, which she commendably did for a siege lasting three months.

On top of the motte there now stands a large square keep, unique for the rows of blank arcading which adorn the outer walls in between the pilaster buttresses. If the masonry looks too fresh it is because the exterior was entirely refaced under Anthony Salvin in the 1830s, but it is clear from old drawings that the new work is a faithful copy of the Caen stone original. No other Norman keep is so decorative – not even Falaise in Normandy, which might be called Norwich's twin. Falaise was built by Henry I and it is likely that Norwich was too. The probable date is 1119–32 when there was a pause in building the cathedral, thus releasing masons with the necessary skills. Some authorities would put the keep later on architectural grounds but there is no recorded expenditure under Henry II. The keep became derelict in the eighteenth century and the old cross-wall has been replaced by a Victorian arcade, inserted when the keep was re-roofed to form part of the Castle Museum. It is now difficult to visualise the original layout. There were three levels, comprising a ground floor for storage and a 'double' storey above, divided by the cross-wall into a hall and solar. Since it lacks an intermediate storey the keep seems rather squat and may be described as a hall-keep. In addition to the main cross-wall there were further subdivisions, as shown by a chapel apse contrived in the south-east corner and a kitchen fireplace in the north-west corner. A feature characteristic of all the greater keeps is the mural gallery running around the upper level. The forebuilding leading up to the ornate first-floor entrance is a Victorian restoration.

Norwich Castle suffered a fate shared by numerous urban castles, degenerating into use as a court house and prison (in the chapel corner are some late medieval carvings said to have been made by prisoners). Nineteenth-century gaol buildings, rehabilitated to serve the museum, occupy the rest of the motte. Edward I built a towered curtain around the summit in 1268–70 but only the footings of the drum towers which flanked the gatehouse are visible now.

The castle was last besieged (and taken) during the Dauphin Louis' invasion of 1216–17. Its subsequent decline was hastened by its position, the construction of the city wall from 1294 onwards leaving the castle in the middle of the city rather than on the perimeter. Much of the city wall can still be followed, the most rewarding stretch being at the south end of the circuit. Near Carrow Bridge is a rare survival: a rounded boom tower on each bank of the River Wensum, once connected by a chain which could be raised to bar the way to hostile shipping. From here the wall ascends Carrow Hill, on top of which is the cylindrical Black Tower – an uncommonly large tower for a city wall and evidently an important vantage point. Beyond this the wall follows the line of Queen's Road, Chapel Field Road and Grapes Hill, curving in a great arc back towards the river. Considerable portions remain, most impressively in Chapel Field Gardens, and there are several rounded and polygonal bastions. In places the parapet was carried on blank arcades, as at Great Yarmouth. The suburb to the north of the Wensum was also walled and there are remains (including two towers) along Bakers Road. All the gatehouses have perished.

The city wall ran for more than two miles but the perimeter of medieval Norwich was considerably longer, its east side relying upon the slender protection afforded by the river. Bishop Bridge – the only medieval crossing – was formerly barred by a gate tower. North of this, where the Wensum bends westwards, stands the Cow Tower, an isolated strongpoint erected by the cathedral monks in 1378. Though it supplemented the city's defences it served in a day-to-day capacity as a toll house. This impressive circular tower, now a shell, is a fine example of early brickwork.

Access: The castle is open regularly (LA). The city wall (LA) and Cow Tower (EH) are freely accessible.

Reference: Castle guidebook by B. Green. Turner for the city wall. *HKW* (II).

Relations: Other keeps attributed to Henry I at Guildford, Portchester, Bamburgh and Carlisle. Compare Great Yarmouth's town wall and the boom towers of Fowey and York.

OXBURGH HALL lies just outside the village of Oxborough, eight miles south-west of Swaffham. This stately brick mansion is surrounded by a wide, water-filled moat. Sir Edmund Bedingfeld obtained a licence to crenellate in 1482 but the house may have been well under way by then, because the licence pardons him for any works already undertaken. However, as we might expect at this late date Oxburgh has only limited pretensions as a defensive structure. In fact it consisted of four purely domestic ranges around a courtyard, the only defensive feature being the gatehouse which dominates the north front. This lofty structure is flanked by semi-octagonal turrets which rise through seven stages, their surfaces enriched with decorative arcading. Cross-slits command the outer gateway and a wide machicolation over-hangs it. The vaulted gate passage preserves its original oak gates. The upper floors are reached by a spiral staircase built entirely of brick, including the moulded handrail. It is possible to cite Oxburgh as the last example of a keep-gatehouse which could have sustained its owner during dangerous episodes. However, there are large windows quite low down on the courtyard side and the whole edifice must have been more for show than anything else. An exaggerated version of this gatehouse in a totally unfortified context is Layer Marney Tower (Essex). The rest of Oxburgh Hall has been modernised by later members of the Bedingfeld family and the hall range was pulled down in the 1770s.

Access: Open regularly in summer (NT).
Reference: Guidebook by H. Bedingfeld.
Relations: The brick castles of Caister, Middleton and Tattershall.

THETFORD CASTLE On the west side of town is a ringwork site (Red Castle), which excavations have shown was thrown up around a church soon after the Norman Conquest. So this was probably the original castle, raised by William de Warenne before his death in 1088. By 1100 Thetford was in the hands of Roger Bigod. It was he who founded the priory and perhaps he also transferred his castle to the stronger site further east on Castle Hill. He utilised the defences of an Iron Age fort but only a section of the double ditch and rampart has survived. The dominant feature in any case is the Norman motte – a classic conical mound rising to nearly seventy feet and as such probably the tallest artificial motte in England. There is no evidence that this castle developed any masonry defences and it came to any early end. The octogenarian Hugh Bigod, Earl of Norfolk, joined Prince Henry's revolt of 1173–74. Henry II's supporters captured and destroyed the castle, though the site remained occupied into the next century.

Access: Castle Hill is freely accessible (LA).
Reference: Renn.
Relations: For William de Warenne see Castle Acre. For the Bigods see Bungay and Framlingham.

THETFORD WARREN LODGE This small tower house stands off the Brandon road, two miles west of Thetford. Though now an empty shell it survives virtually intact. Dating from the fifteenth century, the tower is strongly built but only two storeys high. The windows are kept depressingly small and a murder hole is concealed above the simple entrance doorway. Thetford Warren was a hunting ground of the priors of Thetford and the tower probably served as the residence of the priory's gamekeeper at a time when poaching was rife.

Access: Freely accessible (EH).

WEETING CASTLE, two miles north of Brandon, belonged to the De Plaiz family in Norman times. The remains date from the late twelfth century, making it an early example of a manor house with only limited defensive capability. Instead of the powerful earthworks associated with the castles of this period the house was surrounded by a shallow rectangular moat, though a mound in one corner is probably an altered motte. Inside the enclosure are the fragmentary remains of a hall with a square tower at one end. It is a flinty ruin typical of East Anglia. The tower was, in effect, a small keep, though its connection to a hall looks ahead to the tower houses of the later Middle Ages. Enough remains to show that the tower had a fine apartment on the first floor, i.e. at the level of the hall which stood over an undercroft.

Access: Freely accessible (EH).
Relations: Cranborne Manor is similar.

OTHER SITES A rectangular enclosure at *Old Buckenham* was the predecessor of New Buckenham Castle. Norman motte-and-baileys can be found at *Horsford* and *Wormegay*, the latter deriving much of its strength from surrounding marshland. *Swanton Morley* preserves a moated castle enclosure. *Dilham* (near North Walsham) preserves the stump of a pentagonal castle tower.

Northamptonshire

Northamptonshire has lost a great deal. Of its chief castles Northampton has vanished, Fotheringhay is no more than a grassy mound and even Rockingham only survives in part. Rockingham Castle at least preserves its Edwardian gatehouse, while Barnwell is a little-known castle of the Edwardian type with stout walls, round towers and a towered gatehouse. The tower house at Longthorpe is chiefly interesting for its wall paintings. The main survivors are curiously concentrated at the northern end of the county, as if anticipating invasion from the Wash.

ASTWELL CASTLE About midway between Helmdon and Wappenham rises an embattled gate tower, complete with a tall stair turret and a lower annexe. The archway has been blocked. It formed part of a manor house, probably erected by John Lovett before he disposed of it in 1471. Nothing else is left of the original complex and there is no evidence of fortification. The tower now stands beside a farmhouse which is the only remnant of a Jacobean mansion.

Access: Private.

BARNWELL CASTLE   On the Duke of Gloucester's estate at Barnwell can be seen three successive manorial centres in close proximity. First there are the earthworks of a Norman motte-and-bailey, now hidden in a clump of trees. Then comes the massive stone ruin of Barnwell Castle, built by Berengar le Moine *circa* 1264–66. It seems that Berengar took advantage of Henry III's preoccupation with his barons to build a strong adulterine castle. Berengar later sold his new castle to Ramsey Abbey. It is said that he was compelled to do so by Edward I as a punishment for building it without a licence. Barnwell remained with the abbey until the Dissolution, when it was purchased by Sir Edward Montague. He erected the present house – Barnwell Manor – nearby.

The castle is an interesting example of thirteenth-century military architecture with some delightfully experimental touches. On a smaller scale it anticipates the great castles which Edward I would build in Wales in the following decades, and though it pre-dates Edward's coronation by several years it is a rare English example of a pure 'Edwardian' castle. An unusually thick curtain – well preserved except for the loss of its parapet and a single breach on the west – surrounds an oblong

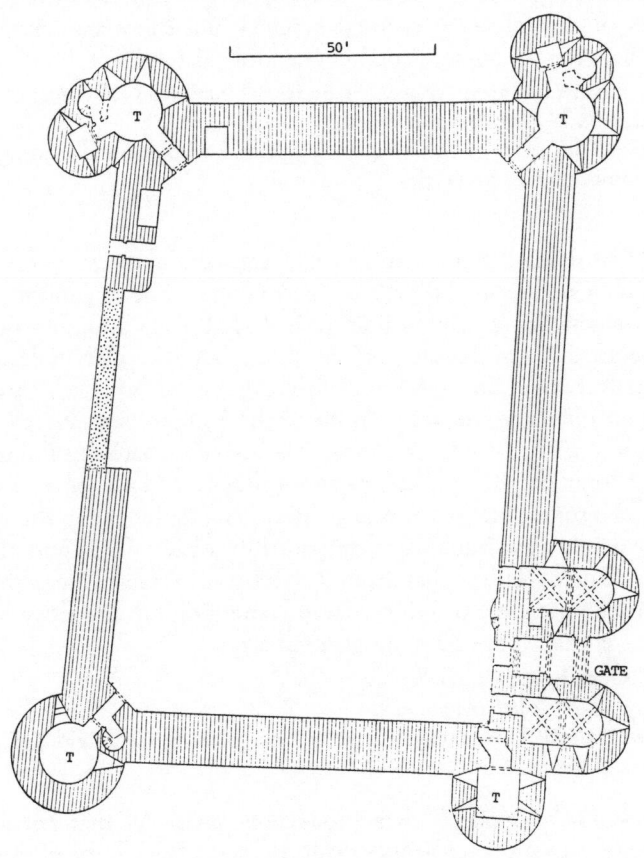

BARNWELL CASTLE

courtyard. Circular towers project boldly at three angles, the fourth being occupied by the gatehouse. The two northern towers are quite eccentric as they both have a smaller round tower projecting from them, resulting in a figure-of-eight plan. The prime function of these subsidiary towers was domestic rather than military. They contained latrines serving the apartments in the main body of the towers. The south-west tower has no projections but its upper floors are square internally for greater domestic convenience. The latrine for this tower was accommodated in a more conventional manner within the thickness of the curtain. Barnwell has an early example of the fully-developed Edwardian gatehouse – a long, vaulted gate passage flanked by U-shaped towers. It is interesting to see how determined the architect was to facilitate flanking fire along every stretch of curtain. As the gatehouse towers only project eastwards he erected a half-round tower at right angles to flank the south curtain. The towers are well provided at ground level with long arrow-slits which have two horizontal slots, special care being taken to ensure that each stretch of curtain was covered from both ends. Nothing remains of the domestic buildings and the bailey now serves as a tennis court. No windows pierce the curtain, showing that the internal buildings were very much lean-to affairs, in contrast with the quadrangular castles of the following century which would show a marked degree of integration between the domestic buildings and the defences.

Access: Private, but open occasionally under the National Gardens scheme.
Reference: VCH *Northamptonshire* (III).
Relations: The similar gatehouse at Rockingham. Leybourne and Mettingham castles also became religious properties.

DRAYTON HOUSE   Set in the middle of a large park to the west of Lowick, near Thrapston, is an architectural jumble of many periods. The core of this mansion is a medieval manor house centred upon a hall. The hall's antiquity is no longer apparent because it was transformed in 1702, but the solar undercroft has a thirteenth-century vault. In 1328 Simon de Drayton obtained a licence to crenellate. He created an oblong courtyard in front of the hall and surrounded it with an embattled curtain. On the sides the curtain has been eliminated by Tudor wings but the entrance front stands complete, its austerity relieved by a series of crenellated buttresses and a square gate tower (the archway was refashioned in the seventeenth century). Evidently no attempt was made to fortify the back of the house. The present turreted facade here is late medieval and it is difficult to regard Simon de Drayton's curtain as anything more than a showy facade. The additions and alterations of later periods have reinforced this domestic atmosphere.

Access: Open by appointment only.
Reference: BOE *Northamptonshire.*
Relations: Fortified manor houses such as Broughton, Stokesay and Aydon.

FOTHERINGHAY CASTLE is a melancholy sight. All that remains of this famous pile are the motte-and-bailey earthworks and a fallen lump of masonry. The earthworks, sited above the River Nene, go back to the castle's foundation – probably by Simon de Senlis (or St Liz), Earl of Northampton, soon after 1100. Edward III gave Fotheringhay to his son, Edmund of Langley, and the castle developed into a favourite seat of the dukes of York who were to contest and win the English throne. It was reconstructed in a sumptuous fashion, though more as a palace than a fortress. The nearby collegiate church, only half preserved, gives some indication of the splendour lost. The castle is chiefly remembered now for its association with two of British history's most enigmatic characters: Richard III, who was born here in 1452, and Mary Queen of Scots, whose long imprisonment was finally ended by execution in the courtyard (1587).

Access: Obtain permission to visit at the farm.
Reference: VCH *Northamptonshire* (II).
Relations: Mary Queen of Scots was imprisoned at Wingfield Manor, Tutbury, Bolton and vanished Sheffield Castle.

LONGTHORPE TOWER, two miles west of Peterborough, is a tower house attached to one corner of a hall. The house dates from the thirteenth century and the tower was added *circa* 1300, when Robert de Thorpe held the manor. Its two lower storeys are vaulted. The ground floor was a store room entered only from outside. It has no connection with the solar above which originally was reached only from the house. There is then a straight stair to the bed chamber above. What distinguishes the tower from many others is the remarkable set of wall paintings adorning the solar, discovered in the 1940s beneath numerous layers of whitewash which had concealed and preserved them since the Reformation. They date from the first half of the fourteenth century. They depict a combination of religious and secular themes and the artistry is surprisingly good. That such fine paintings could adorn the walls of a comparatively modest residence reminds us of the vast amount which has been lost.

Access: Limited opening times in summer (EH).
Reference: Guidebook by E. Clive Rouse.
Relations: Wall paintings at Chester and Belsay.

ROCKINGHAM CASTLE enjoys a commanding position overlooking the valley of the Welland, in idyllic rural surroundings though just two miles north of Corby. The Domesday Book tells us that William I founded the castle. In 1095 it was the venue for the Council of Rockingham which settled the differences between William Rufus and Archbishop Anselm. The castle was basically a royal hunting lodge and popular as such until Edward III's reign. King John came here most years of his reign. A more dramatic episode was the rebellion of the constable, William de Fortibus, in 1221. Hubert de Burgh laid siege and the young Henry III came to watch the fighting. In 1544 the decaying castle was leased to Edward Watson who converted the old residential buildings into a house. During the Civil War the castle's Roundhead garrison withstood several Royalist attacks and sustained a great deal of damage. Evidently the defences were largely demolished afterwards but the house survived and is still occupied.

William the Conqueror's castle consisted of a motte between two baileys. The southern bailey has virtually disappeared and even the motte has been levelled, its circular site now marked by a rose garden. Of the north bailey defences only the east curtain and its gatehouse survive. These remains probably reflect the £200 spent here by King John. The embattled gatehouse is rather a squat structure, only two storeys high but perfectly preserved. It began as a gateway flanked by square bastions. The gap between the towers was then filled in to form an oblong gatehouse, Edward I adding the pair of semi-circular towers pierced by cross-slits. Edward's hall forms the core of the existing house which stands within the bailey. Externally the hall's origin is concealed by Tudor windows and gables, and the interior has been subdivided into several rooms. The other wings are Tudor work with Victorian towers added to improve the skyline.

Access: Limited opening times in summer.
Reference: HKW (II). Souvenir guide.
Relations: Edward I's gatehouses at St Briavels and the Tower of London.

THORPE WATERVILLE CASTLE   Three miles north of Thrapston is the moated site of a castle built by Walter de Langton, Bishop of Lichfield. A licence to crenellate was given in 1301. The castle was quite a sumptuous edifice and the bishop illicitly cut costs by taking all the timber he required from woods belonging to a nearby abbey. Today the site is occupied by a farmhouse and a large barn. The barn was actually the castle hall – hence the octagonal chimney. The carpenters fashioned a noble roof out of the stolen timbers. There are no remains of any defences, if in fact there were any.

Access: Private.
Relations: Bishop Langton's work at Eccleshall and Lichfield.

WOODCROFT CASTLE belonged to the Woodcroft family in the thirteenth century, but a Lawrence Preston was here in 1297 and that date is about right for the castle. Presumably it was a quadrangular stronghold with corner towers, though quite modest in scale. The 'shouldered' lintels of doorways show a close affinity with the Edwardian castles of Wales. However, it is possible that the castle was never finished. All that remains is the entrance front, with a gate tower in the middle and a circular tower at the left end. It survives because a Tudor house backs onto the curtain. Admittedly the gate tower is rather feeble for the Edwardian age. It does not project from the line of the curtain and there was no drawbridge or portcullis. Deprived of its battlements, the castle lacks an appearance of strength. If the other three sides ever did exist they may have disappeared as a result of the Civil War. Woodcroft survived the main conflict without incident, but it was seized during the Royalist uprising of 1648 and had to be stormed by the Roundheads. The castle stands five miles north-west of Peterborough.

Access: Visible from the road.
Reference: Mackenzie (I).
Relations: The Edwardian castle at Barnwell.

OTHER SITES Chief among the vanished castles of Northamptonshire is *North-ampton Castle*. Founded by Simon de Senlis *circa* 1100 but soon taken over by the Crown, the castle was among the most celebrated of medieval strongholds with an exceptionally thick curtain wall. Having been garrisoned by Parliament throughout the Civil War, both castle and town wall were torn down following the Restoration. The last vestiges of the castle were swept away in 1845 to make room for the railway station.

Norman earthworks are scattered across the county though none are particularly impressive. There are ringworks at *Long Buckby*, *Preston Capes*, *Sibbertoft* and *Sulgrave*. Motte-and-baileys include *Lilbourne* and *Castle Dykes* (near Farthingstone). *Clifford's Hill* (near Little Houghton) is a large, isolated motte. Close to Peterborough Cathedral rises *Mount Thorold*, a motte named after the first Norman abbot of Peterborough. Extensive moats mark the position of a castle at *Braybrooke*, while Elizabethan *Castle Ashby* stands near the site of a medieval predecessor.

Northumberland

For much of its history Northumberland has been border country. Hadrian's Wall sweeps across the southern end of the county, while in 1018 the Battle of Carham established the River Tweed as the boundary between England and Scotland. It was a disputed frontier since the English kings claimed overlordship of Scotland and the Scottish kings laid claim to the Border counties. David I (1138) and William the Lion (1174) both took advantage of civil wars in England to make good this claim by force. Nevertheless in Norman times relations between the two kingdoms were *relatively* cordial. Norman castles are not especially numerous in Northumberland, though most of the great ones originated in this period: Alnwick, Bamburgh, Newcastle, Norham, Prudhoe and Warkworth all show their Norman origins.

A 'golden age' of peace in the thirteenth century was shattered by Edward I's determination to bring about a union by force. With the collapse of English aggression at Bannockburn the consequences fell upon northern England, and the Border counties especially. Full-scale invasions were admittedly few, once Robert Bruce had finished venting his fury, but incessant skirmishes devastated the county. It was an era of raids and sieges, and grudge battles such as the moonlit clash at Otterburn (1388). The great barons, notably the Percys, conducted private wars with their counterparts across the Border. Older castles were revamped and new ones appeared. Lightly-fortified Aydon and massive Dunstanburgh are the earliest of the new crop. There followed fortified quadrangles at Chillingham, Etal and Ford, and tower houses such as Belsay, Chipchase and Langley. Sometimes the gatehouse is the dominant feature as at Dunstanburgh, Bothal and Bywell. In Northumberland the fortified house became the rule rather than the exception, even for the lesser gentry who built pele towers in large numbers. A survey commissioned in 1415 lists over a hundred castles and peles in the county, while a survey of the Western and Middle Marches in 1541 shows that the numbers had doubled in the ensuing century. As

169

the clergy enjoyed no immunity from raids some of these towers were 'vicar's peles', as at Corbridge. Even monasteries were fortified, notably Tynemouth Priory which became an important stronghold in its own right.

The prospect of invasion diminished following the destruction of the Scottish army at Flodden in 1513. However, Berwick was given its ring of artillery-proof ramparts under Elizabeth I and conditions remained wild in the elevated western half of the county. Anarchy reigned and the 'Border reivers' made a living out of raiding. In this environment some pele towers continued to be built and the 'bastle' evolved, though these rustic, thick-walled farmhouses can only be classed as defensive in the most rudimentary sense. The union of the Scottish and English crowns in 1603 gradually ushered in more peaceful conditions.

ALNHAM: VICAR'S PELE Alnham, in the upper Aln valley five miles west of Whittingham, was burnt by the Scots on at least one occasion, in 1532. There were two pele towers here but only one survives, close to the church. The survey of 1541 confirms it was a vicar's pele. It is a massive cube of fifteenth-century date, dwarfing the house which has been put up alongside but devoid of original features. It was restored from ruin and re-battlemented in the 1830s.

Access: Visible from the road.
Relations: The vicar's peles at Corbridge, Elsdon, Embleton and Whitton.

ALNWICK ABBEY was a house of Premonstratensian canons founded in 1147. It stands a short distance west of the castle and town of Alnwick, on the opposite bank of the Aln within Hulne Park. The gatehouse is one of the handful of monastic gatehouses designed on keep-gatehouse lines, available as a refuge when required. No attempt was made to defend the entire precinct. Square turrets project boldly at the four corners and a machicolated parapet protects the entrance. The gate arches were blocked after the Dissolution when the building was utilised as a pele tower. The gatehouse was probably built in response to the Black Douglas' raids, heraldic shields on the turrets depicting the Percy arms as they were after 1385.

Access: Exterior only.
Reference: BOE *Northumberland* (2nd edn).
Relations: The fortified monasteries of Hulne, Lindisfarne and Tynemouth.

ALNWICK CASTLE AND TOWN WALL Alnwick's importance stems from its position, guarding what was the main road north across the River Aln. The first castle here is attributed to Ivo de Vescy *circa* 1096. In 1138, when David I of Scotland took possession, the castle was described as 'very strong'. It is doubtful if the defences were yet of stone but stone walls were provided later in the twelfth century under Eustace Fitz John or his son William de Vescy. Another Scottish king, William the Lion, besieged the castle in 1174. This time the castle held firm and the King was captured in an ambush.

When the Vescy line died out Alnwick was bequeathed to the Bishop of Durham, who sold it to Henry de Percy in 1309. A general reconstruction of the castle followed. The Percy lords – every one a Henry – quickly emerged as leading figures in the Border wars but they still found time to participate in the French campaigns and the wider political sphere. The fourth Henry Percy, created Earl of Northumberland, was instrumental in Richard II's downfall and then revolted against Henry IV. Following the Battle of Shrewsbury (1403) the King pursued him to Northumberland and Alnwick Castle surrendered under the mere threat of a cannon bombardment. It changed hands four times during the Wars of the Roses, when Northumberland became a last resort for the defeated Lancastrians. In the 1760s, following a century or more of neglect, the first Duke of Northumberland restored the castle from its semi-ruinous state. In a second great restoration a hundred years later Anthony Salvin swept away this 'Gothick' work, giving the exterior a veneer of rugged austerity while creating a suite of magnificent state apartments inside the keep. The castle is still occupied by the dukes of Northumberland.

The beautiful view from the far bank of the river has been carefully contrived but Alnwick remains an exceptional medieval castle, even if the two restorations have taken their toll on the fabric. It preserves its Norman layout of two baileys with a motte in between. Enough original masonry survives to show that the flattened motte and both baileys were walled even in Norman times, but the towered curtains now date largely from the Percy reconstruction. The first Henry de Percy died six years after purchasing Alnwick and probably got no further than rebuilding the shell keep. This means that the curtain around the baileys must be the work of his son. However, some portions of curtain and several of the towers were rebuilt in the eighteenth and nineteenth centuries, the keep suffering particularly heavy treatment. The stone figures crowning the battlements in various places reflect a Northern tradition, though the ones here are eighteenth-century replacements.

One of the highlights of the castle is the unspoilt outer gatehouse. This is a strong gate tower with polygonal turrets clasping the outer angles. The fine barbican in front has its own flanking turrets and a panel bearing the Percy lion. Only two of the mural towers in the outer bailey are original: The square Abbot's Tower at the north-west corner and the semi-circular Auditor's Tower, which survives amid the accretions built onto the south curtain. The narrow gap between the keep and the south curtain is closed by a much-restored gatehouse leading to the inner bailey. There are three mural towers here: Postern Tower (square), Constable's Tower (D-shaped) and the rebuilt Record Tower. On the north the ends of the curtain once linked up with the keep, but these lengths of wall were demolished in the 1760s when a terrace was created overlooking the river.

The shell keep is the most heavily restored part of Alnwick Castle. Only one of its half-round flanking towers preserves much original material. However, the gatehouse leading into the keep survived both restorations and ranks with the outer gatehouse in terms of interest. It is actually an addition by the second Henry Percy, traditionally financed from the ransom of Scottish prisoners taken at Neville's Cross in 1346. The entrance is flanked by tall octagonal towers with heraldic shields just below the battlements. There is a long, vaulted gate passage beyond. The gatehouse acts as an extension to the original Norman gateway with its sumptuous chevron ornament. Within the compact enclosure of the keep Salvin's Italianate state apartments come as a complete surprise. They have obliterated the medieval residential buildings. Salvin added the lofty Prudhoe Tower which now dominates the castle. Its place was previously occupied by a tall and slender watch tower.

In addition to the river on its north side, the castle is protected to the south and east by a deep ravine. This separates the castle from the town, which developed under the patronage of the Vescys but suffered severely in the Border wars. The townsfolk belatedly obtained the right to collect murage in 1434. Nothing survives of the town wall but two gatehouses bear witness to its course. Pottergate is a sham reconstruction of 1768 but Bondgate is the genuine article. This austere block has shallow towers flanking the gate passage. It is sometimes called Hotspur's Gate after the first Earl of Northumberland's famous son, but he fell at Shrewsbury decades before this gate was built. The Percys actually contributed little to Alnwick's wall and it took the impoverished town half a century to complete it.

> *Access:* The castle precincts and state rooms are open regularly in summer. Two of the towers contain museums. Bondgate (LA) is visible from outside.
> *Reference:* Castle guidebook. BOE *Northumberland* (2nd edn). Turner for the town wall.
> *Relations:* The Percy castles of Warkworth, Cockermouth, Spofforth and Topcliffe. Compare the towered shell keeps at Berkeley and Farnham, and the barbicans at Tynemouth and Warwick.

ANCROFT CHURCH   Northumberland has a number of 'vicar's peles' standing close to their parish churches but Ancroft, five miles south of Berwick, is the only example of a pele which doubles up as a church tower. (Cumberland has a few more instances of this dual role.) St Anne's Church is basically Norman. The massive tower was built into the nave about 1300, clumsily blocking the fine entrance portal. Apart from its location this is a typical pele tower, with a vaulted ground floor entered only from the church and a spiral stair leading to the three upper floors.

> *Access:* The church is normally open.
> *Relations:* The Cumbrian church peles at Burgh-by-Sands, Great Salkeld and Newton Arlosh.

AYDON CASTLE,   two miles north-east of Corbridge, graphically illustrates the collapse of order in Northumberland in the stormy years following Edward I's invasion of Scotland. The entire complex was built in several stages over the course of twenty years or so. It began as a manor house erected in the last years of the thirteenth century. The house had the advantage of a strong setting above the Cor Burn but was otherwise unfortified. The builder was Robert de Reymes, a wealthy Suffolk merchant who purchased the manor in 1296. It proved a disastrous investment. Owing to the shock of Scottish raids it soon became necessary to take defensive measures. De Reymes obtained a licence to crenellate in 1305 and literally crenellated his house, i.e. put battlements on top. He also created a small courtyard in front of the hall. These rudimentary precautions proved ineffective. The Scots sacked the place in 1315 and, in a separate incident, De Reymes was taken prisoner and ransomed. Probably after this raid a curtain wall was built around a large outer courtyard, defending the vulnerable approach from the north. Surprisingly, there was never a pele tower.

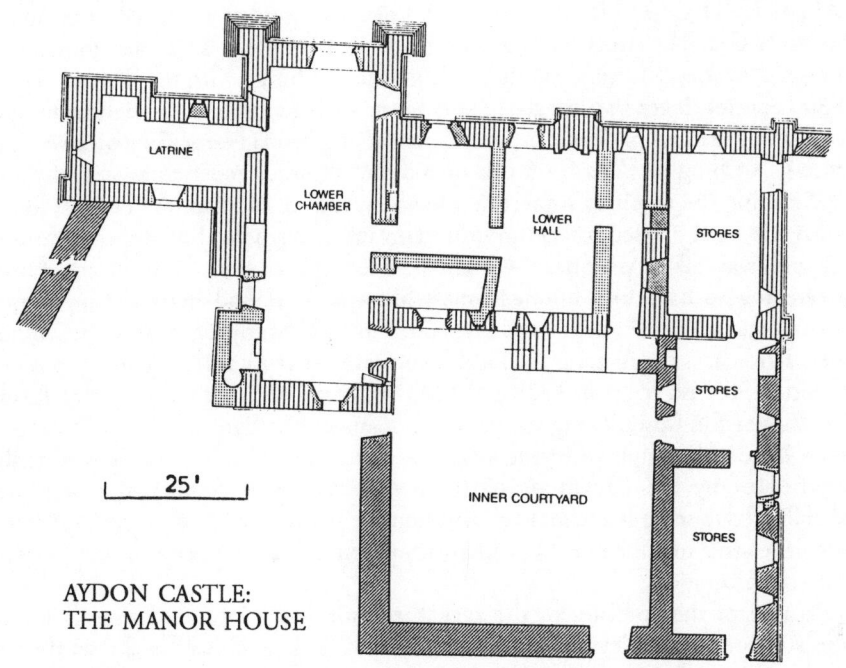

LATRINE

LOWER
CHAMBER

LOWER
HALL

STORES

STORES

INNER COURTYARD

STORES

25'

AYDON CASTLE:
THE MANOR HOUSE

The outer curtain is now quite ruinous. Its northern apex is protected by a U-shaped tower but the entrance is a simple gateway without flanking towers. Ahead lies the inner courtyard which is remarkably well preserved. Aydon is in fact one of the finest surviving manor houses of its era. Later additions to the fabric have been minimal because the castle was let to tenants from the fifteenth century onwards and such people did not have the means to make fashionable changes. The house is L-shaped, the main axis being occupied by the hall with a kitchen wing at right angles to it. The other two sides of the inner courtyard are bounded by a wall with an embattled parapet pierced by arrow-slits. Like many of its contemporaries, the hall stands over an undercroft and is still reached from the courtyard by an external staircase. Beyond the dais end is a projecting solar wing – longer but narrower than the hall – and beyond that a latrine block. A number of two-light windows survive and there are several original fireplaces, notably the reset one in the solar. The fireplace in the hall undercroft has a curious chimney flue overlooking the Cor Burn. There was no fireplace in the hall itself, which must have been heated by a central hearth (the present hall roof is a sixteenth-century replacement).

Access: Standard opening times in summer (EH).

Reference: Guidebook by P. Dixon.

Relations: For Robert de Reymes see also Shortflatt. Compare the contemporary fortified manor houses at Markenfield and Stokesay.

BAMBURGH CASTLE occupies a lofty basalt crag rising up to 150 feet out of the North Sea. The situation makes it one of the strongest – and most romantic – of English castles. Medieval tradition identified Bamburgh with the 'Joyous Garde' of Sir Lancelot. It enters recorded history in the sixth century AD as 'Bebbanburgh', the seat of the kings of Bernicia. The Mercian King Penda besieged it twice without success. Nothing remains from this period and the rock re-emerges as a castle in 1095 during the revolt of Robert de Mowbray, Earl of Northumberland. William Rufus was hard pressed to capture this daunting stronghold, but Robert ventured out and was taken prisoner. William paraded the earl in front of the castle, threatening to have him blinded unless his wife (who had been left in charge) surrendered. Once taken, the castle remained in royal hands for most of the Middle Ages, acting as a check upon the local barons as well as a bastion against the Scots. It resisted Scottish sieges in 1328 and 1333 but changed hands several times during the Wars of the Roses, being battered into ruins by the Earl of Warwick's cannon when Lancastrian fugitives made a last stand here in 1464. The castle was finally disposed of by the Crown in 1610. In the eighteenth century the keep was rehabilitated to serve as a school and almshouses. The rest lay abandoned until 1894, when the arms manufacturer Lord Armstrong purchased the castle and undertook a drastic restoration.

Because of the confines of the rock the castle has a long and narrow layout consisting of three baileys in line. The western bailey is at a lower level than the rest and its walls are fragmentary, while the severe curtain enclosing the middle bailey is now largely Lord Armstrong's. Only the tall, cylindrical Bell Tower (from Henry III's reign) is authentic. It occupies one corner of the bailey and is all the more impressive for rising straight out of the precipice. Beyond the keep stretches the curtain of the eastern or inner bailey. It retains much late Norman masonry, albeit considerably altered owing to the state apartments which back onto it. There are two square flanking towers of different sizes.

Below the eastern tip of the castle are twin semi-circular turrets which flank the outer gateway. From here a steep slope ascends through a restored gate tower towards the summit. Although the curtain has been rebuilt on the seaward side it is clear that this rock-cut approach has never been easy. Attackers could have been bombarded with projectiles from above. The ascent ends at the massive keep, square in plan with corner turrets which rise above parapet level. Though clearly Norman, the keep's precise date is a matter for conjecture. It may be Henry I's work. Some authorities suggest the Scottish King David, since Northumberland was ceded to the Scots during the Anarchy. Others prefer Henry II, though if so the expenditure is not reflected in the royal accounts which survive from his reign onwards. Unusually for a Norman tower keep, the entrance is at ground level and there is no trace of a forebuilding, as if the inaccessibility of the site was considered defence enough! In contrast to the rest of the castle the keep is relatively unspoilt externally, though since it is one of the few Norman keeps to remain habitable the interior has seen many changes. Its four storeys are divided by a cross-wall and a gallery runs around the top level.

Within the inner bailey are grandiose state apartments, entirely rebuilt by Lord Armstrong though the hall preserves the dimensions and some of the masonry of its medieval predecessor. The foundations of an apsidal Norman chapel have been exposed across the courtyard.

Access: Open regularly in summer.
Reference: BOE *Northumberland* (2nd edn). *HKW* (II). Souvenir guide.
Relations: The cliff-top strongholds at Dunstanburgh, Tynemouth and Scarborough. Compare the Norman keeps at Newcastle, Carlisle and Pendragon.

BELLISTER CASTLE overlooks the South Tyne opposite Haltwhistle. The natural mound was used as a ready-made motte by the Normans. On top is the denuded ruin of a thirteenth-century hall with a defensive tower at one corner. John Blenkinsopp took up residence here in the 1480s and the existing castellated house may incorporate his pele tower, though it is unrecognisable after several adaptations over the centuries.

Access: Open by appointment (NT).
Relations: The halls at Aydon, Featherstone and Haughton.

BELSAY CASTLE is often called a pele tower, an impression reinforced by the Jacobean house alongside. However, for centuries the building was a free-standing tower house, and one of considerable grandeur. The walled courtyard which accompanied it has vanished, but the tower itself survives intact and virtually unaltered. It stands in the landscaped grounds of Belsay Hall – a Grecian successor mansion built for Sir Charles Monck in 1815. The castle dates from the fourteenth century but its precise date is unknown. Widdrington once had a very similar tower which was licensed in 1341. If Belsay is contemporary then its builder was Sir John de Strivelyn, a veteran of the Scottish wars. By 1370 the estate was back in the hands of the Middleton family. They had held Belsay previously but forfeited it for spearheading a local revolt against Edward II.

The main body of the tower is oblong and three storeys high, consisting (from the bottom upwards) of a vaulted kitchen, a hall and a solar. It is now entered from the adjoining house. The ground-floor doorway occupies a shallow recess in the middle of the west front, so the tower may be regarded as having two thin projecting wings on this side. In the north 'wing' are four storeys of chambers; in the south the spiral stair and a sequence of tiny rooms, including an oratory. This south-west corner of the tower rises higher than the rest, accommodating six storeys in all. The tower is still roofed over though the floor which divided the hall from the solar has gone. On the walls of the hall are considerable remains of wall paintings, comprising heraldic devices over a floral background. Two tall, traceried windows light this level. The walls are crowned by machicolated parapets, while the corners are capped by round bartizans which have their own machicolations. Thomas Middleton erected the attached house (now a shell) in 1614, as the inscription over the porch tells us.

Access: Standard opening times (EH).
Reference: *An Account of Belsay Castle* by A. E. Middleton.
Relations: Bewcastle is also attributed to John de Strivelyn. Compare the towers at Chipchase and Langley.

BERWICK CASTLE AND TOWN WALL

Berwick-upon-Tweed is said with some justice to have suffered more sieges than any place with the possible exception of Jerusalem. In the Middle Ages it changed hands a bewildering number of times, being a bone of contention between England and Scotland. The town developed as a prosperous port on the north bank of the Tweed under the patronage of the kings of Scotland. Berwick was first ceded to England in 1175 as one of the conditions of release forced on William the Lion following his capture at Alnwick. Richard I sold it back to the Scots to help pay for his Crusade. Although sacked by King John in 1215, Berwick remained in Scottish hands until Edward I invaded in 1296. The native townsfolk were massacred after its fall and English colonists were sent to repopulate the vacant borough. Sir William Wallace temporarily recovered Berwick for the Scots and Robert Bruce seized the town by a ruse in 1318, Edward II failing to recover it. Edward III blockaded the town into surrender (1333) and Berwick remained English for the rest of the fourteenth century, with one brief exception. Then, during Henry Percy's revolt against Henry IV, the rebels handed Berwick over to the Scots in return for support. Henry IV marched north and captured the town after a cannon bombardment (1405). Berwick's last period in Scottish hands was similarly initiated by the deposed Henry VI in a desperate effort to regain his throne. It was recaptured (at the second attempt) by a large English army under Richard, Duke of Gloucester, in 1482. Since then it has changed hands no more, though the existing defences bear witness to the invasion scares of the next three centuries.

Medieval Berwick was strongly defended by its castle and town wall. The stone wall, with a circuit over two miles long, was commenced by Edward I and strengthened after Robert Bruce captured the town. However, little survives of the medieval defences. Instead Berwick is renowned for its Elizabethan fortifications which are among the best of their kind in Europe. They were actually begun in 1558, i.e. late in Queen Mary's reign, when war with France rekindled fears of a Scottish invasion in support of their old ally. Sir Richard Lee, who had worked on the defences of Calais prior to its fall, was brought in to oversee the construction and a number of Italian engineers were consulted. Work proceeded amid several changes in design, since the science of artillery fortification was developing rapidly in this decade. The problems were compounded by the presence of the older town wall, which had been strengthened as recently as Henry VIII's reign. The new enclosure was to be smaller than its predecessor, the northern part of the old walled town being abandoned. After Mary Queen of Scots fled to England the perceived threat from Scotland diminished and the defences were left little more than half complete in 1570. That is why the Elizabethan rampart only guards the landward (north and east) sides of the town. To the south and west, along the Tweed estuary, the medieval wall was left in commission.

Since they are designed for defence by (and against) artillery, the defences of Berwick are very different in conception to medieval town walls. The stone wall is just a low retaining wall backed by a wide earth rampart devised to cushion the shock of cannon fire. Defence was conducted chiefly from the enormous bastions – platforms from which counter-fire could be directed at an attacker. They also allowed cross-fire along the base of the rampart from the gun chambers located in the neck of each bastion. It is these considerations which dictated the peculiar, 'arrow-head' form of these bastions, rare in England but often encountered in artillery fortifications elsewhere. There are five bastions on the ramparts of Berwick: Meg's Mount, Cumberland Bastion, Brass Bastion, Windmill Bastion and King's Mount. The first and last, since they mark the ends of the Elizabethan rampart, are incomplete. The earthen mounds on top of the bastions are a Civil War enhancement. Of the two gates through the defences Scotsgate (north) is a nineteenth-century enlargement but the Cow Port (east) is original. Most of the riverside wall is no longer medieval, having been rebuilt with gun batteries following the Jacobite invasion of 1745. The only exceptions are the stretch between King's Mount and Fisher's Fort and the rounded Coxon's Tower at the south corner of the circuit.

Some fragments of the medieval town wall can be seen in the abandoned north part of the circuit. The main survivors are the octagonal Bell Tower and a semicircular gun battery called Lord's Mount, the latter one of Henry VIII's improvements. Beyond, on a bluff above the river, are the sad remnants of Berwick Castle. Founded in the twelfth century by one of the Scottish kings (probably David I), this celebrated royal stronghold was falling into decay when the Elizabethan town defences were built. Most of what remained was swept away in 1850 to make room for the railway station. Only the ruinous west curtain of the castle was permitted to survive as a boundary wall. It probably incorporates some pre-1296 masonry though the projecting semi-circular tower is an early Tudor gun emplacement. The curtain continues as a spur wall, dropping steeply down the hillside to the remains of another gun tower on the river bank. The wall-walk descends in a series of steps amply justifying their nickname of 'Breakneck Stairs'. Edward I is credited with the spur wall in the years following his conquest of the town.

Access: The castle and town defences are freely accessible (both EH).
Reference: The Fortifications of Berwick-upon-Tweed by I. Macivor. *HKW* (II & IV).
Relations: Carlisle as a Border town. The Elizabethan fortifications at Portsmouth, Carisbrooke and Pendennis.

BITCHFIELD TOWER is a fifteenth-century pele which belonged to the Middleton family. Its relationship with Belsay Castle, their main residence just a mile to the north, is unclear. Larger windows were inserted by Robert Fenwick, who added or rebuilt the attached house in 1622. The authentic exterior of the tower conceals a history of decay followed by a 1930s transformation to make it habitable again.

Access: Private.
Relations: Belsay.

BOTHAL CASTLE is strongly situated on a spur overlooking the River Wansbeck, three miles east of Morpeth. A Norman castle may have occupied the site but the existing structure is the work of Robert de Bertram, who received a licence to crenellate in 1343. Three years later Bertram won distinction for his valour against the Scots at Neville's Cross. On his death Bothal passed to the Ogles, and in 1410 Sir Robert Ogle wrested the castle from his brother in a squabble over their inheritance. After a long period of decay the castle was made habitable again from 1830, the old gatehouse being restored from ruin and the present house put up alongside. The gatehouse was always the principal feature of Bothal Castle, substituting for the tower houses which were more common in the county. The inconvenience of such a keep-gatehouse is evident in the chamber over the gate passage, which suffered the intrusion of drawbridge and portcullis gear as well as murder holes (now blocked) littering the floor. Semi-octagonal towers flank the outer entrance, rising to an embattled parapet which preserves two stone warrior figures in the manner of Alnwick. Just below the battlements a series of shields depicts the arms of Edward III, the Black Prince and prominent local families. The rest of the castle is now very much a ruin, comprising no more than some pieces of curtain which enclosed a narrow, oblong courtyard between the gatehouse and the steep fall to the river.

Access: Visible from the road.
Reference: *Bothal Observed* by R. Bibby.
Relations: Alnwick. The Bertram castle at Mitford.

BYWELL CASTLE rises on a low cliff above the River Tyne, four miles south-east of Corbridge. It is attributed to Ralph Neville, Earl of Westmorland for the long period 1425–84, but Bywell was a relatively minor Neville stronghold. The castle certainly existed by 1464 because in that year it received the deposed Henry VI as a fugitive from the Battle of Hexham. Henry fled on the approach of the Yorkists and Bywell surrendered without a fight. From a distance the castle looks like a typical Northern tower house but it is actually a gatehouse, or rather a combination of the two. This oblong building survives in good condition though it is now an empty shell. The gate passage is flanked by vaulted guard rooms. There is a straight staircase to the first floor with a nasty surprise at the top – a murder hole which could be manned from a window recess above it. The first floor was divided into two living rooms while the large second floor apartment formed the hall. Above the gate arches to front and rear the embattled parapet projects outwards on machicolations, while dainty machicolated turrets rise up at the four corners. Though not a water gate the gatehouse fronted the river, making access to the courtyard more difficult. A survey of 1571 shows that the courtyard defences were left incomplete, but there is still a piece of curtain attached to the gatehouse and the adjacent house incorporates an undercroft.

Access: Visible from the road. Open occasionally.
Reference: BOE *Northumberland* (2nd edn).
Relations: The keep-gatehouses of Bothal and Dunstanburgh. For the Nevilles see Brancepeth, Raby, Middleham and Sheriff Hutton.

CARTINGTON CASTLE is a small but complex ruin. In medieval times it was held by the Cartingtons. The oldest part is the very ruinous curtain with square towers at the eastern corners – a quadrangular castle in miniature. This dates from the early fourteenth century. Later in the century a tower house was added against the north-east corner of the enclosure. It is built of ashlar with a vaulted ground floor and a projecting stair turret. The hall range was added alongside the tower in the fifteenth century – perhaps in 1442 when John Cartington obtained a licence to crenellate. New windows were inserted in Jacobean times, but in 1648 the owners joined the Royalist uprising and the castle was slighted by the Roundheads. Finally, in the 1890s the ruins were restored by Lord Armstrong to provide a romantic vista from his Cragside mansion. Today only the south walls of the tower and the hall stand up high. The remains lie on farm land two miles north-west of Rothbury.

Access: Obtain permission to view at the farm.
Reference: Jackson, *Castles of Northumbria.*
Relations: Small courtyards with tower houses at Edlingham and Mortham.

CHILLINGHAM CASTLE, five miles south-east of Wooler, is an appealing blend of medieval stronghold and Jacobean mansion set in landscaped grounds. The white cattle of Chillingham – the only wild cattle left in England – have roamed the park here since medieval times. In 1296 the Scots descended upon Chillingham and set fire to the manor house, but it was not until 1344 that Sir Thomas de Heaton obtained a licence to crenellate. His castle is one of only two standard quadrangular castles in Northumberland. It is still complete but subsequent alterations have been considerable. The four corners are guarded by massive, oblong towers, none of them projecting at all beyond the curtain. It has been suggested that the south-west tower is an older tower house, though evidently not much older. Except on the north the buildings around the courtyard are all medieval in origin, as their barrel-vaulted undercrofts testify. The south range has always contained the hall but the position of the original entrance to the castle is uncertain.

In the sixteenth century, after Chillingham had passed to the Greys, the internal buildings and the two north corner towers were largely rebuilt. The latter may have been necessary as a result of damage sustained in 1536, when the castle was bombarded by the rebel army of the 'Pilgrimage of Grace'. With the Border still a restless place the reconstruction was undertaken with defensive considerations fully in mind. A different spirit prevailed *circa* 1620 when a second great remodelling commenced. The north range of the castle was rebuilt as a grand entrance front in the Classical idiom, a design attributed doubtfully to Inigo Jones. It was during this phase that the courtyard attained its present appearance, with a peculiar gallery placed in front of the hall range.

Access: Open regularly in summer.
Reference: BOE *Northumberland* (2nd edn).
Relations: The quadrangular castles of Ford, Lumley and Bolton.

CHIPCHASE CASTLE preserves one of the finest of the Northern tower houses. With its machicolated parapet and round bartizans the tower bears a close resemblance to Belsay Castle. Walter Heron acquired Chipchase by marriage in 1348 and he probably built the tower in the ensuing decade. The Herons were responsible for maintaining law and order in the district but on more than one occasion they were accused of complicity with the Scots. Their tower stands on a rise overlooking the North Tyne, two miles south-east of Wark-on-Tyne. It was divided into four storeys – one more than Belsay – comprising a vaulted ground floor with the kitchen, hall and solar occupying the upper floors. The tower is still roofed but the intervening floors have perished. A shallow projection at one corner contains the entrance doorway and the spiral stair. The entrance is still guarded by a wooden portcullis which could be raised from a small chamber on the floor above. Other small rooms occupy this position on the two upper floors and at hall level there is a tiny oratory in the thickness of the wall. Notice the latrine chutes which project from the tower at hall and solar level.

Although an older house stood alongside, the tower now occupies one corner of a mansion built by Cuthbert Heron in 1621, heralding the arrival of more settled conditions even here. When the mansion was remodelled in the eighteenth century dummy windows were set into one side of the tower to match the remainder of the facade.

Access: Limited opening times in summer.
Reference: Guidebook by W. Percy Hedley.
Relations: Belsay. For the Herons see Ford.

COCKLAW TOWER Five miles north of Hexham stands the ruined pele tower of the Errington family, probably built soon after 1415 since it is not mentioned in the survey of that year. Unusually, this tower has entrances both at ground- and first-floor levels. It rises virtually to full height but the parapet has vanished and the ground-floor vault has partly collapsed. In the thickness of the wall is a sinister prison reached only by a hole in the floor above. Standing rather dismally on a farm, the tower continues to decay.

Access: On private land.

COCKLE PARK TOWER This pele tower is attributed to Robert, Lord Ogle, who inherited in 1465. It is oblong with a narrow wing built across the north end, forming a T-plan structure. The north side of the wing presents a martial face to the outside world, with round bartizans connected by a row of machicolations, but the main body of the tower has been transformed by Georgian Gothic windows. It stands three miles north of Morpeth, beyond Hebron.

Access: Exterior visible.
Relations: For the Ogles see Hepple and Tosson.

CORBRIDGE: VICAR'S PELE The long history of Corbridge is attested by its Roman military depot and the Saxon church tower. Not least among the town's attractions is the Vicar's Pele, which stands on the edge of the churchyard and is built of re-used Roman stones. It is the perfect example of a fortified priest's residence, built on a small scale but quite self-contained. The vaulted ground floor is reached through an archway which retains its iron-studded door. From here a straight staircase in the thickness of the wall leads to the first floor, strictly the hall though in a small tower such as this it is better regarded as the priest's dining room. One small refinement usually lacking in the secular lords' dwellings of the period is the stone wash basin at the head of the staircase. Another straight stair leads past a latrine to the solar, which has lost its wooden floor. Despite its small size the tower has a functional parapet with machicolated corner turrets. It was probably built soon after

1300 so it is a survivor from the early years of the Border wars. A second, somewhat altered pele tower exists in Corbridge, attached to Low Hall in Main Street.

Access: Open regularly in summer (LA).
Reference: Toy, *Castles of Great Britain.*
Relations: The vicar's peles at Alnham, Elsdon, Embleton and Whitton.

COUPLAND CASTLE, four miles north-west of Wooler, consists of a lofty pele tower attached to a house of the 1820s. The tower is evidently a late one – this area, so near the Border, remained in a state of chaos well after the union of the two kingdoms – but the date 1619 carved on a fireplace inside is considered a couple of decades too late for a tower of this kind. It is interesting to note that the tower relied upon a conventional parapet for defence whereas in Scotland, the emphasis had by now shifted to gun ports at ground level. A taller wing contains the staircase up to first-floor level, though beyond that the stair is contained in an angle turret, leaving the wing free for extra accommodation. This arrangement shows the influence of the Scottish L-plan, though here the wing projects from the middle of one side. Whatever its date, the tower was built by a member of the Wallis family.

Access: Private.
Reference: BOE *Northumberland* (2nd edn).

CRASTER TOWER, overlooking the little port of Craster, is one of the peles first mentioned in the survey of 1415. It may be a century older. A smaller wing adjoining the tower incorporates the original hall. The present mansion was built in 1769 and the interior of the tower was remodelled in 'Gothick' style at the same time. It is still occupied by the Craster family who have lived here since Norman times.

Access: Open by appointment.

CRESSWELL TOWER is an intact but roofless pele on the coast overlooking Druridge Bay. For long the home of the Cresswell family, it existed by 1415. The tower has the customary ground-floor vault and a stair turret at one corner. The first-floor doorway indicates that a house always stood alongside. It developed in later centuries into a large mansion but only the tower has survived demolition.

Access: On private land.

DALLY CASTLE overlooks the Chirdon Burn, four miles west of Bellingham. In 1237 a Scot, David de Lindsay, was building a castle here without royal approval, and work seems to have been stopped before completion. The remains are of an elongated, oblong building with corner turrets – a fortified hall rather than a tower house, though it was rebuilt on tower house lines by the Swinburnes in the fourteenth century. Little more than footings remain but the bases of several 'fish-tailed' arrow-slits have survived.

Access: Freely accessible.
Relations: Elongated tower houses such as Haughton and Askham.

DILSTON CASTLE, perched above the Devil's Water a mile south-west of Corbridge, is a ruined tower house showing three main stages of development. The main axis of the building is an oblong pele tower attributed to William Claxton who inherited in 1417. The block at the north end, creating an L-plan tower, was added by the Radcliffes over a hundred years later, while the projecting tower at the south end is another addition. Note that the original pele was divided into three storeys whereas the additions have four. New windows and fireplaces were provided throughout in the Jacobean period. At that time Dilston was expanded into a large mansion but the adjacent chapel is the only relic.

Access: Obtain permission to visit at Dilston Hall.
Reference: Jackson, *Castles of Northumbria.*

DUNSTANBURGH CASTLE is spectacularly sited on a basalt headland jutting into the sea. Thomas, Earl of Lancaster, began building here in 1313. During its construction the Scots gained the initiative in their struggle for independence and the north of England lay at their mercy. The blame for this may well be laid at Thomas' door, since his refusal to join Edward II's forces for the campaign which foundered at Bannockburn probably tipped the odds against the King. This incident is typical of Thomas' stormy relations with his royal cousin and suggests that Dunstanburgh was intended more as the remote refuge of a defiant magnate than as a new link in the chain of Border defences. A brief reconciliation between Edward and Thomas accounts for the issue of a licence to crenellate in 1316, though the castle was almost complete by then. As a potential refuge it came to no avail, since Thomas was captured after the Battle of Boroughbridge and put to death by royal command at Pontefract Castle (1322). Dunstanburgh remained a possession of the House of Lancaster but found itself surplus to requirements following the union of the duchy with the Crown in 1399. The castle's decay was hastened by the Earl of Warwick, who twice battered the walls for the Yorkist cause in the 1460s. It is now very much a ruin.

Dunstanburgh's irregular layout was determined by the headland on which it stands. The great courtyard – such a contrast to the compact quadrangles prevalent at the time – could easily have accommodated Earl Thomas' vast retinue. Despite the steep falls there was a curtain on all sides, more strongly built on the south which offers the only level approach. From left to right the south front is defended by the mighty gatehouse and three square flanking towers, the last one (Egincleugh Tower) housing a postern. The only other mural tower is the Lilburn Tower on the west wall, capped by tall corner turrets. On the west and east the curtain has been reduced to its footings, while on the north it has been eaten away by cliffs which drop nearly a hundred feet to Embleton Bay.

The chief feature of the castle is the massive gatehouse, one of the largest in England and typically Edwardian in combining the functions of gatehouse and keep. D-shaped towers flank the entrance passage. The second (top) floor contained the hall, while the silhouette of the gatehouse is dramatised by twin watch turrets. However, the proximity to the gate defences must have proved inconvenient for domestic life. In the 1380s John of Gaunt blocked the gate passage and made a new entrance, protected by a barbican, though the curtain nearby. This had the effect of turning the keep-gatehouse into a keep alone. (The blocking walls were taken down by the Victorians.) John of Gaunt increased his security by creating the tiny walled courtyard immediately behind his keep. Evidently he lived in the keep when he was in residence, since the ruined house in the courtyard formed the constable's lodging.

Access: Standard opening times (EH/NT). The castle is reached by footpath from Craster or Embleton.

Reference: Guidebook by C. Hunter Blair & H. L. Honeyman.

Relations: Pontefract. For situation, compare Bamburgh, Tynemouth and Scarborough. See the Edwardian gatehouses of St Briavels and Tonbridge.

EDLINGHAM CASTLE can be found in a deep valley five miles south-west of Alnwick, overawed by a disused railway viaduct. Only the ruined tower house stands up high, but excavations in 1978–82 uncovered a walled courtyard in front and its footings have been left on view. The castle developed from a hall-house attributed to William de Felton, who purchased the manor in 1295. Polygonal corner turrets show that defence was not entirely absent from the outset, but the curtain was added by one of William's descendants in the fourteenth century. A domestic range lies at right angles to the hall and a long barbican protected the entrance. The tower house rises at the back of the hall, virtually free-standing though it was connected to the hall by a passage. This handsome tower may be the work of Sir Edmund Hastings who inherited in 1402. Note the huge fireplace and the outline of an elaborate vault which covered the lofty apartment, probably the solar, on the first floor. Diagonal corner buttresses (capped by round bartizans) supported its weight, but ultimately the vault collapsed taking part of the tower with it.

Access: Freely accessible (EH).

Reference: BOE *Northumberland* (2nd edn).

Relations: The halls at Aydon, Featherstone and Haughton.

ELSDON CASTLE AND TOWER Elsdon Tower stands close to the village church. It may have been newly built at the time of the 1415 survey, which reveals that it was a vicar's pele. The tower was modified in the sixteenth century, as the gable behind the parapet (in Scottish fashion) suggests, and the interior shows many later changes. A row of machicolations overhangs the original entrance and the arms of the Umfraville family can be seen on the parapet. Their castle, known as Mote Hills, is an impressive motte-and-bailey earthwork just to the east, across the Elsdon Burn. Its ditched motte (with a rampart around the top) and embanked bailey are attributed to Robert de Umfraville in the early twelfth century. Soon after Henry II's accession the Umfravilles abandoned the site for Harbottle Castle, which accounts for the lack of any later masonry here. The village is three miles east of Otterburn.

Access: The tower is visible from the road. The castle is freely accessible.

Reference: BOE *Northumberland* (2nd edn).

Relations: Harbottle. The vicar's peles at Alnham, Corbridge, Embleton and Whitton.

EMBLETON TOWER is a vicar's pele with a nineteenth-century vicarage attached. According to tradition the tower was built in 1395 after the village had suffered in a Scottish raid, but the relatively narrow profile suggests that an older solar block was incorporated. It is a well-preserved example of its kind, its ground floor divided into two vaulted chambers. The corbelled parapet was purely for show as it would have been too low to shield any defenders.

Access: Visible from the churchyard.
Relations: The vicar's peles at Alnham, Corbridge, Embleton and Whitton.

ETAL CASTLE was built by Robert Manners, a licence to crenellate being granted in 1341. Despite its position a few miles from the Border the Manners family seem to have been more preoccupied in feuds with their neighbours, the Herons of Ford Castle. This culminated in a siege in 1428, after which the castle seems to have been abandoned to its hereditary constables, the Collingwoods. There is no record of hostility from the Scots until 1513, when James IV captured it en route to his defeat and death at Flodden nearby. After that a small royal garrison was installed here but by 1564 the castle was uninhabitable.

The castle was protected on two sides by steep banks falling to the River Till. Today the chief features of the ruin are the tower house and gatehouse, which occupied the west and east corners of an irregular quadrangle. The gatehouse, flanked by square towers, bears the Manners arms over the outer archway. In the chamber above are traceried windows and a doorway high up which must have led to a wooden hoarding. The rectangular tower house was entered at ground level through a forebuilding which has largely collapsed. Its four storeys comprised a store room, kitchen (note the big fireplace), hall and solar. A well-preserved length of curtain links the gatehouse to the vaulted stump of the south corner tower. Little else of the curtain survives and the north corner tower, if one existed, has vanished.

Access: Standard opening times in summer (EH).
Reference: BOE *Northumberland* (2nd edn).
Relations: Ford.

FARNE TOWER Inner Farne, the largest of the Farne group of islands, was used as a retreat by the Northumbrian saints Aidan and Cuthbert. Durham Cathedral later established a small Benedictine community in this hallowed place. The chapel of St Cuthbert still remains and beside it rises Prior Castell's Tower, a large pele erected for the safety of the monks *circa* 1500. It serves to show that even this island refuge was not safe. The tower was modernised in the eighteenth century but it retains the usual ground-floor vault. On the first floor is a piscina, suggesting that this room also served as a chapel.

Access: Exterior only (NT). The island is reached by boat from Seahouses in summer.
Relations: Monastic peles at Hulne, Carlisle and Lanercost.

FEATHERSTONE CASTLE is attractively situated in the meadows of the South Tyne, four miles south-west of Haltwhistle. The Featherstonehaugh family lived here at least from the thirteenth century and the buttressed west range of the mansion, overlooking the river, dates back to that era though quite transformed by later alterations. Thus Featherstone began as an unfortified hall but the Border wars compelled Thomas de Featherstonehaugh to provide for his own security. About 1330 he erected a tower at the south end of the hall (part concealed by the nineteenth-century porch). This is one of larger peles, well-preserved externally though the interior has been altered in keeping with the rest of the mansion. The tower is unusual for its projecting wing which is reminiscent of later Scottish L-plan tower houses. However, the Scottish tower wing evolved as a secure place for the entrance whereas here it is purely an annexe. The Featherstonehaughs were involved as much in blood feuds with their neighbours as in fighting the Scots. The other three ranges and their corner towers are now the romantic, castellated vision of Thomas Wallace from 1812 onwards.

Access: Visible from the road.
Reference: BOE *Northumberland* (2nd edn).
Relations: The halls of Aydon and Haughton, and the L-plan pele towers at Lemmington and Arnside.

FORD CASTLE The present serenity of Ford Castle belies its turbulent history. Sir William Heron obtained a licence to crenellate in 1338 and erected a quadrangular stronghold – something of a rarity in the Border counties. This castle was damaged by the Scots on three occasions: First during a raid in 1385, then by James IV before the Battle of Flodden and finally by cannon bombardment as late as 1549. Thomas Carr created an Elizabethan mansion out of the remains – rather an audacious act for the time in this unsettled region. Ford has been restored several times since, most recently by the Marchioness of Waterford who cleared away the neo-Gothic accretions in the 1860s.

Towards the approach the castle presents a castellated wall which is medieval revivalism of the eighteenth century. The courtyard thus enclosed is considerably larger than the medieval quadrangle, which only occupied its north-western quarter. The south and east sides of the original castle have been levelled and the north side is occupied by the mansion. Only the west side is recognisable because its two square angle towers still stand, the five-storey King James' Tower being incorporated into the mansion and the smaller Cow Tower (with a recessed top storey) standing isolated to the south. Another survivor is the old tower house, embedded in the mansion's right wing and no longer recognisable as such. Between the castle and the parish church is the ruined stump of the Parson's Tower, a vicar's pele.

Access: Private, but visible from the churchyard (LA).
Reference: BOE *Northumberland* (2nd edn).
Relations: The quadrangular castle at Chillingham. Another branch of the Herons occupied Chipchase.

HALTON TOWER is a tall and impressive pele, two miles north of Corbridge and barely a mile from Aydon Castle. Like other towers near the line of Hadrian's Wall it is built largely of re-used Roman stones. Rounded bartizans clasp the embattled parapet in the style of Belsay and Chipchase, though the tower is not machicolated. It is recorded that Halton was burnt by the Scots in 1385 and the pele may have been built shortly afterwards by William Carnaby. The adjoining house occupies the normal position alongside, but it dates only from the 1690s and part of a medieval hall stands across the rear of the tower.

Access: Private.
Relations: Belsay and Chipchase.

HARBOTTLE CASTLE overlooks its village in the upper Coquet valley, eight miles west of Rothbury. Odinel de Umfraville, at Henry II's behest, moved here from Elsdon Castle in 1157. The castle surrendered to the Scots during William the Lion's invasion of 1174, resisted John Balliol's supporters in 1296 but fell again to Robert Bruce in 1318. After the Umfraville connection ended in 1436 Harbottle became the headquarters for the Warden of the Middle March, the wildest sector of the Scottish Border. Efforts at repair, however, do not seem to have kept pace with the mounting decay. Today the motte-and-bailey earthworks are still impressive but the masonry remains continue to crumble. Only the western half of the bailey was ever walled in stone and the surviving length of curtain divides the bailey down the middle (with no evidence of an accompanying ditch). At the motte end are vestiges of a gate tower. Bits of wall on the motte denote a late Norman shell keep. The two surviving gun ports here are insertions of Henry VIII's reign, their 'letter-box' form common in contemporary Scotland but not in England.

Access: Obtain permission to visit at the post office.
Reference: Jackson, *Castles of Northumbria.*
Relations: The Umfraville castles of Elsdon, Prudhoe and Cockermouth.

HAUGHTON CASTLE crowns the steep bank of the North Tyne a short distance down-river from Barrasford. This tall and narrow structure is quite unusual among the tower houses of the North. The castle takes this form because it embodies a thirteenth-century hall of the Swinburnes. With the outbreak of Border warfare such houses became easy targets. We have seen how Aydon's hall was expanded into a castle and how a pele tower was added onto the hall at Featherstone. The solution here was novel because the tenant raised the hall into a tower house. This transformation is attributed to Gerard de Widdrington who inherited in 1327. He heightened the walls, putting battlements on top and erecting the square turrets which rise higher still, four at the corners and one corbelled out in the middle of the south front. On the two long sides the parapet was supported on a row of five arches with machicolations on the underside. Such machicolated arcades are rare in England though common in the South of France. Unfortunately the arcades were later walled up so they are now only visible in outline. Haughton was plundered twice by Scottish reivers in Tudor times. It was restored from ruin in the nineteenth century, the lower annexe being an addition by Anthony Salvin.

Access: Private, but visible from the river.
Reference: BOE *Northumberland* (2nd edn).
Relations: Aydon and Featherstone. Compare the machicolated arcades at Southampton.

HEFFERLAW TOWER stands three miles north of Alnwick on a gentle hill overlooking the old course of the Great North Road. This diminutive but well-preserved shell belonged to Alnwick Abbey. It is too small for a genuine pele tower and seems to have served merely as a look-out post, its commanding position allowing early warning of raids. Two carved panels depict the abbot's crozier and the badge of the fourth Percy Earl of Northumberland (1469–89).

Access: On private land.
Relations: Alnwick Abbey.

HEPBURN TOWER, though sometimes called a bastle, is a large and relatively comfortable pele. A tower of the Hepburn family is first mentioned in 1514 and the unusually thick walls suggest a medieval origin, but the windows and the double gable indicate a thorough remodelling in the Elizabethan period. The interior is now filled with trees but the walls still rise to full height, except for one narrow breach caused by the collapse of the spiral stair. It stands in Chillingham Park, a mile south of the castle.

Access: On private land.

HEPPLE TOWER, by the River Coquet at one end of the main village street, is a ruined pele attached to a much later house. Its walls were strong enough to survive an attempt to demolish it in the nineteenth century. Nevertheless one side has fallen, taking some of the barrel vault with it. The tower was held by Sir Robert Ogle at the time of the 1415 survey but it probably dates from the previous century.

Access: Visible from the road.
Relations: For the Ogles see Cockle Park and nearby Tosson.

HEXHAM CASTLE Hexham and its environs ('Hexhamshire') came under the rule of the archbishops of York in medieval times. To the east of the magnificent priory church stand two fortified structures which formed the administrative centre of this little principality. Admittedly the term 'castle' is not in general use. There is an oblong tower known as the Manor Office and a complex gatehouse known as the Moot Hall. According to tradition the courtyard between them was enclosed by a stone wall. The Moot Hall is believed to date from *circa* 1400. It comprises a long gate passage and a machicolated block to one side. The latter contained the archbishop's court house and lodgings for his officials. At each end of the gate passage a square tower rises higher than the rest, the inner and outer gateways being recessed within tall, machicolated arches.

The Manor Office has a double vault at ground level and a continuous line of corbels which once supported a machicolated parapet. There is nothing to distinguish it from many other tower houses of the period, but it was erected in 1330 expressly for use as the archbishop's gaol. As a purpose-built medieval prison it is almost unique but in this wild area there was a pressing need for one. In 1538 a band of reivers managed to break into the tower and free their captive comrades.

Access: The Manor Office contains a museum of Border life. The Moot Hall is only visible from outside (both LA).

Reference: BOE *Northumberland* (2nd edn).

Relations: The archbishops' castle at Cawood. Compare the prison 'keep' at Lydford.

HULNE PRIORY overlooks the River Aln in the idyllic surroundings of Hulne Park, three miles north-west of Alnwick. It was probably the earliest Carmelite friary to be founded in England (*circa* 1240). There are still considerable remains of the church and claustral buildings, but the friary is notable for its surrounding wall which here takes the form of a defensive curtain, with a continuous parapet on top reached by straight stairways from the precinct. The wall survives complete though the battlements have perished. There are two gates, one Tudor and the other a Georgian insertion. A wall such as this is quite exceptional, even in Border country. It suggests the patronage of the Percys of Alnwick. The wall had no flanking towers, however, and must have proved too long to patrol effectively. Hence the prior later turned to the conventional refuge of a pele tower. An inscription in the curtain nearby (now illegible) records that the tower was built by Henry Percy, Earl of Northumberland, in 1488. The tower survives complete to the top of its square corner turrets, though the windows were Gothicised in the eighteenth century when the Duke of Northumberland was landscaping his park.

Access: Obtain permission to visit. Hulne Park can be visited – on foot only – at weekends.

Reference: BOE *Northumberland* (2nd edn).

Relations: The monastic pele at Farne and the fortified monasteries of Lindisfarne and Tynemouth.

LANGLEY CASTLE is an ambitious fourteenth-century tower house commandingly positioned above the Langley Burn, two miles south-west of Haydon Bridge. The main building is an oblong block, its narrowness indicating that the tower has actually developed out of an older hall. Originally there was only one room per floor but the living quarters are augmented by further chambers in the four square angle towers. These towers project to the east and west but not to the north and south, resulting in an H-plan tower house. Only the south-west angle tower was not residential. Instead it contained an elaborate set of latrines, with rows of seats on each level. The chutes discharged through a row of small arches which can still be seen just above ground level. Langley is one of the few later medieval tower houses conserving the Norman idea of a first-floor entrance protected by a forebuilding. This forebuilding, evidently an afterthought, abuts one of the angle towers. Admittedly it contains a spiral stair rather than the straight, wide staircases characteristic of the greater Norman keeps. There is no evidence of any other buildings though some sort of courtyard must have existed.

The castle enters recorded history in 1368 when it was held by Sir Thomas de Lucy. He was probably the builder of the tower house as the windows on the top floor show tracery moving towards the new Perpendicular style. The castle did not remain in use for very long. It passed to the Percy earls of Northumberland and was burnt by Henry IV during Henry Percy's revolt. In 1541 it remained a charred shell. Subsequent decay was minimal, however, and from 1882 the antiquary Cadwallader Bates restored the castle as a residence. This has entailed substantial alterations, such as the insertion of large windows lower down and a more convenient ground-floor entrance. The battlements and turrets are also restoration work.

Access: Now a hotel. Limited access for non-residents.
Reference: BOE *Northumberland* (2nd edn).
Relations: Belsay and Warkworth are comparable tower houses.

LEMMINGTON HALL, five miles south-west of Alnwick, is a Georgian house of 1746 with a large pele tower at one end. Though modernised when the rest of the house was built, the pele remains complete. It is remarkable for its projecting wing, containing the entrance and spiral staircase. This is the only real example of the Scottish L-plan south of the Border, yet few in Scotland can be older. The tower existed by 1415 at the latest. William Beadnell held it at that time and may have been the builder.

Access: Private.
Relations: Towers with projecting wings at Coupland, Featherstone and Arnside.

LINDISFARNE CASTLE AND PRIORY Lindisfarne, or Holy Island, saw its great days in the seventh century when the monastery here was renowned for its learning. Viking raids put an end to this centre of Anglian culture, the monks fleeing with the shrine of St Cuthbert which would ultimately come to rest at Durham. After the Norman Conquest the great monastery of Durham built a Benedictine priory on the site and the present, wind-swept ruins belong to that era. They take the standard form of a cruciform church and claustral buildings. In the fourteenth century, owing to the Border wars, Lindisfarne again fell upon evil times. It is a mark of the priory's impoverishment that, instead of walling the precinct as at Hulne, the monastic buildings themselves were fortified in a rudimentary fashion. An embattled wall survives on the west side of the outer courtyard and the entrance to the cloister was given a protective barbican (now reduced to its footings). The projection with angle turrets on the east resembles a pele tower but seems to have contained the monastic infirmary. Even the church was brought into the sphere of fortification. High up on the west front can be seen two arrow-slits and others once existed along the north side.

Lindisfarne Castle appeared soon after the dissolution of the priory. The survey of 1541 recommended the construction of a fort here to command the harbour. An earthen bulwark was raised a few years later but rebuilding in stone did not occur until 1565–71, i.e. under Elizabeth I. The castle is thus part of the Tudor coastal defence chain but it bears no resemblance to Henry VIII's geometric forts along the South Coast. It owes everything to its position, squatting dramatically on a high basalt crag like a Noah's Ark in stone! The narrow enclosure consists of two stone-faced gun batteries rising straight out of the rock, with a block of lodgings for the garrison between them. A steep ramp ascends to the entrance through the lower battery. The fort saw action once, being seized by the Old Pretender's supporters in 1715. From 1903 the architect Edwin Lutyens made a house out of the garrison's quarters, converting the vaulted Tudor cellars into rather eccentric living rooms.

Access: The castle (NT) is open regularly in summer while the priory (EH) is open at standard times. Holy Island can be reached by causeway from the mainland but only at low tide.

Reference: Priory guidebook by E. Cambridge. *HKW* (IV) for the castle.

Relations: The fortified monasteries at Hulne and Tynemouth. The Elizabethan defences at Berwick.

LONGHORSLEY TOWER stands six miles north-west of Morpeth. It is still a private residence, dominating the other buildings of the village but curiously suburbanised. Apart from the inserted windows this pele is well preserved up to its embattled parapet. It was built by the Horsley family. The tower is a relatively late one but its omission from the 1541 survey is not significant, since that survey did not extend to the more settled south-eastern quarter of Northumberland.

Access: Visible from the road.

MITFORD CASTLE crowns a knoll above the River Wansbeck, two miles west of Morpeth. Natural defence was provided by the Park Burn which curves around the foot of the hill. The castle existed by 1138 when William de Bertram held it against the Scots. This motte-and-bailey stronghold was probably reconstructed in stone soon afterwards. Much featureless curtain still stands around the bailey, except for the southern tip which has been quarried away, and the D-shaped motte is crowned by a shell keep (note the Norman postern at the rear). However, the shell keep surrounds the stump of a tower keep. This keep is often called pentagonal, but it is basically square with one side beaked outwards to a central point, perhaps as a reinforcement against mining. Only the bottom stage of the keep remains, divided by a cross-wall into two vaulted chambers.

The tower keep may have been newly built in 1215, when King John seized the castle from Robert de Bertram. Two years later it resisted a Scottish force under Alexander II. The castle next emerges in 1315 as the refuge of a group of rebels led by Gilbert Middleton. They used it as a base from which to terrorise the countryside. Some loyal barons managed to trick their way into the castle and arrest Gilbert, who was later executed. Soon after, Mitford was sacked during one of Robert Bruce's incursions. The damage was never repaired and the castle sank into ruins.

Access: Freely accessible.

Reference: BOE *Northumberland* (2nd edn).

Relations: For the Bertrams see Bothal. Compare the five-sided tower at Raby.

MORPETH CASTLE is not the huge castellated court house which dominates the southern route into town. That dates only from 1822. The real castle can be seen crowning the hill on the other side of the road. It was an early foundation, suffering its first siege in 1095 during the rebellion of Robert de Mowbray. That siege, however, would have been directed against Ha' (i.e. Hall) Hill, a natural mound in Carlisle Park just to the north of the present site, and separated from it by a ravine. It is uncertain when the castle moved – perhaps after its destruction by King John in 1215. Today the castle has been reduced to some ruinous pieces of bailey curtain and a restored gatehouse, the latter erected by one of the lords Greystoke in the late fourteenth or early fifteenth century. This oblong structure is crowned by a machicolated parapet and corner turrets. There is no record of any hostility from the Scots, but in 1644 the decaying stronghold saw action when the Scottish garrison held out for three weeks before surrendering to a Royalist army.

Access: Exterior visible. Interior by appointment.

Reference: BOE *Northumberland* (2nd edn).

Relations: For the Greystokes see Greystoke. Gatehouses such as Bothal, Bywell and Hylton.

NEWCASTLE UPON TYNE: CASTLE AND TOWN WALL Newcastle owes its importance to the crossing of the Tyne. The first bridge (*Pons Aelius*) was built by the Roman army to provide access to Hadrian's Wall, and one of the Wall forts stood where the castle now stands. The 'New Castle' (presumably called that to distinguish it from the fort) was founded by William I's son Robert Curthose when returning from a Scottish expedition in 1080. Fifteen years later William Rufus wrested the castle from the rebel Robert de Mowbray, and henceforth it was maintained as an important royal garrison. Henry II rebuilt the castle in stone in 1168–78, spending £1100 on the keep and bailey curtain. The Black Gate is an addition of Henry III (1247–50).

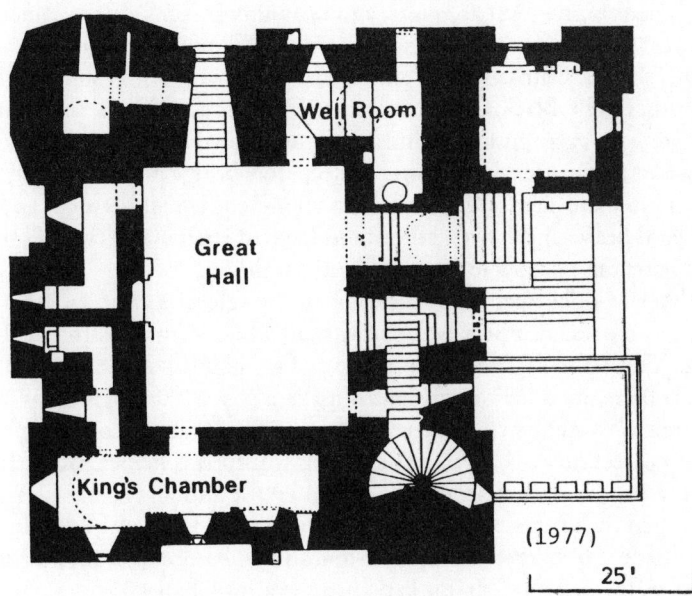

NEWCASTLE: KEEP AT SECOND-FLOOR LEVEL

The triangular site was well protected by nature, with steep falls to the Tyne on the south-east and the vanished Lort Burn on the north-east. Above the river the curtain (pierced by a machicolated postern) has survived in a ruinous condition, but the bailey was cut into two when the railway arrived in 1849. Hence the two main survivors of the castle, the keep and the Black Gate, are separated by the grim arches of a railway viaduct. Days of steam have taken their toll upon the masonry, and although the keep is no longer blackened with soot it is now impaired by patchy modern refacing. In spite of all that the keep is still a fine example of a square Norman keep. It stood in the middle of the bailey but would have been high enough to dominate. Corner turrets rise a little above parapet level, that on the north-west being polygonal rather than square. The existing battlements date from a restoration of 1812 onwards when the keep was restored rather drastically from ruin.

Newcastle's keep is one of the few preserving its forebuilding intact. The broad staircase rises past the modern, first-floor entrance to an elaborate Norman portal level with the second floor. It communicates directly with the principal chamber, i.e. the hall. The hall forms a 'double storey' with a mural gallery surrounding the upper level – a feature characteristic of all the larger Norman keeps. There is no internal cross-wall but a number of residential chambers are contrived within the great thickness of the walls. The solar must have been condensed into the narrow mural apartment known as the King's Chamber. The plainer storey below would no doubt have been the constable's residence, and below that is a grim undercroft, its vault supported on a central pillar. Beneath the grand stair in the forebuilding is an ornate Norman chapel. The second-floor entrance, the integration of the forebuilding with the main body of the keep and the lavish provision of mural chambers are all reminiscent of Henry II's larger keep at Dover. A mason called Maurice is singled out for payment in the royal accounts, and he is almost certainly the same Maurice the Engineer who went on to design Dover in the following decade.

Henry III's Black Gate is an oval gate tower, its upper floors rebuilt as a house in Jacobean times. The Black Gate stands at the end of a barbican, projecting at an angle to the main gatehouse and thus acting as a powerful flanking bastion along the level western approach to the castle. A deep drawbridge pit bars the way into the main gatehouse, and the sudden change in alignment which becomes apparent in the small yard between the two gates would have frustrated assailants all the more. The main gatehouse is now in a fragmentary condition.

In the later Middle Ages the castle sank to the role of a court house and gaol. Militarily its role was usurped by the town wall which contained the castle within its circuit. The right to collect murage was first granted in 1265. In 1280 the Dominican friars obtained permission to make a postern through the wall, so the surviving north-western stretch existed by that time. Building continued well into the fourteenth century – Newcastle's growing wealth was helped rather than hindered by the Border wars. The wall, described by the antiquary John Leland as one of the strongest in Europe, resisted Scottish attacks in 1341 and 1388. However, in 1644 Newcastle surrendered after a three-month bombardment from the Scots, who had joined forces with the English Parliament against Charles I.

Inevitably in a city which became so industrialised, most of the two-mile circuit has disappeared. All the main gatehouses have been pulled down and the fortified bridge across the Tyne collapsed in 1771. Fortunately a substantial length on the north-west escaped destruction, extending from St Andrew's Church along a dingy back lane (West Walls) as far as Westgate Road. It preserves four semi-circular bastions and two intermediate turrets. These corbelled turrets were a distinctive feature of Newcastle's wall. Of the towers, the best preserved is the third one along – the vaulted and embattled Heber Tower. The wall changes direction here and close by can be seen the Dominicans' blocked postern. Clearly the wall and its towers were not particularly high and much of their strength must have derived from the broad accompanying ditch.

Apart from this stretch the town wall is reduced to some interesting fragments. Behind the railway station in Hanover Square an embattled length is preserved, with a ruinous continuation descending steeply to the river. The D-shaped Plummer Tower (Croft Street) is capped by a guildhall of 1750. Off City Road an isolated fragment shows where the wall abruptly changed direction to enclose the suburb of Pandon. Nearby the eighteenth-century Wall Knoll Tower incorporates an original postern.

> *Access:* The keep is open regularly. The other remains of castle and town wall are freely accessible (all LA).
>
> *Reference:* Castle guidebook by B. Harbottle. Turner for the town wall. *HKW* (II).
>
> *Relations:* Dover and the keep at Bamburgh. Compare the barbican at Dover. City walls such as Oxford, Great Yarmouth and Canterbury.

NORHAM CASTLE The area around Norham ('Norhamshire') formed an outlying part of the Durham palatinate in medieval times. This gave the bishops of Durham a sizeable chunk of the Scottish Border to defend. Perched on a hill above the River Tweed, i.e. right on the Border, the castle was founded by Bishop Ranulf Flambard in 1121. David I captured the earth-and-timber stronghold twice in the 1130s, but it remained a possession of the prince-bishops in spite of the Scottish overlordship of Northumberland during the Anarchy. On the resumption of Anglo-Norman rule in 1157 Henry II compelled Bishop Hugh de Puiset to rebuild the castle in stone. It resisted an attack by Alexander II in 1215 and proved its might in the dark years after Bannockburn. Under its constable, Sir Thomas Grey, the castle withstood three prolonged sieges in the years 1318–22, the first of these lasting nearly a year. It earned a reputation for being 'the most dangerous place in England'. In 1327 the Scots managed to storm the castle on returning from a large-scale foray but they soon returned it to the bishop. Norham then enjoyed a respite from Border warfare until 1497, when the old defences stood up to the artillery of James IV. James returned in 1513 on his way to Flodden. This time his powerful cannon, including the famous Mons Meg which can still be seen at Edinburgh Castle, battered down the walls. The castle was left in ruins and a great deal of reconstruction was carried out afterwards under Bishop Ruthall, the castle being adapted to resist the growing power of artillery. The castle was garrisoned until the mid sixteenth century but it was already falling into ruins.

The earthworks of the castle, comprising a low motte and a bailey, are still impressive but the masonry defences are now very ruinous. The keep has fared better than the rest and now dominates the site. One side has collapsed but the other walls stand virtually to full height. It is a rectangular structure of late Norman date –

Bishop Puiset's main surviving contribution – but most of the features date from a remodelling on tower house lines in the 1420s. Two additional floors were squeezed into the former roof space, making five in all. The keep occupies one corner of a curtain which enclosed the motte top. The present wall seems to be entirely Bishop Ruthall's rebuilding – evidence of the damage sustained in 1513. Its great thickness was designed to withstand cannon but not the ravages of time. Most of the wall has been reduced to its footings, including the large, U-shaped Clapham's Tower. Little more survives of the bailey curtain and only towards the river does it attain a substantial height. Erosion of the rampart bank shows that this curtain was constructed over a series of arches – an economical device of no great strength, which makes the castle's performance under siege all the more remarkable. The bailey curtain appears to be of thirteenth-century date but its flanking towers were reconstructed as artillery platforms after 1513. The main gatehouse – walled up for extra security during Robert Bruce's incursions – preserves little more than its vaulted entrance passage.

Access: Standard opening times (EH).
Reference: Guidebook by C. Hunter Blair & H. L. Honeyman.
Relations: Castles of the bishops at Auckland, Durham and Crayke. The Tweed castles of Berwick and Wark.

PRESTON TOWER, a mile east of Ellingham, stands in the grounds of its nineteenth-century successor mansion. In 1415 it was held by the Sheriff of Northumberland, Robert Harbottle, and he is regarded as the probable builder. It was more ambitious than most pele towers – a large oblong with corner turrets rising above the parapet – but only the south end wall remains, together with its flanking turrets and the stumps of the adjoining walls. Small rooms are contrived in the corners. The other three sides were pulled down later but a new rear wall (enclosing a much smaller area) was provided in 1864 when the building was rehabilitated to serve as a clock tower.

Access: Open regularly.
Reference: BOE *Northumberland* (2nd edn).

PRUDHOE CASTLE guarded an important crossing of the River Tyne. Henry I awarded the barony of Prudhoe to Robert de Umfraville and a castle soon rose on the hillside. However, it does not enter recorded history until the time William the Lion, King of Scotland, invaded England. He laid siege to the castle in 1173 and again the following year, but he was unsuccessful on both occasions. These sieges were the highlight of Prudhoe's military history – the later wars with Scotland passed it by. It remained an Umfraville seat until it passed to the Percys by marriage in 1381. Decline set in thereafter. By the seventeenth century the castle had been abandoned, but from 1808 the Duke of Northumberland patched up the ruins and built a house in the bailey.

The castle enjoys a commanding position with steep falls to the river and a deep ditch elsewhere. On the easy south-eastern approach an outer bailey (now levelled) gave extra protection. A ruinous fourteenth-century barbican – the latest defensive addition to the castle – ascends to the well-preserved gate tower. The vaulted gate passage is of simple Norman construction, evidently the oldest masonry in the castle and dating from before 1150. Above the gate is a chapel, added or remodelled early in the following century as shown by the narrow lancet windows. It has an apse which projects on corbels like an oriel window. The top storey is pierced by cross-slits and there are smaller versions of these slits on the embattled parapet. The curtain is late Norman, with an oblong projecting tower at the eastern extremity. At the western angles are early-thirteenth-century towers showing the transition to semi-circular forms. One survives intact but the other has been reduced to its base. The Georgian manor house cuts across the narrow middle of the bailey, connected by the remains of a forebuilding to the Norman keep behind it. This square keep, closely surrounded by the curtain, is one of the smaller Norman keeps and now badly ruined, only one corner (surmounted by a turret) rising to full height. It was probably built by Odinel de Umfraville before William the Lion's attacks. Prudhoe thus shows a typical Norman transition from wooden to masonry defences: First the gateway, then the keep, and finally the surrounding wall.

Access: Standard opening times in summer (EH).
Reference: BOE *Northumberland* (2nd edn).
Relations: The Umfraville castles of Elsdon, Harbottle, Cockermouth and South Kyme. Compare the barbicans at Alnwick and Tynemouth.

SHORTFLATT TOWER is situated between Belsay and Bolam. The Suffolk merchant Robert de Reymes obtained a licence to crenellate both Aydon and Shortflatt in 1305. Aydon Castle is Robert's work but the pele tower of Shortflatt is attributed to a fifteenth-century descendant. Despite later alterations the tower retains its ground-floor vault and embattled parapet. The adjoining house was built or rebuilt in the seventeenth century.

Access: Private.
Relations: Aydon.

THIRLWALL CASTLE stands close to the line of Hadrian's Wall and is constructed entirely from Roman stones. Perched above the Tipalt Burn just to the north of Greenhead, the castle existed by 1369 when John de Thirlwall held it. He may well have been the builder. The Thirlwalls played an active part in the Scottish wars but later degenerated into notorious freebooters. Their large tower house, with thick walls and few windows, is a rare Northumbrian example of the L-plan. The Scots are said to have dismantled the tower in the Civil War and now it is very ruinous, its southern side having collapsed down the slope.

Access: Obtain permission to view at the farm.
Relations: Featherstone and Lemmington for L-plan towers.

TOSSON TOWER (at Great Tosson, two miles west of Rothbury) belonged to the Ogles. This pele does not feature in the list drawn up in 1415 but was already in decay by the time of the 1541 survey. Today the tower is a broken shell but its walls are notable for their unusual thickness. All the facing stones have been robbed from the lower part of the tower but the ashlar facing survives higher up.

Access: Visible from the road.

Relations: The Ogle towers at Cockle Park and Hepple.

TYNEMOUTH CASTLE was a fortified monastery rather than a castle proper. However, it was strong enough to be described as a castle even in the Middle Ages and the defensive role continued after the dissolution of the priory. It occupies a bold promontory at the mouth of the Tyne with cliffs falling sheer into the sea. This forbidding headland first attracted monks in the Anglian period, its natural defences no doubt providing some measure of protection against Viking raids. Robert de Mowbray, Earl of Northumberland, established a Benedictine priory here after the Norman Conquest, but he did not ignore the defensive value of the site. During his rebellion of 1095 he fortified the headland, which held out for two months against William Rufus. The monks obtained a licence to crenellate in 1296, in the wake of Edward I's invasion of Scotland and the first retaliatory raids. The defences were built forthwith, but the cost of the garrison contributed to the priory's impoverishment. Dissolution came in 1539 but the site remained in commission as part of the coastal defence network until the Second World War.

Despite four centuries of purely military occupation the ruins of the priory church still dominate the headland. After 1296 the entire headland was surrounded by a wall, but only on the west and south-west did the terrain demand a serious curtain, and elsewhere the wall has vanished entirely. The west front, facing the town, is dominated by the gatehouse, but the wall to either side of it was replaced in Elizabeth I's reign by the existing stone-cased rampart, designed to support and withstand artillery. At the south-west corner the wall changes to medieval. An embrasured stretch turns inwardly and drops down the hillside, terminating in a shallow turret overlooking Prior's Haven. The gatehouse, though ruined, remains the dominant feature of the defences. As rebuilt by the prior, John of Wheathampstead, in the 1390s this gatehouse was a strong and self-contained structure, with the castellan's hall and solar occupying the two storeys over the gate passage and an annexe containing the kitchen and additional chambers. The gatehouse is preceded by a narrow barbican with angle turrets, probably modelled on the outer gatehouse at Alnwick. In addition there is a shallow barbican on the inner facade, so the gatehouse could be defended from within or without in keep-gatehouse fashion.

Access: Standard opening times (EH).

Reference: Guidebook by A. D. Saunders.

Relations: Alnwick's barbican. The fortified monasteries of Hulne, York and St Michael's Mount.

WARK-ON-TWEED CASTLE There were two Wark castles in Northumberland, one on the Tweed and the other on the Tyne. The castle here, two miles south-west of Coldstream, sits on top of a curious glacial ridge known as The Kaim. Owing to its position on the line of the Border Wark-on-Tweed was frequently besieged. Though garrisoned by the Crown from time to time in response to the pressures from Scotland, Wark was not normally a royal castle. It was founded by Walter l'Espec in Henry I's reign and passed to the Roos family. David I was the first Scottish King to assail its defences. He captured it twice but the castle – rebuilt in stone at Henry II's expense – withstood William the Lion in 1174. In the later Middle Ages Wark was taken by the Scots on several occasions, but they invariably dismantled the castle rather than attempt to hold it. Lord Dacre reinforced the walls to take artillery after the Flodden campaign but it made little difference. The castle was destroyed for the last time in 1549. It was abandoned not long after and too little survives to evoke this illustrious stronghold. Even the motte-and-bailey earthworks are no longer particularly impressive. Rubble walling on the slope of the motte shows where the hexagonal shell keep stood, while some of the bailey curtain is concealed amid gardens facing the river.

Access: Freely accessible.

Reference: BOE *Northumberland* (2nd edn).

Relations: For the Roos family see Helmsley and Belvoir. The Tweed castles at Berwick and Norham.

WARKWORTH CASTLE AND BRIDGE Warkworth lies within a loop of the River Coquet which thus forms a natural moat around it. When the bridge was raised across the river in 1379 the townsfolk saw to their defence by erecting a gate tower at one end. This simple ruin is interesting as the only bridge gate left in England. The Welsh example at Monmouth is better preserved, and more dramatic for rising from one of the bridge piers rather than the bank. However, the gate no doubt served its purpose in deterring casual raiders. Warkworth had suffered its worst assault in 1174, when the Norman church witnessed a massacre of the townsfolk during William the Lion's invasion.

The castle occupies high ground at the neck of the river loop, closing the only dry approach to the village. Today it forms a magnificent ruin. Possibly founded by the Scots during the Anarchy, Henry II granted the castle to the lords of Clavering, who held it until their line came to an end in 1332. Warkworth was then granted to Henry Percy, lord of Alnwick, as a reward for his services in the Scottish wars. It became one of the chief Percy seats. The Scots left the castle alone, except for an abortive siege in 1327, but the walls took a pounding from Henry IV's cannon in 1405, following the Percy revolt. Decline and decay set in from the sixteenth century.

A Norman motte-and-bailey underlies the later masonry. The bailey curtain is a patchwork of various dates, some of it going back to the twelfth century. The south (entrance) front is a grand conception ascribed to Robert de Clavering *circa* 1200. At the west end stands the semi-octagonal Carrickfergus Tower, and in the middle projects a strong gatehouse, its long entrance passage flanked by buttressed turrets. The upper part of the gatehouse, including the machicolations, dates from a general heightening of the defences about a hundred years later. At the eastern end the original tower has been replaced by the square Montague Tower (fifteenth century), which projects eastwards but not southwards. The long east curtain is flanked by the Grey Mare's Tail Tower, similar in plan to the Carrickfergus Tower but part of the late-thirteenth-century improvements. The arrow-slits, with their cross-slits and

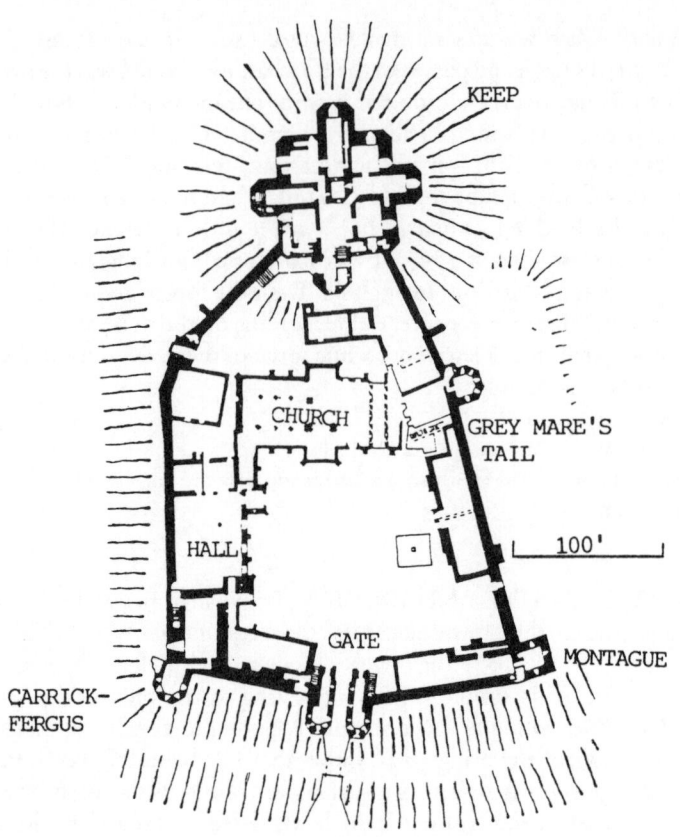

WARKWORTH CASTLE

fish-tails, are worth examining, especially in the Grey Mare's Tail Tower where they attain the incredible length of seventeen feet!

If the bailey defences are largely from the Clavering era, the buildings within reflect the changes wrought by the Percys. Unfortunately most of them have been reduced to their footings. The only exceptions are the Lion Tower and a stair turret which stood at opposite ends of the great hall on the west side of the bailey. The Lion Tower (actually the hall porch) bears the Percy lion above the entrance. It is the work of that Henry Percy who was created Earl of Northumberland in 1377, played a key role in Henry IV's usurpation but led a disastrous revolt against him in 1403. The scale of his ambition is attested by the cruciform church which closed the north side of the bailey. Probably intended as a collegiate establishment on the model of Windsor, it was left unfinished upon his rebellion and is now reduced to foundations.

Warkworth's pride – and the first Earl of Northumberland's chief contribution to the castle – is the massive keep on top of the truncated motte. Like other large tower houses of its era it could have served as a self-contained residence, but the Warkworth keep is more lavish than most and its plan is quite unique. Semi-octagonal towers project from the middle of its four sides, imposing a cruciform arrangement on the interior. The ground floor is divided into a number of vaulted store rooms. Several mural stairs allow convenient access to the floor above, but the principal staircase (located in one of the projecting towers) is a monumental one, reminiscent of those in Norman forebuildings. All the principal apartments stand at first floor level. The hall, the kitchen, and the sanctuary of the chapel (which occupies another of the towers) rose through two stages to benefit from greater height. The other apartments were only one storey high, allowing bed chambers above them and thus a reasonable degree of privacy for the earl's household. A slender watch tower dominates the whole. Though well preserved, the keep is now an empty shell except for one corner which was rehabilitated by Anthony Salvin for the Duke of Northumberland's use. Salvin submitted plans to restore the entire castle, as he had done at Alnwick, but fortunately this did not come to fruition.

> *Access:* The castle is open at standard times (EH). The bridge is freely accessible (LA).
> *Reference:* Castle guidebook by C. Hunter Blair & H. L. Honeyman.
> *Relations:* The Percy castle at Alnwick, St George's Chapel at Windsor and the bridge gate at Monmouth (Wales). Compare the situations of Durham and Shrewsbury.

WELTON HALL is situated beside a reservoir one mile west of Harlow Hill, a little to the south of the Military Road (B6318) which follows the course of Hadrian's Wall. Like several others standing close to the line of the Wall, the pele tower is largely built of Roman stones. This plain edifice, roofless but otherwise intact, was built by the Weltons in the fifteenth century. The house lying at right angles to the tower is actually older than the tower but was remodelled by William Welton in 1614.

> *Access:* Visible from the road.

WHITTON TOWER overlooks the south bank of the River Coquet, opposite Rothbury. The 1415 survey tells us that it was occupied by the rector of Rothbury – in other words a vicar's pele. Owing to the sloping ground the tower has a vaulted basement as well as a vaulted ground floor. This fourteenth-century pele was modernised in Victorian times when it became one corner of a large house.

> *Access:* Private.
> *Relations:* The vicar's peles at Alnham, Corbridge, Elsdon and Embleton.

WILLIMOTESWICK CASTLE, near the South Tyne opposite Bardon Mill in the wild south-west of the county, was the home of the Ridleys. This prominent Border clan indulged in many blood feuds, particularly with the Featherstonehaughs of nearby Featherstone Castle. Nicholas Ridley, the Protestant martyr, was probably born here. The castle does not appear on the list of Northumbrian strongholds drawn up in 1415, but if it did not exist at that time it must have been built soon after. The chief relic is the gatehouse – an oblong block with a vaulted gate passage to one side. Its size (four storeys) suggests that the gatehouse took the place of the more usual tower house. The adjoining farm buildings indicate an oblong enclosure. Two narrow, oblong turrets flank one end of the present farmhouse, which probably occupies the site of the hall.

Access: Exterior visible.
Reference: Jackson, *Castles of Northumbria.*
Relations: Featherstone.

OTHER SITES There are many more pele towers in Northumberland, whether featureless ruins, over-restored or embedded in later houses. The following list is not exhaustive:

Beadnell Tower (now Craster Arms)
Biddlestone Tower (converted into a chapel)
Blanchland Abbey (pele now in Lord Crewe Arms)
Blenkinsopp Castle (near Haltwhistle – ruin)
Burradon Tower (near Newcastle – ruin)
Callaly Castle (near Whittingham)
Cambo Tower
Clennell Hall
Coquet Island Tower (now a lighthouse)
Crawley Tower (near Powburn)
Duddo Tower (ruin)
East Shaftoe Hall (near Bolam)
Fenwick Tower (near Stamfordham – ruin)
Hethpool Tower (near Kirknewton – ruin)
Hetton Hall (near Wooler)

Howtel Tower (ruin)
Kyloe Tower (ruin)
Lilburn Tower (near Wooler – ruin)
Little Harle Tower (near Kirkharle)
Little Swinburne Tower (near Colwell – ruin)
Overgrass Tower (near Longfram-lington – ruin)
Ponteland Tower (now Blackbird Inn)
Rock Hall (near Rennington)
Rudchester Tower (near Harlow Hill)
Shilbottle Tower
Simonburn Castle (ruin)
Stanton Hall
Thornton Tower (Newbrough – ruin)
Whittingham Tower

Norman mottes can be seen at *Gunnerton, Wark-on-Tyne* and *Wooler*, the latter with fragments of a later pele tower on top. Little more than earthworks remain of two thirteenth-century castles, *Nafferton* (near Ovingham) and *Tarset* (near Belling-ham). Nafferton is an example of an unlicensed castle which Henry III ordered to be destroyed. *Staward Pele* was more than a pele tower, but only a fragment survives on a promontory near Haydon Bridge. Quadrangular *Castle Heaton* is represented by a vaulted undercroft while *Ogle Castle* was rebuilt in the seventeenth century. *Widdrington*'s fine tower house has perished. The pele at *Otterburn*, which withstood an attack during the battle there in 1388, was rebuilt in the Victorian era.

Nottinghamshire

Newark is the only castle of any substance remaining in Nottinghamshire, and even that is incomplete. It was once eclipsed by Nottingham Castle, one of the most important of royal strongholds, but Nottingham has suffered the fate of destruction and rebuilding. It is memorable now only for its history and setting.

HALLOUGHTON MANOR HOUSE is a Georgian mansion with a small tower house (now gabled over) at one end. A large traceried window at first-floor level dates the tower to the early fourteenth century. It formed the residence of one of medieval canons serving nearby Southwell Minster. It is strange that a cleric should have chosen to live in a pele tower this far south, especially when his secular neighbours saw no need to.

Access: Visible from the road.

LAXTON CASTLE belonged to the De Caux family, hereditary foresters of Sherwood. King John seized it but the family recovered possession after his death. Their earthwork castle is dominated by a very large mound which has a smaller motte on its summit. Two baileys are attached, the inner once walled though no masonry can be seen now. The fields around Laxton are remarkable because they have preserved the medieval open-field system.

Access: On private land.

NEWARK CASTLE Newark-on-Trent is a handsome town dominated by its church and castle, the latter a seat of the bishops of Lincoln until 1547. It was begun in 1133 by Bishop Alexander – a castle-building prelate like his contemporaries, Roger de Caen and Henry de Blois. At Newark much of the original masonry survives, enough to show that the castle possessed a remarkably symmetrical plan for its date, foreshadowing the quadrangular castles of the later Middle Ages. Alexander built similar castles within his vast diocese at Banbury and Sleaford, but those have perished. Even at Newark, only one and a half sides of the castle still stand. It is fortunate that the Roundheads allowed that much to survive, because Newark proved a formidable obstacle in the Civil War. Twice it resisted Parliamentary assaults and the final, year-long siege was only ended by the King's command. The garrison surrendered with full honours in May 1646. It was the town rather than the castle which bore the brunt of these sieges because the Royalists had enclosed Newark within a ring of artillery-proof earthworks, a portion of them surviving on the southern outskirts of the town.

Despite its incomplete state the castle is still impressive, the long west front surviving virtually intact. The curtain (heightened in the fourteenth century) rises above a low cliff beside the River Trent. The narrow, square tower at the south end is the original Norman one, and presumably the other corner towers once resembled it. According to tradition it was inside this tower that King John died of fever in 1216. Midway along the facade projects a semi-hexagonal tower, part of a remodelling attributed to Bishop Henry de Burghersh (d.1340). His pointed windows piercing the curtain beyond mark the position of the hall. The oriel window is an addition of the 1470s. At the north-west corner rises a strong hexagonal tower, perhaps built after the siege of 1217 when the castle fell to the Dauphin Louis. It contains a sinister bottle dungeon in its rock-cut basement.

The north side of the castle is dominated by Bishop Alexander's gatehouse. Some early Norman castles had a gatehouse rather than a keep as the chief strongpoint, but Newark is probably unique as a twelfth-century example of the theme. Perhaps it should be seen as ahead of its time rather than behind, because the gatehouse here offered ample accommodation, anticipating the keep-gatehouses of Edwardian days. It is now an empty shell but little altered, except for the insertion of some Elizabethan windows. The lofty gate passage leads into the bailey, which is considerably higher than the riverside level. From here it is apparent that the outer wall is just a facade and that the hall and other buildings have disappeared. However, the hall undercroft survives below ground level, with a postern through the curtain leading to the river.

Access: Grounds open daily. The interior is open at certain times (LA).

Reference: BOE *Nottinghamshire*. Mackenzie (I).

Relations: The episcopal castles at Farnham, Sherborne and Wells. Compare the Norman gatehouses at Ludlow, Exeter and Richmond.

NOTTINGHAM CASTLE   occupies a precipitous sandstone rock above the River Leen. Its situation is an impressive one but the present castle is a disappointment, because a Classical mansion has take the place of this famous stronghold. Parliament ordered the destruction of the castle (and Nottingham's town wall) in 1651, and the Duke of Newcastle erected his mansion on the site two decades later. Restored after being gutted during the Reform riots of 1831, the building now houses the municipal museum and art gallery. The medieval castle followed the contours of the site, the highest part of the rock forming a natural motte. Henry II and his successors converted the castle into a mighty stone edifice, with a massive square keep and three walled baileys, but the Cromwellian destruction has been thorough. Henry III's outer gatehouse survives but only one of its rounded flanking towers is original. Beyond lies the site of the middle bailey, preserving an excavated length of curtain and the stump of a round tower added by Edward IV. The palatial inner bailey on the 'motte' has perished entirely.

William the Conqueror established the castle in 1068 and it remained an important royal stronghold throughout the Middle Ages. Several parliaments met here. Despite its strong situation the underlying rock is honeycombed with caves and passages. One of them, known as Mortimer's Hole, is said to have been Edward III's means of entry in 1330 when he seized his mother's lover, Roger Mortimer. Charles I raised his standard here at the start of the Civil War, but he soon moved on for lack of support. Today the castle is chiefly remembered for its legendary associations with Robin Hood.

Access: Grounds and museum open regularly (LA). There are tours of the underground passages.

Reference: HKW (II).
Relations: The strong situations of Beeston and Bamburgh.

OTHER SITES. *Aslockton*, the original home of the Cranmer family, retains a motte known as Cranmer's Mound. Motte-and-bailey castles can also be seen at *Egmanton* and *Cuckney*. A bit of curtain from *Greasley Castle*, a quadrangular stronghold of the Cantilupes near Eastwood, can be seen embedded in the outbuildings of a farm.

Oxfordshire

Oxford has the only surviving Norman stone castle in the county. Apart from a group of motte-and-bailey sites, the other castles of Oxfordshire are fortified houses of the later Middle Ages. They were all properly licensed, reflecting that royal control of castle building was real enough here. Bampton, Shirburn and Grey's Court are altered quadrangular castles. Oxford's city wall – or rather the surviving stretch in the New College gardens – is a worthy sight.

BAMPTON CASTLE The tower of Bampton's fine church must have been brand new when the Empress Matilda's supporters seized and fortified it in 1142. King Stephen laid siege and drove its unwelcome defenders out. This episode apart, Bampton did not possess a castle until 1315 when Aymer de Valence, Earl of Pembroke, obtained a licence to crenellate. He erected a castle of the new quadrangular type, with circular corner towers and two gatehouses facing each other across the bailey. The western gatehouse is incorporated into the Victorian house called Ham Court. This gatehouse is a simple oblong structure, not at all in the Edwardian idiom. Its gate passage is now blocked and the parapet has been gabled over. An embattled piece of curtain stands alongside but the rest of the castle was pulled down after the Civil War.

Access: Private.
Reference: BOE *Oxfordshire.*
Relations: Aymer de Valence's work at Goodrich.

BROUGHTON CASTLE and church stand close together in a delectable setting three miles south-west of Banbury. They are probably both the creation of Sir John de Broughton (d.1315), whose effigy can be seen inside the church. At that time the 'castle' was an undefended manor house and, despite the title, it did not develop much beyond that. It is called a castle because Sir Thomas Wykeham, great-nephew of the Bishop of Winchester, obtained a licence to crenellate in 1405. The surviving length of curtain preserves its battlements but is so low you could almost jump over it! Clearly the wide moat (still water-filled) was a more serious obstacle. A causeway leads across the moat to a simple gate tower which is not especially defensive in character. The house, originally centred upon a hall, was subdivided and remodelled in Tudor splendour by Lord Saye and Sele in the 1550s. The bay windows, gables and plaster ceilings date from that epoch. Only the embattled wing on the left was excluded from the remodelling, remaining a fine example of a medieval solar block. The vaulted undercroft (now a dining room) and the surrounding passages are unusually good work. The solar above has been transformed into a bedroom, but the chapel alongside is perfectly preserved.

Access: Limited opening times in summer.
Reference: BOE *Oxfordshire*. Souvenir guide.
Relations: The fortified manor houses at Drayton, Stokesay and Aydon.

DEDDINGTON CASTLE is chiefly remembered for the abduction of Piers Gaveston, Edward II's arrogant favourite and possible lover, in 1312. Gaveston was being kept in an honourable confinement here by the Earl of Pembroke, but the Earl of Warwick managed to snatch his hated adversary under cover of night and drag him off to summary execution near Warwick. Today the castle site is a playing field south-east of the village, surrounded by the tree-grown Norman rampart of the outer bailey. A small inner bailey once existed – excavations have uncovered its square keep and stone curtain – but nothing is visible now. Several families held the manor in Norman times so the builder is uncertain.

Access: Freely accessible (EH).
Reference: Mackenzie (I).
Relations: For Gaveston's capture see Scarborough.

GREY'S COURT   Three miles west of Henley-on-Thames is an Elizabethan house standing within the remains of a medieval castle. The house was built by Sir Francis Knollys, a favourite of Elizabeth I. John, Lord Grey of Rotherfield, erected the original castle, receiving a licence to crenellate in 1347 following distinguished service during the Crecy campaign. His castle, though not entirely regular, was a large-scale example of the quadrangular plan. However, since the long walls were inadequately flanked by rather small corner towers, it was not designed with serious defensive intentions. Today the remains are scattered among the outbuildings and gardens which surround the house. The southern angle towers, octagonal in form, survive intact but the curtain between them has vanished. In fact, only the east curtain survives to any great extent in the guise of a garden wall. Projecting from this wall is a tall, four-storey tower, known as the keep but not large enough to have contained important residential apartments. Beyond is the stump of the square north-east tower (the fourth angle tower has perished). Several of the outbuildings date from Tudor times, notably the well house with its donkey wheel.

Access: Open regularly in summer (NT).
Reference: NT guidebook.
Relations: The Grey family castles of Codnor and Wilton.

OXFORD CASTLE AND CITY WALL Oxford was already a fortified burgh at the time of the Norman Conquest. The medieval city was periodically torn by violent disputes between the townsfolk and the growing university, 'town and gown' coexisting uneasily within the confines of the defences. These defences were rebuilt in stone from 1226 onwards – an early start signifying the city's importance. The city wall ran for nearly two miles, enclosing an area between the rivers Thames and Cherwell. All the gatehouses have perished but some portions of wall survive. One part stands out from the rest because of its excellent state of preservation. This is the north-east corner of the circuit, running through the grounds of New College. Since its foundation in 1379 the college has honoured its obligation to keep this sector in good repair. As a result the wall stands intact, including its parapet and seven projecting bastions. Five of them are the open-backed, semi-circular type often found on town walls. The other two are square, one rising much higher than the rest because it was built up after 1379 to serve as the college bell tower. Two ruinous bastions survive further west, off Ship Street. Other parts of the circuit have also survived in conjunction with colleges. A long, low stretch with one bastion overlooks Merton Field, while another piece in Brewer Street underlies Pembroke College.

On the west side of the city the wall linked up with Oxford Castle, established by William the Conqueror in 1071. It was nominally a royal castle but even in Norman times the kings of England preferred Beaumont Palace nearby, so the castle was in fact occupied and maintained by its hereditary constables, the D'Oillys. The remains of the castle are intermixed with the grim buildings of a prison. This may seem a lamentable fate but it is fully in keeping with the castle's history, since many urban castles were reduced to prisons and court houses as their defensive role declined. Most of the defences were destroyed after the Civil War. The one remaining tower is St George's Tower – a square, tapering structure probably built soon after the foundation of the castle. It has been suggested that the tower formed the first keep and may even pre-date the motte. The tower would have made an inadequate keep but its austerity makes the alternative view, that it served as the campanile of St George's Chapel, even more unlikely. Robert d'Oilly founded the chapel in 1074. It was the first collegiate establishment inside a castle, and since several scholars were canons here in Norman times it may have been the seed from which Oxford University sprang. (Of the chapel itself only some undercroft columns survive.) Nearby rises a conical Norman motte, over sixty feet high. It has lost its shell keep, but a hexagonal well chamber of the thirteenth century is hidden beneath the summit.

The castle saw its chief military action in 1142 when the Empress Matilda defied King Stephen from its walls. Matilda eventually escaped across the frozen Thames, dressed in white as camouflage in the snow. The only other siege of the castle took place in 1216, when King John wrested the castle from the Magna Carta barons. Charles I made Oxford his headquarters when London declared for Parliament, and an outer ring of ramparts rose around the city to forestall Roundhead attacks. It was here that the Royalists made their last stand, the city surrendering in June 1646 after the King had fled to the Scots

.   *Access:* The castle is only visible from outside (LA). The New College stretch of city wall can be viewed when the college is open, while the other pieces are freely accessible.

Reference: VCH *Oxfordshire* (IV). RCHM *City of Oxford. Oxford Castle* by T. Hassall.
Relations: Castle-prisons at Lincoln and Lancaster. The collegiate churches in castles at Windsor, Leicester and Hastings. Compare the city walls at Canterbury, Great Yarmouth and Newcastle.

SHIRBURN CASTLE is concealed from view in a large park a mile north-east of Watlington. Surrounded by a wet moat, the castle looks like a complete example of the quadrangular type but very much a sham in its features. This is because Shirburn, although a genuine castle, was drastically remodelled in the eighteenth century. A Roundhead siege in 1646 had wrecked the castle. Its two builders were Warine de l'Isle, a veteran of the French wars who obtained a licence to crenellate in 1377; and Thomas Parker, Earl of Macclesfield, who purchased the castle in 1716. Warca's castle was typical of its age, with circular corner towers and domestic ranges against all four walls. It was largely built of brick – an early use of the material – but this is no longer apparent because the entire castle is covered in a veneer of plaster. The north and east sides and the two north corner towers have largely been rebuilt in any case, while an outer range has been added against the south wall and the rest has been pierced by large Georgian windows. The west front is least affected by the changes, though the gate tower has been absorbed by the heightened ranges on either side. Needless to say, the picturesque drawbridge structure dates entirely from the restoration.

> *Access:* Private, and barely visible from outside.
> *Reference:* VCH *Oxfordshire* (VIII).
> *Relations:* Contemporary quadrangular castles such as Bodiam, Cooling and Max-stoke.

OTHER SITES The village of Ascott-under-Wychwood has two castle sites: *Ascott d'Oilly*, where a square Norman keep has been excavated, and the motte-and-bailey known as *Ascott Earl*. Other Norman earthworks exist at *Chipping Norton, Middleton Stoney*, Mixbury (*Beaumont Castle*) and *Swerford*. The important castle at *Banbury*, founded in the 1130s by Alexander, Bishop of Lincoln, was destroyed after the Civil War. It withstood a lengthy siege on the King's behalf in 1644 and finally surrendered in May 1646.

Scilly Isles

The Scilly Isles were frequented by medieval pirates but planned coastal defence only appeared under the Tudors, when it was feared that the Spanish might use them as a base for the invasion of England. Hence artillery fortifications were built on the islands of St Mary's and Tresco under Edward VI, and the defences were augmented after the Spanish Armada scare.

HARRY'S WALLS Despite its name, this fortification goes back to Edward VI, not Henry VIII. It lies on the northern outskirts of Hugh Town on St Mary's, commanding the harbour known as St Mary's Pool. Work started in 1551 but was abandoned at the end of the building season. The remains consist of a low stretch of wall with an arrow-head bastion set diagonally at each end. This is an early use of the arrow-head bastion, an Italian invention which first appeared in England during Henry VIII's last years. The fortunate survival of a designer's plan shows that a square fort with bastions at all four corners was originally intended.

Access: Freely accessible (EH).
Relations: The early arrow-head bastions at Yarmouth and Berwick.

KING CHARLES' CASTLE and its successor, Cromwell's Castle, stand near the northern tip of Tresco, a mile from the harbour of New Grimsby. They command the narrow channel which separates that island from Bryher. King Charles' Castle occupies an elevated position whereas Cromwell's Castle squats by the water's edge. They are separated in time by a hundred years. King Charles' Castle was erected in 1548–51 under Edward VI. It formed an oblong blockhouse with a semi-octagonal gun battery facing seawards. The fort earned its name and its ruinous condition in the Civil War. The Scilly Isles rebelled in favour of the Royalist cause, and Parliament despatched a fleet to subdue them in 1651. Admiral Blake landed on Tresco and stormed the blockhouse, which was blown up by the retreating garrison. Cromwell's Castle – a simple round tower – was built the following year as its replacement.

Access: Freely accessible (EH). Tresco is reached by boat from St Mary's (no motor transport on the island).
Reference: HKW (IV).
Relations: Contemporary Harry's Walls. Sandsfoot Castle is similar.

STAR CASTLE is aptly named, since its plan resembles an eight-pointed star. It stands on the peninsula known as The Hugh overlooking Hugh Town, on St Mary's. Harry's Walls guarded the other side of St Mary's Pool, but Star Castle had the advantage of commanding the channel to the south of the island as well. Essentially the castle consists of a square tower closely surrounded by an outer wall – i.e. a small, concentric unit inspired by the coastal forts of Henry VIII. Both tower and wall have triangular projections from the middle of each side, giving the fort its stellar plan. Despite its austerity the central tower has been adapted to form a residence. Over the entrance are the initials 'E.R.' and the date 1593. They show an Elizabethan attempt to make good the island's defensive deficiencies in the wake of the Spanish Armada. Work progressed quickly and the fort was completed within eighteen months under the guidance of the engineer Robert Adams. The total cost was £959 – more than double the original estimate. Nevertheless this small fortification could not have been a serious obstacle to shipping. More than a century passed before the defences here were expanded, the 'Garrison Walls' which enclose The Hugh being completed in 1746.

Access: Now a hotel.
Reference: HKW (IV).
Relations: Harry's Walls. Robert Adams designed the outer rampart at Pendennis.

OTHER SITES   The one genuine medieval castle of the Scilly Isles is called *Ennor Castle* after the old name for St Mary's. It existed by 1244 and the remains – just a couple of fragments of wall – stand to the north of Old Town. Near Old Grimsby is the stump of the *Old Blockhouse*, one of three small gun towers built on Tresco during Edward VI's reign.

Shropshire

As a Welsh Border county Shropshire has a liberal supply of castles, particularly in the western districts which were the domain of the Marcher lords. Offa's Dyke had defined the frontier since the eighth century but relations between English and Welsh remained hostile at the Norman Conquest. Roger de Montgomery was made palatine Earl of Shrewsbury. He exercised sweeping powers in his little principality, using it as a springboard for penetration into Wales. The palatinate came to an end in 1102 with the rebellion of Roger's son, Robert de Belleme, by which time the Normans had advanced far into Wales. In the thirteenth century Shropshire was to find itself in the front line again as the two Llywelyns, grandfather and grandson, asserted their leadership of a united Welsh principality. With the invasion of Edward I, however, the threat ended.

Shropshire's castles have suffered badly on the whole, some important strongholds having been reduced to earthworks or scraps of masonry. Ludlow is by far the largest and finest of them all. Shrewsbury was a fortress town set in a loop of the River Severn, but its castle was never commensurate with the town's importance. Square keeps at Alberbury, Bridgnorth, Clun, Hopton and Wattlesborough are typical of the late Norman era, while the thirteenth-century transition to round-towered curtains is best illustrated by Whittington, for all its decay. Acton Burnell and Stokesay castles are interesting examples of manor houses with only limited defensive features, reflecting a new optimism just a few years after Edward I's final conquest of Wales.

ACTON BURNELL CASTLE is the work of Robert Burnell, a cleric who rose to become Lord Chancellor and Bishop of Bath and Wells. As chancellor he was responsible for much of Edward I's legislation. The King granted him a licence to crenellate in 1284, and Bishop Burnell rebuilt his birthplace and the church alongside. The castle is an unusual example of a semi-fortified hall-house, recalling the hall-keeps of the Norman era. It is rectangular with square turrets at the corners. The ground floor was divided into several rooms, clearly of a residential nature rather than for storage. Hall and solar stood side by side at first floor level, the hall rising the full height of the building but the solar having a private chamber above it, as shown by the windows. A small annexe between the western corner turrets contained the latrines. This compact medieval house is capped by genuine battlements, but the big hall windows expose its limitations as a fortress. In the absence of any outer defences – even a moat – it is clearly a castle in name only. The Burnell line came to an end in 1420 and the castle fell into disuse. It has survived centuries of decay remarkably well, remaining virtually intact apart from the loss of its roof and flooring. Only the larger north-east turret, which contained the chapel, has collapsed.

Access: Freely accessible (EH).
Reference: Guidebook by C. A. Ralegh Radford. Salter.
Relations: For Bishop Burnell see Holdgate and the palace at Wells.

ALBERBURY CASTLE is one of a group of strongholds guarding the approaches to Shrewsbury from the Welsh Border. The castle was built by Fulk Fitz Warine early in the thirteenth century. Its ruins stand close to the medieval parish church. The dominant part is the keep, now overgrown and largely robbed of its facing stones. It is an oblong structure, somewhat longer than it is high and comprising one residential chamber over an undercroft, i.e. a small version of the hall-keep theme. Rectangular keeps were old fashioned by this time but Shropshire seems to have several late examples. The keep occupies one corner of a walled bailey which was evidently an afterthought. Its curtain is complete except for a rebuilt portion on the south. The wall is low and has lost its parapet, though there are indications of a mural tower. Two simple gateways pierce the curtain, unprotected by flanking towers or gate passages. All in all the castle has the air of a small frontier post erected hurriedly at a time when the Welsh under Llywelyn the Great were threatening the security of the Marches.

Access: Visible from the churchyard.
Reference: Salter.
Relations: For Fulk Fitz Warine see Whittington. Compare the keeps at Bridgnorth, Clun, Hopton and Wattlesborough.

BRIDGNORTH CASTLE Bridgnorth was first fortified as a Saxon burgh, its promontory site on cliffs above the River Severn being well suited for defence. Surprisingly, there was no castle here until 1101 when Robert de Belleme, second Earl of Shrewsbury, abandoned his father's castle at nearby Quatford in favour of this site. The move to a stronger position may have been in preparation for his revolt against Henry I the following year. Henry marched on Bridgnorth at the head of a large force, capturing the castle after a three-week siege. Belleme was banished to

Normandy and Bridgnorth was granted to Hugh de Mortimer. Mortimer's refusal to surrender the castle to Henry II in 1155 resulted in a second great siege, but the outcome was the same as the first. The ringwork on Panpudding Hill to the south of the castle served as the besiegers' camp during one or both of these sieges. Afterwards the castle stayed in royal hands.

The castle occupies the tip of the promontory with the town lying to its north. There were two walled baileys but only the ruinous keep remains – in fact, little more than two sides of it. It is a modest example of a square Norman tower keep, erected in 1166–74 by Henry II, and is only remarkable for its lean. At seventeen degrees the 'Leaning Tower of Bridgnorth' is much more out of perpendicular than its counterpart at Pisa! The keep has been that way since an unsuccessful attempt was made to blow it up after the Civil War. The castle endured a battering from the Roundheads before surrendering in April 1646. The only reminder of Bridgnorth's town wall is the North Gate. It is a rare case of a town gatehouse being rebuilt as a monumental entrance in the eighteenth century – most gates were pulled down at that time.

Access: Freely accessible (LA).
Reference: Bridgnorth Castle by W. Watkins-Pitchford. *HKW* (II).
Relations: Quatford. Shrewsbury was another castle of the earls of Shrewsbury.

BRONCROFT CASTLE, a mile west of Tugford, overlooks Corvedale. This charming house is mainly a castellated sham of the nineteenth century, since the original castle was badly slighted after the Civil War. The two square towers are medieval but much restored, their upper parts and parapets being entirely renewed. These towers, set closely together, originally flanked one end of a vanished hall range (a modern wing now connects them). It is likely that a second pair of towers guarded the other end of the hall. Broncroft was thus a hall with flanking towers which must have been more for effect than real defence. The castle is attributed to Sir Simon Burley, who was executed in 1388 as one of Richard II's unpopular advisers.

Access: Gardens open occasionally.
Reference: Salter.
Relations: The fortified halls at Acton Burnell and Woodsford.

CAUS CASTLE occupies a prominent ridge overlooking the Rea Brook, two miles south-west of Westbury. Roger Fitz Corbet founded the castle after the Norman Conquest, naming it after his native Caux in Normandy. Sadly overgrown and in need of excavation, the castle is an impressive motte-and-bailey, protected by a double ditch and rampart except where the ground falls steeply away. Some masonry shows the position of a round keep on the motte but the bailey curtain is buried in its own rubble. The castle stayed with the Corbets until 1347. It then fell into decay but was garrisoned in the Civil War, falling to the Roundheads in 1645. To the north-west a long outer enclosure marks the site of a failed Norman borough.

Access: On private land.
Reference: Salter.
Relations: For the Corbets see Moreton Corbet and Wattlesborough.

CHENEY LONGVILLE CASTLE   Robert Cheney obtained a licence to crenellate this place, two miles north-west of Craven Arms, in 1395. The surviving buildings show a quadrangular layout once surrounded by a moat, but Cheney Longville barely qualifies as a castle at all. It is really a courtyard mansion lacking the angle towers which would have been a prerequisite for defence. Three ranges survive, but what must have been the hall range on the north has perished. The buildings have largely been adapted for farm purposes, a later farmhouse occupying one corner. Presumably battlements once existed on the outer walls but even these have disappeared.

Access: Visible from the road.
Reference: Salter.

CLUN CASTLE   enjoys a commanding position within a protective bend of the River Clun. The highest part of the site forms a large, natural motte and there are two baileys in succession, a narrow causeway leading from one enclosure into the next. The motte is dominated by the ruin of its keep, rising from the steep slope and thus serving as a powerful flanking tower. This unusual arrangement makes the keep much higher from outside the castle, two of its four storeys being below the summit of the motte. Three sides of the keep rise almost to full height but the wall towards the motte top has vanished. In plan it is the usual oblong keep of the Norman era, an impression verified by the pilaster buttresses and round-headed windows. However, the dynamic positioning suggests a late date around 1200. Fragments survive of a curtain around the motte, including twin half-round gate turrets which are placed rather oddly above the steep slope.

Robert (otherwise called Picot) de Say is said to have founded this castle after the Norman Conquest. It formed the centre of a Marcher lordship known as the Honour of Clun. The Welsh sacked the castle in 1195 and King John captured it during the Magna Carta war. By that time Clun had passed to the Fitzalan lords of Oswestry. It was probably John Fitzalan who built the keep. After becoming earls of Arundel the Fitzalans seem to have neglected their Marcher estates – the castle was already much in need of repair in 1272. Owain Glyndwr attacked it during his revolt but the records fall silent after that episode.

Access: Freely accessible (EH).
Reference: Salter.
Relations: The Fitzalan castles at Oswestry, Shrawardine and Arundel. Norman keeps at Bridgnorth, Hopton and Ludlow.

ELLESMERE CASTLE   is a Norman earthwork on a ridge overlooking The Mere. The large motte lies between two baileys, that to the south-east being more evident now since the north-western bailey has a road running through it. A bowling green occupies the summit of the motte. The castle was raised by Roger de Montgomery, palatine Earl of Shrewsbury. It resisted King Stephen in 1138 while in Peverel hands. Later it was held by Llywelyn the Great but there is no evidence that any masonry existed here.

Access: Visible from the road.
Relations: Roger de Montgomery's castles at Quatford and Shrewsbury.

HOLDGATE CASTLE   lies in the Corve valley, two miles south of Shipton. Beside the parish church is the circular motte of a Norman castle – 'Helgot's Castle' is one of those mentioned in the Domesday Book. Robert Burnell, Lord Chancellor and Bishop of Bath and Wells, purchased the manor before 1284 and was rebuilding Holdgate Castle at the same time as Acton Burnell. The only part still standing is a squat D-shaped tower on the bailey perimeter. It is a flanking tower, indicating an intention to defend which is quite absent at Acton Burnell. No curtain survives and the tower now forms part of a later farmhouse. The tower preserves original arrow-slits but the parapet has given way to a sloping roof.

> *Access:* Private.
> *Reference:* Salter.
> *Relations:* Acton Burnell.

HOPTON CASTLE   On top of a low motte five miles south-east of Clun rise the ruins of a square keep. Pilaster corner buttresses reveal the late Norman origin of the keep but the features show a remodelling in the fourteenth century. This is especially apparent on the upper floor which contains several mural chambers. There were only two storeys, at least in the keep's later medieval form. Today the walls are crumbling. Low earthworks to the west show the position of the bailey. Until the fifteenth century the manor was held by the Hopton family as tenants of the lords of Clun. The castle saw fighting in 1644, suffering a siege on behalf of Parliament. It was the scene of an infamous massacre once the Royalists had broken through, most of the garrison being slaughtered out of hand.

> *Access:* Visible from the road.
> *Relations:* The keeps at Alberbury, Bridgnorth, Clun and Wattlesborough.

LUDLOW CASTLE AND TOWN WALL   Ludlow Castle is one of the finest in the Welsh Marches. Its elevated position above the River Teme adds majesty to a castle with a colourful history and a high degree of architectural interest. The castle is remarkable first and foremost for its early stone defences. The towered curtain surrounding the inner bailey is attributed to Roger de Lacy, who is believed to have raised it in the years between Domesday Book and his banishment, i.e. 1086–95. Dominating the rest is a tall square keep which started off as a gatehouse. The presence of any stone defences, let alone mural towers and a gatehouse, is advanced for the late eleventh century. Admittedly the evidence for its early construction is largely circumstantial and the date could be pushed into the following century. As well as the defences, the castle is notable for its well-preserved residential apartments, particularly the rare circular chapel.

The castle's strength was put to the test in 1138, when King Stephen laid siege but failed to dislodge the supporters of the Empress Matilda who had gathered here. Around the middle of the century Ludlow was a bone of contention between Joce de Dinan and two powerful neighbours who laid claim to the castle. Joce managed to ambush and capture Hugh de Mortimer, but his other rival, Walter de Lacy, seized the castle in his absence. The unfortunate Joce failed to recover it in spite of laying siege. Such was the disorderly life of Marcher barons.

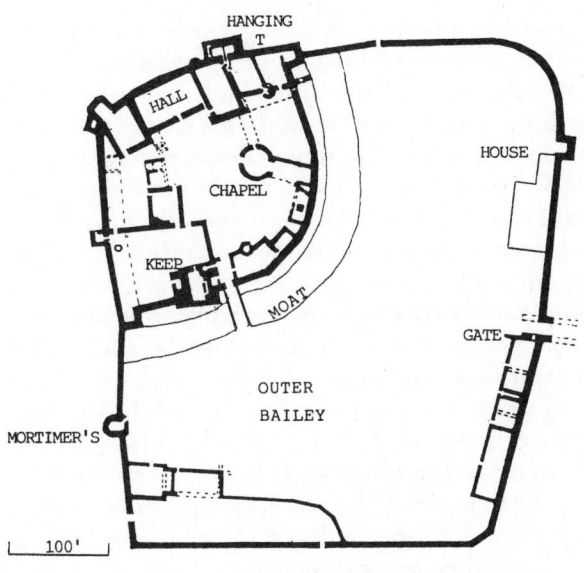

HANGING T

HALL

HOUSE

CHAPEL

KEEP

MOAT

GATE

OUTER
BAILEY

MORTIMER'S

100'

LUDLOW CASTLE

In 1316 Roger Mortimer inherited the castle (he had already occupied it jointly for some years) and the main residential buildings are his. The Mortimers retained their estates beyond Roger's execution (1330) for his part in Edward II's overthrow. When their line died out in 1424 Ludlow passed to Richard, Duke of York. Just outside the town at Ludford Bridge the duke's followers were routed by the Lancastrians in 1459, Ludlow being sacked as a consequence. However, with the accession of Richard's son as Edward IV the castle became the seat of the Council of the Marches, which sought to bring some centralised authority to that baronial wasteland. The King sent his young son (another Edward) to Ludlow to act as a royal figurehead – a precedent followed by Henry VII who sent his eldest son Arthur here. Although the castle sustained considerable damage in the Civil War, not surrendering until June 1646, the council continued to meet here until its abolition in 1689.

Today the castle is a ruin, but an extensive and well-preserved one. From Castle Street a mutilated gatehouse leads into the spacious outer bailey. The surrounding curtain is Norman work which may be attributed to Joce de Dinan or the De Lacys. Immediately south of the gatehouse a Tudor range of retainers' lodgings backs onto the curtain, while to the north is the so-called Beacon Tower. Tradition has it that this square flanking tower featured in the siege of 1138. A grappling iron descended onto the King of Scotland's son and would have hauled him into captivity but for a daring rescue by King Stephen himself. Whether the tower is quite that old is unlikely, but it is the only Norman tower on the outer curtain. Roger Mortimer added a second tower on the opposite (west) side of the bailey. This tall, U-shaped structure is appropriately named after him.

The inner bailey occupies the north-west quadrant of the castle, being isolated from the outer bailey by a steep, rock-cut ditch. The present entrance gateway lies

213

alongside the keep, leading into the bailey through the Elizabethan Judges' Lodgings. When the new entrance was created the old gate passage was blocked up and the Norman gatehouse became a conventional keep. It is assumed that it was converted in the twelfth century – the heyday of the keep – but the present gateway dates only from *circa* 1300. In the Duke of York's time the inner front of the keep was rebuilt on a new alignment, and the interior was remodelled to make a four-storey tower house. Thus today's keep is smaller than the original and towards the courtyard is entirely fifteenth-century work. Roger Mortimer's residential buildings stand against the curtain on the north side of the bailey, securely placed above the steep fall to the river. Although now roofless and empty, these apartments are fine examples of early fourteenth-century domestic architecture, surprisingly little altered by later occupation. All the principal chambers stood at first-floor level. The hall is flanked by projecting wings, the eastern one housing the solar and the west wing containing another important apartment above the buttery and pantry. The kitchen, now very ruinous, occupies an inconveniently detached position. Beyond the east wing is an Elizabethan block. In front stands the circular chapel of St Mary, a gem of late Norman craftsmanship with rich decoration on its archways and capitals. The chapel is one of only five medieval round naves surviving in England – a layout inspired by the church of the Holy Sepulchre in Jerusalem.

It is a measure of confidence in the rock-cut ditch, or perhaps a sign of early experimentation, that the Norman towers are not placed to comprehensively flank the level approach from the outer bailey but instead overlook the north and west fronts which were already well protected by nature. Four towers are original, all square-fronted and open-backed. The largest is the one at the north-west corner, positioned diagonally to provide a shallow flanking role along both faces, while the towers at the other two angles project along one face only. The fifth tower (Hanging Tower), also oblong, is another of Roger Mortimer's additions, containing a suite of latrines which served his residential apartments.

Ludlow did not exist when Roger de Lacy chose this site, so the town is one of those which grew up in the protective shadow of a castle. Defended on two sides by the river, Ludlow's grid of streets is an example of Norman town planning. A walled circuit rose slowly from 1233 onwards, enclosing a near-rectangular area. Although a lot of wall survives, much of it is concealed behind the houses of this old-world town and relatively little can be seen. Redevelopment has led to the exposure of a long portion at the south-east corner of the old circuit, along St John's Street. Nearby Broadgate, astride Broad Street, is the only survivor of the town's seven gatehouses. It preserves its gate passage and one of its rounded flanking towers but the structure has been transformed by conversion into a Georgian house. Ruins of the octagonal south-west angle tower exist in a private garden.

Access: The castle is open regularly except in winter. Parts of the town wall are freely accessible (LA).

Reference: Archaeologia (LXI). Salter. Castle souvenir guide.

Relations: For the De Lacys see Longtown and Lyonshall, and for Roger Mortimer see Wigmore. Richmond is another early Norman castle with a gatehouse and flanking towers.

MORETON CORBET CASTLE consists of the rather meagre remains of a medieval castle juxtaposed with the ruins of a great Elizabethan house. Their battered condition is the legacy of a siege in 1644, when the Roundheads captured the castle. Richard Corbet acquired Moreton in 1203 and it is likely that the small oblong keep was built by him. Little more than one wall stands above the foundations but the remains of a large fireplace at first-floor level confirm an early thirteenth-century date. Some ruinous curtain survives, along with a gate tower which was remodelled to its current gabled form in 1579 (as an inscription relates). That is also the date of Sir Andrew Corbet's grand range at the back of the courtyard. Several Corbet monuments can be seen in the adjacent church.

Access: Freely accessible (EH).
Reference: Salter.
Relations: For the Corbets see Caus and Wattlesborough.

OSWESTRY CASTLE was founded by Reginald de Balliol according to the Domesday Book, but in the twelfth century it passed to the Fitzalans who went on to acquire Clun and Arundel. King John sacked the castle in 1216 and it later withstood an attack from Llywelyn the Last. Finally destroyed after its capture by the Roundheads in 1644, the castle is now reduced to its motte with small fragments of a shell keep on top. The bailey has been built over and Oswestry's town wall has disappeared as well.

Access: Freely accessible (LA).
Relations: For the Fitzalans see Clun and Arundel.

QUATFORD CASTLE was one of those founded by Roger de Montgomery after he became palatine earl in 1073. There is now a sham castle at Quatford but the tree-clad motte of the Norman stronghold can be seen nearby, overlooking a low cliff beside the River Severn. The bailey was overlooked by Roger's collegiate church. No doubt that is one of the reasons why his son Robert de Belleme moved upriver to Bridgnorth in 1101, in preparation for his doomed rebellion against Henry I.

Access: Visible from the road.
Relations: Bridgnorth. Roger de Montgomery's castle at Ellesmere.

SHRAWARDINE CASTLE, one of that group guarding the western routes to Shrewsbury, emerges from obscurity as a royal castle in Henry II's reign. Following destruction by the Welsh in 1216 the castle was restored by John Fitzalan. It resisted the Roundheads in 1644 but succumbed to a ruse the following year. A heavy slighting followed and the remains are correspondingly scanty. The castle is really just a low motte overlooking the River Severn. Three tall fingers of masonry are the only remnants of a shell keep which encased the motte.

Access: Visible from the road.
Relations: The Fitzalans were also at Clun and Oswestry.

SHREWSBURY CASTLE AND TOWN WALL

Shrewsbury occupies a loop of the River Severn, the historic town being entirely surrounded by water except for a narrow neck of high ground at the north end. It was the capital of Roger de Montgomery's short-lived palatinate and, until Edward I's conquest, formed the base for many campaigns into Wales. Llywelyn the Great twice attacked Shrewsbury in retaliatory raids, which prompted the construction of the town wall in 1220–42. The town has preserved many relics of its past but the town wall has suffered the common fate of demolition in recent centuries. One stretch survives along Town Walls, though since it acts as a revetment wall its height can only be appreciated from the river. Just beyond is the only surviving mural tower which has been converted into a house. There is also a postern gate beside the river at the end of St Mary's Water Lane. Of course the wall was a secondary defence to Shrewsbury's natural moat. The present English and Welsh bridges occupy the site of fortified medieval predecessors.

The castle is placed across the neck of the river loop, protecting the only landward approach to the town. It stands on a low cliff above the Severn, though the strong position is now obscured by the railway station. William the Conqueror chose this site within a year of the Norman Conquest, and as early as 1069 the castle resisted a Welsh attack. Unlike Bridgnorth it did not make a stand during Robert de Belleme's rebellion (1102), but its resistance to King Stephen in 1138 resulted in the execution of the entire garrison. Today the castle may seem surprisingly unimpressive, since by the time of its rebuilding in stone it was a minor royal stronghold rather than the seat of a palatine earl. Clearly its counterparts in the Welsh Border towns of Chester and Hereford were more important, so it is ironic that much more survives here. The castle may have appeared more substantial before the outer bailey was swallowed up by the town.

At least the embattled curtain around the inner bailey is more or less intact. This rather low wall can be dated to sporadic expenditure in Henry II's reign though it has been subject to frequent repairs since. The simple gate arch is Norman but the ruined barbican in front is a rare stone fortification of the Civil War period. To the right of the gate rises a high Norman motte. As late as 1270 there was still a wooden keep on top, and the present tower is a folly built by the engineer Thomas Telford before 1800. Telford also remodelled the hall block as a residence for Sir William Pulteney. This building actually dates from Henry III's reign, with a Tudor gallery stage above. The hall block stands against the curtain and has a boldly-projecting circular tower at each end. The only other mural tower (containing a postern) was largely rebuilt during the Civil War. Town and castle were garrisoned for the King but they fell to Parliament in a surprise attack, the Roundheads crossing the river under cover of darkness and pouring through a short gap in the town defences.

Access: The castle is open regularly (LA) – there is a regimental museum in the hall block. The town wall (part NT) is freely accessible.

Reference: Castle guidebook by H. Beaumont. Turner for the town wall. *HKW* (II).

Relations: Chester and Hereford as Welsh Border towns. Compare the positions of Durham and Warkworth. The castles raised by William I at Warwick, Windsor, Lincoln and York.

STOKESAY CASTLE is a classic example of a medieval manor house with certain defensive features. It lies in a hollow a mile south of Craven Arms, beside Stokesay parish church. Most of the existing castle is the work of Lawrence de Ludlow, a wealthy wool merchant who joined the ranks of the landed aristocracy by purchasing the manor in 1281. His lordly aspirations were encouraged by the issue of a licence to crenellate ten years later. It has been said that Lawrence then added defences to his previously-unfortified house, but there is no obvious break between the domestic range and the rest. He did not have long to enjoy his new castle, because he drowned on a mission to Flanders in 1294. It should be noted that the present hall range incorporates an early thirteenth-century tower at its north end, a relic of the previous manor house of the De Say family who gave their name to the village (Stoke Say). The Ludlow family lived here until the sixteenth century and its subsequent history has been mainly one of tenant occupation. For this reason Stokesay is one of those rare medieval houses which have survived the centuries relatively unscathed, neither falling into ruin nor suffering drastic modernisation as a result of changing taste.

The castle is entered through an elaborate, timber-framed gatehouse which is the only substantial addition to the original fabric. It probably replaced the original gate tower in the Jacobean period, which explains why the castle fell so easily to the

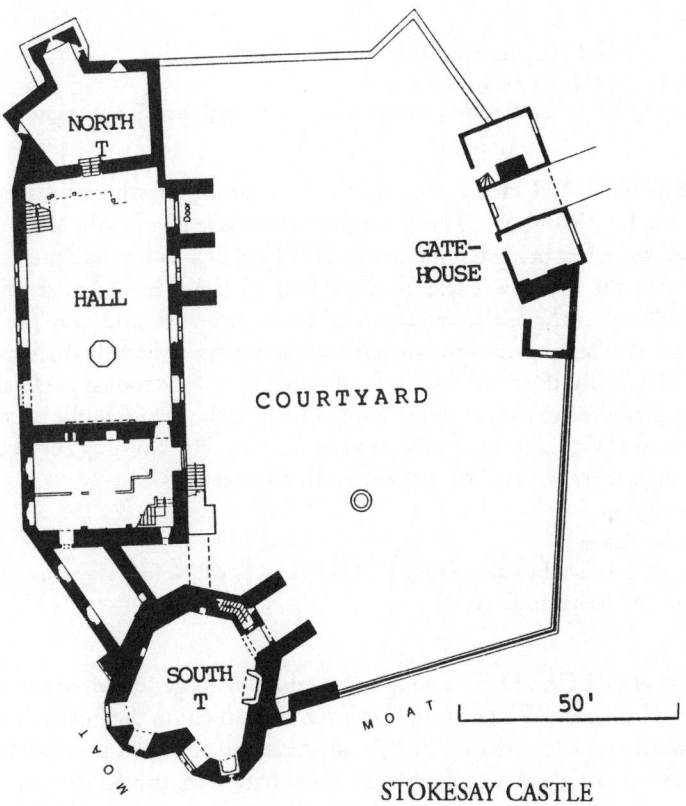

STOKESAY CASTLE

217

Roundheads in 1645. Despite this obvious weakness Parliament ordered the defences to be slighted. Because of this the former curtain has been reduced to little more than a revetment wall bordering the now-dry moat. Only a fragment beside the South Tower shows the original height.

Once inside the courtyard, Lawrence de Ludlow's hall range lies straight ahead. The hall is the outstanding one of its date and exceptionally well preserved. Large traceried windows are set beneath individual gables while the roof is a testament to the skill of medieval carpenters. Its width was quite audacious for the time. A rare survivor is the wooden staircase attached to one end of the hall, ascending to the upper chambers in the northern tower. The picturesque wooden gallery which caps this tower may also go back to Lawrence's era. At the other end of the hall is the solar (with seventeenth-century panelling), standing over an undercroft. Beyond the solar, and isolated from the other residential buildings, rises the embattled South Tower. It is curious for its eccentric plan, semi-octagonal towards the courtyard but presenting a pair of semi-octagonal projections to the outside world. The tower is an early example of the tower house theme, but the emphasis is upon comfort, hence the regular spacing of tall lancet windows. It is from the back of the house that the castle's defensive limitations are most apparent, since Lawrence de Ludlow put large windows on both sides of the hall and only the width of the moat provided protection on this side.

Access: Standard opening times (EH).
Reference: Guidebook by J. Munby.
Relations: The similar fortified manor houses of Broughton, Drayton and Aydon.

WATTLESBOROUGH HALL lies off the Shrewsbury-Welshpool road (A458), two miles north of Westbury. This Georgian farmhouse adjoins the shell of a low square tower, the effect being reminiscent of Northern pele towers and their attached houses. In fact the tower is a late Norman keep as the pilaster buttresses reveal. Despite later neglect the ashlar exterior is still well-preserved and only the parapet has disappeared. The few windows are later enlargements. Evidently there were only two storeys originally, the third floor being formed out of the roof space later. These changes are attributed to the Leighton family who held the manor in the later Middle Ages. Previously Wattlesborough belonged to the Corbets. Nothing survives of the bailey although there is a tradition of three other towers.

Access: Private.
Reference: Salter.
Relations: The nearby Corbet stronghold of Caus. Small Norman keeps at Alberbury, Hopton and Moreton Corbet.

WHITTINGTON CASTLE Though first raised by Roger de Montgomery after the Norman Conquest, Whittington Castle is a monument to the Fitzwarine family. Fulk Fitz Warine, the founder of the dynasty, managed to forfeit it twice. Firstly he was dispossessed for siding with the Magna Carta barons against King John. He paid Henry III a substantial sum to recover his inheritance, and in return the young King granted a licence to crenellate (1221). The same Fulk, much older, died fighting for

Henry at the Battle of Lewes in 1264. Simon de Montfort then gave Whittington to his ally, Prince Llywelyn the Last, and the Fitzwarine heir had to wait thirteen years for Llywelyn's downfall and the recovery of these lands. Eight more Fulks came and went before their line died out in 1415.

Although quite flat the castle site was well protected, by marshland on two sides and by a broad moat (still wet) elsewhere. The only relic of the first castle is a truncated motte lying outside the later defences. Excavations have uncovered the foundations of a square Norman keep inside the present inner bailey. Perhaps it was destroyed by King John. Clearly the keep no longer existed when Fulk Fitz Warine laid out his new castle, since there would not have been enough room for it within the compact bailey. Fulk's rebuilding of the castle was in accordance with the latest defensive principles, no doubt in response to the threat from Llywelyn the Great. The inner bailey, roughly oblong, was surrounded by a thick curtain with rounded towers at three corners and a twin-towered gatehouse at the fourth. In front lay an outer bailey entered through another gatehouse. This outer gatehouse, with its half-round flanking towers, is the only part of the castle to survive intact thanks to neo-Gothic restoration. The inner bailey walls have been reduced to utter ruin. One of the inner gatehouse towers still rises to a fair height (with cross-slits), but the curtain is very ruinous and the other towers are fragmentary. Fortunately, the foundations have been excavated and the site cleared of rubble.

Access: Freely accessible (LA).

Reference: Salter.

Relations: Fulk Fitz Warine's castle at Alberbury. Marcher castles of enclosure such as Goodrich, Pembridge and St Briavels.

OTHER SITES Earthwork castles proliferated in this county after the Norman Conquest, particularly in the Marcher lands to the west. There are numerous small, rather insignificant mounds, since even minor lords had to be on their guard against Welsh reprisal raids. This list gives the more important motte-and-bailey sites:

Bishop's Castle	*Knockin Castle*
Bishop's Moat (near Bishop's Castle)	*Lydham Castle*
Brompton Castle (near Montgomery)	*Minton Castle*
Castell Bryn Amlwg (near Anchor)	*More Castle*
Castle Pulverbatch	*Pan Castle* (near Whitchurch)
Colebatch Castle	*Wilmington Castle* (near Montgomery)
Hodnet Castle	

The Norman keep at *Ruyton* is reduced to a couple of lumps of masonry beside the parish church. *Corfton* and nearby *Corfham* preserve ringworks, while the Norman earthworks of *Brockhurst Castle* overlook Church Stretton. *Red Castle* followed a curious layout on two parallel ridges, taking advantage of the precipitous terrain, but only meagre fragments survive on a rock in Hawkstone Park (near Hodnet). Among later medieval castles, *Charlton* has vanished except for its surrounding moat and *Myddle* preserves only the stump of a stair turret. *Lea Castle* retains part of a small tower house attached to a farmhouse. *Rowton Castle* (near Alberbury) is an eighteenth-century rebuilding of a Corbet stronghold destroyed by Llywelyn the Last.

Somerset

The Normans took advantage of Somerset's hill ranges, leaving behind a few majestically-sited strongholds. Castle Neroche is a formidable earthwork, while Dunster retains its magnificent position but nothing else from the Norman period. In fact, the altered hall at Taunton is the only substantial piece of Norman stonework. Dunster, Taunton and Stogursey show the remains of thirteenth-century towered curtains, but the defences of these castles have suffered much destruction. Better preserved are the contrasting examples of later medieval castles. Farleigh Hungerford is a ruinous quadrangle, Nunney is a striking tower house while the Bishop's Palace at Wells is a fitting neighbour to the beautiful cathedral.

CASTLE NEROCHE occupies a spur of the Blackdown Hills above the village of Curland, six miles south of Taunton. The impressive earthworks comprise a motte-and-bailey stronghold with a triple ditch and rampart guarding the only level approach. Excavations have shown the existing layout to be the result of three phases. First came the outer ditch and rampart, which may date back to the Iron Age. After the Norman Conquest the oblong, embanked bailey was thrown up by Robert, Count of Mortain. The third ditch and rampart followed a few decades later. It is interesting to note that the motte is also a twelfth-century addition and did not belong in the original Norman scheme.

Access: Freely accessible.
Relations: Robert of Mortain's castles at Berkhamsted, Launceston and Trematon.

CLEVEDON COURT is one of the most striking medieval houses in England. The hall, with its flanking porch and chapel, goes back to *circa* 1320 when Sir John de Clevedon held the manor. Attached to the east end of this compact group is an older hall, and adjoining one corner of that is a tall, oblong tower. Because of its crowning gable the tower looks less defensible that it originally was. It is curious that the old hall is set at an angle to the new, and the tower is also out of alignment with the old hall. A length of wall running north from the tower is the remnant of a former curtain, though the present battlements are counterfeit. Evidently the Clevedon family had a small castle here in the thirteenth century, but it was effectively de-fortified by John de Clevedon's reconstruction. The house stands some distance away from the seaside resort, occupying an inland setting at East Clevedon.

Access: Limited opening times in summer (NT).
Reference: NT guidebook.

DUNSTER CASTLE overlooks the picture-book village of Dunster. It is mentioned in the Domesday Book as the 'Castle of Tor'. Dunster Tor is a conical hill which served as a ready-made motte for William de Mohun, who received this estate after the Norman Conquest. In 1376 the Mohun heiress sold the castle to the Luttrell family, who have remained here ever since. Its elevated position lends enchantment but the house itself is a Jacobean mansion, given a picturesque skyline by Anthony Salvin in the 1860s. The medieval castle is now reduced to little more than the inner and outer gatehouses. This is a consequence of the Civil War. After resisting an attack on behalf of Parliament, the castle changed sides and became the staunchest Royalist garrison in Somerset. Under Colonel Wyndham it withstood five months of siege. After its surrender in April 1646 the defences were slighted but the new mansion was left unmolested. The only other recorded siege is an unsuccessful assault by King Stephen's supporters in 1139.

The approach from the village ascends past Tudor stables to the outer gatehouse, added by Sir Hugh Luttrell in 1420. This massive oblong block, with polygonal angle turrets and traceried windows, is the most conspicuous remaining part of the medieval castle. It is placed at right-angles to the inner gate, which is flanked by truncated, half-round towers. These are attributed to Reginald de Mohun (d.1278) though the iron-studded gates are fifteenth-century. Reginald also built a towered curtain around the bailey, sadly reduced to a small portion of wall and one ruinous, semi-circular tower. The bailey now serves as a forecourt to George Luttrell's mansion, commenced in 1617. It occupies the site of the medieval hall range and some older walls are incorporated. A shell keep crowned the Tor but it was landscaped away in the eighteenth century.

Access: Open regularly in summer (NT).

Reference: NT guidebook.

Relations: Round-towered gatehouses such as St Briavels, Rockingham and Beeston.

FARLEIGH HUNGERFORD CASTLE was built by Sir Thomas Hungerford, earliest known Speaker of the House of Commons. He purchased the manor in 1370. His castle existed by 1383 because in that year he was pardoned for crenellating his house without a licence. Thomas erected a quadrangular castle typical of his era, to which his son Sir Walter added an outer courtyard in the 1420s. Except for a period of forfeiture arising from their adherence to the Lancastrian cause during the Wars of the Roses, the Hungerfords lived here until 1686, when declining circum- stances forced them to sell it. The castle quickly sank into ruins after that.

The castle stands on a rise above the River Frome, four miles west of Trowbridge. Sir Walter's outer curtain, enclosing an irregular area in contrast to the inner quadrangle, has one rounded flanking tower guarding the approach and a rather flimsy gate tower with a drawbridge recess. No retainers' lodgings survive, but the chapel and a house for priests have not shared the ruinous fate of the other castle buildings. The chapel, though plain by Somerset standards, is interesting for its group of Hungerford family tombs, including the effigies of Sir Thomas and his wife. The chapel actually predates the castle because it originated as the parish church. Walter built the present church nearby by way of compensation. It is unusual for an outer bailey to be better preserved than the inner, but Thomas' quadrangle now resembles an archaeological site. The layout shows circular corner towers and a round-towered gatehouse in the middle of the south front. However, only the two southern angle towers still rise to near their full height. The rest is reduced to footings and fragments, and the residential buildings which filled much of the courtyard are marked only by incomplete foundations.

Access: Standard opening times (EH).

Reference: EH guidebook.

Relations: Sir Walter Hungerford's gatehouse at Newton. Compare the outer court-yards for retainers at Thornbury and Cooling.

LANGPORT TOWN DEFENCES   Langport enjoyed considerable prosperity as an inland port in the Middle Ages. Like many other small towns its earth ramparts were never strengthened by a continuous stone wall, but the gates – always the most vulnerable parts of a defensive circuit – were rebuilt in stone in the fourteenth century. Only the East Gate survives, near the parish church. This simple gate passage is surmounted by the Hanging Chapel, erected in the new Perpendicular style by one of the town's guilds in 1353. Chapels surmounting town gateways were once quite common.

Access: Visible from outside.

Relations: The chapels on town gates at Bristol and Warwick.

NETHER STOWEY CASTLE is a motte-and-bailey earthwork strongly positioned on a hill overlooking the village. The foundations of a square keep have been uncovered on the summit of the large motte, and its outline is still clearly discernible in the turf. It is likely, but not certain, that this was the castle of William Fitz Odo, burnt down in 1139 by supporters of King Stephen who threw blazing torches through the arrow-slits of the keep. Later the castle was held by the Audleys. It had fallen into decay by the fifteenth century.

Access: Freely accessible.

NEWTON CASTLE   In Newton Park, three miles west of Bath, are a Georgian mansion and two portions of the fortified manor house which preceded it. Only a square tower house and a gatehouse survive, and there is no proof that a walled courtyard ever connected them. The tower was probably built in the fourteenth century by the St Loe family, but its age is difficult to determine owing to the extent of later alterations. Large windows and a stair turret were inserted during a Tudor remodelling. We are on firmer ground with the gate tower, which can be attributed to Sir Walter Hungerford (d.1449). It must be admitted that this gatehouse is by no means a formidable structure, but it has flanking turrets and a row of machicolations to maintain an air of defence. In front of the gatehouse extends a range of Tudor stables with an outer gateway though the middle.

Access: Now part of a college. Obtain permission to view.

Relations: Sir Walter Hungerford added the outer courtyard at Farleigh Hungerford. For the St Loes see Sutton Court.

NUNNEY CASTLE This is the attractive ruin of a fourteenth-century tower house, closely surrounded by a wet moat. It is the work of Sir John de la Mare, who obtained a licence to crenellate in 1373. He was a typical castle-builder of his age – a veteran soldier who made a fortune from ransom and plunder in the Hundred Years War. By the time Sir John built his castle the war was turning sour for the English, and the glut of castle building by veterans may have been motivated at least in part by fears of a French counter-invasion. However, Nunney saw no fighting until 1645, when it fell to the Roundheads after a two-day siege.

The tower house is a rectangular structure with large round turrets at the four corners. It is so narrow in relation to its length that on the shorter sides the turrets almost meet. Tower and turrets were originally surmounted by a continuous machicolated parapet, as the many corbels show. Each turret carries a recessed top stage rising above parapet level. All-round machicolation and recessed inner turrets are more typical of France than England, and the plan is that of a French *bastille*. Sir John must have become familiar with such features during his years of campaigning. The tower house is well preserved except for the north wall, which took a battering during the Civil War siege and finally collapsed in 1910. It is entered on this side through a simple doorway at ground level. A large fireplace shows that this floor housed the kitchen. The first floor was partitioned into service quarters, while the two upper storeys, with their more elaborate windows, contained the hall and solar. Numerous small apartments filled the corner turrets, including a chapel at the level of the solar. The tower contained all the main accommodation. Nevertheless there must have been a courtyard of some sort but no trace remains.

Access: Freely accessible (EH).
Reference: BOE *North Somerset and Bristol.* Mackenzie (II).
Relations: Keeps with corner turrets at Dudley and Rye. For recessed inner turrets see Herstmonceux and Warwick.

STOGURSEY CASTLE lies to the south of the village. The name is a corruption of Stoke Courcy and the castle was founded by the De Courcys in Norman times. Unlike the medieval priory church which has survived the centuries unscathed, the castle is now a ramshackle ruin which reflects its stormy history. It was first destroyed by order of King John. The notorious robber-baron Fawkes de Breaute refortified it, but the castle was destroyed again following his downfall in 1224. Most of the existing masonry dates from *circa* 1300, when the castle was held by the Fitzpayne family. The enclosure is surrounded by a wet moat. Much of the curtain survives, though deprived of whatever flanking towers it once possessed. The base of a round-towered gatehouse is surmounted by a Jacobean cottage. Only one of the cross-slits is original and the drawbridge, of course, is a modern replacement. The castle saw action for the last time in 1455, when a band of Yorkists mounted a surprise attack and sacked it.

Access: Exterior visible from a public footpath.
Reference: VCH *Somerset* (VI).

SUTTON COURT, a mile north-east of Bishop Sutton, suffered heavy restoration in the nineteenth century. The core of the house is a square defensive tower surmounted by a round stair turret. It was probably built by the St Loe family in the fourteenth century and may be compared with their tower house at Newton. The surviving portion of embattled curtain indicates a walled courtyard as well. The rest of Sutton Court is later work, comprising a fifteenth-century hall range and a chapel wing added while Bess of Hardwick was lady of the manor.

Access: Private.
Relations: Newton.

TAUNTON CASTLE is now only a portion of its former self. From Saxon times until 1648 the bishops of Winchester were lords of the manor. Bishop William Giffard (1107–29) built the original hall, some of which survives, but it was his successor Henry de Blois who converted the site into a castle. It was one of several episcopal palaces which Henry fortified during the troubled years of the Anarchy. In the Civil War Taunton endured three sieges on the side of Parliament, and the castle defences were largely destroyed after Charles II's restoration.

The western half of the inner bailey was spared because of its administrative functions. It consists of two converging ranges, forming a triangular layout. The south range is jointly the work of two early-thirteenth-century bishops, Peter des Roches and William Raleigh. A modest round tower projects at the angle and a simple gate tower leads into the bailey. Between the two stood the chapel, but the whole south range has a neo-Gothic veneer owing to renovation in the 1780s, when it was adapted to form the judges' lodging. The long hall range forming the north side of the bailey has a complicated history. Its western half embodies the aisled hall built by Bishop Giffard and the west wall is still recognisably Norman. In the 1240s Bishop Raleigh made the hall narrower than it was before, and it was extended to the east in the eighteenth century. The hall served as a court house for centuries. Judge Jeffreys condemned 508 rebels to death here following the Battle of Sedgemoor in 1685. It now houses the exhibits of the Somerset County Museum. The north front of the hall overlooks the River Tone and still bears the scars of Civil War bombardment. Henry de Blois' oblong keep dominated the destroyed eastern half of the bailey. Some of its footings have been exposed. Originally there was a large outer bailey, but this has vanished with the exception of a much-restored gate tower standing alongside the Castle Hotel.

Access: Open regularly (LA).
Reference: A Brief History of Taunton Castle by T. J. Hunt. BOE *South and West Somerset.*
Relations: Henry de Blois' castle-palaces at Farnham, Bishop's Waltham and Wolvesey (Winchester).

WELLS: BISHOP'S PALACE The cathedral and close at Wells are arguably both the least spoilt and most beautiful in Europe, and the Bishop's Palace complements the ensemble beautifully. It has been the residence of the bishops of Bath and Wells at least since the time of Bishop Jocelin (1206–42). Under the Normans the cathedral church had been transferred to Bath and Jocelin was the first bishop to return fully to Wells again. It is therefore appropriate that the oldest part of the palace goes back to his episcopate and is thus contemporary with the glorious west front of the cathedral. The palace was not fortified until 1341. Riots against the clergy prompted Bishop Ralph of Shrewsbury to obtain a licence to crenellate in that year, and the defences were paid for out of a fine levied on the townsfolk. Ralph's curtain surrounds an irregular, pentagonal enclosure immediately south of the cathedral cloister. The embattled wall has a rounded bastion at each of the five angles. It must be admitted that the curtain is not especially high and the circuit would have been too long to guard effectively. The wide, wet moat (now inhabited by swans) constituted as significant a barrier. Feudal pride is concentrated primarily upon the handsome gatehouse, a lofty block with semi-octagonal flanking turrets to front and rear. Evidently this was the bishop's refuge in times of danger.

Most of the residential buildings stand clear of the curtain, so defence was not compromised by domestic convenience. The central range is Bishop Jocelin's original hall-house. It was heavily restored in the 1840s and the high-pitched, many-gabled appearance is the result of that era. The vaulted undercrofts are original, however, along with the row of windows above. Robert Burnell's chapel projects to the right of Jocelin's wing. A tall, oblong structure with delicate window tracery and a soaring vault, it shows the architectural progress of half a century to good effect. Note the carved roof bosses and the many fragments of medieval glass. Burnell's great hall projects at an angle from the chapel. It has been reduced to little more than two walls, but the size of the building and the tall windows are still impressive. Both hall and chapel are ambitious works for their time, reflecting Bishop Burnell's status as Lord Chancellor under Edward I. Unfortunately the hall was too grand a structure for his successors and it has been roofless since 1550. A century earlier Bishop Beckington built a new wing to the left of Jocelin's range, balancing Burnell's chapel. It formed in effect a new residence on a smaller scale, and its position against the curtain shows that defence was no longer an important consideration.

Access: Limited opening times in summer.
Reference: BOE *North Somerset and Bristol.* Leaflet guide.
Relations: Episcopal castle-palaces such as Sherborne, Wolvesey (Winchester) and Farnham. The great hall resembles Bishop Burnell's castle at Acton Burnell.

OTHER SITES A dramatically-sited Norman castle (mentioned in the Domesday Book) stood on St Michael's Hill at *Montacute*. It did not last long and only an eighteenth-century monument can be seen on this tree-covered hill today. Another important Norman site is *Castle Cary*, where a large Norman keep has been excavated. William de Briwerre's castle at *Bridgwater* was licensed in 1200 and destroyed after the Civil War. The only vestige of this early quadrangular stronghold is the arch of a water gate on West Quay. Fragments of wall mark the site of *Richmont Castle* at East Harptree. Only a mutilated gateway survives from the city wall which surrounded *Bath*.

Staffordshire

The main castles of Staffordshire began as motte-and-bailey strongholds, an origin which has dictated their layout ever since. Norman earthworks underlie Chartley's towered enclosure, while fourteenth-century tower houses crown the mottes at Dudley and Stafford. Tamworth Castle has its residential buildings squeezed into the confines of a Norman shell keep. Even the rebuilding of Tutbury Castle under the Lancastrian kings was constrained by the old rampart. The quadrangular type of the later Middle Ages is represented in an incomplete way by Caverswall, Eccleshall and (unusually) the close wall surrounding Lichfield Cathedral. Most of the county's castles suffered a slighting after the Civil War.

ALTON CASTLE rises from a cliff above the River Churnett. The present house is a Victorian Gothic fantasy of 1847, designed by the architect Pugin for the Earl of Shrewsbury who lived nearby at Alton Towers. However, a real medieval castle occupied the site and the forecourt of the house formed the bailey. It was built by Bertram de Verdun in the 1170s and was provided from the outset with at least one flanking tower. This tower – tall and square – survives in a ruinous condition, with a bit of curtain attached. Note the wide, rock-cut ditch in front.
  Access: Visible from the road.
  Relations: The Norman flanking towers at Windsor and Dover.

CAVERSWALL CASTLE, five miles east of Stoke-on-Trent, was built by William de Caverswall, Sheriff of Staffordshire. He obtained a licence to crenellate in 1275. His castle is an early example of the quadrangular type, and also an early example of the use of octagonal towers instead of square or round. There are four at the corners and another pair flanking the original entrance on the east. Unfortunately the whole ensemble was heavily restored in the Jacobean period. The curtain has been reduced to a revetment wall since the ground level is considerably higher inside the courtyard, and buttresses have been added at regular intervals to reinforce it. The towers rise higher, but their windows are all Jacobean and their crenellated parapets have been replaced by balustrades. The transformation was carried out by Matthew Craddock, a successful merchant and New World pioneer. He purchased the estate around 1615 and built the handsome house which stands on the north side of the courtyard. Presumably he lowered the curtain to allow an unimpeded view into the gardens.
  Access: Private (now a monastery).
  Reference: Salter.
  Relations: The quadrangular castle at Eccleshall.

CHARTLEY CASTLE occupies a hilltop overlooking the A518, approximately midway between Stafford and Uttoxeter. The underlying earthworks, comprising a motte and two baileys in line, are still impressive. They were raised by one of the

Normal earls of Chester. About 1220 another Earl of Chester, Ranulf de Blundeville, built a powerful stone castle here. He raised a strong curtain around the inner bailey with three rounded flanking towers and a round-towered gatehouse. Unfortunately the castle is now very ruinous. The two half-round towers on the south still rise to a commanding height, but the rest has been reduced to footings and lumps of masonry, while the gatehouse has all but disappeared. A large cylindrical keep was placed on top of the earlier motte. Only the base survives, which is unfortunate because round keeps are all too few in England. After Ranulf's death in 1232 Chartley passed to the Ferrers earls of Derby. The castle fell to Henry III after Robert de Ferrers sided with Simon de Montfort, but it seems to have survived to face slow decay in the later Middle Ages. Abandonment finally came in the Tudor period when nearby Chartley Hall was first built.

Access: Freely accessible.
Reference: Salter.
Relations: Ranulf's castles at Beeston and Bolingbroke.

DUDLEY CASTLE was raised by William Fitz Ansculph and is first mentioned in the Domesday Book. The Norman stronghold was destroyed in the aftermath of Prince Henry's revolt. Roger de Somery obtained a licence to refortify the castle in 1264, in return for supporting Henry III against the barons. However, he was taken prisoner soon afterwards so he probably did not get very far. His grandson Sir John de Somery earned notoriety as a robber baron, running a sort of protection racket. It is reported amongst other things that he forced people to assist in building his castles, so the existing keep and curtain are attributed to him. After his death in 1321 the castle passed to the Sutton family. Local squabbles led to an unsuccessful siege in 1330. John Dudley, Duke of Northumberland, transformed the residential buildings into a Tudor mansion. This enterprise was left incomplete on his execution in 1553 for attempting to put Lady Jane Grey on the throne. In 1644 the Roundheads failed to take the castle by storm, but the garrison surrendered without a fight once the Royalist cause was lost. The defences were slighted but the residential buildings remained in use until a fire gutted them in 1750.

The surroundings are now grimly industrial but the limestone ridge on which the castle stands gives it a certain majesty. Today the ruins enjoy the contrast of an accompanying zoo, with animal enclosures in the surrounding ditch. The motte-and-bailey earthworks go back to the Norman era. Some walling and a Tudor gatehouse show the position of a small outer bailey. Sir John de Somery's inner curtain is quite tower-less, which is surprising for the early fourteenth century, and is built in straight sections around the bailey perimeter. Furthermore there is a keep on top of the old motte. Dudley thus has little in common with contemporary quadrangular castles, though the presence of a keep or tower house points to a trend which would increase as the century progressed. The keep was an oblong structure with a rounded bastion at each corner, but the southern half was blasted to its footings at the slighting. Its north facade still towers over the bailey. There were only two storeys, comprising a lofty hall above a store room. The entrance has been consigned to the usual later medieval position at ground level, but there are traces of a chemise wall guarding the approach. At the foot of the motte lies the main gatehouse, now reduced to little more than the vaulted entrance passage and a shattered barbican in front. The gatehouse is also John de Somery's work though it incorporates the side walls of a Norman predecessor.

On the east side of the bailey, following the bends in the curtain, are the residential buildings, now roofless but generally well preserved. Nothing goes back to John de Somery despite the domestic limitations of the keep. The block nearest the gatehouse was built by the Suttons later in the fourteenth century. It contained the chapel and solar over undercrofts, and is relatively little altered. Next comes the hall, rebuilt by John Dudley with a Renaissance loggia facing the bailey. Beyond lie the Tudor kitchen and service wings, the range terminating in a second gateway through the curtain.

Access: Open regularly.
Reference: Guidebook by H. Brakspear & A. Rollason.
Relations: Weoley was another De Somery castle. Compare the tower houses with corner turrets at Stafford and Nunney.

ECCLESHALL CASTLE   The bishops of Lichfield resided here from Saxon times until 1864. Bishop Muschamp obtained an early licence to crenellate in 1200, but the castle was rebuilt to a quadrangular layout by Bishop Walter de Langton *circa* 1310. The chief relic is the shell of the north-east corner tower, a polygonal (nine-sided) structure which has survived virtually intact as a garden folly. Presumably there were other corner towers but only one has been found. The curtain has been reduced to a low revetment wall and the moat (now drained) is crossed by the original stone bridge. Everything else was destroyed during the Civil War, the Roundheads capturing the castle in 1643 after a two-month siege. Bishop Lloyd erected the present mansion on the west side of the courtyard in 1695.

Access: Open occasionally.
Reference: Salter.
Relations: Walter de Langton's close wall at Lichfield and his castle at Thorpe Waterville.

LICHFIELD CLOSE   Lichfield Cathedral was once surrounded by a defensive wall. It was rare for an English cathedral or monastery to develop anything more than a token precinct wall, but Lichfield was not a walled town unlike the majority of cathedral cities. Bishop Walter de Langton, Edward I's Lord Treasurer, obtained a licence to crenellate the cathedral close in 1299. (The west front of the cathedral was built during his episcopate.) The wall enclosed a large rectangle, protecting the canons' houses as well as the cathedral. Today the circuit is reduced to a few isolated stretches, chiefly on the north where the ditch also survives. At the north-east corner stands the hexagonal Bishop's Tower, attached to the Bishop's Palace. A smaller turret (incorporated in St Mary's Vicarage) marks the south-east corner of the circuit. The close became a bone of contention in the Civil War and the cathedral was devastated in the process. It changed hands twice in 1643 and finally fell to the Roundheads after a three-month siege in July 1646. During the first of these sieges the Parliamentary commander, Lord Brooke, was killed by a well-aimed shot from the cathedral's central tower.

Access: The remains are freely accessible.
Reference: VCH *Staffordshire* (XIV).
Relations: The fortified religious precincts at Lincoln and Bury St Edmunds.

LITTYWOOD is a farmhouse surrounded by a ringwork of unusually large proportions, defended by a strong rampart and ditch. It has been suggested that this was the original castle of Roger de Toeni, before his son Robert obtained nearby Stafford Castle. The brick facade of the farmhouse conceals a timber-framed manor house erected later in the Middle Ages. It lies a mile north-east of Bradley on the road to Stafford.

Access: Visible from the road.
Relations: Stafford.

RUSHALL HALL is a modern house occupying the walled enclosure of a medieval manor house. The curtain, not thick but once supporting a parapet, enclosed an oblong courtyard. Residential buildings stood against the curtain, as shown by the fireplace imprints. However, no windows were allowed to pierce the curtain. The angles of the enclosure are quite plain and the only projection is a simple gate tower, its upper chamber now very ruinous. Rushall is relatively late for a structure of such defensive austerity, being the work of the Harper family in the mid fifteenth century. It changed hands twice in the Civil War and afterwards was slighted. The remains stand in Leigh Road.

Access: Exterior only.
Reference: Salter.

STAFFORD CASTLE William the Conqueror raised a castle in the town in 1070. It did not stay with the Crown for long and by the end of the century had passed to Robert de Stafford, whose descendants gradually rose to prominence. For reasons which are quite obscure, the original site was abandoned and a new one chosen a mile to the south-west. Hence the present Stafford Castle is to be found in the suburb of Castlechurch, on a ridge now overlooking the M6 motorway. The impressive earthworks consist of a motte and two baileys. On the motte are the remains of a rectangular tower house with octagonal corner turrets. No doubt it was inspired by the tower on the mound at Dudley. Unfortunately, most of the building is a romantic restoration. Ralph, Lord Stafford, first built the tower house on receipt of a licence to crenellate in 1348. Slighted in the Civil War, it was reconstructed by Baron Stafford early in the nineteenth century but left incomplete. The upper part has been demolished, revealing something of the medieval core.

Access: Freely accessible (LA).
Reference: VCH *Staffordshire* (V). Salter.
Relations: Dudley. Its predecessor, Littywood.

STOURTON CASTLE, overlooking the River Stour, grew out of a royal hunting lodge. Foundations of a towered curtain have been found but the defences were destroyed during the Civil War. The only medieval survivor now is a tall square tower incorporated into an Elizabethan house. The tower was probably built by the Hampton family around 1400. Both tower and house were considerably restored in the nineteenth century.

Access: Private.

TAMWORTH CASTLE Tamworth enters recorded history as the capital of King Offa's Mercia. After the reconquest from the Danes Alfred the Great's daughter Ethelfleda fortified a number of Mercian towns, including Tamworth. According to tradition the castle motte is Ethelfleda's, and this legend is kept alive by a statue in the castle gardens. However, such mounds are a Norman phenomenon and there can be little doubt that the motte was actually raised by Robert de Marmion before the end of the eleventh century. The Marmions held the office of King's Champion, supposedly appearing fully armed at coronations to challenge any would-be opponents of the new monarch. The Frevilles inherited this honour as well as the castle when the Marmion line became extinct in 1294.

The castle and medieval parish church once dominated Tamworth, but now they are overawed by concrete tower blocks. Nevertheless the castle is pleasantly situated in public gardens beside the River Tame. The bailey was already in decay in Tudor times and only the excavated base of a round-towered gatehouse remains to be seen. By contrast, the Norman shell keep on the motte survives intact. It escaped destruction in the Civil War because of the little mansion within. The keep is reached from the former bailey by a thick approach wall, a remarkable example of herringbone masonry dating from *circa* 1100. The keep itself – or rather the irregular, polygonal enclosing wall – is probably a little later. Its battlements are restoration work and much too high for the parapet. A plain square tower projects from the line of the keep and would have commanded the approach. The entrance gateway, surmounted by a Jacobean warder's lodge, is positioned beside the tower.

It is unusual for the main residential buildings of a castle to have stayed within the confines of a shell keep, especially since they remained an aristocratic home until the Victorian era. Indeed, the castle's great attraction is the way in which most of the space inside the keep is crammed with picturesque buildings. The present ones are mainly the work of the Ferrers family, a branch of whom lived here from 1423 to 1688. Their fifteenth-century hall stands in the middle of the keep, thus clear of the surrounding wall. The hall roof is original but the timber-framed walls were filled with brick by Sir John Ferrers, who transformed the keep buildings into an elegant Jacobean house. He rebuilt the solar wing to the south of the hall, creating a suite of private apartments (a portion of the shell keep wall was destroyed in the process). The domestic block to the north of the hall was altered beyond recognition in the nineteenth century.

Access: Open regularly (LA).
Reference: Guidebook. Salter.
Relations: The shell keep at Windsor preserves its interior buildings. Compare the entrance tower on Arundel's shell keep.

TUTBURY CASTLE was founded within five years of the Norman Conquest. Henry de Ferrers received the castle from the King in 1071. Previously it had been held by Hugh d'Avranches, but Hugh relinquished Tutbury in exchange for the Earldom of Chester. One or both of these lords created a powerful motte-and-bailey castle, admirably sited on the edge of an escarpment above the River Dove. Beyond the D-shaped inner bailey are two flanking outer baileys, and there are remnants of a large enclosure surrounding the town. The ruins of the castle look down on the Norman priory church founded by Henry de Ferrers.

As earls of Derby the Ferrers family twice chanced their arms against the Crown, siding with Prince Henry in 1173 and Simon de Montfort in 1264. On both occasions the castle suffered a destructive siege from royal forces. Henry III granted the forfeited Ferrers estates to his son Edmund, Earl of Lancaster. The castle was sacked during Earl Thomas' revolt in 1322, but as a Duchy of Lancaster possession it became royal on Henry IV's accession. Mary Queen of Scots was imprisoned here twice, in some discomfort. The castle saw its last military action in the Civil War. It resisted a Roundhead attack in 1643 but succumbed to a heavy bombardment three years later. A slighting followed.

Owing to its Civil War slighting the castle is very much a ruin. The devastation of previous sieges is perhaps the reason for the absence of early medieval masonry. Apart from the foundations of a Norman chapel, the oldest stone portion is the gate tower at the east end of the inner bailey, built by Earl Thomas in 1313. Only the outer face still stands, and the flanking turrets are fifteenth-century additions. A slow rebuilding of the castle took place under the Lancastrian kings, especially Henry VI who settled Tutbury upon his Queen, Margaret of Anjou. The military character is surprising for royal work of the fifteenth century and may reflect Margaret's unpopularity. South of the gatehouse the curtain is largely buried in the Norman rampart bank. The most conspicuous features are the two handsome square towers flanking the curtain. The North Tower, tall and slender, was half blasted down by the Roundheads. The South Tower comprises two compartments. It appears squat because only the lower two storeys were ever built. Both towers have the characteristics of self-contained tower houses. Beyond the South Tower the curtain survives because it formed the outer wall of the King's Lodging, built on the site of the hall in the 1630s. An eighteenth-century folly tower now crowns the motte. The edge of the escarpment, which runs between the motte and the gatehouse, was once supplemented by a wall but every trace has vanished.

Access: Open regularly.
Reference: Guidebook by R. Somerville.
Relations: Duffield and Oakham were other Ferrers castles. The Lancastrian kings also rebuilt the castles of Leicester and Lancaster.

OTHER SITES *Newcastle-under-Lyme* had an important stronghold of the earls of Chester, with a square Norman keep. A low mound in the Queen Elizabeth Gardens marks the site. A couple of bits of wall crowning a rock are all that remain to be seen of *Heighley Castle*, while nearby *Madeley* preserves a fragment of a castle gateway.

Suffolk

There is an impressive Norman inheritance in the motte-and-bailey earthworks at Clare and Haughley, and the innovative late Norman castles of Framlingham and Orford. Orford Castle preserves its lofty round keep though the towered curtain which accompanied it has perished. Both elements were unusual in the 1160s. Henry II built Orford to check the power of the Bigods, who held sway from their castles of Framlingham and Bungay. Roger Bigod copied Orford's square mural towers in his rebuilding of Framlingham but dispensed with a keep entirely. Little Wenham Hall is interesting both as an early brick building and as a rare example of a crenellated – as opposed to truly fortified – house. Wingfield Castle, though incomplete, is one of the most picturesque of the later medieval quadrangular strongholds.

BUNGAY CASTLE, by the River Waveney, is a testimony to the fortunes of the Bigod family. It was probably first raised by Roger Bigod, the founder of the dynasty, soon after 1100. Roger's son Hugh took advantage of the Anarchy to augment his own power, being created Earl of Norfolk as the price of his eventual loyalty to King Stephen. Henry II confiscated his castles of Bungay and Framlingham, and in 1164 he was obliged to pay a thousand-pound fine in order to regain them. Hugh then built a keep here. It was a massive square edifice, divided into two compartments by a cross-wall and entered via a forebuilding. Clearly at that stage Bungay rather than Framlingham was the chief Bigod seat. In 1173 Hugh enthusiastically took part in Prince Henry's revolt in spite of his advanced age. On the failure of the rebellion Bungay Castle was besieged by Henry II's supporters. The narrow mining tunnel which was driven through the south-west angle of the keep can still be seen. Whether the garrison surrendered before the wooden props were set alight, or whether the mine failed to bring down the keep, is impossible to tell. Despite this escape only the ground-floor stage of the keep remains, and the curtain which closely surrounded it has been reduced to some footings. There can be little doubt that Bungay, like Framlingham, was dismantled by the King's command. It was once assumed that Bungay lay abandoned in favour of Framlingham until 1294, when another Roger, the last of the Bigod earls, obtained a licence to re-crenellate. The twin semi-circular gate towers – the only parts of the castle still rising to nearly full height – are attributed to him. However, the gate towers merely flank an entrance, rather than forming a fully-developed Edwardian gatehouse, so an early-thirteenth-century rebuilding may be postulated. The last Roger Bigod incurred Edward I's wrath by refusing to go to war in Gascony. After his death in 1306 the Bigod lands reverted to the Crown, and Bungay Castle seems to have fallen into ruin.

Access: Freely accessible (LA).
Reference: Bungay Castle by H. Cane.
Relations: Framlingham. Compare the undermining of Rochester keep.

BURY ST EDMUNDS ABBEY Bury was once dominated by one of the greatest of Benedictine abbeys. It grew out of the shrine of St Edmund who was martyred by the Danes. Today the abbey is reduced to scattered ruins and its former magnificence is evoked only by the two gatehouses which led into the abbey precinct from the town. The northern one, known as the Great Gate, is a surprising blend of architectural elegance with defence. The niches and roundels are there for the sake of beauty, but the only openings towards the town are cross-slits and the outer archway is defended by a portcullis. Heraldic shields confirm that the gatehouse was built following the bloody riots of 1327. In that year disputes between the abbey and the townsfolk came to a head. The abbey was plundered freely and several monks were killed. As well as the gatehouse, the Norman precinct wall was heightened and embattled in a rare attempt to convert a monastic precinct into a fortified enclosure. A few portions remain. Even the three arches beneath the Abbot's Bridge, where the precinct wall crosses the River Lark, were sealed with portcullises as the surviving grooves testify. Such contrived defences could never have been effective and they did not prevent the abbey from being sacked again during the Peasants' Revolt.

Access: The remains are freely accessible (EH).
Reference: Guidebook by A. B. Whittingham.
Relations: The defensive monastic gatehouses at Thornton, Tynemouth and Alnwick.

CLARE CASTLE formed the centre of the Honour of Clare, an estate awarded to Richard Fitz Gilbert after the Norman Conquest. It existed by 1090. Fitz Gilbert's descendants took the name De Clare, became earls of Hertford and Gloucester and played a key role in the Norman invasions of Wales and Ireland. The last of their line fell at Bannockburn in 1314 and Clare Castle seems to have fallen into decay after that. A high, conical motte rises above the River Stour in Clare Park. On its summit two sides of a polygonal Norman shell keep still stand. The inner bailey is occupied by a disused railway station and only a length of rampart bank survives.

Access: Open as part of a country park.
Reference: Mackenzie (I).
Relations: The De Clare castles at Tonbridge and Bletchingley.

EYE CASTLE was founded by William Malet according to the Domesday Book. That must have been before his death fighting Hereward the Wake in 1071. His son Robert was banished by Henry I and Eye became a Crown garrison. It was still maintained as such under Henry II. The high motte, covered in trees, can be seen opposite the magnificent Perpendicular tower of the parish church. Some masonry of an approach wall still climbs the motte, but the 'ruin' on top is a nineteenth-century folly. Castle Street preserves the outline of the bailey.

Access: Visible from the road.

FRAMLINGHAM CASTLE was the chief residence of the Bigod earls of Norfolk. It originated soon after 1100, when the first Roger Bigod received a grant of lands in return for supporting Henry I. The earthworks – comprising a large, low, oval motte and an outer bailey – date from his time. Roger's son Hugh Bigod made Bungay the chief stronghold of the family and built his great keep there. Framlingham remained an earth-and-timber stronghold though Hugh did provided some stone residential buildings. After Hugh's revolt in 1173 the defences of Framlingham were dismantled. Hugh's son, another Roger, erected the impressive towered curtain which crowns the motte, no doubt to compensate for the destruction of Bungay. Roger did not recover Framlingham until 1189 and it is likely that he began building immediately. If he had delayed another decade he would probably have employed rounded flanking towers instead of square ones. Presumably the castle was complete by 1215 when it fell to King John, a reprisal for Roger Bigod's involvement with Magna Carta. As there are no signs of damage it would appear that the garrison did not put up much resistance, despite the castle's strength. It was never put to the test again.

Mural towers had appeared sparingly in earlier Anglo-Norman castles, but it was under Henry II that they were first used in a comprehensive way to flank a curtain wall. Those at Framlingham were probably inspired by Henry's destroyed curtain at

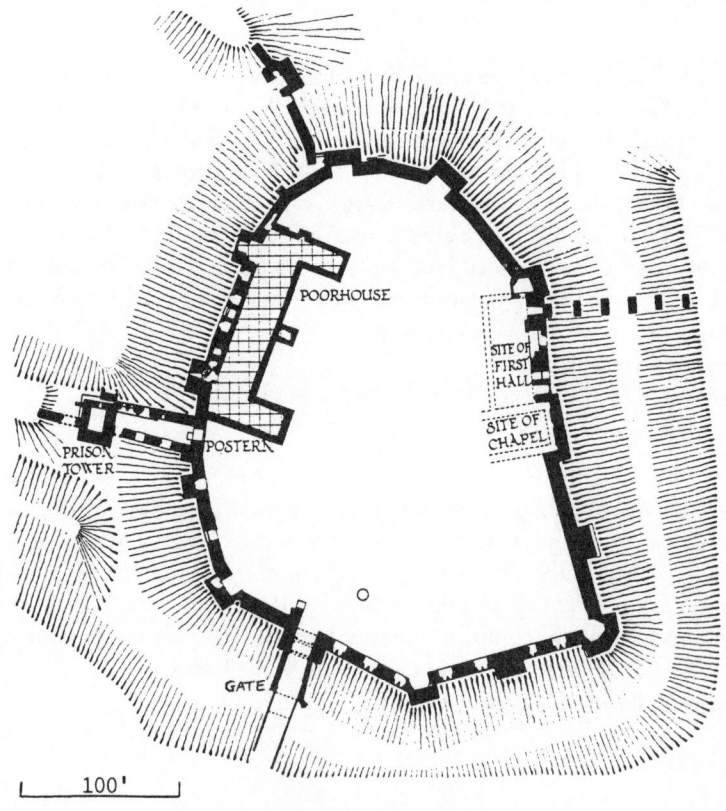

FRAMLINGHAM CASTLE

Orford. Hence they are all square-fronted, and a curtain comprehensively flanked by square towers is something of a rarity since this development coincided with the appearance of round defensive towers. There are thirteen mural towers at Framlingham, three of them solid but the others open-backed. Although they vary in size they are more or less equal in status – not one of them could be described as a keep. In effect the whole enclosure is the keep or there is no keep – another departure from the keep-dominated castles of the twelfth century. Another development is the increased height of the curtain and the greater height of the towers. In conjunction with the motte the walls would have been impossible to scale. It is still possible to do a complete circuit of the wall-walk, though some of the battlements have perished. The open-backed towers were, as now, crossed by wooden bridges which could have been removed if an enemy gained control of one sector of wall. One of the towers contains the entrance gateway.

The same Roger Bigod added an embanked enclosure to the west of the motte. It is only surrounded by an earth rampart but two wing walls link it to the great curtain. The southern wing wall is actually double, enclosing a passage which leads to a postern. This postern is guarded by the square Prison Tower which is actually the largest of the Framlingham towers. Its position allowed it to act as a powerful spur commanding the entire western approach to the castle.

In contrast to the excellent preservation of the surrounding curtain, the residential buildings have almost vanished. A poor house of 1729 occupies the site of the great hall. On the opposite side of the motte one wall of Hugh Bigod's original hall is incorporated in the curtain, and the wide mural tower adjoining it preserves the imprint of Hugh's chapel. These apartments grew into a palace under the Mowbray and Howard dukes of Norfolk, who followed the Bigods in residing at Framlingham. The brick chimneys which surmount most of the towers are an ornamental Tudor addition of the Howards. They also refashioned the main gateway and inserted their arms above it. Only with the execution of the fourth Howard duke in 1572 was the castle abandoned.

Access: Standard opening times (EH).
Reference: Guidebook by F. J. Raby & P. K. Baillie Reynolds.
Relations: Orford. The Bigod castles of Bungay and Thetford. Compare the Norman towered curtains at Windsor and Dover.

HAUGHLEY CASTLE rises behind the village church and green. It is an exceptional Norman earthwork consisting of a huge motte – over sixty feet tall and thus one of the highest in existence – and an oblong bailey, both surrounded by water-filled moats. The bailey is also defended by a massive earth rampart. No masonry is visible and it is unlikely that the castle ever received any stone defences. The earthworks are attributed to Hugh de Montfort before 1100. During Prince Henry's revolt in 1173 the castle, which then had a royal garrison, was destroyed by Hugh Bigod and his ally, Robert de Beaumont. Their rebel army soon succumbed to Henry II's forces but Haughley was never reoccupied.

Access: Freely accessible.
Relations: The mottes at Pleshey and Thetford.

LIDGATE CASTLE is an unusual Norman earthwork. Its motte is roughly oblong in plan and the ditched bailey encloses the parish church of St Mary. The nave of the church is a simple Norman structure which probably originated as the castle chapel. Nearby some featureless walling may mark the site of the hall. It has been suggested that Lidgate was one of the castles raised by King Stephen in 1143 to contain the revolt of Geoffrey de Mandeville, but the masonry suggests a longer period of occupation. The site lies six miles south-east of Newmarket.

Access: Freely accessible.
Relations: Burwell was another of Stephen's castles.

LITTLE WENHAM HALL Seven miles south-west of Ipswich stands one of the most perfect specimens of a thirteenth-century manor house. Apart from its excellent condition, the house is notable as a very early example of English brickwork – probably the earliest to survive. Except for the stone foundations and window dressings, brick is used throughout, even for the vaults which cover the ground-floor undercrofts and the chapel. Sir John de Vallibus is believed to have commenced building. After his death in 1287 it was completed by Petronilla de Nerford, and her namesake St Petronilla is depicted on a boss in the chapel vault. The house follows an L-plan, with the hall occupying the main axis at first-floor level. The chapel stands at right-angles to it and the solar is relegated to the floor above, so the wing is higher than the main block. Higher still is the stair turret in the angle between them. The house is a compact block which may be regarded as an early tower house. Both wings are capped by a crenellated parapet quite suitable for defence. However, the large windows at first-floor level, especially the traceried chapel window, would have detracted from security. In the absence of any outer fortifications the parapet must be regarded as symbolic.

Access: Private.
Reference: BOE *Suffolk*.
Relations: Crenellated manor houses at Acton Burnell and Markenfield.

METTINGHAM CASTLE stands in isolation two miles south-east of Bungay. Sir John de Norwich obtained a licence to crenellate in 1342 as a reward for his services in the Scottish and French wars. Since he was still active on campaign the castle was largely built in his absence. Sir John's effigy can be seen in Mettingham church a mile to the north. Two large, water-filled moats, with a smaller one between them, describe the area of the castle. The northern moat surrounded a walled quadrangle with corner towers, but only the north curtain and its central gatehouse survive. The gatehouse is a tall shell with semi-octagonal flanking turrets. In front are fragments of a barbican. As a secular stronghold Mettingham had only a short life. It was inherited by Sir John's niece, Katherine de Brewes, who happened to be a nun. She made it over to a college of priests in 1382 and they lived here until the Dissolution.

Access: On private land.
Reference: Mackenzie (I).
Relations: Quadrangular Wingfield Castle. Barnwell and Leybourne also ended up in ecclesiastical hands.

ORFORD CASTLE Before its harbour was choked by the great spit known as Orford Ness, Orford enjoyed prosperity as a port. The castle here was erected on a virgin site by Henry II in the years 1165–73. The total cost was £1413. Most of this sum was spent in the first two building seasons, no doubt on the unusual keep which is the only portion still standing. In effect the keep was financed from the fine which Henry II had exacted from Hugh Bigod, Earl of Norfolk. Indeed, although coastal defence must have been a factor, it would seem that Orford was built primarily to check the power of Bigod and other East Anglian barons. Work on a towered curtain then proceeded at a more leisurely pace. Although not the first in a Norman castle, the mural towers were probably the earliest to flank every stretch of wall. No doubt they provided the inspiration for Framlingham Castle, but Orford's curtain has vanished. The castle was complete just in time for Prince Henry's revolt. However, it played no part in the fighting, even though the rebels received reinforcements on the Suffolk coast, and later events passed it by. Edward III finally disposed of the castle by granting it to the Earl of Suffolk.

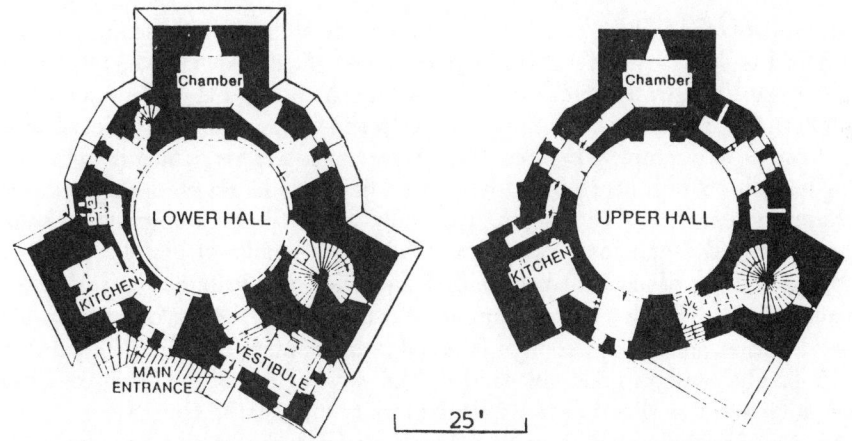

ORFORD CASTLE: KEEP AT FIRST- AND SECOND-FLOOR LEVELS

Only rough earthworks indicate the position of the bailey, but the keep remains intact owing to later preservation as a landmark. It is basically an early example of a circular keep, though not in fact the earliest in England. Admittedly the exterior surface is actually polygonal and the outline is disturbed by the projection of three square towers and a forebuilding. These towers have been the cause of some debate, since their angles would have been more vulnerable to undermining than the circular core. An attempt was clearly made to build a round keep without sacrificing the domestic amenities found in the great square keeps of the late Norman period. As well as providing flanking cover the towers contained subsidiary accommodation for which there was no room in the main body of the keep, and the forebuilding was an obligatory feature in a great Norman keep such as this. Those round keeps which dispensed with projections in favour of security were barely habitable. That is why so few were ever built.

Steps lead up to the forebuilding entrance at first-floor level. Above the vestibule is an ornate little chapel. A wide spiral staircase occupies the tower adjoining the forebuilding. The other towers contain small chambers, arranged so that there are two storeys for each main floor. Evidently the two main apartments formed halls, so the 'solar' in each case must have been reduced to a small chamber in one of the towers. Both halls are served by a kitchen – it is rare to find even one in a Norman keep. Presumably the lower hall at first-floor level was the constable's. The upper (i.e. royal) hall could afford to be better lit. Its present flat roof is misleading and the surviving corbels once supported a conical roof. The keep rose high enough to shield this roof from projectiles, and the towers rise higher still. The ground floor of the keep is the usual storage chamber, with a well in the centre.

Access: Standard opening times (EH).

Reference: Guidebook by R. Allen Brown.

Relations: Framlingham. Round keeps at New Buckenham and Conisbrough, and Henry II's octagonal keep at Chilham.

WINGFIELD CASTLE   The original manor house of the Wingfield family is now Wingfield College. The Wingfield heiress married Michael de la Pole, who made the rare transition from merchant's son to aristocrat. Richard II made him Earl of Suffolk and he obtained a licence to crenellate in 1384. Presumably Wingfield Castle was more or less complete by then. Only three years later his popularity with the King led to his banishment and death in exile. His descendants were as tragic as they were prominent, few of them dying peacefully. Michael's son and grandson were killed during the Agincourt campaign. William, first duke of Suffolk, achieved notoriety for his peace settlement with France, and was beheaded at sea by his enemies (1450). The last duke, Edmund, was regarded as the last claimant to the Yorkist throne, and a long period of exile and imprisonment ended in his execution in 1513. The castle was then dismantled. That was the end of the De la Poles but their affluence is recalled by some splendid tombs in the parish church.

Michael de la Pole built his castle a short distance to the west of the church and college which form the hub of the village. The south front of the castle, reflected in the still water of a broad moat, is an attractive composition. In the middle rises a large gatehouse, its semi-octagonal flanking towers rising higher than the central block. The curtain to either side is pierced by traceried windows, showing that important lodgings once stood against the inner face. Octagonal angle towers (not as high as the gatehouse towers) clasp the ends. Once through the gate passage, it becomes apparent that the south front is now just a facade. The other three sides of the quadrangle have been reduced to a low moat revetment, and nothing has survived of the palatial buildings which must have lined the courtyard. The existing house on the west side, though Tudor, is a comparatively modest dwelling of timber-framed construction, reflecting the castle's subsequent history as the home of tenant farmers.

Access: Private, and barely visible from outside.

Reference: Mackenzie (I).

Relations: The De la Poles also occupied Donnington. Quadrangular castles such as Maxstoke and Bodiam.

OTHER SITES Suffolk has motte-and-bailey sites at *Denham* (near Bury), Great *Ashfield, Lindsey* and *Milden*. The first two retain their wet moats. Two Roman forts of the 'Saxon Shore' were refortified under the Normans. *Burgh Castle* still has its Roman walls but the Norman motte has been levelled, while *Walton Castle* (near Felixstowe) lies submerged beneath the encroaching sea. Nothing is left of *Ipswich*'s medieval town wall.

Surrey

The Norman castles of Surrey stood in a line along the North Downs, guarding the main approaches to London. Farnham Castle is the only one to survive more or less complete, though the royal keep at Guildford makes an impressive ruin. The others have been reduced to earthworks. Surrey is one of those Home Counties where castles never proliferated, and there are hardly any from the later Middle Ages.

BETCHWORTH CASTLE Sir Thomas Browne, Treasurer of the Royal Household, obtained a licence to crenellate his house here in 1449. Despite the licence there are no indications of any serious defence here. The shattered ruin which remains represents the residential wing of Browne's mansion, remodelled in Jacobean times but now quite featureless. It stands on a knoll in Betchworth Park, midway between Betchworth village and Dorking.

Access: On private land.

BLETCHINGLEY CASTLE occupies a ridge to the south of the village, commanding a fine view across the Weald. William the Conqueror granted Bletchingley to Richard Fitz Gilbert, founder of the powerful De Clare family, and the earthworks are probably his. They consist of two baileys with a ringwork between them. No stonework is visible now but excavations have unearthed what appears to have been a hall-keep. The castle was destroyed by Henry III after Gilbert de Clare sided with Simon de Montfort.

Access: On private land.
Relations: The De Clare castles of Tonbridge and Clare.

FARNHAM CASTLE dominates the town from its hilltop site. Until 1927 the castle – a convenient staging post between London and Winchester – was a seat of the bishops of Winchester, and it remains a possession of the English Church. King Stephen's brother, Henry de Blois, first exploited this defensive position during the Anarchy. Around 1138 Bishop Henry fortified all his palaces. He fled into exile on Henry II's accession and his castles were dismantled, but Farnham rose again after the bishop's return in 1158. It is uncertain how far he got in the last thirteen years of his life. He probably at least started the keep but the rest must be the work of his

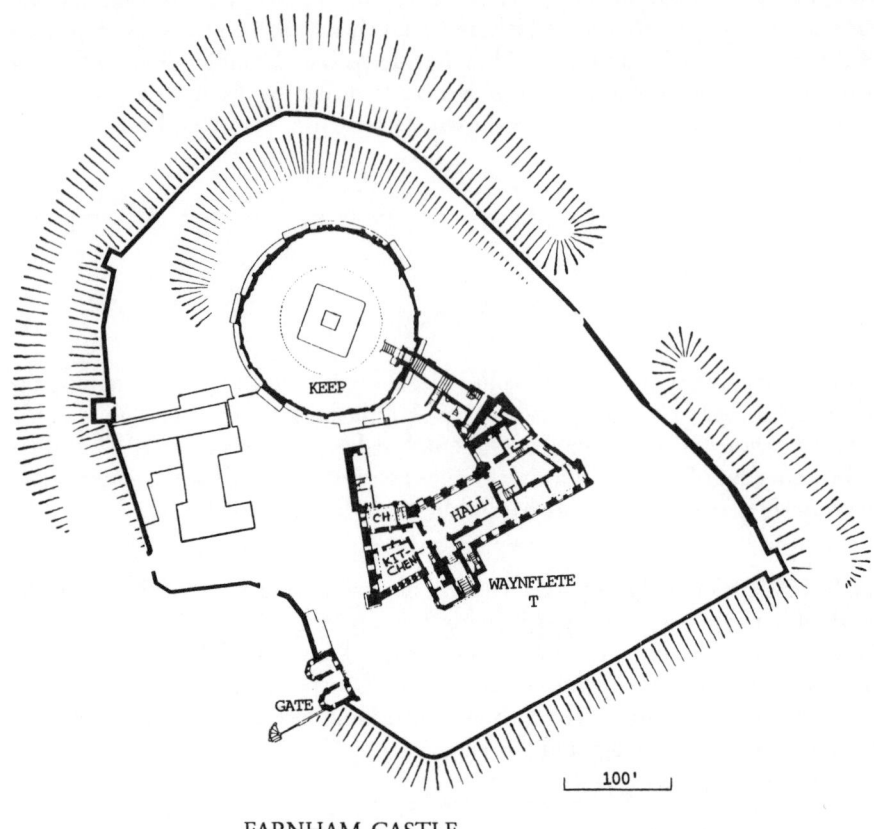

FARNHAM CASTLE

successors, Richard Toclive and Godfrey de Lucy. The castle remains basically a late Norman structure though it has been subjected to many alterations, some of them disfiguring.

The castle was surrounded by an outer curtain intended to keep the defences separate from the residential buildings. Much of the curtain remains though the surrounding ditch must have been as formidable an obstacle. Three square towers still project from the line of the curtain. They are typically late Norman but the truncated gatehouse is of the fully-developed, thirteenth-century type with flanking towers. The inner castle consists of a large shell keep and a small, triangular bailey, together forming a keyhole shape. The main buildings have always occupied the long south range, away from the keep. In 1470–75 William of Waynflete added the brick entrance tower which is now the dominant feature. Its corner turrets and bold parapet (with phoney machicolations) are typical of the last days of castellated architecture. Bishop Waynflete's tower is not a gatehouse but rather a grandiose porch, with steps leading up to the former screens passage between the hall and the kitchen. Bishop Morley reduced the hall in size after the Restoration, but one wooden

240

post from the walled-up Norman arcade can still be seen. The row of lancet windows in the former kitchen shows that the inner bailey was residential rather than defensive in character from the outset. Facing the bailey at a higher level is a Norman chapel, complete with arcade and chancel arch. On the east side the much-altered private apartments of the bishops are arranged around a tiny internal courtyard.

In contrast to the bailey buildings, which are still habitable, the circular shell keep was battered into ruins by order of Parliament. This was a result of the Civil War, when the castle changed hands several times. Despite the slighting, the keep remains a powerful structure with five projections, too shallow to be called towers. A staircase lead up to the entrance through one of the projections. The keep is curious, though not unique, for encasing a motte rather than standing on its summit. This is because of its complex history. Inside the keep it is surprising to find that the motte encloses the stump of a large square tower which was Henry de Blois' original keep. A mound of earth was piled up against it as if to emulate a motte. The tower keep was then demolished and the shell keep wall was erected *around* the mound, the gap between the two being filled in later.

Access: The keep is open at standard times in summer (EH). The residential buildings can be visited at certain times.

Reference: Castle guidebook. Keep guidebook by M. W. Thompson.

Relations: Castle-palaces of the bishops of Winchester at Taunton, Bishop's Waltham and Wolvesey (Winchester). Berkeley and Eynsford are other shell keeps surrounding a motte.

GUILDFORD CASTLE overlooks the River Wey in an elevated defensive position which is typical of Surrey. There is no record of the castle until 1173, when it was garrisoned against Prince Henry's supporters, but it would be surprising if no castle had been founded here after the Norman Conquest. After all, Guildford was a Saxon burgh guarding a gap in the North Downs. Furthermore, there is insufficient expenditure in Henry II's reign to account for the keep, so it probably existed already. King John and Henry III often came here for the hunting. After that the castle declined as a royal residence, serving chiefly as a court house and gaol – a familiar story for a castle in a county town.

The keep is now the only substantial part of the castle. A square Norman structure of average size, it stands on the edge of a large motte which was created out of a natural chalk spur. The keep was stripped of its roof as long ago as 1630, so it is remarkable that it has survived so well in contrast to the rest of the castle. The austerity of the building is relieved only by a few enlarged windows of the Tudor period. This austerity, patches of herringbone masonry and the absence of a forebuilding support a relatively early date. Henry I is the most likely builder. A wooden stair must have led to the first-floor entrance. At this level there is a mural chapel, reached via a passage preserving numerous prisoners' carvings. In addition to the tower keep there was a shell keep around the motte summit, but only a couple of chunks remain. The bailey now forms a municipal garden and little survives. Two sides of a domestic building are a small reminder of Henry III's palace. Nearby the archway of the main gatehouse still leads into the grounds, and a portion of the curtain stands in Castle Cliffe Gardens.

Access: Open regularly in summer (LA).
Reference: Guidebook by F. Holling.
Relations: Probable keeps of Henry I at Portchester, Norwich, Carlisle and Bamburgh.

LAMBETH PALACE, facing Westminster across the Thames, is the historic London residence of the archbishops of Canterbury. First mentioned during the episcopate of Stephen Langton (d.1229), the palace exhibits work from every century since. Its river front is terminated at the northern end by the oblong Lollards' Tower. It gets its name from the tradition that Lollards were incarcerated here, particularly in a small chamber at the top of the projecting turret. The interior is much restored after being gutted during the Blitz. The tower was erected by Henry Chichele in 1434 at a cost of £292, but it seems too small to have served as the tower house of a great ecclesiastic. This is especially apparent when it is realised that the lower annexe is a seventeenth-century addition. Perhaps it was inspired by the Jewel Tower of Westminster Palace, or it may have been intended as a temporary refuge in case of sudden danger. During the Peasants' Revolt of 1381 a frenzied mob had ransacked the palace in search of the then archbishop, who was later hacked to death of Tower Hill. Archbishop Chichele may have feared the worst in the troubled years of Henry VI's minority.

Apart from this tower the palace is quite unfortified. The tower occupies one corner of a small quadrangle known as Cloister Court, containing the archbishops' private quarters. One wing is formed by an early Gothic chapel but the rest has been transformed in later centuries. The large outer courtyard is entered through Cardinal Morton's brick gatehouse of *circa* 1490.

Access: Exterior visible. The interior is open by appointment.
Reference: Guidebook by G. Huelin. VCH *Surrey* (III).
Relations: Palace of Westminster. Saltwood Castle belonged to the archbishops.

REIGATE CASTLE An oval motte (in fact a scarped, natural mound) is the focus of a public garden off the High Street. The castle was probably founded by William de Warenne, Earl of Surrey, after the Norman Conquest. It does not seem to have survived the extinction of the Warenne line in 1347 but the castle was strong enough to suffer a Roundhead siege during the Civil War, after which it was slighted. Not a scrap of original masonry survives – the 'gatehouse' is a folly erected from the old stones in 1777.

Access: Freely accessible (LA).
Relations: The Warenne castles of Lewes, Castle Acre, Conisbrough and Sandal.

OTHER SITES Excavations on the Norman motte at *Abinger* yielded the post holes of two successive wooden towers and a surrounding palisade. *Starborough Castle* (near Edenbridge), a quadrangular castle licensed in 1341, has been reduced to its surrounding moat.

Sussex

It is no coincidence that virtually all Sussex castles stand near the sea. Invasion has always been a threat on the long Sussex coastline – it was here that the Normans landed in 1066. Even before the Battle of Hastings, William the Conqueror had established makeshift castles at Pevensey and Hastings. Sussex therefore has the first English castles to be founded as a result of the Norman Conquest. The chief Norman strongholds formed the administrative centres of the six 'rapes', or districts, into which the county was divided. From east to west they are Hastings, Pevensey, Lewes, Bramber, Arundel and Chichester. Four of them are now ruinous. Arundel has become a stately home, but it has suffered much rebuilding in the process. Only Chichester has lost its castle entirely, but it has the compensation of a complete (if much restored) city wall. The more fragmentary defences of Rye and Winchelsea recall the hazards of the fourteenth century, when coastal towns were regularly devastated by the French and their allies. Amberley Castle and the perfect quadrangular stronghold of Bodiam were built with coastal defence in mind. The same may be true of Herstmonceux Castle, though the latter is a product of the following century and more a brick palace than a fortress. By that time most of the county's ports had become choked with silt. Furthermore there was no sheltered haven suitable for the gathering of a large French or Spanish fleet. Because of this, Camber Castle is only Henrician coastal fort.

AMBERLEY CASTLE rises forbiddingly in the picturesque village of Amberley. It was built by William Rede, Bishop of Chichester, on receipt of a licence to crenellate in 1377. The castle stood near the furthest navigable point of the River Arun, and was probably intended (in conjunction with Arundel Castle down-river) to thwart the raids of French pirates. At the same time it served as a palatial country retreat of the bishops, last used as such in the days of Bishop Sherburne (d.1536). Subsequent decay was hastened, according to tradition, by a Civil War siege. The Duke of Norfolk restored the battered walls from 1908 onwards and made the surviving residential buildings habitable again. His work here is quite restrained when compared with his extensive reconstruction of Arundel.

Amberley is not a standard quadrangular castle and it lacks the perfect symmetry of its near-contemporary, Bodiam. The curtain encloses an elongated space, roughly oblong but narrowing from east to west. At each corner the curtain is raised into a square tower, but these do not project beyond the line of the wall and consequently could not offer any flanking fire. The severity of the curtain is relieved only by narrow window openings, a projecting latrine chute and a simple gatehouse with semi-circular flanking turrets. Bishop Rede's great hall divided the interior of the castle into two unequal courtyards. Half of the hall has vanished though the end wall stands with its three service doorways. The other half and the solar block have been transformed as part of the present house. Beyond is an L-shaped wing embodying the original, thirteenth-century hall of the bishops. Bishop Rede converted it into a chapel but it is now subdivided. Fireplaces and windows in the curtain show that the large western courtyard was surrounded by retainers' lodgings.

Access: Now a hotel. Limited access for non-residents.
Reference: BOE *Sussex.*
Relations: Arundel and Bodiam.

ARUNDEL CASTLE is majestically placed above the River Arun at a gap in the South Downs. It was founded after the Norman Conquest by Roger de Montgomery, Earl of Sussex and Shrewsbury. Roger's earthworks have determined the layout of the castle throughout its history. The plan is similar to Windsor Castle, consisting of two baileys with a conical motte in between. Henry I captured the castle in 1102 when Robert de Belleme, Roger's son, rebelled. Arundel saw action again in 1139 when the Empress Matilda was made welcome here by William d'Albini. King Stephen besieged the castle and forced Matilda to flee to her supporters in the South West. When the Albini (or Aubigny) line died out in 1243 Arundel went to John Fitzalan, whose power base was in the Welsh Marches. As earls of Arundel his descendants enjoyed great wealth and power. They survived two spells of disgrace and dispossession, and several of them are magnificently interred in the Fitzalan Chapel attached to St Nicholas' Church. Since 1580 Arundel has belonged to an equally illustrious family, the Howard dukes of Norfolk. The castle was reduced to ruins after its capture by the Roundheads in 1643. Several restorations followed, culminating in the ambitious reconstruction undertaken by Henry Howard, fifteenth Duke of Norfolk, from 1890 to 1903. His work is much maligned but undeniably magnificent.

The chief medieval survivals are confined to the middle portion of the castle, comprising the gatehouse, a shell keep on the motte and the Bevis Tower. It is curious that the main gatehouse, at the foot of the motte, has always led straight into the inner bailey, where the residential buildings stand. A modern drawbridge crosses into Richard Fitzalan's barbican (*circa* 1295) – a long passage with towers flanking the entrance. The choice of square towers rather than round is unusual for the Edwardian age. The gate tower beyond is an early Norman structure, evidently the first part of the castle to be rebuilt in stone. It may already have stood when the castle was besieged in 1102. From here a wall climbs the slope of the motte to the circular shell keep, generally attributed to William d'Albini. A narrow forebuilding, flanked by a tower, contains the entrance. It must be an early addition because the original keep doorway survives, blocked and partly obscured, alongside. At the foot of the motte in the outer bailey rises the restored Bevis Tower, probably late Norman in origin but with later corner buttresses. From here a much-restored curtain wall loops around the outer bailey.

Palatial residential buildings surround the inner bailey on three sides. The principal rooms and the grandiose exterior are due to the fifteenth duke. An undercroft surviving beneath the west range shows that the Norman hall was somewhat narrower than its Victorian successor. Only on the south front does any medieval work still show. Between the neo-Gothic windows of the Drawing Room some flint masonry of the Norman chapel is still apparent. One blocked window remains complete along with the outline of another.

Access: Open regularly in summer.
Reference: BOE Sussex. Mackenzie (I). Souvenir guide.
Relations: Windsor. See Castle Rising for William d'Albini and Clun for the Fitzalans. Compare the barbicans at Lewes and Warwick.

BODIAM CASTLE is the perfect quadrangular castle of the later Middle Ages. It is set in the middle of a moat sufficiently wide to be considered a lake. The ashlar curtain and its towers are intact, and only the absence of glass betrays the fact that the castle is a ruin. It was built by Sir Edward Dalyngrigge, a veteran of the French wars, in response to a licence to crenellate issued in 1385. Richard II's licence instructs Sir Edward to fortify his manor house 'in defence of the adjacent country and for resistance against our enemies'. Those enemies were the French who, in the previous decade, had gained control of the Channel and wreaked havoc along the South Coast. There were persistent rumours of a full-scale invasion. Although this did not come to fruition, the coastal areas offered easy pickings for French raiders in search of booty and vengeance. The River Rother was then navigable as far as Bodiam, enabling pirates to penetrate some distance inland.

Despite the advances in domestic comfort which characterise its era, the castle manages to present a strong as well as a handsome profile. Tall, cylindrical towers project boldly from the four corners, and to improve flanking cover there is a square tower in the middle of each side, except on the north where the main gatehouse is situated. A modern bridge crosses the moat to an octagonal platform, then continues straight on to the main entrance. The original bridge lay at right angles to it, forcing would-be attackers to expose their unprotected right flanks to hostile fire. It changed direction at the platform, a drawbridge connecting with a barbican which is reduced to a single fragment. A second drawbridge then led to the gatehouse proper. The gateway is flanked by a pair of square towers, both crowned by machicolated parapets. The arrival of firearms is denoted by the provision of 'keyhole' gun ports here in place of traditional arrow-slits. Note the wide machicolation and the display of heraldry over the gate arch. The vaulted gate passage was defended by three portcullises and three sets of gates, the innermost gates being hinged to bar access from the courtyard should the rest of the castle fall into enemy hands – a survival of the keep-gatehouse theme. One portcullis remains in place. Machicolations also crown the central tower on the south front, which contains a water gate leading directly into the hall.

In contrast to the curtain, the buildings inside the castle are now very ruinous. Enough remains, however, to appreciate their layout. There was no outer courtyard, so everything had to be condensed into one small quadrangle. There is a sense of social hierarchy, rather than security, in the way that the garrison's quarters did not communicate with the better accommodation reserved for Sir Edward and his private household. Nevertheless, the chamber over the gateway was controlled from the lord's portion, not the garrison's. Starting at the gatehouse, the garrison's quarters were compressed into the west range and its northern continuation. The south range contained the lord's kitchen and hall. Two large, private chambers and a chapel occupied the east range, the latter projecting a little beyond the line of the curtain and permitted a large east window. Additional accommodation, both for household

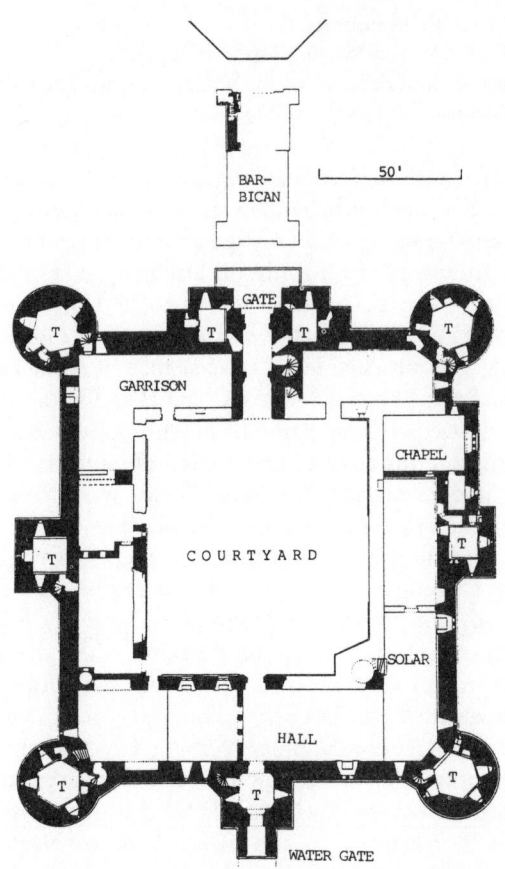

BODIAM CASTLE

and garrison, was provided in the four-storey towers. The castle is well equipped with latrines and fireplaces.

No doubt the castle played its part in national defence but the only recorded incident is a domestic one. After Richard III usurped the throne in 1483 a group of Lancastrians took refuge here, but they were quickly ousted. A Civil War slighting has been suggested, but that makes no sense since it is the residential buildings rather than the outer walls which have suffered. It seems more likely that the interior was robbed following abandonment in Tudor times, while the exterior survived long enough to be appreciated as a landscape feature. Centuries of decay were arrested by Lord Curzon, who repaired and consolidated the remains from 1916 onwards.

Access: Open regularly (NT).

Reference: Guidebook by C. Morton. *Bodiam Castle* by Lord Curzon.

Relations: The quadrangular castles of Herstmonceux, Maxstoke, Wingfield and Bolton. Lord Curzon's restoration of Tattershall.

BRAMBER CASTLE guards a gap where the River Adur cuts through the South Downs. It was established by William de Braose and existed by 1073. The surviving masonry probably dates from before 1100. Though fragmentary, the castle is to be recommended for its marvellous setting. The bailey is formed out of a natural knoll above the river. Several chunks of rubble curtain survive around the edge and a motte is placed oddly in the middle. The most substantial survival is a tall, flint crag dominating the approach. It represents one wall of a square gate tower, large enough to have been the dominant feature of the castle. Several early Norman castles possessed strong gatehouses instead of a keep, but sometimes – as at Ludlow and Richmond – they were later converted into keeps. The same may have happened here. Except for a period of confiscation in King John's reign, Bramber stayed with the Braoses until they died out in 1324. The castle then fell into ruins but was pressed back into service by the Royalists in 1642.

The early Norman church of St Nicholas stands on a small earthwork platform below the gate tower. It was served by a college of priests and no doubt doubled up as the castle chapel and parish church. Originally the church was a cruciform structure but only the nave and the crossing arches survive. The rest was destroyed in the cross-fire of a Civil War siege, the Roundheads installing their guns inside the church to fire upon the castle.

Access: Freely accessible (EH).
Reference: VCH *Sussex* (VI part 1).
Relations: Ludlow and Richmond. The Braose castles of Knepp and Huntington.

CAMBER CASTLE is a Henrician coastal fort located midway between Rye and Winchelsea. At first sight it appears to be typical of Henry VIII's larger forts, its geometrical plan comprising a curtain with rounded bastions closely surrounding a circular tower. In fact the castle is the result of three distinct phases. The central tower belongs to the start of Henry's reign, having been built in 1512 to defend Rye Harbour. As such it is a rare example of public coastal fortification before Henry's great scheme of the 1540s, and a reminder that relations with France were uneasy for most of Henry's reign. The cylindrical tower at Camber was devised to deflect cannon balls and anticipates the rounded design of Henry's later forts.

The outer defences were part of Henry's much larger scheme to counter the threat of invasion from the Catholic powers of Europe. In 1539–40 a curtain was built around the central tower, enclosing an octagonal area. Small gun platforms stood at alternate corners. A corridor runs in the thickness of the curtain, short passages linking the gun platforms to another corridor encircling the central tower. The only bastion at that time was the U-shaped one which contains the entrance. This curious design was adapted in 1542–43 to create a fort more akin to Deal and Walmer castles. The curtain was increased in thickness and the gun platforms were replaced by four semi-circular bastions with large gun ports. Since the original gun ports in the central tower were no longer any use, the tower was heightened to create a two-tier effect. The entire cost of the works here exceeded £24,000.

As a coastal fortification Camber had a short history. By the following century the sea had retreated so far from the castle that it could no longer serve any useful purpose. Charles I authorised its demolition but the order was never carried out.

The sea is now some distance away and the ruined castle squats on the flat landscape like a grounded vessel.

Access: Exterior visible (EH). Interior at certain times.
Reference: HKW (IV).
Relations: Deal and Walmer. For early artillery fortifications see Portsmouth's Round Tower and Dartmouth Castle.

CHICHESTER CITY WALL Chichester began as the Roman city of *Noviomagus*. Occupation continued after the Roman withdrawal and survived the coming of the Saxons. In 895 we hear that the burgesses routed an attacking Danish army, allegedly killing several hundred of them. In common with most other Romano-British towns, Chichester was first enclosed by a defensive wall in the third century. It enclosed an irregular, polygonal area. The existing city wall still follows the Roman alignment throughout and much of the core is no doubt original, but no Roman masonry is visible on the surface. Reconstruction took place from 1261 and French raids prompted a second phase of restoration in the 1370s. The wall remained in commission until the Civil War. In 1642 Chichester was seized by the Royalists and recovered for Parliament by Sir William Waller. Decay and destruction would normally have ensued, but the prosperous Georgian citizens actually repaired their battered wall to create an elevated promenade around the city. This extraordinary behaviour was matched only at Chester. As a result Chichester has one of the best preserved, if most restored, town walls in England. The circuit (well over a mile long) survives intact, except for a gap on the west side, and most of the wall-walk is still accessible. On the other hand it is rather a featureless wall. The restoration was not done in an antiquarian spirit and the four main gatehouses at the compass points, on Roman sites, were replaced by wider archways in the interest of traffic. Most of the semi-circular bastions were lost as well. One survives on the south-east sector and several more can be seen on the south-west. This south-western stretch is now the most impressive part, well seen from Westgate Fields with the Norman cathedral rising in the background.

After the Norman Conquest Roger de Montgomery founded a castle at the north-east angle of the city defences. Only a mutilated motte can be seen in Priory Park. It was destroyed after Henry III's accession and the site was given to the newly-arrived Franciscans (Greyfriars), whose church now dominates the park.

Access: The city wall parapet is freely accessible (LA).
Relations: Chester. Other Roman walls at Canterbury, Colchester and Exeter.

HASTINGS CASTLE stands boldly on Castle Hill, overlooking a seaside town which has an older history as one of the Cinque Ports. After landing at Pevensey, William the Conqueror marched to Hastings and raised a castle even before his clash with King Harold. The Bayeux Tapestry shows a typical motte being raised, and it is likely that the wooden tower and palisade had been shipped ready-to-assemble from Normandy. This first castle probably lay below the hill to protect the harbour and invasion fleet. However, the transfer to the present site must have taken place before long. It may have coincided with the foundation of St Mary's Chapel on the hill top in 1070. The chapel was endowed as a collegiate establishment by Robert, Count of Eu, whose descendants held the castle for most of the Norman period. Thomas Becket was dean of the college before he became Archbishop of Canterbury. King John ordered the destruction of the castle to prevent its fall to the Dauphin Louis, but Henry III refortified it in the 1220s. Hastings was twice sacked by the French in the fourteenth century (little survives of the town wall which was hurriedly built). It appears that the castle had been abandoned as a residence by then but the college remained until the Reformation.

The castle enjoys a superb setting but is now very ruinous. Half of the inner bailey has disappeared into the sea, leaving jagged cliffs behind. Most of the Norman curtain still stands on the remaining two sides, with the footings of Henry III's round-towered gatehouse on the east. The curtain passes straight over the motte (it appears that a tower keep stood elsewhere). West of the motte is the ruin of St Mary's Chapel, mainly Norman though the early Gothic chancel arch is the most prominent feature. The chapel stands in line with the curtain and the mural tower beside it doubled up as the bell tower.

Access: Open regularly (LA).

Reference: VCH *Sussex* (IX). Souvenir guide.

Relations: William I also founded Pevensey after landing. Compare the collegiate castle chapels of Bramber, Windsor and Leicester.

HERSTMONCEUX CASTLE With its quadrangular symmetry, and its tall gatehouse and corner towers reflected in the water of a wide moat, the castle presents immediate affinities with Bodiam. Indeed, if Bodiam is the perfect quadrangular castle of the fourteenth century then Herstmonceux is the most splendid illustration of how this genre developed in the fifteenth century. Like Bodiam, it was built by a veteran of the French wars. Sir Roger Fiennes, Treasurer of the Royal Household, obtained a licence to crenellate in 1441. One obvious contrast is the choice of building material. Sir Roger built his castle in newly-fashionable brick, stone being used only for doorways, windows and corbels. Another difference is the size. The curtain encloses an area nearly twice as large as Bodiam, the better to accommodate the vast household of a prominent baron. Most significantly, the half century in between the construction of the two castles shows a development away from defensive strength towards display. Brick is not necessarily inferior to stone but the curtain is thinner and the flanking towers are slender. Although most of the windows piercing the curtain are later at least some of them were too large to begin with. This is the case even though the castle, overlooking the Pevensey Levels and within sight of the sea, had (for Sussex) the familiar coastal defence purpose.

Despite this change of emphasis the castle retains all the defensive trappings of a medieval stronghold. Octagonal towers project from the four corners and there are three intermediate turrets of semi-octagonal plan on each side. On the south front the place of the middle turret is taken by an imposing gatehouse, reached by a brick bridge which is part of the original fabric. Eighty-four feet high, the gatehouse is a showpiece. The entrance is set within a tall drawbridge recess surmounted by the Fiennes arms. Two narrow slots above the gateway received the beams which raised and lowered the drawbridge. The towers which flank the

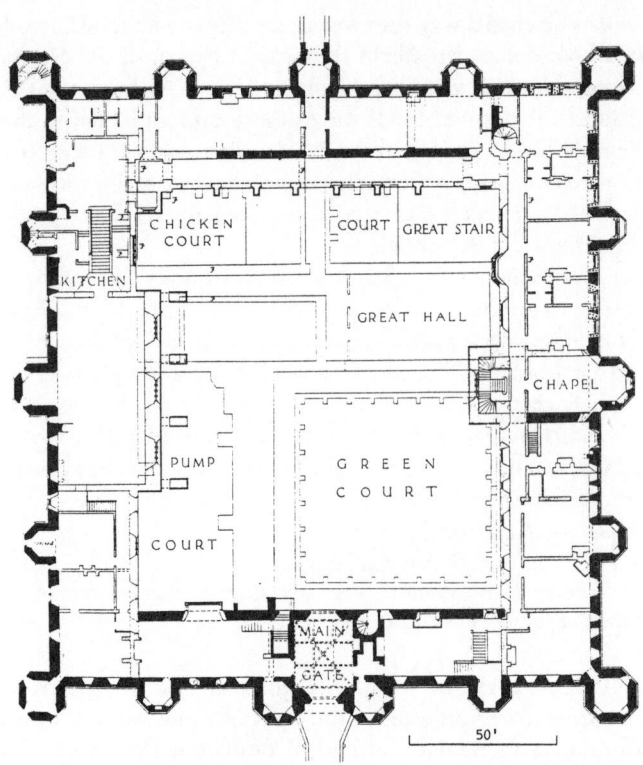

HERSTMONCEUX CASTLE

gatehouse are provided with gun ports and three rows of cross-slits. They begin semi-octagonal like the other intermediate turrets, but near the top they change to round. The whole front of the gatehouse is capped by a machicolated parapet. Above the parapets of the towers rise recessed inner turrets in the French manner. As at Bodiam, the corresponding turret on the north front contains a postern and is also machicolated. The central turret on the east side is pierced by tall windows marking the apse of the chapel.

The castle passed from Sir Roger to a branch of the Dacre family, who lived here until 1708. After that it fell into disuse. In 1777 the residential buildings were demolished to provide materials for nearby Herstmonceux Place. The castle remained a shell until its purchase by Claude Lowther in 1911. He began the task of restoration and rebuilding, continued in the 1930s by Sir Paul Latham. The curtain and its towers only required minor restoration from ruin, but the Tudor-style buildings around the courtyard owe nothing to their predecessors. In fact the single, large courtyard is misleading. The original layout divided the interior into four courtyards. The largest, Green Court, was surrounded by a cloister – an unusual conceit in a secular residence. It must have been a magnificent complex and it is a pity that nothing is left.

Access: Grounds and courtyard open regularly in summer.
Reference: *The History of Herstmonceux Castle* by D. Calvert. VCH *Sussex* (IX).
Relations: Bodiam. For the northern Dacres see Dacre and Naworth. Compare the brick castles at Caister, Oxburgh and Tattershall.

KNEPP CASTLE The present Knepp Castle, seven miles south of Horsham, was built by Nash in 1809. On the edge of a large park overlooking the A24 rises the oval motte (mainly a natural mound) of the original castle. Crowning this motte is the ivy-clad remnant of a late Norman keep. Only one corner still stands, with pilaster buttresses and a fragment of the first-floor doorway. Everything else has vanished. The castle belonged to the De Braose family. King John ordered its demolition after William de Braose joined the Magna Carta barons, but it seems to have survived this episode and there is a tradition of final destruction by the Roundheads.

Access: Visible from the road.
Reference: Mackenzie (I).
Relations: Bramber was another De Braose castle.

LEWES CASTLE AND TOWN WALL On a hill above the River Ouse is the historic town of Lewes. After the Norman Conquest this Saxon burgh and a large estate around it were granted to William de Warenne, Chief Justiciar and sub-sequently Earl of Surrey. He raised a castle on the highest ground and founded England's first Cluniac priory to the south of the town. Lewes Castle is a motte-and-bailey stronghold with the curious feature of two mottes, one at each end of the oval bailey. Only Lincoln can compare with it. It is assumed – but by no means certain – that the smaller Brack's Mount came first, only to be superseded by the larger motte at the west end which is better placed to command the town. Certainly it is the latter which now has a keep but masonry has been found on Brack's Mount as well, so could it be that for some unknown reason the castle was bipolar?

The keep crowning the larger motte was a circular shell keep. Only its southern half remains but patches of herringbone masonry suggest an early date, probably no later than the second William de Warenne (d.1138). The two semi-octagonal flanking towers were added in the late thirteenth century. Much of the curved stretch of curtain between the bailey and the town survives in a ruinous state, again with herringbone masonry. Unfortunately the bailey can no longer be fully appreciated because the town has encroached upon it. A gate tower stood at the foot of the larger motte but only its outer face still stands. In the fourteenth century a short barbican was built in front, terminating in an outer gatehouse which is the best preserved part of the castle. This gatehouse has a machicolated front flanked by circular turrets which project on corbels (one of them has fallen). It was probably built by John, the last of the Warenne earls. On his death in 1347 the Honour of Lewes passed to the Fitzalan earls of Arundel. Lewes Castle fell into decay and the other buildings were ultimately demolished.

Lewes had earthwork defences in Saxon times. The right to collect murage was granted for the building of a stone wall in 1266. Significantly this was just two years

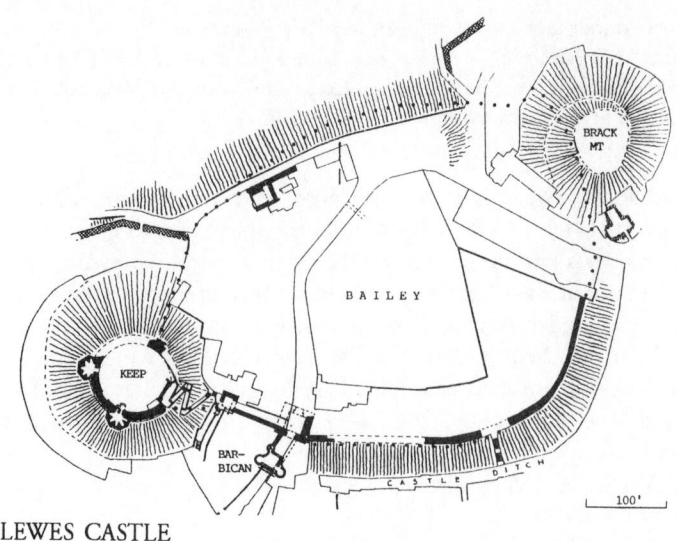

LEWES CASTLE

after the Battle of Lewes, which overspilled into the town after the royal army had been put to flight. The western part of the town wall can still be followed, but it is quite featureless and obscured in parts by later houses. It begins below the castle keep and continues along Pipe Passage to the High Street. One bastion of the West Gate survives concealed behind a house. The wall continues beside Keere Street to the south-west corner of the old circuit.

Access: The castle is open regularly. The town wall is freely accessible (LA).
Reference: Castle guidebook by W. H. Godfrey.
Relations: Lincoln. Reigate, Castle Acre, Conisbrough and Sandal were other Warenne castles.

PEVENSEY CASTLE is an extensive ruin with a very long history. Its outer curtain began as the enclosing wall of *Anderita*, a Roman fort of the 'Saxon Shore'. This chain of defences, stretching from the Wash to the Solent, was raised in the late third century AD. Although there is some debate about their original function, in the following century the forts defended the coast from barbarian raiders in conjunction with the Roman fleet. Pevensey is unlike the others, and unlike Roman forts generally, in being oval rather than rectangular in plan. An early-fourth-century coin found beneath one of the bastions confirms the view that this fort was a later addition to the chain. Unfortunately it lacks the completeness of Portchester Castle. A long stretch of the south wall has collapsed down the slope and there are shorter gaps on the north and east. Nevertheless the surviving portions of Pevensey are the most impressive of any Saxon Shore fort. Ten solid, U-shaped bastions remain, two of them placed closely together to flank the main entrance. The coast is now over a mile away but the flat expanse of the Pevensey Levels once formed an inlet to the sea, the castle occupying a narrow peninsula which could only be approached by land from the west.

252

After the departure of the Romans the fort became a refuge for the beleaguered natives. According to the Anglo-Saxon Chronicle they were overwhelmed and slaughtered here by the invading Saxons in the year 491. After that history falls silent until William the Conqueror landed in Pevensey Bay. Before marching on to Hastings he refortified the site with a strong rampart, perhaps filling in a gap in the Roman wall. This repair job qualifies Pevensey as England's first post-Conquest castle (it should be remembered that a few had been raised by Norman guests before 1066). Once Norman rule had been established William granted Pevensey to his half-brother Robert, Count of Mortain. Presumably it was he who established an inner bailey at the east end of the fort. In 1088 the castle proved strong enough to resist the assaults of William Rufus when the succession to the throne was disputed by Robert Curthose. It only surrendered when Rufus' cause had triumphed, and the garrison had to be starved out again by King Stephen in 1147. The only relic of the Norman castle is the stump of a battered, oblong keep within the inner bailey. The keep is curious for its three rounded bastions. For the time (*circa* 1100) they seem out of character, but clearly they were inspired by the Roman bastions.

The castle is one of those which did not remain for long with any one family. In 1246 Henry III granted it to Peter de Savoy, Earl of Richmond and the Queen's uncle. He should be mentioned because the curtain dividing the inner and outer baileys is attributed to him. It is a good example of thirteenth-century fortification, with a gatehouse and three semi-circular towers providing comprehensive flanking cover. These towers have tall arrow-slits, but they followed the example of the Tower of London in providing accommodation rather than being purely defensive platforms. The gatehouse is an early example of the mature 'Edwardian' type, its round-fronted towers flanking a long gate passage. Unfortunately it is now very ruinous. The curtain was still new when Pevensey endured the most momentous of its sieges. After the Battle of Lewes in 1264 Henry III's defeated supporters took refuge here. Simon de Montfort's son was despatched to lay siege, but all attempts at assault failed and the castle remained defiant until De Montfort's overthrow the following year.

Pevensey withstood one further siege, from the supporters of Richard II at the time of Henry IV's usurpation. The castle was already in decay. With the recession of the sea it played little part in the coastal defence of Tudor times but found itself pressed back into service during the invasion scare of 1940. Machine-gun posts were concealed around the ruins and the towers along the inner curtain were re-roofed to accommodate a new garrison. Thankfully these improvised defences were not put to the test.

Access: Standard opening times (EH).

Reference: Guidebook by C. Peers.

Relations: Portchester. The Tower of London and contemporary towered curtains such as Dover and Corfe. Peter de Savoy's tower at Rye.

RYE CASTLE AND TOWN WALL Rye is an enchanting old town at the mouth of the River Rother, a fine church and quaint streets attesting to its former prosperity. Like its close neighbour, Winchelsea, Rye was admitted to the confederacy of the Cinque Ports in Norman times, so the 'five ports' in fact became seven. These ports played a key role in the naval battles of the Hundred Years War and provided the invasion fleets. Not surprisingly, they became the target for French reprisals, especially in the 1370s when the French wrested control of the Channel. Under the intrepid French adventurer, Jean de Vienne, a number of south-eastern ports were sacked. The worst attack upon Rye came in 1377, when the town was left a charred shell. According to their own account the seafarers were avenged the following year, descending upon the Normandy coast and even recovering the bells which had been taken from their church tower. During this period Rye was enclosed by a town wall. The only substantial part to survive is the ruin of the Land Gate. With its tall entrance portal and rounded flanking towers, this is a worthy piece of late-fourteenth-century fortification. A few pieces of actual wall survive. One stretch can be seen to the west of the Land Gate, along Cinque Ports Road, and there is more overlooking the quay.

The Ypres Tower stands at what was the south-east corner of the walled circuit. This keep is the only remnant of Rye's castle, built by Peter de Savoy when he was overlord of the town in the mid thirteenth century. At that time the very concept of a keep may seem old-fashioned, but Henry III was building one at York. The quatrefoil plan of York's keep is echoed here at Rye: It is a square tower with rounded corner turrets to protect the vulnerable angles. It should be said that this keep is a comparatively modest strongpoint. The townsfolk took it over but impoverishment forced them to sell it in 1430 to John de Ypres – hence its name. In Tudor times, after Rye had recovered from the devastation of the Hundred Years War, it was repurchased and put to use as the town gaol. It now contains the museum of Rye.

Access: Ypres Tower is open regularly in summer. The town wall remains are freely accessible (both LA).
Reference: VCH *Sussex* (IX).
Relations: York. Peter de Savoy's work at Pevensey. Compare the Cinque Port defences of Winchelsea and Sandwich.

WINCHELSEA TOWN WALL 'Old' Winchelsea was submerged in the great storm of 1287, which significantly altered the Sussex coastline. By that time a new town was already being laid out on the present hilltop site under the patronage of Edward I. As a planned medieval town it may be compared with Edward's new foundations in Wales and Gascony. Streets were laid out in a grid centred upon the parish church, and a surrounding wall formed an integral part of the design. The size of the town was ambitious and it was never filled with houses. Now Winchelsea is little more than a village and its lovely church has been reduced to half its intended size. The French tore down the other half and no doubt played their part in stunting the town's development. Winchelsea was the Cinque Port which suffered most at their hands in the fourteenth century. The town was sacked several times, but it was the withdrawal of the sea rather than the French which finished it off. Much of the walled area is now an open field. The three town gatehouses still stand in varying degrees of preservation. The best is the Strand Gate, with its rounded corner turrets, crowning the steep approach from the former harbour. Pipewell Gate, a simple tower, was rebuilt following destruction by the French in 1380. Nearby is the only surviving chunk of the wall itself. The archway of Newgate, now in open country to the south, illustrates the extent of medieval Winchelsea.

Access: The remains are freely accessible (LA).
Reference: VCH *Sussex* (IX).
Relations: Its companion, Rye.

OTHER SITES Ringworks at *Lyminster* and *Patching*, near Arundel, may be associated with the siege of Arundel Castle during the Anarchy. *Aldingbourne* possessed a castle of the bishops of Chichester. Excavations have shown that the 'motte' was actually piled around the lower part of a square keep, as at Lydford Castle. Only the oval, moated platform and a few masonry fragments remain of *Sedgewick Castle*, near Horsham. St Ann's Hill overlooking *Midhurst* once bore another stone castle.

Warwickshire

Just five miles apart stand two of England's finest castles. Warwick has developed into a stately home while Kenilworth is now an imposing ruin. Both illustrate the development of castles from keep to towered enclosure and from fortress to palace, yet it is remarkable how castles so close together can be so far apart in character, layout and building materials. Maxstoke Castle deserves to be better known as one of the best preserved of the later medieval quadrangular castles. Apart from these Warwickshire has a handful of motte-and-bailey sites, notably Brinklow, and some fragmentary later castles.

ASTLEY CASTLE, four miles south-west of Nuneaton, belonged to the Astley family who built the nearby collegiate church. However, a licence to crenellate was awarded in 1266, a year after Thomas de Astley's death at the Battle of Evesham and before his son Andrew was allowed to inherit. The oval site is surrounded by a deep moat, still wet in parts, but the only original masonry is the gate arch with a bit of curtain alongside. Within the bailey stands a collapsed residential block, built after the Greys inherited in 1420 and thoroughly remodelled in Elizabethan times. The defences are said to have been slighted following the uprising to put Lady Jane Grey on the throne.
Access: Exterior visible.
Reference: VCH *Warwickshire* (VI).

BEAUDESERT CASTLE occupies an elongated hill overlooking the Norman parish church, across the River Alne from Henley-in-Arden. It is first mentioned in 1141 when Thurstan de Montfort obtained permission to hold a market here. The castle was seized by the King after Simon de Montfort's defeat but escaped destruction on that occasion. Instead it fell into ruins after the Montfort line died out in 1369. A stone keep and curtain existed here but only extensive earthworks now remain, comprising a ringwork with two baileys in front.
Access: Freely accessible.

BRINKLOW CASTLE is an excellent example of a motte-and-bailey stronghold, standing on high ground beside the parish church. The high, conical motte is surrounded by its own ditch and there are two baileys in line, both defended by strong ramparts and ditches. The earthworks are nearly as good as new and it takes little effort to imagine the wooden palisades back in place. The first mention of the castle comes in 1130 when it was temporarily in royal hands. It was probably raised by the De Mowbrays around 1100, but their tenure was disputed by the Stutevilles. As the castle was never reconstructed in stone it may well have been abandoned by the end of the Norman era.

Access: Freely accessible.
Reference: VCH *Warwickshire* (VI).
Relations: Good motte-and-bailey castles such as Warwick, Haughley and Pleshey.

CALUDON CASTLE An imposing fragment of this castle stands in Caludon Park in the suburb of Stoke, two miles east of Coventry city centre. It represents the outer wall of the hall, which was clearly a lofty apartment over a low undercroft. John de Seagrave obtained the original licence to crenellate in 1305 but John de Mowbray received another in 1354, and the two pointed windows – much too large to pierce the curtain of a genuine fortification – are more likely to be his. The drained moat shows an oval bailey instead of the usual quadrangle. Thomas Mowbray, Duke of Norfolk, set out from here in 1397 to fight Henry of Bolingbroke, but Richard II intervened to stop the duel.

Access: Freely accessible (LA).
Reference: VCH *Warwickshire* (VIII). Salter.
Relations: The Mowbrays' earlier castle at Brinklow.

COVENTRY: CAESAR'S TOWER AND CITY WALL By the fourteenth century Coventry had grown into the fourth largest city in England. The corporation was given the right to collect murage in 1329 but work on the city wall did not begin in earnest until 1364. Construction dragged on for nearly two centuries amid disputes between the citizens and the Prior of Coventry, who ruled half of the city. Building adhered faithfully to the original plan, so that when it was finally completed in 1540 the wall was already obsolete. Coventry resisted a Royalist siege in 1642 and the demolition of the circuit began at the Restoration. Today everything has disappeared except for a fifteenth-century length of wall in Lady Herbert's Garden. At either end of this stretch there is a simple gate tower: Cook Street Gate to the west and the blocked Priory Gate to the east.

The square tower known as Caesar's Tower in Bayley Lane is something of a mystery. It is sometimes said to have formed part of the Norman castle of the earls of Chester, but that probably stood further north. Another suggestion would make it an urban tower house of *circa* 1300, attached Italian-style to the vanished dwelling of a wealthy merchant. It certainly pre-dates the splendid guildhall of St Mary, which has adjoined it since the 1390s. Its vaulted ground floor was used as a strongroom for the guild's treasure. The tower was strong enough to withstand a direct hit during the devastating air raid of November 1940.

Access: The guildhall is open regularly in summer, and the city wall is freely accessible (both LA).

HARTSHILL CASTLE may have been founded by Hugh de Hardreshall, who acquired the manor in 1125. The overgrown motte is a relic of his time. Sometime in the thirteenth century the Hartshill family raised a curtain around a roughly pentagonal bailey. Much of it survives, especially on the south and east, but it is gradually crumbling away. An interesting feature is the regular spacing of cross-slits. Shorn of its parapet, the curtain is not high enough to form an impressive barrier and the lack of flanking towers, even at the angles, is a serious drawback for its time. A brick wall marks the position of an Elizabethan successor mansion.

Access: Visible from the road.
Reference: VCH *Warwickshire* (IV).

KENILWORTH CASTLE, though much ruined, is an extensive and impressive pile. It served in turn as a mighty stronghold and a splendid palace, both roles being enhanced by the artificial lake which once came up to its walls. Founded *circa* 1122 by Geoffrey de Clinton, Henry I's Lord Chamberlain, the castle proved important enough to be taken into royal hands by Henry II. King John spent over £1100 on the outer defences in the years 1210–15, making it one of the largest of English castles. He was then forced to cede it to the baronial opposition as a guarantee of Magna Carta. Henry III showed poor foresight in granting Kenilworth to his son-in-law and future adversary, Simon de Montfort. Following Simon's defeat and death on the battlefield of Evesham, his son (another Simon) made Kenilworth the rallying point for the surviving rebels. In 1266 a momentous siege took place and the castle earned its impregnable reputation. All the King's attempts at assault failed and the large garrison defied excommunication as well. They finally surrendered after six months of resistance when their supplies were exhausted. Despite their desperate condition they still managed to negotiate an honourable withdrawal.

Henry III next awarded Kenilworth to his younger son Edmund 'Crouchback', Earl of Lancaster. So began the castle's association with the Duchy of Lancaster. It was here that Edward II was forced to abdicate before going on to his murder at Berkeley Castle. John of Gaunt transformed the inner bailey into a palatial residence in the 1380s. When his son seized the throne as Henry IV Kenilworth again became a royal castle, but the Lancastrian kings preferred a moated house known as 'the Pleasance' on the far side of the great lake. The last building phase inside the castle took place under Robert Dudley, Earl of Leicester. He enjoyed a special relationship with Elizabeth I and she paid three visits to the castle, notably in 1575 when the entertainments were spectacular even by Tudor standards. Sir Walter Scott's novel *Kenilworth* brilliantly evokes this episode. Unfortunately the splendour came to an abrupt end with the Civil War. Although garrisoned by Parliament throughout, the castle was slighted as a potentially dangerous stronghold in 1649. The great lake was drained at the same time.

The castle consists of an inner bailey on a natural knoll and a large outer bailey which surrounds the inner. Dominating the rest is a massive, oblong keep of Norman

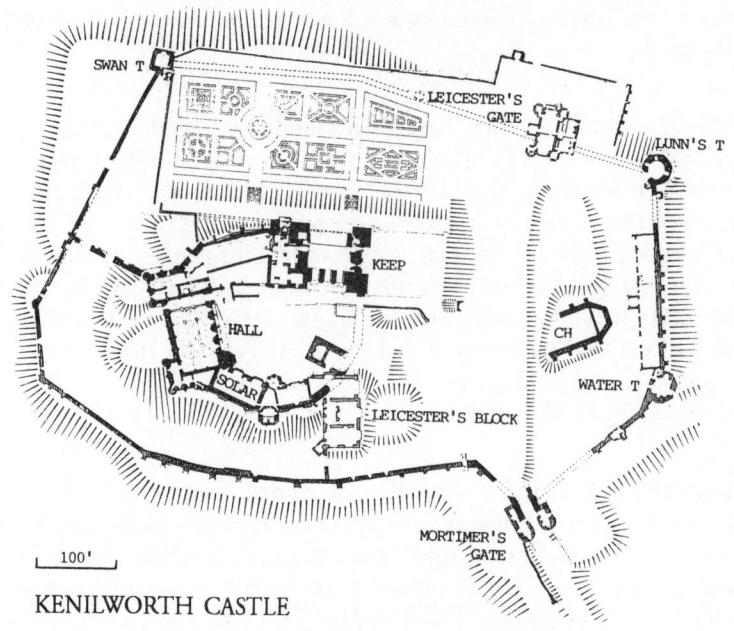

KENILWORTH CASTLE

date. The keep is sometimes attributed to Henry II but there is insufficient royal expenditure to account for it after he took control in 1173. It is therefore more likely that it was built by Henry de Clinton in the previous decade. The keep is longer than it is high, i.e. a hall-keep. Its lowest level, marked by a tall plinth, has always been filled with earth, suggesting that the keep encases the stump of an older motte. Above that there are two storeys, both forming a single apartment. The buttresses which usually clasp the corners of a Norman keep are here exaggerated into projecting towers. Robert Dudley converted the arrow-slits, with one exception, into large windows. The north wall of the keep was blasted down at the slighting. A forebuilding contains the entrance, though Robert Dudley removed the staircase and converted the space into a forecourt.

The keep occupies the north-east corner of the inner bailey. As it now stands this bailey is John of Gaunt's creation, or rather that of his master mason, Robert Skyllington. His work is of the highest standard, befitting such a wealthy and ambitious prince. The buildings back onto a curtain wall – Norman in its core – but the emphasis is residential rather than defensive. The chief apartment is the great hall on the west, magnificent even in ruins. Tall windows to front and rear (including a bay window) made this a very well-lit apartment. The hall stood over an undercroft and an unusually grand staircase led up to the entrance porch. Two square-fronted towers flank the hall, contrived less for defence or domestic convenience than to offer a symmetrical facade from the west. The ranges on either side of the hall are much more ruinous. A kitchen wing linked the great hall to the keep forebuilding. On the other side of the hall two large apartments, identified as the solar and a more private chamber beyond, formed the south range. They are separated by a projecting

258

tower containing latrines. Robert Dudley added a large block for guests (Leicester's Building) at the east end of the south range. His Elizabethan windows contrast with the Perpendicular tracery of John of Gaunt's era. The gap between Leicester's Building and the keep was once filled by a Tudor range and, prior to that, by the Norman curtain.

King John's outer curtain is long and correspondingly low. There are many buttresses but mural towers are provided only sparingly. The castle's real strength derived from its water defences, the vanished lake washing the south and west walls. Consequently there are no towers at all between Mortimer's Gate on the south-east and the ruinous Swan Tower at the north-west angle. The north side was the most vulnerable as there was only a double moat to contend with. The entire curtain here, from the Swan Tower to Lunn's Tower, was destroyed at the slighting. Only the new gatehouse inserted by Robert Dudley was spared. (That and his stable block are the only buildings of the castle to remain intact.) Lunn's Tower is a circular structure at the north-east angle. The next angle is guarded by the semi-octagonal Water Tower, added by Simon de Montfort.

Mortimer's Gate was the main entrance to the castle until Robert Dudley built his new gatehouse. It began as a simple gate tower but was enlarged later, probably under Simon de Montfort. It must have been a fine example of the double-towered type flanking a long entrance passage, but only the lower parts of the gate towers remain. This gatehouse was merely the last in a succession of obstacles. It lies at the head of a narrow causeway which acted both as a barbican and as a dam to control the level of the lake. It was also used for tournaments. The causeway was breached after the Civil War in order to drain the lake. Beyond the causeway stood a second gatehouse (destroyed), and the footings of a third can be found in the earthen outwork known as The Brays.

Access: Standard opening times (EH).
Reference: Guidebook by D. F. Renn.
Relations: Berkeley. King John's work at Corfe, Odiham, Dover and Scarborough. Compare the surviving lake at Leeds Castle.

KINGSBURY HALL occupies a strong site overlooking the River Tame, and separated by a ravine from the parish church. The present house is an early Tudor complex, still extensive but somewhat reduced in dignity. Two ruinous lengths of curtain survive outside. An octagonal turret occupies the angle between them and the curtain is pierced by a simple gateway. The curtain, probably of the fourteenth century, enclosed the original house of the Bracebridge family. It seems that this was a quadrangular castle in miniature.

Access: Exterior only.

MAXSTOKE CASTLE is an excellent example of a later medieval, quadrangular castle. It was built by William de Clinton, whom Edward III made Earl of Huntingdon. As a soldier in the French wars Clinton was a typical castle-builder of his time. He endowed a priory at Maxstoke in 1336, one of the last monastic foundations in England before the Dissolution. There is a tradition of a licence to

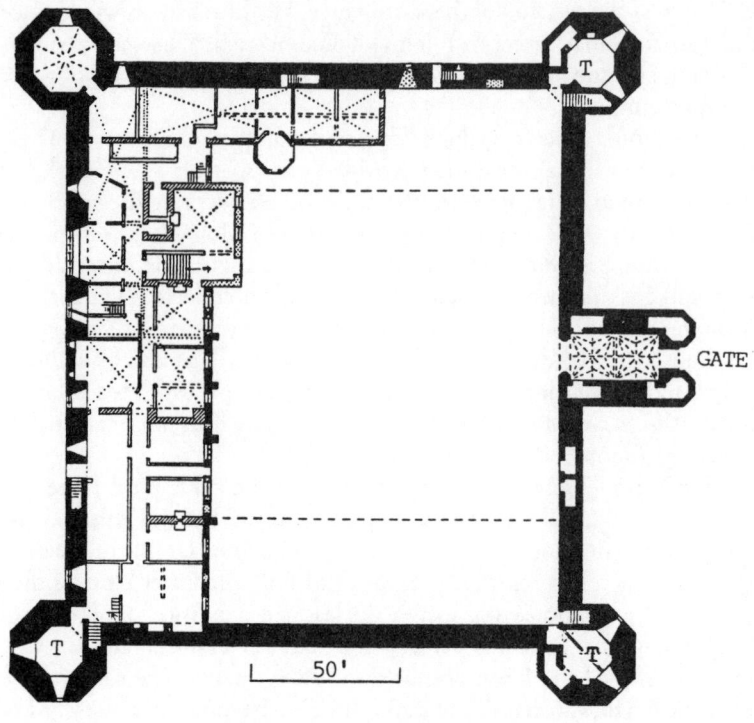

LADY'S TOWER

GATE

T

T

T

50'

MAXSTOKE CASTLE

crenellate being awarded in 1346 but the castle may well have been complete by then. The scattered priory ruins can be seen in the village while the castle occupies a secluded spot two miles further north, i.e. two miles east of Coleshill.

The castle occupies a low-lying site, not at all dominating its surroundings. Its walls and towers are reflected in the water of a broad moat. Although not especially high, the curtain is strongly built and retains its original battlements throughout. At each corner rises an octagonal tower. On the east side these are overshadowed by a striking gatehouse in the middle of the facade. This gatehouse is basically a square tower projecting entirely outside the line of the curtain, but the outer entrance is flanked by octagonal turrets which rise higher than the rest. An intricate lierne vault covers the gate passage, which was defended by a drawbridge, a pair of gates and a portcullis. The surviving gates are studded with iron, bearing the emblem of Humphrey Stafford, Duke of Buckingham. He acquired the castle in the 1440s. Externally the castle has changed remarkably little but it was fortunate to escape the Civil War intact, the owner paying a fine of £2000 to avoid the fate of slighting.

It contrast to the outer walls, the residential buildings have seen many alterations. Only the west range survives, along with a timber-framed Tudor wing which extends some way along the north side. Originally ranges stood against the whole of the north and south walls, as shown by the roof corbels and fireplaces in the curtain. Ranges

260

and curtain were not yet integrated into a single unit as they would be in later quadrangular castles. In fact the curtain was kept free of compromising window openings. The large chapel window in the west wall was inserted by Humphrey Stafford, showing that security was considered less important by his time. The hall (now subdivided) occupied the middle of the west range. Lady's Tower at the north-west corner is a storey higher than the other towers, containing a suite of private rooms reached from the former solar. It may thus be regarded as a tower house.

Access: Private, but there are occasional open days.
Reference: VCH *Warwickshire* (IV). Salter.
Relations: The earlier Clinton castle at Kenilworth. Compare the quadrangular castles at Bodiam, Wingfield (Suffolk) and Bolton.

SECKINGTON CASTLE can be found at the northern apex of the county, four miles north-east of Tamworth. The earthworks of this Norman castle rise a short distance north-west of the parish church. Though not the equal of Brinklow this is nevertheless a well-preserved site, with a prominent motte and a rampart around the bailey. It was probably a short-lived castle of the Anarchy, raised by Robert de Beaumont, Earl of Leicester.

Access: Freely accessible.
Relations: Brinklow. The Beaumont castle at Leicester.

WARWICK CASTLE AND TOWN WALL Warwick Castle, the seat of the earls of Warwick for much of its history, is one of the finest in the land. The view from Castle Bridge has few rivals, with the state apartments perched on a low cliff above the River Avon and the towers of the north-east front rising majestically. The castle has managed to develop into a stately home without sacrificing its medieval form. Its walls and towers have changed little since the late Middle Ages but the sumptuous interiors are the product of more recent centuries, and the whole stands in grounds landscaped by 'Capability' Brown.

Underlying the later stonework are the impressive earthworks of a motte-and-bailey, taking us back to the castle's early days. The high, conical motte is known as Ethelfleda's Mound after Alfred the Great's daughter, but it was actually raised by order of William the Conqueror in 1068. William granted the castle to Henry de Newburgh (or Beaumont), first Norman Earl of Warwick. Little masonry survives from the Norman period. Considerable damage is said to have been wrought by Simon de Montfort's supporters, who raided the castle in 1264 and carried the earl off to captivity at Kenilworth Castle. Four years later castle and earldom passed to the Beauchamps. Thomas Beauchamp became earl in 1331 and began a general reconstruction. It was continued by his son, another Thomas, who joined the baronial opposition to Richard II and endured a period of imprisonment in the Tower of London. He was succeeded by Richard Beauchamp, active in the French wars. Then came Richard Neville, the notorious 'Kingmaker'. After his fall at the Battle of Barnet (1471) Warwick was granted to Richard, Duke of Gloucester, subsequently Richard III. He was the only one of these three Richards to add anything substantial to the fabric of the castle.

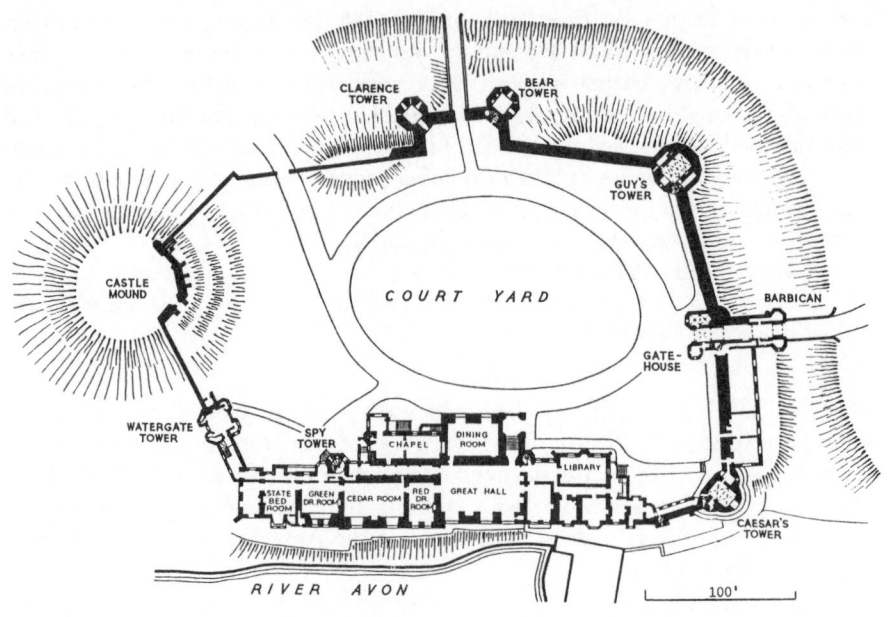

WARWICK CASTLE

The first Thomas Beauchamp began by reconstructing the residential buildings. Only then did he turn to the defences, showing where his priorities lay. The imposing north-east front consists of a strong curtain with a central gatehouse and a magnificent tower at each end. It is very much a show front, but not at all symmetrical because the three towers follow highly individual designs. The gate tower is the oldest part of the scheme (*circa* 1350). Its corner turrets rise above the main parapet and are connected by curious embattled bridges. In front of the gate tower projects a perfect barbican, its outer archway flanked by polygonal turrets. Within the long gate passage can be seen two portcullises and a number of murder holes up in the vault. Caesar's Tower, to the left, is most majestic from the river. From the base of its sloping stone 'apron' to the top of its inner turret the tower rises 147 feet, though about a third of this lies below courtyard level. Steps descend to a grim prison chamber with many Civil War inscriptions. The tower has a unique plan, semi-hexagonal towards the courtyard but tri-lobed on the outside. Above the machicolated parapet rises a recessed inner turret in French style. The tower is said to have been built with the booty Thomas Beauchamp won in the Poitiers campaign (1356). Guy's Tower, named after the Saxon hero Guy of Warwick, is the younger Thomas' work. It is said to have been finished in 1394 at a cost of £395. This handsome tower rises 128 feet from courtyard level, making it somewhat higher than Caesar's Tower. Externally it seems very different, being polygonal (twelve-sided) and lacking a recessed turret. Nevertheless it also has a machicolated crown and the internal arrangements are very similar. Both towers contain five vaulted storeys. Vaulting at all levels is an uncommon extravagance for English towers and shows French

262

influence. The apartments within are square for greater domestic convenience, thus bearing no relationship to the external shape of the towers.

In contrast to the north-east front, the north-west side of the castle is unspectacular. The curtain continues high from Guy's Tower but then descends to join an oblong projection with octagonal corner turrets. This low structure, intended as an artillery tower, was begun by Richard III and left incomplete after his death at Bosworth. The gateway between the turrets is a later insertion. Beyond this tower the wall is a thin and low reconstruction. It ascends the motte, which is crowned by a much-restored segment of a Norman shell keep.

The residential buildings are securely placed on the cliff overlooking the river. Their layout goes back to the first Thomas Beauchamp and fourteenth-century undercrofts underlie the hall, the chapel and a suite of private apartments. However, the main rooms were transformed by Sir Fulke Greville in Jacobean times and there have been several remodellings since, making Warwick one of the most splendid of stately homes with innumerable treasures. The hall was restored after a fire in 1871. It preserves an atmosphere of baronial pride, accentuated by the armour on display. There is more in the Victorian wing between Caesar's Tower and the gatehouse. Indeed, after the Tower of London the castle has the finest collection of arms and armour in England.

There are magnificent Beauchamp tombs in the town's parish church of St Mary. Warwick enters recorded history as one of the burghs fortified against the Danes by Ethelfleda. Her earthwork defences were rebuilt in stone from 1305. Two of the medieval town gates still stand at each end of the High Street. Curiously enough both are surmounted by chapels. The long passage of the West Gate, underlying St James' Chapel, is partly cut out of rock. The chapel tower was added around 1400, and the gate passage had to be extended to support it. Beside the West Gate is the only surviving piece of town wall. The East Gate is a simple gate passage of fifteenth-century date. Its chapel (of St Peter) was rebuilt in 1788.

Access: The castle is open regularly. The town wall remains are freely accessible (LA).
Reference: VCH *Warwickshire* (VIII). Castle souvenir guide.
Relations: The Tower of London. Compare the barbicans at Alnwick, York and Arundel, and Richard III's work at Sudeley. Bristol and Langport have town gates with churches on top.

OTHER SITES Upper *Brailes* and *Kineton* have motte-and-bailey sites. Another motte occupies an unsavoury position beside the M6 motorway at *Castle Bromwich*. The Old Castle at *Studley* is a timber-framed house inside a ringwork. By the River Avon opposite Wolston can be found the concentric enclosure of *Brandon Castle*, with a few stones of a Norman keep. Some lumps of masonry at *Fillongley* mark the site of a castle licensed in 1301. *Baginton Castle* preserves a collapsed undercroft. *Fulbroke Castle* (near Stratford) was built by John, Duke of Bedford, brother of Henry V. Nothing remains on the site, but the hall roof and bay window in the fine Tudor mansion of Compton Wynyates are said to have come from there.

Westmorland and Furness

Where most of Westmorland is concerned the Norman Conquest did not begin until William Rufus invaded in 1092. A group of castles was quickly established but they did not prevent the Scots from occupying this territory during the Anarchy. The square keeps of Appleby, Brough, Brougham and Pendragon rose after Henry II had recovered the disputed Northern counties. These four castles had a common ownership for most of their history and ended up in the hands of the Clifford family. Although not in the front line, Westmorland suffered greatly during the wars which devastated the Scottish Border counties in the fourteenth and fifteenth centuries. It has the pele towers to prove it. Sizergh and Yanwath are the best preserved of this group but there are many others. Fortifications are concentrated in the lowland parts of the county, especially the Eden valley which was the main thoroughfare for Scottish raids. The Furness peninsula is included here for modern geographical convenience. Things were different in the Middle Ages, when it formed part of Lancashire and was most easily approached across the sands of Morecambe Bay. The chief castle here is Piel, the island refuge of the abbots of Furness. Dalton Tower also belonged to the abbey.

APPLEBY CASTLE was founded by Ranulf le Meschin (later Earl of Chester) about the year 1100. It occupies a commanding position overlooking the town and the River Eden. The town, in a protective loop of the river, was probably established at the same time. Appleby descended to Hugh de Morville but he forfeited it for his part in the murder of Thomas Becket. The castle was in royal hands when the Scottish King, William the Lion, invaded the Eden valley in 1174. Its constable surrendered without a fight, Henry II imposing a stiff fine on him in punishment. Afterwards Henry granted the castle to Theobald de Valoignes. Either De Morville or De Valoignes built the tall, square keep which dominates the castle. It is one of the few Norman keeps still intact and roofed over. There is the usual first-floor entrance but no trace of a forebuilding. The first and second floors were the chief apartments, well-lit by pairs of windows. Above that there is a plain top storey – quite unlike the gallery level which might have been expected in a keep of this stature. The walls rise higher to mask the roof and the pilaster buttresses continue above parapet level to form diminutive turrets. Originally there was no internal division; the cross-wall is a later insertion. The keyhole plan of the bailey, which is surrounded by a truncated Norman curtain, suggests that a motte originally occupied the site of the keep. If so it must have been flattened when the keep was built.

In 1269 Appleby was inherited by Roger de Clifford and the castle began its long association with the Clifford family. Their much-altered residential buildings occupy the east side of the bailey, opposite the keep and overlooking the river. A postern passes through the middle of the range (the main gatehouse has disappeared). The great hall is still recognisable beneath its later veneer and each end of the range is built up into a tower. However, the only flanking tower to survive on the curtain is the semi-circular one on the north side. It *may* be the work of Robert de Clifford (d.1314). Appleby town was twice devastated by the Scots in the fourteenth century but they seem to have left the castle well alone. Instead it was dismantled during the Rising of the North (1569) to prevent its use by the rebels. There is little to show for Lady Anne Clifford's restoration of the castle during the Commonwealth period. More evident is the work of her son-in-law, the Earl of Thanet. In 1686–88 he transformed the hall block into the Classical mansion we see today.

Access: Open regularly in summer as part of a conservation centre.
Reference: RCHM *Westmorland.* Curwen.
Relations: The similar keeps of Brough, Brougham and Pendragon, which also became Clifford castles.

ARNSIDE TOWER has a projecting wing, an arrangement common enough in Scotland but rare among English peles. The wing does not contain the entrance so it is not strictly an example of the Scottish L-plan. Instead it housed a kitchen oven at ground level and four storeys of bed chambers above, i.e. one more than the main body of the tower. This pele was built by the Harringtons towards the end of the fourteenth century. Most of it stands to full height but one side collapsed during a gale in 1884. An earlier storm in 1602 caused a fire to sweep through the tower, ending its life as a residence. The vulnerability of this tower to storms is not surprising considering its exposed position on a rise overlooking Morecambe Bay, a mile south of Arnside village.

Access: Obtain permission to view at the nearby farm.
Reference: RCHM *Westmorland.* Curwen.
Relations: For the Harringtons see Gleaston and Wraysholme. Nearby Hazelslack Tower is similar.

ASKHAM HALL is dominated by a tower house which is unusually long in relation to its width. Its shape suggests a building of the hall-keep type, or perhaps a hall block which was subsequently built up into a tower. The tower was built after Edmund Sandford acquired the manor in 1375. A larger hall was attached to the tower before long. Thomas Sandford added two more wings to form an Elizabethan mansion. The tower house was transformed and given a Classical frontage *circa* 1690. The battlements and corner turrets show a Victorian attempt to make the tower look medieval again. It overlooks the River Lowther opposite Lowther Castle – the shell of a castellated mansion begun in 1806.

Access: Private.
Reference: RCHM *Westmorland.*
Relations: The elongated tower houses at Gleaston and Haughton.

BEETHAM HALL deserves better treatment than its use as a farm permits. Standing a short distance south of Beetham village, it was built around 1340 by Thomas de Beetham. His house followed the standard layout of medieval times, comprising a central hall flanked by kitchen and solar wings. Today the hall has been converted into a barn and the kitchen has disappeared. The roofless solar block has a small chapel projecting from it. Large windows mark the dais end of the hall and the chapel sanctuary. The solar block is austere but not secure enough to be regarded as a pele tower. Instead, Thomas or one of his successors raised a stone curtain in front of the house, and portions survive. Arrow-slits and a corbelled parapet emphasise the defensive nature of this wall, though its value must have been limited. The house is said to have been damaged by the Roundheads in 1644 and the existing farmhouse was put up afterwards.

Access: Visible from the road.

Reference: RCHM *Westmorland.*

Relations: Walled manor houses at Burneside, Middleton and Walburn.

BEWLEY CASTLE, three miles west of Appleby, takes its name from Hugh of Beaulieu, Bishop of Carlisle. He first erected a manor house here but the existing ruin was built by an early-fourteenth-century bishop, as indicated by the traceried window in the tower. This tower projects at one end of a hall range, forming an L-plan house. The tower is too small to be called a pele tower, but a pele probably stood at the other end of the hall as suggested by the remains of vaulting. Even bishops needed protection from raids!

Access: On private land.

Relations: For the bishops see Penrith and Rose Castle.

BROUGH CASTLE guards the old route from Carlisle to York at the point where it leaves the Eden valley and begins its climb towards the Stainmore Pass. The Romans defended this route with a chain of forts and one of them stood here. After the Norman invasion of 1092 the site was refortified, perhaps by William Rufus himself. It was put to the test in 1174 when William the Lion invaded. Having easily captured Appleby Castle the Scottish King encountered stern resistance at Brough. Eventually the castle was stormed and burnt. Theobald de Valoignes rebuilt the keep in the 1180s. He probably built the keep at Appleby as well and the two castles are quite similar in layout. Like Appleby, Brough passed to the Clifford family. The castle seems to have been strong enough to deter Scottish attacks but it succumbed to a terrible fire in 1521. Lady Anne Clifford restored her ancestral castles after the Civil War. She reached Brough in 1659 but its derelict state entailed extensive restoration. After this brief revival the castle was abandoned by her successor and is now very much a ruin.

The Roman fort of *Verterae* was laid out on the usual rectangular plan. No Roman masonry survives but the surrounding ditch (deepened in Norman times) is still prominent. It became the outer bailey to the medieval castle which lies across its northern end, overlooking a steep slope. The entrance is through a gate tower which is now an abject ruin. To the right the curtain stands high and includes two windows marking the site of the hall, probably built by Robert de Clifford around 1300. The circular corner tower beyond it is also his work, though much restored by Lady Anne. Elsewhere the curtain is very battered but one portion exhibits herringbone masonry, suggesting that Brough was one of the few Norman castles to be built in stone from the beginning. Within the cobbled bailey only the ruinous hall undercroft survives. The bailey forms a narrow triangle, tapering towards the oblong keep at the west end. The keep is the best preserved part of the castle, still rising to full height apart

266

from two narrow breaches in its walls. It is an austere structure, originally entered at first-floor level though the forebuilding has disappeared. Excavations have shown that this keep replaced an older Norman keep destroyed by William the Lion.

Access: Freely accessible (EH).

Reference: Guidebook by J. Charlton.

Relations: Appleby and the other Clifford castles of Brougham, Pendragon and Skipton. Brougham and Bowes also occupy Roman fort sites.

BROUGHAM CASTLE is an attractive ruin beside the River Eamont, just over a mile south-east of Penrith. As at Brough a Roman fort (*Brocavum*) originally stood on the site and the medieval castle occupies one corner of the rectangular enclosure. There is no record of a medieval castle here until the death of Robert de Vipont in 1228, so although the square keep is typical of the Norman era it is possible that Robert built it after he acquired Brougham in 1203. Square keeps were still being erected in King John's reign. The keep is preceded by a forebuilding in typical Norman fashion. Stairs once led to a doorway at first-floor level but the present ground-floor entrance is an early insertion. From the outset a hall block (destroyed) stood alongside the keep, an arrangement which foreshadows the pele-and-hall houses of the later Middle Ages.

The Clifford family enlarged the castle. Robert de Clifford, who inherit in 1283, became one of the leading soldiers of Edward I's campaigns and met his death at Bannockburn in 1314. He obtained a licence to crenellate in 1309 and constructed a curtain around the quadrilateral bailey. The curtain is defended at its most acute angle by the oblong Tower of League, which is complete except for one collapsed

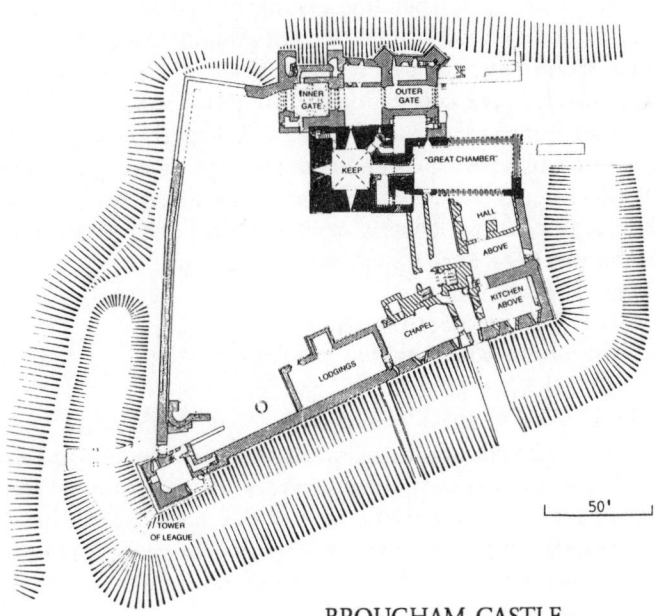

BROUGHAM CASTLE

267

corner. Robert also added the keep's top storey. This is octagonal internally and preserves an ornate oratory in the thickness of the wall. Most interesting of all are the two gatehouses, separated by a small open court and attached to the north side of the keep. Both gatehouses are oblong structures, eschewing the flanking towers more typical of the Edwardian age. The outer gatehouse was flanked by the older hall range and large, traceried windows show how the apartments over the gate passage were put to domestic use. The inner gatehouse was more secure and its portcullis chamber could only be reached from the keep. This arrangement enabled Robert de Clifford or his most trusted henchmen to maintain control over the entrance – a variant of the contemporary Edwardian gatehouse theme. Lord Clifford had his own escape route as well. A spiral stair descends from this gate chamber to a postern beside the river, guarded by a well-positioned arrow-slit in a turret opposite.

Later in the century Roger Clifford (d.1389) erected a new suite of residential buildings on the edge the bailey. The centre piece was a new hall against the east curtain. This adjoined the original hall which in turn connected with the keep. A kitchen stood in the angle of the curtain and there was then a chapel, which is now the best preserved of the residential buildings. Further lodgings once lined the southern and western sides of the curtain. Lady Anne Clifford was the last of her line to reside here, and after her death in 1676 the castle fell into ruin. It should not be confused with the nearby castellated sham known as Brougham Hall.

Access: Standard opening times (EH).
Reference: Guidebook by J. Charlton.
Relations: Brough and the other Clifford castles of Appleby, Pendragon and Skipton.

BURNESIDE HALL, two miles north of Kendal, belonged to the Bellingham family in the later Middle Ages. Their house consists of a modernised hall range and a ruined pele tower of the fourteenth century. The ground floor of the pele is divided into two vaulted rooms separated by a corridor. Evidently they formed the buttery and pantry, the corridor once connecting the hall to the vanished kitchen. Hence this tower was built at the service end of the hall. Perhaps there was a second tower at the solar end but a Tudor wing occupies the site. A portion of curtain survives in front of the house, entered through an Elizabethan gatehouse with is still defensive in tone. Although all pele towers had a small courtyard or 'barmkin' attached the outer defences here were surely more substantial than most.

Access: Visible from the road.
Reference: RCHM *Westmorland*. Curwen.
Relations: The curtains at Beetham and Middleton.

CASTLE HOWE This Castle Howe should not be confused with the one at Kendal or, indeed, a number of other elevated places in Westmorland sharing the name. It is an impressive motte-and-bailey earthwork occupying an elevated site between Tebay and the M6 motorway. Half of the motte has collapsed but the remaining half bears a rampart around the summit. The castle may be associated with the Norman invasion of 1092 but its history is obscure.

Access: On private land.
Relations: Kendal.

CLIFTON HALL belonged to the Wybergh family. Their house developed into a mansion but everything has been demolished with the exception of the squat pele tower. It probably dates from the late fifteenth century and is thus rather late for Westmorland. The tower retains its roof but no intermediate floors. One side has been rebuilt as a Georgian facade with large windows. It stands two miles south of Penrith and close to Brougham Castle.

Access: Standard opening times (EH).

DALTON CASTLE In the Middle Ages most of the Furness peninsula was ruled by Furness Abbey. Monasteries built court houses to administer their estates, but at Dalton-in-Furness in the war-torn years of the early fourteenth century it took the form of a strong tower. Though not strictly for residential purposes the tower is indistinguishable from contemporary pele towers. No doubt it served partly as a gaol from the outset and this became its chief role after the Dissolution. After falling into decay the tower was restored rather too thoroughly in the nineteenth century.

Access: Limited opening times in summer (NT).
Relations: Piel Castle was built by the Abbot of Furness.

GLEASTON CASTLE lies five miles north-east of Barrow-in-Furness, between the villages of Gleaston and Scales. Its predecessor was the nearby motte at Aldingham. The present castle was probably built during the long tenure of Sir John de Harrington (*circa* 1300–47), i.e. at the height of the Border wars. It had an active life of little more than a century, being abandoned after the Harringtons died out in 1458. The castle soon fell into ruins and is now a sorry sight in its farm setting. The curtain enclosed an irregular quadrangle on a sloping site but the rubble masonry has crumbled badly. There are oblong towers at each corner, of different sizes and in varying states of preservation. Today the two south angle towers are the best preserved portions, rising to full height but quite plain and very overgrown. The elongated north-west tower formed a hall-keep, with a gateway through the curtain beside it. Little survives of the north-east tower. Portions of connecting curtain survive except on the north, where it may never have been built.

Access: On private land.
Reference: VCH *Lancashire* (VIII). Curwen.
Relations: The Harrington towers at Arnside and Wraysholme.

HAZELSLACK TOWER This lofty pele ruin, between the villages of Arnside and Beetham, was probably built after 1400. Its commanding position compares with nearby Arnside Tower and the projecting turret flanking the entrance doorway is another similarity. A cross-wall once divided the interior. The east wall is much thicker than the others because it contained a fireplace serving the vanished hall range. The tower belonged to the Stanleys.

Access: On private land.
Relations: Arnside. The Stanley castle at Greenhalgh.

HOWGILL CASTLE overlooks a ravine a short distance east of Milburn village. The symmetrical front and sash windows give the house a Georgian air but appearances are deceptive. They are no more than a veneer over the medieval house of the De Lancasters, first mentioned as a castle in 1354. It shows an adaptation of the normal manor house plan to the uncertainties of Border life. The central block was the hall and the flanking wings were the kitchen and solar, both built up as strong towers. They retain their ground-floor vaults.

Access: Private.

Relations: For the De Lancasters see Kendal. Twin-towered houses such as Askerton and Nappa.

KENDAL CASTLES The first castle at Kendal was the high motte known as Castle Howe on the west side of town. It is now crowned by an obelisk commemorating the 'Glorious Revolution' of 1688. In all likelihood this motte was raised by Ivo de Taillebois, who was granted the barony around 1087. Sometime during the next century one of the De Lancaster family resited the castle on a natural mound (Castle Hill) on the opposite bank of the River Kent. The summit of the mound was enclosed by a strong ringwork bank and surrounded by a wide ditch. The rampart encloses a near-circular courtyard. Towards the end of the century, probably during the lordship of Gilbert Fitz Reinfred, a stone curtain was built along the crest of the rampart. Today the site commands extensive views but the masonry is very ruinous. Portions of curtain still stand along with two small towers, one round and one square, and part of a possible keep at the back. Next to the square tower are later cellars which underlay the hall. During the Scottish wars Kendal suffered several attacks but the castle seems to have remained aloof. Richard II granted Kendal to the Parr family but the castle was seldom occupied after that time, so it was probably not the birthplace of Queen Katherine Parr.

Access: Both sites are freely accessible (LA).

Reference: RCHM *Westmorland.* Curwen.

Relations: The De Lancaster castle at Howgill. Restormel is similar.

KENTMERE HALL is one of the few fortified houses of the upland district, occupying a narrow valley cut out by the River Kent. The fourteenth-century hall has become a ramshackle farmhose and the adjoining pele tower is now roofless but virtually intact. It had a machicolated parapet as the surviving corbels show. This was the home of the Gilpin family and Bernard Gilpin, the 'Apostle of the North', was born here in 1517.

Access: Exterior visible.

LAMMERSIDE CASTLE overlooks the River Eden as it enters the Vale of Mallerstang, three miles south of Kirkby Stephen. It is the ruined stump of a pele tower built by the Warcops or the Whartons in the fourteenth century. The ground floor has a central corridor passing through it with vaulted rooms on either side. They were probably the buttery and pantry of a vanished hall house – an arrangement also found at Burneside Hall.

Access: On private land.
Relations: Burneside.

LEVENS HALL is a splendid mansion beside the River Kent, justly famous for its topiary garden and its unspoilt Elizabethan interior, preserving some notable over-mantels and plaster ceilings. They were inserted in the 1580s when James Bellingham remodelled an older house of the Redman family. The front is divided into four compartments, of which the un-gabled one is a pele tower. It probably dates from the fifteenth century though the large windows are Elizabethan insertions. The solar block forming the east wing is sometimes regarded as a second tower because of its barrel-vaulted ground floor, though it is rather elongated for a pele.

Access: Open regularly in summer.
Reference: RCHM *Westmorland.* Souvenir guide.

MIDDLETON HALL Beside the River Lune, four miles south-west of Sedbergh, stands the fifteenth-century house of the Middleton family. The hall itself has survived the centuries remarkably unspoilt. It is flanked by what is evidently a chamber block rather than a pele tower. As at Beetham Hall, this house relied upon a stone curtain for its defence. There is a small walled courtyard behind the hall and a larger one in front. The parapet is projected out on corbels and the surviving gate arch was the inner end of a gate tower, as the windows above it make clear.

Access: Private.
Relations: Beetham.

PENDRAGON CASTLE According to tradition this was the castle of Uther Pendragon, King Arthur's father. Its position by the River Eden in the bleak Vale of Mallerstang, four miles south of Kirkby Stephen, is suitably romantic. The truth is more prosaic because the square keep which stands here was probably built by Hugh de Morville, one of the four knights who murdered Thomas Becket in Canterbury Cathedral (1170). In spite of this deed he managed to keep hold of Pendragon, and the keep here must have resembled the one at Appleby which may also be Hugh's work. Only the shattered stump remains. Enough is left to show a series of wall passages and a latrine turret projecting diagonally from one corner. The ground-floor entrance, unprotected by any forebuilding, is unusual for a Norman keep. It stands isolated on a natural knoll but there was probably a bailey to the north. Robert de Clifford refortified the castle, a licence to crenellate being granted in 1309. It was sacked by the Scots in 1341. Lady Anne Clifford restored the keep in 1660 but it fell back into ruins after her death.

Access: Freely accessible.
Reference: RCHM *Westmorland.* Curwen.
Relations: Appleby. The keep at Bamburgh.

271

PIEL CASTLE, sometimes known as the Pele of Fouldry, stands on a small island guarding the entrance to the great natural harbour between the Furness peninsula and Walney Island. This castle had an unusual history as a possession of Furness Abbey. A fortification stood here in the Norman period but the present castle was built in the aftermath of Bannockburn. Robert Bruce raided all the way to Furness in 1316. He came again six years later, only to be bought off by Abbot John Cockerham. This abbot obtained a licence to crenellate Piel in 1327 but castle was probably well under way by that time. It formed a secure retreat for the abbot and could have provided a refuge for the Cistercian monks in times of danger. It also served as a depot for the abbey's lucrative export trade in wool.

This very ruinous castle consists of a keep and two square baileys, the inner occupying the south-east corner of the large outer bailey. The outer bailey is represented by a length of curtain and three square corner towers. Much of the inner curtain survives on the north and west, its three flanking towers including a gate tower. By contrast, the south and east sides of the castle have been washed away by the sea and only some fallen chunks of masonry show that a curtain existed here as well. The inner curtain formed a concentric defence around the keep. Although only two storeys high the keep is the dominant feature of the castle. It is also the best preserved part, with the exception of the collapsed eastern end. Diagonal buttresses clasp the corners and a porch covers the ground-floor entrance. It leads into a central corridor with rooms on each side. There is a theory that the keep was not a residence at all but the main warehouse for the abbey's wool. However, this is belied by the provision of fireplaces and ornate windows.

Piel was an ambitious castle for an impoverished monastic community to build and it is possible that the outer bailey was never completed. A later abbot tried to demolish the castle to save the cost of its upkeep, but Henry IV prevented him. Historically the castle is best known as the landing place of the Yorkist pretender Lambert Simnel, en route to his defeat at the Battle of Stoke (1487).

Access: Open regularly in summer (EH). The castle is reached by boat from Roa Island.
Reference: VCH *Lancashire* (VIII). Curwen.
Relations: The abbey's tower at Dalton. Compare the concentric arrangement of keep and curtain at Middleham.

SIZERGH CASTLE has been occupied by the Strickland family since 1239. Nothing here is quite that old, however. The oldest part is the tower house which dominates the rest of the mansion. It dates from the 1340s and must therefore have been built by Sir Thomas de Strickland. Despite the threat from Scotland, Sir Thomas served in the campaigns in Ireland and France. His tower has the usual vaulted ground floor. Original fireplaces and two-light windows survive on the top floor, but the lower levels have been remodelled in keeping with the rest of the house. A turret (the Deincourt Tower) projects from the middle of one side, rising higher than the main tower. Originally it contained a suite of latrines serving the three upper floors. Despite the size of the tower it seems clear that there was an attached hall from the outset. It was largely rebuilt by Walter Strickland in Elizabethan times and has since been given a Georgian front. The plain wings which project in front of the house are also Elizabethan. According to tradition one of them housed the armed

North Wing

Hall

Barracks Wing

Pele

50'

SIZERGH CASTLE

retainers which the Stricklands still found necessary to employ. Not that life was entirely grim here, because the house is notable for its Elizabethan woodwork, including some magnificent overmantels. The castle stands in gardens four miles south of Kendal.

Access: Open regularly in summer (NT).
Reference: Guidebook by H. Hornyold-Strickland.
Relations: Tower houses attached to mansions such as Belsay and Chipchase.

WRAYSHOLME TOWER stands on the Cartmel peninsula, beside a minor road one mile south-west of Allithwaite. This squat, oblong pele is now an empty shell attached to farm buildings. The only feature is a projecting turret containing a latrine. The tower was built – probably in the fifteenth century – by the Harrington family, but they forfeited it for joining Lambert Simnel in his attempt to overthrow Henry VII.

Access: Visible from the road.

YANWATH HALL overlooks the River Eamont, two miles south-west of Penrith. Despite the uncomfortable proximity of the railway line Yanwath is one of the most evocative of the Northern pele-and-hall houses, having been subject to relatively few alterations despite its continued occupation as a farmhouse. As seen from the

273

approach the house consists of a long hall range and a pele tower at the left end. The tower, probably built soon after 1300 when John de Sutton was lord of the manor, has changed little except for the insertion of large Elizabethan windows at first-floor level. Diminutive corner turrets rise above the battlements and the slender octagonal chimney is an original feature. The hall was added or rebuilt in the fifteenth century after the Threlkelds had inherited. It is still recognisable externally and a fine bay window lights the dais end, next to the tower. Internally the hall has been subdivided and the original roof can be seen from what is now the upper floor. Further ranges were put up at the back of the house in Tudor times to enclose a small courtyard.

Access: Exterior visible.
Reference: RCHM *Westmorland.* Curwen.
Relations: The Suttons also held Dudley Castle.

OTHER SITES   As in Cumberland and Northumberland there are a number of lesser pele towers, generally gabled over and attached to later houses:

Broughton Tower (Broughton-in-Furness)	*Ormside Hall* (Great Ormside)
Cowmire Hall (near Windermere)	*Preston Patrick Hall* (near Kendal)
Godmond Hall (near Kendal)	*Skelsmergh Hall* (near Kendal)
Great Asby Rectory	*Thornthwaite Hall* (near Bampton)
Hollin How (near Kendal)	*Wharton Hall* (near Kirkby Stephen)
Killington Hall (ruin)	*Yewbarrow Hall* (near Kendal)
Newbiggin Hall (near Temple Sowerby)	

Hartley Castle is an eighteenth-century house preserving an undercroft from an older stronghold. Among Norman earthwork castles we may single out the motte above the River Lune at *Kirby Lonsdale* and the ringwork at *Pennington.* Excavations at *Aldingham* have shown that the surviving mound began as a ringwork but was later built up into a motte.

Wiltshire

Roger de Caen, Bishop of Salisbury, was the most significant castle builder of Norman Wiltshire. Unfortunately his castles have suffered greatly: Old Sarum, though marvellously positioned, is now extremely ruinous while Devizes has been completely rebuilt. The royal castles of Ludgershall and Marlborough have fared no better. The unusual hexagonal castle of Old Wardour is a later medieval survivor.

CASTLE COMBE   The village of this name is a picturesque place but the castle lies on an elevated spur of land half a mile to the north. Its elongated site is divided into four successive enclosures, separated by strong but overgrown ramparts. Within the innermost bailey is the stump of a square tower, rather small to be called a keep.

The castle was probably raised by Reginald de Dunstanville, Earl of Cornwall (d.1175). It was in ruins by the fifteenth century.

Access: On private land.

Relations: The Dunstanville castles of Tintagel and Trematon.

DEVIZES CASTLE was an important stronghold raised by Roger de Caen in the 1120s. As Bishop of Salisbury and Henry I's Lord Chancellor he was one of a handful of Norman prelates (including Alexander of Lincoln and Henry de Blois) whose castles rivalled anything built by secular lords. Contemporary accounts emphasise its strength and magnificence, but Roger fell from grace when he supported the Empress Matilda. He was seized by King Stephen and Devizes surrendered after the King threatened to have the bishop killed. The castle changed hands several times in the years which followed. Henry II took possession after his accession and the castle remained royal for the rest of the Middle Ages, becoming a retreat for several English queens. It decayed under the Tudors, Parliament ordering the destruction of both the castle and town wall after the Civil War. The present Devizes Castle, occupying the low motte, is a castellated sham dating only from the nineteenth century. During the rebuilding an aisled hall and parts of a massive towered curtain were unearthed, but nothing original seems to have survived above ground.

Access: Exterior visible.

Reference: VCH *Wiltshire* (X). *HKW* (II).

Relations: Roger de Caen's castles at Old Sarum and Sherborne.

LUDGERSHALL CASTLE enters recorded history in 1141, when the Empress Matilda stayed here after being driven from Winchester by King Stephen's supporters. The site is a powerful ringwork enclosed by a double ditch but the only visible stonework is one flint wall of a square Norman tower. Excavations have shown that it overlies a demolished square keep, probably of the Anarchy. Henry III took possession in 1225. He often visited Ludgershall and Marlborough castles for the hunting. Extensive residential buildings of his reign have been unearthed but none are visible. After Henry's death the castle fell into disuse. The remains lie on the north side of the town.

Access: Freely accessible (EH).

Reference: *HKW* (II).

Relations: Marlborough.

MARLBOROUGH CASTLE An impressive, conical mound (nearly sixty feet high) rises in the grounds of Marlborough College. Tradition has made it Merlin's burial mound but it is in fact a Norman motte, once crowned by a round keep. The site of the bailey is occupied by Castle House, built in the eighteenth century and part of the college since its foundation in 1843. The castle was a royal one, probably founded under William I though it first enters history in 1110 when Henry I celebrated Easter here. Richard I wrested the castle from Prince John in 1194, and it fell to the Dauphin Louis in 1216. Both John and Henry III came here frequently to hunt in Savernake Forest. Decline set in afterwards and little of the castle remained by the time Marlborough saw fighting during the Civil War.

Access: Freely accessible.
Reference: HKW (II).
Relations: Ludgershall was another royal hunting lodge.

OLD SARUM CASTLE Old Sarum is Old Salisbury, looking down upon its successor city from a chalk hilltop two miles to the north. The oval site is enclosed by a mighty ditch and rampart first dug in the Iron Age. Thanks to its later history Old Sarum is in fact the most impressive of the ancient hillforts dotted around Salisbury Plain. The last British occupants were driven out by the Saxon invaders in the year 552. Later it was the Saxons' turn to take refuge here to escape the onslaught of the Danes, the hillfort being utilised as one of the burghs or fortified towns which guarded Wessex. It was strong enough to repulse the Danish King Sweyn in 1003. A royal castle was founded here within a few years of the Norman Conquest and a cathedral soon joined it on the hilltop. These great structures displaced the town to the adjoining slopes, the hillfort area becoming in effect the outer bailey of the castle. During the Norman period there was a gradual drift to the much more convenient site in the valley below. The acrimonious relationship between the castle garrison and the cathedral canons prompted the bishop to seek a new home there as well. The present Salisbury Cathedral was begun in 1220 and Old Sarum quickly became deserted except for the castle. Even the castle had been abandoned by the fifteenth century, though this classic 'rotten borough' continued to be represented in Parliament until the Reform Act of 1832.

Today Old Sarum is a bare hill with no evidence of the Saxon town it once contained. There are just the foundations of the Norman cathedral in the north-west quadrant of the hillfort enclosure and the denuded remains of the castle in the centre. The castle stands on a circular mound which is so large and low that it is better described as an elevated ringwork than a motte. Although still nominally in royal hands, Bishop Roger de Caen undertook the rebuilding of the castle in stone. He showed his priorities by erecting a palace inside the ringwork before erecting any defences. (Another possibility is that the defences were built after Roger's downfall in 1139, in which case Old Sarum is the only stone castle which can be attributed to King Stephen.) Later stone-robbing has been intense and the castle is now very much an archaeological site. The foundations have been excavated but little stands to any appreciable height. Roger's palace surrounds a square inner courtyard in the same way as his other castle-palace at Sherborne. The curtain follows the edge of the ringwork with the footings of a gate tower on the east. A square keep stood astride the curtain on the opposite side of the bailey. It is the best preserved portion of the castle though it rises no higher than its sloping plinth.

Access: Standard opening times (EH).
Reference: Guidebook by H. de S. Shortt. HKW (II).
Relations: Devizes and Sherborne for Roger de Caen. Dover, Elmley and Almondbury castles occupy hillfort sites.

OLD WARDOUR CASTLE was built by John, Lord Lovell. He obtained a licence to crenellate in 1393. It is more than likely that the eminent architect William Wynford was responsible for the design. His keep follows a unique hexagonal plan with a small courtyard at the centre, in effect a revival of the Norman shell keep theme. One of the six sides projects outwards to form an impressive entrance front, its gateway flanked by twin square towers. This front is now the best preserved part of the keep. Internally the accommodation was arranged with typical late medieval intricacy. The hall lies above the gateway on the entrance front, its tall windows even on the outer facade showing that comfort was always an important factor. The flanking towers contain a number of small chambers. As seen from the courtyard, the segment of the hexagon to the left of the hall contained the solar, and that to the right the kitchen – both standing over vaulted undercrofts. In contrast to the well-preserved front, the rear portion of the keep has largely disappeared, only its courtyard wall surviving to some extent. This portion suffered most from Civil War damage. The outer gate arch and the principal doorway from the courtyard are handsome Renaissance portals contrasting with the Gothic nature of the keep. They were two of the alterations made by Sir Matthew Arundell when he modernised the keep from 1578. Presumably the concentric courtyard always existed but its enclosing wall is also Tudor.

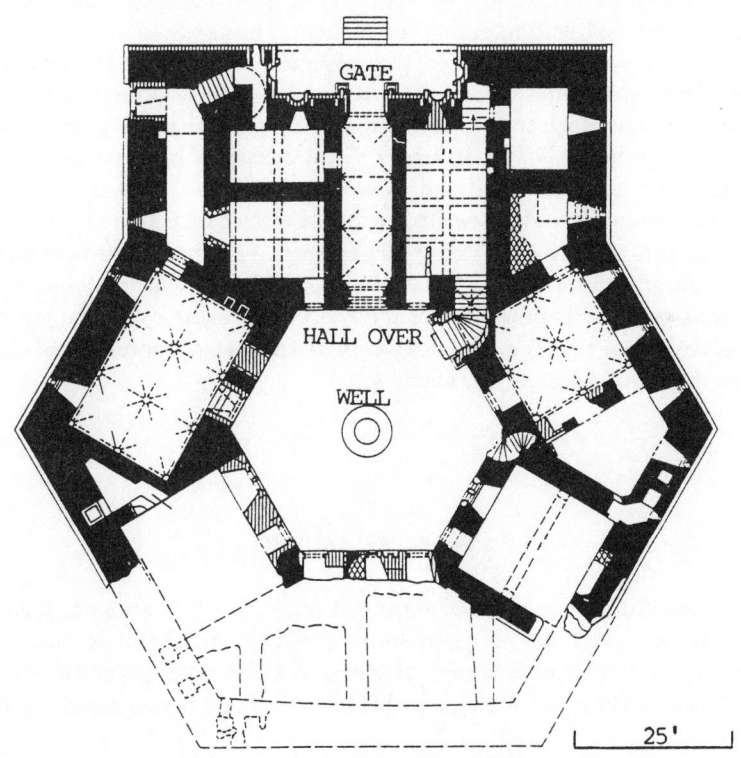

OLD WARDOUR CASTLE AT GROUND LEVEL

Despite the Elizabethan modifications the castle put up a valiant resistance in the Civil War. It endured a siege from both sides in turn, showing that the Royalists did not have a monopoly of stubborn defenders. Lady Arundell tried in vain to keep the Roundheads at bay in 1643. Once they had occupied the castle, however, they soon found themselves isolated in Royalist territory. For four months the castle suffered a heavy bombardment and by the time it surrendered in March 1644 it had been reduced to something near its present state. The Arundells returned here and built the 'new' Wardour Castle – a stately mansion – in the 1770s. After the fashion of the time Old Wardour was preserved as a romantic ruin in the park, set amid woods and overlooking an ornamental lake. These beautiful surroundings happily remain. The castle can be found two miles south of Tisbury.

Access: Standard opening times (EH).
Reference: Guidebook by A. D. Saunders & R. B. Pugh.
Relations: Compare the arrangement of domestic buildings in the keeps at Restormel and Windsor.

OTHER SITES Roger de Caen built another of his castles uncomfortably close to *Malmesbury* Abbey. It was demolished in 1216 and nothing survives. Nor is anything left of a castle raised at *Downton* by Roger's episcopal neighbour, Henry de Blois. Wiltshire saw a lot of fighting during the Anarchy. During those war-torn years the great neolithic mound of *Silbury Hill* (near Avebury) was drummed into service as a motte. King Stephen himself converted *Wilton Abbey* (now Wilton House) into a temporary fortress, much to the annoyance of the resident nuns. A stone keep of this era has been unearthed at *Membury*. Great *Somerford* has a motte-and-bailey site; *Castle Orchard* (Stourton) and *Norwood Castle* (near Oaksey) are others. Nothing survives of the oblong, walled enclosure erected on Castle Hill above *Mere* by Richard, Earl of Cornwall (Henry III's brother). *Longford Castle* near Salisbury deserves a mention as a unique Elizabethan replica of a medieval castle. It was a fantasy creation of Sir Thomas Gorges and is also remarkable for its triangular plan. The massive round towers at the three corners convey an impression of strength belied by the thin walls and large windows.

Worcestershire

Relatively few castles exist in Worcestershire. Even Worcester Castle was abandoned at an early date, leaving the marvellously-sited Elmley, which is now just an earthwork, and the episcopal castle at Hartlebury, which still exists as a mansion but not at all as a fortification. Weoley Castle makes an interesting archaeological site.

ELMLEY CASTLE overlooks the picturesque village of the same name from the northern slope of Bredon Hill. The earthworks are extensive and impressive. There are two baileys, the inner basically a ringwork though one end tapers to a point.

These lie within an Iron Age rampart which follows the contours of the hill. Excavations have uncovered some of the stone curtain which crowned the ringwork bank. Inside the ringwork are the rubble footings of a square structure, probably the forebuilding of a vanished keep. The castle was probably raised by the D'Abitots before 1100. It passed to the Beauchamps, but its elevated site can never have been convenient and they abandoned it after acquiring Warwick Castle in 1268.

Access: Freely accessible.
Reference: VCH *Worcestershire* (III).
Relations: Warwick. Old Sarum, Dover and Almondbury are other examples of castles within hillforts.

HARTLEBURY CASTLE The bishops of Worcester have had a palace here since Saxon times. Bishop Godfrey Giffard obtained a licence to crenellate in 1268. Apparently it was an early example of a quadrangular castle with corner towers, but nothing is left of the defences except for the wide stretch of moat behind the house. The castle was dismantled after its capture by the Roundheads in 1646, and the residential buildings at the back of the courtyard were adapted as a mansion by several eighteenth-century bishops. The low central range embodies the hall, rebuilt by Bishop Carpenter (d.1476). The southern wing is the chapel, which may go back to Bishop Giffard's time, while the matching north wing is entirely eighteenth century. Everything now has a 'Gothick' air as a result of the Georgian renovations.

Access: There is a museum (LA) in the north wing. The state rooms are open at certain times.
Reference: VCH *Worcestershire* (III). Souvenir guide.
Relations: Episcopal castles at Eccleshall, Newark and Wells.

HOLT CASTLE, five miles north of Worcester, stands between the River Severn and a fine Norman church. It was held by a junior branch of the Beauchamp family. The slender, square tower in front of the present house is the relic of a larger castle begun by John, Lord Beauchamp of Kidderminster. Perhaps only this tower had been built when he was executed in 1388 as one of Richard II's unpopular favourites. The hall-house behind was built in the following century, an entrance passage being cut through the tower to convert it into an entrance porch. This house still exists but has been Georgianised. By contrast the tower is little altered, retaining its original windows and battlements.

Access: Visible from the road.
Reference: VCH *Worcestershire* (III). Salter.
Relations: The Beauchamp castles of Elmley and Warwick. Compare the position of Bishop Waynflete's tower at Farnham.

WEOLEY CASTLE lies in the suburb of the same name four miles south-west of Birmingham city centre. Before excavations began in the 1930s only a few fragments of masonry could be seen, but now the entire walled circuit has been uncovered. Roger de Somery obtained a licence to crenellate in 1264 (he received a licence for Dudley Castle at the same time). However, his subsequent captivity and death make the builder of Weoley more likely to be his son, another Roger, in the 1270s. The courtyard is enclosed by a curtain which is now no higher than a moat revetment. It includes a gate tower at the north-west corner and four projecting towers – unusual in the Edwardian era for being square-fronted rather than round. Best preserved is the tower at the north-east corner, its pointed arch marking the bottom of a latrine chute. The other three towers stand mid-wall rather than at the angles. Various domestic buildings which stood rather haphazardly around the courtyard are marked out on the ground. They have been identified with the help of a survey compiled in 1424. The hall stood detached from the curtain on the east side of the courtyard. Finds from the excavations can be seen in a small site museum.

Access: Limited opening times in summer (LA).
Reference: Guidebook by A. M. Burchard.
Relations: Dudley.

WORCESTER CITY WALL   Worcester was enclosed by a stone wall from 1224 but it did not face the test of siege until the Civil War. The city held out for the King until July 1646 and was stormed again by Cromwell's troops after the Battle of Worcester (1651). The city wall had almost vanished but the construction of a by-pass has revealed a considerable stretch of the eastern wall, visible along City Walls Road. It does not stand very high and the only feature is the base of a half-round bastion. All six gates have vanished, as well as the fortified bridge which crossed the River Severn. Worcester's castle has vanished as well. William I raised it beside the river within the precinct of Worcester Cathedral. The site was returned to the monks in 1216 when they allowed King John to be buried inside their cathedral church. However, the motte remained until 1833.

Access: The remains are freely accessible (LA).
Reference: Salter.

OTHER SITES   There are Norman mottes at *Castlemorton* and *Leigh* (near Bransford), and a ditched enclosure on a spur above *Beoley*. *Hanley Castle* was built by King John as a hunting lodge. It was later a retreat of the Despensers and the Beauchamps, but only the semi-circular bailey platform remains. Lower *Strensham* preserves the concentric double moat of a castle licensed in 1388.

Yorkshire: East Riding and York

Of the three ridings of Yorkshire the East Riding is by far the poorest for castles. Its distance from the Scottish Border made them less necessary, and much has been destroyed. Wressle is the only stone castle of any substance remaining, and even that is incomplete. Skipsea is a impressive motte-and-bailey earthwork. York is included here for convenience, though strictly it does not belong to any of the ridings. York is full of medieval fortifications, not only its famous city wall but two Norman mottes (one bearing a later keep) and even a fortified abbey.

BEVERLEY TOWN DEFENCES The townsfolk requested permission to have defences in 1321, when fear of Scotland may have been felt even here. No stone wall was ever built, the town making do with a ditch and rampart for its protection, but the five gatehouses were masonry structures. The only survivor is the North Bar. It spans the street of the same name close to St Mary's Church – the lesser of the two magnificent churches for which Beverley is famous. This gate tower was rebuilt in 1409. It is an outstanding example of early brickwork, with a ribbed vault and a stepped parapet all of brick. The building accounts record that over 112,000 bricks (curiously long and narrow by later standards) were used in the construction. A portcullis groove is provided in the outer archway.

Access: Exterior visible (LA).
Reference: Turner.

PAULL HOLME lies near the north bank of the Humber, six miles south-east of Hull and a mile beyond the village of Paull. It was the medieval home of the Holme family. They built their house in pele tower form in the late fifteenth century. It is a reminder that the Humber estuary was not entirely immune from French raids, though this ruin is virtually the only structure of its type left in the East Riding. Characteristically of this area, the building material is brick, even for the ground-floor vault.

Access: Visible from the road.

SKIPSEA CASTLE is an unusual motte-and-bailey stronghold. The narrow bailey is bounded by a rampart but the ditched motte is curiously remote from it. This is because the land surrounding the motte was once a marsh. Excavations have unearthed the wooden causeway which connected the motte with the bailey. The castle was raised by Drogo de Bevrere, a Flemish knight who came to England with the Normans. It existed by 1086, when he was banished for murdering his wife. It passed to the counts of Aumale and was destroyed by order of Henry III in 1221, following the revolt of William de Fortibus. The earthworks lie a short distance west of the village at Skipsea Brough.

Access: Freely accessible (EH).
Relations: For William de Fortibus see Castle Bytham and Cockermouth.

WRESSLE CASTLE   This handsome ruin stands close to the River Derwent, six miles east of Selby. It was built from *circa* 1380 by Sir Thomas Percy, brother of the redoubtable Henry Percy, Earl of Northumberland. He became commander of the fleet and Earl of Worcester under Richard II, but lost his head for siding with his brother at the Battle of Shrewsbury (1403). The castle was later restored to the Percys and became a popular retreat. Wressle was a mature quadrangular castle, comprising four ranges around a courtyard and a large, oblong tower at each corner. It would thus have resembled its contemporary, Bolton Castle. Unfortunately the castle was slighted by order of Parliament in 1648 and three sides were demolished either then or later. The slighting was precautionary, since Wressle had been garrisoned by the Roundheads throughout the Civil War. Apart from the isolated gate arch only the south range survives, along with its twin flanking towers. This portion escaped the slighting because it was still inhabited, and it remained so until a fire gutted the interior in 1796. The fine ashlar exterior remains virtually intact and unspoilt but the interior is wildly overgrown. Note the tall windows which pierce the range at first-floor level, denoting the position of the hall. The solar would thus have occupied the spacious chamber at the same level in the western tower, with a more private apartment above. The east tower housed a chapel at this level, as shown by the ambitious windows, and two chambers above it. Both towers were served by spiral staircases, located at what would have been the corners of the courtyard.

> *Access:* Obtain permission to visit at the farm.
> *Reference:* BOE *Yorkshire – York and the East Riding.* Mackenzie (II).
> *Relations:* Bolton. The Percy castles of Spofforth, Cockermouth, Alnwick and Wark-worth.

YORK CASTLES, CITY WALL AND ABBEY   The history of York begins with the Romans. About AD 71 the advancing Ninth Legion chose this site as its base. The Sixth Legion soon replaced the Ninth but *Eburacum* remained one of the three legionary fortresses of Roman Britain, along with Chester and Caerleon. It was here that Constantine was first proclaimed emperor (306). After the departure of the Romans the old defences were utilised by new invaders. In turn York became the capital of the Anglian Kingdom of Northumbria and the Danish Kingdom of *Jorvik.* By the Norman Conquest it was surpassed in size only by London.

Among other great monuments York is renowned for its medieval city wall. Not only does the walled circuit remain nearly complete (some two and a half miles of it), but the city also preserves its original gatehouses, here known as bars. Fortunately the defences were not slighted following the siege of the city during the Civil War. York surrendered to a combined Scottish and Parliamentary force in July 1644, after Prince Rupert's relieving army had been routed at Marston Moor. The Roundhead commander, Sir Thomas Fairfax, treated the city with respect (it is largely thanks to him that the York churches preserve so much medieval glass). The Jacobite scare of 1745 kept the city wall in commission for a while longer. Systematic demolition began in 1807, but the Archbishop of York raised legal objections and became the saviour of the circuit. There followed a rather heavy-handed restoration, particularly of parapets.

Medieval York was divided into three sectors by the River Ouse and its tributary, the Foss. The northern sector between the rivers, now dominated by the Minster, is the site of the Roman fortress. It followed, on a grand scale, the usual rectangular layout of Roman forts. The fortress wall has vanished on two sides, towards the rivers. However, on the north-west and north-east the Roman and medieval defences coincide. Here the Roman wall lies buried beneath a mighty rampart first constructed in the tenth century, during the Danish occupation. The two 'suburbs' beyond the rivers are also delimited by ramparts. A stone wall was built on top of these ramparts in the thirteenth and fourteenth centuries. The circuit preserves thirty-seven projecting bastions (round, square and polygonal) which are irregularly spaced. This figure includes a handful of larger towers situated at key points. The four bars are striking edifices, but it should be admitted that the older ramparts form the major obstacle and the stone wall would be quite puny without them. In places the wall-walk is only a few feet above the crest of the rampart. Furthermore, except in Micklegate the wall as first constructed was so thin that the wall-walk must have projected on corbels. The present walkway supported by arcades dates from a substantial remodelling of the defences in Henry VII's reign. This is a late example of city wall strengthening, motivated less by the continuing threat from Scotland than by the county's pro-Yorkist sympathies. However, the city fell to the rebels during the 'Pilgrimage of Grace' (1536).

Our tour around the wall takes the traditional starting point of Bootham Bar, in the shadow of the Minster's towers. It occupies the site of the north-west gate of the legionary fortress. Though somewhat restored the gatehouse is typical of York's bars: a tall gate tower with rounded corner bartizans corbelled out higher up. The upper floors date from the early fourteenth century but the round-headed entrance passage is Norman. From Bootham Bar the city wall follows the line of the Roman fortress wall as described above. This portion, built *circa* 1250–70, affords fine views of the Minster. A number of bastions survive, though the largest (at the northern angle) is a Victorian reconstruction. The next gatehouse, Monk Bar, is the tallest of the four, featuring a two-tier parapet and numerous cross-slits. Every floor except the top one is vaulted. There is no Norman gate passage here, the gatehouse having been rebuilt on a new site after 1330 to allow an expansion of the Minster close. The two doorways leading nowhere at first-floor level are a reminder that all the bars once had barbicans in front. Beyond Monk Bar the ruins of a Roman angle tower show where the fortress and city walls part company. The Roman wall turned right towards the Ouse, while the city wall continues to the Foss. The tower which ended this portion of the circuit has disappeared.

There follows a half-mile gap which was never walled, as the narrow River Foss once broadened into a lake here. We regain the city wall at the Red Tower, an oblong brick structure of 1490. Here the Walmgate sector of the wall begins. Walmgate was a late developer. Its rampart is entirely Norman and the stone wall on top was not begun until 1345. This sector is the lowest of the three and has few bastions, but Walmgate Bar is a compensation. It is the only one to retain its barbican – a narrow walled passage. By contrast, the inner face of the bar forms a handsome Elizabethan house. The wall continues past the triple arch of Fishergate Bar to the Fishergate Postern Tower, a tall, square tower which is another early Tudor addition.

At this point we have returned to the River Foss. On the opposite bank are the remains of York Castle. It is a reflection of the city's importance that William the

Conqueror should raise not one but two motte-and-bailey castles, both guarding the approach along the River Ouse. The first castle rose upon William's arrival in 1068 and the second appeared the following year. A few months later a Danish fleet sailed up the Ouse and destroyed both castles, but they soon rose again. That called York Castle was always the more important of the pair. Its heyday was Edward II's reign when the threat from Scotland meant that the King and his court were frequently in residence. It sits on the narrow tongue of land between the two rivers. The surviving portions belong to a general reconstruction under Henry III in 1245–70, i.e. concurrently with much of the city wall. The total cost was £2600. A stretch of bailey curtain and two open-backed, semi-circular bastions survive. The rest of the curtain and its two gatehouses have vanished. So have the palatial residential buildings which occupied the bailey (now Castle Green). Eighteenth-century assize courts and prison blocks have taken their place. They show how the castle degenerated into a court house and gaol, though the prison buildings have been adapted to serve as the excellent Castle Museum.

The chief relic of York Castle is the keep, crowning William I's great motte. It is known as Clifford's Tower from the mangled corpse of Roger Clifford which dangled here after the Battle of Boroughbridge. The quatrefoil plan (like a four-leaf clover) is unique in England and probably derives from the French keep at Etampes. It was devised by the master mason Henry de Reynes, the architect of Westminster Abbey. The keep is only two storeys high. Turrets are corbelled out at the junctions of three of the lobes, while a forebuilding projects from the fourth side. This forebuilding, the only part still roofed, has been rebuilt at least once owing to subsidence. Indeed, cracks in the masonry demonstrate that the tower is a little too heavy for the artificial mound beneath it. Clifford's Tower is something of a rarity for its time, as Henry III's reign was the apogee of the keep-less enclosure. Considering the importance of this royal stronghold it is surprising that no stone keep had been built earlier. A wooden keep still occupied the motte in 1190. In that year York's prosperous Jewish community, fearing a pogrom, took refuge inside it and refused to come out. In the ensuing siege the Jews set fire to the tower – and themselves – rather than face the fury of the mob.

Beyond the Ouse rises the other Norman motte. This fortification is known as the Old Baile. It became the responsibility of the archbishops of York and was still being maintained in the fourteenth century. On two sides the former bailey is bounded by the city wall. We are now in Micklegate, the other medieval suburb. Micklegate began as a Roman civilian town and the rampart here is Danish, as in the northern sector. The wall which crowns it dates from the mid-to-late thirteenth century. Micklegate Bar bears the arms of Edward III but incorporates a Norman gate passage, like Bootham Bar. The main road from London passed under this gatehouse so it became the chief location for displaying rebels' heads, including Henry Percy ('Hotspur') in 1403 and the Duke of York in 1460. The next section of wall is pierced by several Victorian arches. At the end of the Micklegate stretch we reach the River Ouse again. Two U-shaped boom towers flank the river. Lendal Tower is the larger, but both are much restored.

Across the Ouse we are back in the northern sector of the defences. The wall returning to Bootham Bar is incomplete, but the grounds of the Yorkshire Museum preserve two towers of great antiquity. First comes the Multangular Tower – the west angle tower of the Roman fortress, rebuilt in polygonal form about AD 300. This tower was incorporated in the medieval defences and its embrasured upper part was rebuilt in the thirteenth century. The rampart bank has been removed beyond this tower to reveal the Roman fortress wall. There follows the Anglian Tower, erected by one of the Northumbrian kings to close a gap in the Roman wall. At a time when fortifications were invariably built of timber this vaulted stone tower is unique, though undeniably modest where compare with the mighty Roman tower nearby. The longest gap in the city wall follows. It was demolished in the 1830s to make way for St Leonard's Place.

From Bootham Bar another defensive wall extends along the thoroughfare known as Bootham, then makes a right-angled turn towards the Ouse. This wall is flanked by slender U-shaped bastions, larger towers (two round and one square) guarding the corners. St Mary's Tower at the north corner displays a fissure caused by undermining during the 1644 siege. A Norman gatehouse leads inside. This was in fact the precinct wall of York Abbey, a Benedictine house. The wall was raised to a defensible height and given its flanking towers after the abbot obtained a licence to crenellate in 1318. At that time Robert Bruce's raids threatened even York and this extra-mural abbey must have felt insecure.

> *Access:* The city wall parapet is freely accessible, though it may be closed in wet weather (LA). The abbey defences are visible from the road. The Castle Museum is open regularly (LA), while Clifford's Tower can be visited at standard times (EH).
>
> *Reference:* RCHM *City of York* (II). *The Bars and Walls of York* by R. M. Butler. *Clifford's Tower* by D. F. Renn. *HKW* (II).
>
> *Relations:* The city wall at Chester incorporates another legionary fortress. London also had two castles. Compare Henry III's work at Windsor, Dover and the Tower of London, and the fortified monastery at Tynemouth.

OTHER SITES Mottes remain at *Cottingham* and Great *Driffield*. At *Roos* some earthwork survive of a castle of the Roos family, while *Leconfield Castle* (licensed 1308) was a Percy stronghold, marked by its large moated enclosure. The *Danish Tower* at Flamborough is the stump of a pele tower. *Kingston upon Hull* was founded by Edward I in the angle between the Humber and the River Hull. Its late-four-teenth-century town wall was unique for being constructed entirely of brick. Unfortunately nothing remains above ground, and the ditch in front of the wall was later widened to form the chain of town docks. Nor is there anything left of the Citadel, which lay opposite the town on the east bank of the Hull. It was the most northerly of Henry VIII's coastal forts with a plan reminiscent of Southsea Castle.

Yorkshire: North Riding

Yorkshire suffered badly with the arrival of the Normans. William the Conqueror's heavy-handed suppression of revolt (the Harrying of the North) laid much of it waste. There was a sporadic threat from Scotland, culminating in David I's unsuccessful invasion of 1138. Earthwork castles are quite common but Norman masonry castles are relatively few. The earliest is Richmond – a castle so advanced that it had a gatehouse and a towered curtain within two decades of the Norman Conquest, as well as England's earliest stone hall. Bowes and Scarborough preserve contrasting keeps of Henry II, while Middleham has a contemporary baronial example. Helmsley Castle, though much ruined, shows an early use of round flanking towers. After that there is little to show for the comparatively peaceful thirteenth century.

The period after Bannockburn was the most devastating for the region. Robert Bruce led his countrymen on daring raids deep into northern England. After Bruce's death the English recovered their morale. The Scots were seldom a menace this far south again, but the threat remained and the barons of the county were frequently involved in Scottish campaigns. This warlike aristocracy took pride in castle building, with comparatively little interference from royal officialdom. There is some royal work of this era, i.e. the outer curtain at Pickering and Scarborough's barbican. Bolton Castle is the archetypal baronial quadrangle, consisting of four ranges around a courtyard and square towers at the corners. Sheriff Hutton and Danby castles are less complete examples of the same theme, and at Middleham the Nevilles built a quadrangular castle around the older keep. The most ambitious tower house is the truncated one at Gilling. Among pele towers may be singled out Mortham and the twin towers of Nappa Hall. However, Yorkshire did not become another Northumberland and peles are relatively few. Castles of the fifteenth century (such as Snape and Crayke) show the general trend towards greater comfort to the detriment of strength. Today the major castles of the North Riding survive as battered but noble ruins, pushed along that path in some cases by Civil War slighting.

ASKE HALL Midway between Richmond and Gilling West is the large park surrounding Aske Hall. This mansion has two wings terminating in towers. That in front of the east wing is actually a pele tower, originating in the fifteenth century but transformed by later alterations. The other tower has been added for the sake of symmetry. From Norman times until 1512 the manor belonged to the Aske family.

Access: Open by appointment.
Relations: Danby Hall is similar.

AYTON CASTLE sits on the bank of the River Derwent at West Ayton, four miles south-west of Scarborough. This ruined pele tower is attributed to Sir Ralph Eure *circa* 1400. It is divided into two vaulted rooms at ground level. Twin stairs led to the upper floors but little more than one side now rises to full height. The surviving corbels at the wall-head are evidence of a machicolated parapet.

Access: Exterior only (LA).
Relations: For Ralph Eure see Witton Castle.

BOLTON CASTLE dominates the Wensleydale village of Castle Bolton, five miles west of Leyburn. It is one of the most complete examples of a quadrangular castle remaining. The castle was built by Richard, Lord Scrope, steward of the Royal Household under Richard II. A licence to crenellate was awarded in 1379 but it is likely that the castle was almost complete by then. A contract for building the east range and its flanking towers had been drawn up the previous year with the master mason John Lewyn. Since this is the most accessible side it is reasonable to assume that the rest of the castle had already been built, otherwise the east range would have impeded the construction of the other three. From the uniformity of design it is also likely that John Lewyn was the architect of the entire castle.

The castle is a tall and compact structure, its curtain backed by ranges of buildings on all four sides. Bolton is one of those mature quadrangular castles which can be described as consisting of four ranges around a courtyard, as opposed to having a set of lean-to buildings against the curtain. Massive rectangular towers rise up at the corners. They project very little beyond the curtain so they are not flanking towers in the traditional sense. Small turrets project in the middle of the two longer sides. Although ruined, the castle survives in a fine state of preservation except for the collapsed north-east tower. This was the main victim of the Civil War slighting. John Scrope, still in his teens, held Bolton for the King during that conflict. The castle endured a year-long siege before surrendering to the Roundheads in November 1645. The west range and south-west tower escaped the slighting and remain habitable.

A long gate passage pierces the east range immediately beside the south-east tower. Any attacker who managed to penetrate the obstacles within the gate passage would have found himself in a death trap, as the courtyard of the castle is unusually well geared towards providing a second line of defence. Most of the windows are small, and suitable for use by archers. The five doorways into the domestic apartments were each barred by a portcullis. Four of them – concealed in the corners of the courtyard – are protected by overhanging machicolations.

The ground floors of the towers and connecting ranges are divided into barrel-vaulted compartments in typical Northern fashion. They housed stores, workshops and stables. In contrast to these grim chambers, the two upper floors contained handsome living quarters. There was indeed a surprisingly large amount of private accommodation, augmented by the five-storey towers. The hall in the north range rose through two storeys, giving this chamber suitably lofty proportions. To the east lay the domestic offices, including a kitchen in the destroyed north-east tower. Presumably the solar occupied the room adjacent to the hall in the north-west tower. The west range contains two spacious apartments forming a separate residential suite, presumably for guests. According to tradition Mary Queen of Scots occupied the south-west tower during her stay here in 1568. The most important room in the south range is the chapel at second-floor level. There follows the south-east tower. This tower and the adjacent portions of the connecting ranges (including the chamber over the gate passage) formed a self-contained unit. This is sometimes described as the garrison's quarters but it is more likely to have been occupied by the

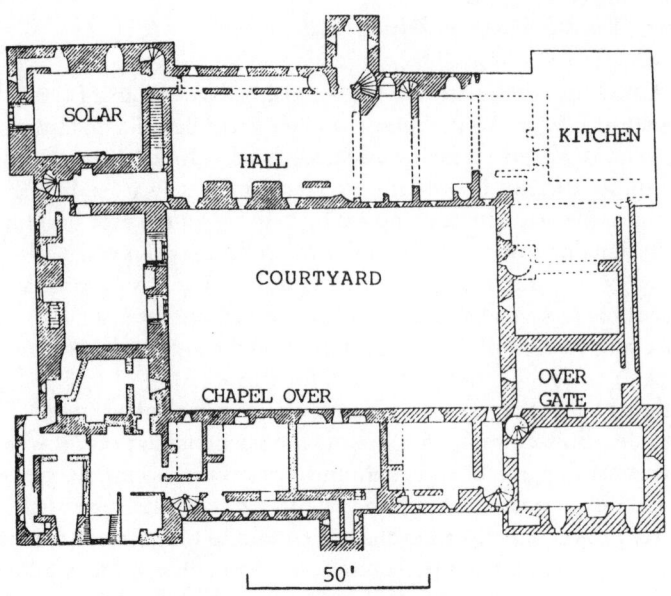

BOLTON CASTLE AT FIRST-FLOOR LEVEL

constable, or even by the Scropes themselves during emergencies. In that way someone trustworthy could maintain control over the entrance. The garrison must therefore have been squashed into the remainder of the east range.

Access: Open regularly except in winter.
Reference: Guidebook by G. Jackson. VCH *Yorkshire, North Riding* (I).
Relations: For Mary Queen of Scots see Fotheringhay, Tutbury and Wingfield Manor. Compare the quadrangular castles of Danby, Sheriff Hutton, Wressle and Lumley.

BOWES CASTLE stands in the valley of the River Greta, guarding the eastern approach to the Stainmore Pass over the Pennines. Like its western counterpart at Brough, the castle occupies the site of a Roman fort (*Lavatrae*). The stone defences of this fort have vanished, leaving only an earth rampart behind, and its northern end has been obscured by the medieval castle and parish church. Henry II built the oblong keep which survives as an imposing ruin. The royal accounts show that most of the work was done in 1171–74, as if in anticipation of William the Lion's invasion during Prince Henry's revolt. After William's capture the urgency diminished, only small sums being spent for the rest of Henry's reign. The keep is a rare example of a hall-keep, somewhat longer than it is high. The hall was entered directly at first-floor level, though the forebuilding which protected the entrance has been reduced to its foundations. Originally the hall occupied two-thirds of the keep's length, with a solar beyond it at the west end, but the cross-wall which stood between them has fallen. Beneath were dimly-lit undercrofts, now open to the sky. The north-west corner of the fort was cut off by a ditch to form a small bailey around the keep, but there was

288

never a stone curtain. No doubt the fort site was utilised as an outer bailey. The castle's later history is uneventful, except for its capture by rebels in 1322. It was already falling into ruins at that time.

Access: Freely accessible (EH).
Reference: VCH *Yorkshire, North Riding* (I).
Relations: Brough. Henry II also built the keep at Scarborough. Compare the hall-keeps at Middleham and Castle Rising.

COWTON CASTLE crowns a hill overlooking South Cowton church, five miles north-east of Catterick. Sir Richard Conyers is said to have built the castle, along with the church, towards the end of the fifteenth century. The castle is an oblong tower – large enough to be regarded as a free-standing tower house rather than a pele tower. Several original windows remain. Indeed, the tower is quite unspoilt despite its continued use as a farmhouse. A taller stair turret projects near one end.

Access: Private.
Relations: The Conyers castle at nearby Hornby.

CRAYKE CASTLE and village occupy a hill overlooking the Vale of York. Crayke belonged to the bishops of Durham and a castle is said to have existed here in Norman times. However, the two remaining portions date from the fifteenth century. The main survivor is a tall chamber block, rather narrow in relation to its length. It was built by Bishop Robert Neville in 1441 but thoroughly restored in the eighteenth century following Civil War damage (the castle was besieged by the Roundheads). Projecting from this block is the vaulted undercroft of the former kitchen. Beyond lay the hall, which has vanished. Nearby, but detached from the domestic range, lies the ruined stump of a tower house which seems to have been the only defensive portion. It may also be Bishop Neville's. Only the ground floor, divided into two vaulted compartments, survived the slighting of the castle in 1647.

Access: Visible from the road.
Reference: VCH *Yorkshire, North Riding* (II).
Relations: The bishops' castles at Auckland, Durham, Norham and Somerton.

DANBY CASTLE This gaunt, moorland ruin is dramatically sited on a ridge overlooking the River Esk, a mile south-east of Danby village. By analogy with quadrangular strongholds such as Bolton and Sheriff Hutton, this castle is believed to date from the late fourteenth century. Danby passed from the Latimers to the Nevilles in 1380 or thereabouts, so it is not certain which family was responsible for its construction. It became the seat of a junior branch of the Neville dynasty. They assumed the title of Lord Latimer. Compared with the complexity of Bolton, Danby is a modest quadrangle surrounding a small oblong courtyard. The accommodation was limited to one main chamber in each range: hall on the east, kitchen (with an immense fireplace) on the north and solar on the south, all surmounting undercrofts. Much still remains of these three ranges but the west range, which contained the entrance, has perished. The square corner towers are unusual because they project diagonally. These towers survive in conditions varying from the fragmentary south-west tower to the impressive south-east tower which is incorporated into the present farmhouse.

Access: Private, but well seen from the road.
Reference: VCH *Yorkshire, North Riding* (II).
Relations: Bolton and Sheriff Hutton. Snape was another castle of the Neville lords Latimer.

DANBY HALL, no relation to Danby Castle, lies within a spacious park beside the River Ure, two miles east of Middleham. It is basically a much-restored Elizabethan mansion. However, as at Aske Hall an older pele tower is attached to one of the flanking wings. This embattled tower was built by a member of the Kilham or Conyers families, who resided here successively in the later Middle Ages.

Access: Private.
Relations: Aske. For the Conyers family see Cowton and Hornby.

GILLING CASTLE crowns a hill above the village of Gilling East. This dignified mansion consists of a square central block and two long flanking wings. The wings are eighteenth-century and the rest was given a substantial facelift at the same time. However, the central block is actually a large tower house, built by Thomas de Etton in the late fourteenth century. Only the ground floor retains its original appearance. Doorways at the front and rear of the tower lead into a central passage with three vaulted cellars on each side. The upper floors have been transformed and only the outer walls are medieval. Today the tower is notable for its solar, the product of an earlier restoration by William Fairfax in Elizabethan times. The splendid panelling and heraldic glass have been restored to their original setting after twenty years' exile in America.

Access: Now a school, but the solar is open regularly.
Reference: VCH *Yorkshire, North Riding* (I).

HARLSEY CASTLE, four miles north-east of Northallerton, is marked by a row of three vaulted undercrofts which probably formed the ground floor of a tower house. It is the only surviving part of a castle which stood within a large outer enclosure, still bounded on three sides by a wide ditch. According to the antiquary Leland the castle was built by Sir James Strangeways, a judge who bought the manor in 1423.

Access: On private land.

HELMSLEY CASTLE guarded the valley of the River Rye. Walter l'Espec, the founder of nearby Rievaulx Abbey, is believed to have had a castle here. However, the existing earthworks and masonry are attributed to Robert de Roos, lord of the manor from 1186 to 1227. The Roos family held it until 1508. The castle comprises an oblong bailey, surrounded by a formidable double ditch which is cut out of solid rock on the west side. Though extremely ruinous, Helmsley is a good example of the revolution which was taking place in castle-building in the early thirteenth century. It features a strong curtain with circular towers guarding three of the four corners. Only the south-east corner was not so well defended, because here stood a simple gate tower which did not act as a flanking bastion. A stronger entrance, flanked by semi-circular towers, was provided on the north front. The largest tower is the D-shaped one projecting on the east. Clearly this was the keep, and the only D-shaped tower in England which can be called a keep. It was probably Robert de Roos' son William who strengthened the entrances. He built an outer gatehouse in front of the north gate and a large barbican beyond the south-east gate. All these works can still be seen in outline, but the curtain and most of its towers have been reduced to their footings. In 1644 the castle suffered a three-month siege before surrendering to the Roundhead commander, Sir Thomas Fairfax. Its subsequent slighting was a severe one.

The only portions of the castle to stand up high are the keep, the barbican and the west range. At a time when round towers were replacing square ones, the D-shaped keep at Helmsley was a compromise between defensive strength and domestic convenience. The curved outer portion of the keep has been blasted down to its footings, but the courtyard front stands entire. As first built the keep consisted of a single apartment over an undercroft, so its use must have been limited. The two upper floors and the twin surmounting turrets were added *circa* 1300, in the time of the second William de Roos. The first William de Roos' barbican consists of a screen wall on the rampart between the inner and outer ditches. A semi-circular tower flanks each end of this wall and a round-towered gatehouse stands in the middle. The west range, largely Elizabethan, is the only part of the castle to retain its roof. It remained in use after the slighting but was later abandoned for Duncombe Park. At one end is the shell of a large square tower guarding a 'kink' in the west curtain. Though remodelled in the Elizabethan period to form part of the west range, this tower contained a suite of chambers, including the solar. Some foundations beyond mark the site of the hall.

Access: Standard opening times (EH).·
Reference: Guidebook by G. Coppack.
Relations: The Roos castles of Belvoir and Wark-on-Tweed. There is another D-shaped keep at Ewloe across the Welsh Border.

HORNBY CASTLE began as a medieval stronghold, developed into a mansion but has suffered the fate of twentieth-century demolition. Only the square St Quintin Tower escaped. The name of this tower is a reminder of the St Quintin family. They probably built it in the fourteenth century, though the windows indicate a remodelling towards 1500 under William, Lord Conyers. An original gateway adjoins the tower but the truncated range beyond is neo-Gothic. The later mansion occupied a quadrangle and it is likely that the original castle followed the same lines. It can be found two miles south of Catterick.

Access: Visible from the road.
Relations: Cowton was another Conyers castle. Nearby Ravensworth was similar.

KILTON CASTLE stands within a wooded estate two miles south-west of Loftus. The main attraction of the castle is its precipitous situation on a spur overlooking the Kilton Beck. The only level approach is cut off by a deep ditch, overlooked by a fragment of curtain and an angle turret. Owing to the confines of the site the courtyard was long and narrow. In the middle stands one ruinous wall from a square Norman keep. Beyond that another stretch of curtain survives, terminating in a D-shaped tower with arrow-slits. It is the best preserved part of these meagre ruins but seems rather superfluous, perched as it is on the cliff's edge. This tower dates from the thirteenth century, after the castle had been acquired by the Thweng family.

Access: Obtain permission to visit from the estate warden.
Reference: VCH *Yorkshire, North Riding* (II).

MIDDLEHAM CASTLES The imposing ruin of the present castle is hemmed in by the Wensleydale town of Middleham. Its predecessor was the impressive earthwork known as William's Hill, on higher ground to the south-west. This, with its embanked ringwork and narrow bailey, was probably raised soon after the Norman Conquest by Alan the Red, Lord of Richmond. In the 1170s or thereabouts Ribald Fitz Ranulf moved down to the present site. He built the rectangular keep which forms the centre of the castle. The emphasis is upon length and there is no intermediate floor, so it can be described as a hall-keep. Over a hundred feet long, it is a surprisingly large structure for a relatively humble knight. Divided lengthways by a cross-wall, the keep contained a hall and solar standing over undercrofts. The present entrance is through a gap at ground level, but originally a stone staircase (now cut away) led to a first-floor doorway. There is no sign of a protective forebuilding. The vaults which covered the undercrofts have fallen, and the arcade which ran down the middle of the wider undercroft (i.e. below the hall) has been reduced to its column bases. Otherwise the keep is well preserved. A large fireplace in the cross-wall shows that part of the undercroft served as the kitchen. At first-floor level small chambers are contrived in the angle turrets, except for the one housing the spiral staircase. On two sides of the keep central projections contain latrines. A new solar was created above the hall in the fifteenth century, during the Neville occupation.

Middleham was acquired by the Nevilles in 1270. They were emerging as a major family in the North. It must have been Ralph Neville who enlarged the castle *circa* 1300, making it the earliest of the Neville castles to have survived. Ralph built a curtain around the keep, creating in effect a quadrangular castle with a keep in the middle. The curtain surrounds the keep quite closely, so this was a concentric castle inspired by the Edwardian castles of Wales. Archers on the keep parapet could easily have shot over the heads of defenders on the curtain, especially since that curtain was originally lower than it is now. However, Ralph's angle towers show little regard for Edwardian principles. Three of them are oblong and they hardly project beyond the curtain at all. Only the south-west corner was given a modest, half-round flanking tower. The original entrance to the castle was through a gate tower in the middle of the east side. Like most of the east curtain, this gatehouse has been reduced to its foundations. A ruinous chapel block connects it to the keep.

The curtain was heightened in the fifteenth century, partly for effect and partly to accommodate the new lodgings which were built against it on three sides. They leave just a narrow corridor around the keep. Evidently these were retainers' lodgings, the chief residential apartments remaining in the modernised keep. The north-east corner tower was adapted to form a new gate tower. It has a vaulted gate passage and a row of machicolation corbels at the top. These works are attributed to Ralph Neville, Earl of Westmorland, and perhaps his son Richard, Earl of Salisbury. The second Richard Neville is more famous as the 'Kingmaker'. Middleham formed his Northern power-base and he earned his nickname by holding Edward IV prisoner here in 1469. After his death at Barnet two years later the castle was granted to Richard, Duke of Gloucester. It was his favourite residence during the years he spent as viceroy in the North, but following his short reign as Richard III the castle fell into a terminal state of decay.

Access: Standard opening times for the castle (EH). William's Hill is on private land.
Reference: Guidebook by J. Weaver.
Relations: The Neville castles at Sheriff Hutton, Brancepeth, Raby and Penrith. For Alan the Red see Richmond. Compare the hall-keeps of Bowes and Castle Rising.

MORTHAM TOWER is an evocative little stronghold overlooking the River Greta near its junction with the Tees, two miles south-east of Barnard Castle. It consists of a pele tower occupying one corner of a small enclosure. The tall tower is attributed to Sir Thomas Rokeby, who fought at Neville's Cross in 1346. During his absence the original house here was sacked by the Scots, thus giving the impetus for rebuilding as a pele. Corner bartizans add distinction to the parapet. The crenellations are unusual, forming rows of square apertures just below the wall top. Wooden shutters would have suspended from the lintels. Another Thomas Rokeby added the courtyard in Henry VII's reign. It is a quadrangular castle in miniature. His hall block survives as a barn on the north side but later buildings occupy the flanks. The south front is an embattled length of curtain, pierced by a simple gateway.

Access: Private.
Reference: VCH *Yorkshire, North Riding* (I).
Relations: Towers with bartizans at York and Belsay. The walled enclosures at Walburn and Beetham halls.

MULGRAVE CASTLE Four miles north-west of Whitby, just outside Lythe, is the Georgian house known as Mulgrave Castle. A footpath leads through the Mulgrave Woods to the ruins of the original castle, nearly a mile south-west of its successor. It was built by Peter de Maulay, who acquired the manor by marriage in 1214. De Maulay stood high in royal favour owing to his part in the murder of Prince Arthur, King John's nephew and a rival contender to the English throne. His castle stands on a ridge, the buttressed curtain forming a revetment around the bailey. The only level approach is cut off by a ditch and the entrance is flanked by a broken drum tower. Within the bailey are the remains of a square tower house, added about a century later by another Peter de Maulay. Its circular corner turrets have collapsed and one wall is pierced by a large Elizabethan window. The castle was reduced to its melancholy state by slighting after the Civil War.

Access: The site is accessible at weekends (on foot from Sandsend).

Reference: VCH *Yorkshire, North Riding* (II).
Relations: Compare the tower houses at Dudley and Nunney.

NAPPA HALL Beneath a rocky crag in Wensleydale, on a minor road a mile east of Askrigg, stands the old home of the Metcalfes. Thomas Metcalfe is said to have built this house in the 1450s. It is a fine example of the pele-and-hall houses commonly found in the North, but here the hall has two flanking towers. The taller of the two is a handsome structure, with original windows and a stair turret rising above the battlements. It contained the solar at first-floor level and private apartments on the two upper floors. The lower tower housed the kitchen and domestic offices, but a new kitchen was added beyond it in the seventeenth century. The hall itself has been partitioned for use as a farmhouse. Mary Queen of Scots is said to have stayed here a night or two during her spell of imprisonment at Bolton Castle.

Access: Visible from the road.
Reference: VCH *Yorkshire, North Riding* (I).
Relations: Twin-towered hall-houses such as Askerton, Howgill and Lympne.

PICKERING CASTLE is a good example of a Norman motte-and-bailey stronghold, occupying a commanding position above the Pickering Beck. Its two baileys are dominated by the conical motte which rises up between them. The motte has its own ditch. Pickering was one of those royal castles frequented by monarchs for the local hunting. In all likelihood the castle was founded by William the Conqueror but it only emerges from obscurity in Henry II's reign. Small sums recorded in the royal accounts during the 1180s are sufficient to account for the plain curtain enclosing the inner bailey. The only mural tower commanded the entrance to the bailey and guarded the approach wall up the side of the motte. During the Magna Carta war the castle suffered damage, necessitating some repairs under Henry III. The shell keep on top of the motte is attributed entirely to Henry, and thus rather late for a keep of this type. Both keep and curtain are now very ruinous. Within the inner bailey, two successive halls have been reduced to their footings. By contrast the thirteenth-century chapel survives intact and roofed, though its east end is a modern rebuilding.

In 1267 Henry III gave Pickering to his son Edmund 'Crouchback'. It formed part of the vast estate accompanying his creation as Earl of Lancaster. After the revolt and execution of Edmund's son Thomas (1322) the Lancastrian estates were confiscated. At that time Yorkshire lay exposed to Robert Bruce's raids and Edward II ordered the strengthening of the castle. In 1323–26 the palisade enclosing the outer bailey was replaced by a stone curtain costing nearly £1000. The outer curtain, unlike the inner, has come down to us in a good state of preservation. Its three towers are known (from west to east) as the Mill Tower, Diate Hill Tower and Rosamund's Tower. Although these towers act as flankers they are not numerous enough to be totally effective. They also follow the Northern preference for square instead of round. Such factors show that the Edwardian age of impregnable castle building was over. The depleted royal resources would not allow anything more ambitious. All three towers contained suites of apartments for resident officials or visiting dignitaries, a function as important as their defensive role. Rosamund's Tower also houses a postern, reached from the ditch between the inner and outer baileys. The main gateway formed the inner side of a gatehouse which has otherwise disappeared.

The outer bailey was barely complete when Edward II was overthrown. Pickering and the other Lancastrian estates were restored to Earl Thomas' brother. The castle thus remained one of the numerous Duchy of Lancaster strongholds, reverting to the Crown and decaying into ruin after Henry IV usurped the throne.

Access: Standard opening times (EH).
Reference: Guidebook by L. Butler.
Relations: Fortified royal hunting lodges such as Rockingham, St Briavels and Odiham. Edward II rebuilt Knaresborough Castle.

RAVENSWORTH CASTLE, five miles north-west of Richmond, is a sombre ruin. Encompassed by a dry moat, this was once a castle of some grandeur. It may have been founded in Norman times but the existing masonry dates from the fourteenth century. The castle formed an irregular quadrangle with angle towers. Only one square tower now stands, virtually intact except for its parapet. The fragment of curtain adjoining the tower contains the entrance gateway, retaining the groove for a portcullis. A few other pieces of curtain indicate the position of the courtyard. The castle belonged to the Fitzhugh family.

Access: Visible from the road.
Relations: Tanfield was another Fitzhugh castle.

RICHMOND CASTLE crowns a high cliff above the River Swale. Commenced by Alan 'the Red' soon after the Norman Conquest, the castle was the centre of a great estate known as the Earldom of Richmond. Castle and title passed, through Alan's nephew, to the dukes of Brittany, who held them intermittently for the next three centuries. The dukes frequently lost and regained Richmond owing to their shifting allegiance between the kings of England and France. The connection was finally severed in 1384 during the Hundred Years War. Fifteenth-century owners included the Nevilles, the Duke of Bedford, Edmund Tudor (Henry VII's father) and the future Richard III. However, the castle was seldom in use by then. A report of 1538 recommended that it be restored to a defensible condition, but nothing was done and the castle sank into ruins. It is ironic that this impressive pile never stood the test of siege.

The castle is remarkable because it is largely an early Norman masonry stronghold. Alan the Red received Richmond in 1071 and the castle was probably complete before his death in 1089. The absence of earth ramparts, layers of herringbone masonry and the rudimentary architecture all suggest that it was a stone structure from the beginning. Few castles were built in stone before the twelfth century. Richmond is interesting because, in its original form, it did not possess a keep but relied instead upon a towered curtain and a gatehouse. A few other early Norman castles had gatehouses in lieu of a keep but the flanking towers here are the oldest in any English medieval castle. Ludlow Castle, far away on the Welsh Border, offers a near-contemporary parallel, but towers flanking a curtain would not become

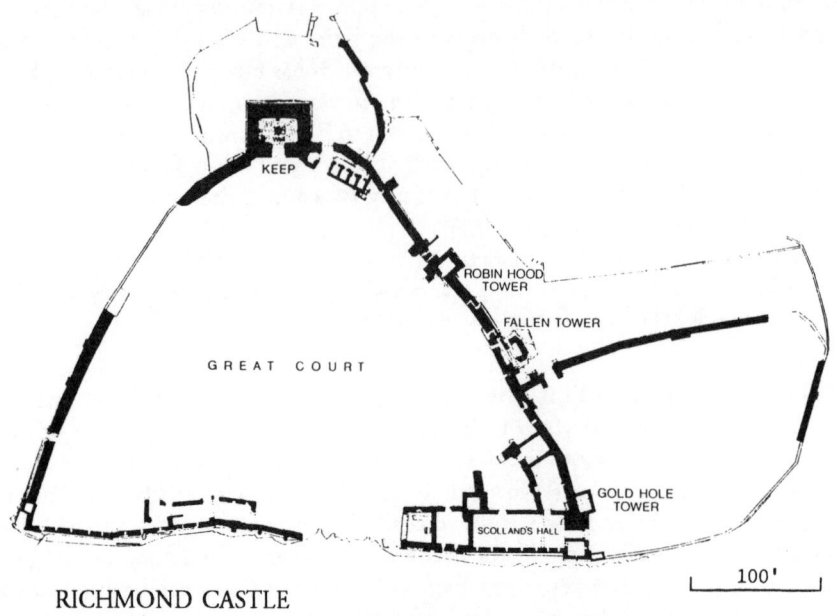

RICHMOND CASTLE

common for another century. Richmond's triangular hilltop was originally walled on two sides only, the cliff above the river being considered more than adequate protection on the third. (The ruinous curtain on that side is a later Norman addition.) The western approach is also quite steep, so this stretch of curtain is tower-less except for a narrow turret overlooking the river. It was on the vulnerable east front that three square mural towers were provided, a gatehouse occupying the northern apex of the bailey.

The splendid keep which now dominates the rest occupies the site of the original gatehouse. Ludlow's early gatehouse was adapted to become a keep, but here the rebuilding was almost total. Only the inner gate arch survives to show what stood here previously, its rubble masonry contrasting with the ashlar above. This archway now leads into the vaulted ground floor. The upper floors are reached via a doorway at first-floor level, but there is no sign of a forebuilding. Each floor is linked by a straight staircase rather than the more customary spiral. The keep rises a hundred feet to an embattled parapet and angle turrets. It is the only part of the castle to remain intact and roofed. Conan the Little, Duke of Brittany, built the keep, though Henry II provided the finishing touches after the duke's death in 1171. A new entrance gateway was cut through the curtain immediately beside the keep, additional protection being provided by a barbican which is now fragmentary.

We follow Alan the Red's east curtain from the keep to Robin Hood's Tower, housing a vaulted chapel at ground level. The second tower has collapsed. Immediately beyond it a gateway leads into the outer bailey, surrounded by a later Norman curtain. The main bailey at Richmond is exceptionally large, which explains the peculiarity of this smaller outer bailey. Next comes the Gold Hole Tower, third and last of Alan the Red's mural towers. It is attached to Scolland's Hall, justly claimed to be the oldest hall in England. Named after Alan the Red's steward, Scolland's Hall is an instructive example of early Norman craftsmanship, still intact though now a roofless shell. The hall proper stood at first-floor level. There is an undercroft below, one end containing a postern which leads to the outer bailey. Originally the east end of the hall was partitioned off to form a solar. The present solar block, at right angles to the hall, was added by John, Duke of Brittany. He embarked on a limited remodelling of the castle early in the fourteenth century, also heightening the towers on the east curtain. His contribution represents the only significant post-Norman work in the castle. A town wall was also built in those stormy years but the only relic is a postern spanning the steep lane known as The Wynd.

Access: Standard opening times (EH).

Reference: Guidebook by C. Peers.

Relations: Ludlow. Compare the early Norman gatehouses at Bramber and Exeter, and the similar layout of Scarborough. The hall at Chepstow Castle (just across the Welsh Border) may be older than Scolland's.

SCARBOROUGH CASTLE occupies a dramatic headland rising three hundred feet out of the North Sea. This formidable site was first occupied in the Iron Age, while the Romans built a signal station on the edge of the cliff to give early warning of pirate raids. It did not become a castle until William le Gros, Count of Aumale (or Albemarle) settled here during the Anarchy. He led the Northern barons to victory against the Scots at the Battle of the Standard in 1138, and was made Earl of York as a reward. It is likely that work had started on the great curtain by that time. So strong was the site that Henry II took it off William soon after his accession, and henceforth Scarborough was to remain a royal fortress. Henry built the keep in the years 1157–64.

The first of several sieges took place in 1312 when Piers Gaveston, Edward II's haughty favourite, took refuge here. The rebel barons were unable to storm the castle, but Gaveston's supplies eventually ran out and he was forced upon their mercy. His captivity ended in summary execution at Warwick. Six years later the Scots sacked the town, though they did not attempt to take the castle. (Scarborough's town wall has vanished.) There was an abortive siege of the castle during the Pilgrimage of Grace (1536) and a group of rebels briefly seized the castle in 1557, in protest at Queen Mary's Spanish marriage. However, the greatest of the sieges took place during the Civil War. In fact there were two. The first lasted eighteen months, finally ending – with full honours for the garrison – in August 1645. Scarborough's church was used as a redoubt by the besiegers and was half blasted down in the cross-fire. The Roundhead governor changed sides during the Royalist uprising of 1648. This time the damaged castle only lasted four months, but the two sieges are a remarkable testimony. The castle was reduced to ruins in these sieges and the keep suffered a slighting afterwards, but the headland remained in military occupation for a few more centuries. The castle endured a further bombardment in 1914 when Scarborough was shelled by the German fleet.

The castle headland is roughly triangular, with precipitous drops to the sea on the east and north-west. On the south-west there is merely a wide and deep ravine separating the castle from the town. It was along this side that William le Gros built his curtain. Initially there was no keep, but a gate tower probably stood on the line of the present entrance. Thus Scarborough seems to have been modelled on Richmond Castle in its original form. At first no flanking towers existed. The semi-circular projecting bastions date from King John's reign. Eight survive and a ninth has perished, but they cannot account for all the £2000 that John spent on this castle. That was an enormous sum and much of his work must have vanished. Admittedly he also built the Mossdale Hall which stands midway along the curtain. That is hard to appreciate now because the hall is faced in eighteenth-century brickwork.

Only a narrow causeway at the west angle connects the castle headland to the town. On the townward side stands the barbican, a small enclosure with a round-towered outer gatehouse. It was added by Edward III as a precaution against French raids during the Hundred Years War. It is thus the latest part of the castle's defences. The narrowest part of the causeway was closed by a thirteenth-century gate tower, now reduced to its base. There are deep drawbridge chasms (now crossed by stone bridges) to front and rear. After that comes the steep ascent to the keep.

Henry II's keep is the dominant feature of the castle. Unlike Richmond the keep is not a conversion of the original gatehouse, but it is placed in a commanding position overlooking the entrance to the castle. This tall, square tower was a little larger than Richmond's keep. It does not compare so well now because one wall was blasted down by the Roundheads. A flight of steps leads to the first-floor entrance, but the forebuilding has been reduced to its footings. Though generously provided with windows, the upper floors do not have the profusion of mural chambers which characterise Henry II's later keeps. A ruined curtain around the keep creates a small inner bailey. Near Mossdale Hall are the foundations of William le Gros' original hall. Further east on the edge of the cliff some fragments of a medieval chapel overlie the Roman signal station.

Access: Standard opening times (EH).

Reference: Guidebook by G. Port. *HKW* (II).

Relations: Richmond. William le Gros' work at Castle Bytham and Sutton Valence. Other keeps of Henry II can be seen at Bowes, Newcastle, Orford, Chilham and Dover.

SCARGILL CASTLE overlooks the River Greta, four miles south of Barnard Castle. The gate tower is rudely incorporated into farm buildings. This modest structure is badly mutilated, its archway blocked and its parapet gabled over. A residential range at right angles survives in a ruinous condition. The castle was occupied by the Scargill family. They entertained Edward II here but the remains indicate a lightly-fortified quadrangle of the fifteenth century.

Access: Visible from the road.

SHERIFF HUTTON CASTLE The name of the village recalls Bertram de Bulmer, Sheriff of York in Stephen's reign. He raised the first castle here – a square motte near the church. However, the masonry castle occupies a different site south-east of the village. John, Lord Neville, obtained a licence to crenellate in 1382. Perhaps he began building here once Raby Castle was complete. It formed one of an impressive chain of Neville strongholds. John's son Ralph became Earl of

Westmorland, and on his death in 1425 the Neville estates were partitioned. The younger Ralph retained the title and the Durham estates while Richard inherited the Yorkshire estates. Thus Sheriff Hutton descended to the younger Richard Neville, Earl of Warwick, better known as the 'Kingmaker'. When he fell in 1471 his lands were conferred on Richard, Duke of Gloucester, subsequently Richard III. All three Richards seem to have alternated between Middleham and Sheriff Hutton. Richard III's young son is buried in the parish church here. Thomas Howard obtained the castle as a reward for his victory at Flodden, but decline seems to have set in about this time and the castle was a ruin by the following century.

The castle is one of those desolate monuments which deserve better treatment. Its farmyard setting is quite beneath its dignity. Although ill-treated by time, the four oblong corner towers still stand high and retain their ground-floor vaults. They show that the castle formed a large quadrangle. Unfortunately, the connecting walls and ranges have disappeared and even the courtyard faces of the towers have been ripped away. The north-west tower is the best preserved, rising five storeys to nearly a hundred feet. Most fragmentary is the north-east tower, reduced to one precarious stone finger. The south-east tower formed one of a pair guarding the entrance. Its partner survives in a fragmentary state.

Access: On private land.
Reference: VCH *Yorkshire, North Riding* (II).
Relations: Middleham, Raby and the Neville castle at Brancepeth. Compare the quadrangles at Bolton and Lumley.

SNAPE CASTLE, two miles south of Bedale, is part ruin and part inhabited. George Neville, Lord Latimer, first built the castle before his death in 1469. It was always a small-scale quadrangle but in its present form the castle owes much to Thomas Cecil, Lord Burghley – son of Elizabeth I's famous minister. The three slender corner towers date entirely from his time. The south range and the larger tower at the south-east corner incorporate original work, but later occupation has resulted in many alterations. There is also a row of vaulted cellars denoting the east range, but the best preserved portion of the Neville castle is the chapel. It projects beyond the east range, negating the defensive strength of the castle in a manner typical of the fifteenth century. This embattled chapel is a small but handsome structure standing over an undercroft. Its Perpendicular windows retain some original glass, while the Verrio ceiling (sadly damaged) recalls the Georgian era, when Snape was still a country mansion.

Access: The chapel can be visited and the rest is clearly visible.
Reference: VCH *Yorkshire, North Riding* (I).
Relations: The Latimers castle of Danby.

TANFIELD CASTLE A gate tower at West Tanfield, known as the Marmion Tower, is the only relic of this castle. The Marmions lived here in the fourteenth century but this structure is attributed to Sir Henry Fitzhugh (d.1424). It stands in uncomfortable proximity to the parish church. Though now roofless, the gate tower is structurally intact. The vaulted gate passage is placed off-centre to accommodate a porter's lodge on one side. Above the gate projects an oriel window of delicate tracery – typical of the fifteenth-century drift towards luxury. The top floor has a latrine projection and the building is capped by an embattled parapet. Nothing survives of the rest of the castle and its defensive character is questionable.

Access: Freely accessible (EH).
Reference: VCH *Yorkshire, North Riding* (I).
Relations: The Fitzhugh castle at Ravensworth.

TOPCLIFFE CASTLE can be found a mile south-east of the village, where the Cod Beck joins the River Swale. This impressive motte-and-bailey site is known as the Maiden's Bower. The high motte is encircled by its own ditch. William de Percy may have founded the castle after the Norman Conquest but there is no mention of it until Prince Henry's revolt, when it was fortified for the King. In the fourteenth century the Percys built a new manor house beside the old earthworks. It was here in 1489 that a mob murdered the Earl of Northumberland.

Access: On private land.
Relations: The Percy castles of Spofforth, Cockermouth, Alnwick and Warkworth.

WALBURN HALL stands four miles north of Leyburn, beside the road to Richmond. The house is fronted by a length of late medieval wall, capped by an embattled parapet and pierced by an arched gateway. Like certain other Northern manor houses with a curtain facing the outside world, there is no evidence that a pele tower stood here. The house at the back of the courtyard is basically early Tudor, with a long east wing added in the Elizabethan era. Walburn belonged to a branch of the Scrope family. Despite its limitations as a fortress it was held against the Roundheads in 1644.

Access: Visible from the road.
Relations: Bolton Castle was the main seat of the Scropes. Compare the curtains at Beetham and Mortham.

WHORLTON CASTLE was founded by the Meynells in Norman times. The ditched enclosure goes back that far. It passed to the Darcy family and the existing masonry is probably the work of Philip, last of the Darcy lords, who died in 1419. The main relic is the oblong gatehouse which rises out of the ditch. This is now an empty shell. Carved shields above the gateway depict the arms of the Meynells, the Darcys and the Greys. The gate passage has lost its side walls and vault. Originally there were two storeys on either side of it. A hall occupied the whole of the top floor. At the back of the bailey are two vaulted cellars, probably representing the base of a large tower house. There is no evidence that a stone wall ever surrounded the bailey. The castle stands on a hill to the north-east of Swainby.

Access: Freely accessible.
Reference: VCH *Yorkshire, North Riding* (II).

OTHER SITES Norman earthworks include motte-and-bailey sites at *Cropton* and *Pickhill*, and isolated mottes such as *Castle Levington* (near Kirklevington) and *Yafforth*. *Cotherstone*'s motte, overlooking the River Tees, retains small fragments of a shell keep on top. *Killerby Castle* and *Castle Hills*, both near Catterick, have impressive rampart banks. The castle of the bishops of Durham at *Northallerton* has vanished. So has *Malton Castle*, which occupied a Roman fort site. It was abandoned after Robert Bruce sacked it in 1322.

Moving on to the later Middle Ages, the Scrope castle at *Kirkby Fleetham* (licensed in 1314) has been reduced to a couple of pieces of wall. *Slingsby Castle* is a Jacobean ruin on an older site. Later houses have also displaced the Cleveland castles of *Skelton* and *Wilton*. *Sigston Castle* (Kirkby Sigston) is marked by its moated enclosure, while *Bolton Old Hall* (at Bolton-on-Swale) incorporates a pele tower.

Yorkshire: West Riding

Much of this large riding is upland, which explains why there are not more castles here. At the south end, quite close together, are the majestic motte-and-bailey earthworks of Tickhill and the even more majestic keep at Conisbrough. Another pair are the once-mighty castles of Pontefract and Sandal, both slighted severely in the aftermath of the Civil War but resuscitated as places of interest thanks to excavation. Further north ruinous Knaresborough and restored Skipton (also victims of the Civil War) are contrasting examples of early-fourteenth-century fortification. Those were the big six. The tower house of Harewood Castle deserves a mention, along with embattled Markenfield Hall. For some reason there are several medieval houses in the riding which bear the courtesy title of castle but appear to have no fortifications.

ALMONDBURY CASTLE Castle Hill dominates its industrial surroundings, rising to the west of Almondbury with steep falls on all sides but one. This lofty hill is crowned by Iron Age ramparts forming a double line of defence all the way around the promontory. During the Anarchy Henry de Lacy created a triangular inner bailey, surrounded by its own rampart, at the south end of the enclosure. A Victorian folly tower stands within. The castle survived Henry II's accession but was dismantled by order of Henry III during the Barons' Wars.

Access: Freely accessible (LA).

Relations: Castles utilising hillforts such as Elmley, Old Sarum and Dover. For the De Lacys see Pontefract.

BARDEN TOWER occupies a beautiful setting in Wharfedale, three miles north-west of Bolton Abbey. The centre is a fourteenth-century tower house of the Clifford family, enlarged and transformed by Henry Clifford, the 'Shepherd Lord'. He is called that because of his upbringing on the Cumbrian fells, in hiding from the

Yorkists who had killed his father and grandfather. Restored to his estates by Henry VII, Lord Clifford spent a lot of time here, researching into astronomy. His remodelling turned it into an unfortified house with shallow flanking wings and large windows. A period of decay was temporarily halted by Lady Anne Clifford in 1658, but the building is now a ruin.

Access: Exterior visible.
Relations: For Henry Clifford see Skipton.

BOLLING HALL On Bowling Hall Road, a mile south-east of Bradford city centre, is a large country mansion now engulfed in an urban setting. The austere tower on the left of the long facade is a medieval pele tower – something of a rarity in the West Riding. It was built in the fifteenth century by a member of the Bolling family. Nothing survives of the original hall. The rest of the mansion dates from later centuries, including the matching tower on the right.

Access: Open regularly (LA).

CAWOOD CASTLE, on the River Ouse, was a favourite residence of the arch-bishops of York in the later Middle Ages. It was magnificent enough to be called 'the Windsor of the North'. The main quadrangle, built in the fourteenth century, was pulled down after its capture by the Roundheads in 1644. Despite the Civil War siege it is doubtful if it was ever a genuine fortification. The surviving brick range, which formed one side of an outer courtyard, is entirely domestic in character. In the centre is a stone gatehouse, enriched with oriel windows and a decorative parapet. Gatehouse and range were built by Archbishop John Kempe in the 1440s.

Access: Exterior visible.
Reference: Mackenzie (II).
Relations: Hexham has another castle of the archbishops.

CONISBROUGH CASTLE crowns a hill above the River Don. This stronghold of the earls of Surrey was probably founded by William de Warenne after the Norman Conquest, but nothing is known about the original castle. The mighty round keep and towered curtain were raised by Hamelin Plantagenet, Henry II's half-brother, who inherited the Warenne title and estates by marriage. They probably date from the last two decades of the twelfth century, making Conisbrough an advanced castle for its day.

Conisbrough's magnificent keep dominates the rest. Undoubtedly the finest of England's few round keeps, it is built of ashlar masonry and rises to nearly a hundred feet. Only the battlements are missing. The tall plinth gave greater stability against mining and would have caused rocks hurled from the parapet to ricochet outwards. Unlike some of its contemporaries the keep is not a perfect cylinder because six turrets project from the outer face. These taper outwards to form semi-hexagonal or wedge-shaped flankers. This shape reduced the amount of 'dead ground' invisible to defenders at the wall-head, and represents a halfway stage between the square flanking towers prevalent at that time and the rounded ones which would soon appear on the curtain

302

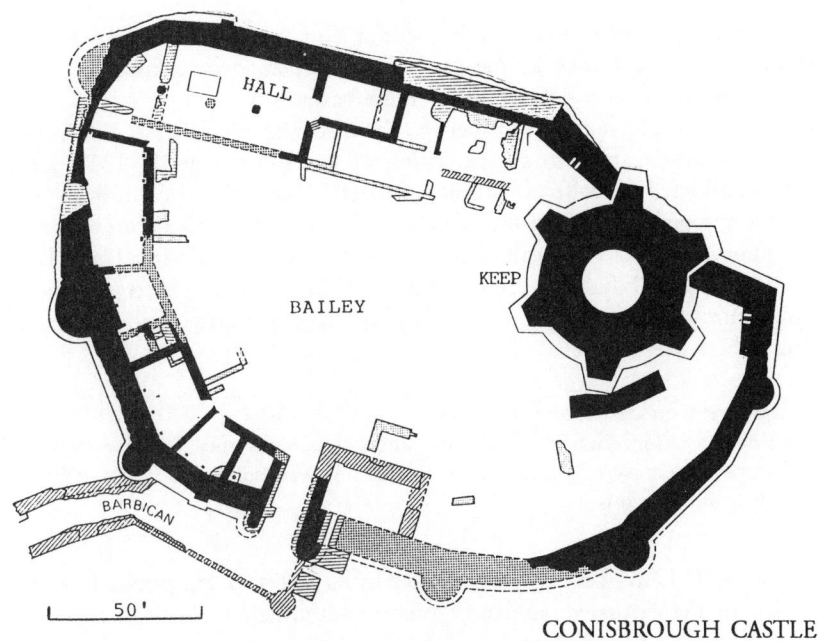

HALL

KEEP

BAILEY

BARBICAN

50'

CONISBROUGH CASTLE

here. Hamelin may have been influenced by his half-brother's round keep at Orford, which has three square turrets. Unlike Orford there is no forebuilding to break the symmetry of the outline. The entrance to the keep is in the conventional position at first-floor level, but it is approached by an outside staircase.

The keep is so well preserved that it has been possible to insert a new roof and floors after centuries as an empty shell. The entrance floor and the floor beneath it were both used for storage. A hole in the roof of the ground-floor vault enabled water to be hoisted up from the well below. Staircases following the curvature of the wall connect all floors. On the second floor was the hall, heated by a large fireplace with an immense hood. The less ostentatious fireplace on the top floor marks the position of the solar. At this level an ornate little chapel occupies one of the turrets. It is the only mural chamber, in contrast to Orford or some of Henry II's square keeps which are honeycombed with them. Even the window provision in the keep is minimal. Clearly it was primarily a fortification, and the Warennes must usually have occupied the residential buildings whose foundations lie against the curtain.

Evidently the keep came first and the curtain second, since the curtain abuts the keep but is not bonded into it. The ruined curtain surrounding the compact, oval bailey is notable for its solid, half-round projecting bastions. In the late twelfth century flanking towers of any kind were an innovation, and when used they were generally square-fronted. Ignoring a handful of Roman forts, Conisbrough has probably the earliest English example of a curtain flanked at regular intervals by rounded towers. Admittedly they are too shallow to be very effective and towers would improve in the following century. Three bastions survive out of the original six. The best preserved stretch of curtain is on the north. Unfortunately this side has no flanking towers because of the steepness of the terrain. On the south a portion

303

of curtain has slid down the hillside and the gate tower has been reduced to its foundations. The entrance to the castle is strengthened by a narrow barbican, commanded by the most slender of the mural bastions.

The castle must have been complete by the time Hamelin died in 1202. Its later history was uneventful with the exception of one short siege. In 1317 John de Warenne abducted the wife of Thomas, Earl of Lancaster, and Conisbrough soon fell to the enraged earl. When the Warennes died out the castle became a property of the dukes of York. The castle was more or less abandoned after Duke Edward seized the throne as Edward IV. It was a ruin by 1538. Sir Walter Scott gave the castle literary fame by making it – quite fictitiously – the residence of the Saxon thane Cedric in his novel *Ivanhoe*.

Access: Standard opening times (EH).
Reference: Guidebook by S. Johnson.
Relations: Orford. Sandal, Castle Acre and Lewes were other Warenne strongholds. Compare the towered curtains of Framlingham, Windsor and Dover, and Berkeley's early round bastions.

HAREWOOD CASTLE is overshadowed by its successor, Harewood House. The castle lies in the extensive parkland which surrounds that Georgian masterpiece. Though ruinous and neglected, the castle is still an impressive tower house. It was built by Sir William Aldburgh, a licence to crenellate being awarded in 1367. He bequeathed the castle to his two daughters equally, so for the next two centuries it was shared by the Redmans and the Rythers. Some of their tombs can be seen in the adjacent church. Essentially the tower house is an oblong structure with angle turrets, rising from the steep slope overlooking the River Wharfe. It is only two storeys high, comprising a hall at ground level and a solar above. However, the layout is elaborated by the projection of a large kitchen from the western side, resulting in an L-plan structure. Owing to the sloping terrain there is a cellar beneath the kitchen. The north-west corner turret contains the entrance, surmounted by a small portcullis chamber. Above that is a tiny chapel which was reached from the solar. Small chambers occupy the other turrets too. Presumably there was some kind of courtyard but every trace has vanished.

Access: Although Harewood House is open there is no access to the castle.
Reference: Mackenzie (II).
Relations: Northern tower houses such as Belsay and Langley.

HAZLEWOOD CASTLE lies near the A64, three miles south-west of Tadcaster. The castle was a standard medieval house centred upon a hall, but the complex has been Georgianised beyond recognition. Only the little chapel at the east end escaped this treatment. It contains monuments to the Vavasour family, who continued Roman Catholic worship here after the Reformation. Sir William Vavasour obtained a licence for a chapel in 1286. Four years later he received a licence to crenellate as well. At the back of the house is a modest projection which could be a flanking tower, but there is no other evidence of fortification. If there was ever a defensive courtyard in front of the house it has vanished.

Access: Private.
Reference: BOE *Yorkshire – The West Riding.*

KNARESBOROUGH CASTLE is superbly sited on a rock high above the River Nidd, with steep falls on all sides but the east. It first emerges as a royal castle in 1130. King John strengthened the castle but only some of the townward ditch survives from his building campaign. The remains we see belong to Edward II's reconstruction of the castle in 1307–12. Presumably it was intended as a depot for the ongoing wars with Scotland. The master mason was Hugh of Titchmarsh and the works cost a total of £2174. Though built with royal money Edward immediately conferred the castle upon his hated favourite, Piers Gaveston. A more popular occupant was Queen Philippa of Hainault. She made it her home, thus maintaining a royal presence in the North during Edward III's long absences on campaign in France. In 1372 the Honour of Knaresborough became part of the Duchy of Lancaster. It returned to royal control with the usurpation of Henry of Bolingbroke in 1399, but neglect ensued. The castle was refortified by the Royalists during the Civil War. It withstood the Roundheads for six months before surrendered on honourable terms in December 1644. A thorough slighting followed.

Owing to the slighting and later stone robbing the castle is fragmentary. The enclosure, divided into two baileys by a cross-wall, has been reduced to fragments of curtain and the slender, half-round flanking turrets of the outer gatehouse. Only the ruined keep and an Elizabethan courthouse are more substantial. The keep stood on the north side of the castle, at the junction of the two baileys. It is an early example of the tower house theme which would soon dominate Northern castle building. The keep is oblong but its outer (north) face forms a semi-octagonal projection. Much of this side was blasted down at the slighting, but the courtyard front stands almost to full height. The ground-floor kitchen and the sinister prison beneath it have stone vaults supported on a central column. Above was the hall, its long wash basin revealing an unusual regard for hygiene. At this level a large doorway overlooks the courtyard. A solar occupied the very ruinous top floor.

Access: Grounds accessible daily. The keep is open regularly in summer (LA).
Reference: Guidebook by J. Symington. *HKW* (II).
Relations: Edward II's work at Pickering.

LAUGHTON CASTLE Laughton-en-le-Morthen formed the original centre of the barony which became the Honour of Tickhill. It seems likely therefore that Roger de Busli founded the castle in the late eleventh century, before a new and stronger castle was raised at Tickhill. The site is a well-preserved but overgrown earthwork, featuring a conical motte and an oval bailey surrounded by rampart and ditch.

Access: Freely accessible.
Relations: Tickhill.

MARKENFIELD HALL is reached via an un-signposted track off the A61, three miles south of Ripon. This unspoilt medieval mansion is surrounded by a wet moat. The buildings around the courtyard are overshadowed by the main residential block, which occupies the north-east corner. This L-plan complex is the oldest part. Its features are consistent with the year 1310, when John de Markenfield obtained a licence to crenellate. With its hall, solar and chapel, all at first-floor level over undercrofts, the building is emphatically a manor house, not a tower house. The large windows, particularly in the chapel, would have been vulnerable to assault. However, the block is capped by a genuine crenellated parapet with cross-slits. John de Markenfield seems to have interpreted his licence quite literally by putting battlements on top of his house. No further defences materialised, even though this was the era of Scottish raids.

Access: Limited opening times in summer.
Reference: BOE *Yorkshire – The West Riding*. Mackenzie (II).
Relations: Aydon and Little Wenham are similar.

PONTEFRACT CASTLE formed the centre of the Honour of Pontefract, a vast estate granted to Ilbert de Lacy after the Norman Conquest. The castle is mentioned in the Domesday Book. The De Lacys lived here for over two centuries, but on the death of Henry de Lacy in 1311 the Honour came into the hands of Thomas, Earl of Lancaster. This acquisition strengthened Thomas' hand in the struggle with his cousin, Edward II, but the tables were turned at the Battle of Boroughbridge in 1322. Ironically, the captured earl was brought to Pontefract for summary execution. An even more illustrious victim was Richard II, who languished here after his overthrow in 1399. Richard died in the castle, whether by deliberate murder or calculated neglect. As a Duchy of Lancaster stronghold Pontefract now belonged to the Crown and ceased to be a regular residence, but its importance as a garrison post and prison lasted well into the Tudor period.

The castle proved its strength in the Civil War, suffering three sieges on the King's behalf. A Royalist relieving force broke the first siege (1644) but the Roundheads returned the following year, finally obtaining the surrender of the weakened castle after a three-month bombardment. During the Royalist uprising of 1648 the castle again declared for the King, and it took another six months to subdue it. Oliver Cromwell took charge of operations, his report to Parliament emphasising the exceptional strength of the castle. Indeed, it only surrendered after Charles I's execution, when all hope was lost. Afterwards the castle was ruthlessly slighted.

A painting in Pontefract Museum provides an eyewitness record of the castle as it appeared shortly before the slighting. It is sad to compare this majestic sight with the fragmentary ruins on the hilltop. The only portions standing to any height are the stump of the keep and an adjacent length of curtain. Excavations have laid bare the foundations of the inner bailey. The curtain dates from the De Lacy period but large square towers were added under Earl Thomas and his successors. There are footings of three on the line of the curtain, and a fourth oddly placed in the ditch. Within the bailey are two domestic undercrofts and the foundations of an apsidal Norman chapel. The keep crowns a rocky knoll which formed a natural motte. Owing to its incomplete state the date and original appearance of the keep are still debated. About half the circumference survives, with three rounded projections of different sizes. It therefore seems likely that the keep was circular, but had six bastions projecting in an astonishingly irregular manner. Two walled outer baileys have vanished entirely.

Access: Freely accessible (LA).
Reference: BOE *Yorkshire – The West Riding*. Mackenzie (II).
Relations: The De Lacy castles of Clitheroe, Halton and Longtown. Duchy of Lancaster work at Dunstanburgh, Kenilworth and Leicester. Compare the royal murders at Berkeley and the Tower of London.

RIPLEY CASTLE, four miles north of Harrogate, stands on a rise above the Thornton Beck. It is the ancestral seat of the Ingilby family. The oldest part is the detached, fifteenth-century gate tower. The house itself is a Georgian mansion but one of the corner towers is older. Inscriptions on the top floor tell us that Sir William Ingilby built it in 1548–55. That is unusually late for a tower house anywhere south of the Scottish Border. As such it is a curious piece of Tudor conservatism, but the large windows confirm that it is a tower house in form rather than substance. Even the gatehouse is not overtly defensive and there is no evidence for a walled courtyard, so as a genuine castle Ripley is doubtful.

Access: Open regularly in summer.
Reference: BOE *Yorkshire – The West Riding*. Souvenir guide.

SANDAL CASTLE Before 1157 one of the Warenne earls of Surrey abandoned a castle at Wakefield in favour of Sandal Magna, two miles further south. The new motte-and-bailey castle took advantage of a strong position above the River Calder. Conversion to stone may have begun under Hamelin Plantagenet, after he had completed Conisbrough Castle. However, Hamelin died in 1202 and most of the masonry is attributed to his son William and his grandson John (d.1305). After the last Warenne earl died in 1347 Sandal, like Conisbrough, passed to Edmund of Langley, thus becoming a property of the dukes of York. On the last day of 1460 Duke Richard rashly sallied out of the castle to fight the Lancastrians before his army had fully assembled. The Battle of Wakefield, fought in sight of the castle, resulted in the rout of the Yorkists and the slaughter of the duke and his eldest son. Though ruined by the Elizabethan period, the castle distinguished itself in the Civil War. The Roundheads captured it – at the second attempt – in 1645 and a severe slighting followed.

As a result of the slighting little more than earthworks appeared to remain, but a thorough series of excavations in 1963–72 removed the accumulation of earth and rubble, uncovering the entire plan. Although little stands to any height the exposed footings show that Sandal was an unusual and powerful castle. On the motte is the base of a shell keep, remarkable for the elaborate defences in front of it. A walled entrance passage descends the steep slope of the motte, its lower end guarded by twin round turrets preserving ashlar plinths. Beyond the drawbridge chasm is the massive base of a D-shaped barbican, projecting deeply into the bailey and surrounded by its own ditch. The bailey forms a narrow concentric strip around it.

Unfortunately the bailey curtain has been destroyed to its foundations. Apparently there were no mural towers, but the entrance is preceded by a narrow barbican. The two bits of wall still standing in the bailey belonged to the hall block.

Access: Freely accessible (LA).
Reference: Guidebook by P. Mayes. Fry.
Relations: Conisbrough and the other Warenne castles of Castle Acre and Lewes. Excavated castle sites such as Pontefract, Bolingbroke and Weoley.

SKIPTON CASTLE was founded by Robert de Romille *circa* 1090. The castle incorporates Norman masonry but is largely the work of the powerful Clifford family. Robert de Clifford, already a big lord in Westmorland, received Skipton in 1310. He immediately set to work on rebuilding the castle, but it must have been incomplete when he fell at Bannockburn four years later. Work probably continued under his son Roger, who was executed for supporting Earl Thomas of Lancaster against Edward II. The Clifford ownership saw one other interruption, during the Wars of the Roses. Two Cliffords died fighting for the Lancastrians and the young heir Henry was brought up in hiding on the Cumbrian fells to escape Yorkist retribution. Reinstated by Henry VII, he became known the 'Shepherd Lord'. Skipton was one of a group of Yorkshire castles which stood firm for the Royalist cause, surrendering in December 1645 after a long siege. A half-hearted slighting followed, and just a decade later the damage was made good thanks to Lady Anne Clifford. She restored all the old Clifford castles and occupied them in the manner of her ancestors. Most of her castles were abandoned after her death in 1676, but Skipton survives in as good a state as she left it.

The castle is strongly situated on a cliff above the Eller Beck. It is clear that an outer bailey existed because the outer gatehouse still stands. This gatehouse, with its rounded flanking towers, is part of Robert de Clifford's reconstruction, but the building was remodelled by Lady Anne. Hers is the balustraded parapet bearing the Clifford motto 'Desormais' ('Henceforth'). Beyond the gatehouse lies the inner curtain with its cluster of towers. To the right extends a Tudor range added in 1535 by the Earl of Cumberland. The range terminates in a tower which is actually another relic of the outer bailey defences. Unlike the other towers it is octagonal.

It is best to regard the inner curtain as a shell keep, since it encases a low motte and has a small circumference. Its Norman origin is attested by the round-headed archway in the gate passage. Otherwise this keep is a notable and (for England) rare example of Edwardian military architecture. It is a D-shaped enclosure surrounded by a thick curtain. The flat north side rests on the cliff's edge, while the curve of the 'D' is defended by six closely-spaced towers. These stout round towers – and the stretches of curtain between them – rise from a massive plinth which was proof against mining. Two of the towers are set together to flank the entrance, but the front of this gatehouse is masked by a Tudor porch. It prepares us for the delightful atmosphere of the tiny Conduit Court, which is filled by an ancient yew tree. Most of the limited space is occupied by residential buildings. Against the north curtain stands the medieval domestic block, comprising a kitchen, hall and solar above undercrofts. The east wing with its twin bay windows was added by the Shepherd Lord, who inserted new windows elsewhere in the courtyard as well. Further accommodation was provided in the towers. Lady Anne rebuilt the tops of the towers after Civil War damage. The junction between the thick medieval walling and her thin, non-military masonry is quite apparent within.

Access: Open regularly.
Reference: BOE *Yorkshire – The West Riding.* Souvenir guide.
Relations: The Clifford castles of Appleby, Brough, Brougham and Pendragon. Compare the closely-packed shell keep at Tamworth.

SPOFFORTH CASTLE belonged to the Percy family from Norman times. Henry de Percy obtained a licence to crenellate in 1308. The following year he purchased the barony of Alnwick, thus beginning a new phase for the Percys as Border war lords. Alnwick Castle was strongly rebuilt but Spofforth did not receive similar treatment, in spite of the Scottish raids which were beginning to have an impact this far south. Indeed, it is a castle in name only. The surviving range, which formed the west side of a quadrangle, is purely domestic in character. Nevertheless, even in ruins it is a fine example of a medieval house. The hall has a thirteenth-century undercroft, partly cut out of rock, but the superstructure is fifteenth century. Henry de Percy's portion is the solar wing, including a narrow chapel and a latrine block. In 1461 the house was sacked by the Yorkists.

Access: Standard opening times (EH).
Reference: EH guidebook.
Relations: Alnwick and the other Percy castles of Topcliffe, Warkworth and Cockermouth.

TICKHILL CASTLE The vast estate known as the Honour of Tickhill was awarded to Roger de Busli after the Norman Conquest. He raised his first castle at Laughton, but Tickhill existed by the time of his death in 1098. It passed to Robert de Belleme, Earl of Shrewsbury, and was confiscated following his rebellion in 1102. From that time onwards Tickhill was normally a royal stronghold, though often held in dower by the queens of England. In 1372 Tickhill and Knaresborough were given to John of Gaunt as Duke of Lancaster, but they reverted to the Crown when his son usurped the throne as Henry IV. The castle has witnessed three sieges. The first took place when Prince John's supporters were driven out by Richard I, following his return from captivity. The next siege occurred in 1322, during the showdown between Edward II and his cousin Thomas, Earl of Lancaster. Thomas was unable to take the castle by assault, and it held out for three weeks until being relieved by the King's supporters. The castle did not distinguish itself during the Civil War, surrendering to the Roundheads after only a two-day siege in 1644.

The prodigious earthworks of the castle rise up near the majestic parish church. They are among the most impressive in England, the motte being over seventy feet high. A massive rampart and a deep ditch – still partly filled with water – surround the bailey. A long stretch of plain curtain crowns the rampart bank, but the chief masonry survivor is the simple Norman gate tower which is now an empty shell. Gatehouse and curtain are attributed to Henry I, as the solitary royal account surviving for the year 1130 records building activity here. The short barbican in front of the gatehouse is a later addition. The present house inside the bailey incorporates part of the old residential buildings. Excavations have revealed that an unusual eleven-sided tower keep stood on the motte. It was built by Henry II in 1178–80 and may have influenced the design of the keep at nearby Conisbrough.

Access: Private, but well seen from the road.
Reference: HKW (II). Mackenzie.
Relations: Conisbrough and Laughton.

OTHER SITES Norman earthworks are scattered around the riding. Motte-and-baileys can be seen at *Barwick-in-Elmet*, *Burton-in-Lonsdale*, *Langthwaite* (near Doncaster), *Mexborough* and *Mirfield*. Bailey Hill at *Bradfield* is another, while the site in Clarence Park at *Wakefield* was the predecessor on Sandal Castle. *Aldborough* has a ringwork on Studforth Hill. The turreted *Farnhill House* has a probable pele tower attached. *John of Gaunt's Castle* in Haverah Park (near Harrogate), has been reduced to its foundations. This tower house was a hunting lodge of the dukes of Lancaster. *Sheffield Castle*, an important stronghold by the River Don, is best known as the prison of Mary Queen of Scots for some of her time in England. It was destroyed after the Civil War. The footings of a round tower have been uncovered but the site is now occupied by Castle Market.

GLOSSARY

Adulterine castles are those erected without permission – i.e. without a royal licence to crenellate. They proliferated during the Anarchy owing to the breakdown of the King's authority. Many of these castles were demolished when Henry II set about restoring order. Even in later centuries, however, castles were often unlicensed. There are several instances of licences being granted retrospectively in the form of a pardon (e.g. *Bolton, Dunstanburgh, Farleigh Hungerford*). Less fortunate barons, such as the builder of *Barnwell*, were forced to surrender their unlicensed castles.

Apse A semi-circular projection, commonly found at the sanctuary end of a Norman church. Sometimes the apse is surrounded by an arcaded passage or *ambulatory*, as at St John's Chapel in the *Tower of London*. An apsidal tower is a round-fronted one, characteristic of thirteenth-century developments in military architecture.

Arcade A row of arches mounted on columns, dividing a building into two or more sections. Arcades are a standard feature of medieval churches but they are often found in domestic buildings as well, e.g. in the keep at *Rochester* and the halls of *Oakham* and *Winchester* castles.

Arrow-slits frequently pierce curtain walls and towers, enabling archers to fire upon the enemy without. Primitive versions can be found even in the earliest stone castles. It should be noted that not all narrow openings in walls are arrow-slits; some provided a little much-needed light and ventilation. Genuine arrow-slits are typically tall and very narrow (little more than the width of an arrow head). Sometimes there are cross-slits to allow lateral fire and 'fish tails' at the base to cover the ground outside more effectively. The Grey Mare's Tail Tower at *Warkworth Castle* has the most spectacular slits in England, reaching a length of seventeen feet! The embrasure behind the arrow-slit had to be tall enough to accommodate a bowman and wide enough for him to manoeuvre. Because of the restricted space crossbows were usually preferred to the six-foot English longbow. Crossbows were more powerful in any case and the archer did not suffer the disadvantage of being exposed to counter-fire while he reloaded his cumbersome weapon.

Bailey or Ward The courtyard of a castle, i.e. the area enclosed by the rampart or curtain. All castles had at least one bailey because it was impossible to condense all the necessary accommodation into a single great tower or keep. In Norman times the keep or motte (if one existed) was the lord's domain and the bailey contained such essential buildings as barracks, stables and workshops. Sooner or later the lord migrated to more comfortable quarters in the bailey and the garrison sometimes found itself relegated to an outer enclosure or 'base court'. Many earthwork strongholds of the Norman era had several baileys.

Baileys are usually sequential (i.e. one in front of the other) in order to present a succession of obstacles to an attacking force. However, concentric layouts appear sporadically throughout the Middle Ages. There was a tendency to keep the bailey to a manageable size, thus reducing the length of the perimeter and the number of men necessary to defend it. Large outer baileys were seldom walled in stone, though there are exceptions – big enough to house a medieval army – at *Beeston, Dunstanburgh* and *Scarborough*.

Barbican An outer extension to a gateway, increasing the number of barriers which a besieger had to force his way through. The commonest type of barbican is a walled passage projecting from the front of the gatehouse proper, perhaps with corner turrets as in the fine examples at *Alnwick, Arundel, Lewes* and *Warwick* castles. This kind was often found on town walls as well, but Walmgate Bar at *York* has the only survivor. The barbican was left unroofed so that attackers caught inside could be showered with arrows from above – a veritable death trap. The outer entrance would have been closed by massive doors, a portcullis and perhaps a drawbridge as well, thus duplicating the defences of the main gatehouse. Sometimes the barbican takes the form of a small outer enclosure beyond the moat, as at *Scarborough*. *Goodrich* has a semi-circular example which would have involved besiegers in an awkward turning manoeuvre while under arrow fire.

Barmkin The term used in northern England and Scotland to describe the small courtyards accompanying pele towers. Most peles must have had some sort of outer enclosure but stone curtains are rare.

Bartizan A small turret corbelled out at parapet level, usually at the corners of a tower. They are found in Northern tower houses such as *Belsay* and *Chipchase*, and on the bars of *York* city wall.

Bastion A flanking tower. The term is especially used for towers which have a purely defensive purpose, such as the open-backed variety often found on town walls (e.g. *Canterbury, Oxford*). It is also used to describe the arrow-headed projections from artillery fortifications.

Battlements *see* Crenellations.

Berm A narrow ledge between the curtain and the edge of the ditch. The berm could be controlled by surprise sorties from a postern but, if the defenders lacked initiative, this ledge might prove a useful foothold for the enemy. Consequently some later castles, such as *Bodiam*, rise straight out of the moat.

Blockhouse A small artillery fortification, such as the lesser coastal forts of Henry VIII.

Boom A chain extending across a river to keep out enemy vessels. The raising and lowering of the chain was sometimes controlled by a tower on either bank, hence the 'boom towers' at *Fowey, Norwich* and *York*.

Bridges were fortified in medieval times when they led into walled towns. Their defence consisted of one or perhaps two gate towers barring the way across. At Monmouth (Wales) the gate stands on one of the bridge piers, but England's only surviving example – at *Warkworth* – occupies solid ground at the townward end. It is unfortunate that so many have disappeared, but narrow bridge gates were too much of an obstacle to the traffic of later centuries.

Building materials The earliest castles were earthworks with wooden palisades. During the twelfth century most castles of substance acquired stone defences. The residential buildings often remained of timber, but hardly any survive. Stone is the enduring material of castles. Geography naturally influenced what kind of stone was used and how far it had to be transported. Fine *ashlar* masonry is generally a sign of good building stone nearby, though in some cases it was conveyed a long way, even from the Caen quarries in Normandy. Such stone is only a veneer covering a rubble core. In East Anglia and other places where there is no good stone locally, builders had to make the most of flint.

Not surprisingly, it was in East Anglia that bricks first became popular. *Little Wenham Hall* is perhaps the earliest brick building extant, but the material did not become popular until the fifteenth century. Bricks can be just as strong as stone, so their use is by no means an indication of weakness. However, the emergence of brick coincided with the decline of the castle. Some of the last castles were built in the new material, including quadrangular strongholds such as *Caister* and *Herstmonceux*, the tower house at *Tattershall* and *Oxburgh*'s gatehouse.

Burgh In England, burghs were Saxon towns fortified by Alfred the Great and his successors as strongpoints against the Danes. Some burghs utilised Roman town defences but a number of new towns were founded. Their layouts are surprisingly regular, showing that town planning did not die out with the Romans. The defences of most burghs were later rebuilt in stone, but *Wallingford* and *Wareham* preserve their original earth ramparts.

Buttery The room in which beer and wine were stored. It was often located between the hall and the kitchen, and reached by one of the three doorways from the screens passage. Enormous quantities of beer were consumed in a medieval household but imported wine was a more expensive taste.

Cannon first appeared in England in the early fourteenth century. Initially these unstable devices could be as dangerous to the user as to the enemy, firing a bolt or a stone with much less accuracy than the conventional catapult. The thunderous din of such weapons *could* frighten a garrison into surrender, as Henry IV discovered when he took his guns into Northumberland to crush the Percy revolt. The science of artillery developed in the fifteenth century with the manufacture of longer barrels and the appearance of iron cannon balls. Very little account was taken of the new weapon, though gun ports became more common. A handful of new strongpoints on the South Coast (notably *Dartmouth Castle*) took the lead in being specifically designed for defence by cannon.

The impact of the new weapon was not fully appreciated until the Scottish invasion of 1513, when 'Mons Meg' blasted down the walls of *Norham Castle*. Norham and a few other Scottish Border castles were reconstructed with extra-thick curtains to withstand artillery, but as private castle building was coming to an end in England it is in the sphere of public fortification that most new developments are found. Henry VIII's coastal forts are distinguished in the main by their rounded, geometrical layouts, based on principles devised in northern Europe (e.g. *Deal, Walmer, St Mawes*). However, a contrasting design originating in Italy soon prevailed. Defence reverted to earth ramparts to cushion the impact of enemy fire, though usually with a stone revetment. Large, 'arrow head' bastions – angular rather than square – formed defensive gun emplacements. *Berwick* was refortified in the new manner during the 1560s, and *Carisbrooke* and *Pendennis* castles were enlarged to counter the threat of Spanish invasion. The principles of artillery defence remained basically the same until they were rendered obsolete by nineteenth-century advances in fire power.

Castle The term derives from the Latin *castellum*, meaning 'little fort'. Its restriction to private strongholds of the Middle Ages is a specialist definition not embraced by most dictionaries, yet if a suitable word did not exist one would have to be invented. It is best to regard the castle as a fortified house, because the combination of residential and defensive roles is a feature common to most medieval fortifications but not to those of earlier and later periods. This does not imply that castles were constantly occupied or that they were intended to be impregnable in the event of siege. Our definition is flexible enough to include those later medieval strongholds which are sometimes dismissed as 'fortified manor houses' because of their concessions to domestic comfort. Nor is there any size restriction. Castles range from vast complexes covering many acres to single towers. However, not every medieval fortification was the private home of an individual. Towns were defended as they had been in earlier times and a minority of 'castles' actually served a purely military function.

Chapels are a ubiquitous feature of medieval times and most castles had at least one. Often there was a private oratory for the lord's use in the keep and a larger chapel in the bailey. The forebuilding was a convenient place in Norman keeps, as at *Dover* and *Newcastle*. In the *Tower of London* the beautiful chapel of St John has an apse which projects out of the White Tower. Bailey chapels tended to be free-standing in Norman times, but later they were integrated into the main residential block. Most castle chapels are simple oblongs but more complex plans – with side aisles and a chancel – appear occasionally, while *Ludlow* has a rare circular example. The principal constraint (seldom ignored) was the liturgical requirement to place the altar at the east end. The chapel would have been the most lavishly appointed room of any castle. Even if the architecture now seems plain, we can be sure that the interior was once richly coloured with brilliant wall paintings and stained glass.

A few castle chapels were served by colleges of secular priests. *Hastings* and *Oxford* had early Norman foundations, but by far the greatest of the collegiate chapels is St George's in *Windsor Castle*. As rebuilt under Edward IV this is a building of cathedral proportions and one of the finest examples of Perpendicular architecture. Three canons' cloisters lie around it, occupying most of the lower ward.

Chemise or **Mantlet** A concentric outer wall.

Concentric castles are those having two parallel lines of defence, the outer wall closely surrounding the inner. In addition to providing a double obstacle against attackers, the inner curtain rises higher than the outer so that defenders could fire upon the enemy from two levels simultaneously. Furthermore, besiegers who had forced their way into the outer courtyard would find themselves in a narrow space under fire from the parapets on either side. The idea, like so much else, originated in the East and came to western Europe through the Crusades. *Dover Castle* became a concentric fortress early in the thirteenth century but the concept did not reach maturity until Edward I's reign, with the enlargement of the *Tower of London* and the erection of his famous Welsh castles. Apart from the Tower of London there are actually very few English examples. *Middleham* has a concentric curtain surrounding the keep, *Goodrich* is concentric on two sides, and there are later echoes of the theme at *Raby* and *Compton* castles. The principles of concentricity were revived in some of Henry VIII's coastal forts, such as *Deal* and *Walmer*, in order to provide gun fire at several levels.

Constable or **Castellan** The official in charge of a castle during the owner's absence. Many castles, particularly royal ones, were occupied by the constable and a small caretaker household for long periods. The constable had quarters which were distinct from the lord's, often in the keep. The constableship of a great castle such as *Dover* or the *Tower of London* was a prestigious post granted to men of high rank. They were usually elsewhere, leaving the day-to-day administration in the hands of a deputy or lieutenant.

Courtyard *see* Bailey.

Crenellations Battlements. In a medieval fortification defence was conducted primarily from the wall-head, so crenellated parapets were a feature of even the earliest stone castles. Battlements are divided into two parts: the solid bits (merlons) shielding the defenders and the gaps (crenels) from which they could fire at the enemy. Crenels were often shuttered over for greater protection, and the pivot holes for these shutters can be seen occasionally. Since they are inherently the weakest part of the wall, battlements rapidly succumb to decay.

Often they have disappeared or been rebuilt. It should also be appreciated that, while crenellations are the essential hallmark of medieval fortifications, they are used symbolically in many unfortified buildings as well. Phoney battlements are usually quite easy to detect, since genuine merlons are tall enough to cover a man's head and considerably wider than the crenels.

Kings gave their approval for private castle building by means of a *licence to crenellate*. This was a charter permitting a subject to crenellate or fortify his manor house. At times it reads like a peremptory command to strengthen the defences of the realm. For example, Richard II ordered the erection of *Bodiam Castle* 'for resistance against our enemies'. Sometimes licences were an unsolicited reward for loyal service. Frequently these were not acted upon, as the list of extant licences reveals. Generally, however, licences must have been granted to those who had applied for them. There were many unlicensed or adulterine castles, presumably the work of barons who could not be bothered to apply or did not feel they needed to. As a gesture of royal favour the licence to crenellate outlasted the need for private fortification. The last ones were granted by Henry VIII.

Cross-wall An interior dividing wall. Many Norman keeps were divided into two or more parts by cross-walls. They could be very substantial: when *Rochester* keep was undermined in 1215, the garrison took refuge behind the cross-wall and continued their defence.

Curtain The wall surrounding a bailey. Its chief characteristic is the embattled parapet on top. Curtains had to be thick enough (generally six to ten feet) to withstand the pounding of siege engines and high enough (up to forty feet) to frustrate attempts at scaling them. Flanking towers were a great advantage for protecting stretches of wall against attack. Owing to the threat of undermining the curtain was most vulnerable at its base, so the wall was often made stronger here by means of a projecting plinth or a 'batter'. Sometimes the curtain is pierced by arrow-slits. There may be windows if the domestic buildings back onto the curtain, but this was ill-advised from a defensive point of view unless that particular stretch was inaccessible from outside owing to steep falls (as at *Durham*, *Warwick*, etc.). Later medieval castles tend to have more (and larger) openings cut through the curtain – a big concession to comfortable living at the expense of security. They also have thinner curtains, but this is not necessarily a weakness because walls of this era are usually better constructed than their rubble-filled Norman predecessors.

Ditch *see* Moat.

Donjon The Norman-French term for a keep. Our word 'dungeon' derives from it, suggesting that many Norman keeps became prisons once they had been abandoned as residences. *Lancaster's* keep still is!

Drawbridge The early Norman drawbridge was a simple wooden structure spanning the moat, but capable of being hauled back into the gate passage when necessary. Before long the raised drawbridge appeared, alternating as a bridge and as a barrier. A popular variety was the turning bridge, which pivoted half in and half out of the gate passage. When the outer part was raised, the inner part sank into a deep pit which would present a further obstacle to assailants who had succeeded in smashing their way through. Later medieval drawbridges were often raised by means of a winch operated from the chamber above the gateway, or by a pair of wooden beams which raised the drawbridge when their inner halves were lowered. You can see the recesses for these beams at *Herstmonceux*. Inevitably, the drawbridge was never long enough to span the full width of a moat, and its outer end connected with a fixed bridge projecting from the far side.

Drum towers are rounded or D-shaped ones, especially common in the thirteenth century.

Edwardian Where castles are concerned this term refers to the reign of Edward I (1272–1307). It is the age of the high curtain wall, comprehensively flanked by towers (usually round) and entered through a strong gatehouse. Keeps were seldom built, except for keep-gatehouses such as *St Briavels* or *Tonbridge*. Occasionally there is a concentric outer curtain (notably the *Tower of London*). It should be noted that the 'Edwardian' castle is something of a misnomer, since all these elements had appeared before Edward's succession (e.g. *Barnwell, Dover*). England has few castles to compare with the mighty group erected by the King and his barons to consolidate the conquest of Wales. The type is exemplified by *Goodrich*, but that is a Welsh Marcher castle in spirit. They represent the apogee of the medieval castle as a military instrument. In the following century there was a trend – much more evident in England – towards less expensive castles drawing a fine line between defence and comfort. The quadrangular castle became common, and both keeps and square towers enjoyed a revival.

Embrasure An opening through a wall, i.e. a window or the recess behind an arrow-slit.

Fireplaces are a common feature of castles, even in Norman times. Early fireplaces discharged their smoke through vents in the outer wall, but *Christchurch* has a remarkable Norman chimney and this type of outlet quickly became the norm, except in halls which often retained the traditional central hearth. The fireplace itself developed through ponderous hoods to intricate Gothic overmantels. Fireplaces multiplied in the later Middle Ages as living standards rose and private chambers proliferated.

Forebuilding Tower keeps of the Norman era were usually entered at first-floor level, access being gained by an external flight of steps. A forebuilding encased this approach in stone, putting a series of barriers in the path of a besieger. The staircase was left open to the sky so that assailants could be exposed to fire from the parapet. Most square keeps had forebuildings but many have perished. Those at *Dover* and *Newcastle* are the best, forming an integral part of the keep and rising (unusually) to a second-floor entrance. This is the signature of Henry II's architect Maurice. The forebuilding at *Castle Rising* is extremely well preserved. Forebuildings occasionally appear on other types of keep, as at *Orford* (circular) and *Berkeley* (shell).

Garrison In Norman times military service equated with the feudal system. A magnate owed so many men for garrison duty in the King's castles, and could claim similar services from his own vassals. This system was not very flexible, since feudal levies could return home once their term had ended. As a result war lords came to rely upon paid mercenaries to supplement the feudal levy, and this expedient became the norm following the outbreak of chronic warfare with Scotland and France. By the fifteenth century each great baron had his own private army, at least in times of danger. Sometimes, as at *Thornbury*, their barracks may still be seen, but it is a misconception to imagine castles filled with armed retainers. In times of peace a large garrison would be an unnecessary and costly conceit. Even in wartime too many soldiers would prove a liability, consuming provisions without contributing effectively to defence. A castle required enough men – mostly archers – to maintain a healthy resistance from the wall-head and arrow-slits. Any more was superfluous.

Gatehouse The most vulnerable parts of any fortification are the entrances. It is therefore no surprise to find that the gateways of an earthwork castle or town enclosure were often the first parts to be rebuilt in stone. Some Norman curtains are pierced by simple gate arches, but the entrance was considerably increased in strength if it could be lengthened into a passage containing several obstacles. Usually, this passage formed the lowest floor of a square tower. There are some surprisingly large gate towers of the early Norman era, notably *Exeter*, *Ludlow* and *Richmond*. Less emphasis was placed upon the gatehouse in the keep-dominated castles of the twelfth century (except at *Newark*). Only with the arrival of multi-towered curtains towards the end of the century did the gatehouse receive more attention.

The evolution of the flanking tower had a dramatic impact upon gatehouse development. Norman gate towers were still vulnerable to close-up assault because the gateway was out of sight to the defender stationed on the battlements, unless he leant so far forward that he became an easy target for enemy archers. If the outer archway were flanked by towers, however, this 'blind' ground would be well covered. Early examples of the new style, notably the two gatehouses along the inner curtain at *Dover Castle*, are simple gateways flanked by shallow, square towers. Before long the towers became deeper, creating a long gate passage between them. Since this was the age of rounded defensive forms, most thirteenth-century gatehouses have round-fronted or U-shaped flanking towers. The gatehouse developed from effective but unpretentious examples such as *Beeston* to the mighty Edwardian keep-gate-houses of *Dunstanburgh* and *Tonbridge*.

At its best the gatehouse was a formidable obstacle. Even if there was no barbican requiring a preliminary assault, it would be necessary to cross the moat somehow and batter down the drawbridge. Behind the drawbridge there was likely to be a portcullis and a heavy pair of gates, and such barriers would repeat themselves at the inner end of the gate passage. The passage itself might prove to be a death trap, with 'murder holes' in the vault and arrow-slits in the side walls.

By the Edwardian period the gatehouse had developed from its three separate elements – i.e. the gate passage and its twin towers – into a unified whole. As a result of this unity, the gatehouse reverted in the fourteenth century to a square or rectangular shape. Flanking towers were generally still employed, whether square, round or polygonal according to the builder's preference, but they became adjuncts rather than an integral part of the structure. This transition is illustrated well by *Saltwood Castle* and the West Gate on *Canterbury*'s city wall. The next stage was the elimination of towers altogether, or their demotion to ineffectual turrets. This process, and the disappearance of essential features such as the drawbridge and portcullis, epitomise the decline of castles in the fifteenth century. However, the simple gate tower remained an economical alternative to the twin-towered gatehouse throughout the age of castles, and the arrival of machicolations provided another means of controlling blind ground. Gatehouses remained a spectacular symbol of aristocratic pride well into the Tudor period, and they feature in medieval manor houses and monasteries as well, so they are not in themselves proof of a fortified residence.

Gun ports first appear in fortifications on the South Coast in the fourteenth century, doubtless in response to French raids. These early gun ports resemble an inverted keyhole, consisting of a small, circular opening and a slit for sighting above (see instances at *Canterbury*, *Southampton*, *Bodiam* and *Cooling*). The opening is just above floor level because early cannon had no mountings. The guns of the era were not very powerful weapons and their range was extremely limited. Splayed openings for larger cannon, permitting a wider range of fire, appear at *Dartmouth Castle* in the 1480s and are widely used in Henry VIII's series of coastal forts. Firing these primitive devices in the confined space of a castle guardroom must have been a very unpleasant experience, and hazardous as well!

Hall The hall was the centre of medieval domestic life. Medieval houses consisted of a 'great' or main hall flanked on one side by the owner's private chamber (solar) and on the other by a group of service apartments, notably the kitchen. This plan would be elaborated, especially in the later Middle Ages, with a chapel and additional private rooms beyond the solar. It should be stressed that this standard layout was not always strictly adhered to, particularly in a castle where defensive considerations prevailed. In Norman times and beyond the components of the hall-house were often up-ended into a tower keep. However, lords always preferred more spacious accommodation within the bailey whenever possible, and the hall at *Richmond Castle* was built not long after the Norman Conquest. When residential buildings did escape from the keep into the bailey, they tended to be placed against the curtain on the side where the castle is least accessible. Windows could then be cut through the curtain without much loss of security. Some later castle builders placed the hall across the courtyard to permit large windows on either side.

The hall itself was the largest of the castle's domestic buildings. It was the centre of administration and justice as well as being the chief dining area. The lord and his personal household occupied a platform or *dais* at the solar end of the hall, while the rank and file sat on benches 'below the salt'. Most of the retainers actually slept in the hall, at least in Norman times. Heating was increasingly provided by means of fireplaces, though the traditional hearth in the middle of the floor was sometimes preferred even in the later Middle Ages, smoke escaping through a hole or 'louvre' in the roof. The main entrance to the hall was located at the service end. Draughts were kept at bay to some extent by a long wooden screen and the outer doorways were sheltered by projecting porches. Many halls stand over an undercroft and are reached by a flight of steps.

The domestic buildings were as much a part of a castle as the fortifications, but in many cases they have vanished leaving only a defensive shell. Needless to say the outer walls are stouter, and therefore more likely to last. Furthermore it is clear that many domestic buildings were of timber, and these have rarely survived. Nevertheless, some excellent halls still remain. By far the greatest is Westminster Hall (*Palace of Westminster*), but this is exceptional because it was intended from the outset as a magnificent setting for royal ceremonial. *Oakham* and *Winchester* castle halls are the outstanding examples of Norman and early Gothic work. Both have arcades dividing the interior into a 'nave' and aisles, like a church, but later medieval halls tend to be aisleless with the entire width of the building spanned by a pitched timber roof. The roof is the crowning glory of halls such as *Berkeley*, *Stokesay* and *Penshurst Place*. By contrast, the halls at *Kenilworth* and *Wells* are magnificent even in ruins. As the focus of the medieval house the hall lasted well into the Tudor period, but with the appearance of separate dining rooms for family and servants it declined to the status of an entrance hall.

Hall-keep A minority of Norman keeps cannot strictly be described as towers because they are somewhat longer than they are high. Basically they form strongly-built hall-houses, with the hall, solar and other chambers at first-floor level over an undercroft. *Castle Rising* and *Middleham* have the outstanding examples of such hall-keeps.

Henrician Pertaining to the reign of Henry VIII. Henrician castles are his series of artillery forts along the South Coast.

Herringbone masonry is laid in alternate diagonal courses so that it resembles a row of fish bones. This peculiar form of stone-laying was employed frequently (but not exclusively) in early Norman times.

Hoarding or Brattice In a medieval castle there was a certain amount of 'blind' ground at the foot of the curtain, where defenders on the battlements could not look down or throw things without exposing themselves to enemy fire. Consequently, a covered wooden gallery or hoarding was sometimes positioned in front of the battlements, with holes in the floor through which assailants could be observed and fired upon. You can sometimes see sockets in the masonry for the beams which supported these hoardings. Inevitably such structures were vulnerable to fire, and in the later Middle Ages the hoarding was translated into stone with the appearance of machicolations.

Keep Many castles have one tower which dominates the rest. It may be the only tower, or the chief tower of many. This is the keep, donjon or great tower. It contained the principal accommodation, at least in the Norman period, and provided a last refuge for defence in the event of siege. Sometimes, to all intents and purposes, the keep *is* the castle, but a bailey was invariably necessary for barracks, stables, workshops etc. Keeps come in various shapes and sizes but the vast majority are square or rectangular in plan. A keep may stand isolated within the bailey, so that it could only be assaulted once the rest of the castle had fallen, or on the line of the curtain where it could double up as a mural tower.

Although the motte-and-bailey earthwork remained the commonest type of castle for many years after the Norman Conquest, a few castles received stone keeps in William I's lifetime. William himself commenced the *Tower of London*'s White Tower and was responsible for an even bigger keep at *Colchester*. Interestingly enough, keeps of this magnitude were seldom attempted again. From the twelfth century only Henry II's keep at *Dover* can compare, though *Bamburgh* and *Rochester* are nearly as ambitious. Large keeps such as these are divided internally into two or more sections by cross-walls. This enabled the hall, solar and chapel to be located at the same level, but sufficiently high up to allow reasonably large windows without loss of security. Such keeps are four or even five stages high, though the principal floor is actually a 'double' storey with a gallery running around the walls at the upper level. (The gallery was evidently an amenity, not a military feature.) Domestic arrangements are surprisingly advanced for the period, with fireplaces, mural chambers, latrines and a well – the latter vital if the keep were to be truly self-contained. In less ambitious Norman keeps the conventional layout of the medieval house was up-ended to fit into a tower. Service quarters filled the dimly-lit lower floor(s), the hall formed a lofty apartment above them and the solar occupied the top storey for maximum security. Such keeps can also be very well appointed (e.g. *Hedingham*, *Newcastle*), but there are a number of modest keeps of the *Clitheroe* type which only provided basic accommodation. In Norman keeps large and small the entrance was usually positioned on the first (or even second) floor for greater security, and protected by a forebuilding.

Square keeps continued to be built beyond the Norman period, but as round towers made an appearance, so some keeps were built in circular or polygonal form. The earliest round keep (*New Buckenham*, of *circa* 1150) was well ahead of its time for England. From a defensive point of view a pure cylinder was the ideal, though *Conisbrough* and *Orford* keeps are elaborated with projecting turrets. Round keeps were popular in the Welsh Marches where defence remained an overriding priority. They did not catch on in England because they were inconvenient for domestic purposes, and lords were already abandoning their cramped keeps for more luxurious quarters in the bailey. It has even been suggested that reliance on the keep as a last resort had proved a flawed strategy, since defenders might hold on to the bailey with less tenacity! For these reasons, some new castles of the thirteenth century do not have a keep at all. They are castles of enclosure, relying wholly upon the curtain and a number of self-contained flanking towers for defence. It should be noted that some early Norman castles lacked a keep as well (*Ludlow*, *Richmond*), so the concept of the keep-less stronghold was not entirely new.

Nevertheless the demise of the keep should not be exaggerated. Henry III provided a quatrefoil keep on the old motte at *York Castle*, and new castles of the later Middle Ages often did have a keep. These later keeps are usually called 'tower houses' to emphasise that they are not just a throw-back to the Norman keep theme. It has been argued that the use of mercenaries forced lords into a secure place where they could be safe in the event of mutiny. Some of these towers evidently were intended as refuges for times of trouble, because the main residential buildings stood in the bailey. However, the main reason for the revival may be a matter of status as much as defence. Keeps were always a striking symbol of lordship and they contained a suite of private apartments kept separate from the public eye of the bailey. Tower houses were sometimes appended to unfortified manor houses in this period, especially in the wild North.

Later medieval tower houses usually revert to the oblong plan of the Norman keep, though turrets are often found at the vulnerable angles. Tower houses range in size from impressive piles such as *Ashby, Nunney* and *Warkworth* to the many small pele towers characteristic of Scottish Border country. In the fourteenth century they are self-contained and defensible, often standing apart from the other buildings of the castle even if they lack the complex entrance arrangements which were the hallmark of the Norman keep. In the next century we sometimes see the triumph of appearances over genuine defence. Even *Tattershall*'s great tower was merely a glorious adjunct to the bailey buildings. It was not isolated from the rest of the castle and the absurdly large windows invited assault.

Keep-gatehouse The gatehouse of a castle is often situated close to the commanding presence of a keep. It was a logical step to combine these two structures, enabling the lord or his deputy to maintain control over the gateway in times of danger. Because of the problems associated with hired levies, the keep-gatehouse is sometimes cited as an innovation of the Edwardian period (good English examples can be seen at *Dunstanburgh* and *Tonbridge*). However, the type appears much earlier: at *Newark* in the twelfth century, and at *Ludlow* and *Richmond* as far back as the late eleventh. A characteristic of the fully-developed keep-gatehouse is that the inner gates were barred from the gate passage, not the courtyard, so that the building could be isolated from the rest of the castle if the need arose. The living accommodation lay in the upper storeys, though the floor immediately above the gate passage would be inconvenienced by the portcullis and drawbridge mechanisms. Because of the domestic limitations keep-gatehouses, like circular keeps, never became popular, and in a few of the above examples the gate passage was later blocked to create a conventional keep.

Kitchens often stood detached from the rest of the house in the early Middle Ages to prevent the spread of fire. Even later, in the standard plan of the medieval house, the kitchen kept a safe distance from the hall, being reached via a corridor from the screens passage. Castle kitchens can be impressive buildings in their own right, with massive fireplaces (at least two) and a lofty roof. Sometimes the kitchen is substantial enough to serve as a mural tower, as at *Raby Castle* and Wolvesey Palace (*Winchester*). There is no standard position for the kitchen in keeps. It may occupy one of the lower floors, or it is sometimes condensed rather awkwardly into a turret or mural chamber.

Latrines in castles are often called 'garderobes', though that term literally means a wardrobe. Castles are surprisingly well equipped with latrines. Often the seat and shaft have disappeared, but any wall passage coming to a dead end is likely to have been one. Sanitation was not as sophisticated as in the monastic *reredorter*. Unless the chute could be positioned directly over a river it discharged into the ditch or a cesspit, which would have to be cleaned out from time to time! The latrine was one of those residential aspects which could undermine the strength of a castle. In 1204 Chateau Gaillard was captured by an intrepid band of soldiers who climbed up the latrine shaft.

Machicolations feature on many later medieval fortifications. They are a reworking in stone of the wooden hoardings described above. The embattled parapet projects out from the wall face on corbels, and in the gap between each corbel is a hole through which objects could be dropped onto the enemy. Machicolations appear most commonly over the gateways to a castle or town, since these were the most vulnerable spots. Sometimes the entire parapet of the gatehouse, keep or flanking towers was machicolated, as at *Lancaster, Tattershall* and *Warwick*, but expense normally prohibited their use along the curtain. The corbels of Tattershall support a covered gallery emulating contemporary French castles. Since machicolations are one of those features which lend a distinctive air to any tower, some late medieval mansions possess phoney examples which are there merely for show.

Master mason In medieval times the role of master mason was synonymous with that of architect. Often we do not know who the architect was, especially in the Norman period for which records are more scanty. Gundulf, Bishop of Rochester, is said to have been the architect of the White Tower in the *Tower of London*, while the royal accounts known as the Pipe Rolls tell us that Maurice 'the Engineer' designed the keeps at *Dover* and *Newcastle*. We know more about later master masons, especially those employed by the Crown. Such men were equally proficient in religious and secular architecture. Thus, Henry de Reynes was engaged at *Windsor* and *York* castles while simultaneously undertaking the reconstruction of Westminster Abbey. Henry Yevele worked at *Cooling* and *Saltwood* castles as well as building Westminster Hall (*Palace of Westminster*) and Canterbury Cathedral nave.

Merlons are the solid parts of a crenellated parapet. They are sometimes pierced by arrow-slits.

Moat The moat surrounding a castle or town was as vital for defence as the curtain or rampart bank. Indeed, it is the combination of the two which made defence credible. Most medieval manor houses had moats – they only went out of fashion at the end of the sixteenth century – but a moat by itself was insufficient protection. A wall is equally vulnerable on its own, because without a moat in front there is nothing to hinder the operations of siege towers, battering rams and miners. It should be emphasised that moats do not have to be wet. Although some Norman castles took advantage of water defences, the majority of them, being situated on elevated ground, had to make do with a dry ditch. A ditch with steep sides is just as effective a barrier – try clambering up one! Water-filled moats were the natural choice for the low-lying quadrangular castles of the later Middle Ages. By this period the water works were as much an amenity as a defence, and the fish-ponds accompanying moats were an important source of food. *Bodiam* and *Leeds* have lakes rather than moats around them, while *Kenilworth Castle* was once renowned for its great artificial mere.

Monasteries were often fortified in medieval Europe but England has few examples. Only on the Scottish Border was there a serious need for defence, and even here a communal pele tower might be all that the impoverished inmates could afford. The priory at *Tynemouth* became a formidable stronghold in its own right and *York Abbey* is surrounded by a towered curtain. Further south a few cathedrals and abbeys fortified their precincts in response to the hostility of neighbouring townsfolk, who resented the wealth and privileges of the Church. Such enclosures were too large for the religious community to patrol effectively and defence focused upon a stately but secure gatehouse, as at *Bury St Edmunds* and *Thornton*. The latter even has a barbican.

Motte The large, flat-topped mound forming the citadel of many Norman earthwork castles is called a 'motte'. Mottes became a feature of the English landscape straight after the Norman Conquest. The Bayeux Tapestry shows a motte being thrown up at *Hastings* just after the Normans first landed. They were relatively cheap and quick to build – especially with a pressed labour force of conquered Saxons – but it is wrong to imagine them as the product of a few days' work. Excavations at *York Castle* have shown how the motte was gradually built up, layer upon layer. Sometimes nature provided a ready-made motte which just required a little scarping. *Lincoln* and *Lewes* castles possess the oddity of two mottes each. There are hundreds of motte-and-bailey castles scattered across England. It is reasonable to associate many of them with the Anarchy, when England was divided between Stephen and Matilda and adulterine castle building was rife. Although stone castles became increasingly common during the course of the twelfth century, the earth-and-timber stronghold lasted at least until Henry II's reign.

The classic motte is tall and conical, as at *Arundel*, *Berkhamsted*, *Warwick*, etc. However, many mottes were never raised to such a height, resulting in a lower mound with a larger summit. Nor are they all circular in plan. Often the motte was surrounded by a ditch, thus isolating it from the bailey. The motte was the earthwork counterpart of the stone keep, and on its summit would be a wooden tower or a palisade surrounding the lord's house. The palisade was sometimes rebuilt in stone, thus creating a shell keep. Tower keeps could not be erected on top of artificial mounds because of their immense weight. A lot of the more important motte-and-bailey castles were later given stone defences, but at *Brinklow*, *Haughley*, *Pleshey* and *Thetford*, to name a handful of the best examples, the earthworks are not distorted by masonry and their power can be fully appreciated. *Mountfitchet Castle* goes further by providing a reconstruction of the wooden palisades and buildings.

Murder holes are openings in a floor through which unpleasant surprises could be dropped on the heads of assailants. Blocks of stone would have been the most likely weapon, not boiling oil – oil was too precious a commodity to waste. Murder holes are most often found in the vault of a gate passage. In this position they could also be useful for pouring water onto bonfires if a besieger attempted to set the gates alight.

Offset As castle walls increase in height they generally decrease in thickness. This reduction occurs in stages and there is a discernible 'offset' at each interval, often used in towers to support the main floor joists.

Parapet The embattled wall shielding defenders on the wall walk.

Pele tower A small tower house most common in the Scottish Border counties, where protracted warfare in the latter Middle Ages led to their proliferation. Some pele towers were free-standing units but most were accompanied by a hall. In effect the pele was a fortified solar block, with an undercroft (often vaulted) beneath the solar proper and one or two bed chambers above it. In some cases, as at *Nappa Hall*, there is a second tower at the service end of the hall. Pele towers are invariably simple oblong structures, though a few possess a projecting wing inspired by the Scottish L-plan. The largest 'peles', such as *Belsay* and *Dacre*, are better regarded as self-contained tower houses. *Halton Tower*, *Yanwath Hall* and the Vicar's Pele at *Corbridge* are more typical.

Perpendicular The last (and uniquely English) phase of Gothic architecture, originating in the 1320s and finally dying out in the Elizabethan period. It is characterised by its parallel uniformity, in contrast to the flowing tracery which had flourished previously.

Pilaster Shallow buttress frequently found in Norman architecture.

Plinth Sloping projection at the base of a wall. This is a common architectural feature but in fortifications it gave greater stability against undermining. Furthermore, objects thrown from the battlements would ricochet dangerously onto a besieging force.

Portcullis One of the standard defensive features of a medieval gatehouse, the portcullis was a grille which could be lowered to block the entrance passage. Usually it was made of wood but reinforced with metal strips. Raising and lowering was accomplished by means of a windlass located in the chamber above the gate passage. Only a few examples remain in situ (*Tower of London, Warwick, Windsor*), but you can often see the grooves into which the portcullis slotted.

Postern or **Sallyport** In addition to the gatehouse castles were often provided with one or more subsidiary entrances. Such posterns took the form of small gateways cut through the curtain or its flanking towers. Convenience of access may sometimes have been a factor but their chief purpose was to act as outlets for counter-attacking the enemy. We can discern a typical dilemma in the provision of posterns, for while they were ideal for aggressive defence they also presented the besieger with a comparatively easy way in.

Prisons did exist in medieval castles, but there is a tendency to misrepresent any dimly-lit undercroft as a dungeon when it was really a store room. Purpose-built prisons are not all that common in English castles. Those which exist are grim chambers in the basements of towers, as at *Newark* and *Warwick*. High-ranking prisoners enjoyed better conditions, and the *Tower of London* became the most exclusive prison of all. Many urban castles degenerated into gaols and assize courts when they ceased to have any other purpose.

Putlog holes are sometimes visible in the masonry. They received the ends of wooden beams which supported scaffolding during initial construction, or (if just below the parapet) a hoarding.

Quadrangular castles There are a few forerunners of the quadrangular plan, such as *Newark*, but Norman castles on the whole were laid out irregularly to take advantage of the terrain. In the thirteenth century castle builders began to recognise the advantages of a simple, rectangular layout, in which the curtain could be effectively flanked by a minimal number of towers (generally one at each corner). This is best illustrated in England at *Barnwell*. After 1300 the majority of new castles are distinguished by their quadrangular plans. The layout was particularly suited to level ground where there was a reliance upon water defences instead of natural strength. The corner towers may be square, round or polygonal, and the gatehouse is generally placed in the middle of one side. Although the later Middle Ages saw the revival of the keep theme there is rarely a keep in a quadrangular castle, where the emphasis was rather on residential buildings arranged around the court-yard. During the fourteenth century there was a gradual increase in the integration of the domestic buildings. Nearly a century after Barnwell, castles such as *Maxstoke* still had residential buildings leaning against the curtain. By the end of the fourteenth century, however, the quadrangular castle had become in effect four ranges around a courtyard, with the outer wall of each range doubling up as the curtain. This is apparent at *Bodiam* and *Bolton*. In the fifteenth century defensive pretensions are increasingly abandoned. We are left with spectacular, quasi-fortified palaces such as *Herstmonceux*.

Rampart A wall, especially one of earth, with a walkway on top. Most Norman earthwork castles have a rampart immediately behind the ditch.

Ringwork Some Norman earthwork castles have no motte, leaving the inner bailey as the last line of defence. Such motte-less enclosures are often called ringworks, a term at least appropriate when the bailey is round or oval in shape. They are the earthwork equivalent of the keep-less stone castles sometimes found even in the Norman period. Invariably they are surrounded by a strong rampart and ditch. Excavations have found examples of ringworks which were later built up into mottes.

Screens passage The entrance to a medieval hall was situated at its 'lower' or service end, the doorway from the courtyard admitting to a passage cut off from the main body of the hall by a wooden screen. Often this screen was surmounted by a gallery, as at *Berkeley* and *Haddon Hall*. The screens passage communicated with the service quarters. In the standard manor house plan there are three doorways, those on either side communicating with the buttery and pantry, and the middle one leading to the kitchen via a corridor. In a castle this layout might be modified to fit in with the confines of the site, but the screen would normally have been present.

Shell keep An alternative to the tower form of keep was the 'shell' keep, so called because it is a circular or polygonal enclosure surrounded by a wall. They were relatively cheap to build, serving as a direct replacement of the wooden palisade on top of a Norman motte. Most shell keeps do stand on the motte top, though the examples at *Berkeley* and *Farnham* encase the mound instead. These two are also unusual for their flanking towers. Sometimes a tower guards the entrance, as at *Arundel* and *Tamworth*, but the majority of shell keeps are plain walls entered through simple gateways. The residential buildings within have survived only rarely, since in most cases they later came down into the bailey. *Windsor* retains a suite of apartments backing onto the wall, while at *Tamworth* the buildings are crammed around a central hall. Shell keeps were a Norman phenomenon though a few later examples exist. *Old Wardour* is an interesting late medieval revival of the type.

Sieges Some castles and fortified towns never stood the test of siege. This reflects the comparatively peaceful nature of England even in the Middle Ages, and its success (after the Norman Conquest) in averting foreign invasion. A land with many castles was difficult to conquer because each one could delay the invader for months. Nevertheless, no fortification was truly impregnable because, without any prospect of outside relief, it was only a matter of time before provisions ran out.

The medieval besieger had two basic options – direct assault or a slow containment. Starving out the garrison would inevitably be successful if the besieger was strong enough to enforce an effective blockade, but it might prove too ambitious a task for his overstretched resources, particularly in the earlier Middle Ages when the fixed-term feudal levy was the main source of recruitment. Consequently, a direct assault was invariably attempted first. Castles developed their defences in response to increasingly powerful weapons of assault. Most of these weapons originated in ancient times, but the twelfth century witnessed great advances in siege craft. The whole process was accelerated in western Europe by the lessons learned in the Crusades. Needless to say the besieger's aim was to penetrate a castle's defences, whether by climbing over, breaking through or undermining. Entrances became so well defended that it was often easier to attack a vulnerable stretch of curtain, preferably one on level ground and unprotected by flanking towers. Most methods of attack could not begin until the assailants had reached the base of the wall. This meant that the ditch or moat must first be crossed by making a causeway of earth or rocks – a difficult enterprise when under fire from defenders at the wall head.

It was possible to reach the parapet by means of scaling ladders or siege towers. Climbing a scaling ladder must have been a risky undertaking and it would have taken many men to overwhelm the defenders. Siege towers were more formidable. Once a section of the ditch had been filled they were wheeled up to the curtain, a drawbridge being lowered onto the parapet so that attackers could cross *en masse*. Sometimes they were high enough to overawe the castle bailey, and there might be a catapult positioned on top to further demoralise the defenders. Siege towers were covered in damp animal skins to allay the threat of fire. The remedy to ladders and siege towers was to build higher walls, though the battle for height was one which a determined besieger was always likely to win.

Before the appearance of firearms castle walls could only be battered by rams and catapults. The battering ram, suspended from its protective 'cat', was an effective weapon if concentrated upon a particular spot for long enough. Defenders could respond by lowering a great hook from the battlements, attempting to grasp the head of the ram and lift it out of action. Catapults had the advantage of being operable from a distance. The arm was pulled back by means of a windlass, then suddenly released to dispatch a boulder with force. They were used primarily to hammer curtains. However, a variety of other projectiles might cause mayhem if hurled into the bailey, such as Greek fire or even dead horses! A variant of the catapult was a device like a huge crossbow for discharging bolts. This is sometimes called a *ballista*, and the stone-throwing engine a *mangonel*, but such terms are used haphazardly by medieval chroniclers. Castle builders responded by making walls thicker, though a thick curtain might still be breached if it was filled with poorly-mortared rubble.

If other methods failed the besieger was left with the option of undermining. This entailed digging a tunnel towards the castle walls and excavating a wide hollow beneath the foundations. A mining tunnel still exists at *Bungay*. Tunnel and hollow were carefully supported by wooden props to prevent their premature collapse. Once complete the tunnel would be filled with combustible materials which were set alight, resulting in the collapse of the wall above. The corners of square towers were especially vulnerable to undermining, as demonstrated by the collapse of *Rochester* keep in 1215. Defenders sometimes attempted to intercept mining tunnels by digging a counter-mine of their own, resulting in some fierce fighting under ground. Undermining offered a high chance of success but it was a slow process demanding skilled personnel. Sometimes, of course, a besieger would be fortunate enough to succeed without serious fighting. We often read of tricks and betrayals. Alternatively the garrison might simply realise the futility of resistance. It was manifestly better to surrender on good terms than endure months of siege, only to starve or hang as a reward.

Many sieges took place in the confused years of the Anarchy, when Stephen and Matilda vied for supremacy. This was an exceptionally long period of civil strife for England and castles frequently changed hands. At that time the majority of castles were still made of earth and timber and siege techniques were relatively primitive, involving a lot of hand-to-hand fighting. We know very little about siege operations during Prince Henry's revolt in 1174, but there were some notable sieges during the Magna Carta war (1215–16), when the *trebuchet* made its debut in England. This stone-throwing engine was rather like a giant sling, dispatching a stone with considerably more force than the traditional catapult. The Dauphin Louis' trebuchets breached several curtains, and undermining caused devastation at *Dover* and *Rochester* castles. The thirteenth century was the climax of the castle as an instrument of warfare. Desperate rebels brought about prolonged sieges at *Bedford* and *Kenilworth* which severely tested the resources of the Crown. By contrast there was little siege warfare in later medieval England, even during the Wars of the Roses. Though becoming expert at siegecraft in their wars with Scotland and France, the English settled their domestic disputes on the battlefield. Only Scottish Border castles were periodically attacked.

The introduction of cannon did not have a dramatic impact upon the declining castle. Ironically, however, many medieval fortifications were later bombarded by artillery. The Civil War brought chaos to the country and old castles were dragged into the conflict as garrison posts by both sides. Most castles were quite unprepared for hostilities. Many were already in a ruinous condition and those which were still inhabited had generally been weakened from a defensive point of view in the interest of greater comfort. Nevertheless, where there was a will to resist some castles and towns held out remarkably well, in memorable sieges at *Ashby, Corfe, Pontefract* and *Scarborough*, to name but a few. It must be admitted that sometimes the old defences were supplemented by artillery-proof earthworks, as at *Basing House* and *Donnington*.

Siege fort   In Norman times it was customary for a besieging force to protect themselves from sudden counter-attack by digging a ditch and rampart around their camp. Such siege forts can still be seen at *Bridgnorth* and *Corfe*.

Slighting   The process of rendering a fortification untenable to prevent its future use. This was achieved by breaching walls and undermining towers, or (later) by blowing them up with gunpowder. Total destruction was seldom attempted because of the great effort involved, and later stone robbers have often done far more damage. Parliament ordered the slighting of many Royalist castles after the Civil War but there are earlier instances, such as the reduction of adulterine castles by Henry II.

Solar   The solar or great chamber was the chief private room of the medieval house, to which the lord and his immediate family could retire when they wanted to escape from the bustle of the hall. It is located beyond the *dais* end of the hall, often forming a cross-wing over a vaulted undercroft. In Scottish Border territory, and occasionally elsewhere, the solar wing is built up into a pele tower. In the later Middle Ages the accommodation requirements of a great lord's household became more complex, resulting in the provision of a whole suite of apartments for family and guests. In tower keeps the solar was positioned on the top floor, though in the largest Norman keeps there is room for it alongside the hall.

Stairs   communicated between the different levels of towers and provided access from the courtyard to the wall walk. Straight stairs are sometimes found in the thickness of the wall but the spiral staircase was more practical in towers. It occupies a hollow cylinder, usually contrived at the corner of a building or some other point where the wall is reinforced, e.g. by a buttress. Each step radiates from a central post or *newel*. Spiral stairs are often steep and narrow, but in larger keeps they can be quite spacious.

Towers   are a feature of most masonry castles, whether they appear singly in the form of a keep or as a series of flankers along the curtain. Tower keeps rose from the early Norman period but the use of flanking towers caught on more slowly. *Ludlow* and *Richmond* castles employed mural towers in the generation after the Norman Conquest, and such towers appeared sporadically for a century afterwards. However, it is only from Henry II's reign that they were spaced closely enough to flank a curtain comprehensively. *Windsor's* upper ward preserves the earliest surviving group, albeit much restored, and the multi-towered curtains at *Dover* and *Framlingham* followed. Each section of curtain was covered by a pair of towers, so that besiegers could not get close without being fired upon from either side.

These Norman castles have square-fronted mural towers, but round defensive towers appeared in England about this time. The earliest is the keep at *New Buckenham*. Circular structures were less vulnerable to undermining, since it was the angles of square structures that tended to collapse. An alternative remedy was to make the foundations so massive that a mining tunnel would have little effect, so we sometimes encounter the paradox of round towers rising from square bases. Thirteenth-century mural towers are often semi-circular or U-shaped rather than cylindrical, with their curved faces towards the outside world. Sometimes they are purely fighting platforms and open towards the bailey, as at *Dover*. However, in ambitious enclosures such as *Goodrich* and the *Tower of London* each tower is a defensible unit which could be held independently in the event of siege. This trend, plus the domestic awkwardness of round rooms, contributed to the decline of the keep. Mural towers often interrupt the wall walk, so that attackers who had stormed one sector could not overrun the entire circuit.

The move towards self-contained mural towers coincided with a need for more private accommodation within castles. Each tower became a residential unit as well as a defensive bastion, containing three or four storeys of apartments served by fireplaces and latrines. The inconvenience of circular rooms surfaced again. Square towers had never died out completely even in the thirteenth century, and in later medieval castles they were often preferred. By that time the defensive advantage of round towers were less persuasive, since castles of this era were not intended to face a siege long enough for undermining to be attempted. Octagonal or other polygonal shapes were an acceptable alternative to round towers, as demonstrated in early days by the *Tower of London*'s Bell Tower and later at *Maxstoke* and *Wingfield* castles. As the Middle Ages drew to a close towers ceased to have any defensive purpose, though they were often built for show.

Tower house *see* Keep.

Town walls The fifty or so chief towns of medieval England were walled in stone. Some towns inherited stone fortifications left by the Romans. *Colchester* and *Exeter* retain town walls which are largely Roman despite later occupation, while *Chester* and *York* incorporate the defences of Roman legionary fortresses. New towns of the Saxon period were protected by earth ramparts and ditches, as at *Wallingford* and *Wareham*. Earthworks remained the usual town defence throughout the Norman period and some towns could never afford anything more, except perhaps for stone gates. Most Saxon burghs were saddled with castles after the Norman Conquest, and Norman lords encouraged the development of new boroughs outside their castle gates. As a result most fortified towns had a castle as well, usually located on the perimeter where it could play a part in the overall defence of the town.

The thirteenth and fourteenth centuries were the heyday of reconstructing town defences in stone. This was an era of growing prosperity, towns becoming conscious of their wealth and status. Fortification was normally the responsibility of the burgesses themselves. They had to obtain royal permission to charge a levy known as *murage* to finance the construction and repair of town walls. A circuit a mile or two long took several decades to build and could rarely have been patrolled effectively. Flanking towers were an essential feature of the age. They were usually the open-backed, semi-circular variety for greater economy, though larger towers might appear at key points. Economy is also evident in the way that a river was often considered sufficient defence on one side. This was even the case in *London*. A potential source of weakness was the number of roads leading into the town from the outside world. Each one had to be barred by a gatehouse, preferably of the type with twin flanking towers like *Canterbury*'s West Gate or *Southampton*'s Bargate, though many town gates are simpler structures. A few even have churches on top! Needless to say, a town wall was not a very plausible obstacle unless it had a wide ditch in front.

By the time of the Black Death most towns had completed their defences. A few up-and-coming towns were walled in the fifteenth century, and *Berwick* was given its artillery-proof circuit as late as Elizabeth I's reign. Afterwards the story is one of decay and destruction, sometimes hastened by deliberate slighting in the Civil War. As towns expanded their walls were gradually pulled down, and gates were often demolished because they obstructed the road. Considering England's urban expansion in the eighteenth and nineteenth centuries it is a wonder that there is anything left at all. Fortunately a few cities preserved their defensive circuits as amenities. That is how *York*'s city wall has come down to us more or less intact. *Chester* and *Chichester* have complete but much-restored circuits, deprived of their gatehouses. Some towns retain impressive sections of wall with flanking towers, as at *Canterbury, Newcastle, Oxford* and *Southampton*. More often there is just a short stretch left, or perhaps a gate or two.

Undercroft The main apartments of medieval houses often stand above undercrofts, which were useful for storage and other menial functions. Undercrofts are not strictly cellars because most of them are above ground level. They are often vaulted.

Vault An arched roof of stone. Vaults served to prevent the spread of fire, but as a rule only undercrofts and small mural chambers are vaulted in English domestic architecture. The commonest type is the barrel or tunnel vault, of one continuous section. In more complex vaults stone ribs cover the intersections, junctions between ribs being marked by carved bosses. Wide vaults had to be supported on one or more rows of columns. In the late Middle Ages elaborate rib patterns gave way to the fan vault – so called because each component resembles an open fan.

Ward *see* Bailey.

Water gate A gate leading directly to water – either a river or the sea. Many castles were supplied this way at a time when water transport was easiest, especially for bulky goods. In some cases boats could be unloaded inside the gate passage, as formerly at the Traitors' Gate in the *Tower of London*.

Wells Every castle needed a reliable supply of drinking water, so there was sure to be at least one well. It might be necessary to dig a long way to reach an underground source of water, especially in a hilltop castle, so wells can be major engineering achievements in their own right. *Dover*, a castle exceptional in so many ways, has England's deepest well, plunging 350 feet into the North Downs chalk. Here and at *Newcastle* a network of lead piping supplied water to various parts of the keep, and *Rochester*'s well ascended the keep in a shaft which could be accessed at each level. The most celebrated courtyard well is the one at *Carisbrooke* which is still operated by donkey wheel.

Windows The provision of windows could seriously weaken a castle, but some windows were inevitable in a complex which was residential as well as defensive. Even in Norman times the greater keeps were generously lit on the upper floors. In later medieval castles, with domestic ranges against the curtain and apartments in the flanking towers as well, it was impossible to eliminate windows in the outer walls entirely. As a general rule, windows were small at ground level but grew progressively larger on upper floors. There is evidence for protective iron grilles, but the large windows of some fifteenth-century castles were clearly incompatible with genuine defensive capability.

Round-headed Norman windows gave way to the pointed 'lancet' towards the year 1200. These windows are narrow, frequently appearing in pairs divided by a mullion. Internal splays maximised the amount of light which could enter. Window tracery appeared in the second half of the thirteenth century, the inventiveness of geometrical and curvilinear patterns being supplanted about a century later by the regularity of Perpendicular tracery. Note that tracery is always more elaborate in churches and chapels than in secular building.

Yett A strong gate which resembles a portcullis insofar as it takes the form of an iron grille. Unlike other gates it was not vulnerable to fire. Yetts are a feature of tower houses in northern England and Scotland (see surviving instances at *Dalston Hall* and *Naworth*).

BIBLIOGRAPHY

This list is restricted to the more important books out of the many published. It includes the standard works and some very useful regional guides. Individual guidebooks are available for many castles which are open to the public, ranging from scholarly handbooks to glossy but less informative souvenir guides. Where justified they are cited in the gazetteer. Otherwise references have been taken from the *Victoria County Histories* (**VCH**) and the volumes of the *Royal Commission on Historical Monuments* (**RCHM**). Unfortunately both series are far from complete. *The Buildings of England* (**BOE**) has the advantage of completeness, though some of the volumes are more detailed than others. *The History of the King's Works* (**HKW**) is a vital historical source for royal castles. Beyond that there is an enormous wealth of historical and archaeological periodicals to consult, many of them very old. Cathcart-King's book should be consulted for comprehensive reference details.

Anderson W. & Swaan W., *Castles of Europe* (London, 1970)
Armitage E. S., *Early Norman Castles of the British Isles* (London, 1912)
Braun H., *The English Castle* (London, 1947)
Brown R. Allen, *Castles from the Air* (London, 1989)
————, *English Castles*, 3rd edn (London, 1976)
————, *The Architecture of Castles* (London, 1984)
Burke J., *Life in the Castle in Medieval England* (London, 1978)
Cathcart-King D. J., *Castellarium Anglicanum* (New York, 1983)
Clark G. T., *Medieval Military Architecture in England* (London, 1884) 2 vols
Curwen J. F., *Castles and Fortified Towers of Cumberland, Westmorland and Lancashire North of the Sands* (Kendal, 1913)
Fry P. S., *Castles of the British Isles*, 2nd edn (Newton Abbot, 1990)
Guy J., *Kent Castles* (Gillingham, 1980)
Hugill R., *Borderland Castles and Peles* (Newcastle, 1970)
————, *Castles of Cumberland and Westmorland* (Newcastle, 1977)
————, *Castles of Durham* (Newcastle, 1979)
Jackson M. J., *Castles of Cumbria* (Carlisle, 1990)
————, *Castles of Northumbria* (Carlisle, 1992)
Long B., *Castles of Northumberland* (Newcastle, 1967)
Mackenzie J. D., *The Castles of England* (London, 1897) 2 vols
Matarasso F., *The English Castle* (London, 1993)
McNeil T., *Castles* (London, 1992)
Morley B., *Henry VIII and the Development of Coastal Defence* (London, 1976)
O'Neil B. H. St John, *Castles*, 2nd edn (London, 1973)
————, *Castles and Cannon* (Oxford, 1960)
Platt C., *The Castle in Medieval England and Wales* (London, 1982)
Renn D. F., *Norman Castles in Britain*, 2nd edn (London, 1973)
Salter M., *The Castles and Moated Mansions of Shropshire* (Wolverhampton, 1988)
————, *The Castles and Moated Mansions of Staffordshire* (Wolverhampton, 1989)
————, *The Castles and Moated Mansions of Warwickshire* (Malvern, 1992)

————, *The Castles of Herefordshire and Worcestershire* (Wolverhampton, 1989)

Simpson W. Douglas, *Castles from the Air* (London, 1949)

————, *Castles in Britain* (London, 1966)

————, *Castles in England and Wales* (London, 1969)

————, *Exploring Castles* (London, 1957)

Sorrell A., *British Castles* (London, 1973)

Taylor A. J., 'Military Architecture', *Medieval England*, ed. A. L. Poole (Oxford, 1958)

Thompson A. Hamilton, *Military Architecture in England during the Middle Ages* (Oxford, 1912)

Thompson M. W., *The Decline of the Castle* (Cambridge, 1987)

————, *The Rise of the Castle* (Cambridge, 1991)

Toy S., *A History of Fortification* (London, 1955)

————, *The Castles of Great Britain*, 4th edn (London, 1966)

Turner H. L., *Town Defences in England and Wales* (London, 1971)

Warner P., *The Medieval Castle* (London, 1971)

Wood M., *The English Mediaeval House* (London, 1983)

INDEX OF SITES

Main entries are highlighted by an asterisk. Ordnance Survey grid references are given (usually the six-figure number, but only four figures where entries cover a wider area). The modern county, if different, is shown in brackets.